# McDougal Littell
# CLASSZONE

## Visit **classzone.com** and get connected.

*ClassZone* resources provide instruction, practice and learning support for students and parents.

### Animated History & Geography

- Brings history to life with interactive activities and visuals
- Provides interactive maps, charts, and graphs

### Current Events

- Takes you beyond the text and keeps you up-to-date on world events
- Reflects the most recent political, economic, and social issues
- Provides weekly current events quizzes to help check comprehension

### Interactive Review

- Provides a unique way to review key concepts and events
- Includes geography games, crossword puzzles, and matching games
- Helps ensure lesson comprehension through graphic organizers, animated flipcards, and review/study notes

### Research and Writing

- Includes links to primary sources, chapter resources, biographies, and state-specific resources
- Provides support for your writing assignments through complete writing models, rubrics, and research guides

### Access the online version of your textbook at **classzone.com**

Your complete text, along with animated maps, charts and infographics, is available for immediate use!

# McDougal Littell
### Where Great Lessons Begin

# NEW JERSEY EDITION

McDougal Littell

# American HISTORY

BEGINNINGS THROUGH RECONSTRUCTION

C. Fred

# Senior Consultants

**Dr. Robert Dallek** is an acclaimed historian of the American presidency and an authority on leadership and crises. His biography of President John F. Kennedy, *An Unfinished Life*, spent eight weeks on *The New York Times* bestseller list. A former professor of History at Boston University, Dr. Dallek also spent three decades as a professor at UCLA, and a year as a visiting professor at Oxford. In recent years he has also been a visiting professor at Dartmouth College. In addition to his books, he is the author of more than 100 publications and the recipient of numerous honors and awards. He is a frequent commentator on radio and television networks, including NPR, CNN, and NBC, on subjects concerning the presidency, current events, and foreign policy.

**Dr. Jesus Garcia** is professor of Curriculum and Instruction at the University of Nevada, Las Vegas, and past president of the National Council for the Social Studies. A former social studies teacher, Dr. Garcia has co-authored many books and articles on subjects that range from teaching social studies in elementary and middle schools to seeking diversity in education. Dr. Garcia has also worked for both the Chicago and Washington, D.C., public schools and the Arkansas Department of Education as a consultant on social studies standards.

**Dr. Donna Ogle** is professor of Reading and Language at National-Louis University in Chicago, Illinois, and is a specialist in reading in the content areas, with an interest in social studies. She is past president of the International Reading Association and a former social studies teacher. Dr. Ogle is currently directing two content literacy projects in Chicago schools and is Senior Consultant to the Striving Readers Research Project. She continues to explore applications of the K-W-L strategy she developed and is adding a Partner Reading component—PRC2 (Partner Reading and Content 2).

**C. Frederick Risinger** is the former Director of Professional Development and coordinator for Social Studies Education at Indiana University. He is past president of the National Council for the Social Studies as well as past president of the National Social Studies Supervisors Association. Mr. Risinger also served on the coordinating committee for the National History Standards Project. He writes a monthly column on technology in the social studies classroom for *Social Education* and is the current president of the Social Science Education Consortium.

ISBN-10: 0-618-92161-3
ISBN-13: 978-0-618-92161-4

01 02 03 04 05 06 07 08 09 DWO 12 11 10 09 08 07

Internet Web Site: http://www.mcdougallittell.com

# Consultants and Reviewers

##  NEW JERSEY REVIEWERS

**Jeff Ballin**
Union School District
Union, NJ

**John Boland**
Point Pleasant Beach High School
Point Pleasant Beach, NJ

**Edward Canzanese**
Rosa International Middle School
Cherry Hill, NJ

**William J. Colley**
Social Studies Supervisor
Jersey City Public Schools
Jersey City, NJ

**Nick DiGregory**
Delsea Regional High School
Franklinville, NJ

**Suzanne Diszler**
Hamilton Township
Board of Education
Hamilton, NJ

**Lisa Ann Robinson**
Manalapan Englishtown
Middle School
Manalapan, NJ

**Cynthia A. Smith**
Williamstown Middle School
Williamstown, NJ

# Student Panel

The following Middle School Student Panel reviewed textbook materials and technology products for this program.

Jessica Baker
Nelly Benitez
Ameer Cannon
Katie Conley
Murad Dajani
Will DiFrancesca
Tom Foydel
Philippa Gillette
Jenny Gorelick
Michael Grassle
Danielle Jackson
DeJauna Jackson
Mark Johnson
David Lenz
Andrew Mack

Madelaine Martin
Jabari McIntyre
Victoria Meliska
Sarah Peters
Brianna Ransom
Andrés Rivera-Thompson
Simone Samuels
Ben Shoaf
Gabriel Siegal
Kyle Siegal
Brock Snider
Hank Strickler
Jasmine Wright
Hannah Wyler

# Teacher Consultants

The following educators provided ongoing review of key components
or contributed teaching ideas and activities for this program.

**Venise N. Battle**
Shady Hill School
Cambridge, Massachusetts

**Paul C. Beavers**
J.T. Moore Middle School
Nashville, Tennessee

**Cristy Berger**
Wilkinson Middle School
Madison, Michigan

**Holly West Brewer**
Buena Vista Paideia Magnet
Nashville, Tennessee

**David Brothman**
North Chicago School District
North Chicago, Illinois

**Ron Campana**
United Federation of Teachers
New York, New York

**Patricia B. Carlson**
Swanson Middle School
Arlington, Virginia

**Meg DeWeese**
Thoreau Academy-Tulsa Public
School System
Tulsa, Oklahoma

**Kelly Ellis**
Hamilton Middle School
Cypress, Texas

**James Grimes**
Middlesex County Vocational-
Technical High School
Woodbridge, New Jersey

**Julie Guild**
Carl Albert Junior High
Oklahoma City, Oklahoma

**Brent Heath**
De Anza Middle School
Ontario, California

**Suzanne Hidalgo**
Serrano Middle School
Highland, California

**Cathryn Mahan Hinesley**
Seneca Ridge Middle School
Sterling, Virginia

**Alan Hornbecker**
Walt Whitman Middle School
Alexandria, Virginia

**Barbara Kennedy**
Sylvan Middle School
Citrus Heights, California

**Pamela Knifflin**
Navasota Junior High
Navasota, Texas

**Tammy Leiber**
Navasota Junior High
Navasota, Texas

**Lori Lesslie**
Cedar Bluff Middle School
Knoxville, Tennessee

**Christine Loop**
Glasgow Middle School
Alexandria, Virginia

**Brian McKenzie**
Buffalo Public School #81
Buffalo, New York

**Kayne Miller**
Longfellow Middle School
Falls Church, Virginia

**Ronnie Moppin**
Sunny Vale Middle School
Blue Springs, Missouri

**Caroline Ona**
Washington Irving Middle School
Springfield, Virginia

**Jean Price**
St. John's School
Houston, Texas

**Meg Robbins**
Wilbraham Middle School
Northampton, Massachusetts

**Philip Rodriguez**
McNair Middle School
San Antonio, Texas

**Leslie Schubert**
Parkland School
McHenry, Illinois

**Robert Sisko**
Carteret Middle School
Carteret, New Jersey

**Jim Sorenson**
Chippewa Middle School
Des Plaines, Illinois

**Amy Smith**
Lanier Middle School
Fairfax, Virginia

**Marci Smith**
Hurst-Euless-Bedford ISD
Bedford, Texas

**Nicholas Sysock**
Carteret Middle School
Carteret, New Jersey

**Susan Weber**
Maple Point Middle School
Langhorne, Pennsylvania

**Becky Wedeking**
Eisenhower Middle School
Topeka, Kansas

**Lisa Williams**
Lamberton Middle School
Carlisle, Pennsylvania

# NEW JERSEY

# OVERVIEW
**New Jersey Student Edition**

**New Jersey Edition Table of Contents**     NJ6

**New Jersey Steps To Success**     NJ29

- Guide to Understanding New Jersey's Core Curriculum Content Standards for Social Studies
- Guide to Test-Taking Strategies and Practice

**Lessons with Embedded New Jersey Cumulative Progress Indicators**

 Look for the New Jersey symbol throughout this book. It highlights targeted cumulative progress indicators to help you succeed on your test.

**Complete New Jersey Core Curriculum Content Standards for Social Studies**     R81

**NEW JERSEY CONTENTS**

*Ocean City Beach, Ocean City, New Jersey © Corbis*

# UNIT 1 NEW JERSEY

# Three Worlds Meet

| | |
|---|---|
| Reading for Understanding | NJ20 |
| Strategies for Reading American History | NJ20 |
| Themes of American History | NJ24 |
| Exploring History Online | NJ26 |
| Guide to Test-Taking Strategies and Practice | S1 |
| Geography Handbook | A1 |
| Rand McNally World Atlas | A20 |

## Chapter 1 (Beginnings–1500)
## The World Before 1500 — 2

| | |
|---|---|
| 1 Societies of the Americas | 4 |
| 2 Societies of Africa | 12 |
| 3 Societies of Europe | 16 |
| New Jersey Standards-Based Assessment | 23 |

## Chapter 2 (1492–1650)
## European Exploration of the Americas — 24

| | |
|---|---|
| 1 Spain Claims an Empire | 26 |
| 2 European Competition in North America | 34 |
| 3 The Spanish and Native Americans | 40 |
| *Reading Primary Sources* The Iroquois Great Law of Peace | 46 |
| 4 Beginnings of Slavery in the Americas | 48 |
| New Jersey Standards-Based Assessment | 55 |

## Online Activities
at **CLASSZONE.COM**

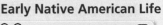

### Animated HISTORY
**Early Native American Life**

Experience the activity and commerce of a Native American market, p. 10.

### Interactive Review

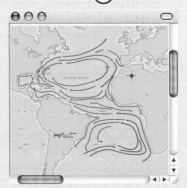

Play the GeoGame to test your knowledge of the European explorations of North America, p. 21.

### Online Test Practice
Review test-taking strategies and practice your test, pages 23, 55.

# UNIT 2 NEW JERSEY

# The English Colonies

**Chapter 3** (1585–1732)

## The English Establish
## 13 Colonies      58

| | |
|---|---|
| 1 Early Colonies Have Mixed Success | 60 |
| 2 New England Colonies | 66 |
| *Reading Primary Sources* The Mayflower Compact; The Fundamental Orders of Connecticut | 74 |
| 3 The Southern Colonies | 76 |
| 4 The Middle Colonies | 82 |
| New Jersey Standards-Based Assessment | 91 |

**Chapter 4** (1651–1753)

## The Colonies Develop      92

| | |
|---|---|
| 1 New England: Commerce and Religion | 94 |
| 2 The Southern Colonies: Plantations and Slavery | 102 |
| 3 The Middle Colonies: Farms and Cities | 110 |
| 4 The Backcountry | 116 |
| New Jersey Standards-Based Assessment | 123 |

**Chapter 5** (1689–1763)

## Beginnings of an American
## Identity      124

| | |
|---|---|
| 1 Early American Culture | 126 |
| *Climate and Building Traditions* Housing & Climate | 134 |
| 2 Roots of American Democracy | 136 |
| 3 The French and Indian War | 142 |
| New Jersey Standards-Based Assessment | 151 |

## Online Activities
at **CLASSZONE.COM**

**Animated HISTORY**
**A New England Seaport**

Visit a busy New England seaport in the 1700s, p. 108.

**Interactive Review**

American writer, publisher, scientist, inventor, and diplomat

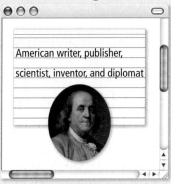

Use Interactive Flipcards to review key people, places, and events in the American colonies, p. 149.

## Online Test Practice

Review test-taking strategies and practice your test, pages 91, 123, 151.

# Creating A New Nation

**Chapter 6** (1763–1776)

## The Road to Revolution  **154**

1 Tighter British Control  156
2 Colonial Resistance Grows  160
  *The American Spirit* The Spirit of Liberty  167
3 The Road to Lexington and Concord  168
  *Connect to Literature* Johnny Tremain  175
4 Declaring Independence  176
  *Reading Primary Sources*
  The Declaration of Independence  184
  New Jersey Standards-Based Assessment  191

**Chapter 7** (1775–1783)

## The American Revolution  **192**

1 The Early Years of the War  194
2 The War Expands  204
3 The Path to Victory  212
  *The American Spirit* Rallying to the Cause  220
4 The Legacy of the War  222
  New Jersey Standards-Based Assessment  231

**Chapter 8** (1776–1791)

## Confederation to Constitution  **232**

1 The Confederation Era  234
  *Connect Geography & History* The Northwest Territory  240
2 Creating the Constitution  242
3 Ratification and the Bill of Rights  248
  *Reading Primary Sources* The Federalist, No. 51;
  Objections to the Constitution  255
  New Jersey Standards-Based Assessment  259

**Constitution Handbook:**
**The Living Constitution**  260
Seven Principles of the Constitution  262
*Reading Primary Sources*
The Constitution of the United States  266
New Jersey Standards-Based
Assessment  299

**Citizenship Handbook**  300
The Role of the Citizen  300
Building Citizenship Skills  304
Practicing Citizenship Skills  307

## Online Activities
at CLASSZONE.COM

**Animated HISTORY**
Battle Tactics

See a Revolutionary War battle come alive, p. 202.

**Interactive Review**

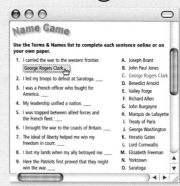

Play the Name Game to test your knowledge of the Revolutionary War, p. 229.

## Online Test Practice

Review test-taking strategies and practice your test, pages 191, 231, 259, 299.

# UNIT 4 NEW JERSEY

# The Early Republic

**Chapter 9** (1789–1800)
## Launching a New Republic     310
1 Washington's Presidency     312
2 Challenges to the New Government     318
  *The American Spirit* New Styles for a New Nation     324
3 The Federalists in Charge     326
  New Jersey Standards-Based Assessment     335

**Chapter 10** (1800–1816)
## The Jefferson Era     336
1 Jeffersonian Democracy     338
  *Supreme Court* Marbury v. Madison     342
2 The Louisiana Purchase and Exploration     344
  *Connect Geography & History*
  American Landscapes     350
3 The War of 1812     352
  New Jersey Standards-Based Assessment     361

**Chapter 11** (1800–1844)
## National and Regional Growth     362
1 Early Industry and Inventions     364
2 Plantations and Slavery Spread     372
3 Nationalism & Sectionalism     378
  *Supreme Court* McCulloch v. Maryland     380
  *Reading Primary Sources* The Monroe Doctrine     385
  New Jersey Standards-Based Assessment     389

## Online Activities
at CLASSZONE.COM

 **HISTORY**
### An American Textile Mill

Experience what life was like in an 1800s mill town, p. 370.

### Interactive Review

Play the GeoGame to test your knowledge of the new republic, p. 333.

### Online Test Practice

Review test-taking strategies and practice your test, pages 335, 361, 389.

# UNIT 5 NEW JERSEY

# A Changing Nation

**Chapter 12** (1824–1840)
## The Age of Jackson                          **392**

1 Jacksonian Democracy & States' Rights          394
2 Jackson's Policy Toward Native Americans        402
3 Prosperity & Panic                             408
New Jersey Standards-Based Assessment            415

**Chapter 13** (1821–1853)
## Manifest Destiny                             **416**

1 Trails West                                    418
2 The Texas Revolution                           426
3 The War with Mexico                            432
4 The California Gold Rush                        438
*The American Spirit* The Spirit of '49          444
New Jersey Standards-Based Assessment            447

**Chapter 14** (1830–1860)
## A New Spirit of Change                       **448**

1 The Hopes of Immigrants                        450
2 Reforming American Society                     456
*Reading Primary Sources*
Report to the Massachusetts Legislature          462
3 Abolition and Women's Rights                   464
*Connect to Literature*
*The True Confessions of Charlotte Doyle*        472
New Jersey Standards-Based Assessment            475

## Online Activities
at CLASSZONE.COM

**Animated HISTORY**
The Journey West

Endure the hardships and dangers of the westward journey across America's wilderness, p. 424.

**Interactive Review**

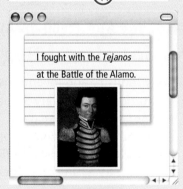

I fought with the *Tejanos* at the Battle of the Alamo.

Use Interactive Flipcards to review key people, places, and events of the mid-1800s, p. 445.

## Online Test Practice
Review test-taking strategies and practice your test, pages 415, 447, 475.

# A Nation Divided and Rebuilt

**Chapter 15** (1846–1861)

## The Nation Breaking Apart     **478**

| | |
|---|---|
| 1 Tensions Rise Between North and South | 480 |
| *Connect Geography & History* Land Use & Slavery | 488 |
| 2 Slavery Dominates Politics | 490 |
| *Supreme Court* Dred Scott v. Sandford | 494 |
| 3 Lincoln's Election and Southern Secession | 498 |
| New Jersey Standards-Based Assessment | 507 |

**Chapter 16** (1861–1862)

## The Civil War Begins     **508**

| | |
|---|---|
| 1 War Erupts | 510 |
| 2 Life in the Army | 516 |
| 3 No End in Sight | 522 |
| *Connect to Literature* Across Five Aprils | 530 |
| New Jersey Standards-Based Assessment | 533 |

**Chapter 17** (1863–1865)

## The Tide of War Turns     **534**

| | |
|---|---|
| 1 The Emancipation Proclamation | 536 |
| 2 War Affects Society | 542 |
| 3 The North Wins | 548 |
| 4 The Legacy of the War | 558 |
| *Reading Primary Sources* | |
| The Gettyburg Address; Lincoln's Second Inaugural | 563 |
| New Jersey Standards-Based Assessment | 567 |

**Chapter 18** (1865–1877)

## Reconstruction     **568**

| | |
|---|---|
| 1 Rebuilding the Union | 570 |
| 2 Reconstruction Changes Daily Life | 576 |
| 3 The End of Reconstruction | 582 |
| New Jersey Standards-Based Assessment | 591 |

## Online Activities
at CLASSZONE.COM

### Animated HISTORY
**Naval Action at Vicksburg**

See Union naval power in action at Vicksburg, p. 556.

### Interactive Review

Slave States

Play the GeoGame to test your knowledge of the history and geography of the Civil War, p. 505.

### Online Test Practice

Review test-taking strategies and practice your test, pages 507, 533, 567, 591.

# Epilogue

**Epilogue 1** (1860–1914)
## America Transformed
592

**Epilogue 2** (1914–1929)
## World War I and Its Legacy
594

**Epilogue 3** (1929–1960)
## Depression, War, and Recovery
596

**Epilogue 4** (1954–1975)
## Civil Rights, Vietnam, and Watergate
598

**Epilogue 5** (1976–Present)
## America in a Changing World
600

### Reference Section

| | |
|---|---|
| Skillbuilder Handbook | R1 |
| Facts About the States | R40 |
| Presidents of the U.S. | R42 |
| Gazetteer | R45 |
| English Glossary | R49 |
| Spanish Glossary | R56 |
| Index | R65 |
| Acknowledgments | R76 |
| Complete List of New Jersey Core Curriculum Content Standards for Social Studies | R81 |

## Animated HISTORY

| | |
|---|---|
| Early Native American Life | 10 |
| A New England Seaport | 108 |
| Battle Tactics | 202 |
| An American Textile Mill | 370 |
| American Trails West | 424 |
| Naval Action at Vicksburg | 556 |

## CONNECT Geography & History

| | |
|---|---|
| Climate and Building Traditions | 134 |
| The Northwest Territory | 240 |
| American Landscapes | 350 |
| Land Use and Slavery | 488 |

## American Spirit

| | |
|---|---|
| Popular Resistance | 167 |
| Rallying to the Cause | 220 |
| New Styles for a New Nation | 324 |
| California's Gold Rush | 444 |

## Connect to Literature

| | |
|---|---|
| *Johnny Tremain,* by Esther Forbes | 175 |
| *The True Confessions of Charlotte Doyle,* by Avi | 472 |
| *Across Five Aprils,* by Irene Hunt | 530 |

## SUPREME COURT

| | |
|---|---|
| *Marbury v. Madison (1803)* | 342 |
| *McCulloch v. Maryland (1819)* | 380 |
| *Dred Scott v. Sandford (1857)* | 494 |

## COMPARING

| | |
|---|---|
| Early Societies of the Americas | 7 |
| Aztec and Inca Civilizations | 32 |
| Religion in the Early Colonies | 78 |
| Slave Populations | 105 |
| Class Systems | 128 |
| Prewar and Postwar Boundaries, 1754–1763 | 146 |
| Revolutionary Leaders | 165 |
| Symbols of Freedom | 181 |
| Prewar and Postwar Boundaries, 1775–1783 | 225 |
| Plans for Government | 245 |
| Military Responsibilities | 272 |
| Roles of the President | 278 |
| Federal and State Powers | 282 |
| Political Parties | 329 |
| Sectional Interests | 399 |
| Push and Pull Factors | 452 |
| Free States, Slave States, and Territories | 486 |
| North and South | 514 |
| Northern and Southern Inflation | 545 |
| Images of Battle | 560 |
| Southern Agriculture | 579 |
| Contract System and Sharecropping | 580 |
| Political Representation | 584 |

## COMPARING Perspectives

| | |
|---|---|
| Religious Tolerance vs. Intolerance | 70 |
| Patriots and Loyalists | 196 |
| Antifederalists and Federalists | 250 |
| Jefferson and Satanta | 348 |
| Life in the Mills | 366 |
| For and Against Settlements in Texas | 428 |
| Images of Slavery | 484 |

# FEATURES

## CONNECTING History

| | |
|---|---|
| Warfare and Exploration | 18 |
| New Englanders Oppose the King | 173 |
| Wars and Social Change | 546 |

## CONNECT To Today

| | |
|---|---|
| Piracy | 97 |
| Military Communication | 214 |
| The Cherokee Nation of Oklahoma | 406 |
| Economic Opportunity | 442 |
| Political Debate | 495 |
| Richmond, Virginia | 578 |

## CONNECT Economics and History

| | |
|---|---|
| Mercantilism | 62 |
| Triangular Trade | 98 |
| Paying for the War | 224 |
| How Banks Work | 316 |
| The Business Cycle | 410 |
| Investment | 482 |

## CONNECT Citizenship and History

| | |
|---|---|
| Voting Rights | 64 |
| Trial by Jury | 138 |
| Debate and Free Speech | 252 |
| Exercising the Vote | 397 |
| Reaching Compromise | 496 |

## ANALYZING Political Cartoons

| | |
|---|---|
| Two Historical Cartoons | 170 |
| The Present State of Great Britain | 206 |
| The XYZ Affair | 330 |
| Footrace to the White House | 501 |
| Freedom to the Slave | 539 |

## Reading Primary Sources

| | |
|---|---|
| The Iroquois Great Law of Peace; A Relation of Maryland | 46 |
| The Mayflower Compact; The Fundamental Orders of Connecticut | 74 |
| Declaration of Independence | 184 |
| *The Federalist*, No. 51, James Madison; Objections to the Constitution, George Mason | 255 |
| The Constitution of the United States | 266 |
| The Monroe Doctrine | 385 |
| Report to the Massachusetts Legislature, Dorothea Dix | 462 |
| The Gettysburg Address, Abraham Lincoln; Lincoln's Second Inaugural Address, Abraham Lincoln | 563 |

## Daily Life

| | |
|---|---|
| In the Colonies | 85 |
| The Colonial Marketplace | 162 |
| At Valley Forge | 208 |
| On the Trail | 422 |

## History Makers

| | |
|---|---|
| Christopher Columbus | 28 |
| Mary Dyer | 71 |
| Ben Franklin | 132 |
| Samuel Adams | 165 |
| John Adams | 165 |
| Abigail Adams | 172 |
| George Washington | 197 |
| James Madison | 244 |
| Alexander Hamilton | 315 |
| John Marshall | 342 |
| Sacagawea | 351 |
| Nat Turner | 376 |
| Andrew Jackson | 396 |
| James Beckwourth | 420 |
| Juan Seguín | 430 |
| Horace Mann | 460 |
| Dorothea Dix | 462 |
| Frederick Douglass | 466 |
| Elizabeth Cady Stanton | 469 |
| Harriet Beecher Stowe | 485 |
| Roger Taney | 494 |
| Abraham Lincoln | 512 |
| Ulysses S. Grant | 552 |
| Robert E. Lee | 552 |
| Andrew Johnson | 572 |

## History through Art

| | |
|---|---|
| Elizabeth I | 37 |
| A Changing Puritan World | 100 |
| The Surrender of Lord Cornwallis | 217 |
| The Women of Les Halles Marching to Versailles | 322 |
| Portrait of George Washington, Gilbert Stuart | 357 |
| The Peninsula Campaign | 527 |

## TECHNOLOGY of the TIME

| | |
|---|---|
| GIS & GPS | A4 |
| Thomas Jefferson | 340 |
| Industrialization | 368 |
| Civil War Technology | 520 |

# PRIMARY SOURCES

## Chapter 1

| | |
|---|---|
| Montezuma | 5 |
| Mansa Musa, as told by historian Al-Umari | 13 |
| Queen Isabella | 17 |

## Chapter 2

| | |
|---|---|
| Bernal Díaz del Castillo, quoted in *Notable Latin American Women* | 27 |
| Henry Hudson, quoted in *Discoverers of America* | 35 |
| Guamán Poma, *Letter to a King* | 41 |
| The Iroquois Great Law of Peace | 46 |
| A Relation of Maryland | 47 |
| Olaudah Equiano, quoted in *Great Slave Narratives* | 50 |
| Bernal Díaz del Castillo, from *The Conquest of New Spain* | 55 |

## Chapter 3

| | |
|---|---|
| from **John White's Journals** (1590) | 61 |
| John Winthrop, *"Model of Christian Charity"* | 67 |
| Richard Saltonstall | 70 |
| Nathaniel Ward | 70 |
| Roger Williams | 70 |
| John Cotton | 70 |
| The Mayflower Compact | 74 |
| The Fundamental Orders of Connecticut | 75 |
| Letter to Lord Baltimore from the Maryland Assembly | 77 |
| Letter from a South Carolina doctor, quoted in *American Colonies* | 79 |
| Peter Stuyvesant, from a letter of 1661 | 83 |
| from **The Frame of the Government of Pennsylvania**, 1682 | 86 |

## Chapter 4

| | |
|---|---|
| Captain Thomas Smith, poem in self-portrait | 95 |
| Increase Mather, from the sermon "The Day of Trouble is Near," 1674 | 100 |
| George Mason, quoted in *Common Landscape of America* | 103 |
| Edward Kimber, quoted in *White over Black* | 106 |
| William Penn, Letter to the Native Americans, 1681 | 111 |
| Peter Kalm, quoted in *America at 1750* | 112 |
| James Logan, letter of Nov. 18, 1729 | 117 |

## Chapter 5

| | |
|---|---|
| Eliza Lucas Pinckney, quoted in *Colonies and Revolution* | 127 |
| Jonathan Edwards, "Sinners in the Hands of an Angry God" | 131 |
| Increase Mather, quoted in *The Last American Puritan* | 137 |
| Magna Carta, translated in *A Documentary History of England* | 138 |
| *New York Weekly Journal*, quoted in *Colonial America, 1607–1763* | 141 |
| Pontiac, quoted in *Pontiac and the Indian Uprising* | 143 |
| Major General Jeffrey Amherst, quoted in *The Conspiracy of Pontiac* | 148 |
| Pontiac, 1763 | 151 |

## Chapter 6

| | |
|---|---|
| Sally Franklin, quoted in *Founding Mothers* | 157 |
| William Pitt, quoted in *Patriots* | 159 |
| Anonymous, account of the Boston Massacre | 161 |
| John Dickinson, *Letters from a Farmer in Pennsylvania* | 163 |
| George Hewes, quoted in *A Retrospect of the Boston Tea-Party* | 166 |
| John Robbins, quoted in *Redcoats and Rebels* | 169 |
| Patrick Henry, quoted in *Patriots* | 172 |
| Margaret Kemble Gage, quoted in *Paul Revere's Ride* | 177 |
| Thomas Paine, *Common Sense* | 180 |
| Thomas Jefferson, from The Declaration of Independence | 183 |
| Thomas Jefferson, The Declaration of Independence | 184 |
| from **The Declaration of Rights of the Stamp Act Congress** | 191 |

## Chapter 7

| | |
|---|---|
| John Singleton Copley, letter to Henry Pelham | 195 |
| A lady from Philadelphia | 196 |
| Samuel Adams | 196 |
| Mather Byles | 196 |
| *Massachusetts Gazette, and Boston News-Letter* | 196 |
| Thomas Paine, *The American Crisis* | 199 |
| Dr. Harris, a veteran of the Battle of Rhode Island | 205 |
| James P. Collins, quoted in *The Spirit of Seventy-Six* | 213 |
| Joseph Plumb Martin, quoted in *The Revolutionaries* | 219 |
| Anonymous, patriotic curses | 220 |
| Phillis Wheatley, poem | 221 |
| Joseph Brant, 1783 | 226 |
| Temperance Smith | 231 |

## Chapter 8

| | |
|---|---|
| Plough Jogger, quoted in *The People Speak: American Voices, Some Famous, Some Little Known* | 235 |
| Edmund Randolph, quoted in *Edmund Randolph: A Biography* | 243 |
| Roger Sherman, June 11, 1787 | 246 |
| Mercy Otis Warren, quoted in *Mercy Otis Warren* | 249 |
| Alexander Hamilton, *The Federalist* "Number 1" | 250 |
| Patrick Henry | 250 |
| George Mason | 250 |
| Alexander Hamilton | 250 |
| John Jay | 250 |
| *The Federalist* "Number 51" | 255 |
| Thomas Jefferson, December 20, 1787 | 259 |

## Constitution Handbook

| | |
|---|---|
| The Constitution of the United States | 266 |

## Chapter 9

| | |
|---|---|
| Charles Thomson, quoted in *George Washington's Papers, Library of Congress, 1741–1977* | 313 |
| Little Turtle, quoted in *The Life and Times of Little Turtle* | 319 |
| Alexander Hamilton, *The Works of Alexander Hamilton* | 321 |
| Benjamin Banneker, *letter to Thomas Jefferson 1791* | 327 |
| George Washington, Farewell Address | 335 |

## Chapter 10

James Callender, quoted in *American Aurora* 339
Thomas Jefferson, First Inaugural Address 341
Chief Justice John Marshall, *Marbury v. Madison* (1803) 342
William Clark, journal entry, October 19,1805 345
Thomas Jefferson, Speech to a Delegation
    of Indian Chiefs, January 4, 1806 348
Satanta, Kiowa Chief, September 1876 348
Stephan Decatur, 1816 353

## Chapter 11

Harriet Hanson Robinson, from *Loom and Spindle;*
    *or, Life among the Early Mill Girls* 365
A Description of Factory Life by an Associationist, 1846 366
Charles Dickens, *American Notes*, 1842 366
Catherine Beale, quoted in *Slave Testimony* 373
Wes Brady, quoted in *Remembering Slavery* 375
Frederick Douglass, *Narrative of the Life*
    *of Frederick Douglass* 376
Henry Clay, *The Life and Speeches of Henry Clay* 379
Thomas Cobb, quoted in *Henry Clay:*
    *Statesman for the Union* 382
James Monroe, The Monroe Doctrine 385
Thomas Jefferson, April 22, 1820 389

## Chapter 12

Margaret Bayard Smith, *The First Forty*
    *Years of Washington Society* 395
Daniel Webster, a speech in the U.S.
    Senate, January 26, 1830 400
Anonymous traveler, quoted in the *Advocate* 403
John G. Burnett, quoted in *The Native Americans,*
    edited by Betty and Ian Ballantine 406
Martin Van Buren, from a letter to Congress
    dated September 4, 1837 409
Martin Van Buren, from a letter to Congress
    dated September 5, 1837 415

## Chapter 13

Jim Clyman, quoted in *The West*, by Geoffrey C. Ward 419
Ezra Meeker, pioneer 422
Mary Austin Holley, *Texas: Observations Historical,*
    *Geographical and Descriptive*, 1833 427
Attributed to Mexican Soldier José Maria
    Sanchez, April 1828 428
Stephen Austin, ca. 1837 428
James K. Polk, Inaugural Address, 1845 433
John O'Sullivan, *The Annals of America*, Vol 7 434
Elizabeth Keegan 444
Frederick Douglass, in *The North Star,* January 21, 1848 447

## Chapter 14

John Downe, letter to his wife, August 12, 1830 451
Mary Lyon, letter, October 7, 1836 457
Harriet Hanson, quoted in Howard Zinn's
    *A People's History of the United States* 459
Dorothea Dix, Report to the Massachusetts
    Legislature 462
Frances Ellen Watkins Harper, "The Slave Mother" 465
Declaration of Sentiments and Resolutions, 1848 469
Frederick Douglass, 1852 475

## Chapter 15

Alexis de Tocqueville, *Journey to America* 481
Harriet Beecher Stowe, *Uncle Tom's Cabin* 485
Abraham Lincoln, Springfield, Illinois, June 16, 1858 495
Mary Boykin Chesnut, *A Diary from Dixie* 499
Abraham Lincoln, First Inaugural Address 504
E. B. Heyward, South Carolina, Nov. 20, 1860 507

## Chapter 16

Emma Holmes, *The Diary of*
    *Miss Emma Holmes, 1861–1866* 511
Major Peter Vredenburgh, Jr., quoted in
    *Upon the Tented Field* 517
William Keesy, quoted in *The Civil War Infantryman* 519
Sarah Morgan, *The Civil War Diary of a*
    *Southern Woman* 523
John B. Gordon, quoted in *Voices of the Civil War* 529
General George McClellan, quoted in
    *Civil War Journal: The Leaders* 533

## Chapter 17

Frederick Douglass, quoted in *Battle Cry of Freedom* 537
Abraham Lincoln, from the *Emancipation Proclamation* 538
Agnes, quoted in *Reminiscences of Peace and War* 543
Union officer, quoted in *Sherman: Fighting Prophet* 544
Tillie Pierce, quoted in *War Between Brothers* 549
Walt Whitman, *This Dust Was Once the Man* 559
Booker T. Washington, *Up from Slavery* 562
Abraham Lincoln, The Gettysburg Address (1863) 563
Abraham Lincoln, Second Inaugural Address (1865) 564
Frederick Douglass, quoted in *Passages to Freedom* 567

## Chapter 18

Thaddeus Stevens, the *Congressional Globe,*
    December 18, 1865 571
B., *The New National Era,* July 23, 1874 577
Bayley Wyat, quoted in *Reconstruction:*
    *America's Unfinished Revolution* 579
Robert B. Elliott, quoted in *The Glorious Failure* 583
Joseph Rainey, quoted in *The Trouble They Seen* 585
U.S. Representative Robert Elliott of South Carolina 591

# HISTORICAL MAPS

| | |
|---|---|
| Land and Resources | A9 |
| Climate Zones | A10 |
| Destruction of Original Forests | A15 |
| Domestic Migration, 2000–2004 | A16 |
| The Atlantic World, 1490 | 3 |
| The Americas Before 1500 | 7 |
| Africa, 1100–1500 | 14 |
| North America | 25 |
| Columbus' Explorations, 1492–1504 | 29 |
| Treaty of Tordesillas | 30 |
| European Exploration of the Americas, 1500–1550 | 30 |
| Hudson's Explorations | 36 |
| European Settlements in the Americas, 1650 | 38 |
| Spain's American Empire, 1700 | 42 |
| Jamestown and Roanoke, 1607 | 59 |
| New England Colonies, 1630 | 69 |
| New England Colonies, 1640 | 72 |
| Southern Colonies, 1740 | 80 |
| New Netherland | 82 |
| American Colonies, 1740 | 86 |
| Colonial Trade Routes, 1750 | 93 |
| The New England Colonies, 1750 | 96 |
| The Southern Colonies, 1750 | 107 |
| Middle Colonies, 1750 | 113 |
| The Backcountry, 1750 | 118 |
| Eastern North America, 1750 | 125 |
| French and Indian War | 145 |
| Comparing Prewar and Postwar Boundaries, 1754–1763 | 146 |
| Boston, 1775 | 155 |
| News of the Fighting Spreads | 178 |
| Revolutionary America | 193 |
| War in the Middle States, 1776–1777 | 198 |
| War in the North, 1777 | 200 |
| War on the Frontier, 1778–1779 | 209 |
| War in the South, 1778–1781 | 215 |
| Battle of Yorktown, 1781 | 216 |
| Comparing Prewar and Postwar Boundaries, 1775–1781 | 225 |
| U.S. Population, 1790 | 233 |
| Western Land Claims, 1789 | 237 |
| Slave Population, 1790 | 246 |
| Ratification in the Middle States, 1790 | 258 |
| Early America, 1776–1800 | 311 |
| Trans-Appalachian West, 1791–1795 | 320 |
| Map of North America Drawn in 1802 | 337 |
| Lewis and Clark, 1804–1807 | 347 |
| Pike's Route | 349 |
| The War of 1812 | 355 |
| Transportation Systems, 1814 | 363 |
| The Cotton Kingdom, 1840 | 375 |
| The Missouri Compromise, 1820–1821 | 382 |
| Settled Areas, 1800–1830 | 393 |
| Removal of Southeast Tribes, 1820–1840 | 405 |
| The Western Wilderness, 1850s | 417 |
| Trails West, 1850 | 421 |
| Texas Revolution, 1836 | 431 |
| Oregon Territory, 1846 | 434 |
| The War with Mexico, 1846–1847 | 435 |
| Growth of the United States, 1783–1853 | 436 |
| Emigration to America, 1831–1860 | 449 |
| Underground Railroad | 467 |
| North-South Divide, 1846 | 479 |
| Election of 1860 | 500 |
| Secession, 1860–1861 | 507 |
| The Early Years of the War, 1861–1862 | 509 |
| States Choose Sides, 1861 | 513 |
| The Civil War, 1861–1862 | 524 |
| Major Battles, 1862 | 525 |
| Battles in the East, 1862 | 526 |
| The Confederacy Falls, 1863–1865 | 535 |
| Battle of Gettysburg, 1863 | 551 |
| Vicksburg and Sherman's March, 1863–1864 | 553 |
| Grant's Virginia Campaign, 1864–1865 | 554 |
| The Struggle for Vicksburg, 1863 | 556 |
| Farmland in the South | 569 |
| Southern Military Districts, 1867 | 574 |

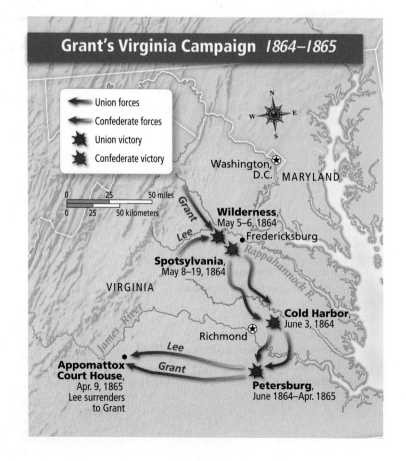

## Grant's Virginia Campaign *1864–1865*

Union forces
Confederate forces
Union victory
Confederate victory

0   25   50 miles
0   25   50 kilometers

Washington, D.C.  MARYLAND

Grant

Wilderness, May 5–6, 1864

Lee

Fredericksburg

Rappahannock R.

Spotsylvania, May 8–19, 1864

VIRGINIA

Cold Harbor, June 3, 1864

Richmond

James River

Lee

Grant

Appomattox Court House, Apr. 9, 1865 Lee surrenders to Grant

Petersburg, June 1864–Apr. 1865

## Graphs

| | |
|---|---|
| Slaves Imported to the Americas, 1451–1810 | 54 |
| Population of the 13 Colonies, 1650–1750 | 90 |
| Comparing Slave Populations | 105 |
| Ethnic Groups in the Middle Colonies | 115 |
| Slave Importation Estimates, 1701–1750 | 122 |
| New England Exports | 123 |
| American Casualties, 1775–1783 | 230 |
| Financial Problems, 1789–1791 | 334 |
| U.S. Presidential Election, 1796 | 335 |
| Foreign Trade, 1800–1812 | 361 |
| The Cotton Kingdom, 1840 | 375 |
| Southeastern People Relocated | 405 |
| Population of United States and West of Appalachia | 446 |
| Foreign-Born Population, 1860 | 453 |
| Northern and Southern Inflation | 545 |
| African Americans and Women in Congress | 584 |
| National Debt, 1861–1869 | 590 |

## Tables and Charts

| | |
|---|---|
| Sedentary, Semisedentary, and Nonsedentary Civilizations | 7 |
| Founding the Colonies | 87 |
| Powers Granted and Denied Congress | 236 |
| Comparing Plans for Government | 245 |
| Goals of the Preamble | 266 |
| Comparing Federal Office Terms and Requirements | 268 |
| Views of Democracy | 398 |
| California Water Rights | 443 |
| Comparing Push and Pull Factors | 452 |
| Comparing Southern Agriculture | 579 |

## Essential Question Charts

| | |
|---|---|
| Chapter 1 Essential Question Chart | 19 |
| Chapter 2 Essential Question Chart | 51 |
| Chapter 3 Essential Question Chart | 88 |
| Chapter 4 Essential Question Chart | 119 |
| Chapter 5 Essential Question Chart | 147 |
| Chapter 6 Essential Question Chart | 182 |
| Chapter 7 Essential Question Chart | 218 |
| Chapter 8 Essential Question Chart | 253 |
| Chapter 9 Essential Question Chart | 331 |
| Chapter 10 Essential Question Chart | 356 |
| Chapter 11 Essential Question Chart | 383 |
| Chapter 12 Essential Question Chart | 411 |
| Chapter 13 Essential Question Chart | 442 |
| Chapter 14 Essential Question Chart | 470 |
| Chapter 15 Essential Question Chart | 503 |
| Chapter 16 Essential Question Chart | 528 |
| Chapter 17 Essential Question Chart | 561 |
| Chapter 18 Essential Question Chart | 587 |

## Timelines

| | |
|---|---|
| Chapter 1 Opener | 2 |
| Chapter 2 Opener | 24 |
| Chapter 3 Opener | 58 |
| Chapter 4 Opener | 92 |
| Chapter 5 Opener | 124 |
| Chapter 6 Opener | 154 |
| Chapter 7 Opener | 192 |
| Chapter 8 Opener | 232 |
| Constitutional Amendments | 296 |
| Chapter 9 Opener | 310 |
| Chapter 10 Opener | 336 |
| Chapter 11 Opener | 362 |
| Technology of the Time | 368 |
| Chapter 12 Opener | 392 |
| Chapter 13 Opener | 416 |
| Chapter 14 Opener | 448 |
| Chapter 15 Opener | 478 |
| Chapter 16 Opener | 508 |
| Chapter 17 Opener | 534 |
| Wars and Social Change | 546 |
| Chapter 18 Opener | 568 |

## Infographics

| | |
|---|---|
| The Columbian Exchange | 44 |
| Religion in the Early Colonies | 78 |
| Colonial Governments | 140 |
| Paying for the War | 224 |
| How a Bill Becomes a Law | 270 |
| Electoral College | 276 |
| Checks and Balances | 281 |
| Federal and State Powers | 282 |
| Amending the Constitution | 283 |
| How Banks Work | 316 |
| The Business Cycle | 410 |
| Investment | 482 |
| Election of 1856 | 492 |
| Comparing Contract System and Sharecropping | 580 |

# Reading for Understanding

These pages explain how the *American History* chapters are organized. By using the four key strategies on the right, you will become a more successful reader of history, and more knowledgeable about your state's standards.

**Take a look at each strategy, using pages from Chapter 7, *The American Revolution*.**

## FOUR STEPS TO BEING A STRATEGIC READER

1. **Set a Purpose for Reading**
2. **Build Your Social Studies Vocabulary**
3. **Use Active Reading Strategies**
4. **Check Your Understanding**

## ① Set a Purpose for Reading

**Key features at the beginning of each chapter help you set a purpose for reading.**

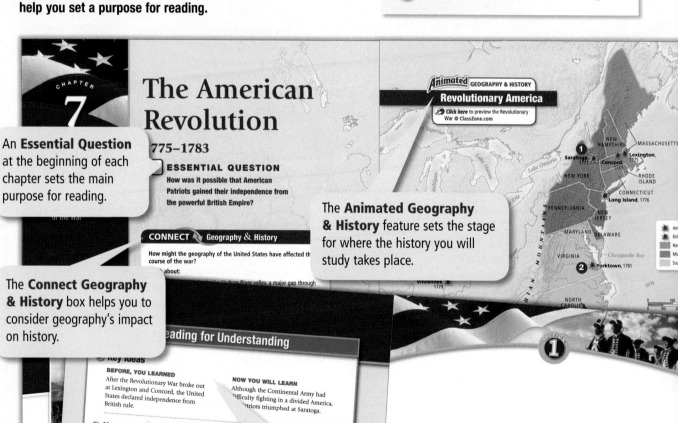

### CHAPTER 7

# The American Revolution
### 1775–1783

**ESSENTIAL QUESTION**
How was it possible that American Patriots gained their independence from the powerful British Empire?

**CONNECT** Geography & History

How might the geography of the United States have affected the course of the war?

**Animated GEOGRAPHY & HISTORY**
**Revolutionary America**
*Click here* to preview the Revolutionary War @ ClassZone.com

An **Essential Question** at the beginning of each chapter sets the main purpose for reading.

The **Animated Geography & History** feature sets the stage for where the history you will study takes place.

The **Connect Geography & History** box helps you to consider geography's impact on history.

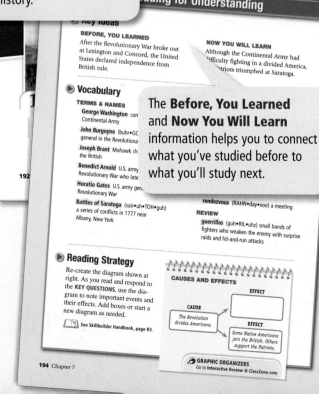

## Reading for Understanding

### Key Ideas

**BEFORE, YOU LEARNED**
After the Revolutionary War broke out at Lexington and Concord, the United States declared independence from British rule.

**NOW YOU WILL LEARN**
Although the Continental Army had difficulty fighting in a divided America, Patriots triumphed at Saratoga.

### Vocabulary

**TERMS & NAMES**
**George Washington** com... Continental Army

**John Burgoyne** (buhr•GO... general in the Revolutiona...

**Joseph Brant** Mohawk ch... the British

**Benedict Arnold** U.S. army... Revolutionary War who late...

**Horatio Gates** U.S. army gen... Revolutionary War

**Battles of Saratoga** (sair•uh•TOH•guh) a series of conflicts in 1777 near Albany, New York

**rendezvous** (RAHN•day•voo) a meeting

**REVIEW**
**guerrillas** (guh•RIL•uhz) small bands of fighters who weaken the enemy with surprise raids and hit-and-run attacks

### Reading Strategy

Re-create the diagram shown at right. As you read and respond to the **KEY QUESTIONS**, use the diagram to note important events and their effects. Add boxes or start a new diagram as needed.

See Skillbuilder Handbook, page R3.

**CAUSES AND EFFECTS**

**CAUSE**
The Revolution divides Americans.

**EFFECT**

**EFFECT**
Some Native Americans join the British. Others support the Patriots.

**GRAPHIC ORGANIZERS**
Go to Interactive Review @ ClassZone.com

The **Before, You Learned** and **Now You Will Learn** information helps you to connect what you've studied before to what you'll study next.

Each topic covered in the chapter is followed by a ▶ **Key Question** that sets your purpose for reading about that topic.

...end during the Bo... ea Party. Copley's wi... (in the blue dress) l... r infant son during the siege of Boston. In t... ckground stands Copley himself—an America... o became one of the great... est painters in the B... Empire.

Copley was bor... d raised in Boston. Before the war, he left Bo... to study overseas. When he received news of t... ghting in America, he wrote to his half-brothe...

**PRIMARY SO... CE**

❝ Could anythi... e more fortunate than the time of my leavin... oston? Poor America. I hope for the best, but I fear the worst. Yet c... ain I am she will finally emerge from her present calamity and become... mighty empire. ❞

—John Singleton Copley, letter to Henry Pelham

*The Copley Family, by John Singleton Copley*

Copley wo... ried about his family as he traveled through Europe. Eventually, he foun... them safe in London. They had arrived with the first wave of Loyalist ref... gees. Copley painted this portrait after their reunion.

### Americans Divided

▶ **KEY QUESTION** In what ways was the Revolution like a civil war?

The issue of separating from Britain divided American society. Historians estimate that 20 to 30 percent of Americans were Loyalists, 40 to 45 percent were Patriots, and the rest were **neutral**, or not favoring any one side.

## ② Build Your Social Studies Vocabulary

The Reading for Understanding pages provide three important ways to build your vocabulary.

The **Terms & Names** cover the most important events, people, places, and social studies concepts in the section.

**Visual Vocabulary** features provide visual support for some definitions.

The **Background Vocabulary** lists words you need to know in order to understand the basic concepts and ideas discussed in the section.

### ② Reading f

#### ▶ Key Ideas

**BEFORE, YOU LEARNED**
Despite the Continental Army's difficulties, the Patriots triumphed at Saratoga.

Br... by forcing them to spread their m... ry resources around the world.

#### ▶ Vocabulary

**TERMS & NAMES**

**Marquis de Lafayette** (mahr•KEE•deh laf•eye•EHT) French aristocrat who volunteered to serve in Washington's army

**Valley Forge** site in southeast Pennsylvania where Washington and his army camped in the winter of 1777–1778

**George Rogers Clark** frontiersman who helped defend the Western frontier

**John Paul Jones** sea commander who attacked British ships near the British coast

**Wilderness Road** a trail into Kentucky

**BACKGROUND VOCABULARY**

**ally** (AL•eye) a country that agrees to help another country achieve a common goal

**desert** (duh•ZERT) to leave military duty without permission

**privateer** (pry•vuh•TEER) a privately owned ship that has been granted permission by a wartime government to attack an enemy's merchant ships

Visual Vocabulary
privateer

photograph courtesy of Peabody Essex Museum

#### ▶ Reading Strategy

Recreate the diagram shown at right. As you read and respond to the **KEY QUESTIONS**, use the center box to record the main idea; use the outer ovals to note important details. Add ovals or start a new diagram as needed.

📖 See Skillbuilder Handbook, page R2.

**MAIN IDEAS AND DETAILS**

Other nations join the war.

The War Expands

**GRAPHIC ORGANIZERS**
Go to **Interactive Review @ ClassZone.com**

**204** Chapter 7

---

**Connecting History**

**Expansion**
Europeans would continue to settle and claim lands in the West until they reached the Pacific Ocean. You will see this theme emerge when you study westward expansion in later chapters.

**Ame...**
and his men set out for Vincennes from K...
...ilton wasn't expecting an attack because th...
But Clark's men slogged through miles o...
chest-deep water. They caught the British...

When Hamilton and his troops trie...
pretended to have a larger force than he re...
Native American allies of the British in pla...
to do the same to the British unless they s...
gave up.

Clark's victory gave the Americans a...
the Great Lakes and the Ohio River (ever...
remained in the hands of the British). Thi...
size of the original 13 states. The expansi...
had another consequence: it forced the B...
over a larger area and further weakened t...

🔺 **CAUSES AND EFFECTS** Explain why the war spread to the frontier.

### War on the Waves

🔻 **KEY QUESTION** How did Americans expand the naval w...

The war expanded not only west into the frontier bu...
high seas. By 1777, Britain had over 200 warships off th...
allowed Britain to control the Atlantic trade routes to...

**Terms & Names** and **Background Vocabulary** are highlighted and defined in the main text so that you'll understand them as you read and study.

**British Trade Disrupted** Because the America...
Congress encouraged American **privateers** to attack B...
A privateer is a privately owned ship...
permission by a wartime governmen...
merchant ships. After capturing a... the crew of
a privateer sold its cargo and ... d the money.
America commissioned more ... n 1,000 privateer...
to prey on the British. The... ...ptured hundreds o...
ships, causing British m... chants to call on their
government to end t!... war.

Though outnum!... ered, the Continental Navy
scored several victories. A daring officer named
**John Paul Jones** inspired Americans by sailing
across the Atlantic to attack British ships along
the coast of Britain itself.

**"I Have Not Yet Begun to Fight"** In 1779,
Jones became the commander of a ship named
*Bonhomme Richard*. With four other ships, he
patrolled the English coast. In September, Jones's
vessels approached a convoy in which two British
warships were guarding a number of supply ships.

James Forten, who later became famous for his efforts to end slavery, joined a privateer at the age of 14.

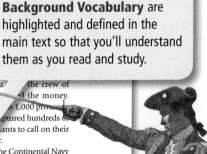

# READING FOR UNDERSTANDING

## ③ Use Active Reading Strategies

Active reading strategies help you note the most important information in each section.

**(A)** **Reading Strategy** Each Reading for Understanding page contains a Reading Strategy diagram to help you track and organize the information you read.

**(B)** **Skillbuilder Handbook** Every Reading Strategy is supported by a corresponding lesson in the Skillbuilder Handbook at the back of this book.

**(C)** **Active Reading Strategies** in the Skillbuilder Handbook will help you to read and study *American History*.

---

**BACKGROUND VOCABULARY**
**redoubt** (re•DOWT) a small fort

**Battle of Charles Town** British siege of Charles Town (Charleston), South Carolina, in May 1780, in which the Americans suffered their worst defeat of the war

**Lord Cornwallis** (korn•WAHL•ihs) British general whose campaigns in the South led to his defeat at Yorktown

**Battle of Yorktown** final battle of the war, in which French and American forces led by George Washington defeated British General Cornwallis

**Visual Vocabulary**
redoubt at Yorktown

▶ **Reading Strategy**

Re-create the diagram shown at right. As you read and respond to the **KEY QUESTIONS**, use the diagram to record important events in the order in which they occurred.

📖 **See Skillbuilder Handbook, page R5.**

**(A)**

**SEQUENCE EVENTS**

| British capture Savannah, 1778. | British capture Charles Town, 1780. | |
|---|---|---|

| | British capture Georgia. | |
|---|---|---|

**GRAPHIC ORGANIZERS**
Go to **Interactive Review @ ClassZone.com**

**212** Chapter 7

---

## Skillbuilder Handbook

**(B)** ### Table of Contents

**Reading and Critical Thinking**

1.1 Taking Notes with Graphic Organizers
1.2 Summarizing
1.3 Finding Main Ideas
1.4 Sequencing Events
1.5 Categorizing
1.6 Analyzing Causes and Effects
1.7 Comparing and Contrasting
1.8 Identifying Problems and Solutions
1.9 Making Inferences
1.10 Making Generalizations
1.11 Drawing Conclusions
1.12 Making Decisions
1.13 Evaluating
1.14 Analyzing Point of View
1.15 Distinguishing Fact from Opinion
1.16 Analyzing Primary Sources
1.17 Recognizing Bias and Propaganda
1.18 Synthesizing

**Reading Maps, Graphs, and Other Visu**

2.1 Reading Maps
2.2 Reading Graphs and Charts
2.3 Analyzing Political Cartoons
2.4 Creating a Map
2.5 Creating a Model

**Research, Writing, and Presentation S**

3.1 Formulating Historical Questions
3.2 Identify and Use Primary and Secondary Sources
3.3 Using a Database
3.4 Paraphrasing
3.5 Outlining
3.6 Forming and Supporting Opinions
3.7 Essay
3.8 Constructed Response
3.9 Extended Response

---

**(C)** ## 1.3 Finding Main Ideas

### Defining the Skill

The **main idea** is a statement that summarizes the main point of a speech, an article, a section of a book, or a paragraph. Main ideas can be stated or unstated. The main idea of a paragraph is often stated in the first or last sentence. If it is the first sentence, it is followed by sentences that support that main idea. If it is the last sentence, the details build up to the main idea. To find an unstated idea, you must use the details of the paragraph as clues.

### Applying the Skill

The following paragraph describes the role of women in the American Revolution. Use the strategies listed below to help you identify the main idea.

### How to Find the Main Idea

**Strategy ①** Identify what you think may be the stated main idea. Check the first and last sentences of the paragraph to see if either could be the stated main idea.

**Strategy ②** Identify details that support that idea. Some details explain the main idea. Others give examples of what is stated in the main idea.

**WOMEN IN THE REVOLUTION**

① Many women tried to help the army. Martha Washington and other wives followed their husbands to army camps. ② The wives cooked, did laundry, and nursed sick or wounded soldiers. ② A few women even helped to fight. ② Mary Hays earned the nickname "Molly Pitcher" by carrying water to tired soldiers during a battle. ② Deborah Sampson dressed as a man, enlisted, and fought in several engagements.

### Make a Chart

Making a chart can help you identify the main idea and details in a passage or paragraph. The chart below identifies the main idea and details in the paragraph you just read.

*Main Idea:* Women helped the army during the Revolution.

*Detail:* They cooked and did laundry
*Detail:* They nursed the wounded and sick soldiers
*Detail:* They helped to fight.
*Detail:* One woman, Molly Pitcher, carried water to soldiers during battles.

### Practicing the Skill

Turn to Chapter 5, Section 2, "Roots of American Democracy." Read "Parliament and Colonial Government" on page 137, and create a chart that identifies the main idea and the supporting details.

# ④ Check Your Understanding

One of the most important things you'll do as you study *American History* is to check your understanding of events, people, places, and issues as you read.

**Ⓐ Connect to the Essential Question**
This chart summarizes the information that will help you understand the most important ideas in the chapter.

**Ⓑ Interactive Review** includes a Name Game and provides two online activities to test your knowledge of the history you just studied.

**Ⓒ Section Assessment** reviews the section Terms & Names, revisits your Reading Strategy notes, and provides key questions about the section.

large segments of the population were actively involved in a poli
Even if the British had succeeded in defeating an American army,
would never have been able to conquer the American people.

## Ⓐ CONNECT ➤ to the Essential Question

How was it possible that American Patriots gained their independence from the powerful British Empire?

| AMERICAN STRENGTHS | | BRITISH WEAKNESSES |
|---|---|---|
| Patriots fought for their lives, their property, and their political ideals. | **Motivation** | The British and their Hessian mercenaries fought merely for p |
| Many civilians actively supported the Revolutio technique Rebellion | **Popular support** | The British were unprepared for popular uprising. There was no w |
| Ameri mistakes patriotism | | |
| France su and Spai expandin French m | | |
| America | | |

## Ⓑ CHAPTER 7 Interactive ✪ Review

### Chapter Summary

**① Key Idea**
Although the Continental Army had difficulty fighting in a divided America, the Patriots triumphed at Saratoga.

**② Key Idea**
The expansion of the war weakened the British by forcing them to spread their military resources around the world.

**③ Key Idea**
The Continental Army, their allies, and the American people brought about an American victory.

**④ Key Idea**
Americans emerged from the Revolution as citizens of a unified nation that valued the ideal of liberty.

To create Review and Study Notes go to **Interactive Review** @ ClassZone.com

### Name Game

Use the Terms & Names list to comple your own paper.

1. I carried the war to the western frontie George Rogers Clark
2. I led my troops to defeat at Saratoga. __
3. I was a French officer who fought for America. __
4. My leadership unified a nation. __
5. I was trapped between allied forces and the French fleet. __
6. I brought the war to the coasts of Britain. __
7. The ideal of liberty helped me win my freedom in court. __
8. I lost my lands when my ally betrayed me. __
9. Here the Patriots first proved that they mig win the war. __
10. Here the Continental Army endured a diffic winter. __

## Activities

### CROSSWORD PUZZLE

Complete the online crossword puzzle to show what you know about the American Revolution.

**ACROSS**
1. _____ captured the British warship *Serapis*.

### GEOGAME

Use this online map to reinforce your understanding including the locations of important battles and geo drop each place name in the list at its location on th you keep track of your progress online.

Trenton
Saratoga
Lake Ontario
Valley Forge
Hudson River

More place names online

---

**Defining Religious Freedom** For many Americans, central to the
liberty was the idea that religion is a private matter and that people
have the right to choose and practice their personal religious beliefs
such as James Madison and Thomas Jefferson called for a "sepa
church and state," meaning that the state should not be involved in
affairs.

In 1777 Thomas Jefferson proposed his **Virginia Statute for Religious**
In it, he claimed that people have a "natural right" to freedom o
including religious opinion. Jefferson opposed state laws that p
Jews or Catholics from holding public office. He also opposed the
using tax money to support churches, because, he wrote, "to com
to furnish contributions of money for the propagation of opini
he disbelieves, is sinful and tyrannical."

Jefferson's statute was eventually adopted as law in Virgin
became the basis of the religious rights guaranteed by the Bill
the U.S. Constitution.

**Uniting the States** For almost two centuries each colony ha
erned independently of its neighbors. The colonies had been
and often uncooperative. However, as the war turned colonie
Americans saw how important it was for these states to work
nation. The great challenge that lay ahead was how to remai
nation of independent states, despite regional and religious d

🔺 **SUMMARIZE** Describe the ideals that emerged from the Revoluti

## Ⓒ

**ONLINE Q**
For test practi
Interactive

**TERMS & NAMES**
1. Explain the importance of
   • Treaty of Paris        • Richard Allen
   • Elizabeth Freeman   • Virginia Statute for Religious Freedom

**USING YOUR READING NOTES**
2. **Categorize** List and categorize the major results of the Revolutionary War.

**KEY IDEAS**
3. What groups gained least from
4. How did the goals of the Revol toward a more just society afte

**CRITICAL THINKING**
5. **Connect Economics & History** Treaty of Paris protect America's economic interests?
6. **Causes and Effects** How did the Patriot victory affect Native Americans?
7. **Historical Perspective** What might have happened if, during the peace negotiations, each state had tried to negotiate independently?
8. **Writing** **Citizenship Report** Use the Internet

## Themes of American History

Themes are ideas and issues that arise and reappear through American history. Understanding these themes will help you to connect the past and the present and to make sense of U.S. history. *American History* focuses on nine of these themes.

### Democratic Ideals

Americans have built their society around the principles of democracy. In a democracy, power lies with the people, and every individual enjoys basic rights that cannot be taken away. Throughout the nation's history, however, some Americans— mainly women and minorities—have had to struggle to gain their full rights. Still, the ideals of democracy remain the guiding principles of this land.

### Citizenship

The citizens of the United States enjoy rights and freedoms found in very few other places in the world. Yet Americans know that with such freedoms come responsibilities and duties. Whether they stand in line to vote or spend a weekend to clean up a local river, Americans recognize that citizen participation is what keeps a democracy strong.

### Diversity and Unity

The United States has been a land of many peoples, cultures, and faiths. Throughout the nation's history, this blend of ethnic, racial, and religious groups has helped to create a rich and uniquely American culture. The nation's many different peoples are united in their belief in American values and ideals.

### Impact of the Individual

The history of the United States is the story not only of governments and laws but of individuals. Indeed, individuals have made the United States what it is today through their extraordinary and ordinary achievements. American history provides a variety of examples of the impact of the individual on society in both the United States and the world.

### Immigration and Migration

This country was settled by and has remained a magnet for immigrants. Also, within the United States, large numbers of people have migrated to different regions of the country. However, movements to and within the United States have not always been voluntary. Africans were brought against their will to this country. Native Americans were forced from their homelands in order to make room for European settlers.

Martin Luther King, Jr.

## Economics in History

Economics has had a powerful impact on the course of U.S. history. For example, the desire for wealth led thousands to join the California Gold Rush in 1849. The nation as a whole has grown wealthy, thanks to its abundant resources and the hard work of its citizens. An important economic issue, however, has been how to make sure that all people have opportunities to share fully in the nation's wealth. This issue will continue to be important in the 21st century.

**Mid-1800s telegraph**

## Science and Technology

Americans have always been quick to embrace inventions and new ways of doing things. After all, this country was settled by people who turned away from old ways and tried new ones. In the past two centuries, new inventions, new technologies, and scientific breakthroughs have transformed the United States—and will continue to do so in our lifetimes and beyond.

## America and the World

As the power and influence of the United States have grown, the nation has played a much more active role in world affairs. Indeed, throughout the 20th century, the United States focused much of its energy on events beyond its borders. The nation fought in two world wars and tried to promote democracy, peace, and economic growth around the globe. As one of the world's political and economic leaders, the United States continues to be a key player in world affairs.

## Expansion

When the United States declared its independence from Great Britain, it was only a collection of states along the Atlantic Ocean. But the new country would not remain that way for long. Many Americans shared a sense of curiosity, adventure, and a strong belief that their destiny was to expand all the way to the Pacific Ocean. Driven by this belief, they pushed westward. Americans' efforts to increase the size of their nation is a recurring theme in early U.S. history.

## Exploring History Online

***American History*** provides a variety of tools to help you explore history online. See history come to life in the Animation Center. Find help for your research projects in the Research and Writing Center. Review for tests with the Interactive Review, or create your own activities in the Activity Center. Go to ClassZone.com to make *American History* interactive!

## ClassZone.com

is your gateway to exploring history. Explore the different **ClassZone Centers** to help you study and have fun with history.

**A** **Interactive Review** provides you with flip cards, a crossword puzzle, section quizzes, drag-and-drop map activities, and more.

**B** **Activity Center** You'll find a variety of interactive tools that will help you engage with history *your* way.

**C** **Activity Maker** lets you create your own activities so that you can focus on what *you* need to review.

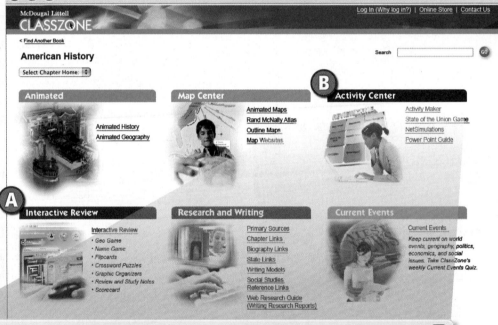

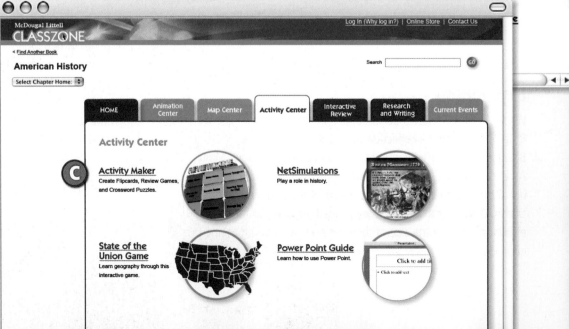

# Animation Center

A rich collection of interactive features and maps on a wide variety of historical eras and topics

**A** **Roll-overs**
Explore the illustration by clicking on areas you'd like to know more about. This Battle Tactics animation links to features about tactics, cannon loading, a soldier's gear, and more.

**B** **3D models**
Study this soldier's gear by rotating the 3D model.

**C** **In-depth Views and Information**
Click each box to find out what a soldier carried during the war.

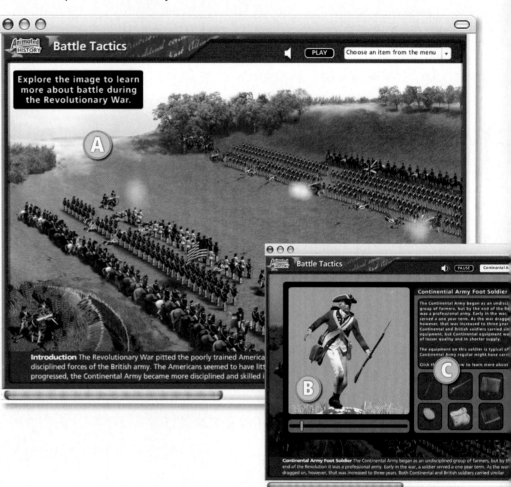

# Review Game

- Create your own review game to study history *your* way.

- Select your own topics from any chapter to help you focus on specific people, places, or events to review.

- Help your friends to explore history online. Challenge them to play a review game that you create and modify!

# NEW JERSEY

NEW JERSEY CORE CURRICULUM CONTENT STANDARDS

## STEPS TO SUCCESS

*Guide to Understanding*

**New Jersey's Core Curriculum Content Standards for Social Studies** NJ31

- New Jersey's Core Curriculum Content Standards for Social Studies are organized into six standards. Each standard includes strands that are divided into cumulative progress indicators.

*Guide to*

**Test-Taking Strategies and Practice** S1

- These test-taking strategies and practice are designed to help you tackle many of the items you will find on a standardized test.

 For a complete list of the New Jersey Core Curriculum Content Standards for Social Studies, see page R81.

Ocean City Beach, Ocean City, New Jersey © Corbis

TEST-TAKING STRATEGIES AND PRACTICE

# Why Study History?

When you study U.S. history, you will see how the past informs your everyday life. Many things, such as the clothes you wear and the music you listen to, have been influenced by America's past.

Learn how to think like a historian! Dive into the dramatic events of America's past and uncover the lives of the people who shaped our nation's history.

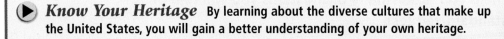

▶ *Be An Informed Citizen*  Your textbook will show you how the United States were founded, and how our current government came into existence.

Your textbook will also encourage you to be a more active participant in your community and to make a difference in our nation's future.

▶ *Become a Better Critical Thinker*  Many questions throughout this book will encourage you to form your own opinion.

For example, what would *you* have done during the Civil War if fighting for what you believed in meant fighting against your own family?

▶ *Know Your Heritage*  By learning about the diverse cultures that make up the United States, you will gain a better understanding of your own heritage.

# *What Will I Learn?*

*Guide to Understanding*
## New Jersey's Core Curriculum Content Standards for Social Studies

New Jersey's Core Curriculum Content Standards for Social Studies are organized into six standards.

| | |
|---|---|
| **6.1** | **Social Studies Skills** |
| **6.2** | **Civics** |
| **6.3** | **World History** |
| **6.4** | **United States and New Jersey History** |
| **6.5** | **Economics** |
| **6.6** | **Geography** |

Each standard includes strands that are divided into cumulative progress indicators.

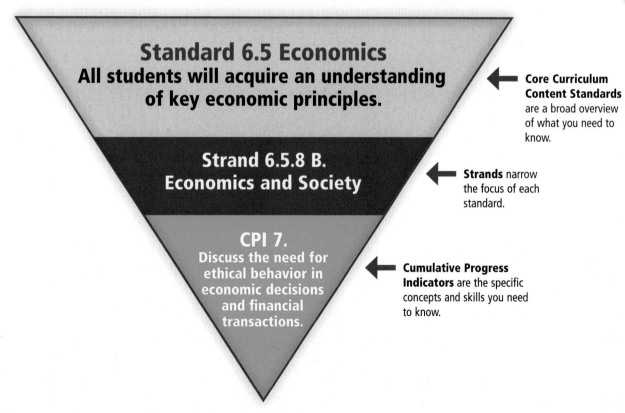

**Standard 6.5 Economics**
**All students will acquire an understanding of key economic principles.**

← **Core Curriculum Content Standards** are a broad overview of what you need to know.

**Strand 6.5.8 B.**
**Economics and Society**

← **Strands** narrow the focus of each standard.

**CPI 7.**
Discuss the need for ethical behavior in economic decisions and financial transactions.

← **Cumulative Progress Indicators** are the specific concepts and skills you need to know.

## Overview
# New Jersey Core Curriculum Content Standards for Social Studies

The charts that follow provide a brief overview of each standard and its strands and cumulative progress indicators. The cumulative progress indicators are the concepts and skills addressed by each strand. Look for them at the beginning of each section.

For a full list of the New Jersey Core Curriculum Content Standards for Social Studies, see page R81.

---

**6.1**  **SOCIAL STUDIES SKILLS: All students will utilize historical thinking, problem solving, and research skills to maximize their understanding of civics, history, geography, and economics.**

| Strand and Cumulative Progress Indicators | What It Means to *You* |
| --- | --- |
| **6.1.8 A. Social Studies Skills**<br><br>1. Analyze how events are related over time.<br><br>2. Use critical thinking skills to interpret events, recognize bias, point of view, and context.<br><br>10. Distinguish fact from fiction by comparing sources about figures and events with fictionalized characters and events. | • Social studies skills provide the basis to understand and appreciate the knowledge gained through the other five standards.<br><br>• The ability to see how events are related, recognize bias, and distinguish fact from fiction is crucial to the study of people, places, events, and issues. |

---

**6.2**  **CIVICS: All students will know, understand and appreciate the values and principles of American democracy and the rights, responsibilities, and roles of a citizen in the nation and the world.**

| Strand and Cumulative Progress Indicators | What It Means to *You* |
| --- | --- |
| **6.2.8 C. The Constitution and American Democracy**<br><br>1. Discuss the major principles of the Constitution, including shared powers, checks and balances, separation of church and state, and federalism.<br><br>2. Compare and contrast the purposes, organization, functions, and interactions of the legislative, executive, and judicial branches of national, state, and local governments and independent regulatory agencies. | • Preparing informed, active, and responsible citizens is an important goal of social studies education.<br><br>• Understanding the historical foundations, values, and principles of the United States system of government prepares us to make effective choices as voters, workers, consumers, and members of our local, state, and national communities. |

**WORLD HISTORY: All students will demonstrate knowledge of world history in order to understand life and events in the past and how they relate to the present and the future.**

| Strand and Cumulative Progress Indicators | What It Means to *You* |
| --- | --- |
| **6.3.8 D. The Age of Global Encounters (1400–1750)**<br><br>1. Discuss factors that contributed to oceanic travel and exploration in the 15th and 16th centuries, including technological innovations in ship building, navigation, naval warfare, navigational inventions such as the compass, and the impact of wind currents on the major trade routes. | • In the 1400s, Europeans sailed from their shores in search of distant lands. Curiosity as well as a desire for new markets and wealth gave them courage, and new sailing technologies made their voyages possible. These voyages laid the foundation for the world we live in today. |

**UNITED STATES AND NEW JERSEY HISTORY: All students will demonstrate knowledge of United States and New Jersey history in order to understand life and events in the past and how they relate to the present and future.**

| Strand and Cumulative Progress Indicators | What It Means to *You* |
| --- | --- |
| **6.4.8 F. Expansion and Reform (1801–1861)**<br><br>1. Describe the political, economic, and social changes in New Jersey and American society preceding the Civil War, including the early stages of industrialization, the growth of cities, and the political, legal, and social controversies surrounding the expansion of slavery.<br><br>8. Discuss sectional compromises associated with westward expansion of slavery, such as the Missouri Compromise (1820) and the continued resistance to slavery by African Americans (e.g., Amistad Revolt). | • The North and the South developed different economic systems that led to political differences between the regions. While the North industrialized, the South relied on agriculture. This reliance on agriculture fueled the growth of slavery in the South. As the country expanded westward, the spread of slavery became a matter of debate that eventually led to war. The Civil War ended slavery, but different regions of the country continue to have differing political and economic interests today. |

 **6.5**  **ECONOMICS: All students will acquire an understanding of key economic principles.**

| Strand and Cumulative Progress Indicators | What It Means to *You* |
| --- | --- |
| **6.5.8 A. Economic Literacy** 1. Discuss how needs and wants change as one ages and the impact of planning, spending and saving. 2. Explain the law of supply and demand. 3. Compare ways to save money, including checking and savings accounts, stocks and bonds, and the relationship between risk and return in investments. 4. Describe the role credit plays in the economy and explain the difference in cost between cash and credit purchases. | • We are called on to make economic decisions every day as consumers, producers, savers, and investors. Our decision-making is improved if we understand economic concepts and their applications. • Understanding economic concepts helps us plan our careers, manage our finances, and deal with an increasingly global economy. |

 **6.6**  **GEOGRAPHY: All students will apply knowledge of spatial relationships and other geographic skills to understand human behavior in relation to the physical and cultural environment.**

| Strand and Cumulative Progress Indicators | What It Means to *You* |
| --- | --- |
| **6.6.8 A. The World in Spatial Terms** 1. Distinguish among the distinct charcteristics of maps, globes, graphs, charts, diagrams, and other geographical representations, and the utility of each in solving problems. 2. Translate maps into appropriate spatial graphics to display geographical information. 3. Explain the spatial concepts of relative and absolute location and distance. | • Maps, globes, graphs, charts, and diagrams are effective ways to represent and compare geographical and historical information. They allow you to quickly see relationships between places, events, and characteristics. Being able to use and understand these geographical tools is an important social studies skill. |

# Guide to
# TEST-TAKING STRATEGIES AND PRACTICE

This section of your book helps you develop and practice the skills you need to study history and to take standardized tests

    The **Test-Taking Strategies and Practice** offer specific strategies for tackling many of the items you'll find on a standardized test. It gives tips for answering multiple-choice, constructed-response, extended-response, and document-based questions. In addition, it offers guidelines for analyzing primary and secondary sources, maps, political cartoons, charts, graphs, and timelines. Each strategy is followed by a set of questions you can use for practice.

## CONTENTS Test-Taking Strategies and Practice

Multiple Choice . . . . . . . . . . . . . . . . . . . . . . S2

Primary Sources . . . . . . . . . . . . . . . . . . . . . S4

Secondary Sources . . . . . . . . . . . . . . . . . . . S6

Political Cartoons . . . . . . . . . . . . . . . . . . . . S8

Charts . . . . . . . . . . . . . . . . . . . . . . . . . . . . . S10

Line and Bar Graphs . . . . . . . . . . . . . . . . . . S12

Pie Graphs . . . . . . . . . . . . . . . . . . . . . . . . . . S14

Thematic Maps . . . . . . . . . . . . . . . . . . . . . . S16

Timelines . . . . . . . . . . . . . . . . . . . . . . . . . . . S18

Reading Visuals . . . . . . . . . . . . . . . . . . . . . . S20

Document-Based Questions . . . . . . . . . . . . S24

The chart below provides a guide to the test-taking strategies and practice that will help prepare you for standards-based assessments.

**Find online test practice @ ClassZone.com**

- **Learn** each strategy by reviewing the numbered steps on the page listed in the column.

- **Practice** the strategy on the following page.

- **Apply** the strategies you learned in the **New Jersey Standards-Based Asessment** at the end of each chapter.

| Strategy | Learn | Practice | Apply |
|---|---|---|---|
| Multiple Choice | p. S2 | p. S3 | end of every chapter |
| Primary and Secondary Sources | pp. S4, S6 | pp. S5, S7 | p. 55, Chapter 2<br>p. 231, Chapter 7<br>p. 335, Chapter 9 |
| Political Cartoons | p. S8 | p. S9 | p. 361, Chapter 10<br>p. 415, Chapter 12 |
| Charts | p. S10 | p. S11 | p. 22, Chapter 1<br>p. 334, Chapter 9 |
| Line and Bar Graphs | p. S12 | p. S13 | p. 335, Chapter 9<br>p. 361, Chapter 10 |
| Pie Graphs | p. S14 | p. S15 | p. 123, Chapter 4 |
| Thematic Maps | p. S16 | p. S17 | p. 447, Chapter 13<br>p. 507, Chapter 15<br>p. 533, Chapter 16<br>p. 591, Chapter 18 |
| Timelines | p. S18 | p. S19 | p. 360, Chapter 10 |
| Constructed and Extended Response | pp. S20, 22 | pp. S21, 23 | p. 23, Chapter 1<br>p. 55, Chapter 2<br>p. 91, Chapter 3 |
| Document-Based Questions | pp. S24–25 | pp. S26–27 | p. 231, Chapter 7<br>p. 361, Chapter 10 |

# Primary Sources

Primary sources are materials written or made by people who took part in or witnessed historical events. Letters, diaries, speeches, newspaper articles, and autobiographies are all primary sources. So, too, are legal documents, such as wills, deeds, and financial records.

**❶** Look at the source line and identify the author. Consider what qualifies the author to write about the events discussed in the passage.

**❷** Skim the document to form an idea of what it is about.

**❸** Note special punctuation. Ellipses indicate that words or sentences have been removed from the original passage. Brackets indicate words that were not in the original. Bracketed words often are replacements for difficult or unfamiliar terms.

**❹** Carefully read the passage and distinguish between facts and the author's opinions.

**❺** Consider for whom the author was writing. The intended audience may influence what and how an author writes.

**❻** Before rereading the passage, skim the questions to identify the information you need to find.

## The Flight from the White House

*Wednesday Morning, twelve o'clock.* Since sunrise I have been turning my spy-glass in every direction, . . . but alas! I can see **❸** only groups of military, wandering in all directions, as if there **❹** was a lack of arms, or of spirit to fight for their own fireside.

**❷** *Three o'clock.* Will you believe it, my sister? We have had a battle, or skirmish, near Bladensburg, and here I am still, within sound of the cannon!. . . Two messengers covered with dust come to bid me fly. . . . At this late hour a wagon has been [found], and I have had it filled with plate and the most valuable portable articles belonging to the house. Whether it will reach its destination . . . or fall into the hands of British soldiery, events must determine. Our kind friend, Mr. Carroll, has come to hasten my departure, and is in a very bad humor with me, because I insist on waiting until the large picture of General Washington is secured. . . . It is done! and the precious portrait placed in the hands of two gentlemen of New York, for safe keeping. And now, dear sister, I must leave this house. . . . When I shall again write to you, or where I shall be tomorrow, I cannot tell!

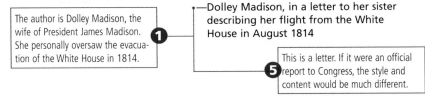

The author is Dolley Madison, the wife of President James Madison. She personally oversaw the evacuation of the White House in 1814. **❶**

—Dolley Madison, in a letter to her sister describing her flight from the White House in August 1814

This is a letter. If it were an official **❺** report to Congress, the style and content would be much different.

**❻ 1.** Dolley Madison's letter describes her preparations to flee the White House in advance of a British attack. In which war did this attack take place?

    **A.** War of Jenkins' Ear

    **B.** French and Indian War

    **C.** Revolutionary War

    **D.** War of 1812

**2.** Why might Dolley Madison be considered a good source of information on the British attack on Washington, D.C.?

    **A.** She was the wife of President James Madison.

    **B.** She was an eyewitness to the attack.

    **C.** She helped her husband develop military policy.

    **D.** She had intercepted British war plans.

answers: 1 (D), 2 (B)

**Directions:** Use this passage and your knowledge of U.S. history to answer questions 1 through 4.

### Life in Texas, Mid-1800s

I wish that I could emphasize this feature of our early Texan life. *The spirit of helpfulness and friendly fellowship always prevailed. It was one of the best of the good things of the new country.* We were all strangers together, always willing to lend or borrow. . . . Once Mr. Van Zandt was called away from home . . . [and] another man came and took our gun and killed a deer, for he knew we needed meat. . . . When our need for things was pressing, we usually found a way for making them. One time Mr. Van Zandt needed a saddle—he made it, having only a drawing knife from which to fashion the saddle-tree from a dead sassafras tree which he cut down for the purpose. His shoes were gone and he could get no others. He bought some red leather, made a last [a foot-shaped, wooden block] and manufactured some very respectable shoes.

—Frances Cook Lipscomb Van Zandt,
Texas settler, 1839–1846

1. What was a good thing about the new Texas country that the author writes was important to her?

   A. being hungry

   B. being a stranger

   C. the spirit of helpfulness and friendliness

   D. getting deer meat whenever she wanted it

2. Mr. Van Zandt used leather, wood, and simple tools to

   A. build a wagon.

   B. make goods to trade for meat.

   C. build a spinning wheel.

   D. make a saddle and shoes.

3. According to the passage, the Van Zandts and their Texas neighbors got their supplies in all of the following ways *except* by

   A. lending or borrowing things.

   B. making them by hand with simple tools.

   C. buying them from mail-order catalogs.

   D. volunteering to help each other.

4. Frances Van Zandt wrote, "We were all strangers together," to explain that hardships on the Texas frontier

   A. left people isolated and alone.

   B. drew people together to help each other.

   C. were shared only by close friends and relatives.

   D. made people suspicious of one another.

Passage from "Frances Cook Lipscomb Van Zandt Reminisces About the Early Years in Texas, 1839–1846," from the Van Zandt Folder, Mary Daggett Lake Papers, series IV, box 3, Fort Worth Public Library, Fort Worth, Texas. Courtesy of the Fort Worth Public Library, Fort Worth, Texas.

## Secondary Sources

Secondary sources are descriptions or interpretations of historical events made by people who were not at those events. The most common types of written secondary sources are history books, encyclopedias, and biographies. A secondary source often combines information from several primary sources.

**❶** Read titles to preview what the passage is about.

**❷** Look for topic sentences. These, too, will help you preview the content of the passage.

**❸** As you read, use context clues to help you understand difficult or unfamiliar words. (You can tell from the description of the battle in the previous sentences that the word *fiasco* must mean something like "disaster," "failure," or "blunder.")

**❹** As you read, ask and answer questions that come to mind. You might ask: Why did Dolley Madison take a bed with her? Why would the British burn public buildings?

**❺** Before rereading the passage, skim the questions to identify the information you need to find.

**❶ The British Offensive**

**❷** Ironically, Britain achieved a far more spectacular success in an operation originally designed as a diversion from their main thrust down Lake Champlain. In 1814 a British army sailed from Bermuda for Chesapeake Bay, landed near Washington, and met a larger American force . . . at Bladensburg, Maryland, on August 24. The Battle of Bladensburg quickly became the "Bladensburg races" as the American militia fled, almost without firing a shot. The British then descended on Washington. Madison, who had **❸** witnessed the Bladensburg fiasco escaped into the Virginia hills. His wife, Dolley, pausing only long enough to load her silver, a bed, and a portrait of George Washington onto her carriage, hastened to join her husband, while British troops ate the supper prepared for the Madisons at the presidential **❹** mansion. Then they burned the mansion and other public buildings in Washington. A few weeks later, the British attacked Baltimore, but after failing to crack its defenses, they broke off the operation.

—Paul S. Boyer, et al., *The Enduring Vision*

**❺ 1.** Why do you think the authors refer to the Battle of Bladensburg as a "fiasco"?

    **A.** because the American forces fled almost without a fight

    **B.** because President Madison had to flee the White House

    **C.** because it allowed the British to attack Washington, D.C.

    **D.** because it was a famous victory for the British forces

**2.** What, according to the authors, did the British raid on Washington, D.C., accomplish?

    **A.** It paved the way for the British capture of Baltimore.

    **B.** It drove all the American militia out of the city.

> Remember to be wary of choices that contain absolutes, such as *all, every,* or *only.*

    **C.** It helped the British offensive on Lake Champlain.

    **D.** It burned down the presidential mansion and other public buildings.

answers: 1 (A), 2 (D)

**PRACTICE**

**Directions:** Use this passage and your knowledge of U.S. history to answer questions 1 through 3.

### African-American Sailors

African Americans contributed greatly to the growth of maritime commerce in the United States. Beginning in colonial times, slaves, with their masters' permission, hired themselves out as sailors. Some served as translators on slave ships. Merchant ships also offered a means of escape for runaway slaves. A few escapees even took to the sea as pirates.

Seafaring was one of the few occupations open to free African Americans. They served on clippers, naval vessels, and whaling ships from the 1700s into the late 1800s. Federal crew lists from Atlantic seaports show that during this time, African Americans made up 10 percent or more of sailors on American ships. Seafaring was an especially dangerous line of work for free blacks. They risked capture in southern ports, where they were often thrown in jail or sold into slavery.

1. What records show that African Americans made up 10 percent or more of sailors on American ships?

   A. shipyard records
   B. family bibles
   C. federal crew lists
   D. ships' logs

2. The passage implies that free and enslaved African Americans went to sea for all of the following reasons *except* to

   A. escape slavery.
   B. live as pirates.
   C. earn wages as sailors.
   D. discover new lands.

3. The author states that life was especially dangerous for free African-American sailors because

   A. American prosperity depended on their work alone.
   B. the worst jobs on board ship were always assigned to them.
   C. they ran the risk of capture and enslavement in southern ports.
   D. they were more likely than white sailors to contract scurvy.

# Political Cartoons

Political cartoons are drawings that express views on political issues of the day. Cartoonists use symbols and such artistic styles as caricature—exaggerating a person's physical features—to get their message across.

**1** Identify the subject of the cartoon. Titles and captions often indicate the subject matter.

**2** Identify the main characters in the cartoon. Here, the main character is Horace Greeley, a candidate in the 1872 presidential election.

**3** Note the symbols—ideas or images that stand for something else—used in the cartoon.

**4** Study labels and other written information in the cartoon.

**5** Analyze the point of view. How cartoonists use caricature often indicates how they feel. The exaggeration of Greeley's physical appearance— short and overweight— makes him appear comical.

**6** Interpret the cartoonist's message.

The cartoonist shows Tammany Hall, New York's Democratic political machine, as a tiger. Uncle Sam, a symbol for the United States, is shown looking on.

The writing on the wall suggests that Tammany Hall wants reform. The "Whitewash" label on the bucket suggests that the tiger's true, corrupt, stripes are just being covered up.

Thomas Nast, *Harper's Weekly*, August 31, 1872

**1** "What are you going to do about it, if 'Old Honesty' lets him loose again?"

1. Based on the cartoon, what do you think was Horace Greeley's major issue in the 1872 presidential campaign?

   **A.** political reform

   **B.** states' rights

   **C.** abolition

   **D.** temperance

2. Which one of the following statements do you think *best* represents the cartoonist's point of view?

   **A.** Horace Greeley is an honest man.

   **B.** Tammany Hall supports political reform.

   **C.** Tammany Hall, regardless of Greeley's view, is still corrupt.

   **D.** Horace Greeley, like most Tammany politicians, is corrupt.

answers: 1 (A), 2 (C)

Cartoon: The Granger Collection, New York

**PRACTICE**

**Directions:** Use the cartoon and your knowledge of U.S. history to answer questions 1 through 3.

Anonymous, 1858

1. Stephen A. Douglas is portrayed as a gladiator armed with the sword and shield of

   A. Congress and the rule of law.

   B. freedom of speech and the press.

   C. constitutional and property rights of slaveholders.

   D. voting rights and self-government for the territories.

2. Popular sovereignty was used in the 1850s to address the issue of

   A. states' rights.

   B. federalism.

   C. slavery.

   D. voting rights.

3. The cartoon illustrates the fight over whether to

   A. admit Kansas into the Union as a free state or a proslavery state.

   B. grant freedom of the press to newspapers in the territories.

   C. allowed sword fighting and dueling as legal activities in the 1850s.

   D. replace a system of majority rule with a monarchy.

# Charts

Charts present information in a visual form. History textbooks use several types of charts, including tables, flow charts, Venn diagrams, and concept webs. The type of chart most commonly found in standardized tests is the table. It organizes information in columns and rows for easy viewing.

**❶** Read the title and identify the broad subject of the chart.

**❷** Read the column and row headings and any other labels. This will provide more details about the subject of the chart.

**❸** Compare and contrast the information from column to column and row to row.

**❹** Try to draw conclusions from the information in the chart. Ask yourself: What trends does the chart show?

**❺** Read the questions, and then study the chart again.

**❶ Trails West, 1850**

| Trail | Start/End Point | Distance | Time Taken | Average Daily Distance | Best Time to Travel |
|-------|-----------------|----------|------------|------------------------|---------------------|
| California Trail | Fort Hall, Id./Sutter's Fort, Calif. | 700 miles | About 6 weeks | 15 miles | Summer months |
| Mormon Trail | Nauvoo, Ill./Great Salt Lake, Ut. | 1,300 miles | 2–3 months | 15–20 miles | May–September |
| Old Spanish Trail | Santa Fe/Los Angeles | 1,200 miles | 10–12 weeks | 12–15 miles | Spring–early summer |
| Oregon Trail | Missouri/Oregon | 2,000 miles | 4–6 months | 10–15 miles | April–September |
| Santa Fe Trail | Missouri/Santa Fe | 800 miles | 6–8 weeks | 12–20 miles | Early spring–early summer |

**❸** Compare and contrast the distance, time taken, and average daily distance traveled for each trail.

**1.** What was the best time of year for travel on most of the trails?

**A.** spring and summer

**B.** summer and fall

**C.** April

**D.** September

**2.** On which trails did travelers sometimes average 20 miles per day?

**A.** California and Oregon trails

**B.** Santa Fe and Old Spanish trails

**C.** Mormon and Santa Fe trails

**D.** Oregon and Mormon trails

answers: 1 (A), 2 (C)

**Directions:** Use the chart and your knowledge of U.S. history to answer questions 1 through 4.

## Percentage of Population Free and Enslaved, by States and Territories *1790*

| North | | | South | | |
|---|---|---|---|---|---|
| **States/Territories** | **Free** | **Enslaved** | **States/Territories** | **Free** | **Enslaved** |
| Connecticut | 98.9 | 1.1 | Georgia | 64.5 | 35.5 |
| Delaware | 85.0 | 15.0 | Kentucky | 83.1 | 16.9 |
| Maine | 100.0 | 0.0 | Maryland | 67.8 | 32.2 |
| Massachusetts | 100.0 | 0.0 | North Carolina | 74.5 | 25.5 |
| New Hampshire | 99.9 | 0.1 | South Carolina | 57.0 | 43.0 |
| New Jersey | 93.8 | 6.2 | Virginia | 60.9 | 39.1 |
| New York | 93.8 | 6.2 | | | |
| Pennsylvania | 99.1 | 0.9 | | | |
| Rhode Island | 98.6 | 1.4 | | | |
| Vermont | 100.0 | 0.0 | | | |

Source: Inter-University Consortium for Political and Social Research

1. Which state had the highest percentage of enslaved people?

   A. New Hampshire

   B. North Carolina

   C. Rhode Island

   D. South Carolina

2. Which of the following best describes most states in the North?

   A. The population was more than 98 percent free.

   B. More than 10 percent of the population was enslaved.

   C. Less than 60 percent of the population was free.

   D. The population was more than 20 percent enslaved.

3. Which statement about the percentage of enslaved people is true?

   A. It is much lower in the South.

   B. It is much higher in the South.

   C. There is no difference between the regions.

   D. There is a slight difference between the regions.

4. What economic factor best explains the population differences between the regions?

   A. The North focused on manufacturing.

   B. The North was wealthy enough to free enslaved people.

   C. The South focused on plantation agriculture.

   D. The South needed enslaved people for factory work.

# Line and Bar Graphs

Graphs show statistics in a visual form. Line graphs are particularly useful for showing changes over time. Bar graphs make it easy to compare numbers or sets of numbers.

**1** Read the title and identify the broad subject of the graph.

**2** Study the labels on the vertical and horizontal axes to see the kinds of information presented in the graph. Note the intervals between amounts and between dates. This will help you read the graph more efficiently.

**3** Look at the source line and evaluate the reliability of the information in the graph. Government statistics on education tend to be reliable.

**4** Study the information in the graph and note any trends.

**5** Draw conclusions and make generalizations based on these trends.

**6** Read the questions carefully, and then study the graph again.

**1** **United States Population, 1800–1850**

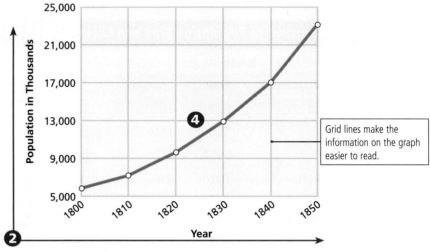

Grid lines make the information on the graph easier to read.

**3** Source: *Historical Statistics of the United States*

**6** **1.** The United States population rose above 10,000,000 between what years?

   **A.** 1810 and 1820

   **B.** 1820 and 1830

   **C.** 1830 and 1840

   **D.** 1840 and 1850

**1** **United States Urban Population, 1800–1850**

A generalization you might make here is that urban population grew markedly between 1840 and 1850.

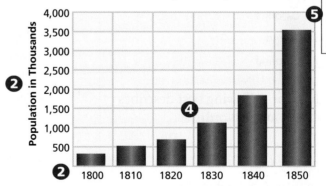

**3** Source: *Historical Statistics of the United States*

**6** **2.** Which of the following sentences *best* describes the trend shown in the bar graph?

   **A.** United States urban population steadily increased.

   **B.** United States urban population showed little change.

   **C.** United States urban population rose and fell.

   **D.** United States urban population decreased steadily.

answers: 1 (B), 2 (A)

**Directions:** Use the graphs and your knowledge of U.S. history to answer questions 1 through 4.

### Growth of the African-American Population, 1820–1860

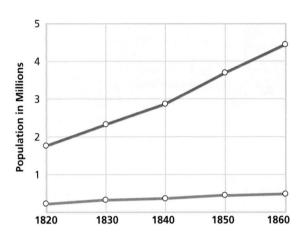

- ■ Total Population
- ■ Free Population

Source: Gilder Lehrman Institute of American History

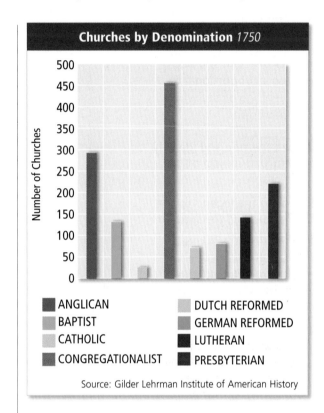

**Churches by Denomination** *1750*

- ■ ANGLICAN
- ■ BAPTIST
- ■ CATHOLIC
- ■ CONGREGATIONALIST
- ■ DUTCH REFORMED
- ■ GERMAN REFORMED
- ■ LUTHERAN
- ■ PRESBYTERIAN

Source: Gilder Lehrman Institute of American History

**1.** In which decade did the total African-American population first exceed 3.5 million?

A. 1820–1830

B. 1830–1840

C. 1840–1850

D. 1850–1860

**2.** About how many times larger than the free African-American population was the total population in 1860?

A. four

B. five

C. six

D. eight

**3.** Which one of the following statements accurately reflects information in the graph?

A. There were more Congregationalist churches than all other denominations combined.

B. There were more Presbyterian churches than Anglican churches.

C. The Baptists had the fewest churches.

D. The Congregationalists had the most churches.

**4.** Which denomination had the fewest churches?

A. Anglican

B. Catholic

C. German Reformed

D. Lutheran

# Pie Graphs

A pie, or circle, graph shows relationships among the parts of a whole. These parts look like slices of a pie. The size of each slice is proportional to the percentage of the whole that it represents.

**1** Read the title and identify the broad subject of the pie graph.

**2** Look at the legend to see what each of the slices of pie represent.

**3** Read the source line and note the origin of the data shown in the pie graph.

**4** Compare the slices of the pie and try to make generalizations and draw conclusions from your comparisons.

**5** Read the questions carefully and review difficult or unfamiliar terms.

**6** Eliminate choices that you know are wrong.

**1** The Popular Vote in the 1860 Presidential Election

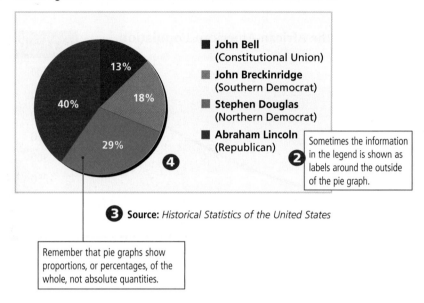

- **John Bell** (Constitutional Union)
- **John Breckinridge** (Southern Democrat)
- **Stephen Douglas** (Northern Democrat)
- **Abraham Lincoln** (Republican)

**2** Sometimes the information in the legend is shown as labels around the outside of the pie graph.

**3** Source: *Historical Statistics of the United States*

Remember that pie graphs show proportions, or percentages, of the whole, not absolute quantities.

1. Which of these describes Abraham Lincoln's victory in the 1860 presidential election?

   A. landslide
   B. majority of the votes cast
   C. plurality of the votes cast
   D. narrow margin

   **5** In electoral terms, the word *landslide* refers to an overwhelming victory, *majority* means "more than 50 percent," and *plurality* means "the most but less than 50 percent."

2. What political situation in 1860 does the pie graph show?

   A. The Democratic Party was split into northern and southern wings before the 1860 election.

   B. The Republican Party was not yet an important force in national politics.

   C. Douglas won fewer popular votes than Lincoln but won more electoral votes.

   D. Because no candidate won a majority of the popular votes, the House of Representatives decided the election.

   **6** You can eliminate **B** when you notice that the Republican Party received more votes than any other.

answers: 1 (C), 2 (A)

PRACTICE

**Directions:** Use the pie graph and your knowledge of U.S. history to answer questions 1 through 4.

### Ethnic Makeup of the Colonial Population, 1775

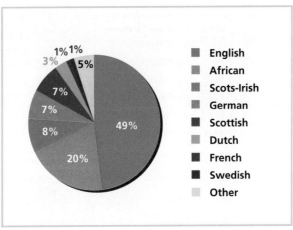

**Source:** http://www.digitalhistory.com

1. What was the largest ethnic group in the colonial population of 1775?

   A. African

   B. Dutch

   C. English

   D. French

2. What percentage of the colonial population came from Africa?

   A. 5%

   B. 8%

   C. 20%

   D. 48%

3. What percentage of the colonial population came from the Netherlands?

   A. 1%

   B. 3%

   C. 7%

   D. 8%

4. What was the largest group of non-English-speaking Europeans to settle in the colonies?

   A. Swedes

   B. Dutch

   C. Germans

   D. French

# Thematic Maps

A thematic map, or special-purpose map, focuses on a particular topic. The location of baseball parks, a country's natural resources, election results, and major battles in a war are all topics you might see illustrated on a thematic map.

**1** Read the title to determine the subject and purpose of the map.

**2** Examine the labels on the map to find more information about the map's subject and purpose.

**3** Study the legend to find the meaning of the symbols and colors used on the map.

**4** Look at the colors and symbols on the map and try to identify patterns.

**5** Use the compass rose or North arrow to determine directions on the map.

**6** Use the scale to estimate distances between places shown on the map.

**7** Read the questions and then carefully study the map to determine the answers.

**1** **Southern Military Districts, 1867**

**3** While a thematic map focuses on one topic, it often offers several kinds of information on that topic. Therefore, the legend for a thematic map is usually very detailed.

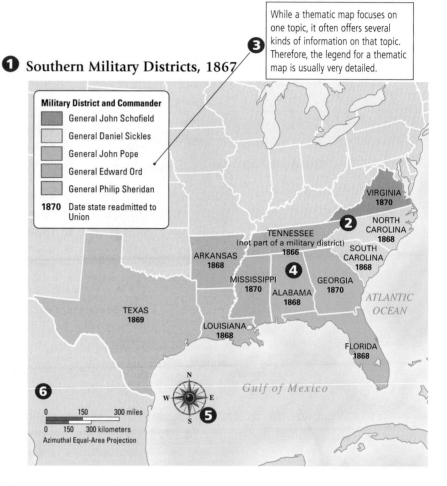

**Military District and Commander**
- General John Schofield
- General Daniel Sickles
- General John Pope
- General Edward Ord
- General Philip Sheridan

**1870** Date state readmitted to Union

VIRGINIA 1870
NORTH CAROLINA 1868
TENNESSEE (not part of a military district)
1866
ARKANSAS 1868
SOUTH CAROLINA 1868
MISSISSIPPI 1870
GEORGIA 1870
ALABAMA 1868
TEXAS 1869
LOUISIANA 1868
FLORIDA 1868
ATLANTIC OCEAN
Gulf of Mexico

0   150   300 miles
0   150   300 kilometers
Azimuthal Equal-Area Projection

**7** **1.** Which former Confederate state was the first to be readmitted to the Union?

    **A.** Tennessee

    **B.** South Carolina

    **C.** Florida

    **D.** Alabama

**2.** Who commanded the military district in which Texas was located?

    **A.** General Edward Ord

    **B.** General John Pope

    **C.** General Philip Sheridan

    **D.** General Daniel Sickles

answers: 1 (A), 2 (C)

**Directions:** Use the map and your knowledge of U.S. history to answer questions 1 through 4.

## The Battle of San Jacinto, 1836

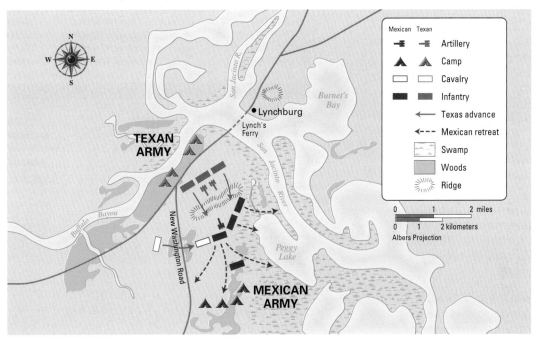

1. The Texan camp was located in what type of area?

   A. swamp

   B. ridge

   C. woods

   D. open plains

2. In which direction did the Texan forces move to attack the Mexican army?

   A. directly south

   B. northeast

   C. directly east

   D. southeast

3. Which of these forces attacked the Mexican forces from the west?

   A. Texan artillery

   B. Texan cavalry

   C. Texan infantry

   D. Texan artillery, cavalry, and infantry

4. What was the importance of the Battle of San Jacinto?

   A. Texas won its independence from Mexico.

   B. It avenged the defeats at Goliad and the Alamo.

   C. Texas gained U.S. support in the struggle for freedom.

   D. It proved that the Texans were better fighters than the Mexicans.

# Timelines

A timeline is a type of chart that lists events in the order in which they occurred. In other words, timelines are a visual method of showing what happened when.

**❶** Read the title to discover the subject of the timeline.

**❷** Identify the time period covered by the timeline by noting the earliest and latest dates shown. On vertical timelines, the earliest date is shown at the top. On horizontal timelines, it is on the far left.

**❸** Read the events and their dates in sequence. Notice the intervals between events.

**❹** Use your knowledge of history to develop a fuller picture of the events listed in the timeline. For example, place the events in a broader context by considering what was happening elsewhere in the world.

**❺** Note how events are related to one another. Look particularly for cause-effect relationships.

**❻** Use the information you have gathered from the above strategies to answer the questions.

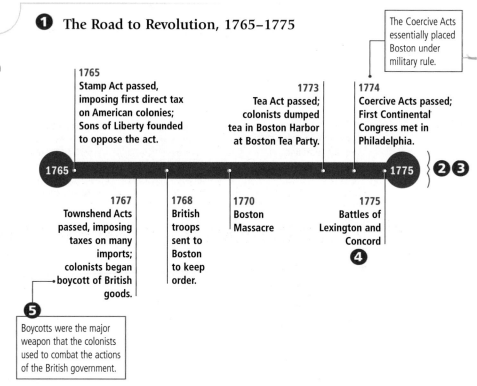

**❶** **The Road to Revolution, 1765–1775**

The Coercive Acts essentially placed Boston under military rule.

**1765**
Stamp Act passed, imposing first direct tax on American colonies; Sons of Liberty founded to oppose the act.

**1773**
Tea Act passed; colonists dumped tea in Boston Harbor at Boston Tea Party.

**1774**
Coercive Acts passed; First Continental Congress met in Philadelphia.

1765 — 1775 **❷❸**

**1767**
Townshend Acts passed, imposing taxes on many imports; colonists began boycott of British goods.

**1768**
British troops sent to Boston to keep order.

**1770**
Boston Massacre

**1775**
Battles of Lexington and Concord
**❹**

**❺**
Boycotts were the major weapon that the colonists used to combat the actions of the British government.

**❻** **1.** How did the colonists respond to the passage of the Townshend Acts?

    **A.** They founded the Sons of Liberty.

    **B.** They dumped British tea in Boston Harbor.

    **C.** They began a boycott of British goods.

    **D.** They called the First Continental Congress.

**2.** About how much time passed between the Coercive Acts and the first battles of the Revolutionary War?

    **A.** one year

    **B.** three years

    **C.** seven years

    **D.** nine years

answers: 1 (C), 2 (A)

**PRACTICE**

**Directions:** Use the timeline and your knowledge of U.S. history to answer questions 1 through 3.

**The Erie Canal, 1816–1840s**

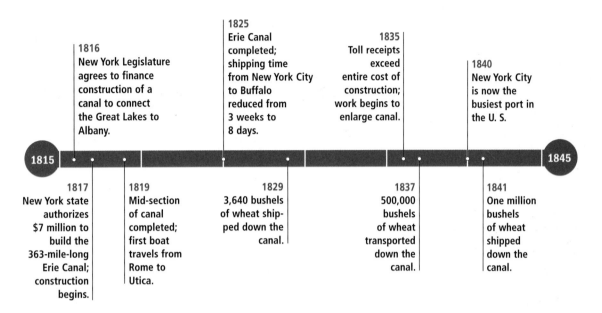

1825
Erie Canal completed; shipping time from New York City to Buffalo reduced from 3 weeks to 8 days.

1816
New York Legislature agrees to finance construction of a canal to connect the Great Lakes to Albany.

1835
Toll receipts exceed entire cost of construction; work begins to enlarge canal.

1840
New York City is now the busiest port in the U. S.

1815 — 1845

1817
New York state authorizes $7 million to build the 363-mile-long Erie Canal; construction begins.

1819
Mid-section of canal completed; first boat travels from Rome to Utica.

1829
3,640 bushels of wheat shipped down the canal.

1837
500,000 bushels of wheat transported down the canal.

1841
One million bushels of wheat shipped down the canal.

---

**1.** The Erie Canal was completed and ready for water traffic between Buffalo and Albany in what year?

    **A.** 1817

    **B.** 1819

    **C.** 1825

    **D.** 1840

**2.** About how many years after the canal was finished did work begin to enlarge it?

    **A.** 4 years

    **B.** 6 years

    **C.** 11 years

    **D.** 21 years

**3.** Which of the following statements about the Erie Canal is *not* true?

    **A.** The canal greatly reduced the time it took to ship goods between the Great Lakes and New York.

    **B.** From 1837 to 1841, the volume of wheat shipped through the canal doubled.

    **C.** The cost of building the canal was greater than the amount of tolls collected.

    **D.** The mid-section of the canal was completed in 1819.

# Constructed Response

Constructed-response questions focus on various kinds of documents. Each document is usually accompanied by a series of questions. These questions call for short answers that, for the most part, can be found directly in the document. Some answers, however, require knowledge of the subject or time period addressed in the document.

**1** Read the title of the document to discover the subject addressed in the questions.

**2** Study and analyze the document. Take notes on what you see.

**3** Read the questions and then study the document again to locate the answers.

**4** Carefully write your answers. Unless the directions say otherwise, your answers need not be complete sentences.

**1** List of Purchases Made by Meriwether Lewis for the Expedition

| Item | Cost |
|------|------|
| Mathematical Instruments | $ 412.95 |
| Arms, Ammunition, & Accouterments | 182.08 |
| Medicine, etc. | 94.49 |
| Clothing | 317.73 |
| Provision, etc. | 366.70 |
| Indian Presents | 669.50 |
| Camp Equipage | 116.68 |
| | $2,160.13 |

**Source:** National Archives and Records Administration

**2** Constructed-response questions use a wide range of documents, including short passages, cartoons, charts, graphs, maps, time lines, posters, and other visual materials. The information in this chart is taken from the records kept by Meriwether Lewis.

**3** 1. What was the largest expense for Lewis and Clark's expedition to the West?

**4** _Indian presents_

2. Why were arms and ammunition needed for the expedition?

_for protection and for hunting for food_

3. Why did Lewis and Clark carry mathematical instruments with them on their expedition to the West?

_President Thomas Jefferson asked Lewis and Clark to make charts and to carry out scientific studies during the expedition._

**PRACTICE**

**Directions:** Use the chart and your knowledge of U.S. history to answer questions 1 through 3.

### First Amendment Rights: the Five Basic Freedoms

| | |
|---|---|
| Freedom of Religion | People have the right to practice the religion of their choice. |
| Freedom of Speech | People have the right to state their ideas. |
| Freedom of the Press | People have the right to publish their ideas. |
| Freedom of Assembly | People have the right to meet peacefully in groups. |
| Freedom to Petition | People have the right to make requests and complain to the government. |

1. Does the First Amendment guarantee you the right to belong to any religion you like?

2. You write a letter to the mayor asking for a stop sign to be placed at an intersection near your school. Which of the five basic freedoms are you exercising?

3. What specific activities are covered by freedom of speech, and what activities are covered by freedom of the press? How are the two freedoms related?

# Extended Response

Extended-response questions, like constructed-response questions, usually focus on one kind of document. However, they are more complex and require more time to complete than typical short-answer constructed-response questions. Some extended-response questions ask you to present information from the document in a different form. Others require you to apply your knowledge of history to information contained in the document.

**1** Read the title of the document to get an idea of the subject.

**2** Study and analyze the document. Take notes on your ideas.

**3** Carefully read the extended-response questions.

**4** If the question calls for a graph or some other kind of diagram, make a rough sketch on scrap paper first. Then make a final copy of your drawing on the answer sheet.

**5** If the question requires a written response, jot down ideas in outline form. Use this outline to write your answer.

**1** **Ratifying the Constitution**

| State | Date Ratified |
|-------|---------------|
| Connecticut | January 9, 1788 |
| Delaware | December 7, 1787 |
| Georgia | January 2, 1788 |
| Maryland | April 28, 1788 |
| Massachusetts | February 6, 1788 |
| New Hampshire | June 21, 1788 |
| New Jersey | December 18, 1787 |
| New York | July 26, 1788 |
| North Carolina | November 21, 1789 |
| Pennsylvania | December 12, 1787 |
| Rhode Island | May 29, 1790 |
| South Carolina | May 23, 1788 |
| Virginia | June 25, 1788 |

**2**

**4** For time lines and other diagrams, remember to include a title and all appropriate labels.

**3** **1.** Use the information in the chart and your knowledge of U.S. history to create a time line for the ratification of the Constitution.

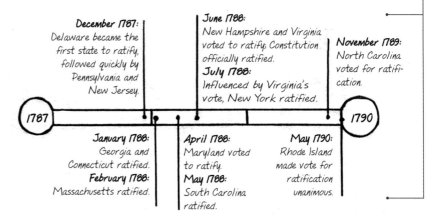

The Ratification of the Constitution

**December 1787:** Delaware became the first state to ratify, followed quickly by Pennsylvania and New Jersey.

**June 1788:** New Hampshire and Virginia voted to ratify; Constitution officially ratified.

**July 1788:** Influenced by Virginia's vote, New York ratified.

**November 1789:** North Carolina voted for ratification.

1787 — 1790

**January 1788:** Georgia and Connecticut ratified.
**February 1788:** Massachusetts ratified.

**April 1788:** Maryland voted to ratify.
**May 1788:** South Carolina ratified.

**May 1790:** Rhode Island made vote for ratification unanimous.

**3** **2.** Write a brief essay explaining the significance of the Bill of Rights to the ratification of the Constitution.

**5** **Essay Rubric** The best essays will point out that the promise of a Bill of Rights was key to getting enough support to ensure ratification of the Constitution. The vote for ratification by Virginia—the largest of the states—was contingent upon the passage of a Bill of Rights.

**Directions:** Use the passage and your knowledge of U.S. history to make a chart like the one below. Complete the chart by providing the information requested at the end of the paragraph.

### A Country Dividing

As the United States grew during the 1800s, Congress and the people argued about what form of government each new territory and state would have. The differences of opinion centered on one issue more than any other: slavery. Eventually, those sectional arguments led to the Civil War. The left side of the chart below lists three acts of Congress that addressed the issue of slavery in the West. Describe at least three provisions of each of these acts. (Note that the first provision of each act has been written for you.)

| Act | Provisions |
|---|---|
| **Missouri Compromise, 1820–1821** | 1. Slavery was to be prohibited in the Louisiana territory north of the 36° 30′ parallel.<br><br>2.<br><br>3. |
| **Compromise of 1850** | 1. The territories of New Mexico and Utah were created without restrictions on slavery.<br><br>2.<br><br>3. |
| **Kansas-Nebraska Act, 1854** | 1. Two new territories, Kansas and Nebraska, were created.<br><br>2.<br><br>3. |

# Document-Based Questions

A document-based question focuses on several documents— both visual and written. These documents often are accompanied by short-answer questions. You then use the answers to these questions and information from the documents to write an essay on a specified subject.

**1** Carefully read the "Historical Context" to get an indication of the issue addressed in the question.

**2** Note the action words used in the "Task" section. These words tell you exactly what the essay question requires.

**3** Study and analyze each document. Think about how the documents are connected to the essay question. Take notes on your ideas.

**4** Read and answer each of the document-specific questions.

## Introduction

**1** **Historical Context:** During President George Washington's first term, political parties started to develop around the beliefs of two members of Washington's cabinet, Secretary of the Treasury Alexander Hamilton and Secretary of State Thomas Jefferson. Despite Washington's opposition to political parties, they had a great influence in American domestic and foreign policy.

**2** **Task:** (Discuss) the role of the Federalist and the Democratic-Republican parties in the early republic, and (explain) why George Washington believed that political parties were divisive.

## Part 1: Short Answer

Study each document carefully and answer the questions that follow.

### Document 1: A Warning on Political Parties

**3** Let me . . . warn you in the most solemn manner against the baneful [harmful] effects of the spirit of party generally. This spirit, unfortunately, is inseparable from our nature, having its root in the strongest passions of the human mind. . . .

It serves always to distract the public councils and enfeeble [weaken] the public administration. It agitates the community with illfounded jealousies and false alarms; kindles the animosity [hatred] of one part against another; foments occasionally riot and insurrection. It opens the door to foreign influence and corruption, which find a facilitated access [easy entry] to the government itself through the channels of party passions.

—George Washington, Farewell Address

**4** **Why did Washington believe that political parties would harm the nation?**

*He believed that political parties would have a bad effect on the nation by playing upon the jealousies of different factions and stirring up considerable trouble for the nation. Foreign governments might also find it easy to use political parties to influence our national affairs.*

## Document 2: Positions of the First United States Political Parties

| Federalist Party | Democratic-Republican Party |
|---|---|
| Strong central government | Weak central government |
| Loose interpretation of the Constitution | Strict interpretation of the Constitution |
| Government should pay states' Revolutionary War debts | Each state should pay its own debts |
| Favored a national bank | Opposed a national bank |
| Favored business interests | Favored agricultural interests |
| Pro-British foreign policy | Pro-French foreign policy |

**How were the policies favored by the Federalists different from those favored by the Democratic-Republicans?**

*The parties held opposite views on major policy issues.*

## Document 3: Policy Dispute in Congress Hall, Philadelphia

Prints Division, The New York Public Library, Astor, Lenox, and Tilden Foundations.

**The cartoon shows the two parties fighting over foreign policy. What does it imply about their ability to settle disagreements?**

*Their disputes, if not settled by debate, threatened to destroy the federal government.*

## Part 2: Essay

**5** Using information from the documents, your answers to the questions in Part 1, and your knowledge of U.S. history, write an essay in which you discuss the different views the first political parties held on major issues between 1789 and 1801, and explain why Washington believed that political parties were divisive. **6**

**5** Carefully read the essay question. Then write an outline for your essay.

**6** Write your essay. Be sure that it has an introductory paragraph that introduces your argument, main body paragraphs that explain it, and a concluding paragraph that restates your position. In your essay, include extracts or details from specific documents to support your ideas. Add other supporting facts or details that you know from your study of American history.

**Essay Rubric** The best essays will point out the differences between the Federalists and the Democratic-Republicans (Document 2) and will show how political disagreements, such as those portrayed in the cartoon (Document 3), supported Washington's warning in his Farewell Address (Document 1). Essays should draw upon information not specifically included in the documents that illustrates an understanding of the political debate during the Washington and Adams administrations. Students may also refer to the Alien and Sedition Acts passed by the Federalist Congress during Adams's presidency and the opposing viewpoint expressed in the Kentucky and Virginia Resolutions authored by Jefferson and Madison, respectively.

## Introduction

**Historical Context:** In 1775, Great Britain had an army of 48,647 men located throughout the world, more than 8,500 of them in the Americas. A rebellion by the small group of 13 colonies in America did not scare the keepers of such a large colonial empire.

**Task:** Discuss how the colonists' beliefs and military actions contributed to their victory in the Revolution. Include the significance of the American alliances with European nations.

## Part 1: Short Answer

Study each document carefully and answer the questions that follow.

### Document 1: First Georgia Regiment of Infantry Continental Line, 1777

The hunting shirt, or rifle dress, shown here was recommended by George Washington in his general order of July 24, 1776. Declaring it a practical item to be given to the troops, he also claimed that ". . . it is a dress justly supposed to carry no small terror to the enemy, who think every such person a complete marksman."

Source: New York Historical Society

**What unusual military tactics did patriots like the man in the picture use to surprise and outsmart the British during the Revolution?**

Document 1: *Uniforms of the American Revolution: 1st Georgia Regiment Continental Infantry, 1777, Private Field Dress*, Charles Lefferts. Watercolor, gouache on paper. Copyright © Collection of the New York Historical Society.

### Document 2: Philadelphia, September 12, 1777

I close this paper with a short address to General Howe. . . . We know the cause which we are engaged in, and though a passionate fondness for it may make us grieve at every injury. . . . We are not moved by the gloomy smile of a worthless king, but by the ardent glow of generous patriotism. We fight not to enslave, but to set a country free, and to make room upon the earth for honest men to live in. In such a case we are sure that we are right; and we leave to you the despairing reflection of being the tool of a miserable tyrant.

—Thomas Paine, *The American Crisis No. IV*

**Although this excerpt is addressed to the British General Howe, how might it also have encouraged the colonists to continue their fight against the British?**

### Document 3: The Battle of Yorktown, 1781: Winning the American Revolution

**Estimated American, French, and British Forces and Casualties**

| Generals and Their Divisions | Forces | Casualties |
|---|---|---|
| General Washington (American colonies) | 11,100 | 76 |
| General Rochambeau (France) | 7,800 | 186 |
| General Cornwallis (Britain) | 8,000 | 482 |

Source: U.S. Army Center of Military History

**Estimated French and British Naval Strength\***

| French and British Fleets | Ships | Guns on Board Ship |
|---|---|---|
| Admiral Graves (Britain) | 19 | 1,450 |
| Admiral DeGrasse (France) | 24 | 2,610 |

*D++small craft or transport ships

**What support was provided by the French in the Battle of Yorktown?**

## Part 2: Essay

Using information from the documents, your answers to the questions in Part 1, and your knowledge of U.S. history, write an essay that discusses how the colonists' beliefs and military actions contributed to their victory in the Revolution. Include in your essay the significance of American alliances with European nations.

# The Landscape of America

The best place to begin your study of American history is with the geography of America. Geography is more than the study of the land and people. It also involves the relationship between people and their environment.

The United States is part of the North American continent. The United States ranks third in both total area and population in the world. It is filled with an incredible variety of physical features, natural resources, climactic conditions, and people. This handbook will help you to learn about these factors and to understand how they affected the development of the United States.

Chicago's waterways—its river system, canals, and location on Lake Michigan—have made it the commercial hub of the Midwest.

Turbines in a California "wind farm" use coastal winds to generate electricity. California is the birthplace of both windsurfing and America's first wind farms.

ROCKY MOUNTAINS

WEST

NORTHEAST

MIDWEST

APPALACHIAN MOUNTAINS

SOUTH

Rhode Island is world-renowned for its commercial fishing.

The climate and soil of Alabama are well-suited for growing cotton. The United States grows over 4 million tons of cotton annually.

*The Landscape of America* **A1**

# Themes of Geography

One useful way to think about geography is in terms of major themes or ideas. These pages examine the five major themes of geography and show how they apply to Boston, Massachusetts.

## Location

"Where am I?" Your answer is your location. One way to answer is to use absolute location. That means using the coordinates of longitude and latitude (see page A6). For example, if you're in Boston, your absolute location is approximately 42° north latitude and 71° west longitude.

More likely, however, you'll use relative location to answer the question. Relative location describes where an area is in relation to another area. For example, Boston lies in the northeast corner of the United States, next to the Atlantic Ocean.

**THINKING ABOUT GEOGRAPHY** What is the relative location of your school?

One of the world's best natural ports, Boston has been a center of international shipping for more than 300 years.

## Region

Geographers can't easily study the whole world at one time. So they break the world into regions. A region can be as large as a continent or as small as a neighborhood. A region has certain shared characteristics that set it apart. These characteristics might include political division, climate, language, or religion. Boston is part of the northeast region. It shares a climate—humid continental—with the cities of New York and Philadelphia.

**THINKING ABOUT GEOGRAPHY** What characteristics does your city or town share with nearby cities or towns?

## Place

"What is Boston like?" Place can help you answer this question. Place refers to the physical and human factors that make one area different from another. Physical characteristics are natural features, such as physical setting, plants, animals, and weather.

Human characteristics include cultural diversity and the things people have made—including language, the arts, and architecture. For instance, Boston includes African Americans, as well as people of Irish, Italian, Chinese, and Hispanic ancestry.

**THINKING ABOUT GEOGRAPHY** What physical and human characteristics make where you live unique?

The dragon dance is a holiday tradition in Boston's vibrant Chinatown neighborhood.

# Movement

Movement refers to the shifting of people, goods, and ideas from one place to another. People constantly move in search of better places to live, and they trade goods with one another over great distances. Movement also causes ideas to travel from place to place. In recent years, technology has quickened the movement of ideas and goods.

Boston became known as the Cradle of Liberty because of the movement of ideas. The concepts of freedom and self-government that developed in Boston spread to the other colonies and helped to start the American Revolution.

**THINKING ABOUT GEOGRAPHY** What are some of the different ways you spread information and ideas?

Boston's subway system, which runs both above and below ground, is the oldest in the nation.

# Human-Environment Interaction

Human-environment interaction refers to ways people interact with their environment, such as building a dam, cutting down a tree, or even sitting in the sun.

In Boston, human-environment interaction occurred when officials filled in swampy areas to make the city larger. In other ways, the environment has forced people to act. For example, people have had to invent ways to protect themselves from extreme weather and natural disasters.

**THINKING ABOUT GEOGRAPHY** What are ways that people in your city or town have changed their environment?

## Themes of Geography **Assessment**

### MAIN IDEAS

**1.** What is the relative location of your home?

**2.** What are three characteristics of the region in which you live?

**3.** What are at least three ways in which you have recently interacted with the environment?

### CRITICAL THINKING

**4. Forming and Supporting Opinions** Which aspect of geography described in these themes do you think has most affected your life? Explain.

#### Think about

• ways that you interact with your environment

• how you travel from place to place

# Map Basics

Geographers use many different types of maps, and these maps all have a variety of features. The map on the next page gives you information on a historical event—the final two years of the Civil War. But you can use it to learn about different parts of a map, too.

## Types of Maps

**Physical maps** Physical maps show mountains, hills, plains, rivers, lakes, oceans, and other physical features of an area. (See Atlas p. A29.)

**Political maps** Political maps show political units, such as countries, states, provinces, counties, districts, and towns. Each unit is normally shaded a different color, represented by a symbol, or shown with a different typeface. (See Atlas p. A28.)

**Historical maps** Historical maps illustrate such things as economic activity, migrations, battles, and changing national boundaries.

## TECHNOLOGY *of the* TIME

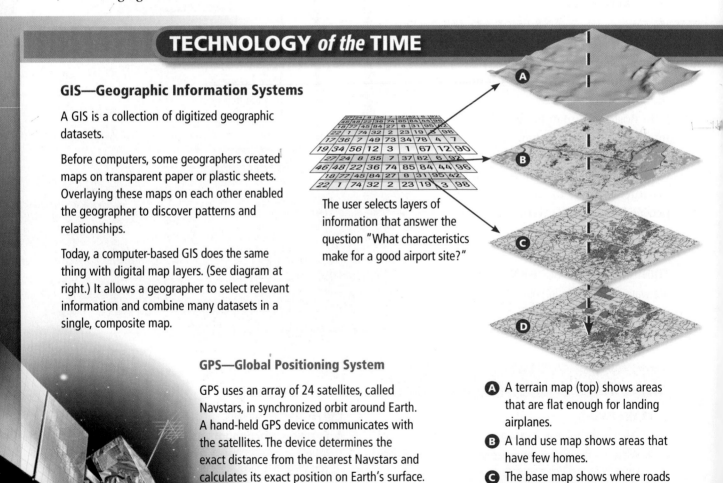

### GIS—Geographic Information Systems

A GIS is a collection of digitized geographic datasets.

Before computers, some geographers created maps on transparent paper or plastic sheets. Overlaying these maps on each other enabled the geographer to discover patterns and relationships.

Today, a computer-based GIS does the same thing with digital map layers. (See diagram at right.) It allows a geographer to select relevant information and combine many datasets in a single, composite map.

The user selects layers of information that answer the question "What characteristics make for a good airport site?"

### GPS—Global Positioning System

GPS uses an array of 24 satellites, called Navstars, in synchronized orbit around Earth. A hand-held GPS device communicates with the satellites. The device determines the exact distance from the nearest Navstars and calculates its exact position on Earth's surface.

**A** A terrain map (top) shows areas that are flat enough for landing airplanes.

**B** A land use map shows areas that have few homes.

**C** The base map shows where roads are located.

**D** The layers are combined to create a composite map showing possible sites for the airport.

# Reading a Map

**A** **Lines** Lines indicate political boundaries, roads and highways, human movement, and rivers and other waterways.

**B** **Symbols** Symbols represent such items as capital cities, battle sites, or economic activities.

**C** **Labels** Labels are words or phrases that explain various items or activities on a map.

**D** **Compass Rose** A compass rose shows which way the directions north (N), south (S), east (E), and west (W) point on the map.

**E** **Scale** A scale shows the ratio between a unit of length on the map and a unit of distance on the earth. A typical one-inch scale indicates the number of miles and kilometers that length represents on the map.

**F** **Colors** Colors show a variety of information on a map, such as population density or the physical growth of a country.

**G** **Legend or Key** A legend or key lists and explains the symbols, lines, and colors on a map.

**H** **Lines of Longitude** These are imaginary, north-south lines that run around the globe.

**I** **Lines of Latitude** These are imaginary, east-west lines that run around the globe. Together, latitude and longitude lines form a grid on a map or globe to indicate an area's absolute location.

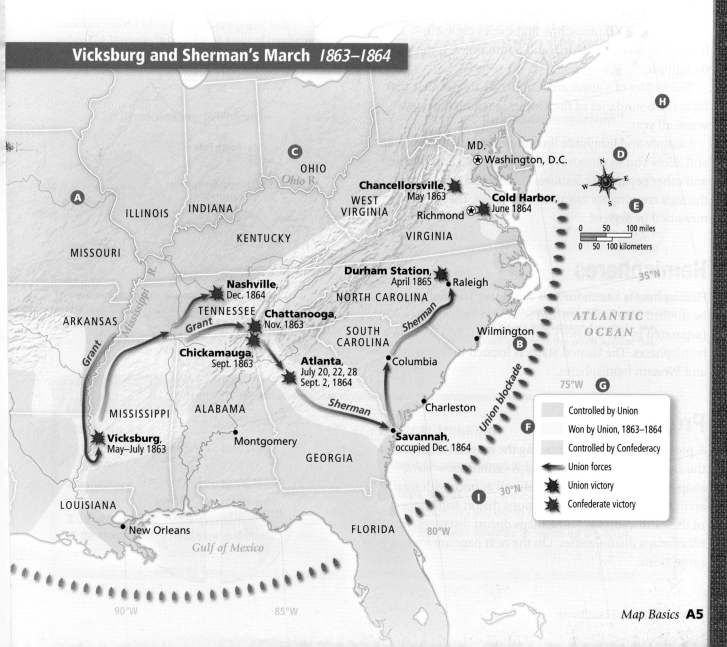

## Vicksburg and Sherman's March 1863–1864

**Legend:**
- Controlled by Union
- Won by Union, 1863–1864
- Controlled by Confederacy
- Union forces
- Union victory
- Confederate victory

Battle sites and locations shown on map:
- Washington, D.C. (MD.)
- Chancellorsville, May 1863 (WEST VIRGINIA)
- Cold Harbor, June 1864
- Richmond (VIRGINIA)
- Durham Station, April 1865
- Raleigh (NORTH CAROLINA)
- Nashville, Dec. 1864 (TENNESSEE)
- Chattanooga, Nov. 1863
- Chickamauga, Sept. 1863
- Atlanta, July 20, 22, 28 Sept. 2, 1864
- Columbia (SOUTH CAROLINA)
- Wilmington
- Charleston
- Vicksburg, May–July 1863 (MISSISSIPPI)
- Montgomery (ALABAMA)
- Savannah, occupied Dec. 1864 (GEORGIA)
- New Orleans (LOUISIANA)
- Grant, Sherman (Union forces routes)
- Union blockade
- ATLANTIC OCEAN
- Gulf of Mexico

States labeled: ILLINOIS, INDIANA, OHIO, MISSOURI, ARKANSAS, KENTUCKY, TENNESSEE, MISSISSIPPI, ALABAMA, GEORGIA, LOUISIANA, FLORIDA, VIRGINIA, WEST VIRGINIA, NORTH CAROLINA, SOUTH CAROLINA

Lines of latitude/longitude: 35°N, 30°N, 75°W, 80°W, 85°W, 90°W

Scale: 0–50–100 miles; 0–50–100 kilometers

# Physical Geography of the United States

Physical geography involves all the natural features on the earth. This includes the land, resources, climate, and vegetation.

## Land

Separated from much of the world by two oceans, the United States covers 3,717,796 square miles and spans the entire width of North America. To the west, Hawaii stretches the United States into the Pacific Ocean. To the north, Alaska extends the United States to the Arctic Circle. On the U.S. mainland, a huge central plain separates large mountains in the West and low mountains in the East. Plains make up almost half of the country, while mountains and plateaus make up a quarter each.

An abundance of lakes—Alaska alone has three million—and rivers also dot the landscape. Twenty percent of the United States is farmed. Urban areas cover only about two percent of the nation.

These sandstone buttes in Monument Valley Navajo Tribal Park (Utah) are nicknamed "the Mittens."

**THINKING ABOUT GEOGRAPHY** What is the land like around your city or state?

## Resources

The United States has a variety of natural resources. Vast amounts of coal, oil, and natural gas lie underneath American soil. Valuable deposits of lead, zinc, uranium, gold, and silver also exist. These resources have helped the United States become the world's leading industrial nation—producing more than 20 percent of the world's goods and services.

These resources have also helped the United States become both the world's largest producer of energy (natural gas, oil, coal, nuclear power, and electricity) and the world's largest consumer of it. Other natural resources include the Great Lakes, which are shared with Canada. They contain about 20 percent of the world's total supply of fresh surface water. Refer to the map on the next page to examine the nation's natural resources.

**THINKING ABOUT GEOGRAPHY** What are the different natural resources that you and your family use in your daily lives?

Coal mining is an important industry in parts of the Northwest, the Southwest, and the East.

Melting glaciers thousands of years ago left deposits of sand and gravel in ridges, called eskers, like this one in North Dakota.

# Land and Resources

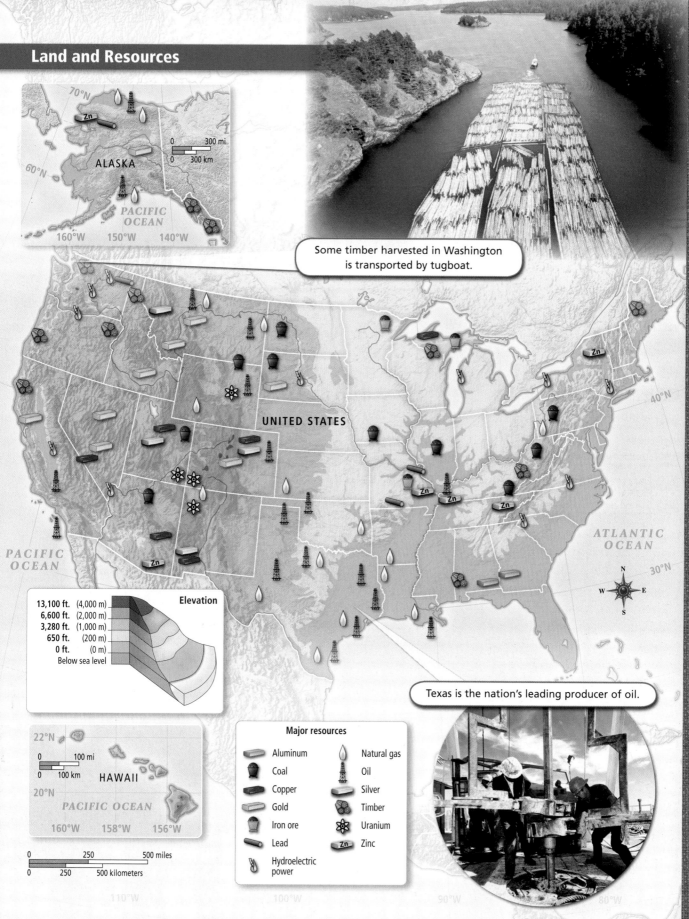

**ALASKA**

PACIFIC OCEAN

Some timber harvested in Washington is transported by tugboat.

**UNITED STATES**

PACIFIC OCEAN

ATLANTIC OCEAN

| | Elevation |
|---|---|
| 13,100 ft. | (4,000 m) |
| 6,600 ft. | (2,000 m) |
| 3,280 ft. | (1,000 m) |
| 650 ft. | (200 m) |
| 0 ft. | (0 m) |
| Below sea level | |

Texas is the nation's leading producer of oil.

**HAWAII**

PACIFIC OCEAN

0     250     500 miles
0     250     500 kilometers

**Major resources**

| | |
|---|---|
| Aluminum | Natural gas |
| Coal | Oil |
| Copper | Silver |
| Gold | Timber |
| Iron ore | Uranium |
| Lead | Zinc |
| Hydroelectric power | |

*Physical Geography of the United States* **A9**

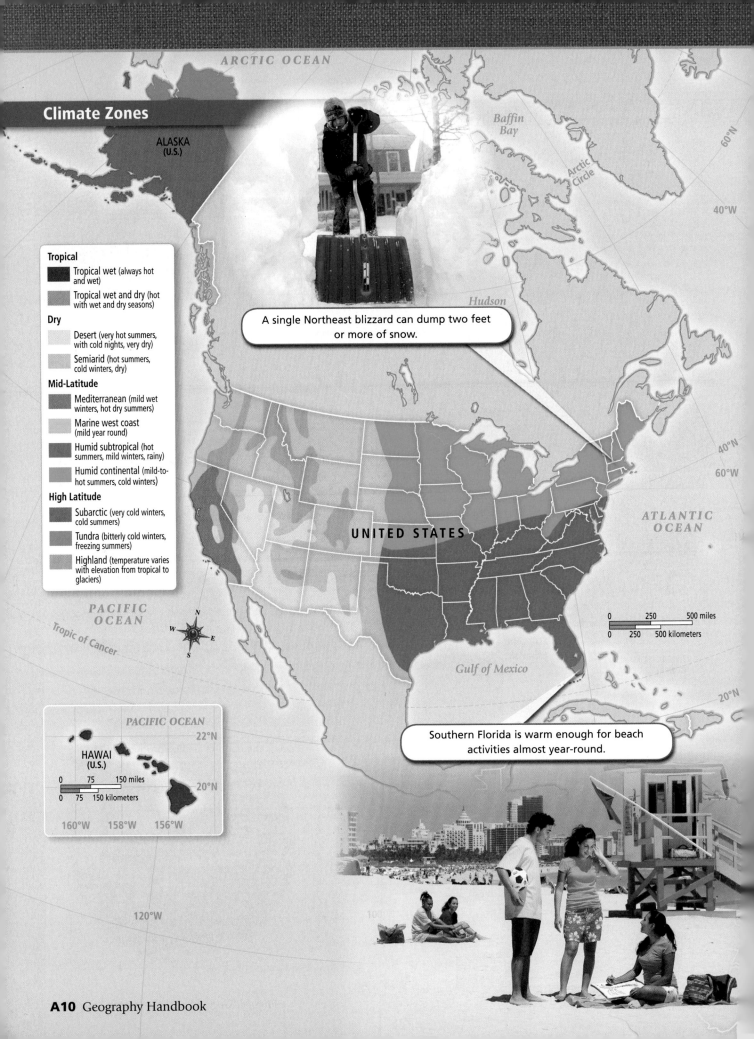

# Climate Zones

**Tropical**

Tropical wet (always hot and wet)

Tropical wet and dry (hot with wet and dry seasons)

**Dry**

Desert (very hot summers, with cold nights, very dry)

Semiarid (hot summers, cold winters, dry)

**Mid-Latitude**

Mediterranean (mild wet winters, hot dry summers)

Marine west coast (mild year round)

Humid subtropical (hot summers, mild winters, rainy)

Humid continental (mild-to-hot summers, cold winters)

**High Latitude**

Subarctic (very cold winters, cold summers)

Tundra (bitterly cold winters, freezing summers)

Highland (temperature varies with elevation from tropical to glaciers)

A single Northeast blizzard can dump two feet or more of snow.

Southern Florida is warm enough for beach activities almost year-round.

Spanish moss grows in coastal areas from Virginia south to Venezuela. This scene is of Cumberland Island, Georgia.

## Climate

The United States contains a variety of climates. For example, the mean temperature in January in Miami, Florida, is 67°F, while it is 11°F in Minneapolis, Minnesota. Most of the United States experiences a continental climate, or distinct change of seasons. Some regional climatic differences include hot and humid summers in the Southeast versus hot and dry summers in the Southwest. Harsh winters and heavy snow can blanket parts of the Midwest, the Northeast, and the higher elevations of the West and Northwest. Refer to the map on the previous page to see the nation's climatic regions.

Human activities have affected the climate, too. For example, pollution from cars and factories can affect local weather conditions and are contributing to a dangerous rise in the earth's temperature.

**THINKING ABOUT GEOGRAPHY** How would you describe the climate where you live?

## Vegetation

Between 20,000 and 25,000 species and subspecies of plants and vegetation grow in the United States—including over 1,000 different kinds of trees. Climate often dictates the type of vegetation found in a region. For instance, cold autumns in the Northeast contribute to the brilliantly colored autumn leaves. Rain nourishes the forests in the Northwest and Southeast. The central plains, where rainfall is less heavy, are covered by grass. Cactus plants thrive in the dry southwestern deserts.

Along with natural vegetation, climate dictates the nation's variety of planted crops. For example, temperate weather in the Midwest helps wheat to grow, while warm weather nourishes citrus fruit in Florida and California.

**THINKING ABOUT GEOGRAPHY** What kinds of trees or plants grow in your region?

### Physical Geography Assessment

**MAIN IDEAS**

1. What are the different aspects of physical geography?

2. Which state contains the largest variety of climates?

3. What two states contain most of the country's oil resources?

**CRITICAL THINKING**

5. **Drawing Conclusions** What do you think are the advantages of living in a country with diverse physical geography?

**Think about**
- the different resources available in your region
- the variety of recreational activities in your region

# Geography Dictionary

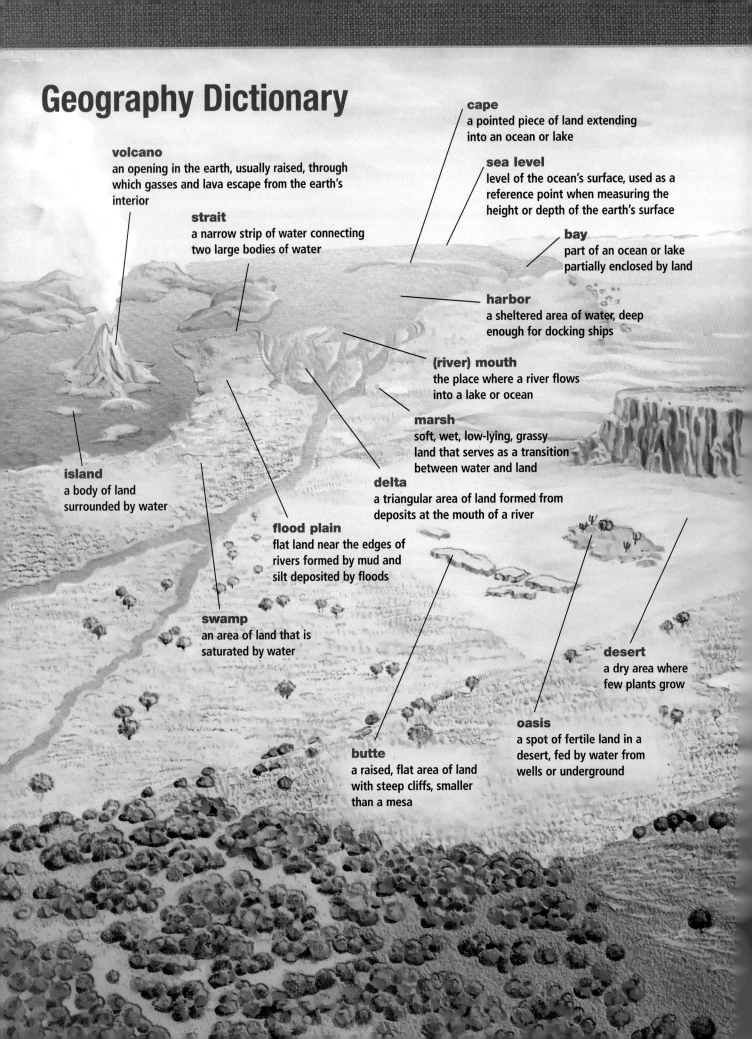

**cape**
a pointed piece of land extending into an ocean or lake

**sea level**
level of the ocean's surface, used as a reference point when measuring the height or depth of the earth's surface

**bay**
part of an ocean or lake partially enclosed by land

**volcano**
an opening in the earth, usually raised, through which gasses and lava escape from the earth's interior

**strait**
a narrow strip of water connecting two large bodies of water

**harbor**
a sheltered area of water, deep enough for docking ships

**(river) mouth**
the place where a river flows into a lake or ocean

**marsh**
soft, wet, low-lying, grassy land that serves as a transition between water and land

**island**
a body of land surrounded by water

**delta**
a triangular area of land formed from deposits at the mouth of a river

**flood plain**
flat land near the edges of rivers formed by mud and silt deposited by floods

**desert**
a dry area where few plants grow

**swamp**
an area of land that is saturated by water

**oasis**
a spot of fertile land in a desert, fed by water from wells or underground

**butte**
a raised, flat area of land with steep cliffs, smaller than a mesa

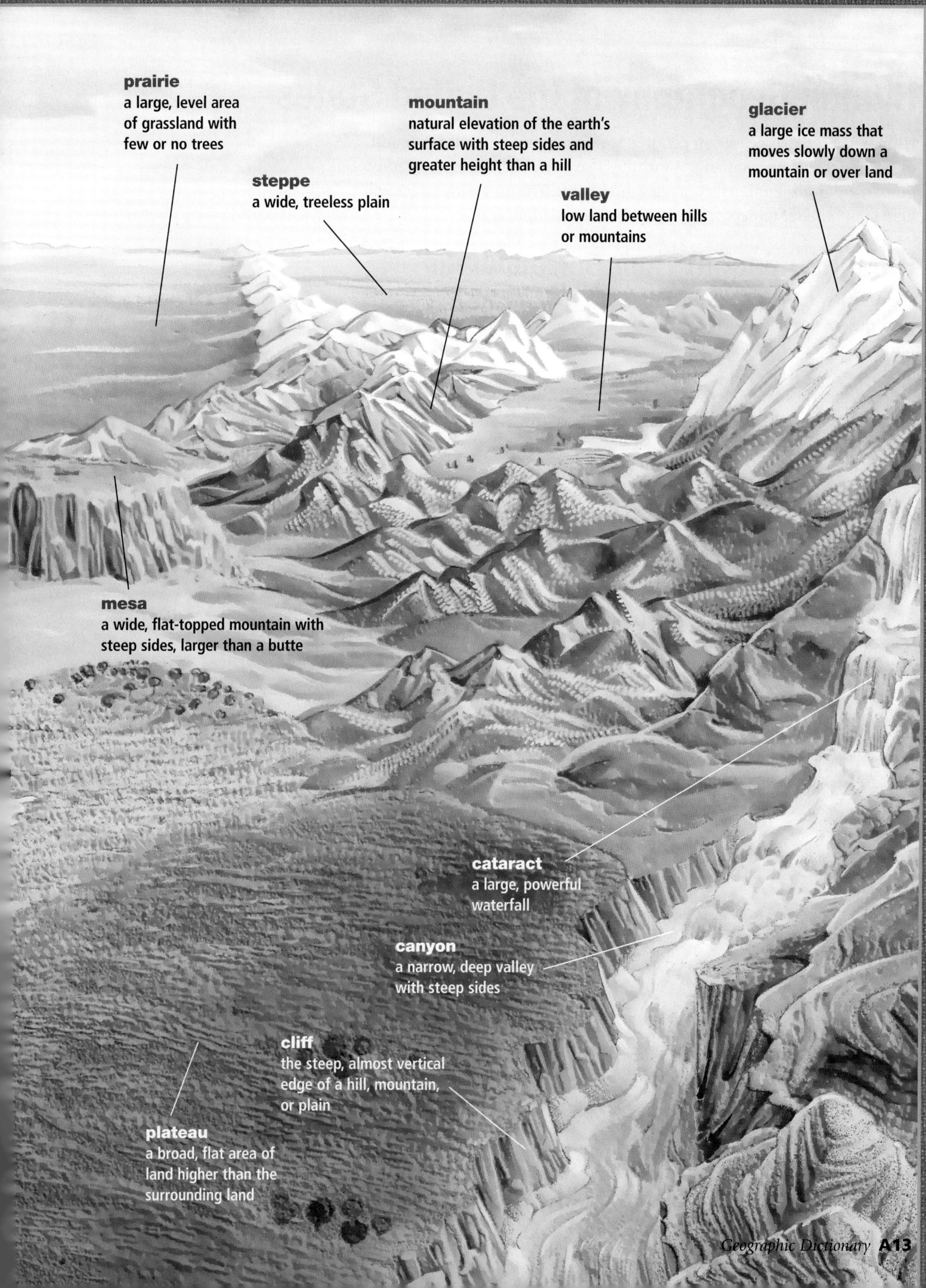

**prairie**
a large, level area
of grassland with
few or no trees

**steppe**
a wide, treeless plain

**mountain**
natural elevation of the earth's
surface with steep sides and
greater height than a hill

**valley**
low land between hills
or mountains

**glacier**
a large ice mass that
moves slowly down a
mountain or over land

**mesa**
a wide, flat-topped mountain with
steep sides, larger than a butte

**cataract**
a large, powerful
waterfall

**canyon**
a narrow, deep valley
with steep sides

**cliff**
the steep, almost vertical
edge of a hill, mountain,
or plain

**plateau**
a broad, flat area of
land higher than the
surrounding land

# Human Geography of the United States

Human geography focuses on people's relationships with each other and the surrounding environment. It includes two main themes of geography: human-environment interaction and movement. The following pages will help you to better understand the link between people and geography.

## Humans Adapt to Their Surroundings

Humans have always adapted to their environment. For example, in North America, many Native American tribes burned forest patches to create grazing area to attract animals and to clear area for farmland. In addition, Americans have adapted to their environment by building numerous dams, bridges, and tunnels. More recently, scientists and engineers have been developing building materials that will better withstand the earthquakes that occasionally strike California.

**THINKING ABOUT GEOGRAPHY** What are some of the ways in which you interact with your environment on a daily basis?

The Fred Hartman Bridge, completed in 1995, crosses the Houston Ship Channel, connecting two suburbs of Houston, Texas.

The multi-level cliff dwellings of Mesa Verde, Colorado, were built by Ancestral Pueblo people between 700 and 900 years ago.

# Humans Affect the Environment

When humans interact with the environment, sometimes nature suffers. In the United States, for example, major oil leaks or spills occur each year—fouling shorelines and harming wildlife. Building suburbs and strip malls has also destroyed forests, farmland, and valuable wetlands.

**THINKING ABOUT GEOGRAPHY** What are some of the environmental problems in your city or town?

Workers use heavy equipment to attack a Gulf of Mexico oil spill.

# Preserving and Restoring

In 2003, Americans recycled more than 30% of their garbage—about 72 million tons. In 2005, the Kyoto Protocol began to take effect, requiring the signing countries to limit or reduce greenhouse gas emissions. As of 2006, 165 nations had ratified Kyoto.

**THINKING ABOUT GEOGRAPHY**
What are some of the ways in which you help the environment?

## Destruction of Original Forests

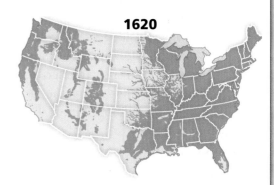

**1620**

**1850**

**1926**

This maps show that, over the years, human beings have nearly cut down all the original forests in the United States. Each dot represents 25,000 acres.

More than 3,000 volunteers each year participate in Hands on Miami Day by planting trees and cleaning up neighborhoods.

*Human Geography of the United States* A15

# Human Movement

In prehistoric times, people roamed the earth in search of food. Today, people move from place to place for many different reasons. Among them are cost of living, job availability, and climate. Since the 1950s, many Americans—as well as many new immigrants—moved to the Sunbelt. This region runs through the southern United States from Virginia to California. Since 1990 the nation has seen a population shift from the North and East to the South and West.

- The fastest growing county in the United States—Riverside—and three of the country's ten fastest growing cities are in Southern California. Yet the state has seen a steady outmigration.

- Cities such as Dallas-Forth Worth, Atlanta, and Minneapolis-St. Paul show net outmigration while their surrounding suburbs have net immigration.

**THINKING ABOUT GEOGRAPHY**

Has your family ever moved? If so, what were some of the reasons?

**Clark County,** home to Las Vegas, is one of the nation's fastest growing metropolitan areas. In just six years (1999 to 2005), school enrollments grew from about 217,000 to 291,000—more than one third.

## Domestic Migration *2000–2004*

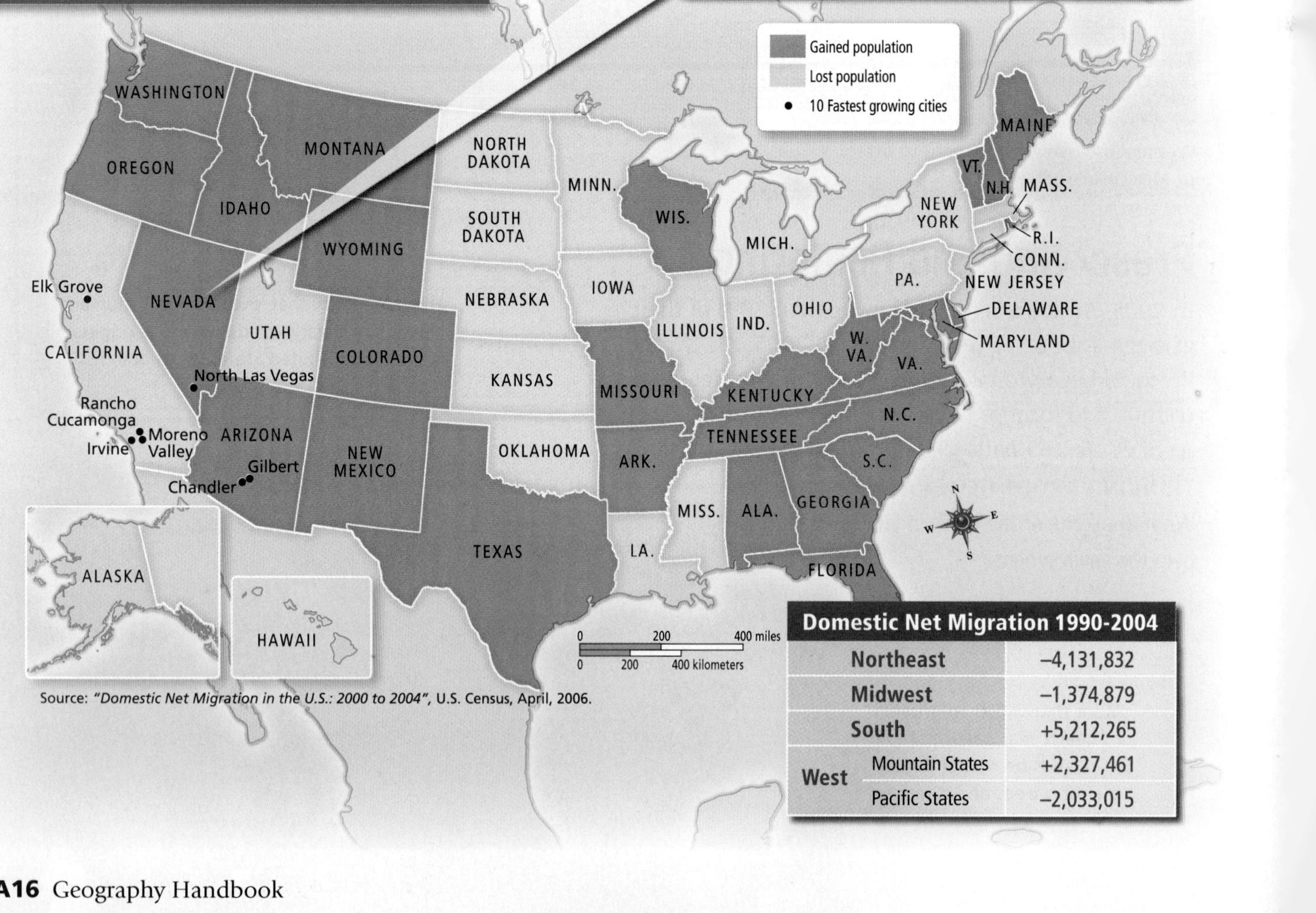

Legend:
- Gained population
- Lost population
- • 10 Fastest growing cities

States labeled on map: WASHINGTON, OREGON, MONTANA, IDAHO, WYOMING, NEVADA, UTAH, CALIFORNIA, ARIZONA, NEW MEXICO, COLORADO, NORTH DAKOTA, SOUTH DAKOTA, NEBRASKA, KANSAS, OKLAHOMA, TEXAS, MINN., IOWA, MISSOURI, ARK., LA., WIS., ILLINOIS, IND., MICH., OHIO, KENTUCKY, TENNESSEE, MISS., ALA., GEORGIA, FLORIDA, S.C., N.C., VA., W. VA., PA., NEW YORK, MAINE, VT., N.H., MASS., R.I., CONN., NEW JERSEY, DELAWARE, MARYLAND, ALASKA, HAWAII

Cities: Elk Grove, North Las Vegas, Rancho Cucamonga, Irvine, Moreno Valley, Gilbert, Chandler

Scale: 0 200 400 miles / 0 200 400 kilometers

Source: "Domestic Net Migration in the U.S.: 2000 to 2004", U.S. Census, April, 2006.

| Domestic Net Migration 1990-2004 | | |
|---|---|---|
| Northeast | | −4,131,832 |
| Midwest | | −1,374,879 |
| South | | +5,212,265 |
| West | Mountain States | +2,327,461 |
| | Pacific States | −2,033,015 |

# Humans Spread Ideas and Information

Throughout U.S. history, people from all over the world have come to the United States. They have brought with them food, music, language, technology, and other aspects of their culture. As a result, the United States is one of the most culturally rich and diverse nations in the world. Look around your town or city. You'll probably notice different people, languages, and foods.

Today, the spreading of ideas and customs does not rely solely on human movement. Technology—from the Internet to television to satellites—spreads ideas and information throughout the world faster than ever. This has created an ever-growing, interconnected world. As the 21st century continues, human geography will continue to play a key role in shaping the United States and the world.

**THINKING ABOUT GEOGRAPHY** How have computers and the Internet affected your life?

American consumer products are for sale around the globe.

*Puertorriqueños* celebrate the National Puerto Rican Day Parade in New York City.

## Human Geography Assessment

### MAIN IDEAS

1. What are some of the ways that people have helped to restore the environment?

2. What are some of the ways that residents of your region have successfully modified their landscape?

3. What are some of the reasons that people move from place to place?

### CRITICAL THINKING

4. **Recognizing Effects** In what ways has technology helped bring people in the world together?

   **Think about**
   • the different ways in which people communicate today
   • the speed in which people today can communicate over long distances

# Geography Handbook Assessment

## TERMS

**Briefly explain the significance of each of the following.**

1. physical map
2. political map
3. longitude
4. latitude
5. hemisphere
6. projection
7. flood plain
8. sea level
9. human geography
10. human movement

**Compare and contrast each pair of terms.**

11. place; location
12. parallel; meridian
13. climate; temperature

## REVIEW

**Themes of Geography (pages A2–A3)**

14. What is the difference between absolute location and relative location?

15. What is meant by the theme of place?

16. What are the themes of movement and human-environment interaction?

**Map Basics (pages A4–A7)**

17. What do you think are some of the benefits of using technology to study geography?

18. What are the three major kinds of maps?

19. What are latitude and longitude lines?

**Physical Geography (pages A8–A11)**

20. How have the natural resources in the United States helped its economic development?

21. What are the different climates within the United States?

**Human Geography (pages A14–A16)**

22. How is human geography different from physical geography?

23. What aspects of human geography might cause people to move?

## CRITICAL THINKING

24. **Forming and Supporting Opinions** Which of the five themes of geography do you think has had the most impact on history? Why?

25. **Causes and Effects** How do the climate and natural resources of an area affect its economy?

26. **Categorizing** Create a diagram to organize information from this Handbook about the regions of the United States.

|  | West | South | Midwest | Northeast |
|---|---|---|---|---|
| Landforms | Rocky Mountains | Mississippi Delta |  |  |
| Resources |  |  |  |  |
|  |  |  |  |  |

27. **Drawing Conclusions** How have computers helped geographers make more accurate maps?

28. **Making Inferences** Why do you think the Mercator projection is used for all types of navigation?

**Use the photograph below to answer 29–31.**

29. What region of the United States is pictured here?

30. What are some of the physical features of this area?

31. What is the climate of the area pictured?

## MULTIPLE CHOICE

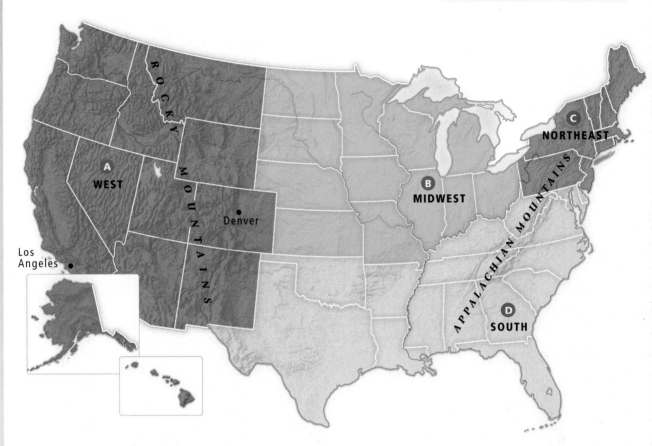

**Use the map and your knowledge of geography to answer questions 1–3.**

1. **Which describes the absolute location of Denver?**

   **A.** approximately 39°N 105°W, elev. 5,280 feet

   **B.** 844 miles ENE of Los Angeles

   **C.** mountainous; highland climate

   **D.** state capital of Colorado

2. **Which region is a source for uranium ore?**

   **A.** Ⓐ    **B.** Ⓑ    **C.** Ⓒ    **D.** Ⓓ

3. **Which region has a primarily humid subtropical climate?**

   **A.** Ⓐ    **B.** Ⓑ    **C.** Ⓒ    **D.** Ⓓ

**Read each question and choose the best answer.**

4. **The United States is located in which hemispheres?**

   **A.** Northern and Western

   **B.** Southern and Western

   **C.** Northern and Eastern

   **D.** Southern and Eastern

5. **Constructing a breakwater in Boston harbor is an example of how humans—**

   **A.** adapt to their environment.

   **B.** affect their environment.

   **C.** spread ideas and information.

   **D.** restore their environment.

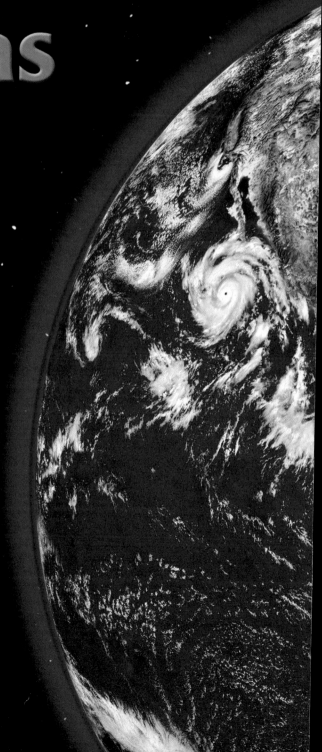

# ❄ RAND M℃NALLY
# World Atlas

## CONTENTS

Human Emergence on Earth .................... A22
World: Political ....................................... A24
World: Physical ...................................... A26
North America: Physical ........................ A28
South America: Physical ........................ A29
Mexico, Central America,
   and the Caribbean: Political .............. A30
Native America to 1525 ........................ A32
United States: Political ......................... A34
United States: Physical ......................... A36
U.S. Territorial Expansion ...................... A38

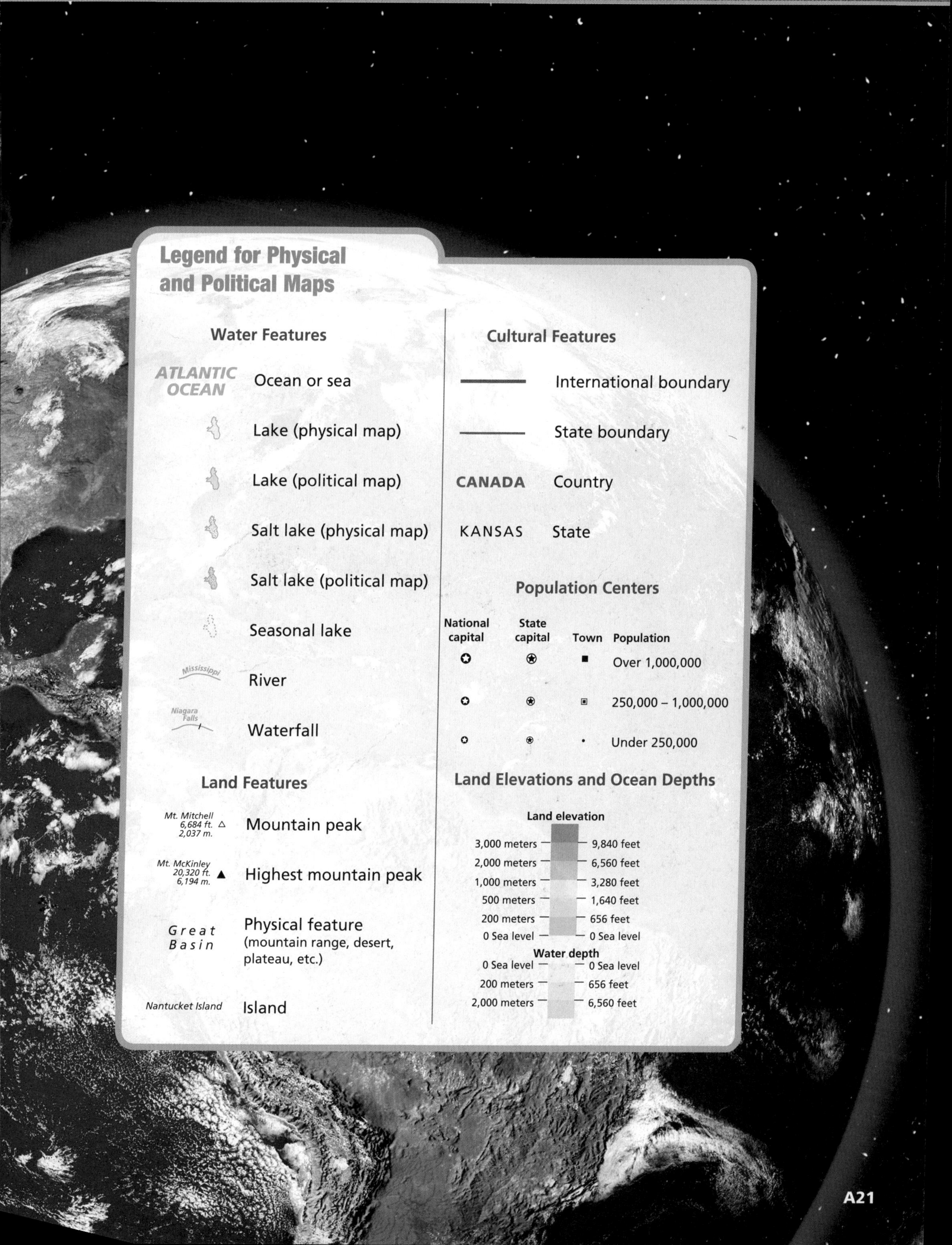

# Legend for Physical and Political Maps

## Water Features

*ATLANTIC OCEAN*    Ocean or sea

    Lake (physical map)

    Lake (political map)

    Salt lake (physical map)

    Salt lake (political map)

    Seasonal lake

 *Mississippi*    River

 *Niagara Falls*    Waterfall

## Land Features

*Mt. Mitchell 6,684 ft. 2,037 m.* △    Mountain peak

*Mt. McKinley 20,320 ft. 6,194 m.* ▲    Highest mountain peak

*Great Basin*    Physical feature (mountain range, desert, plateau, etc.)

*Nantucket Island*    Island

## Cultural Features

──────    International boundary

────    State boundary

**CANADA**    Country

KANSAS    State

## Population Centers

| National capital | State capital | Town | Population |
|---|---|---|---|
| ✪ | ✪ | ■ | Over 1,000,000 |
| ✪ | ✪ | ◙ | 250,000 – 1,000,000 |
| ✪ | ✪ | • | Under 250,000 |

## Land Elevations and Ocean Depths

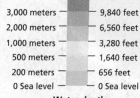

**Land elevation**

| 3,000 meters | 9,840 feet |
| 2,000 meters | 6,560 feet |
| 1,000 meters | 3,280 feet |
| 500 meters | 1,640 feet |
| 200 meters | 656 feet |
| 0 Sea level | 0 Sea level |

**Water depth**

| 0 Sea level | 0 Sea level |
| 200 meters | 656 feet |
| 2,000 meters | 6,560 feet |

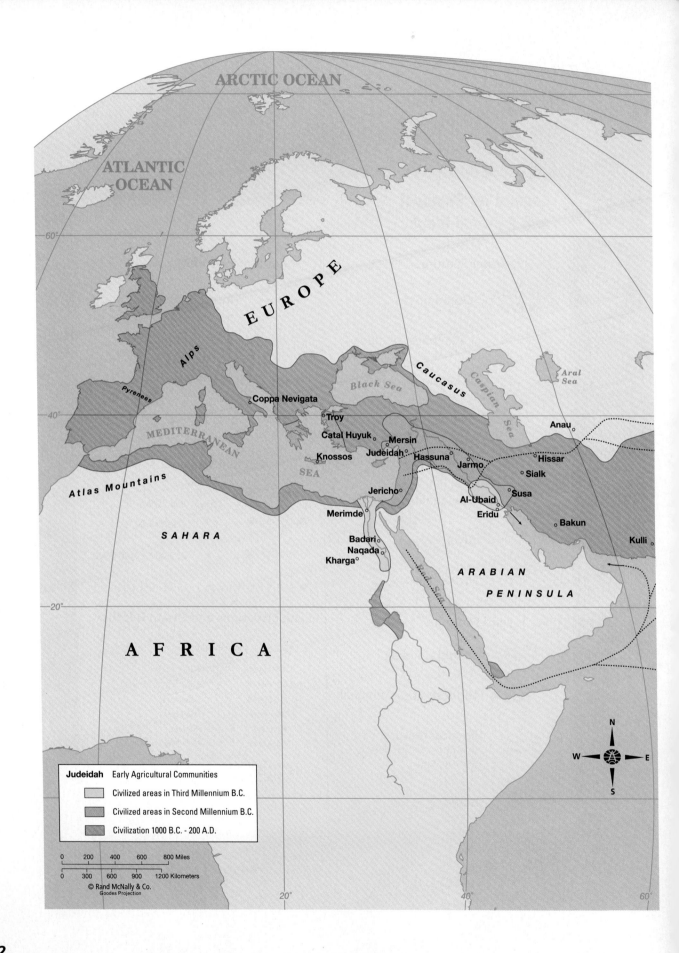

ARCTIC OCEAN

ATLANTIC
OCEAN

EUROPE

Alps

Pyrenees

Caucasus

Black Sea

Caspian Sea

Aral Sea

Coppa Nevigata

Troy

Catal Huyuk
Mersin
Judeidah
Knossos
Hassuna
Jarmo
Anau

Hissar

Sialk

MEDITERRANEAN

SEA

Jericho

Al-Ubaid
Susa

Eridu

Bakun

Atlas Mountains

Kulli

Merimde

SAHARA

Badari
Naqada
Kharga

ARABIAN

PENINSULA

AFRICA

N
W        E
S

Judeidah    Early Agricultural Communities

Civilized areas in Third Millennium B.C.

Civilized areas in Second Millennium B.C.

Civilization 1000 B.C. - 200 A.D.

0    200    400    600    800 Miles

0    300    600    900    1200 Kilometers

© Rand McNally & Co.
Goodes Projection

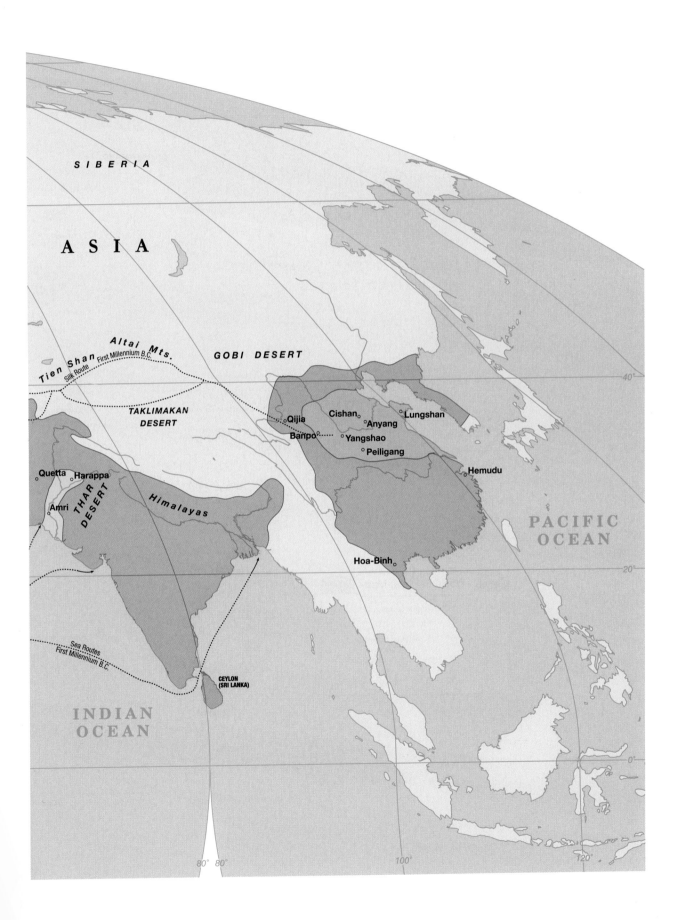

SIBERIA

ASIA

Altai Mts.

Tien Shan

GOBI DESERT

Silk Route First Millennium B.C.

TAKLIMAKAN
DESERT

Qijia

Cishan

Anyang

Lungshan

Baripo

Yangshao

Peiligang

Hemudu

Quetta

Harappa

THAR
DESERT

Himalayas

Amri

PACIFIC
OCEAN

Hoa-Binh

Sea Routes
First Millennium B.C.

CEYLON
(SRI LANKA)

INDIAN
OCEAN

40°

20°

0°

80° 80°

100°

120°

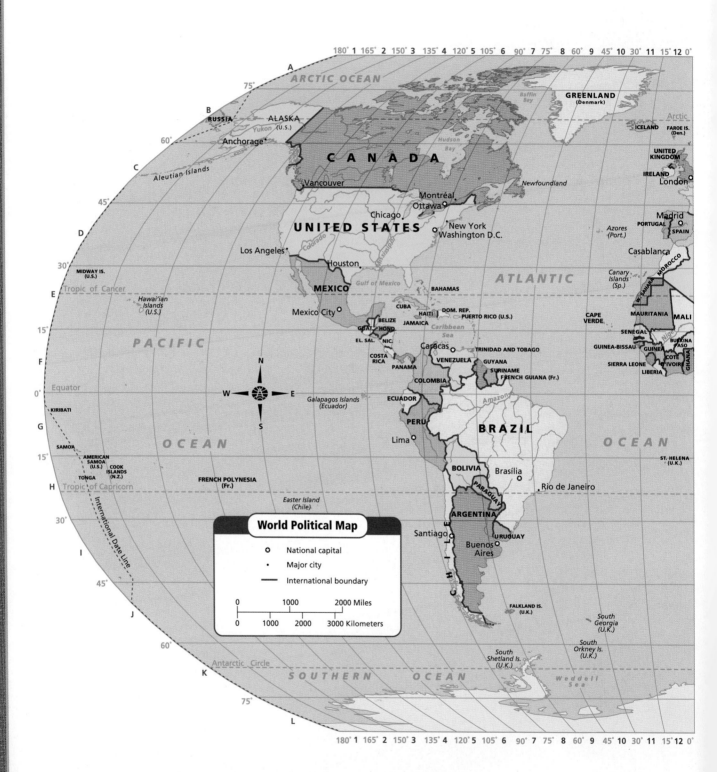

RAND McNALLY

13 15° 14 30° 15 45° 16 60° 17 75° 18 90° 19 105° 20 120° 21 135° 22 150° 23 165° 24 180°

*Franz Josef Land*

ARCTIC OCEAN — A

*Spitsbergen (Nor.)*

75° B

*Novaya Zemlya*

Circle

NORWAY

FINLAND

SWEDEN EST.
LAT.
LITH. ○ Moscow

Novosibirsk

R U S S I A

60° 
*Bering Sea*

C

*North Sea* DEN.

NETH. GERMANY POLAND BELARUS
FRANCE CZ. SVK. UKRAINE
AUS. HUNG. MOLD.
ITALY SLVN. ROM.
Rome BUL.
GREECE

*Volga*

*Black Sea*

KAZAKHSTAN

GEO.
ARM. AZER.
UZBEKISTAN
TURKMENISTAN KYRG.
TAJIK.

MONGOLIA

*Sea of Okhotsk*

45° 

*Sea of Japan*

NORTH KOREA

Beijing ○

C H I N A

SOUTH KOREA Seoul ○

JAPAN
Tōkyō ○

D

30° E

TUNISIA
*Crete* CYPRUS LEB. SYRIA
ISRAEL IRAQ
JORDAN

TURKEY

○ Tehrān

I R A N

AFGHANISTAN

*Yangtze*

Shanghai

PACIFIC

ALGERIA LIBYA EGYPT

KUWAIT
Cairo ○

SAUDI
ARABIA QATAR
U.A.E.

PAKISTAN
Karachi

Mumbai
(Bombay)

NEPAL
BHU.
BNG.

I N D I A

MYANMAR LAOS

TAIWAN

Hong Kong

NORTHERN MARIANA ISLANDS
(U.S.)

Tropic of Cancer

WAKE ISLAND
(U.S.)

15°

NIGER CHAD SUDAN

*Red Sea*

*Nile*

ERITREA
DJIBOUTI

OMAN

YEMEN

*Arabian Sea*

*Bay of Bengal*

SRI LANKA

*South China Sea*

Bangkok THAILAND
CAMBODIA

VIETNAM
Manila

PHILIPPINES

PALAU

GUAM
(U.S.)

F

FED. STATES OF
MICRONESIA

MARSHALL
ISLANDS

0° Equator

NIGERIA
Lagos
CAMEROON
EQUATORIAL
GUINEA
GABON

CENTRAL
AFRICAN
REPUBLIC

ETHIOPIA

Addis
Ababa

SOMALIA

UG.
KENYA

*Congo*

MALDIVES

SEYCHELLES

SINGAPORE

BRUNEI
MALAYSIA

*Borneo*

*Sumatra*

Jakarta ○

I N D O N E S I A

*Java*

EAST TIMOR

New Guinea

PAPUA
NEW GUINEA

OCEAN

SOLOMON
ISLANDS

G

CONGO
DEM. REP.
OF THE CONGO

RWANDA
BURUNDI

TANZANIA

COMOROS

I N D I A N

15° 
*Coral Sea*

VANUATU

ANGOLA
ZAMBIA

MALAWI
MOZAMBIQUE

ZIMBABWE

MADAGASCAR

MAURITIUS

NEW CALEDONIA
(Fr.)

FIJI

H

NAMIBIA
BOTSWANA

REUNION
(Fr.)

Tropic of Capricorn

OCEAN

A U S T R A L I A

Brisbane

30°

Johannesburg

SWAZILAND

SOUTH
AFRICA LESOTHO

Perth

*Darling*

Sydney

Auckland

Melbourne

NEW ZEALAND

I

*Tasmania*

45°

*Îles Kerguélen
(Fr.)*

J

60°

S O U T H E R N     O C E A N

Antarctic Circle

K

75°

A N T A R C T I C A

© Rand McNally & Co.
Made in U.S.A.
N-CLA10000-P1- -9-9-11

L

13 15° 14 30° 15 45° 16 60° 17 75° 18 90° 19 105° 20 120° 21 135° 22 150° 23 165° 24 180°

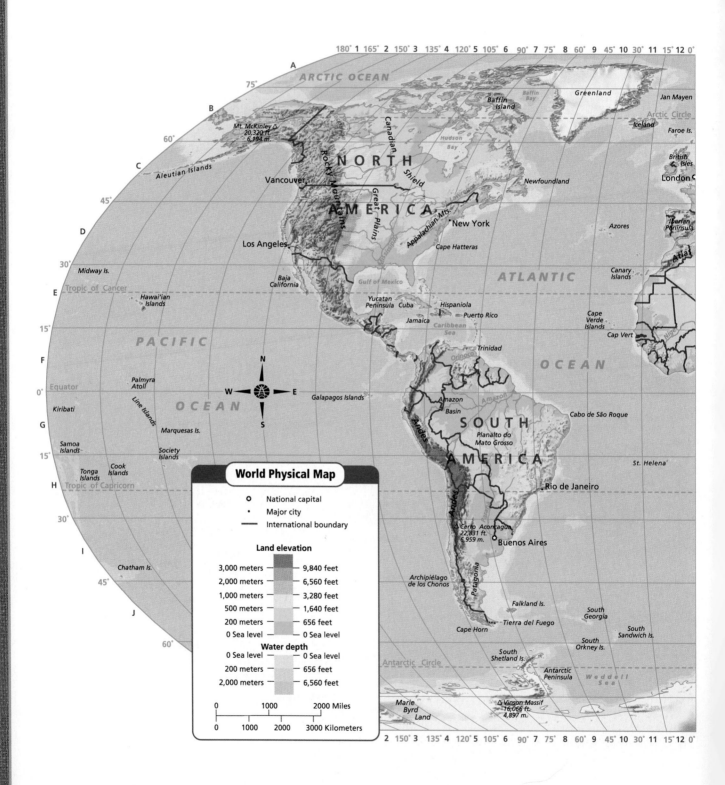

**World Physical Map**

⊙ National capital
• Major city
— International boundary

**Land elevation**

| | |
|---|---|
| 3,000 meters | 9,840 feet |
| 2,000 meters | 6,560 feet |
| 1,000 meters | 3,280 feet |
| 500 meters | 1,640 feet |
| 200 meters | 656 feet |
| 0 Sea level | 0 Sea level |

**Water depth**

| | |
|---|---|
| 0 Sea level | 0 Sea level |
| 200 meters | 656 feet |
| 2,000 meters | 6,560 feet |

0    1000    2000 Miles

0   1000   2000   3000 Kilometers

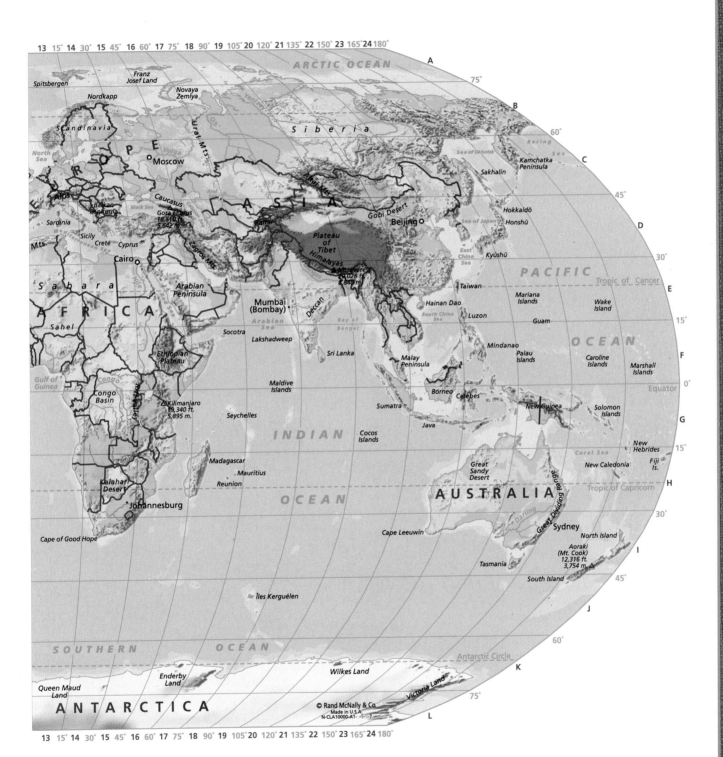

13 15° 14 30° 15 45° 16 60° 17 75° 18 90° 19 105° 20 120° 21 135° 22 150° 23 165° 24 180°

ARCTIC OCEAN

75°

Spitsbergen
Franz
Josef Land
Nordkapp
Novaya
Zemlya
Siberia
60°
Bering
Sea
Scandinavia
Ural Mts.
Ob
Yenisey
Kamchatka
Peninsula
North
Sea
Moscow
Volga
Don
ASIA
Sakhalin
Sea of Okhotsk
45°
Alps
Balkan
Peninsula
Caucasus
Gora Elbrus
18,510 ft.
5,642 m.
Black Sea
Aral
Sea
Pamir
Altai Mts.
Gobi Desert
Beijing
Sea of Japan
Hokkaidō
Honshū
Sardinia
Sicily
Crete Cyprus
Zagros Mts.
Plateau
of
Tibet
Himalayas
Mt. Everest
29,028 ft.
8,848 m.
East
China
Sea
Kyūshū
30°
Mts.
Mediterranean Sea
Cairo
Nile
Red Sea
Arabian
Peninsula
Deccan
Taiwan
PACIFIC
Tropic of Cancer
Sahara
AFRICA
Mumbai
(Bombay)
Arabian
Sea
Hainan Dao
South China
Sea
Mariana
Islands
Wake
Island
15°
Sahel
Socotra
Lakshadweep
Bay of
Bengal
Luzon
Guam
OCEAN
Ethiopian
Plateau
Sri Lanka
Mindanao
Palau
Islands
Caroline
Islands
Marshall
Islands
Gulf of
Guinea
Congo
Basin
Kilimanjaro
19,340 ft.
5,895 m.
Maldive
Islands
Malay
Peninsula
Borneo
Celebes
Equator 0°
Great Rift Valley
Seychelles
Sumatra
New Guinea
Solomon
Islands
15°
INDIAN
Cocos
Islands
Java
Coral Sea
New
Hebrides
Fiji
Is.
Madagascar
Mauritius
Reunion
Great
Sandy
Desert
New Caledonia
Kalahari
Desert
OCEAN
AUSTRALIA
Great Dividing Range
Tropic of Capricorn
30°
Johannesburg
Darling
Sydney
Cape of Good Hope
Cape Leeuwin
North Island
Aoraki
(Mt. Cook)
12,316 ft.
3,754 m.
Tasmania
45°
Îles Kerguélen
South Island
60°
SOUTHERN
OCEAN
Antarctic Circle
Queen Maud
Land
Enderby
Land
Wilkes Land
Victoria Land
75°
ANTARCTICA
© Rand McNally & Co.
Made in U.S.A.
N-CLA10000-A1- -5- -7

13 15° 14 30° 15 45° 16 60° 17 75° 18 90° 19 105° 20 120° 21 135° 22 150° 23 165° 24 180°

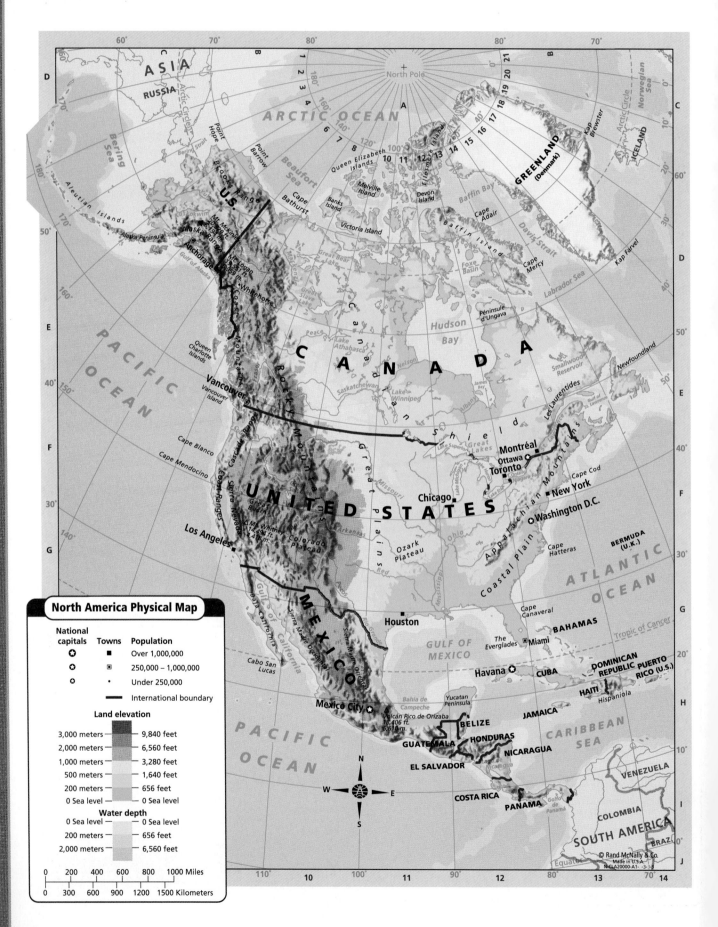

## North America Physical Map

**National capitals** ⊕ / ⊙ / ⊙
**Towns**
■ Over 1,000,000
▣ 250,000 – 1,000,000
• Under 250,000
—— International boundary

### Land elevation
3,000 meters — 9,840 feet
2,000 meters — 6,560 feet
1,000 meters — 3,280 feet
500 meters — 1,640 feet
200 meters — 656 feet
0 Sea level — 0 Sea level

### Water depth
0 Sea level — 0 Sea level
200 meters — 656 feet
2,000 meters — 6,560 feet

0 200 400 600 800 1000 Miles
0 300 600 900 1200 1500 Kilometers

© Rand McNally & Co.
Made in U.S.A.
N-CLA20000-A1- -3- 8

RAND McNALLY

## South America Physical Map

**National capitals**
⊛ Over 1,000,000
⊕ 250,000 – 1,000,000
⊙ Under 250,000

**Towns**
■ Over 1,000,000
▣ 250,000 – 1,000,000
• Under 250,000

**Population**

International boundary

**Land elevation**
| 3,000 meters | 9,840 feet |
| 2,000 meters | 6,560 feet |
| 1,000 meters | 3,280 feet |
| 500 meters | 1,640 feet |
| 200 meters | 656 feet |
| 0 Sea level | 0 Sea level |

**Water depth**
| 0 Sea level | 0 Sea level |
| 200 meters | 656 feet |
| 2,000 meters | 6,560 feet |

0 200 400 600 800 1000 Miles
0 300 600 900 1200 1500 Kilometers

© Rand McNally & Co.
Made in U.S.A.
N-CLA40000-A1- -4- -4

RAND M²NALLY

A29

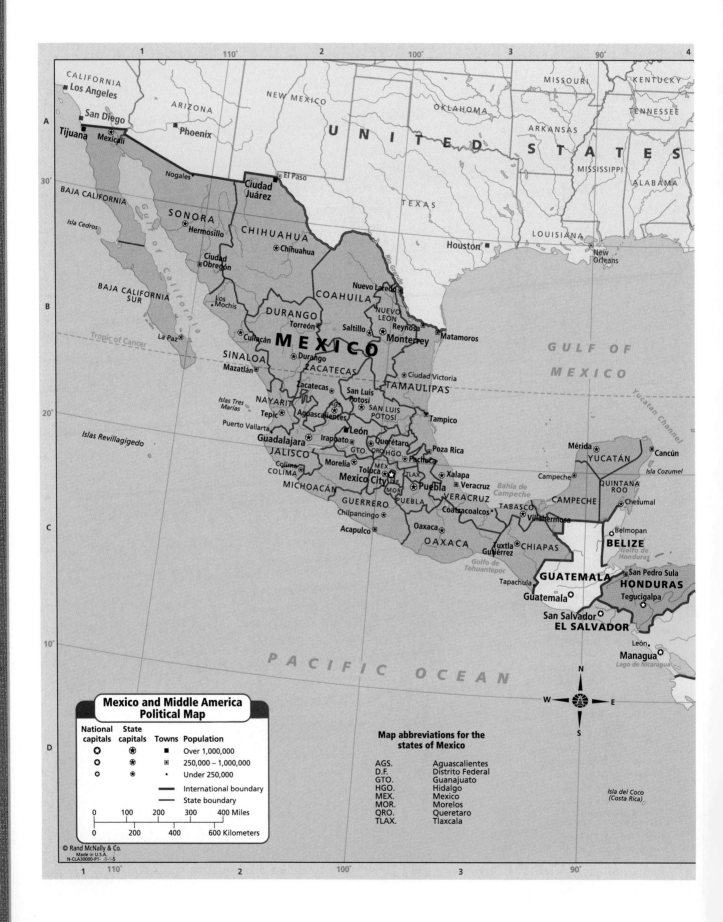

## Mexico and Middle America Political Map

| National capitals | State capitals | Towns | Population |
|---|---|---|---|
| ✪ | ✪ | ■ | Over 1,000,000 |
| ✪ | ✪ | ▣ | 250,000 – 1,000,000 |
| ✪ | ✪ | • | Under 250,000 |

International boundary
State boundary

0   100   200   300   400 Miles
0      200      400      600 Kilometers

© Rand McNally & Co.
Made in U.S.A.
N-CLA30000-P1- -5- -5

### Map abbreviations for the states of Mexico

| AGS. | Aguascalientes |
|---|---|
| D.F. | Distrito Federal |
| GTO. | Guanajuato |
| HGO. | Hidalgo |
| MEX. | Mexico |
| MOR. | Morelos |
| QRO. | Queretaro |
| TLAX. | Tlaxcala |

Isla del Coco
(Costa Rica)

RAND MCNALLY

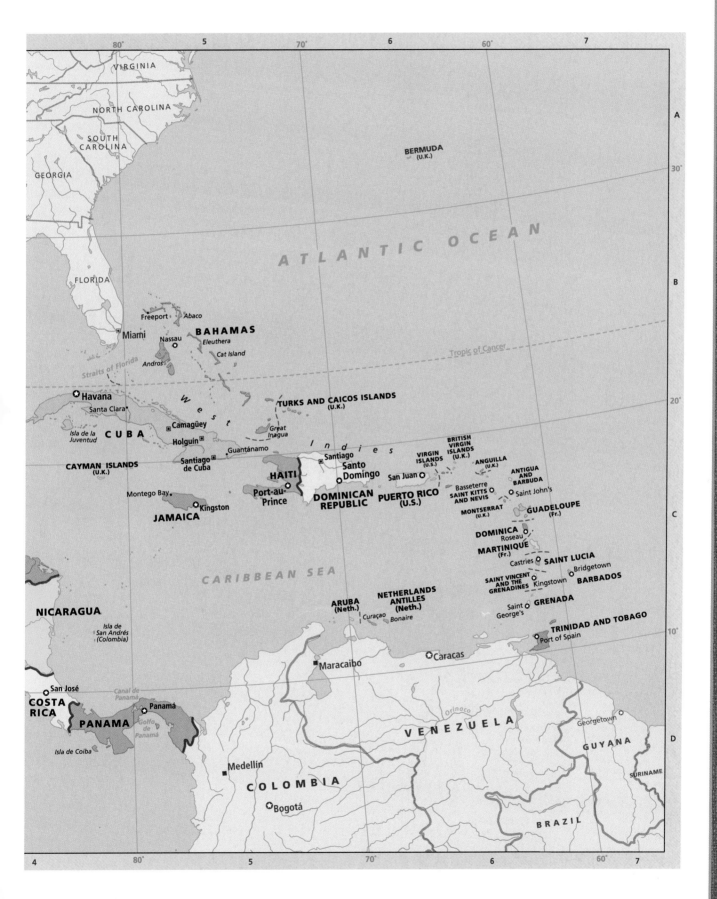

ATLANTIC OCEAN

VIRGINIA

NORTH CAROLINA

SOUTH CAROLINA

GEORGIA

FLORIDA

BERMUDA
(U.K.)

30°

Freeport  Abaco
Miami
Nassau   Eleuthera
Straits of Florida   Cat Island
Andros

BAHAMAS

Tropic of Cancer

Havana
Santa Clara          TURKS AND CAICOS ISLANDS          20°
Camagüey                                (U.K.)
Isla de la                          Great
Juventud   CUBA   Holguín         Inagua

CAYMAN ISLANDS   Santiago   Guantánamo          BRITISH
(U.K.)           de Cuba                        VIRGIN
                               Santiago        ISLANDS   ANGUILLA
Montego Bay        HAITI      Santo   VIRGIN   (U.K.)   (U.K.)   ANTIGUA
                            Domingo   ISLANDS                    AND
                   Port-au-          (U.S.)   San Juan          BARBUDA
Kingston           Prince   DOMINICAN  PUERTO RICO  Basseterre  Saint John's
JAMAICA                     REPUBLIC    (U.S.)    SAINT KITTS
                                                  AND NEVIS   GUADELOUPE
                                         MONTSERRAT           (Fr.)         C
                                          (U.K.)
                                        DOMINICA  Roseau
CARIBBEAN SEA                           MARTINIQUE
                                          (Fr.)
                                        Castries   SAINT LUCIA
                                                        Bridgetown
                            NETHERLANDS  SAINT VINCENT  Kingstown  BARBADOS
NICARAGUA        ARUBA      ANTILLES     AND THE
                (Neth.)     (Neth.)      GRENADINES
Isla de                Curaçao  Bonaire   Saint   GRENADA
San Andrés                              George's            10°
(Colombia)                                       TRINIDAD AND TOBAGO
                                                 Port of Spain

San José                    Maracaibo      Caracas

COSTA      Canal de
RICA       Panamá   Panamá
           PANAMA                                   Georgetown
Isla de Coiba  Golfo de                VENEZUELA              GUYANA   D
               Panamá
                                Orinoco
           Medellín                                           SURINAME

           COLOMBIA
                Bogotá                              BRAZIL

RAND M℠NALLY

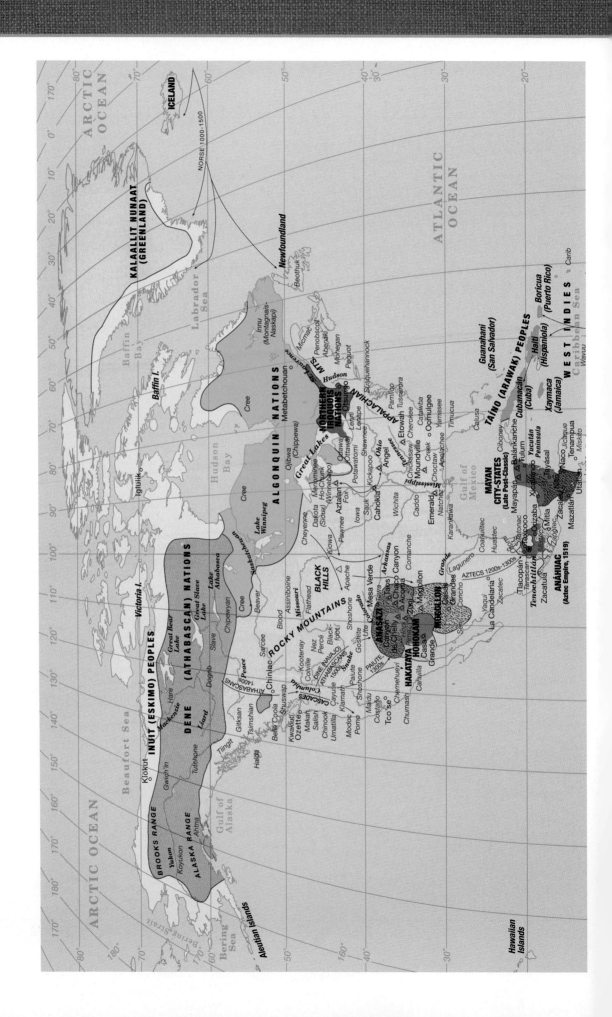

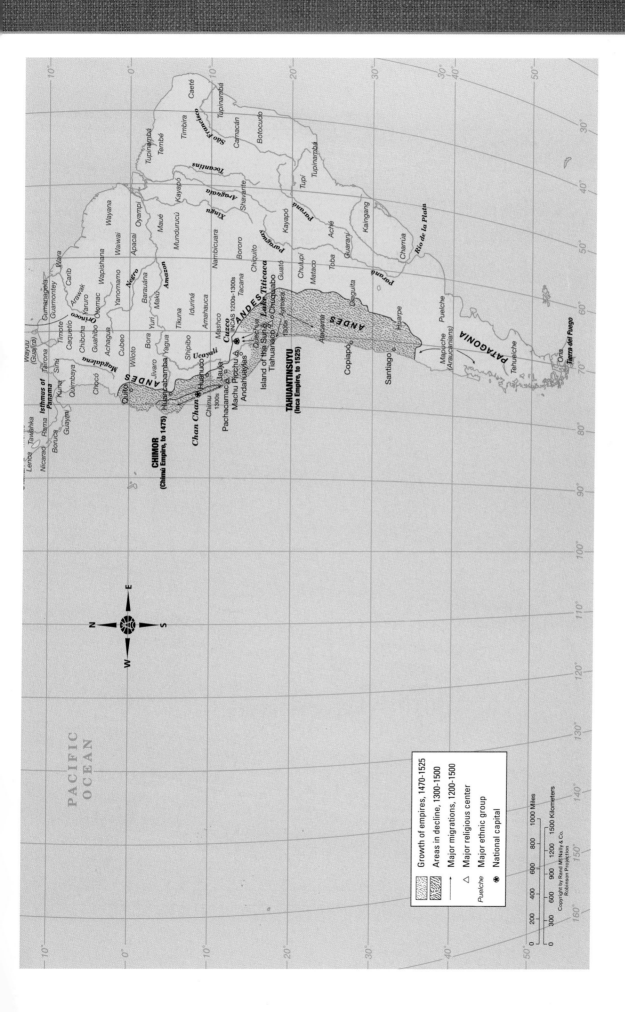

PACIFIC
OCEAN

N E S W

CHIMOR
(Chimú Empire, to 1475)

Chan Chan

CUZCO
INCAS 1200s–1300s

TAHUANTINSUYU
(Inca Empire, to 1525)

ANDES

PATAGONIA

Tierra del Fuego

**Legend:**
- Growth of empires, 1470–1525
- Areas in decline, 1300–1500
- → Major migrations, 1200–1500
- △ Major religious center
- *Puelche* Major ethnic group
- ✸ National capital

0  200  400  600  800  1000 Miles
0  300  600  900  1200  1500 Kilometers

Copyright by Rand McNally & Co.
Robinson Projection

RAND McNALLY

A33

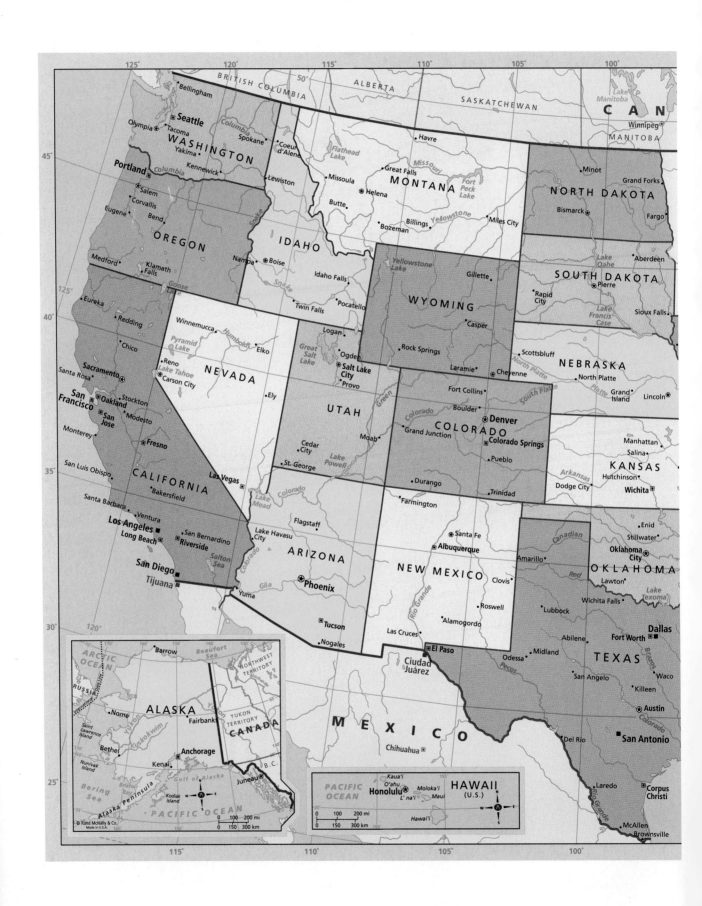

RANDMNALLY

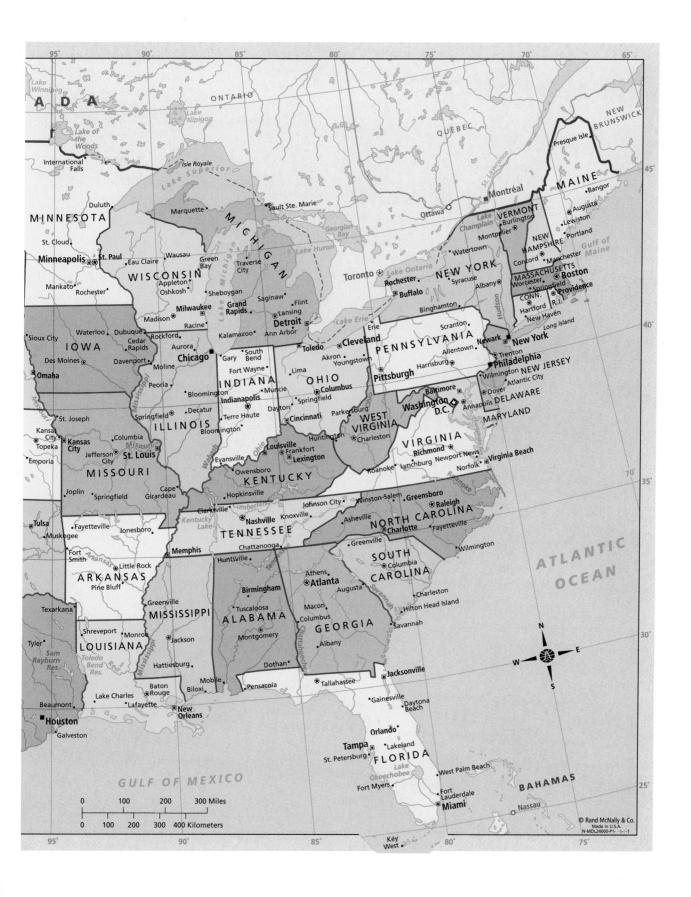

CANADA

ONTARIO

QUÉBEC

Lake Winnipeg
Lake of the Woods
International Falls
Duluth
Isle Royale
Marquette
Sault Ste. Marie
Lake Superior
Lake Nipigon
Ottawa
Montréal
MAINE
Presque Isle
NEW BRUNSWICK
Bangor
Augusta
Lewiston
Portland
Gulf of Maine

MINNESOTA
St. Cloud
Minneapolis  St. Paul
Mankato
Rochester
Eau Claire  Wausau
WISCONSIN
Appleton  Oshkosh
Madison  Milwaukee
Racine
Green Bay
Sheboygan
MICHIGAN
Traverse City
Saginaw  Flint
Grand Rapids  Lansing
Kalamazoo  Ann Arbor
Lake Michigan
Lake Huron
Georgian Bay
Toronto
Lake Ontario
Rochester
Buffalo
Lake Erie
Erie
VERMONT
Burlington
Montpelier
Watertown
NEW YORK
Syracuse
Albany
NEW HAMPSHIRE
Concord  Manchester
Portland
MASSACHUSETTS
Worcester  Boston
Springfield
CONN.  Providence
Hartford  R.I.
New Haven
Binghamton
Scranton
Long Island

IOWA
Sioux City
Waterloo  Dubuque
Cedar Rapids
Des Moines  Davenport
Omaha
Rockford  Aurora
Moline  Chicago
Peoria
Bloomington
Springfield
ILLINOIS
Decatur
Terre Haute
Bloomington
Gary  South Bend
Fort Wayne
INDIANA
Muncie
Indianapolis
Lima
OHIO
Columbus
Springfield
Dayton
Cincinnati
Toledo
Akron
Youngstown
Cleveland
PENNSYLVANIA
Pittsburgh
Harrisburg
Allentown
Newark  New York
Trenton
Philadelphia
Wilmington  NEW JERSEY
Atlantic City
Dover  DELAWARE
Baltimore
Washington D.C.
Annapolis  MARYLAND

Missouri
St. Joseph
Kansas City
Topeka
Emporia
Columbia
Jefferson City
St. Louis
MISSOURI
Joplin
Springfield
Cape Girardeau
Wabash
Evansville
Owensboro
Louisville  Frankfort
Lexington
KENTUCKY
Hopkinsville
Ohio
Parkersburg
WEST VIRGINIA
Charleston
Huntington
VIRGINIA
Richmond
Roanoke  Lynchburg  Newport News
Norfolk  Virginia Beach
Roanoke

Tulsa
Muskogee
Fort Smith
Fayetteville
Jonesboro
ARKANSAS
Little Rock
Pine Bluff
Arkansas
Clarksville
Nashville  Knoxville
Johnson City
Winston-Salem  Greensboro
Raleigh
Asheville
NORTH CAROLINA
Charlotte  Fayetteville
Wilmington
TENNESSEE
Memphis
Chattanooga
Huntsville
Greenville
SOUTH CAROLINA
Columbia
Charleston
Hilton Head Island

Texarkana
Tyler
Sam Rayburn Res.
Shreveport  Monroe
LOUISIANA
Toledo Bend Res.
Red
Jackson
MISSISSIPPI
Greenville
Hattiesburg
Birmingham
Tuscaloosa
ALABAMA
Montgomery
Dothan
Athens  Atlanta
Augusta
Macon
Columbus
GEORGIA
Albany
Savannah
Chattahoochee
Savannah

Beaumont
Houston
Galveston
Lake Charles  Lafayette
Baton Rouge
New Orleans
Biloxi  Mobile
Pensacola
Tallahassee
Jacksonville
GULF OF MEXICO

Gainesville
Daytona Beach
Orlando
Tampa  Lakeland
St. Petersburg
FLORIDA
Lake Okeechobee
West Palm Beach
Fort Myers
Fort Lauderdale
Miami
Key West

ATLANTIC OCEAN

BAHAMAS
Nassau

Lake Champlain
Hudson
St. Lawrence

N
W  E
S

0  100  200  300 Miles
0  100  200  300  400 Kilometers

© Rand McNally & Co.
Made in U.S.A.
N-MOL24000-P1- -1-1- -1

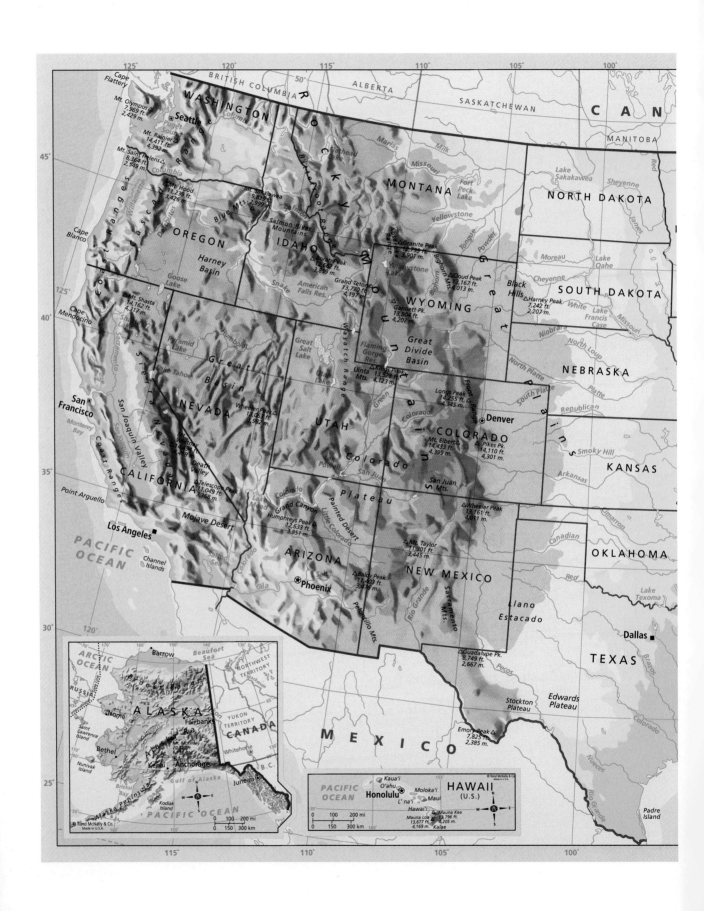

RAND McNALLY

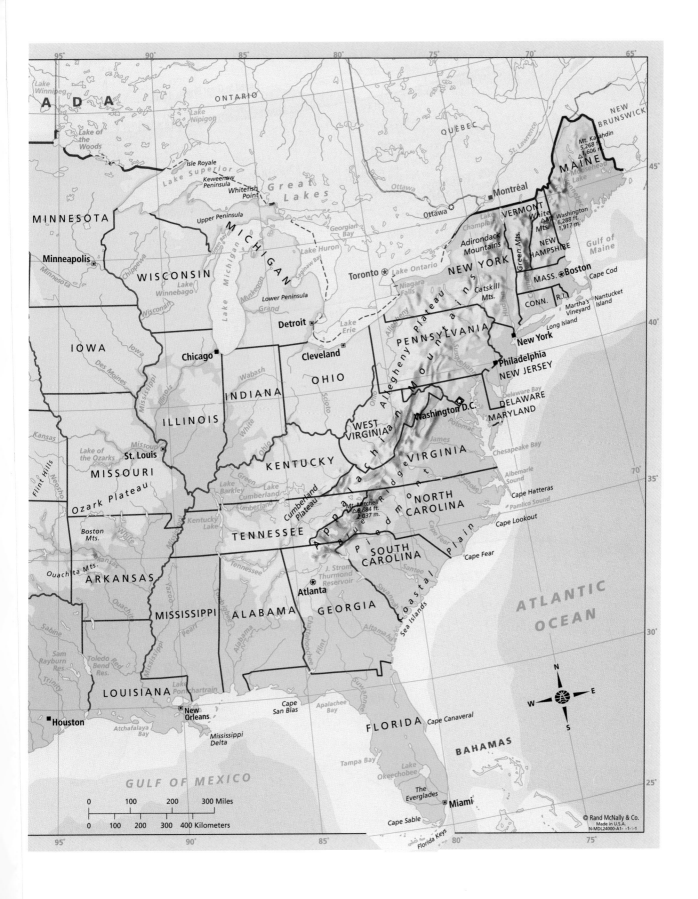

CANADA

**MINNESOTA**

Lake Winnipeg
Lake of the Woods
Isle Royale
Keweenaw Peninsula
Whitefish Point
Lake Superior
Upper Peninsula

ONTARIO

QUÉBEC

Lake Nipigon

Ottawa

St. Lawrence

NEW BRUNSWICK

MAINE
Mt. Katahdin 5,268 ft. 1,606 m.
Moosehead Lake

Montréal

Ottawa

Lake Champlain

VERMONT
White Mts.
Mt. Washington 6,288 ft. 1,917 m.

NEW HAMPSHIRE

Gulf of Maine

Minneapolis

Minnesota

WISCONSIN

MICHIGAN

Lake Huron

Georgian Bay

Saginaw Bay

Lower Peninsula
Grand
Muskegon

Lake Michigan

Lake Winnebago

Wisconsin

Chippewa

Toronto
Lake Ontario
Niagara Falls

Adirondack Mountains

NEW YORK

Catskill Mts.

Green Mts.

Hudson

MASS. Boston
Cape Cod

CONN.
R.I.
Martha's Vineyard
Nantucket Island

IOWA

Des Moines

Chicago

Cleveland

Detroit
Lake Erie

OHIO

Allegheny Plateau

PENNSYLVANIA

Appalachian Mountains

Susquehanna

New York
Long Island

Philadelphia
NEW JERSEY

DELAWARE
Delaware Bay

ILLINOIS

INDIANA

Wabash

White

Ohio

WEST VIRGINIA

Washington D.C.
Potomac

MARYLAND

Chesapeake Bay

Missouri

Lake of the Ozarks

St. Louis

MISSOURI

Ozark Plateau

Green

Lake Barkley

KENTUCKY

Cumberland

Kentucky Lake

VIRGINIA
James

Roanoke

Albemarle Sound

Cape Hatteras

Flint Hills

Kansas

Neosho

Boston Mts.

White

Cumberland

Cumberland Plateau

Mt. Mitchell 6,684 ft. 2,037 m.

NORTH CAROLINA

Pamlico Sound

Cape Lookout

Ouachita Mts.

ARKANSAS

Ouachita

TENNESSEE

Tennessee

Blue Ridge

Piedmont

SOUTH CAROLINA

Cape Fear

Cape Fear

Coastal Plain

Sabine

Yazoo

Pearl

MISSISSIPPI

ALABAMA

Alabama

GEORGIA

J. Strom Thurmond Reservoir

Atlanta

Santee

Savannah

Sea Islands

ATLANTIC OCEAN

Sam Rayburn Res.

Toledo Bend Res.

Trinity

Red

LOUISIANA

Lake Pontchartrain

Mississippi

Chattahoochee

Flint

Altamaha

Houston

New Orleans
Atchafalaya Bay
Mississippi Delta

Cape San Blas

Apalachee Bay

FLORIDA
Cape Canaveral

Suwannee

N
W E
S

GULF OF MEXICO

Tampa Bay

Lake Okeechobee

BAHAMAS

The Everglades

Miami

Cape Sable

Florida Keys

0 100 200 300 Miles
0 100 200 300 400 Kilometers

© Rand McNally & Co.
Made in U.S.A.
N-MDL24000-A1- -1-1-1

# Three Worlds Meet

**Beginnings–1650**

**1 The World Before 1500**
Beginnings–1500 pages 2–23

**2 European Exploration of the Americas**
1492–1650 pages 24–55

## Why It Matters Now

In the 1400s, brave men from Europe crossed uncharted waters to find new trade routes and to discover their destiny. Their actions would write a new chapter in world history. Their story—of their interactions with other peoples and of how they learned from those peoples—is our story, and has made us who we are today.

Until lions have their historians,
tales of the hunt shall always
glorify the hunters.
—African Proverb

# The World Before 1500

## Beginnings–1500

 **ESSENTIAL QUESTION**

How did American, African, and European societies differ from one another before 1500?

## CONNECT ↻ Geography & History

How did world geography both divide and connect the different cultures of the Americas, Africa, and Europe?

**Think about:**

**1** how the Atlantic Ocean's currents affected early navigation, exploration, and trade

**2** how people might have first arrived in the Americas

**3** ways in which Africans and Europeans might have come into contact

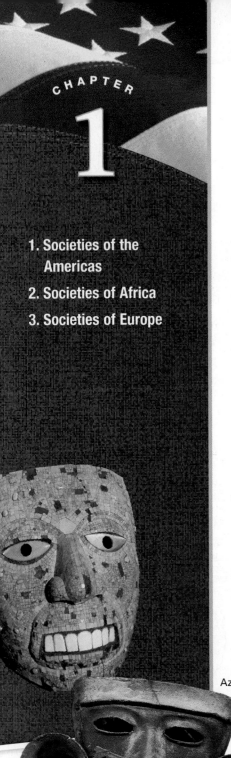

Aztec masks

**A.D. 1200s** Kingdom of Mali takes over Ghana.

▼

**Effect** Islam spreads through West Africa.

Victims of the Black Death that killed millions in the 1300s

**35,000 B.C.**

The "first Americans" migrate from Asia.

▼

**Effect** Native peoples spread throughout the Americas, forming numerous societies.

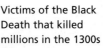

Inca figure

**1300s** The Inca and Aztec Empires expand in the Americas.

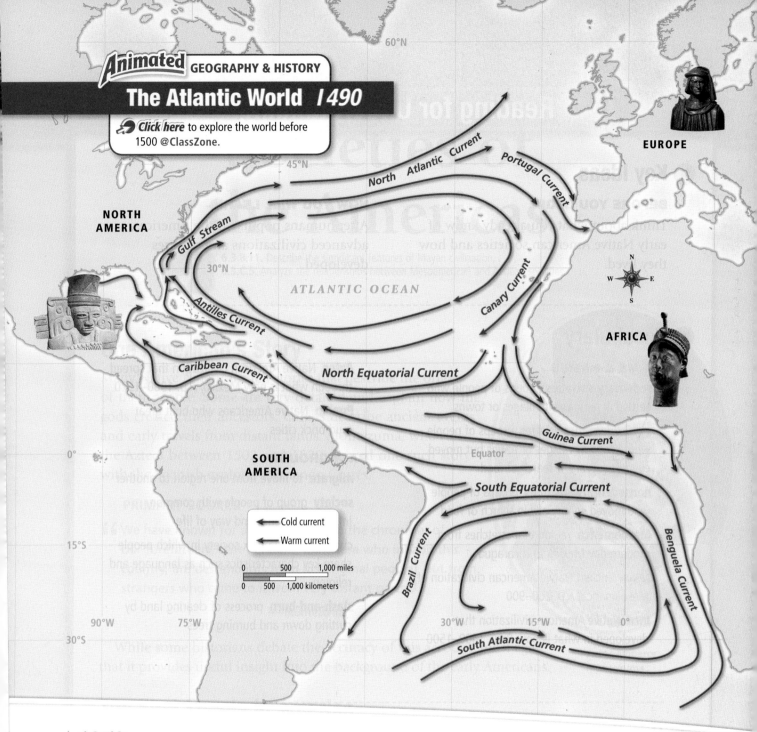

EUROPE

NORTH
AMERICA

Gulf Stream

North Atlantic Current

Portugal Current

45°N

30°N

ATLANTIC OCEAN

Antilles Current

Canary Current

AFRICA

Caribbean Current

North Equatorial Current

Guinea Current

0°

SOUTH
AMERICA

Equator

South Equatorial Current

15°S

Brazil Current

Benguela Current

— Cold current
— Warm current

0   500   1,000 miles
0   500   1,000 kilometers

90°W   75°W

30°W   15°W   0°

30°S

South Atlantic Current

---

**1350** The Renaissance begins
in Italy.

▼

**Effect** New ideas about the world, science,
and human nature spread throughout Europe.

late **1400s**

**1400s** European sailors begin to
understand the Atlantic Ocean's currents.

▼

**Effect** Routes to Africa and the Americas
open for exploration.

Kongo and Ndongo rule
Central Africa.

*The World Before 1500* **3**

time, three basic types of societies developed throughout North, Central, and South America. (See chart on next page.)

- **sedentary societies** created permanent towns or villages. These towns were densely populated and included wide streets, large farms, markets, and hundreds of dwellings.
- **semisedentary societies** built towns or villages, but moved them every few years in search of migrating animals and new land for farming.
- **nonsedentary societies** did not construct permanent villages or towns but created small, temporary camps that could be easily moved in a continual search for large game, fish, and edible plants.

▲ **CATEGORIZE** Describe the early societies of the Americas.

**Connect** *to the* **World**

**Social Organization**
As you will see in the next section, similar patterns of social development occurred in Africa.

## The Rise of Civilizations

▼ **KEY QUESTION** What led people to form complex civilizations?

Around 1200 B.C. the first Americans began to form larger communities. This occurred when several small societies joined one another through political alliance or military takeover. Over time, some of these communities grew into vast **civilizations**—complex societies in which people share important characteristics such as language, religion, art, dress, and political structure.

**The Growth of Complex Societies** The first great American civilization emerged in **Mesoamerica**, a region that stretches from modern-day Mexico to Nicaragua. Between 1200 B.C. and 400 B.C., the Olmec people dominated the region by creating large farms on the region's rich soil. There they grew enough maize, or corn, to feed thousands of people.

After the Olmec, Mesoamerica was ruled by the **Maya** peoples. During the period from A.D. 250 to 900, the Maya made many advances in art and architecture that endured through the centuries. They constructed large cities that included giant temples, numerous shrines, vast marketplaces, and even ball courts for games and contests.

Perhaps the most recognizable pieces of Olmec art are the colossal heads carved of stone. Some are over ten feet tall and weigh thousands of pounds.

**Early Civilizations Fall** Living in a complex civilization had many advantages. With more workers available, it became possible to build bigger cities, cultivate larger farms, store extra food, and form immense armies for protection. But despite these advantages, each of these early civilizations declined before Europeans reached the Americas in 1492.

No one knows why the early civilizations fell. Some historians blame major environmental changes such as rivers drying up or volcanic eruptions. Others suggest that catastrophic weather, disease, warfare, widespread famine, or internal political revolt are more likely causes.

▲ **SUMMARIZE** Identify the advantages and disadvantages of living in complex civilizations.

## EARLY SOCIETIES OF THE AMERICAS

By 1500, Native American societies displayed a variety of customs, languages, cultures, and ways of life. These societies can be categorized into three major groups.

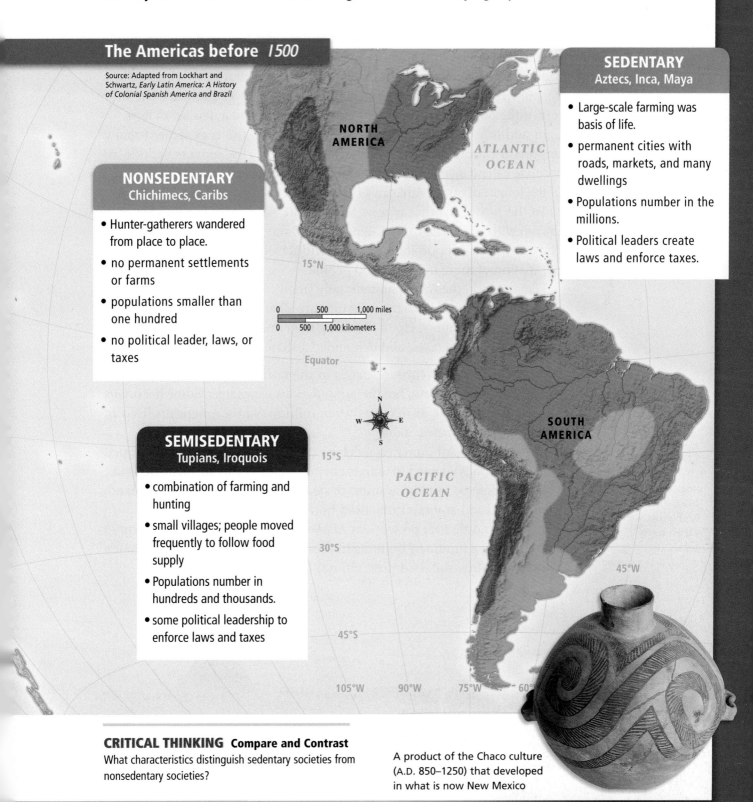

### The Americas before 1500

Source: Adapted from Lockhart and Schwartz, *Early Latin America: A History of Colonial Spanish America and Brazil*

NORTH AMERICA

ATLANTIC OCEAN

15°N

Equator

PACIFIC OCEAN

SOUTH AMERICA

15°S

30°S

45°S

45°W

105°W    90°W    75°W    60°

0    500    1,000 miles
0    500    1,000 kilometers

#### NONSEDENTARY
Chichimecs, Caribs

- Hunter-gatherers wandered from place to place.
- no permanent settlements or farms
- populations smaller than one hundred
- no political leader, laws, or taxes

#### SEMISEDENTARY
Tupians, Iroquois

- combination of farming and hunting
- small villages; people moved frequently to follow food supply
- Populations number in hundreds and thousands.
- some political leadership to enforce laws and taxes

#### SEDENTARY
Aztecs, Inca, Maya

- Large-scale farming was basis of life.
- permanent cities with roads, markets, and many dwellings
- Populations number in the millions.
- Political leaders create laws and enforce taxes.

### CRITICAL THINKING  Compare and Contrast
What characteristics distinguish sedentary societies from nonsedentary societies?

A product of the Chaco culture (A.D. 850–1250) that developed in what is now New Mexico

## Pre-Contact Societies

🔻 **KEY QUESTION** How did the environment affect the way native peoples lived?

When the great civilizations declined, native peoples broke apart into small, self-governing societies. But these groups faced difficult times. Often they had to fight one another for land, crops, and valuable trade goods. Once again, people sought the advantages of living in larger communities.

**Aztec and Inca Empires** Between 1300 and 1500, two great empires dominated Mesoamerica. In what is now Peru, the **Inca** people created a vast civilization that included as many as ten million inhabitants. Originally these people were part of smaller, independent groups. Over the years, the Inca united the population under a single government and a new set of laws.

In addition to creating a new political system, the Inca created many important cultural and scientific advances. Inca achievements include an accurate calendar, an early clock, and a system of paved roads that ran most of the length of South America's Pacific coast.

To the north, in what is now Mexico, the **Aztec** people also created a major civilization. The capital, Tenochtitlán, was an island in Lake Texcoco. The city was built upon logs and mud and served as a natural fortress for a population of more than 140,000 people.

Like the Inca, the Aztecs united many small communities under a single government. They did this by using military alliances and warfare to control their weaker neighbors. Upon defeating their enemies, the Aztecs enforced new laws, collected taxes, and demanded a share of crops and labor.

**Native North Americans** Societies to the north were not as complex as those in Mexico and Peru, but their populations were larger. Some historians believe that by 1400, as many as seven million Native Americans lived in what is now the United States.

Throughout North America, a diverse range of native societies developed as various groups adapted to unique environments—whether arctic ice fields, scorching deserts, muddy swamps, or dense forests. In each case, the land, plants, and local animals influenced how native peoples lived.

In the far north, near present-day Alaska, the Inuit (IHN•yoo•iht) peoples lived on frozen tundra by building homes made of ice. They hunted whales, seals, and walrus and used these animals for food, fuel, and clothing.

*(top)* Inca earrings, A.D. 200 *(bottom)* Macchu Picchu ruins can be visited today, high in the Andes. *(inset)* close up of typical Inca stonework

Toward the southwest—in modern-day Arizona and New Mexico—the **Pueblo** people made their homes. Pueblo people used irrigation to build large farms in the valley regions near the desert. In addition, they constructed multi-storied mud-brick houses under steep mountain cliffs. This design provided both shade from the sun and protection from enemies.

In the Northeast, between the Great Lakes and the Atlantic Ocean, lived the Iroquois and Algonquin peoples. In this region, Native Americans built large villages and farms using **slash-and-burn** agriculture, a process of chopping down trees and burning the land to clear it. Often, this method was repeated annually—clearing large tracts of land for only one season of farming.

Native American religions were also influenced by the environment. Native Americans worshipped many gods whom they believed controlled the sun, moon, sky, crops, rivers, and animals.

**An Isolated World** Although Native Americans interacted extensively with their neighbors, and sometimes traveled great distances, they remained isolated from the rest of the world. As a result, before the 1400s, people throughout the Americas had no experience of European technology, warfare, culture, or disease.

Built by the Pueblo people, Mesa Verde stands in present-day Colorado.

 **SYNTHESIZE** Explain why the natural environment was so important to early societies.

---

**New Jersey Core Curriculum Content Standards** *Review*

 **ONLINE QUIZ** For test practice, go to **Interactive Review @ ClassZone.com**

### TERMS & NAMES

1. Explain the significance of
   - sedentary societies
   - semisedentary societies
   - nonsedentary societies
   - Mesoamerica
   - Maya
   - Inca
   - Aztec
   - Pueblo

### USING YOUR READING NOTES

2. **Categorize** Complete the diagram you began at the beginning of this section.

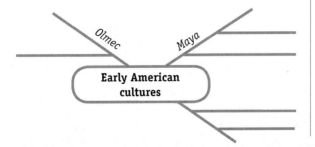

Olmec   Maya

Early American cultures

### KEY IDEAS

3. How did ancient people migrate to the Americas?

4. How did the natural environment affect the development of early societies?

### CRITICAL THINKING

5. **Analyze** How did sedentary societies differ from semisedentary societies and nonsedentary societies?

6. **Causes and Effects** How did warfare and military alliances affect early societies?

7. **Connect** *to* **Today** What are the advantages of living in a modern civilization?

8. **Art** Research the civilizations that developed in the Americas. Then draw a picture representing some aspect of an early Native American civilization.

**Click here** for more information on the Aztec market
@ ClassZone.com

## Aztec Market

As the sun rises over the Aztec capital at Tenochtitlán, merchants and customers begin arriving at the city's largest market. The market, in an area called Tlatelolco, attracted around 25,000 people each day to buy and sell gold, silver, flowers, cloth, food, and slaves.

**Click here** Modern Mexico City, which stands on the site of the Aztec capital.

**Click here** A woman at a Mexico City market prepares *nopales*, or cactus pads, a traditional food.

**Click here** Diagram of the city of Tenochtitlán.

## Activity

### Build a Model of Tenochtitlán

1. In groups of 2 or 3 students, use the internet to research the layout and buildings of Tenochtitlán.

2. With your group, build a model of an important building in the city.

3. Present the model to the class, explaining its place and importance in the city.

## ▶ Key Ideas

**BEFORE, YOU LEARNED**
After humans migrated to the Americas, a variety of civilizations developed.

**NOW YOU WILL LEARN**
In Africa, complex and simple societies competed for resources and trade in three geographical zones.

## ▶ Vocabulary

**TERMS & NAMES**

**Sahara** a large desert in Northern Africa

**Islam** religion that teaches there is one God, named Allah, and Muhammad is his prophet

**Muslim** follower of the religion of Islam

**Ghana** West African kingdom that prospered between A.D. 700 and 1000

**Mali** West African kingdom that ruled from about 1200 to 1400

**Kongo** Central African kingdom in the 1400s that engaged in warfare and slavery

**Ndongo** Central African kingdom that ruled during the 1400s

**BACKGROUND VOCABULARY**

**savanna** flat grassland with abundant wildlife, thorny bushes, and scattered trees

**slave** someone who is captured for use in forced, unpaid labor

**Visual Vocabulary** Sahara

## ▶ Reading Strategy

Re-create the cluster diagram shown at right. As you read and respond to the **KEY QUESTIONS**, use the outer circles to record important information about how each cultural group adapted to its environment.

 **Skillbuilder Handbook, page R4.**

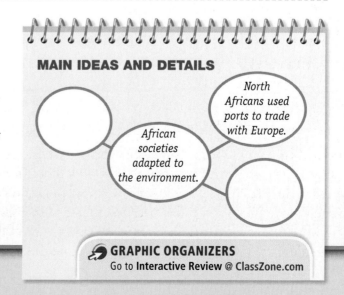

**MAIN IDEAS AND DETAILS**

North Africans used ports to trade with Europe.

African societies adapted to the environment.

**GRAPHIC ORGANIZERS**
Go to **Interactive Review** @ ClassZone.com

# Societies of Africa

**6.3.C.2.** Discuss the spread of Islam in . . . Northern Africa and the influence of Islamic ideas and practices on other cultures and social behavior, including the significance of the Quran and the Five Pillars of Islam.

**6.3.C.4.** Analyze the rise of the West African Empires of Ghana, Mali, and Songhay and compare with changes in Asia, Europe, and the Americas.

## One African's Story

As early as the 1300s, Africans were exploring the Atlantic Ocean, traveling north to Europe and west into the uncharted sea. In 1324, emperor Mansa Musa of Mali told the historian Al-Umari of the previous emperor's attempt to discover the edge of the Atlantic Ocean.

Mansa Musa

### PRIMARY SOURCE

❝ The ruler who preceded me would not believe that it was impossible to discover the limits of the neighboring sea. . . he had 200 ships equipped and filled them with men. . . water and supplies in sufficient quantity to last for years. . . . They went away; their absence was long before any of them returned. ❞

—Mansa Musa, as told by historian Al-Umari

As the story goes, only one ship returned to Mali. No one knows what happened to the others. But Musa's account shows that Africans looked westward into the Atlantic Ocean in hopes of finding new lands to conquer and goods to trade.

## African Kingdoms Before 1200

🔻 **KEY QUESTION** How did Africa's three geographic zones influence the development of early societies?

Although geographically isolated from Europe and Asia, early African societies were connected to the world through extensive trade and commerce.

**Geography and Culture** The African continent consists of three large geographic zones. In the north is the **Sahara**, a huge, hot desert area with little or no vegetation. In the south is a vast **savanna**, a long and flat grassland with abundant wildlife, thorny bushes, and scattered trees. And in the middle, in Central and Western Africa, is a great transitional, or midway, zone where dense rain forests and broad rivers meet the Atlantic Ocean.

CHAPTER

2

1. Spain Claims an Empire

2. European Competition in North America

3. The Spanish and Native Americans

4. Beginnings of Slavery in the Americas

# European Exploration of the Americas

## 1492–1650

 **ESSENTIAL QUESTION**

How did Europeans transform life in the Americas?

**CONNECT** Geography & History

How might the physical geography of the Americas have affected European exploration?

**Think about:**

1. the major landforms and rivers

2. the distances covered. For example, the distance between Spain and the east coast of North America is almost 4,000 miles

3. the harsh conditions under which people traveled

This map of the Americas was drawn about 200 years after European settlement began.

Christopher Columbus

**1492**

Columbus lands in the Americas.

**1494** Treaty of Tordesillas signed.
▼
**Effect** Set boundary for Spanish and Portuguese exploration.

**1521** Cortés conquers the Aztec Empire for Spain.

**1531** Pizarro conquers the Inca Empire for Spain.

**1534** Cartier explores the St. Lawrence in search of the Northwest Passage.

16th-century Inca goblet

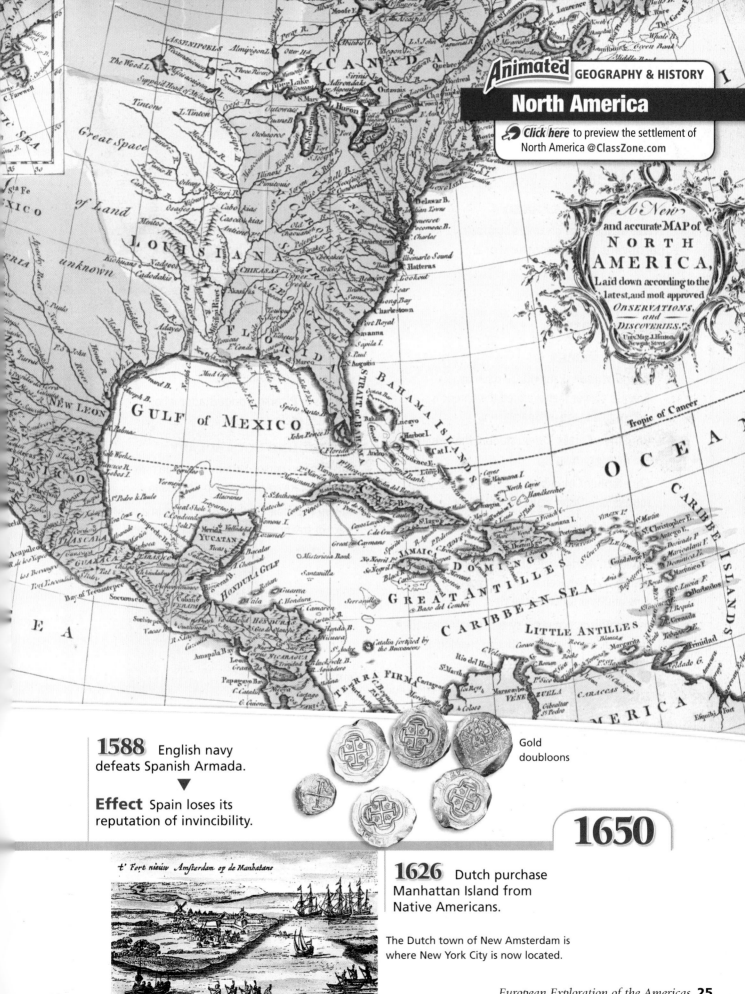

*A New and accurate MAP of NORTH AMERICA, Laid down according to the latest, and most approved OBSERVATIONS, and DISCOVERIES. Univ. Mag. J. Hinton, Newgate Street.*

**1588** English navy
defeats Spanish Armada.

▼

**Effect** Spain loses its
reputation of invincibility.

Gold
doubloons

**1650**

**1626** Dutch purchase
Manhattan Island from
Native Americans.

The Dutch town of New Amsterdam is
where New York City is now located.

't Fort nieüw Amfterdam op de Manhatans

*European Exploration of the Americas* **25**

# Reading for Understanding

## ▶ Key Ideas

**BEFORE, YOU LEARNED**
Trade and social changes spurred Europeans to explore the world.

**NOW YOU WILL LEARN**
After Columbus' voyages, the Spanish quickly conquered the Native American empires of the Aztecs and the Inca.

## ▶ Vocabulary

**TERMS & NAMES**

**conquistador** (kahn•KEES•tuh•dawr) Spanish soldier that explored the Americas and claimed land for Spain

**Hernando Cortés** *conquistador* who brought the Aztecs to ruin

**Christopher Columbus** Italian navigator who looked for a faster water route to Asia

**Treaty of Tordesillas** (tawr•day•SEEL•yahs) 1494 treaty in which Spain and Portugal agreed to divide lands of the Western hemisphere between them and moved the Line of Demarcation to the west

**mercantilism** economic system that increased money in a country's treasury by creating a favorable balance of trade

**Amerigo Vespucci** Italian sailor who explored what is now the Americas

**Francisco Pizarro** *conquistador* who defeated the Inca

**BACKGROUND VOCABULARY**

**missionary** person sent by the Church to convert Native Americans to Christianity

**alliance** people or nations involved in a pact or treaty

**Visual Vocabulary**
Amerigo Vespucci

## ▶ Reading Strategy

Re-create the diagram shown at right. As you read and respond to the **KEY QUESTIONS**, use the diagram to record important events in sequence.

 **See Skillbuilder Handbook, page R5.**

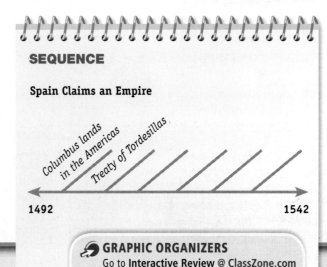

**SEQUENCE**

**Spain Claims an Empire**

Columbus lands in the Americas

Treaty of Tordesillas

1492                    1542

**GRAPHIC ORGANIZERS**
Go to **Interactive Review** @ ClassZone.com

# Spain Claims an Empire

 **6.3.D.3.** Compare the social and political elements of Incan and Aztec societies, . . . .
**6.4.C.4.** Discuss the characteristics of the Spanish and Portuguese exploration and conquest of the Americas, including Spanish interaction with the Incan and Aztec empires, . . . .

## One European's Story

In 1519, soldiers known as *conquistadors* (kahn•KEES•tuh•dawrz), or conquerors, explored the Americas and claimed them for Spain. **Hernando Cortés** was a leading *conquistador*. He led a Spanish army into Tabasco, an Aztec province in southeastern Mexico.

Cortés took advantage of the weaknesses of the Aztec Empire. He relied on a young Aztec woman, named Doña Marina, or Malinche (mah•LEEN•kay), to help him. One of the Spanish foot soldiers wrote about Malinche.

Malinche acted as translator and guide to Cortés for the Spanish conquest of the Aztecs.

**PRIMARY SOURCE**

❝ Doña Marina . . . although she had . . . seen us surrounded in the late battles, and knew that all of us were wounded and sick, yet never allowed us to see any sign of fear in her, only . . . courage. ❞

—Bernal Díaz del Castillo, quoted in *Notable Latin American Women*

Malinche played a key role in the Spanish conquest of the Aztecs. Spanish colonists followed to create a rich new empire in the Americas.

## Exploring the Americas

🔻 **KEY QUESTION** Why did the Europeans want to explore the Americas?

In the 1400s, Italian and Arab merchants ran the trade with Asia. Other Europeans, envious of Italian wealth, began to look for different routes to Asia.

**Shortcuts to Asia** Sailors seeking a route to Asia depended on the skill of their navigator. A navigator plans the course of a ship by using maps and nautical instruments to find its position. In the 1400s, a Portuguese prince,

Henry the Navigator, began a school of navigation. He paid for sailing expeditions to explore the Atlantic and the west coast of Africa. His ships traveled further down the African coast than Europeans had ever gone. Those voyages began Europe's age of discovery. This age of discovery eventually led Europeans to the Americas.

Under the sponsorship of Henry the Navigator, the Portuguese developed an improved ship called the caravel. The caravel had triangular sails as well as square sails. Square sails carried the ship forward when the wind was at its back. Triangular sails allowed the caravel to sail into the wind. The caravel was better than other European ships of the time at sailing into the wind.

In January 1488, Bartolomeu Días (DEE-uhs), a Portuguese explorer, reached the southern tip of Africa. After sailing around it, he returned to Portugal at the urging of his crew. Días is said to have named the tip the Cape of Good Hope because he hoped they had found a route to Asia.

**A Water Route to Asia** Ten years later, another Portuguese explorer, Vasco da Gama, followed Días's route around the Cape. He continued north along the eastern coast of Africa. Then he sailed east across the Indian Ocean to India. At last, someone had found an all-water route to Asia.

This route meant that the Portuguese could now trade with Asia without dealing with Muslim or Italian traders. Portugal took control of the valuable spice trade. Portuguese merchants grew wealthy. Spain and other European rivals wanted to take part in this rich trade. They began to look for their own water routes to Asia.

**Christopher Columbus** Before da Gama's voyage, an Italian sailor and navigator named **Christopher Columbus** thought he knew a faster way to reach Asia by sailing west across the Atlantic, which he calculated to be a shorter journey.

Spain's rulers, King Ferdinand and Queen Isabella, liked Columbus' plan because they wanted a share of the rich Asian trade. The Queen also welcomed a chance to spread Christianity. After years of waiting, Columbus assembled his ships —the *Niña,* the *Pinta,* and the *Santa María*—at the port of Palos de la Frontera in southern Spain. His fleet left the harbor on August 3, 1492.

## History Makers

### Christopher Columbus    1451–1506

Genoese sailor Christopher Columbus thought he had found a faster way to reach Asia by sailing west across the Atlantic. But he underestimated the distance around the globe. In 1484, Columbus asked the king of Portugal to finance his voyage. The king refused, citing Columbus' miscalculations and the promising progress of his own explorers. Columbus then asked the Spanish court. In January 1492, his plan was accepted, and on August 3, 1492, Columbus set out on a voyage that changed history.

With one voyage to present-day Hispaniola, Columbus changed European views of the world. People soon realized that he had reached continents that had been unknown to them. Thanks to Columbus, the Atlantic Ocean became a bridge that connected Europe, Africa, and the Americas. Columbus completed a total of four voyages.

**CRITICAL THINKING** **Evaluate** What qualities and character traits, shown in Columbus' actions, may have made him a good leader?

 **ONLINE BIOGRAPHY** For more on Christopher Columbus, go to the **Research & Writing Center @ ClassZone.com**

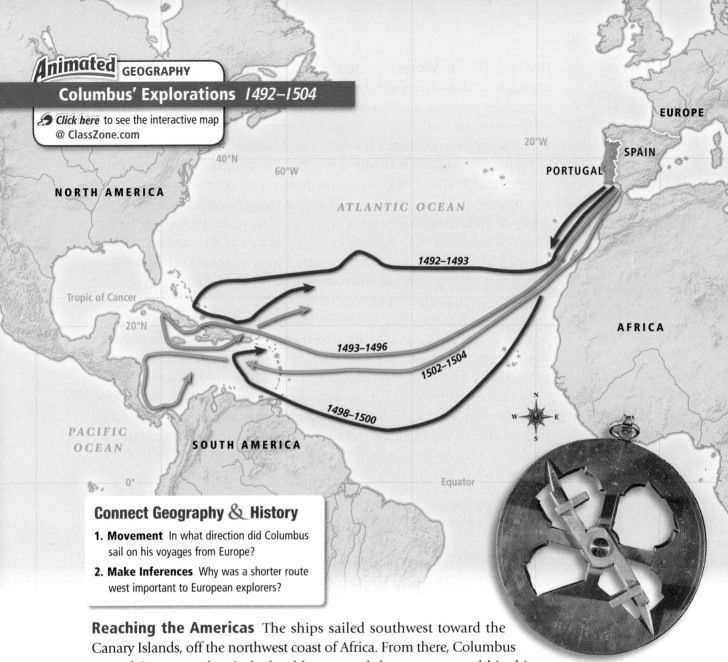

EUROPE

SPAIN

PORTUGAL

20°W

40°N

60°W

NORTH AMERICA

ATLANTIC OCEAN

1492–1493

Tropic of Cancer

20°N

AFRICA

1493–1496

1502–1504

1498–1500

PACIFIC OCEAN

SOUTH AMERICA

N
W   E
S

0°

Equator

### Connect Geography & History

1. **Movement** In what direction did Columbus sail on his voyages from Europe?

2. **Make Inferences** Why was a shorter route west important to European explorers?

The astrolabe was invented by the ancient Greeks. Sailors used it to help find their latitude.

**Reaching the Americas** The ships sailed southwest toward the Canary Islands, off the northwest coast of Africa. From there, Columbus was relying on trade winds that blew toward the west to speed his ships across the ocean. (See map on page 1.) But by October 10, he had been at sea for about four weeks and had not sighted land during that time. The crew were close to mutiny, or open rebellion, when they finally saw land.

The ships landed on an island in the Caribbean Sea. Columbus believed he had reached somewhere in India, or Asia, where spices grew. Columbus named the island San Salvador and claimed it for Spain. Eager to reach the rich country of Japan, which he believed to be nearby, he left San Salvador with a group of islanders. For the next three months he visited several of the Caribbean islands.

Finally he reached an island he named La Española, which today is called Hispaniola. There, Columbus and his men found gold and pearls. This convinced Columbus that he had reached Asia. He decided to return home. In 1493 he sailed back to Spain. Believing that he had found a water route to Asia, he wrote to Ferdinand and Isabella. No one suspected that Columbus had landed near continents entirely unknown to Europeans.

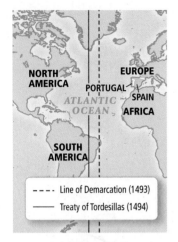

Line of Demarcation (1493)
Treaty of Tordesillas (1494)

The Line of Demarcation between Spain and Portugal was adjusted by the Treaty of Tordesillas.

**Dividing Up the World** Due to the surge in explorations, in 1493, Pope Alexander VI drew an imaginary line around the world to decide who would control the lands that sailors were exploring. It was called the Line of Demarcation. Portugal could claim all non-Christian lands to the east of the line. Spain could claim the non-Christian lands to the west.

Portugal's King John II was unhappy—he believed the line favored Spain. He demanded that the Spanish rulers meet with him to change the pope's decision. In June 1494, the two countries agreed to the **Treaty of Tordesillas** (tawr•day•SEEL•yahs). This treaty moved the Line of Demarcation more than 800 miles farther west. The change later allowed Portugal to claim much of eastern South America, which later became the Portuguese colony of Brazil. This agreement led to an increase in Spanish and Portuguese voyages of exploration.

Europeans had three main goals during this age of exploration: first, they wanted to spread Christianity beyond Europe. Many expeditions included **missionaries**, or people sent to covert the native people to Christianity. Second, they wanted to expand their empires. Third, they wanted riches.

By increasing their wealth, European countries could gain power and security. An economic system called **mercantilism** was the way Europeans enriched their treasuries. For example, colonies provided mines that produced gold and silver. They also produced goods, such as crops, that could be traded for gold and silver. Finally, they served as a market for the home country.

## European Exploration of the Americas *1500–1550*

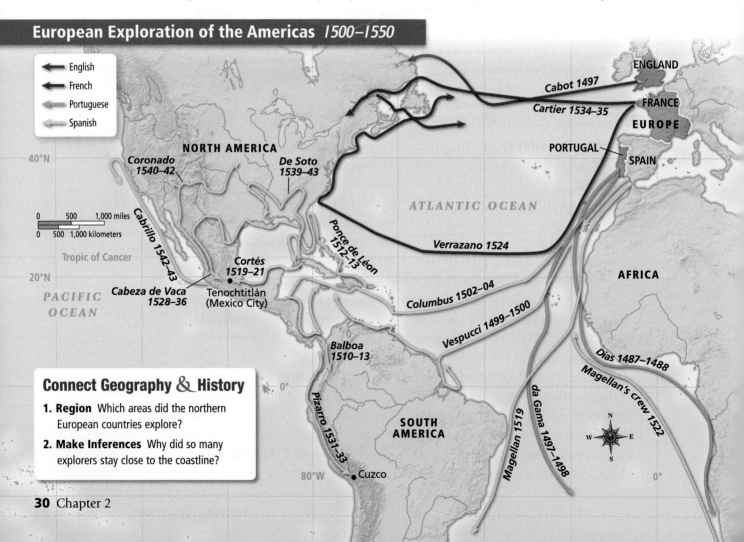

**Connect Geography & History**

1. **Region** Which areas did the northern European countries explore?
2. **Make Inferences** Why did so many explorers stay close to the coastline?

**Europeans Explore New Lands** After Columbus' first voyage, many explorers went to sea. **Amerigo Vespucci** (vehs•POO•chee) was one of the first. He was an Italian sailor who set out in 1501 to find a sea route to Asia. Vespucci realized, however, that the land he saw on this voyage was not Asia. A German mapmaker, impressed by Vespucci's account of the lands, named the continent "America" after him.

This is a 1596 engraving of the historic voyage of Amerigo Vespuccl.

Another famous explorer was the Spaniard Vasco Núñez de Balboa. Balboa heard Native American reports of another sea and a province rich in gold. In 1513, he led an expedition through the jungles of Panama and reached the Pacific Ocean. Balboa claimed the ocean and all the lands around it for Spain.

But perhaps no explorer was more capable than the Portuguese sailor Ferdinand Magellan. He proposed to reach Asia by sailing west around South America. The Spanish king agreed to fund Magellan's voyage. In 1519, Magellan set out from Spain with five ships and about 270 men. After a stormy passage around South America, Magellan entered the Pacific Ocean. For several months his crew crossed the Pacific, suffering great hardship.

Eventually, Magellan reached the Philippines, where he became involved in a local battle and was killed. But his crew traveled on. In 1522, the one remaining ship arrived back in Spain. The sailors in Magellan's crew were the first people to sail around the world.

▲ **ANALYZE MOTIVES** Explain why Europeans wanted to explore the Americas.

## Conquering the Americas

▼ **KEY QUESTION** Why did Native American civilizations fall so quickly?

When Columbus arrived in the Caribbean, Native Americans had been living in the Americas for tens of thousands of years. In what is now Mexico and Peru, complex civilizations had developed. But these civilizations were unprepared for the Spanish attacks that began in the early 16th century.

**The Invasion of Mexico** While Magellan's crew was sailing around the world, the Spanish began their conquest of the Americas. Hernando Cortés landed on the Mexican coast with 508 *conquistadors* in 1519. He already knew that the Aztec Empire was not a single unified nation. Rather it was made up of several hundred mini-states who fought one another and hated their conquerors—the Aztecs.

The Spanish arrival shook the Aztec Empire, which ruled most of Mexico. The Aztec emperor Montezuma II feared that Cortés was an Aztec god sent to reclaim the throne. Montezuma sent Cortés precious gifts to get him to leave. But the gifts only excited Spanish dreams of riches.

The Spaniards marched inland and formed pacts or treaties, called **alliances**, with the native peoples who hated Aztec rule. After a few months,

Cortés reached the Aztec capital, Tenochtitlán (teh•nawch•tee•TLAHN). Montezuma welcomed Cortés with great ceremony. However, Cortés took Montezuma captive and tried to rule the Aztec by giving commands through the Aztec emperor.

But the Aztecs rebelled and trapped the Spanish in Tenochtitlán. On June 30, 1520, the Aztecs caught the Spaniards trying to escape, and fighting broke out. About 1,800 Spaniards and their allies were killed. The Spaniards called the event *La Noche Triste* (lah NAW•cheh TREES•teh)—the Sad Night.

Despite this defeat, Cortés led his forces back to Tenochtitlán in May 1521. At this point, the Spaniards got help from an unusual source—disease. Many Aztecs fell victim to an outbreak of smallpox, which severely weakened their ranks. The germs that caused this disease had been brought to America by the Europeans.

On his return, Cortés placed Tenochtitlán under siege for several months. When Tenochtitlán finally fell in August 1521, the empire lay in ruins. On the rubble of the Aztec capital, the Spanish built Mexico City. Over time, the populations and cultures of Spain and Mexico merged and produced a new society, that of the present-day nation of Mexico.

Aztec calendar

## COMPARING Aztec & Inca Civilizations

In 1521, Cortés conquered the Aztecs. Pizzarro had subdued the Inca by the mid-1530s. Both were powerful empires for about 400 years and left a rich cultural heritage to their regions.

| | Beliefs | Social structure | Economy | Writing | Agriculture |
|---|---|---|---|---|---|
| **Aztec** (Present-day Northern Mexico; capital: Tenochtitlán) | Supreme sun god; total loyalty to the king | 1. king 2. nobles (military and priests) 3. commoners 4. slaves | State-controlled: provinces pay tribute in gold, food, and other products | Pictographic (picture) writing on paper made of deerskin or fiber | Terraced farming; floating gardens, causeways, aqueducts |
| **Inca** (Parts of present-day Argentina, Bolivia, Chile, Ecuador, and Peru; capital: Cuzco) | Supreme sun god; total loyalty to the emperor | 1. emperor 2. royal families 3. small units of commoners | State-controlled: provinces pay tribute in labor | No known writing system; kept records on knotted cords, or *quipus*. | Terraced farming; steep mountainous region |

## CRITICAL THINKING

1. **Compare and Contrast** What were the biggest differences between the Aztec and Inca societies?

2. **Make Inferences** Why did the Aztecs demand tribute in goods rather than labor?

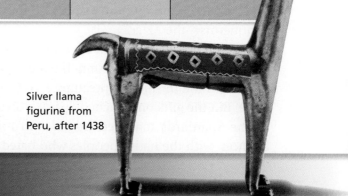

Silver llama figurine from Peru, after 1438

**The Inca Empire Falls** Despite the fall of the Aztec, the Inca still had a powerful empire in the Cuzco Valley in what is now Peru. By 1525, the Inca ruled a 2,000-mile-long territory in the Andes Mountains along the western coast of South America. The Inca also possessed much gold and silver. Stories of Incan wealth reached the Spanish. In 1531, a *conquistador* named **Francisco Pizarro** led 180 men into Peru.

Incan emperor Atahualpa (ah•tuh•WAHL•puh) went to greet the Spaniards, but the Spanish killed thousands of Inca and took him captive. To free himself, Atahualpa gave the Spanish a treasure of gold, but the Spaniards killed him anyway. With the Incan emperor dead, the Inca Empire collapsed. Then Pizarro took control of this area for Spain, which he had already called Peru.

How did the great Aztec and Inca empires fall to such small groups of *conquistadors*? Spanish success can be explained by three major reasons.

- The Spanish weakened the Aztec and Inca empires by making alliances with their enemies
- The spread of European diseases killed millions of Native Americans
- Over time, the Spanish acted brutally toward the Native Americans under their control.

Spain conquered the major Native American empires in Central and South America. Then the Spaniards began to look at other parts of the Americas.

 **CAUSES AND EFFECTS** Describe the impact Europeans had on native societies.

**Connecting History**

**Highway System**
The Inca highway system consisted of two main north-south roads, each about 2,250 miles long. Ironically, the Inca roads greatly aided the Spanish in their attempts to conquer the empire in 1532.

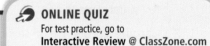

**New Jersey Core Curriculum Content Standards *Review***

**ONLINE QUIZ**
For test practice, go to
**Interactive Review @ ClassZone.com**

### TERMS & NAMES

**1.** Explain the importance of

- *conquistador*
- mercantilism
- Hernando Cortés
- Amerigo Vespucci
- Christopher Columbus
- Francisco Pizarro
- Treaty of Tordesillas

### USING YOUR READING NOTES

**2. Sequence** Complete the diagram you started at the beginning of this section.

**Spain Claims an Empire**

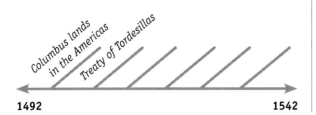

1492                                    1542

### KEY IDEAS

**3.** Why did Europeans set their sights on reaching Asia?

**4.** Why did Spain succeed in conquering so much of the Americas?

### CRITICAL THINKING

**5. Evaluate** How effective was the Treaty of Tordesillas?

**6. Summarize** What factors enabled the Spanish to conquer the Aztecs?

**7. Connect to Today** How are Spanish and Native American traditions present in North American culture today?

**8. Writing Journal** Imagine you are a sailor on Columbus' first voyage. Write a journal entry about reaching Hispaniola.

## ▶ Key Ideas

**BEFORE, YOU LEARNED**
Following Columbus' voyages, the Spanish conquered the Native American empires of the Aztecs and the Inca.

**NOW YOU WILL LEARN**
Competition for the riches of the Americas led to tension and conflict among European powers.

## ▶ Vocabulary

**TERMS & NAMES**

**Henry Hudson**  English explorer who sailed for the Dutch and landed at the coast of present-day New York

**John Cabot**  Italian sailor who sailed for the English and is believed to have landed in Newfoundland, Canada

**Giovanni da Verrazzano**  Italian sailor who sailed for the French with hopes of finding an all-water route to Asia

**Jacques Cartier**  French sailor who sailed up the St. Lawrence River to present-day Montreal

**Spanish Armada**  large fleet of ships sent to invade England and restore Catholicism

**Samuel de Champlain**  founder of fur-trading post at Quebec

**New France**  first permanent French colony in North America

**New Netherland**  first permanent Dutch colony in North America

**BACKGROUND VOCABULARY**

**galleon**  sailing ship

**Visual Vocabulary**  Spanish Armada

## ▶ Reading Strategy

Re-create the diagram shown at right. As you read and respond to the **KEY QUESTIONS**, use the diagram to record important events in this section.

 See Skillbuilder Handbook, page R6.

| CATEGORIES | |
|---|---|
| England | *Sent Cabot to find a western route across the Atlantic (1497)* |
| France | *Founded Fort Caroline (1564)* |
| Netherlands | |
| Spain | |

**GRAPHIC ORGANIZERS**
Go to **Interactive Review** @ ClassZone.com

# European Competition in North America

 **6.3.D.1.** Discuss factors that contributed to oceanic travel and exploration in the 15th and 16th centuries, . . . .
**6.4.C.1.** Discuss factors that stimulated European overseas explorations between the 15th and 17th centuries and the impact of that exploration on the modern world.

## One European's Story

In 1609, the Englishman **Henry Hudson** set sail from Europe. He sailed under the Dutch flag and hoped to find a route to China. Arriving at the coast of present-day New York, he sailed up the river that now bears his name. In his journal, Hudson described what he saw.

### PRIMARY SOURCE

❝ The land is the finest for cultivation that I ever in my life set foot upon, and it also abounds in trees . . . . These natives are a very good people; for when they saw that I would not remain, they supposed that I was afraid of their bows, taking their arrows, they broke them in pieces and threw them into the fire. ❞

—Henry Hudson, quoted in *Discoverers of America*

Henry Hudson sailed into Hudson Bay, Canada, in 1610. The bay became the center of a thriving fur-trading region.

Hudson did not find a route to Asia, but continued to try. In 1610, while sailing for the English, his crew rebelled and set Hudson adrift in a small boat. Hudson, his son, and seven others were never heard from again.

## The Race to Explore North America

🔻 **KEY QUESTION** What drew European explorers to North America?

Dazzled by Spain's success, other European nations hoped to enjoy the riches of the Americas. As England and France searched for a Northwest passage, Spanish explorers sought a Native American civilization in North America as rich as the ones they had discovered in South and Central America.

# Reading for Understanding

## ▶ Key Ideas

**BEFORE, YOU LEARNED**
European powers faced conflict and tension as they competed for riches in North America.

**NOW YOU WILL LEARN**
Native Americans' lives were transformed as Spain grew rich from its new empire.

## ▶ Vocabulary

**TERMS & NAMES**

***encomienda*** (en•koh•mee•YEN•duh) grant of Native American slave labor

***hacienda*** (HAH•see•YEN•duh) large farm or estate

**mission** settlement created by the Spanish church in order to convert Native Americans to Christianity

**Bartolomé de Las Casas** Spaniard who fought for Native American rights

**Columbian Exchange** transfer of plants, animals and diseases between the Western and Eastern hemispheres

**BACKGROUND VOCABULARY**

**plantation** large farm that raises cash crops

**export** to send abroad for trade or sale

**Visual Vocabulary** Mission

## ▶ Reading Strategy

Re-create the diagram shown at right. As you read and respond to the **KEY QUESTIONS**, use the diagram to note important details that support the main idea of this section. Add ovals as needed.

 See Skillbuilder Handbook, page R4.

**MAIN IDEAS AND DETAILS**

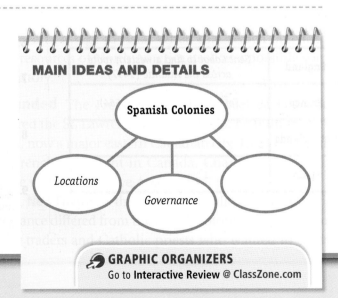

Spanish Colonies

Locations

Governance

**GRAPHIC ORGANIZERS**
Go to **Interactive Review** @ ClassZone.com

# The Spanish and Native Americans

**6.4.C.3.** Compare the political, social, economic, and religious systems of Africans, Europeans, and Native Americans who converged in the western hemisphere after 1492 . . . .
**6.4.D.1.** Analyze the political, social, and cultural characteristics of the English colonies.

## One American's Story

Guamán Poma de Ayala, a Peruvian Native American, wrote to King Philip III of Spain in the early 1600s. He described the treatment of Native Americans at the hands of the Spanish.

### PRIMARY SOURCE

❝ It is their [the Spanish] practice to collect Indians into groups and send them to forced labor without wages, while they themselves receive the payment. ❞

—Guamán Poma, Letter to a King

In his letter, Poma de Ayala asked the king to help the Native Americans and uphold the rule of law in Peru. If the king actually read the letter, it made no difference. Spanish colonists continued to mistreat Native Americans as the Spanish Empire expanded in the Americas.

A Spanish missionary forces a Native American woman to work at a loom.

## Spanish Colonies in the Americas

🔽 **KEY QUESTION** How did Spain draw wealth from its new lands?

The Spanish Empire grew rapidly, despite competition from other European countries. Eventually, Spain controlled much of the Americas. Spain took several steps to establish an effective colonial government. It also transformed the landscape and reorganized societies throughout the Americas.

**Organizing the Empire** First, Spain divided its American empire into two provinces called New Spain and Peru. Each province was called a viceroyalty. The top official of each viceroyalty, called the viceroy, ruled in the king's name.

The Spanish also built new roads to transport people and goods across the empire. These roads stretched outward from the capitals at Mexico City and Lima. The roads helped Spain control the colonies by allowing soldiers to

## Spain's American Empire 1700

NORTH AMERICA

ATLANTIC OCEAN

30°N

Tropic of Cancer

WEST INDIES

15°N

Mexico City

CENTRAL AMERICA

PACIFIC OCEAN

Equator 0°

Lima

SOUTH AMERICA

Tropic of Capricorn

30°S

Viceroyalty of New Spain

Viceroyalty of Peru

0   500   1,000 miles
0   500   1,000 kilometers

45°S

105°W   90°W   60°W   45°W   30°W

Aztec two-headed snake

### Connect Geography & History

1. **Location** Which viceroyalty included the West Indies?

2. **Draw Conclusions** What advantage did Spain have by dividing its empire into two provinces?

move quickly from place to place. Roads also improved the Spanish economy because materials, such as gold and silver, could be transported efficiently to the coast and then to Spain.

The Spaniards made sure that people with Spanish backgrounds held power in the colonies. Spanish-born colonists such as Cortés made up the top layer of colonial society. Just below the Spanish were the Creoles—people of Spanish descent who were born in the colonies. The next step down the social order were the *mestizos*. *Mestizos* are people of mixed Spanish and Native American ancestry. The people with the least power and fewest rights were Native Americans and enslaved Africans.

**Making the Colonies Productive** Spanish colonists received **encomiendas** as a way of collecting tribute from the conquered peoples. An *encomienda* was a grant of forced Native American labor. The *encomienda* system helped the Spanish colonies become more productive.

The Spanish rulers also created large estates, called **haciendas**, to provide food for the colony. *Haciendas* usually became large farms where Native Americans worked to grow cash crops, such as coffee and cotton. The *encomienda* and *hacienda* systems put much of the power and land in the hands of a few people. The Spanish also forced Native Americans to work on **plantations**, large farms that raised cash crops. These crops were usually **exported**, or sent to Europe. The most important crop was sugar.

Although sugar was in great demand in Europe, there was not much land there to grow it. The demand led to the development of sugar plantations in the Americas. On his second voyage to the Americas, in 1493, Columbus brought sugar cane to Hispaniola, one of the Caribbean islands he had landed on in 1492. He found ideal conditions for sugar production. Spanish planters expanded operations to the nearby islands that Spain colonized.

Sugar plantations required many workers, so the Spanish planters turned to native peoples, such as the Taino. Through *encomiendas*, the Spaniards forced thousands of Taino to work in the fields. The plantations thrived, but many of the Taino suffered and died.

▲ **SUMMARIZE** Explain how the Spanish got wealthy from their new lands.

# The Church in the Spanish Colonies

▼ **KEY QUESTION** How did the Church contribute to colonization?

The Spanish monarchs did not intend for the *conquistadores* to destroy the native populations of the Americas. In fact, the Spanish crown wanted Native Americans to become tax-paying subjects and adopt Spanish culture. The Catholic Church played an important role in this process.

**The Church Sets Up Missions** The Spanish church leaders were key players in Spanish colonial society. In places like New Mexico and California, the Church built **missions**, settlements that included a church, a town, and farmlands. The goal of the missions was to convert Native Americans to Christianity. The missions also increased Spanish control over the land.

Missions helped the Native Americans to create a better supply of food. They also offered Native Americans protection against enemies. Many Native Americans learned how to read and write in the missions. Others developed skills such as carpentry and metalworking.

Over time, however, many Native Americans grew increasingly unhappy. The missionaries often worked them as if they were slaves. The missionaries also tried to replace Native American religions and traditions. As a result, some Native Americans ran away, while others rebelled. Some destroyed churches and killed missionaries.

**Las Casas Condemns Abuse** Most Spaniards treated the Native Americans as little more than beasts of burden. Fray Toribio de Benavente, a Catholic missionary, wrote that the Spanish "do nothing but command. They are the drones who suck the honey which is made by the poor bees, the Indians."

Not all Spaniards approved of this treatment. One man in particular fought for better treatment of Native Americans. His name was **Bartolomé de Las Casas**. Las Casas had come to Hispaniola in 1502 and taken part in the conquest of Cuba a decade later. For his part in the conquest, he received an *encomienda*. Las Casas was also a Catholic priest, however, and he soon faced a moral dilemma: How can a person serve God and enslave Native Americans at the same time?

In 1514, Las Casas gave up his claim to the Native Americans who worked for him. For the next 50 years, he fought for Native Americans, earning the title "Protector of the Indians."

Because of his efforts, the Spanish king issued the New Laws in 1542. These laws ordered the gradual freeing of all enslaved Native Americans.

*Conquistador* armor

Holders of *encomiendas* who were found guilty of mistreating Native Americans had their *encomiendas* taken away from them. However, Spanish colonists strongly protested against the New Laws, and the king eventually gave in and reversed many of them.

🔺 **DRAW CONCLUSIONS** Explain how the church played a part in Spanish colonization.

## The Columbian Exchange

🔻 **KEY QUESTION** What were the effects of the Columbian Exchange?

The arrival of the Spanish in the Americas brought more than a clash of peoples and cultures. It also brought a movement of plants, animals, and diseases between the Eastern and Western hemispheres. This movement of living things between hemispheres is called the **Columbian Exchange**.

**Trade Brings Disease** One result of the Columbian Exchange was the transfer of germs from Europe to the Americas. Before the Europeans arrived, Native American farmland stretched all along the eastern seaboard of what is now the United States. Many of the communities that farmed these lands were wiped out by European diseases before the settlers began arriving in large numbers. The Native Americans had no immunity to the germs that caused such diseases as smallpox, measles, and influenza.

Exact numbers are unknown, but historians estimate that diseases brought by Europeans killed more than 20 million Native Americans in Mexico in the first century after conquest. The population of Native Americans in Central

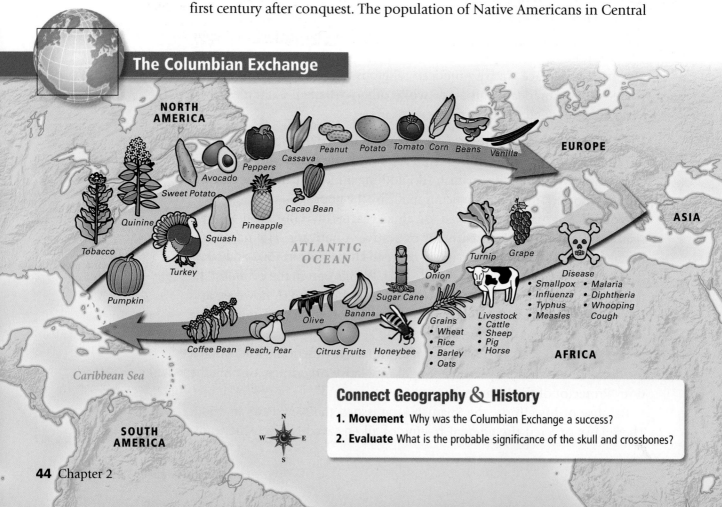

**The Columbian Exchange**

NORTH AMERICA — Tobacco, Quinine, Sweet Potato, Avocado, Peppers, Cassava, Peanut, Potato, Tomato, Corn, Beans, Vanilla — EUROPE

Turkey, Squash, Pineapple, Cacao Bean

Pumpkin

ATLANTIC OCEAN

ASIA

Coffee Bean, Peach, Pear, Olive, Banana, Citrus Fruits, Honeybee, Sugar Cane, Onion, Turnip, Grape

Grains • Wheat • Rice • Barley • Oats

Livestock • Cattle • Sheep • Pig • Horse

Disease • Smallpox • Influenza • Typhus • Measles • Malaria • Diphtheria • Whooping Cough

AFRICA

Caribbean Sea

SOUTH AMERICA

### Connect Geography & History

1. **Movement** Why was the Columbian Exchange a success?

2. **Evaluate** What is the probable significance of the skull and crossbones?

America may have decreased by 90 to 95 percent between the years 1519 and 1619. The result was similar in Peru and other parts of the Americas. Bernardino de Sahagún, a Spanish missionary in Mexico, described the effects of smallpox on the Aztecs: "Very many died of it. . . . They could not move: they could not stir. . . . And if they stirred, much did they cry out. Great was its destruction."

**Positive Effects of the Exchange** Other effects of the Columbian Exchange were more positive. The Spanish brought many plants and animals to the Americas. European livestock—cattle, pigs, and horses—all thrived in the Americas. Crops from the Eastern Hemisphere, such as grapes, onions, and wheat, also thrived in the Western Hemisphere.

The Columbian Exchange benefited Europe, too. Many American crops became part of the European diet. Two that had a huge impact were potatoes and corn. Potatoes, for example, became an important food in Ireland, Russia, and other parts of Europe. Without potatoes, Europe's population might not have grown as rapidly as it did.

By mixing the products of two hemispheres, the Columbian Exchange brought the world closer together. Of course, people were also moving from one hemisphere to the other, blending their cultures in the process.

 **RECOGNIZE EFFECTS** Explain the effect of the Columbian Exchange on the Eastern and Western hemispheres.

---

**New Jersey Core Curriculum Content Standards** *Review*

 **ONLINE QUIZ**
For test practice, go to
**Interactive Review @ ClassZone.com**

**TERMS & NAMES**

**1.** Explain the importance of

- *encomienda*
- *hacienda*
- mission
- Bartolomé de Las Casas
- Columbian Exchange

**USING YOUR READING NOTES**

**2. Main Ideas and Details** Complete the diagram you started at the beginning of this section.

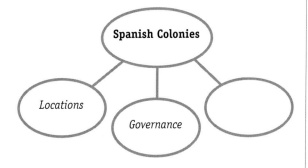

**KEY IDEAS**

**3.** How did Spain establish a new colonial government in the Americas?

**4.** How did the Columbian Exchange connect the Eastern and Western hemispheres?

**CRITICAL THINKING**

**5. Analyze Motives** Why do you think the Spaniards chose to utilize Native Americans in the new colonies?

**6. Draw Conclusions** Over time, do you think the Catholic Church's missions were more helpful or harmful to the Native Americans? Explain.

**7. Evaluate** How did the missions transform the Native American way of life?

**8. Connect** *to* **Today** How is the Columbian Exchange put into effect today?

**9. Art Collage** Make a collage that illustrates the plants and animals involved in the Columbian Exchange.

## ▶ Key Ideas

**BEFORE, YOU LEARNED**
As the Spanish Empire expanded in the Americas, Native Americans' lives were transformed.

**NOW YOU WILL LEARN**
Slavery was introduced on a large scale to provide cheap labor for the colonies.

## ▶ Vocabulary

**TERMS & NAMES**

**slavery** practice of one person being owned by another

**middle passage** middle leg of the triangular trade route that brought captured Africans to the Americas to serve as slaves

**slave codes** law passed to regulate the treatment of slaves

**racism** belief that some people are inferior because of their race

**BACKGROUND VOCABULARY**

**maroon** runaway or fugitive slave

**Visual Vocabulary** Middle Passage

## ▶ Reading Strategy

Re-create the diagram shown at right. As you read and respond to the **KEY QUESTIONS**, use the diagram to compare the experiences of Native Americans and Africans under slavery.

 **See Skillbuilder Handbook, page R8.**

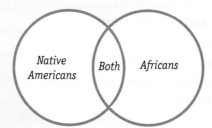

**COMPARE AND CONTRAST**

Native Americans | Both | Africans

**GRAPHIC ORGANIZERS**
Go to **Interactive Review** @ ClassZone.com

# Beginnings of Slavery in the Americas

**6.4.C.7.** Analyze the cultures and interactions of peoples in the Americas, Western Europe, and Africa after 1450 . . . .
**6.4.C.8.** Discuss how millions of Africans, brought against their will from Central Africa to the Americas, . . . , retained their humanity, their families, and their cultures during enslavement.

## One American's Story

In 1546, Diego de Campo was the leader of 7,000 **maroons**, or runaway slaves, on the island of Hispaniola. There were only about 1,000 European men on the island. The Spanish planters greatly feared de Campo. When the Spanish attacked the maroons, de Campo and his followers defeated the Spanish.

Eventually the Spaniards captured de Campo. He offered to lead the fight against the maroons. The Spanish accepted the offer. With de Campo's help, the Spanish defeated the maroons, and slavery in Hispaniola grew. In this section you will read how slave labor expanded in the Americas.

## Slavery Takes Hold in the Colonies

🔽 **KEY QUESTION** How did slavery bring wealth to Europeans but suffering to millions of Africans and Native Americans?

By the 1600s, **slavery**, the practice of one person being owned by another, was firmly established in the Americas. But slavery was not new. It was a very ancient institution.

Maroons often joined Native American groups.

**Origins of American Slavery** In some societies, slaves were mainly domestic servants in wealthy households. Some labored in mines and fields. People were enslaved when they were captured in battle or sold to pay off debts. Some slaves were treated with some respect. Some were allowed to marry and own property. The children of some slaves were allowed to go free.

Slavery began to change with the rise of sugar plantations. To work these plantations, Europeans had used slaves in southern Europe since the 1100s. Then, in the 1400s and 1500s, Portugal and Spain set up sugar plantations on islands in the eastern Atlantic. To work these plantations, they used African slaves bought from traders in Africa.

When the Spanish and Portuguese founded their colonies in the Americas, they brought the plantation system with them. At first they tried to enslave Native Americans to work in the fields and mines. But the Native Americans quickly died from overwork and disease. In some cases, they rebelled with the help of local allies.

The Spaniards then looked to other sources of slave labor, including Spanish slaves, black Christian slaves, and Asian slaves. But there was not enough of any of these groups to meet demand.

**The Slave Trade** The Spanish and Portuguese enslaved Africans to provide plantation labor. Africans proved to be their best resource. They enslaved Africans for four basic reasons.

- Africans were immune to most European diseases.
- Africans had no friends or family in the Americas to help them resist or escape enslavement.
- Enslaved Africans provided a permanent source of cheap labor. Even their children could be held in bondage.
- Many Africans had worked on farms in their native lands.

Over time, the colonies came to depend on slave labor. European slave traders ran the shipment of Africans to the Americas. On the coast of West Africa, local kings captured inland Africans. The kings then traded these captives for European goods, such as textiles, ironware, wine, and guns. This trade made the coastal kingdoms rich while weakening inland African societies. Before the slave trade ended in the late 1800s, between 12 and 15 million Africans had been enslaved and shipped to the Western Hemisphere. Of these, perhaps two million died during the voyage.

**The Middle Passage** The voyage from Africa to the Americas was called the **middle passage** because it was the middle leg of the triangular trade. The triangular trade refers to the movement of trade ships between Europe, Africa, and the Americas.

Olaudah Equiano (oh•LOW•duh•ehk•wee•AHN•oh) was one of those captured Africans. He made the journey in the 1700s. He was about 11 years old when he was taken from his home and sold into slavery. Later, after he bought his freedom, he wrote about the beginning of the middle passage.

**PRIMARY SOURCE**

❝ The first object which saluted my eyes when I arrived on the coast, was the sea, and a slave ship . . . waiting for its cargo. These filled me with astonishment, which was soon converted into terror, when I was carried on board. ❞

—Olaudah Equiano, quoted in *Great Slave Narratives*

Olaudah Equiano was brought to the West Indies from West Africa in the 1700s.

Equiano saw a row of men shackled in chains. He also saw a large boiling kettle. He feared that he was going to be cooked and eaten "by those white men with horrible looks, red faces, and long hair."

The scene on the slave deck below was even worse. Several hundred slaves were crammed into a space so small that there was not even enough room to stand up. Foul smells and disease, along with the shrieks and groans of the dying, made the middle passage a terrifying experience.

Many enslaved Africans died from disease or from cruel treatment at the hands of slave traders. Many others committed suicide by plunging into the ocean. It is believed that between 15 and 20 percent of the Africans aboard each slave ship perished during the brutal trip. The captives who did not die faced new horrors in the Americas.

▲ **CAUSES AND EFFECTS** Discuss the results of the African slave trade.

## Slavery in the Americas

▼ **KEY QUESTION** What were the long-term effects of slavery in the Americas?

Once the enslaved Africans arrived in the colonies, they were sold at auction. Some worked as house servants. Most were forced to do hard labor in *haciendas* or mines. They were fed and housed poorly.

## CONNECT to the Essential Question

### How did Europeans transform life in the Americas?

| CAUSES | EFFECTS |
|---|---|
| **Europeans explore** | Expansion of colonial empires, destruction of Aztec and Inca Empires; growth of wealth and power |
| **establish colonies** | Spread of disease; spread of Christianity; brutal oppression of conquered peoples; establishment of *encomiendas, haciendas,* and missions |
| **compete for colonies** | Treaty of Tordesillas (1494); establishment of New France and New Netherland; defeat of Spanish Armada; growth of English colonies |
| **introduced the Columbian Exchange** | **Brought**—to Americas: disease; livestock, grains, onions, citrus fruits, olives, grapes, bananas, sugar cane |
| | **Taken**—to Eastern Hemisphere: tobacco, squash, turkey, peppers, cocoa, peanuts, potatoes, corn |
| **introduced slavery** | Provides labor in mines and plantations; slave trade expands quickly between Africa and the Americas; millions of captives die; racism grows |

**CRITICAL THINKING** **Make Inferences** What were the effects of European colonization on the daily lives of native peoples?

# One American's Story

In 1546, Diego de Campo was the leader of 7,000 **maroons**, or runaway slaves, on the island of Hispaniola. There were only about 1,000 European men on the island. The Spanish planters greatly feared de Campo. When the Spanish attacked the maroons, de Campo and his followers defeated the Spanish.

Eventually the Spaniards captured de Campo. He offered to lead the fight against the maroons. The Spanish accepted the offer. With de Campo's help, the Spanish defeated the maroons, and slavery in Hispaniola grew. In this section you will read how slave labor expanded in the Americas.

# Slavery Takes Hold in the Colonies

 **KEY QUESTION** How did slavery bring wealth to Europeans but suffering to millions of Africans and Native Americans?

By the 1600s, **slavery**, the practice of one person being owned by another, was firmly established in the Americas. But slavery was not new. It was a very ancient institution.

**Origins of American Slavery** In some societies, slaves were mainly domestic servants in wealthy households. Some labored in mines and fields. People were enslaved when they were captured in battle or sold to pay off debts. Some slaves were treated with some respect. Some were allowed to marry and own property. The children of some slaves were allowed to go free.

Slavery began to change with the rise of sugar plantations. To work these plantations, Europeans had used slaves in southern Europe since the 1100s.

---

**New Jersey Core Curriculum Content Standards** *Review*

**ONLINE QUIZ**
For test practice, go to
**Interactive Review @ ClassZone.com**

### TERMS & NAMES
1. Explain the significance of
   - slavery
   - slave codes
   - middle passage
   - racism

### USING YOUR READING NOTES
2. **Compare and Contrast** Complete the diagram you started at the beginning of this section.

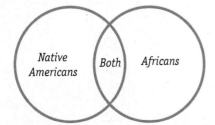

### KEY IDEAS
3. Why did Europeans bring Africans to the Americas?
4. What are three examples of bad conditions faced by enslaved Africans?

### CRITICAL THINKING
5. **Point of View** Why do you think the slave traders were so cruel to the slaves they transported across the ocean?
6. **Connect Economics & History** How did the enslaved Africans contribute to the Columbian Exchange?
7. **Connect** *to* **Today** What are some of the long-term effects of slavery in the Americas today?
8. **Writing** **Report** Research the contributions of Olaudah Equiano to our knowledge of slavery.

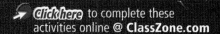

## Chapter Summary

**1** **Key Idea**
After Columbus' voyages, the Spanish quickly conquered the Native American empires of the Aztecs and the Inca.

**2** **Key Idea**
Competition for the riches of the Americas led to tension and conflict among European powers.

**3** **Key Idea**
Native Americans' lives were transformed as Spain grew rich from its new empire.

**4** **Key Idea**
Slavery was introduced on a large scale to provide cheap labor for the colonies.

For detailed Review and Study Notes go to **Interactive Review** @ **ClassZone.com**

## Name Game

**Use the Terms & Names list to complete each sentence online or on your own paper.**

1. _____ led an army to conquer the Aztec empire.
   Hernando Cortés

2. _____ moved the Line of Demarcation to the west.

3. America is named after _____.

4. The large fleet of ships sent to restore Catholicism to England is called the _____.

5. _____ founded a fur trading post in Quebec.

6. _____ was a grant of Native American labor.

7. A large farm or estate is called a _____.

8. _____ earned the title of "Protector of the Indians."

9. For enslaved Africans, the voyage from Africa to the Americas is the _____.

10. _____ is a belief that some people are inferior because of their race.

A. Samuel de Champlain
B. Columbian Exchange
C. Treaty of Tordesillas
D. Bartolomé de Las Casas
E. plantations
F. *encomienda*
G. Jacques Cartier
H. Hernando Cortés
I. Amerigo Vespucci
J. racism
K. slavery
L. Francisco Pizarro
M. *hacienda*
N. middle passage
O. Spanish Armada

## Activities

### CROSSWORD PUZZLE

Complete the online crossword to show you know about European exploration of the Americas.

**ACROSS**
**1.** An instrument used to find latitude.

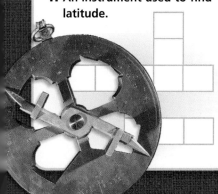

### FLIPCARD

Use the online flipcards to quiz yourself on the terms and names introduced in this chapter

I landed in the Americas in 1492.

ANSWER:
Christopher Columbus

## VOCABULARY

**Explain the significance of each of the following.**

1. Christopher Columbus
2. Columbian Exchange
3. Bartolomé de Las Casas
4. Henry Hudson
5. John Cabot
6. Spanish Armada
7. mercantilism
8. Treaty of Tordesillas
9. Amerigo Vespucci
10. Hernando Cortés
11. Francisco Pizarro
12. Jacques Cartier
13. Samuel de Champlain
14. Giovanni da Verrazzano

**Explain how the terms and names in each group are related.**

15. *encomienda, hacienda*
16. plantation, mission
17. middle passage, slavery
18. *conquistador*, missionary

## KEY IDEAS

**❶ Spain Claims an Empire (pages 26–33)**

19. Why did Europeans seek new trade routes to Asia?
20. Who conquered the Aztecs and Incas?
21. What are three reasons that explain Spain's success in building an empire in the Americas?

**❷ European Competition in North America (pages 34–39)**

22. What was the Northwest Passage?
23. Why did the Spanish Armada attack England?
24. What did the French and Dutch colonists trade?

**❸ The Spanish and Native Americans (pages 40–45)**

25. How did Spanish rule affect Native Americans?
26. How did the Columbian Exchange affect Europe?

**❹ Beginnings of Slavery in the Americas (pages 48–52)**

27. Why did the Spanish and Portuguese use slave labor in their colonies?
28. How did the slave trade work?

## CRITICAL THINKING

29. **Analyze Leadership** What leadership qualities helped the *conquistadors* and early explorers succeed in their efforts?

30. **Synthesize** Despite the competition from other nations, how did the Spanish Empire in the Americas grow so quickly?

31. **Causes & Effects** Create a chart to show the causes and effects of European exploration of the Americas.

| Causes | Effects |
|---|---|
| *national competition* | *European colonies* |
| *spread of Christianity* | |

32. **Compare and Contrast** How did France and the Netherlands differ in the way they set up colonies in North America?

33. **Recognize Bias and Propaganda** How did slavery influence racial attitudes among Europeans?

34. **Interpret Charts** Read the chart below. About how many slaves were imported to the Americas between 1493 and 1810?

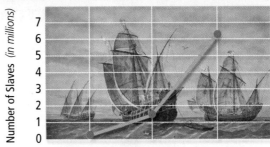

**Slaves Imported to the Americas** *1451–1810*

Number of Slaves (in millions)

7
6
5
4
3
2
1
0

1451–1600  1601–1700  1701–1810

Years

Source: Philip D. Curtin, *The Atlantic Slave Trade*

**✔ TEST PRACTICE**

• **Online Test Practice** @ ClassZone.com
• **Test-Taking Strategies & Practice** at the front of this book

## DOCUMENT-BASED QUESTIONS

### Part 1: Short Answer

**Study each document carefully and answer the questions that follow.**

**DOCUMENT 1**

**1.** This image illustrates the meeting of Montezuma and Cortés. What does the picture tell you about the meeting between the Spaniards and the Aztecs?

**DOCUMENT 2**

**PRIMARY SOURCE**

❝ On our arrival . . . Montezuma was awaiting our Captain [Cortés]. Taking him by the hand, the prince led him to . . . the hall where he was to lodge. . . . Montezuma had ready for him a very rich necklace, made of golden crabs, a marvellous piece of work, which he hung round Cortés' neck. His captains were greatly astonished at this sign of honour. ❞

—Bernal Díaz del Castillo,
from *The Conquest of New Spain*

**2.** What can you tell about Montezuma and the Spaniards from this passage?

### Part 2: Essay

**3.** Using information from the documents, your answers to the questions in Part 1, and your knowledge of U.S. history, write an essay that discusses how the Spanish invaders betrayed the trust of the Aztecs and the Inca.

## YOU BE THE HISTORIAN

**35. Evaluate** How did advances in shipbuilding and seamanship affect European exploration?

**36. Make Inferences** Why do you think it took France and the Netherlands so long to set up colonies in the Americas?

**37. Economics & History** What were some of the positive and negative effects of the Columbian Exchange?

**38. WHAT IF?** Suppose Spain did not choose to support Columbus in his expedition. How do you think this would have affected colonization?

**39. Citizenship** What kind of values did Las Casas demonstrate in his actions? How effective was he in improving his society?

**40. Connect to Today** How have advances in technology changed exploration?

Answer the
## ESSENTIAL QUESTION

**How did Europeans transform life in the Americas?**

**Written Response** Write a two- to three-paragraph response to the Essential Question. Be sure to consider the key ideas of each section as well as the most significant factors that led to the European exploration of the Americas.

### Response Rubric

**A strong response will**

• demonstrate an understanding of life in the Americas prior to European exploration
• provide analysis of European motives
• compare European and Native American values
• discuss economic, religious, and social changes brought out by European settlement

# The English Colonies

## 1585–1763

**3** The English Establish
13 Colonies
1585–1732 pages 58–91

**4** The Colonies Develop
1651–1753 pages 92–123

**5** Beginnings of
an American Identity
1689–1763 pages 124–151

## Why It Matters Now

The American identity was initially shaped by the English, both as colonies developed and as tensions arose with British powers. Why England, and not other nations that sought wealth and influence in the new land? The answer lies in the traditions, values, and character of early English settlers, and in their determination to forge a new life in the colonies. Yet just as England established firm roots in early America, it also set the colonies on the path to the freedom and independence that we cherish today.

The history of every country begins
in the heart of a man or a woman.
—Willa Cather

CHAPTER

3

1. Early Colonies Have Mixed Success
2. New England Colonies
3. The Southern Colonies
4. The Middle Colonies

# The English Establish 13 Colonies

## 1585–1732

 **ESSENTIAL QUESTION**

How did the experience of the early colonists shape America's political and social ideals?

---

**CONNECT** ⟳ **Geography & History**

What were the advantages and disadvantages of the location of the first English colonies?

**Think about:**

1 why these early settlements were not established directly on the coast

2 the poor, sandy soil of Roanoke Island

3 the sand bars and shallow waters that made it difficult for Spanish ships to attack the colonists

---

A replica of the *Mayflower*

**1607**
**Jamestown** founded.

**1620**
*Mayflower* arrives in **Plymouth**.

**1630** Puritan settlers found the **Massachusetts** Bay Colony.

## 1585

The unsuccessful colony of **Roanoke** is founded in Virginia.

tobacco plant

**1614** Virginia sends the first shipment of tobacco to England.

▼

**Effect** To meet consumer demand, tobacco plantations spread throughout the Chesapeake Bay.

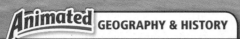
Lands of Powhatan people

VIRGINIA

Jamestown

James River

York River

Werowocomoco

Chesapeake Bay

Albemarle Sound

76°W

Roanoke

ATLANTIC OCEAN

37°N

36°N

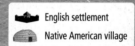

English settlement

Native American village

Scale varies across perspective view.

ATLANTIC OCEAN

SPANISH

William Penn meets with Native Americans.

**1681** Pennsylvania is founded.

# 1732

James Oglethorpe founds Georgia.

British royal seal

**1664** The English seize the Dutch colony of New Netherland and rename it New York.

▼

**Effect** English colonies now stretch from New England through the South.

*The English Establish 13 Colonies* **59**

# Reading for Understanding

## ▶ Key Ideas

**BEFORE, YOU LEARNED**

European nations competed to explore the Americas, where they conquered native peoples and introduced slavery.

**NOW YOU WILL LEARN**

Of the three earliest English colonies in North America, only Jamestown managed to survive.

---

## ▶ Vocabulary

**TERMS & NAMES**

**Sir Walter Raleigh** (RAW•lee) founder of England's first American colony

**mercantilism** (MUR•kuhn•tee•LIHZ•uhm) economic system that European nations used to enrich their treasuries

**Jamestown** first permanent English settlement in North America

**John Smith** leader of the Jamestown colony

**headright** land grant given to one who could pay his or her way to the colonies

**indentured servant** one who worked for a set time without pay in exchange for a free passage to America

**House of Burgesses** the Virginia assembly, which was the first representative assembly in the American colonies

**BACKGROUND VOCABULARY**

**joint-stock company** company funded by a group of investors

**investor** person who puts money into a project to earn a profit

**charter** written contract giving the right to establish a colony

**royal colony** colony ruled by the king's appointed officials

---

## ▶ Reading Strategy

Re-create the diagram shown at right. As you read and respond to the **KEY QUESTIONS**, use the boxes to compare and contrast the benefits and risks of colonization.

 See Skillbuilder Handbook, page R8.

**COMPARE AND CONTRAST**

**COLONIZATION**

| Benefits | Risks |
|---|---|
| *wealth created for mother country* | |

 **GRAPHIC ORGANIZERS**
Go to **Interactive Review** @ ClassZone.com

# SECTION 1

# Early Colonies Have Mixed Success

**6.4.D.1.** Analyze the political, social, and cultural characteristics of the English colonies.
**6.4.D.2** Describe the political, religious, social, and economic institutions that emerged in Colonial America, including New Netherland and colonial New Jersey.

## One American Story

In 1587 John White was the governor of the English colony at Roanoke, an island off North Carolina. It was here that White's daughter Eleanor gave birth to Virginia Dare—the first English child born in North America.

White went back to England and did not see Roanoke again until 1590. He was shocked by what he found on his return.

### PRIMARY SOURCE

❝ We found the houses taken down, and the place very strongly enclosed with a high [fence] of great trees, and one of the chief trees. . . had bark taken off, and five foot from the ground in fair capital letters was [carved] CROATOAN, without any cross or sign of distress. ❞

—from John White's *Journals* (1590)

One of John White's drawings of Native Americans

*Croatoan* was the name of a local tribe and a nearby island. However, White never discovered the fate of the colonists or his family. Although Roanoke failed, later English settlements in America were successful.

## The First English Colonies

🔻 **KEY QUESTION** What were the benefits and risks of colonizing America?

In the late 1500s, the English government was envious of the wealth that Spain had taken from its American colonies. The English people, faced with few job opportunities at home, hoped to find riches in America. Most were unaware of the dangers waiting for them on America's eastern shores.

**Early Colonies Fail** Queen Elizabeth I gave **Sir Walter Raleigh** (RAW•lee) permission to sponsor England's first American colony. Raleigh, a soldier and adventurer, established the colony in 1585 on Roanoke Island. He named the colony Virginia after the unmarried, or virgin, queen. But troubles with local tribes and lack of food forced the colonists to return to England. Raleigh tried to establish Roanoke again in 1587, with the results described in One American Story (previous page). No one knows what happened to this "lost colony." Some historians think that the starving colonists joined a local tribe of Native Americans. Others believe that they were killed.

In 1607, the English tried to found the Sagadahoc colony on the Kennebec River in Maine. Again, hunger forced most colonists to return to England.

**Financing a Colony** Raleigh lost his investment when his colony failed. Later, other merchants tried financing a colony through a **joint-stock company**. Joint-stock companies were funded by **investors**, people who put money into a project to earn profits. Each investor owned a portion of the company, called shares of stock. Investors shared profits and risk.

Merchants formed two joint-stock companies to colonize America: the Virginia Company of London and the Virginia Company of Plymouth. These companies sought permission to colonize from James I, who had become king after Queen Elizabeth's death. Colonies were important in **mercantilism** (MUR•kuhn•tee•LIHZ•uhm)—an economic system that European nations used to enrich their treasuries.

## CONNECT ➦ *Economics and History*

### MERCANTILISM

In mercantilism, a nation would increase its wealth through selling more products to foreign nations than it bought from them.

Colonies helped a nation achieve a favorable balance of trade between exports and imports.

Colonists created a demand, or market, for the mother country's goods and supplied the mother country with cheap raw materials. In this way, the mother country would not have to buy expensive raw materials from rival nations.

RAW MATERIALS

FINISHED GOODS

**COLONIES**
- provide raw materials to England
- buy finished goods from England
- could trade only with England

**ENGLAND**
- imports cheap raw materials from the colonies
- exports finished goods to colonies and other nations

### CRITICAL THINKING

1. **Make Inferences** How did colonies enrich a nation?

2. **Connect** *to* **Today** What do you think would happen if, for several years, your family collected less money than it paid for goods? How might such a situation affect a nation?

King James granted charters to both companies in 1606. A **charter** was a written contract, issued by a government, giving the company the right to establish a colony. Because a charter also gave the company the right to govern the colony, each charter was like a primitive constitution.

▲ **COMPARE AND CONTRAST** Compare the benefits and risks of colonization.

## Jamestown Is Founded in 1607

▼ **KEY QUESTION** What democratic tradition was planted in Jamestown?

In 1607 100 colonists, sent by the Virginia Company of London, sailed into the Chesapeake Bay. They traveled up the James River until they found a spot that seemed safe from a Spanish attack. The settlement was named **Jamestown** in honor of King James I. This became the first permanent English settlement in North America.

**Jamestown Struggles to Survive** The colony's early years were troubled. Colonists became ill from diseases carried by water or insects. To make matters worse, the London Company had promised that the colony would be rich with gold, like the Spanish colonies. Settlers searched for treasure instead of building houses and planting crops.

The climate was also a hardship. The English were not prepared for Virginia's hot, humid summers and bitterly cold winters. As one colonist recalled, "There were never Englishmen left in a foreign country in such misery as we were in this newly discovered Virginia."

By January 1608, only 38 of the colonists remained alive. Later that year, **John Smith**, a soldier and adventurer, took control. Smith brought order to the colony. But when Smith returned to England, the colony fell back into confusion. During this "starving time" the colonists ate rodents and snakes. Fortunately, the colony was saved when relief ships arrived in 1610. Lord De La Warr, the new governor, imposed discipline. More attention was paid to farming, and the colony survived.

Although the local Powhatan tribe had traded corn to the colonists, relations between the two groups were tense and sometimes violent. The situation did not improve until 1614, when Chief Powhatan's daughter, Pocahontas, married a colonist named John Rolfe. The Virginia Company brought the couple to England to advertise the colony. Sadly, Pocahontas died there, when she was about twenty-one.

**Tobacco Transforms the Colony** Unable to find gold, the colonists discovered another product that could bring them wealth—tobacco. In 1614 John Rolfe sent the first shipment of tobacco to England. It became popular in Europe and ensured the colony's survival.

The success of tobacco growing changed the colony. When the colonists demanded a share of the profits, the company responded by allowing them to own land. Settlers worked harder once the land became their own.

**Connect** *to the* **World**

**Colonization**
In 1608, a year after the first permanent English colony was established at Jamestown, the French founded their first permanent colony at Quebec.
*Chapter 2, p. 38.*

Pocahontas in English dress

Tobacco farms began spreading along the James River. This established the pattern for the entire Chesapeake Bay—the region's many rivers allowed planters to ship their crops directly to England.

To attract settlers, the Virginia Company offered a **headright**, a 50-acre land grant for anyone who could pay his or her way to the colony. Those who could not afford passage to America often became **indentured servants**. These men and women agreed to work without pay for a landlord if the landlord paid for their passage to America. After they had served for the time specified in the contract—usually about 4 to 6 years—the landlord restored their freedom.

In 1619 the first Africans arrived in Jamestown. It is not known whether they arrived as indentured servants or as enslaved workers. In the colony's first decades, planters relied more on European indentured servants. Slavery did not become widespread until the late 1600s.

**The House of Burgesses Is Formed** Settlers soon became frustrated at the lack of self government. So the Virginia Company decided that burgesses, or elected representatives, would meet once a year. The **House of Burgesses**, created in 1619, was the first representative assembly in the colonies.

The House of Burgesses had the authority to pass local laws and to raise taxes. Throughout the colonial period, the power of a local government to raise taxes remained a closely guarded right.

## CONNECT ⟳ *Citizenship and History*

### VOTING RIGHTS

The creation of the Virginia House of Burgesses did not establish democracy in the modern sense—only male landowners had the right to vote. But it was a step in a long process that gradually extended voting rights to larger and larger sections of the population.

Today, all citizens aged 18 and over have the right to vote. But in order to vote, citizens must first register. This can be done by mail, in person, or in some states, at the Department of Motor Vehicles. Information about voter registration can also be found on the "Rock the Vote" website. Rock the Vote aims to boost voter turnout. Kids who are too young to vote can still participate in America's democracy by educating others.

#### Activity

**Contribute to Voter Education!**

1 Let your parents and older relatives know how they can register to vote.

2 As local elections are due, work with your classmates to make signs informing people how to register to vote. Display these signs in public places.

3 With a parent or older relative, speak to people in your neighborhood about the importance of registering to vote

4 Go to the "Rock the Vote" website and send the link via email to people you know.

See Citizenship Handbook, page 303.

**Representative Government** The colony's government and its very existence were threatened by a Native American uprising in 1622. The local Native American tribe, the Powhatan, were alarmed by the expanding tobacco plantations and the growing English population. On March 22, the Powhatan launched an attack on settlements all along the James River. A quarter of the English population was killed.

Jamestown survived, but the Virginia Company did not. After the uprising, King James I took back the company's charter and turned Virginia into a **royal colony**. A royal colony is ruled by the king's appointed officials.

James I, who opposed the idea of elected governments, also got rid of the assembly. This act outraged the colonists. They protested fiercely, sending requests and petitions for the assembly to be restored. After King James's death, his son, Charles I granted the colonists' wishes, and by 1629 the House of Burgesses was meeting once again. In 1639, the King commanded that the governor call an assembly every year.

Thus, the Virginia colonists won for themselves the right to participate in government. As more English colonies were planted on America's eastern seaboard, the political traditions of liberty and representative government took root in America's fertile ground.

 **SUMMARIZE** Identify the democratic tradition planted at Jamestown.

A member of the Powhatan watches an English ship; from the film *The New World*.

**Connect** *to the* **World**

**Representative Government**
In the colonies of other European nations, elected assemblies were not allowed.

---

**New Jersey Core Curriculum Content Standards** *Review*

 **ONLINE QUIZ**
For test practice, go to
**Interactive Review** @ ClassZone.com

### TERMS & NAMES
**1.** Explain the importance of
- Sir Walter Raleigh
- John Smith
- mercantilism
- House of Burgesses
- Jamestown

### USING YOUR READING NOTES
**2. Compare and Contrast** Complete the diagram that you started at the beginning of this section.

**COLONIZATION**

| Benefits | Risks |
|---|---|
| *wealth created for mother country* | |

### KEY IDEAS
**3.** Why did the English want to colonize America?

**4.** What events saved Jamestown from destruction?

**5.** What powers belonged to the House of Burgesses?

### CRITICAL THINKING
**6. Connect Economics & History** How did the success of tobacco growing change Virginia?

**7. Problems and Solutions** Why were the settlers unprepared for colonizing Virginia?

**8. Connect** *to* **Today** What modern democratic traditions can be traced back to the Jamestown colony?

**9. Art** You want indentured servants to work on your plantation. Design an advertisement that will attract people to the colony of Virginia.

## ▶ Key Ideas

**BEFORE, YOU LEARNED**

In Jamestown, Virginia, the first permanent English colony in North America, settlers established representative government.

**NOW YOU WILL LEARN**

English colonists settled New England, where they planted many political and religious traditions.

## ▶ Vocabulary

**TERMS & NAMES**

**John Winthrop** Puritan leader who became the first governor of the Massachusetts Bay Colony

**Pilgrims** Separatist group that traveled to America to gain religious freedom

**Mayflower Compact** document that helped establish the practice of self-government

**Puritans** English dissenters who wanted to reform the Church of England

**Great Migration** the movement of tens of thousands of English settlers to New England during the 1630s

**Roger Williams** Puritan dissenter who established Rhode Island

**Anne Hutchinson** Puritan dissenter who was banished from Massachusetts

**Fundamental Orders of Connecticut** document that has been called the first written constitution in America

**Quakers** group of Protestant dissenters

**BACKGROUND VOCABULARY**

**dissenter** (dih•SEHN•tuhr) person who disagrees with an official church

**persecute** (PUR•sih•KYOOT) to mistreat

**tolerance** acceptance of different opinions

**congregation** group of people who belong to the same church

**banish** to force someone to leave a place

## ▶ Reading Strategy

Re-create the diagram shown at right. As you read and respond to the **KEY QUESTIONS**, use the boxes to show why the Pilgrims settled in America.

 See Skillbuilder Handbook, page R3.

**CAUSES AND EFFECTS**

| Cause | Effect |
|---|---|
|  | *Pilgrims settled in America.* |

 **GRAPHIC ORGANIZERS**
Go to **Interactive Review** @ ClassZone.com

# New England Colonies

**6.4.D.1.** Analyze the political, social, and cultural characteristics of the English colonies.
**6.4.D.2.** Describe the political, religious, social, and economic institutions that emerged in Colonial America, including New Netherland and colonial New Jersey.

## One American's Story

One Sunday morning in 1630, **John Winthrop**, a Puritan leader, gave a sermon to a congregation gathered on a ship's deck. The ship was called the *Arbella*, and it was one of four carrying hundreds of English colonists across the Atlantic Ocean to Massachusetts Bay. In his sermon Winthrop stated that success would come only if the settlers worked together as a community to achieve their common goals.

### PRIMARY SOURCE

❝ We must be knit together in this work. . . . We must delight in each other, make others' conditions our own and rejoice together, mourn together, labor and suffer together. . . . For we must consider that we shall be as a City upon a Hill; the eyes of all people are on us. ❞

—John Winthrop, "Model of Christian Charity"

*John Winthrop, by Charles Osgood*

Tens of thousands of English settlers soon followed Winthrop and tried to create a religious society dedicated to the common good.

## The Voyage of the Mayflower

🔻 **KEY QUESTION** Why did the Pilgrims want to settle in America?

In the early 1500s, King Henry VIII of England broke his country's ties with the Catholic Church and established the Church of England. Although English Protestants approved of separation from the Catholic Church, many disagreed with certain aspects of the English church. Those who disagreed with England's official church were called **dissenters** (dih•SEHN•tuhrz).

**Religious Freedom and Self-Government** In the early 1600s, another dissenting group called the Separatists wanted to separate from the Church of England. They thought it was still too much like the Catholic Church. King James **persecuted** (PUR•sih•KYOOT•ted), or mistreated, the Separatists for rejecting England's official church. To escape this persecution, they fled to Holland, a country known for its **tolerance**, or acceptance of different

A reenactment of preparation for a Thanksgiving feast. **Why would the Pilgrims need Native Americans' help in order to survive?**

opinions. Eventually the Separatists approached the Virginia Company and gained permission to settle in America. Because this group of Separatists traveled far to gain religious freedom, they later became known as the **Pilgrims**. A pilgrim is a person who goes on a religious journey.

**The Pilgrims Found Plymouth** On a cold November day in 1620, the Pilgrims, traveling on a ship called the *Mayflower*, arrived off Cape Cod on the Massachusetts coast. Blown north off its course, the *Mayflower* landed in an area that John Smith had mapped and called New England. The Pilgrims settled on the site of an abandoned Native American village. They called their settlement Plymouth.

Because the Pilgrims landed beyond the limits of the Virginia Company, their charter did not apply. They were far from government authority and the laws of England. So most of the men aboard the *Mayflower* signed an agreement called the **Mayflower Compact**. The Mayflower Compact helped establish the practice of self-government and majority rule. (See Reading Primary Sources, page 74.)

Like the settlers at Jamestown, the Pilgrims at Plymouth endured a "starving time." Half the group died during the first winter. However, they were saved by Native Americans who had learned to speak English. Squanto, a Native American, taught the Pilgrims how to plant native crops.

Sometime in the fall of 1621 the Plymouth settlement celebrated a good harvest by holding a three-day feast. It was the first Thanksgiving in New England. This Thanksgiving came to represent the peace that existed at that time between the Native Americans and Pilgrims.

▲ **CAUSES AND EFFECTS** Explain why the Pilgrims settled in America.

## The Puritans Come to Massachusetts Bay

▼ **KEY QUESTION** What kind of society did the Puritans hope to create?

By the late 1620s, England was troubled by religious and political conflict. Many groups of dissenters were speaking out against the king and the Church of England. The **Puritans** were one such group. Unlike the Separatists, who wanted to break away from the English church, the Puritans wanted to reform, or "purify" its practices. The Puritans faced increasing persecution in England. Many decided to leave and set up a Puritan society in America.

**The Great Migration** In 1629, the Massachusetts Bay Company, a joint-stock company owned by Puritan merchants, received a royal charter to settle New England. The charter also gave the colony freedom to govern itself. In 1630, 11 ships carried about 1,000 passengers to the Massachusetts Bay Colony. There the Puritans founded Boston, which became the most important town in New England. Between 1630 and 1640 about 20,000 more settlers crossed the Atlantic Ocean in what is known as the **Great Migration**.

**The New England Way** The Puritans set up their ideal society—a religious "commonwealth" of tightly-knit communities. Instead of a church governed by bishops and king, they created self-governing **congregations**. A congregation is a group of people who belong to the same church. Because Puritan congregations were self-governing, their churches came to be called "Congregationalist." This Congregationalist way of organizing churches became known as "the New England Way."

Each congregation chose its minister and set up its own town. The town's most important building was the meetinghouse, where religious services were held. Everyone had to attend these services. The meetinghouse was also used for town meetings, a form of self-government.

Puritan values helped the colonists organize their society and overcome the hardships of colonial life. Puritan colonists valued:

- **hard work** as a way of honoring God. The Puritan work ethic contributed to the colony's rapid growth and success.
- **education.** Because the Puritans wanted everyone to be able to read the Bible, laws required that all children learn to read.
- **representative government.** Puritans brought their traditions of town meetings and local self-government with them to America.

Democratic rights were quickly expanded. The colony's charter allowed only "freemen" or investors to vote. But when the colonists arrived in America, Winthrop, the colony's first governor, changed the definition of "freeman" to mean any male church member. Although this covered only a limited number of people, it was a major step in expanding voting rights.

▲ **SUMMARIZE** Describe the kind of society the Puritans hoped to create.

## Massachusetts Bay "Seeds" New England

▼ **KEY QUESTION** Why did some colonists leave Massachusetts?

The Puritans worked hard to create an orderly society and felt threatened by those who questioned their ways. But dissenters within their ranks soon began challenging Puritan leaders. Disagreements within Massachusetts forced many to leave and found other colonies. In this way, Massachusetts became a "seed colony" out of which other New England colonies grew.

**New England Colonies** *1630*

MASSACHUSETTS BAY COLONY
• Boston (1630)
*Massachusetts Bay*
Connecticut River
Merrimack River
• Plymouth (1620)
PLYMOUTH COLONY
*Cape Cod*
ATLANTIC OCEAN
*Nantucket*
*Martha's Vineyard*
42°N
41°N
72°W   71°W   70°W   69°W

0   25   50 miles
0   25   50 kilometers

The first colonists built houses with roofs of thatch, or straw, like this one.

**Connect Geography & History**

1. **Place** How far is Plymouth from Boston?
2. **Make Inferences** Why do you think that Boston became the most important port in New England?

**Rhode Island Welcomes Dissenters** In Salem, Massachusetts, the minister **Roger Williams** shocked Puritan authorities by insisting that

- the colonists had no right to take Native American lands by force;
- no one should be forced to attend church;
- the Puritans should not impose their religious beliefs on others; and
- church and state should be kept separate.

Because of his beliefs, the Puritans had Williams **banished**, or forced to leave the colony. In 1636 he fled south and founded Rhode Island, a colony that guaranteed religious tolerance and separation of church and state. Williams also established the first Baptist Church in America.

**Anne Hutchinson** was another dissenter. She believed that many of the clergy were not among the "elect"—those chosen by God for salvation. She held discussions that challenged church authority. Hutchinson was also tried and banished from Massachusetts. In 1638 she fled to Rhode Island. That same year, John Wheelwright, Anne Hutchinson's brother-in-law and supporter, also fled. He established the town of Exeter, in what is now New Hampshire. The town's founders wrote the Exeter Compact, which was based on the Mayflower Compact. New Hampshire became a separate colony in 1679.

**ONLINE PRIMARY SOURCE**

Hear the debate at the **Research & Writing Center** @ ClassZone.com

# COMPARING *Perspectives*

## RELIGIOUS TOLERANCE VS. INTOLERANCE

Puritans began arguing over religious matters almost as soon as they had set up the Massachusetts Bay Colony. Those who disagreed with Puritan leaders were sometimes brought to trial and punished. Issues of religious freedom were widely debated as some colonists argued for and others argued against tolerance.

### FOR TOLERANCE

" It doth not a little grieve my spirit to hear what sad things are reported daily of your tyranny and persecutions in New England, as that you fine, whip, and imprison men for their consciences.
—*Richard Saltonstall*

Forced worship stinks in God's nostrils. "
—*Roger Williams, minister*

### AGAINST TOLERANCE

" He that is willing to tolerate any religion. . . either doubts of his own [religion] or is not sincere in it.
—*Nathaniel Ward, minister*

We have here Presbyterian churches as well as Congregational. . . .Only we are [reluctant] to be blown up and down. . . by every wind of new notions. "
—*John Cotton, minister*

### CRITICAL THINKING

**Connect** *to* **Today** Which group might feel more at ease in modern American society and why?

**Connecticut Extends Voting Rights** Conservative Puritans also set up new colonies. In 1636, Thomas Hooker moved his congregation to the Connecticut Valley. There settlers wrote the **Fundamental Orders of Connecticut** in 1639. (See pages 74–75.) The Orders extended voting rights to non-church members. This expanded representative government.

 **SUMMARIZE** Explain why some colonists left Massachusetts.

## The Fight for Tolerance

🔻 **KEY QUESTION** Why did the Quakers protest against the Puritans?

Although Puritans had come to America to find religious freedom for themselves, they would not allow all faiths to worship freely. They were particularly intolerant of the **Quakers**, another group of Protestant dissenters.

**Puritans Persecute Quakers** The name "Quakers" came from a leader's statement that they should "tremble [quake] at the word of the Lord." Quaker beliefs angered the Puritans. The Quakers believed God could be known directly through an "inner light," and that Puritan sermons and ministers were obstacles to the direct experience of God. Because Quakers believed that women were spiritually equal to men, Quaker women served as preachers and as missionaries. These beliefs and practices threatened the very foundations of the New England Way. For this, Quakers were jailed, whipped, or banished from Puritan colonies.

Although often banished, Quaker missionaries defied the authorities, returning repeatedly to Puritan colonies to speak openly about their faith. In frustration, Puritan leaders passed laws with increasingly brutal punishments. Finally Puritans began executing Quakers who returned after being banished.

In response, Quakers became martyrs, people who choose to die for a religious principle. One of the most famous Quaker martyrs was a woman named Mary Dyer. Despite her banishment from the colony, Dyer returned to Massachusetts, determined to "look the bloody laws in the face." Although she was executed, her death led to greater religious tolerance.

 **CAUSES AND EFFECTS** Explain why the Quakers protested against the Puritans.

## History Makers

### Mary Dyer   *?–1660*

Mary Dyer, the religious martyr, came to Massachusetts with her husband, William Dyer, in 1635. She supported her friend Anne Hutchinson during Hutchinson's trial. When Hutchinson was banished from Massachusetts, Dyer followed her to Rhode Island. Returning to England, Dyer met George Fox, the founder of the Quakers. In 1657 she was back in New England as a Quaker missionary. For speaking openly about her faith, Dyer was banished once from New Haven before being imprisoned and banished three times from Massachusetts.

Determined to protest against religious intolerance, Dyer again returned, this time to face the sentence of death. She was hanged on June 1, 1660. As she had hoped, her execution helped end the Puritan persecution of the Quakers.

**CRITICAL THINKING** Make Inferences Why do you think the Puritans felt threatened by the Quakers?

 **ONLINE BIOGRAPHY** For more on the life of Mary Dyer, go to the **Research & Writing Center** @ ClassZone.com

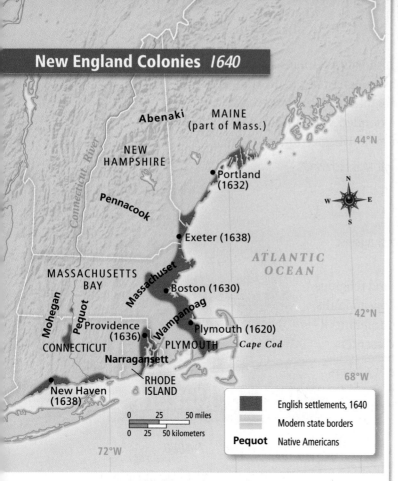

## New England Colonies *1640*

MAINE (part of Mass.)

Abenaki

NEW HAMPSHIRE

Connecticut River

Pennacook

Portland (1632)

Exeter (1638)

ATLANTIC OCEAN

MASSACHUSETTS BAY

Massachuset

Boston (1630)

Mohegan

Pequot

Wampanoag

Providence (1636)

Plymouth (1620)

CONNECTICUT

PLYMOUTH

Cape Cod

Narragansett

New Haven (1638)

RHODE ISLAND

44°N

42°N

68°W

72°W

0    25    50 miles
0    25    50 kilometers

☐ English settlements, 1640
☐ Modern state borders
**Pequot** Native Americans

### Connect Geography & History

1. **Place** Why did the colonies grow mainly north-south?
2. **Make Inferences** Why did most early settlements develop along rivers and the coast?

## Creating a New England

🔻 **KEY QUESTION** What did the New England colonies have in common?

By the 1650s, settlers had fanned out across New England, bringing their beliefs, religious disagreements, and political traditions with them. Although a number of colonies were established throughout the region, the New England colonies had much in common.

**New England Foundations** Many New England settlers came from the densely-populated eastern counties of England. They were used to living in towns and established similar settlements in America. Most New England settlers were also religious dissenters who disagreed with the practices of both the Catholic and the Anglican churches. The New England population was mainly Puritan, but had large numbers of other Protestant groups such as Quakers, Separatists, Baptists, and other dissenters in Rhode Island.

Most New England settlers came from the middle ranks of English society. Many were highly skilled and educated. As they were wealthier than most of the early settlers in the South, they were able to pay their own way across the Atlantic. Few were forced to become indentured servants, who sold their freedom in exchange for passage to America. Unlike the first Jamestown colonists, who were mostly young men, the Puritans traveled in "companies" with their families, friends, and neighbors.

**Questions About an Established Church** In all the New England colonies, settlers were aware that they were creating new societies in what was, for them, a new world. It is not surprising that they often argued about what direction these new societies should take.

A major argument revolved around a single question: should each colony have one, dominant, "established" church, funded by the taxpayer? In Europe, each national government supported only one established religious group. Other groups might face persecution from the religious group in power.

When the Puritans set up their society in Massachusetts, their church became the only established church in the colony. Other New England colonies were also dominated by Puritans, who tolerated some Christian groups but persecuted others. Only Rhode Island tolerated all Christian denominations, as well as Judaism.

**Democratic Traditions** Throughout the New England colonies, settlers established democratic practices and self-government. Colonists wove democratic practices into both their local government and their church life.

- The Congregational churches of the Puritans were self-governing.
- In Massachusetts, Puritan men elected the governor and the legislature.
- Voting rights were expanded in Massachusetts and Connecticut.
- In the New England countryside, towns controlled their own affairs.

A modern town meeting

Because of this democratic tradition in the region, the New England town meeting became a symbol of local self-government. At a time when very few Europeans had the right to vote, New England became famous for its democratic practices.

During these early decades of settlement, Massachusetts had the largest population and the greatest influence in the region. Its democratic political trends, its religious beliefs, and the conflicts of its early years influenced the course of American history.

▲ **COMPARE AND CONTRAST** Describe the features that the New England colonies had in common.

---

**New Jersey Core Curriculum Content Standards Review**

**ONLINE QUIZ**
For test practice, go to
**Interactive Review @ ClassZone.com**

**TERMS & NAMES**

1. Explain the importance of
   - John Winthrop
   - Pilgrims
   - Mayflower Compact
   - Puritans
   - Great Migration
   - Roger Williams
   - Anne Hutchinson
   - Fundamental Orders of Connecticut
   - Quakers

**USING YOUR READING NOTES**

2. **Causes and Effects** Complete the diagram that you started at the beginning of this section.

| Cause | Effect |
|-------|--------|
|       | *Pilgrims settled in America.* |

**KEY IDEAS**

3. Why did the Puritans leave England?

4. Why was Rhode Island founded?

5. In what ways were New England settlers different from the settlers of Jamestown?

**CRITICAL THINKING**

6. **Analyze Point of View** Why was religious tolerance an important issue for the early settlers?

7. **Make Generalizations** How did the Puritans weave democracy into their political and religious life?

8. **Connect to Today** What modern American values might be familiar to a 17th-century Puritan?

9. **Writing** **Research Report** Mary Dyer broke Puritan laws by returning to Massachusetts. This was an act of civil disobedience. Write a paper about other historical figures who used this form of protest.

# Reading Primary Sources

# The Mayflower Compact

**SETTING THE STAGE** In 1620, 41 colonists aboard the *Mayflower* drew up the Mayflower Compact. This document refers to the area where they landed as "Virginia" because the land grants of the Virginia Company extended into New England. The colonists provided for self-government under majority rule of the male voters.

### Reasons for Voyage

The three reasons the colonists give for their voyage to the eastern seaboard of North America are the glory of God, the advancement of Christianity, and the honor of the king.

**1. Might there have been more practical reasons for the voyage? Explain.**

### Guiding Purpose

In signing the compact, the colonists' guiding purpose is the general good of the colony.

**2. What does this suggest about the relationship between the individual and the community?**

We, whose names are underwritten, . . . having undertaken for the glory of God, and advancement of the Christian faith, and the honor of our King and country, a voyage to plant the first colony in the northern parts of Virginia, do by these presents, solemnly and mutually in the presence of God and one another **covenant**[1] and combine ourselves together into a civil **body politic**,[2] for our better ordering and preservation; and furtherance of the ends aforesaid . . . do enact, constitute, and frame such just and equal laws, ordinances, acts, constitutions, and offices from time to time as shall be thought most [proper] and convenient for the general good of the colony unto which we promise all due submission and obedience. In witness whereof we have hereunto subscribed our names at Cape Cod the eleventh of November, in the year of our **sovereign**[3] lord King James of England . . . Anno Domini 1620.

From B. P. Poore, ed., *The Federal and State Constitutions,* Part I, p. 931.

------------------------------------------------------------------------

1. **covenant:** promise in a binding agreement
2. **body politic:** the people of a politically organized group
3. **sovereign:** supreme

# The Fundamental Orders of Connecticut

**SETTING THE STAGE** In January 1639, male citizens of three townships in Connecticut (Hartford, Windsor, and Wethersfield) assembled and drew up the Fundamental Orders of Connecticut. This document is often called the first written constitution in America. It contains a preamble, or introduction, and a set of laws.

## Preamble

Forasmuch as it has pleased the Almighty God by the wise disposition of His Divine Providence so to order and dispose of things that we, the inhabitants and residents of Windsor, Hartford, and Wethersfield are now cohabiting and dwelling in and upon the river of Conectecotte [Connecticut] and the lands thereunto adjoining; and well knowing where a people are gathered together the Word of God requires that, to maintain the peace and union of such a people, there should be an orderly and decent government established according to God, to order and dispose of the affairs of the people at all seasons as occasion shall require; do therefore associate and **conjoin**[1] ourselves to be as one public state or commonwealth. . . . As also in our civil affairs to be guided and goverened according to such laws, rules, orders, and decrees as shall be made, ordered, and decreed as follows:

## Laws, Rules, and Orders

**1.** It is ordered, sentenced, and decreed that there shall be yearly two general assemblies or courts. . . . The first shall be called the Court of Election, wherein shall be yearly chosen . . . so many magistrates and other public officers as shall be found **requisite**[2]. . . .

**4.** It is ordered . . . that no person be chosen governor above once in two years, and that the governor shall be always a member of some approved congregation. . . .

**5.** It is ordered . . . that to the aforesaid Court of Election the several towns shall send their deputies. . . . Also, the other General Court in September shall be for making of laws, and any other public occasion which concerns the good of the Commonwealth. . . .

---

**1. conjoin:** unite **2. requisite:** required

### Good Government

In the eyes of the colonists, good government is pleasing to God. An orderly and decent government helps to maintain peace and order within a community and between people.

**3. How would you define good government today?**

### The Governor's Role

The person serving as governor can serve only once every two years and must be a member of an approved church or congregation.

**4. Why might the colonists have wished to limit the power of the chief executive?**

### The Courts

The Court of Election chooses officials to serve; the General Court makes laws.

**5. Why might it be a good idea to separate these two functions?**

## DOCUMENT-BASED QUESTIONS

### Short Answer
**1.** Whose rights did the Mayflower Compact protect?

**2.** In what ways were the Fundamental Orders based on religion?

### Extended Answer
**3.** How do you think these documents reveal the English foundation of American democracy?

## ▶ Key Ideas

**BEFORE, YOU LEARNED**

The first permanent English colony in North America was founded in Virginia.

**NOW YOU WILL LEARN**

New Southern colonies were settled by fortune-seekers, religious refugees, enslaved Africans, and the poor.

## ▶ Vocabulary

**TERMS & NAMES**

**Lord Baltimore** Catholic owner of the colony of Maryland

**Margaret Brent** attorney of the governor of Maryland

**Act of Toleration** Maryland law that forbade religious persecution

**Huguenots** French Protestants

**James Oglethorpe** the founder of Georgia

**BACKGROUND VOCABULARY**

**proprietary colony** colony governed by a single owner, or proprietor

**elite** highest-ranking social group

Visual Vocabulary
statue of James Oglethorpe

**diversity** variety

**region** distinct area of land

**Tidewater** flat land along the coast

## ▶ Reading Strategy

Re-create the diagram shown at right. As you read and respond to the **KEY QUESTIONS**, use the boxes to show how each colony was founded because of social or political problems in England.

 **See Skillbuilder Handbook, page R9.**

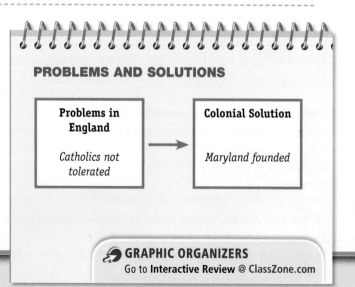

**PROBLEMS AND SOLUTIONS**

| Problems in England | Colonial Solution |
|---|---|
| *Catholics not tolerated* | *Maryland founded* |

**GRAPHIC ORGANIZERS**
Go to **Interactive Review** @ ClassZone.com

# The Southern Colonies

**6.4.D.1** Analyze the political, social, and cultural characteristics of the English colonies.
**6.4.D.2** Describe the political, religious, social, and economic institutions that emerged in Colonial America, including New Netherland and colonial New Jersey.

## One American's Story

In the 1640s fear and confusion spread through Maryland. A Puritan rebellion had been followed by the governor's death. Soldiers demanded their pay, but there was no money to pay them. No one had time to wait for instructions from the colony's owner, **Lord Baltimore**, who lived in England. So **Margaret Brent**, the governor's attorney, took action. First she rose before the Assembly to demand the right to vote. Because she was a woman, her request was denied. However, as the governor's attorney, she still had power. So to raise money to pay the troops, she sold Lord Baltimore's cattle. When Baltimore heard of this sale he was furious. The Assembly defended Brent's actions:

Margaret Brent demands the right to vote.

**PRIMARY SOURCE**

❝ It was better for [the] colony's safety at that time in her hands than in any man's else in the province. She rather deserved favor and thanks from your Honor. ❞

—letter to Lord Baltimore from the Maryland Assembly

Margaret Brent acted decisively at a time when few women had political power or many legal rights. But the colonies were a new world, where unusual circumstances often led colonists to play unfamiliar roles.

## Lord Baltimore Founds Maryland

🔽 **KEY QUESTION** What kind of society was planned for Maryland?

In 1634, the second Southern colony, Maryland, was settled on the Chesapeake Bay. Maryland was also intended to be a new kind of society, free from the religious conflicts of Europe.

**The Act of Toleration** When Maryland was founded, Catholics and Protestants in Europe had been fighting each other for a century. In England many Anglicans, including King Charles I, sympathized with the Catholics. Charles supported the Catholic Lord Baltimore's plan for a colony where

Catholics would not be persecuted. He gave Maryland to Lord Baltimore as a **proprietary colony**, a colony governed by a single owner, or proprietor.

The first settlement, St. Mary's City, located on the Chesapeake Bay, became the capital. Colonists were allowed to elect an assembly, and in 1649 the **Act of Toleration** forbade religious persecution.

Maryland based its economy on growing tobacco, which required backbreaking work. The tobacco crop quickly used up nutrients in the soil, and workers had to clear more land. Planters were always searching for laborers. Most tobacco workers were either indentured servants or slaves.

**Religious Conflict In Maryland**  The colony did not develop as planned. Some Catholics, such as Margaret Brent, did settle in Maryland. But they were outnumbered by Protestants. In 1645 Puritans tried to seize power in Maryland. Although order was restored, in 1654 Puritans dismissed Maryland's governor. They got rid of the Act of Toleration and replaced it with an anti-Catholic law. Eventually the act was restored. However, it was clear that achieving religious tolerance would be a difficult struggle.

▲ **PROBLEMS AND SOLUTIONS**  Describe the kind of society planned for Maryland.

## COMPARING  *Religious Groups*

## RELIGION IN THE EARLY COLONIES

In the 17th century, conflict between Catholics and Protestants divided Europeans. In England and its colonies, there were also disagreements among Protestants. These disagreements created a variety of religious groups.

| Protestants (do not recognize Pope's authority) | | | | Catholic (Pope leads church.) |
|---|---|---|---|---|
| **Quakers** | **Baptists** | **Puritans** | **Anglicans** | |
| Kings and bishops have no authority. | Church & state should be separate. | No bishops; congregations make decisions. | King heads church. Bishops rule. | Bishops help govern. |
| silent prayer important | sermon important | sermon important | sermon & Catholic-style ritual | ritual important |

**CRITICAL THINKING  Compare and Contrast**  Which Protestant denomination was most similar to Catholicism?

# The Carolinas

▼ **KEY QUESTION** What attracted settlers to the Carolinas?

During the 1640s England was torn by civil war and colonization stopped. In 1649, a Puritan republic was set up in England. Then, in 1660, the monarchy was restored, and Charles II became king. He rewarded eight supporters by giving them land for a new colony named Carolina.

**Proprietors Plan Their Colony** The proprietors, or owners, hoped to attract settlers by offering religious toleration, large land grants, and political representation. The northern part of Carolina was already populated by colonists from Virginia. The southern area was settled by English colonists who had been living in the West Indies. It was in this region that English settlers from Barbados built Charles Town (later called Charleston) in 1670.

The proprietors offered religious toleration to all Christians and Jews. After 1685, Charleston became a refuge for **Huguenots**, or French Protestants. Many Huguenots fled France to seek religious freedom in America.

**Rice and Slavery** In the 1690s, Carolina's colonists started exporting rice. They learned how to cultivate this crop from enslaved Africans, who had grown it in West Africa. Growing rice required a large labor force. So planters imported more enslaved Africans to do the work.

Reenactors portray slave life in the South.

### PRIMARY SOURCE

❝ Our Staple Commodity for some years has been Rice, and Tilling, planting, Hoeing, Reaping, Threshing, Pounding have all been done merely by the poor Slaves here. ❞

—letter from a South Carolina doctor, quoted in *American Colonies*

Slave labor helped make Carolina planters the richest **elite**, or high-ranking group, on the eastern seaboard. However, because they were so outnumbered by their slaves, this elite lived in constant fear of revolt.

Colonists also captured and enslaved Native Americans. As a result of this, and the taking of tribal lands, wars broke out between the settlers and Native American tribes, including the Tuscarora and Yamasee. The wars killed so many Native Americans that more lands were opened for the settlers.

**The Colonists Rebel** In 1691 a group of settlers forced the proprietors to establish a separate government and assembly in "North Carolina." Colonists were unhappy that the proprietors did not provide enough military protection from the Spanish and Native Americans. To gain more military support from the king, in 1719 the colonists overthrew the colony's proprietary rule. In 1729, both North Carolina and South Carolina became royal colonies, ruled by governors appointed by the king.

▲ **CAUSES AND EFFECTS** Explain what attracted settlers to the Carolinas.

# Georgia

▼ **KEY QUESTION** Why was Georgia founded?

In 1732, **James Oglethorpe** received a charter for Georgia, named after King George II. A year later Oglethorpe built the first settlement at Savannah.

**Ethnic and Religious Diversity** The colony was meant as a place where debtors and the poor could make a fresh start. It was hoped that such settlers would protect the English colonies against Spanish Florida to the south and French Louisiana to the west.

A population of great **diversity**, or variety, settled in Georgia. English, German, Swiss, and Scottish colonists arrived. All Protestant groups, as well as Jews, were welcome. However, Catholics were banned in case they might sympathize with Spanish Catholics in Florida.

**Oglethorpe's Policies** Oglethorpe set strict rules. He opposed large plantations and slavery because he wanted to help poor settlers establish small farms. He believed that a free population could better defend the colony against attack. He also feared that slave revolts might weaken the colony.

The colonists were unhappy with Oglethorpe's policies. They were envious of South Carolina's prosperity, which came from slave labor. In response, the trustees legalized slavery, and Georgia became a royal colony. Georgia turned into a plantation society like that of South Carolina.

▲ **SUMMARIZE** Explain why Georgia was founded.

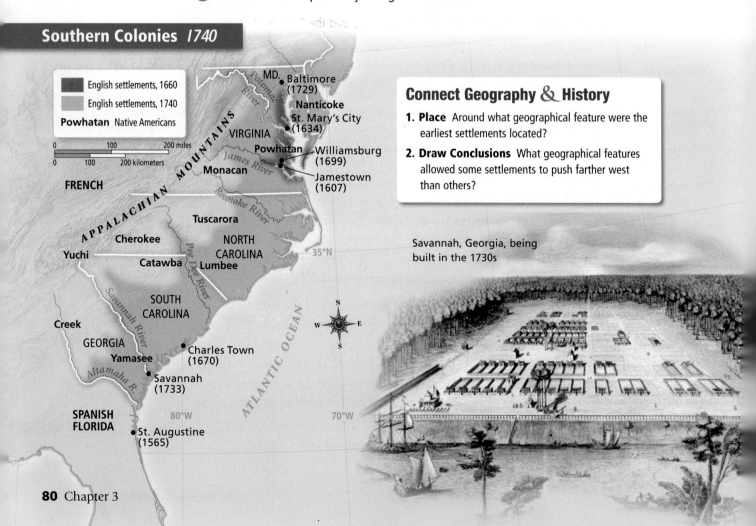

## Southern Colonies *1740*

**English settlements, 1660**
**English settlements, 1740**
**Powhatan** Native Americans

0          100          200 miles
0     100     200 kilometers

FRENCH

APPALACHIAN MOUNTAINS

MD. Baltimore (1729)
Nanticoke
St. Mary's City (1634)
VIRGINIA
Powhatan — Williamsburg (1699)
James River
Monacan
Jamestown (1607)
Roanoke River
Tuscarora
Cherokee
NORTH CAROLINA
Yuchi
Catawba   Lumbee
35°N
Pee Dee River
SOUTH CAROLINA
Savannah River
Creek
GEORGIA
Charles Town (1670)
Yamasee
Altamaha R.
Savannah (1733)
SPANISH FLORIDA
80°W
St. Augustine (1565)
70°W
ATLANTIC OCEAN
N W E S

### Connect Geography & History

1. **Place** Around what geographical feature were the earliest settlements located?

2. **Draw Conclusions** What geographical features allowed some settlements to push farther west than others?

Savannah, Georgia, being built in the 1730s

# The Region of the South

 **KEY QUESTION** What features did the Southern Colonies have in common?

With the addition of Georgia, the Southern Colonies now formed a **region**, or distinct area of land. This Southern region stretched from the borders of the Spanish colony of Florida north through the Carolinas, Virginia, and Maryland. The Southern Colonies shared a common climate and culture.

**Southern Culture Develops** The Appalachian Mountains bordered these colonies in the west. In the east, the flat land along the coast was known as the **Tidewater**. The soil and climate of the Tidewater encouraged the planting of warm-weather crops such as tobacco, rice, and indigo. These crops required a large labor force, so the region became home to the largest population of enslaved Africans in the colonies.

As large plantations formed along the rivers in coastal areas, landowners became rich from exporting cash crops. A wealthy elite soon developed, especially in Virginia and South Carolina. Meanwhile, poorer settlers were forced west onto the frontier.

Although the Anglican church was the established religion throughout the South, religious diversity increased. Many of the Southern Colonies promised religious toleration in order to attract settlers.

Colonists throughout the South demanded greater say in how they were governed. Eventually, every Southern colony was allowed an elected representative assembly.

 **COMPARE AND CONTRAST** Describe the features that the Southern Colonies had in common.

## Connecting History

**Social Conflict**
Disagreements between the rich planters of the coast and poorer settlers of the frontier would lead to Bacon's Rebellion in 1676. *Chapter 4, p. 104.*

---

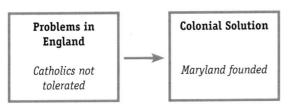

**New Jersey Core Curriculum Content Standards** *Review*

**ONLINE QUIZ**
For test practice, go to
**Interactive Review @ ClassZone.com**

### TERMS & NAMES
**1.** Explain the importance of
- Lord Baltimore
- Margaret Brent
- Act of Toleration
- Huguenots
- James Oglethorpe

### USING YOUR READING NOTES
**2. Problems and Solutions** Complete the diagram you began at the beginning of this section.

| Problems in England | | Colonial Solution |
|---|---|---|
| *Catholics not tolerated* | → | *Maryland founded* |

### KEY IDEAS
**3.** Why did Lord Baltimore found the colony of Maryland?

**4.** What drew settlers to the Carolinas?

**5.** What kind of society did Oglethorpe want for Georgia?

### CRITICAL THINKING
**6. Analyze Causes and Effects** Why did slavery expand in the Southern Colonies?

**7. Connect Economics & History** Why did South Carolina planters become such a wealthy elite?

**8.** **Writing** **Letter** Write a persuasive letter to a London newspaper, describing opportunities in the Carolinas and urging other settlers to join you there.

*The English Establish 13 Colonies* **81**

England and the colonies. Penn founded Pennsylvania to provide a place where Quakers could practice their beliefs, free of persecution. It was also meant to be a colony where the world could see Quaker ideals at work. Penn declared that Pennsylvania would be a "holy experiment" in Quaker religious tolerance and an "example to the Nations." But unlike the Puritan colonies in New England, Pennsylvania would have no tax-supported church.

The Quakers welcomed those of different religions and ethnic groups. This Quaker ideal of tolerance was written into the Frame of Government of Pennsylvania, which declared

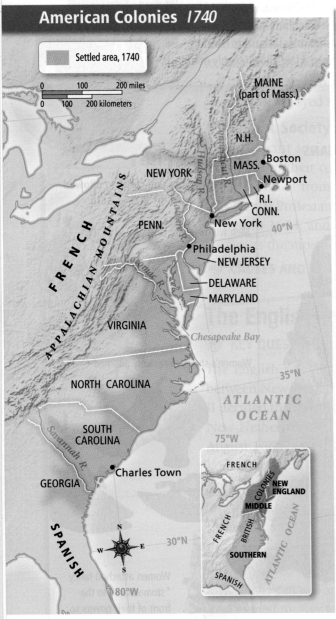

**American Colonies 1740**

Settled area, 1740

0    100    200 miles
0   100   200 kilometers

MAINE (part of Mass.)

N.H.

MASS. •Boston

NEW YORK

Newport

R.I.

CONN.

PENN. New York

40°N

•Philadelphia

NEW JERSEY

DELAWARE

MARYLAND

VIRGINIA

Chesapeake Bay

35°N

NORTH CAROLINA

ATLANTIC OCEAN

SOUTH CAROLINA

75°W

•Charles Town

GEORGIA

FRENCH

COLONIES NEW ENGLAND

MIDDLE

FRENCH

BRITISH

SOUTHERN

SPANISH

ATLANTIC OCEAN

30°N

80°W

FRENCH APPALACHIAN MOUNTAINS

Hudson R.

Savannah R.

SPANISH

N W E S

## Connect Geography & History

1. **Place** What geographical feature acted as a barrier to settlers traveling west?
2. **Make Generalizations** Which settlements were in more frequent contact with the outside world?

**PRIMARY SOURCE**

❝ [All persons] shall, in no ways, be molested or prejudiced for their religious persuasion, or practice, in matters of faith and worship, nor shall they be compelled at any time, to frequent or maintain any religious worship. ❞

—from The Frame of the Government of Pennsylvania, 1682

In Pennsylvania, Penn extended religious freedom and equality to all. Because of this, settlers from many European countries came to Pennsylvania seeking religious freedom and a better life. Penn himself designed the colony's capital. It was named Philadelphia, meaning "city of brotherly love."

Like the Puritans of New England, the Quakers valued hard work and thrift, or the careful management of money. These Quaker values, combined with Penn's policies, helped poor immigrants become rich. With its long growing season and fertile soil, Pennsylvania became one of the wealthiest American colonies.

**Thirteen Colonies** By the 1730s, 13 English colonies were thriving along the eastern seaboard of North America. The colonial economies were growing and the population was increasing dramatically. In fact, the American population was doubling every twenty-five years.

In many ways, the earliest English colonies in Virginia and Massachusetts set the pattern of development for the later Northern and Southern Colonies. Virginia, in the South, saw the development of a plantation economy. Massachusetts, in the North, created towns that relied on shipping to produce wealth.

Separated by great distances, distinct colonial cultures developed. But despite differences in climate, religion, and social organization, the colonies had much in common.

Many colonies were born of political events in England. The chart below shows how conditions in England affected the settlement of America.

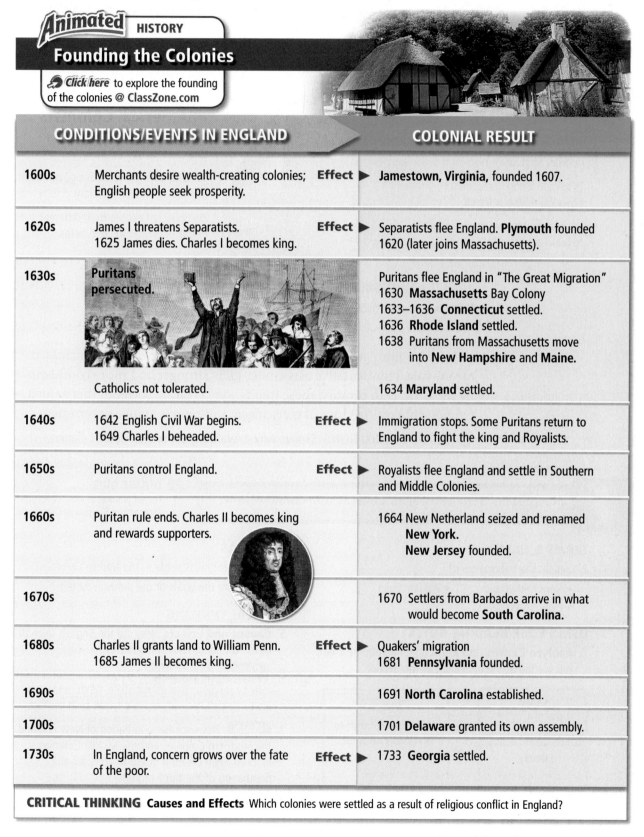

**Animated HISTORY**

## Founding the Colonies

*Click here* to explore the founding of the colonies @ ClassZone.com

| CONDITIONS/EVENTS IN ENGLAND | | COLONIAL RESULT |
|---|---|---|
| **1600s** | Merchants desire wealth-creating colonies; English people seek prosperity. | **Effect** ▶ | **Jamestown, Virginia,** founded 1607. |
| **1620s** | James I threatens Separatists. 1625 James dies. Charles I becomes king. | **Effect** ▶ | Separatists flee England. **Plymouth** founded 1620 (later joins Massachusetts). |
| **1630s** | Puritans persecuted. Catholics not tolerated. | | Puritans flee England in "The Great Migration" 1630 **Massachusetts** Bay Colony 1633–1636 **Connecticut** settled. 1636 **Rhode Island** settled. 1638 Puritans from Massachusetts move into **New Hampshire** and **Maine.** 1634 **Maryland** settled. |
| **1640s** | 1642 English Civil War begins. 1649 Charles I beheaded. | **Effect** ▶ | Immigration stops. Some Puritans return to England to fight the king and Royalists. |
| **1650s** | Puritans control England. | **Effect** ▶ | Royalists flee England and settle in Southern and Middle Colonies. |
| **1660s** | Puritan rule ends. Charles II becomes king and rewards supporters. | | 1664 New Netherland seized and renamed **New York. New Jersey** founded. |
| **1670s** | | | 1670 Settlers from Barbados arrive in what would become **South Carolina.** |
| **1680s** | Charles II grants land to William Penn. 1685 James II becomes king. | **Effect** ▶ | Quakers' migration 1681 **Pennsylvania** founded. |
| **1690s** | | | 1691 **North Carolina** established. |
| **1700s** | | | 1701 **Delaware** granted its own assembly. |
| **1730s** | In England, concern grows over the fate of the poor. | **Effect** ▶ | 1733 **Georgia** settled. |

**CRITICAL THINKING** Causes and Effects Which colonies were settled as a result of religious conflict in England?

The colonies were not only connected through their relationship with England. The early colonists shared the same experiences and concerns.

## CONNECT to the Essential Question

### How did the experience of the early colonists shape America's political and social ideals?

**Colonists Left Their Homelands**

in order to create a new kind of society.

to escape being persecuted by a more powerful religious group.

in order to improve their lives or to make a fresh start.

**In America, Colonists**

struggled with issues of religious tolerance.

established representative government and respect for English law.

encountered people from different ethnic backgrounds and faiths.

### CRITICAL THINKING

**Make Inferences** Which experiences helped the colonists value tolerance?

As more immigrants arrived, religious and ethnic diversity increased. Meanwhile, representative assemblies grew stronger and more confident. By the early 18th century, these trends were creating societies that valued religious liberty, freedom of conscience, and representative government.

▲ **DRAW CONCLUSIONS** Explain why toleration grew in the Middle Colonies.

**New Jersey Core Curriculum Content Standards** *Review*

**ONLINE QUIZ**
For test practice, go to **Interactive Review @ ClassZone.com**

### TERMS & NAMES

**1.** Explain the importance of
- New Netherland
- William Penn
- Peter Stuyvesant

### USING YOUR READING NOTES

**2. Analyze Causes and Effects** Complete the chart you started at the beginning of this section.

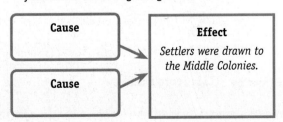

### KEY IDEAS

**3.** Why did colonists settle in the Middle Colonies?

**4.** What were the goals of the patroon system?

### CRITICAL THINKING

**5. Causes and Effects** Why did the English seize the Dutch colony of New Netherland?

**6.** **Connect** *to* **Today** Many modern nations are torn by religious and ethnic strife. What values and ideals helped America move beyond such conflicts?

**7.** **Math** Research the population of New England, the Southern Colonies and the Middle Colonies in 1700. Then create a graph to compare the population of the three regions.

## Chapter Summary

**1** **Key Idea**
Of the three earliest English colonies, only Jamestown managed to survive.

**2** **Key Idea**
English colonists settled New England, where they planted many political and religious traditions.

**3** **Key Idea**
New Southern colonies were settled by fortune-seekers, religious refugees, enslaved Africans, and the poor.

**4** **Key Idea**
Religious tolerance and ethnic diversity characterized the Middle Colonies.

For detailed Review and Study Notes go to **Interactive Review @ ClassZone.com**

## Name Game

**Use the Terms & Names list to complete each sentence online or on your own paper.**

1. I became leader of the Jamestown colony.
   John Smith 👆

2. I founded a colony to protect the other English colonies from attack. ____

3. I founded England's first American colony. ____

4. I wanted to create a colony where Catholics would not be persecuted. ____

5. I was a minister who was banished from the Massachusetts Bay Colony. ____

6. I helped set the Middle Colonies on the road to tolerance and diversity. ____

7. I was a woman who questioned the authority of the clergy. ____

8. This document helped establish the practice of self-government. ____

9. I governed the city that would become New York. ____

10. I acted as attorney for the governor of Maryland. _____

A. James Oglethorpe
B. Mayflower Compact
C. Roger Williams
D. William Penn
E. Jamestown
F. Sir Walter Raleigh
G. House of Burgesses
H. Margaret Brent
I. Peter Stuyvesant
J. New Netherland
K. John Smith
L. mercantilism
M. Anne Hutchinson
N. Puritans
O. Lord Baltimore
P. William Penn

## Activities

### FLIP CARD

Use the online flip cards to quiz yourself on the terms and names introduced in this chapter.

The first governor of Massachusetts Bay colony.

ANSWER
John Winthrop

### GEOGAME

Use this online map to reinforce your understanding of the early English colonies. Drag and drop each label in the list at its location on the map. A scorecard helps you keep track of your progress online.

Chesapeake Bay

York River

James River

Roanoke

Jamestown

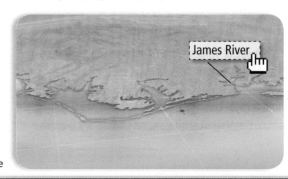

James River 👆

More items online

1. New England: Commerce and Religion

2. The Southern Colonies: Plantations and Slavery

3. The Middle Colonies: Farms and Cities

4. The Backcountry

# The Colonies Develop

## 1651–1753

 **ESSENTIAL QUESTION**

What factors allowed each colonial region to grow and prosper?

**CONNECT** ⟲ **Geography & History**

How did the Atlantic Ocean help bring prosperity to American colonists?

**Think about:**

**1** the importance of trans-Atlantic trade

**2** how the slave trade fit into the Atlantic trade network

**3** the way communities in different regions used natural resources to create wealth

detail from *Jamestown: N. Bacon, 1676* by Howard Pyle

**1676** Nathaniel Bacon leads a rebellion in Virginia.

▼

**Effect** After the rebellion ends, the House of Burgesses limits the governor's power.

**1651** Parliament passes the first of the Navigation Acts.

seal of Parliament

**1675** King Philip's War begins in New England.

**1692** The Salem witchcraft trials begin in Massachusetts.

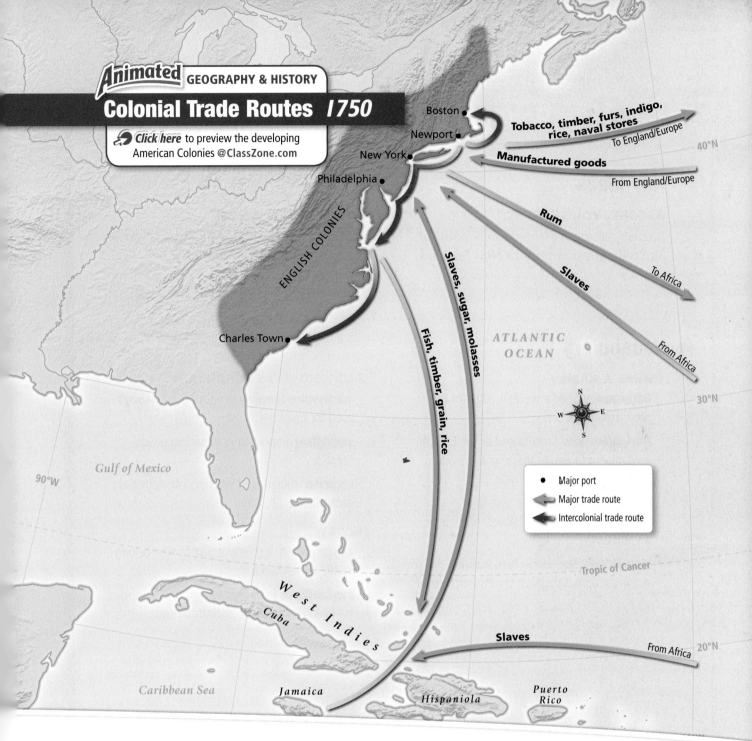

# Colonial Trade Routes *1750*

🖱 **Click here** to preview the developing
American Colonies @ClassZone.com

Boston

Newport

New York

Philadelphia

Tobacco, timber, furs, indigo, rice, naval stores
To England/Europe

40°N

Manufactured goods
From England/Europe

ENGLISH COLONIES

Rum
To Africa

Slaves
From Africa

Slaves, sugar, molasses

Charles Town

ATLANTIC OCEAN

Fish, timber, grain, rice

30°N

Gulf of Mexico

90°W

N
W    E
S

• Major port
⬅ Major trade route
⬅ Intercolonial trade route

Tropic of Cancer

West Indies

Cuba

Slaves
From Africa    20°N

Caribbean Sea

Jamaica

Hispaniola

Puerto Rico

**1739** The Stono Rebellion, a slave uprising, takes place in South Carolina.

▼

**Effect** Southern Colonies make slave codes even stricter.

**1712** Enslaved Africans rebel in New York City.

# 1753

A young officer named George Washington is sent to warn the French to leave the Ohio territory.

slave market on Wall Street, New York in the early 18th century

# Reading for Understanding

## Key Ideas

**BEFORE, YOU LEARNED**

English colonists planted many political and religious traditions in New England.

**NOW YOU WILL LEARN**

Prosperity and religious diversity brought changes to Puritan New England.

## ▶ Vocabulary

**TERMS & NAMES**

**Backcountry** the far western edges of the other colonies

**Navigation Acts** laws passed by the English government to ensure that England made money from its colonies' trade

**triangular trade** complex system of transatlantic exchange of slaves, rum, sugar, and molasses

**King Philip's War** 1675–1676 Native American uprising against the Puritan colonies

**BACKGROUND VOCABULARY**

**subsistence farming** producing just enough food for one's needs

**smuggling** importing or exporting goods illegally

**common** shared land where public activities took place

**REVIEW**

**congregation** a group of people who belong to the same church

**mercantilism** economic system that European nations used to enrich their treasuries

## ▶ Reading Strategy

Re-create the diagram shown at right. As you read and respond to the **KEY QUESTIONS**, use the diagram to record the causes and effects of the Navigation Acts.

 **See Skillbuilder Handbook, page R7.**

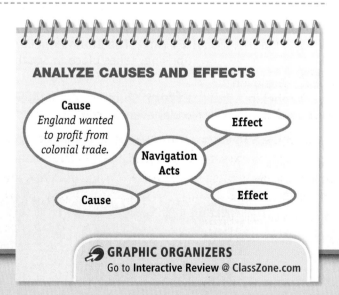

**ANALYZE CAUSES AND EFFECTS**

Cause
*England wanted to profit from colonial trade.*

Effect

Navigation Acts

Cause

Effect

**GRAPHIC ORGANIZERS**
Go to **Interactive Review** @ ClassZone.com

# New England:
## Commerce and Religion

**6.4.D.1.** Analyze the political, social, and cultural characteristics of the English colonies.
**6.4.D.6.** Identify factors that account for the establishment of African slavery in the Americas.

## One American's Story

Like many other New England Puritans, Captain Thomas Smith had grown rich through commerce. In this self-portrait from 1680, he displays his wealthy clothes and surroundings. He was proud of his achievements: the painting includes a scene of a naval battle in which he may have fought. Smith enjoyed his worldly success. But as a Puritan, he was also torn between the joys of this world and the need to prepare for the next. So under the skull appears a religious poem that begins

**PRIMARY SOURCE**

❝ Why why should I the World be minding
  Therein a World of Evils finding.
  Then Farewell World: Farewell thy Jarres [conflicts]
  Thy Joies thy Toies thy Wiles thy Warrs ❞

—poem in Captain Thomas Smith's self-portrait

Captain Thomas Smith
Self–Portrait, Worcester
Art Museum

The poem reveals a man who was aware of both the "evils" and the "joys" and "toys" of this world. Like other New Englanders, Captain Smith struggled to balance his religious life with his commercial success.

## The Resources of New England

🔻 **KEY QUESTION** Why did England pass the Navigation Acts?

By the 1700s, the colonies formed several distinct regions: New England, the Middle Colonies, the Southern Colonies and the **Backcountry**, which ran through the far western edges of the colonies. Of all the colonial regions, New England was the most populated. Its people grew rich by cleverly exploiting the region's resources.

**Farms and Towns** Farming in New England was not easy. The growing season was short, and the soil in many places was rocky. Most farmers practiced **subsistence farming**. That is, they produced just enough food for themselves and sometimes a little extra to trade in town.

Most New England farmers lived near a town. Colonial officials sold large plots of land to groups of people—often to a Puritan **congregation**. The congregation settled the town and divided the land among its members.

This pattern of settlement led New England towns to develop in a unique way. Usually, a cluster of farmhouses and a meetinghouse were built around a **common**—shared land where public activities took place. Because people lived together in small towns, a diverse economy developed. Farmers sold produce to shopkeepers; shopkeepers had enough customers to make a living. Along the coast, seaport towns shipped farm products and provided a marketplace for goods coming into New England.

**Harvesting the Sea** The Atlantic Ocean offered many economic opportunities. Near New England's coast were some of the world's best whaling and fishing grounds for mackerel, halibut, cod, herring, and other fish.

New England's forests provided everything needed to harvest these "pastures" of fish. Wood from oak trees made excellent ship hulls. Hundred-foot-tall white pines were ideal for masts. Shipbuilders used about 2,500 trees to produce just one ship!

The forests were a valuable resource. Soon New England was exporting timber, as well as fish, to the world. As merchants grew rich from exporting these goods, their ships began carrying goods produced in other places as well. New England's ships became an important part of international trade.

Throughout New England, the population benefitted from the wealth being created in the seaports. The colonists were soon competing with England's fishermen, shipbuilders, and merchants. As coastal towns like Boston, Salem, and Newport grew rich, the English government began to take notice.

**The Navigation Acts** According to the economic theory of **mercantilism**, the mother country was supposed to profit from its colonies. As the American colonists prospered, England wanted to make sure that it profited

**The New England Colonies** *1750*

MAINE
(part of Mass.)

Claimed by
N.Y. & N.H.

NEW
HAMPSHIRE

Portsmouth

Salem
Boston

MASSACHUSETTS

Newport

CONNECTICUT

RHODE
ISLAND

ATLANTIC
OCEAN

Connecticut River

Hudson River

70°W

40°N

**Major Exports**

- Furs and skins
- Cattle and grain
- Fish
- Iron
- Ships
- Rum
- Timber
- Whaling Products

0    50    100 miles
0   50   100 kilometers

## Connect Geography & History

1. **Location** All of the New England colonies are located to the east of what major river?

2. **Make Inferences** Why do you think New Englanders exported so many ocean-related products?

from colonial prosperity. So the English government began passing the **Navigation Acts** in 1651. The Navigation Acts had four major provisions designed to ensure that England made money from its colonies' trade.

1. All goods had to be carried on English ships or on ships made in the English colonies.
2. Products such as tobacco, wood, and sugar could be sold only to England or its colonies.
3. European imports to the colonies had to pass through English ports.
4. Officials were to tax any colonial goods not shipped to England.

The colonists resented these laws. Merchants ignored the acts whenever possible. England had trouble controlling colonial shipping and patrolling the long coastline of the colonies. **Smuggling**—importing or exporting goods illegally—was common. England also had great difficulty preventing pirates, like the legendary Blackbeard, from interfering with colonial shipping.

▲ **CAUSES AND EFFECTS** Explain why England passed the Navigation Acts.

## CONNECT To Today

### PIRACY

In the late 1600s, England faced a problem that it had helped create—Atlantic piracy. For decades, England had encouraged pirates to attack Spanish shipping. But as England itself grew rich from commerce, pirates began attacking English ships. They also smuggled goods into and out of colonial ports.

Pirates in colonial times

Rich cargoes have always attracted pirates. Today, piracy flourishes in southeast Asia, especially in the busy Malacca Strait between Indonesia and Malaysia.

Each year 50,000 ships, carrying half the world's oil shipments, pass through the strait. Hundreds of ships are attacked annually. Vessels are often hijacked and the crew held to ransom. In 2004, Indonesia, Singapore, and Malaysia agreed to fight piracy in their waters.

Modern coastguard on the lookout for piracy near Guam

### CRITICAL THINKING

1. **Make Inferences** Why was piracy a threat to the mercantilist system?
2. **Draw Conclusions** Why are modern pirates attracted to the Malacca Strait?

# Atlantic Trade

**KEY QUESTION** How did New Englanders profit from the triangular trade?

New England settlers engaged in three types of trade. First was the trade with other colonies. Second was the exchange of goods with Europe. But the third type, known as the **triangular trade**, had a sinister, or evil, aspect—because it involved trade in human beings.

**Human Cargo** Triangular trade describes a complex system of trans-Atlantic trade used to exchange slaves, rum, sugar, and molasses. For example, a ship might leave New England with a cargo of rum and iron. In Africa, the captain would trade his cargo for slaves. Slaves then endured the cruel voyage to the West Indies, where they were exchanged for sugar and molasses. Traders then took the sugar and molasses back to New England. There, colonists used the molasses to make rum, and the sequence began again.

New Englanders not only brought slaves to the West Indies but also sent fish to feed the huge slave population there. In this way, the economies of New England and the West Indies were closely tied. This trading system brought prosperity to both New England and the West Indies.

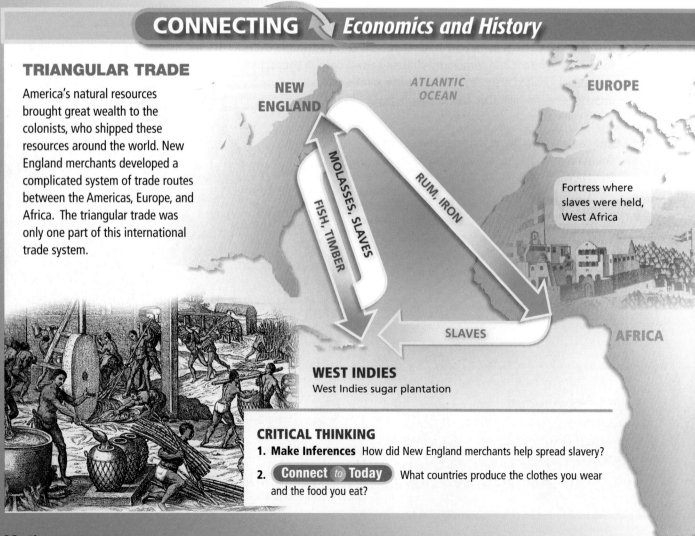

## CONNECTING ⟳ Economics and History

### TRIANGULAR TRADE

America's natural resources brought great wealth to the colonists, who shipped these resources around the world. New England merchants developed a complicated system of trade routes between the Americas, Europe, and Africa. The triangular trade was only one part of this international trade system.

NEW ENGLAND

ATLANTIC OCEAN

EUROPE

MOLASSES, SLAVES

FISH, TIMBER

RUM, IRON

Fortress where slaves were held, West Africa

SLAVES

AFRICA

**WEST INDIES**
West Indies sugar plantation

### CRITICAL THINKING

1. **Make Inferences** How did New England merchants help spread slavery?

2. **Connect** *to* **Today** What countries produce the clothes you wear and the food you eat?

**Africans in New England** Despite New Englanders' involvement in the slave trade, there were few slaves in New England. In 1700 slaves made up only 2 percent of New England's population. New England had no large plantations, so there was no need for a large labor force on each farm. This is why a large slave population never developed in New England.

Some New Englanders who lived in larger towns and cities did own slaves. Enslaved people worked as house servants, cooks, gardeners, and stable-hands. In the 1700s, New England slave owners seldom had enough room to house more than one or two slaves. Instead, more and more slave owners hired out their slaves to work on the docks or in shops or warehouses. Slave owners sometimes allowed their slaves to keep a portion of their wages.

Occasionally, the enslaved were able to save enough to buy their freedom. In fact, New England had more free blacks than any other region. A free African American man might become a merchant, sailor, printer, carpenter, or landowner. Even so, white colonists did not treat free African Americans as equals.

🔺 **SUMMARIZE** Explain how New Englanders profited from the triangular trade.

# King Philip's War

🔽 **KEY QUESTION** How did Native Americans react to colonial growth?

Europeans and Native Americans had different attitudes about land ownership. Europeans believed that land could be owned. Native Americans had a more communal attitude to land use. Conflict over land resulted in warfare.

**Fighting for Survival** Native American tribes in New England were alarmed by the increasing numbers of settlers on their hunting grounds and near their crops. They were also troubled by the growing influence of European culture on their people. In 1675–1676, they carried out an uprising against the Puritan colonies. This was known as **King Philip's War**. "King Philip" was the English name of Metacom, leader of the Wampanoag tribe, who led the first attacks against the colonists.

The Wampanoag were soon joined by other tribes. For both sides, the war was a fight for survival. Twelve Puritan towns were destroyed. Forty other towns, including Plymouth and Providence, were attacked. For a while, it seemed as if the New England colonies might be destroyed.

In desperation, the English colonists turned to other Native American peoples for help. Southern New England tribes such as the Pequot and the Mohegan showed the New Englanders how to track down and ambush the rebel tribes. In the summer of 1676 the uprising collapsed. Many Native Americans were killed, while others were sold into slavery in the West Indies. English settlers expanded even farther into Native American land.

🔺 **MAKE INFERENCES** Explain how Native Americans reacted to colonial growth.

Why might King Philip (*shown above*) have been outraged by European attitudes about land use?

*The Colonies Develop* **99**

# Changes in Puritan Society

▼ **KEY QUESTION** What factors helped weaken Puritan religious control?

New England society was changing rapidly by the late 1600s. One of the most noticeable changes was the decline of Puritan power.

**Economic Success and Religious Diversity** The Puritan values of hard work made many New Englanders rich. But some colonists now seemed to care more about business and material possessions than about religion. Puritan ministers noticed the change and used their sermons to condemn the new interest in worldly success.

## History *through* Art

Portraits of Elizabeth, Mary, and John Freake by an unidentified artist, from the collection of the Worcester Art Museum.

### A Changing Puritan World

These portraits, painted a few years before King Philip's War, are windows onto a changing Puritan world. Elizabeth, (shown with her daughter Mary) and John Freake were in their 30s when these portraits were painted in the 1670s. Elizabeth was one of the children of the first generation of Puritans, who arrived during the Great Migration. Elizabeth and John enjoyed the fruits of the prosperous society that their parents had created. Their clothes are richly decorated and expensive. For example, John's elaborate lace collar, gloves, and ruffled sleeves display his wealth.

**CRITICAL VIEWING** How do Elizabeth's clothes and surroundings reveal the wealth of Puritan society in the late 1600s?

The arrival of non-Puritan immigrants also threatened Puritan control. The success of the colony began attracting different kinds of immigrants. Baptists and Anglicans established churches in Massachusetts and Connecticut, where Puritans had once been the most powerful group.

Political changes further weakened Puritan domination. In 1691, a new royal charter for Massachusetts guaranteed religious freedom for all Protestants, not just Puritans. The charter broke Puritan power by ending the churches' control of elections. The loss of power created great uncertainty for many Puritans, which may have contributed to one of the strangest episodes in American history—the Salem witchcraft trials.

**The Salem Witchcraft Trials** In 1692, a year after the new charter broke Puritan power, a terrifying series of events occurred in Salem Village, Massachusetts. Several girls, pretending to be bewitched, began accusing others of witchcraft.

Hysteria spread through the community. Those accused were forced to name others as witches. More than 100 people were arrested and dozens were tried. Of those, 19 were found guilty and put to death by hanging, including a popular minister. In addition, two dogs were hanged, and a man was pressed to death when he refused to cooperate with the court.

Eventually, important ministers intervened, and the governor stopped the executions. Within a few years, several of the accusers admitted that they had made false accusations. In 1697 one of the judges begged public forgiveness for his part in the trials.

**Puritan Legacy** Although Puritan power declined, Puritan values survived. These values have influenced American culture. Americans have inherited:

- the Puritan work ethic
- a high regard for education
- opposition to royal power and support for representative government
- the practice of voting on decisions affecting the community

Many of these Puritan values helped put America on the road to independence.

An elderly women being arrested for witchcraft in Salem
**Why do you think the girls accused so many people of witchcraft?**

 **CAUSES AND EFFECTS** Describe how Puritan religious control was weakened in the later 1600s.

---

**New Jersey Core Curriculum Content Standards** *Review*

 **ONLINE QUIZ**
For test practice, go to
**Interactive Review @ ClassZone.com**

### TERMS & NAMES

1. Explain the importance of
   - Backcountry
   - triangular trade
   - Navigation Acts
   - King Philip's War

### USING YOUR READING NOTES

2. **Causes and Effects** Complete the diagram you started at the beginning of this section to show the causes and effects of the Navigation Acts.

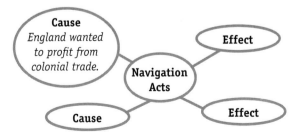

### KEY IDEAS

3. How did England profit from colonial shipping?
4. What changes did prosperity bring to New England?

### CRITICAL THINKING

5. **Make Inferences** How do you think the enslaved were able to save money if they were not paid for their labor?

6. **Connect Economics & History** Why did New England come to depend on fishing and shipbuilding?

7. **Connect** *to* **Today** New Englanders took economic advantage of their environment. Describe modern examples of people using natural resources to gain wealth.

8. **Writing** **Letter** Write a letter from Metacom to the English colonists. Explain the reasons for the war that is about to be launched against them.

Because most plantations were largely self-sufficient, large urban centers were unnecessary in the South. The port city of Charles Town (later called Charleston) in South Carolina was an early exception.

**The Planter Class** The owners of the plantations were considered the **elite** of this society. In the early colonies, this class was drawn from the noble families of the south and west of England.

The planter class was relatively small compared to the rest of the population. However, they soon gained control of political and economic power in the South. A foreign traveler in the South commented that the planters "think and act precisely as do the nobility in other countries."

The planters formed the highest level of a class system that included large numbers of poor freemen, indentured servants, and slaves. The social system in the South was dramatically different from New England, where numerous middle-class families had settled. In the South, tension between social groups led to a major conflict in the late 17th century.

**Bacon's Rebellion in 1676** The desire for land and wealth had drawn settlers to America, so it is not surprising that many of the early conflicts in the South were over land. By the 1670s many indentured servants had completed their service and demanded land. Because the wealthy planters controlled the Tidewater region, these poorer freemen were forced into the western frontier, where they battled Native Americans for land.

*Jamestown: N. Bacon, 1676* by Howard Pyle

Nathaniel Bacon and a group of landless frontier settlers were already angry with Virginia Governor William Berkeley. They complained about high taxes and Governor Berkeley's favoritism toward large plantation owners. Bacon demanded that Berkeley help defend frontier settlements against Native Americans. Berkeley's refusal of Bacon's demand sparked **Bacon's Rebellion** in 1676.

Bacon entered Jamestown, took control of the House of Burgesses, and burned Jamestown to the ground. However, Bacon's sudden illness and death ended the rebellion. Berkeley hanged 23 of Bacon's followers. Angered by Berkeley's actions, King Charles II recalled the governor to England. Afterwards, the House of Burgesses passed laws to prevent a royal governor from assuming such power again. The burgesses had taken an important step against tyranny.

▲ **COMPARE AND CONTRAST** Explain what tensions developed between Tidewater and frontier settlers.

## The Search for Cheap Labor

🔻 **KEY QUESTION** Why did planters turn to slavery?

In the early Southern Colonies, there were few Africans, either enslaved or free. In 1665, fewer than 500 Africans had been brought into Virginia. At that time, African and European indentured servants worked in the fields together.

In the 1660s, the labor system began to change as indentured white servants left the plantations. Their terms of service were finished, and many moved west in order to buy their own farms. At the same time, fewer European laborers were emigrating to the Southern Colonies. Landowners had to find another source of labor.

**Planters Turn to Slavery** At first planters tried to enslave Native Americans. But many Native Americans either died of diseases brought by Europeans or were able to escape into the forests that they knew so well.

To meet their labor needs, the planters turned to enslaved Africans. As a result, the enslaved population grew rapidly. By 1750, there were over 235,000 enslaved Africans in America. About 68 percent lived in the Southern Colonies. By 1750 enslaved Africans made up about 40 percent of the South's population.

As the slave population increased, laws were passed to define slavery and to control the growing numbers of people being held against their will. Local militia patrolled the countryside to check that any traveling Africans were carrying passes. Slave quarters were checked regularly for weapons.

**Living in Slavery** On large Southern plantations, slaves usually toiled in groups of about 20 to 25 under the supervision of **overseers**. Overseers were people who watched over and directed the work of others. Enslaved people performed strenuous and exhausting work, often for 15 hours a day at the peak of the harvest season. If slaves did not appear to be doing their full share of work, they were often whipped by the overseer. If they defied their masters, they could be tortured or mutilated.

Enslaved people usually lived in small one-room cabins with straw for bedding. For a week's food, a slave might receive only around a quarter bushel of cornmeal and around 3 pounds of pork. Some planters allowed their slaves to raise their own food.

In spite of the brutal living conditions, Africans preserved many customs and beliefs from their homelands. These included music, dances, stories, and, for a time, African religions—including Islam. African kinship customs became the basis of African-American family culture.

🔺 **CAUSES AND EFFECTS** Explain why planters turned to slavery.

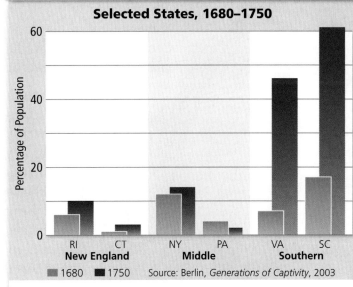

**COMPARING** *Slave Populations*

**Selected States, 1680–1750**

■ 1680   ■ 1750   Source: Berlin, *Generations of Captivity*, 2003

**CRITICAL VIEWING** Analyze Charts What percentage of the population was enslaved in the South in 1710?

# Expansion of Plantations Brings Resistance

🔽 **KEY QUESTION** How did African Americans resist their enslavement?

Slavery allowed plantation farming to expand in South Carolina and Georgia. Without slave labor, there probably would have been no rice plantations in the lowcountry—the region's swampy lowlands.

**Backbreaking Labor** Rice cultivation required great skill. Because West Africans had these skills, planters sought out slaves who came from Africa's rice-growing regions. Rice growing involved backbreaking labor. Enslaved workers drained swamps, raked fields, burned stubble, and broke ground before planting. They also had to tend the fields and harvest the crop.

On higher ground, planters grew **indigo**, a plant that produces a deep blue dye used to dye clothes. A young woman named **Eliza Lucas** had introduced indigo as a successful plantation crop after her father left her to supervise his South Carolina plantations when she was 17.

**The Enslaved Fight Back** Although they were kept in bondage, people of African origin found ways to resist their enslavement. They sometimes worked slowly, damaged goods, or deliberately carried out orders the wrong way. A British traveler in 1746 noted that many slaves pretended not to understand tasks they often had performed in West Africa.

Reenactors portray slave labor.

**PRIMARY SOURCE**

❝ You would really be surpriz'd at their Perseverance; let an hundred Men shew him how to hoe, or drive a wheelbarrow, he'll still take the one by the Bottom, and the other by the Wheel; and they often die before they can be conquer'd. ❞

—Edward Kimber, quoted in *White over Black*

**Connecting History**

**Slavery**
In the next century, South Carolina's continuing dependence on slavery would lead the state to secede from the Union in 1860—the event that led to the Civil War.
*See Chapter 15, p. 502.*

In South Carolina, the enslaved vastly outnumbered whites, who lived in fear of slave rebellions. Their fears came true in the late 1730s when a revolt occurred in South Carolina.

**The Stono Rebellion** In September 1739, an uprising known as the **Stono Rebellion** took place. The revolt began when about 20 slaves gathered at the Stono River just southwest of Charles Town. Wielding weapons, they killed planters and marched south, beating drums and chanting "Liberty!" They called out for other slaves to join them in their plan to seek freedom in Spanish-held Florida. Many joined them, and their numbers grew until there were perhaps one hundred in open rebellion. Seven plantations were burned along their route and twenty whites were killed. By late that afternoon, however, a white militia had surrounded the escaping slaves. The two sides clashed, and many slaves died in the fighting. Those captured were executed.

Stono and similar revolts led planters to make slave codes even stricter. Slaves were now forbidden from leaving plantations without written permission. The laws also made it illegal for slaves to meet with free blacks. Such laws made the conditions of slavery even more inhumane.

**Economy of the South** The Southern Colonies' plantation economy and large slave population helped create a unique Southern identity. In northern colonies, with their diverse economies, wealth was more evenly distributed. Southern economies were less diverse, based on crops such as tobacco, rice, and indigo. The wealth from these crops was concentrated in the hands of an elite.

The different economic systems of Northern and Southern Colonies were reflected in the landscape: the north had smaller farms and larger, more numerous towns. The South had scattered settlements, few towns, and self-sufficient plantations. The contrast between northern and southern landscapes, settlement patterns, and economic systems emerged very early in American history. Distinct regionalisms were developing that continue to influence American culture and politics.

 **SUMMARIZE** Describe how African Americans resisted their enslavement.

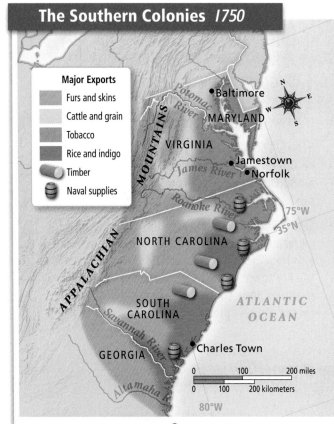

## The Southern Colonies 1750

**Major Exports**
- Furs and skins
- Cattle and grain
- Tobacco
- Rice and indigo
- Timber
- Naval supplies

### Connect Geography & History

1. **Place** Which Southern Colonies grew both rice and indigo?
2. **Draw Conclusions** Where would planters have built their plantations if they wanted to keep transportation costs low?

---

**New Jersey Core Curriculum Content Standards** *Review*

 **ONLINE QUIZ**
For test practice, go to
**Interactive Review @ ClassZone.com**

### TERMS & NAMES

1. Explain the importance of
   - Bacon's Rebellion
   - Eliza Lucas
   - Stono Rebellion

### USING YOUR READING NOTES

2. **Compare and Contrast** Complete the diagram you started at the beginning of this section.

| Tidewater *wealthy planters* | Western Frontier |
|---|---|

### KEY IDEAS

3. Where were most of the early plantations located?
4. How did planters meet their labor needs?

### CRITICAL THINKING

5. **Make Inferences** Why did South Carolina's colonists live in fear of a slave revolt?
6. **Summarize** How did the House of Burgesses strengthen colonists' rights after Bacon's Rebellion?
7. **Writing** **Research Report** Use the internet to research the Virginia House of Burgesses. Write a paragraph on the importance of the House of Burgesses in the history of American democracy.

# Animated HISTORY
## A NEW ENGLAND SEAPORT

 **Click here** to learn more about how New Englanders created wealth through trade @ ClassZone.com

In New England, densely settled towns developed on the coast. These towns became centers of a worldwide commerce, exporting many different products, such as fish, lumber, and foodstuffs.

This commerce brought wealth to an elite of merchants, bankers, and insurers. However, trade also benefitted the population of New England's smaller towns, rural villages, and farms. For several centuries, New England's sea trade was the basis for the region's prosperity.

## COMPARING Economies

By 1700 two economic systems had developed in the colonies—one in the North and one in the South. Both systems created wealth, but in very different ways.

Drayton Hall, near Charleston, South Carolina

### Northern Seaport and Southern Plantation

• New England towns had many free workers who bought and sold products among themselves and shipped goods to other places.

• In contrast, the South had few towns. Economic life centered on the plantations. Each plantation exported a limited number of crops.

   A Southern plantation was so self-sufficient that it was like a small town in itself. Plantation slaves produced food and made products in the workshops.

## Activity

### Seaport and Plantation

**1** Divide the class into two groups. Have one group research the layout of an 18th-century plantation. Have the other reseach the types of buildings and businesses found in a New England seaport.

**2** Let the plantation group draw a plan of a typical plantation, identifying the various service buildings. Have the seaport group draw the plan of a coastal town.

**3** Present the research to the class.

## ▶ Key Ideas

**BEFORE, YOU LEARNED**

The Middle Colonies attracted a diverse population who favored religious tolerance.

**NOW YOU WILL LEARN**

Rich farmland and a climate of tolerance helped the Middle Colonies prosper.

## ▶ Vocabulary

**TERMS & NAMES**

**Philadelphia** settlement on the Delaware River that became the fastest growing city in the colonies

**Conestoga wagons** covered wagons introduced by German immigrants

**BACKGROUND VOCABULARY**

**artisans** skilled craftspeople, such as blacksmiths and cabinet makers

**denomination** distinct religious group

**REVIEW**

**Quakers** group of Protestant dissenters

**tolerance** acceptance of different opinions

Visual Vocabulary
blacksmith

## ▶ Reading Strategy

Re-create the diagram shown at right. As you read and respond to the **KEY QUESTIONS**, use the diagram to note important details that support the Main Idea of this section.

📖 **See Skillbuilder Handbook, page R4.**

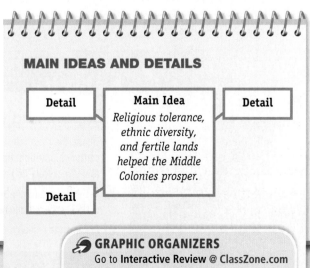

**MAIN IDEAS AND DETAILS**

| Detail | **Main Idea** *Religious tolerance, ethnic diversity, and fertile lands helped the Middle Colonies prosper.* | Detail |
|---|---|---|

Detail

**GRAPHIC ORGANIZERS**
Go to **Interactive Review** @ ClassZone.com

# The Middle Colonies:
## Farms and Cities

**6.4.D.1.** Analyze the political, social, and cultural characteristics of the English colonies.
**6.4.D.2.** Describe the political, religious, social, and economic institutions that emerged in Colonial America, including New Netherland and colonial New Jersey.

## One American's Story

William Penn, who established Pennsylvania, was aware that earlier English colonists had not treated Native Americans with respect. Writing from England, Penn promised Native Americans that the people of his colony would behave differently.

**PRIMARY SOURCE**

❝ I am very sensible to the unkindness and injustice which have been too much exercised toward you by the people of these parts of the world. . . . I have a great love and regard toward you, and desire to win and gain your love and friendship by a kind, just and peaceable life; and the people I send are of the same mind. ❞

—Letter from William Penn to the Native Americans, 1681

*Penn's Treaty with the Indians* by Edward Hicks

The **Quakers**, a group of Protestant dissenters, did develop a good relationship with tribes in Pennsylvania. The Quakers also accepted people who had different religious beliefs. This helped to create a climate of **tolerance**, or acceptance of different opinions, in the prosperous Middle Colonies of New York, New Jersey, Pennsylvania, and Delaware.

## A Prosperous Region

▼ **KEY QUESTION** Why did the cities of the Middle Colonies grow so rapidly?

The Middle Colonies had much to offer in addition to a climate of tolerance. Immigrants were drawn to the region's productive land.

Among the immigrants who came to the Middle Colonies were Dutch and German farmers. Their skills, knowledge, and hard work produced an abundance of foods.

**Productive Farms** The Middle Colonies enjoyed a longer growing season than New England and a soil rich enough to grow cash crops. These were crops raised to be sold for money. Common cash crops included fruits, vegetables, and, above all, grain. In fact, the Middle Colonies produced so much grain that people began calling them the "breadbasket" colonies.

**Growing Cities** The excellent harbors of the Middle Colonies were ideal sites for cities. New York City grew at the mouth of the Hudson River, and **Philadelphia** was founded on the Delaware River. The merchants who lived in these growing port cities exported grain and other cash crops from local farms and imported manufactured goods from England.

Because of its enormous trade, Philadelphia became the fastest growing city in the colonies. By the 1750s, it was home to a dozen large shipyards—places where ships are built or repaired.

The city's wealth also brought many public improvements. Large and beautiful buildings, such as Philadelphia's statehouse—which was later renamed Independence Hall—graced the city's streets. In 1748, a Swedish visitor was impressed by the city's beauty and wealth.

**PRIMARY SOURCE**

❝ And yet . . . its natural advantages, trade, riches, and power are by no means inferior to . . . any, even of the most ancient, towns in Europe. ❞

—Peter Kalm, quoted in *America at 1750*

New York could also thank trade for its rapid growth. This bustling port handled flour, bread, furs, and whale oil. At midcentury, an English naval officer admired the city's elegant buildings and paved streets. "Such is this city," he said, "that very few in England can rival it in its show."

🔺 **MAIN IDEAS & DETAILS** Explain why the cities of the Middle Colonies grew.

(*below*) A late 18th-century view of Philadelphia.
**In what other respects did Philadelphia grow in the 1700s?**

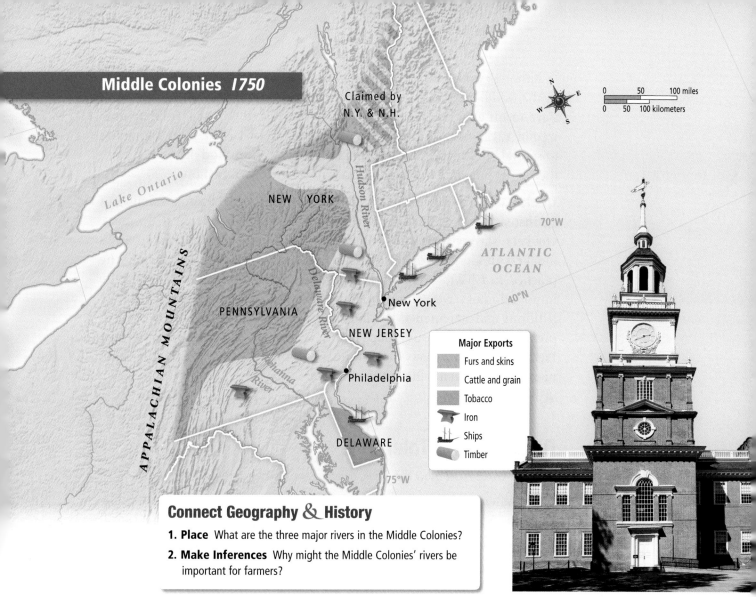

## Middle Colonies *1750*

Claimed by
N.Y. & N.H.

Lake Ontario

NEW YORK

Hudson River

ATLANTIC
OCEAN

70°W

40°N

APPALACHIAN MOUNTAINS

PENNSYLVANIA

Delaware River

NEW JERSEY

New York

Mohawk River

Philadelphia

DELAWARE

75°W

**Major Exports**

| | |
|---|---|
| | Furs and skins |
| | Cattle and grain |
| | Tobacco |
| | Iron |
| | Ships |
| | Timber |

Independence Hall,
Philadelphia

### Connect Geography & History

1. **Place** What are the three major rivers in the Middle Colonies?
2. **Make Inferences** Why might the Middle Colonies' rivers be important for farmers?

# African Americans in the Cities

▼ **KEY QUESTION** How did African Americans help build the cities?

Unlike the economy that developed in the South, the economy of the Middle Colonies did not depend on a large slave population. In 1750, only about 7 percent of the Middle Colonies' population was enslaved. Most of these enslaved people lived in the cities.

**Racial Tension in New York City** New York City had a larger number of people of African descent than any other Northern city. Its African American population was divided between the enslaved and the free.

The slave trade was an important part of the city's economy. Many Africans were brought to New York City in order to serve wealthy families. Enslaved people worked as manual laborers, servants, drivers, and as assistants to **artisans**, or craftspeople. Before New York came under English control, enslaved Africans had built roads, houses, and public buildings—the very foundations of the colony.

A free black community developed in New York City as early as 1644. Free African-American men and women worked as laborers, servants, and sailors. For a time free blacks had the right to own property.

Although both free and enslaved African Americans enjoyed some rights in the Middle Colonies, their lives were harsh. As in the South, fears of a slave revolt grew as the slave population increased. Those fears were realized in 1712 when a group of African-born slaves rebelled. After setting fire to several buildings, the rebels suffered defeat, torture, and death. However, their cruel punishments did not prevent other slave rebellions.

**Quakers Condemn Slavery** Some white colonists began speaking out against slavery. The Quakers were the first group to condemn it. To many Quakers, slavery was immoral and against Christian principles. In 1688 Quakers in Germantown, Pennsylvania, issued a statement against the practice. In 1712 the Pennsylvania government attempted to discourage the importation of slaves. Throughout the 1700s, Quakers published antislavery petitions and statements. The antislavery efforts of the Quakers were supported by other religious groups in the Delaware Valley, such as the German Pietists. These antislavery ideals influenced immigrants in the Middle Colonies—and eventually the entire nation.

▲ **SUMMARIZE** Explain how African Americans helped build the cities.

# Diversity and Tolerance

▼ **KEY QUESTION** How did ethnic diversity encourage tolerance?

Many different immigrant groups arrived in the port cities of the Middle Colonies. Soon the region's population became remarkably diverse.

**A Diverse Population** The Germans formed one of the largest immigrant groups in the region. Many Germans arrived between 1710 and 1740. Most came as indentured servants fleeing religious intolerance. They were particularly attracted to Pennsylvania because the colony did not tax its people in order to support a particular **denomination**, or distinct religious group. Like the Puritans before them, German immigrants arrived in family groups and tended to settle together in distinct communities. Many moved to the western frontier of Pennsylvania, where land was cheaper.

Famous for their farming skills, these immigrants soon influenced the culture of the Middle Colonies. Germans also brought a strong tradition of skilled crafts to the Middle Colonies. For example, it was German gunsmiths who first developed the long rifle. Other German artisans, or craftspeople, became ironworkers and makers of glass, furniture, and kitchenware.

Reenactors in Pennsylvania portray life on a colonial German farm.

Germans built **Conestoga wagons** to carry their produce to town. These wagons used wide wheels suitable for dirt roads, and the wagons' curved beds prevented spilling when climbing hills. Another important feature of this type of wagon was the canvas covering that offered protection from rain.

**Diversity Leads to Tolerance** The Dutch in New York and the Quakers in Pennsylvania were two groups that practiced religious tolerance. That is, they honored the right to worship without interference. This laid the foundation for the well-known religious tolerance of the Middle Colonies.

In contrast to New England, where the English Puritans dominated religious life, many different religious groups settled in the Middle Colonies. Because of this diversity, the various religious groups had to learn to accept, or at least tolerate, one another. The tolerance that developed in the Middle Colonies would one day serve as a model for the nation.

Like the other colonial regions, the Middle Colonies have left a lasting legacy. New York City is still a center of commerce and of ethnic and religious diversity. Colonial Pennsylvania produced the model of a society based on tolerance. Although slavery existed in the Middle Colonies, as it did in other colonial regions, some were beginning to raise their voices against it. In fact, throughout the colonial period the Middle Colonies were moving closer to modern America's civil ideals—of a society based on diversity, tolerance, and religious freedom.

 **CAUSES AND EFFECTS** Explain how ethnic diversity encouraged tolerance.

**Connect** *to the* **World**

**Tolerance**
Attitudes in parts of the Middle Colonies may have been influenced by the earliest Dutch settlers. These settlers came from the Dutch Republic, a country famous for its religious tolerance.

---

**New Jersey Core Curriculum Content Standards** *Review*

**ONLINE QUIZ**
For test practice, go to
**Interactive Review** @ ClassZone.com

**TERMS & NAMES**

**1.** Explain the importance of
- Philadelphia
- Conestoga wagons

**USING YOUR READING NOTES**

**2. Main Ideas and Details** Complete the diagram you started at the beginning of this section.

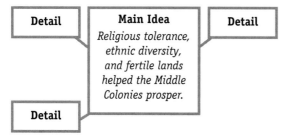

**KEY IDEAS**

**3.** What factors allowed large coastal cities to develop in the Middle Colonies?

**4.** How did religious tolerance develop in the Middle Colonies?

**CRITICAL THINKING**

**5. Analyze Graphs** Study the graph below of ethnic groups in the Middle Colonies. What two languages might you have heard most frequently?

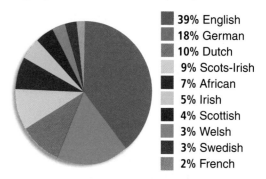

- 39% English
- 18% German
- 10% Dutch
- 9% Scots-Irish
- 7% African
- 5% Irish
- 4% Scottish
- 3% Welsh
- 3% Swedish
- 2% French

Source: Population of the British Colonies in America Before 1776, *1975*

**6.** **Math** Use the graph shown above to calculate the number of people speaking each language, given that the Middle Colonies had a population of roughly 297,000. Then create a table to show the results.

# Reading for Understanding

## ▶ Key Ideas

**BEFORE, YOU LEARNED**

Poorer settlers moved into the far western parts of Virginia and other colonies.

**NOW YOU WILL LEARN**

Settlers in the Backcountry developed their own regional traditions and culture.

## ▶ Vocabulary

**TERMS & NAMES**

**Appalachian Mountains** mountain range stretching from eastern Canada south to Alabama

**Scots-Irish** the name given to people from the borderlands of Scotland and England and from the region of northern Ireland

**BACKGROUND VOCABULARY**

**fall line** the point at which waterfalls prevent large boats from moving farther upriver

**Piedmont** the broad plateau that lies at the foot of the Blue Ridge Mountains of the Appalachian range

**clans** large groups of families that claim a common ancestor

**Visual Vocabulary**
Appalachian Mountains

## ▶ Reading Strategy

Re-create the diagram shown at right. As you read and respond to the **KEY QUESTIONS**, use the diagram to compare Backcountry life with life in the other colonies.

 See Skillbuilder Handbook, page R8.

**COMPARE AND CONTRAST**

Backcountry Life

Life in Other Colonies

Common Features

*many resources*

**GRAPHIC ORGANIZERS**
Go to **Interactive Review** @ ClassZone.com

# The Backcountry

 **6.4.D.1.** Analyze the political, social, and cultural characteristics of the English colonies.
**6.4.D.2.** Describe the political, religious, social, and economic institutions that emerged in Colonial America, including New Netherland and colonial New Jersey.

## One American's Story

In Pennsylvania, the provincial secretary, James Logan, had received instructions from William Penn, the proprietor of the colony. Penn wanted Logan to welcome all religious groups who had suffered persecution in Europe. When Presbyterians from the troubled region of northern Ireland started arriving in the colony, Logan took advantage of their fighting skills. He placed them on the western frontier where they could defend the colony from attack. Years later, Logan recalled his decision.

Scots-Irish arrive in Pennsylvania

**PRIMARY SOURCE**

❝ About that time [1720] considerable numbers of good, sober people came in from Ireland, who wanted to be settled. . . . I therefore thought it might be prudent to plant a settlement of such men . . . as a frontier, in case of any disturbance. ❞

—James Logan, letter of Nov. 18, 1729

The frontier land where the Presbyterians of Northern Ireland were settled was known as the Backcountry. The Backcountry was one of the four major regions of the English colonies.

## Settling the Backcountry

🔻 **KEY QUESTION** What made Backcountry life unique?

The Backcountry extended through the western parts of many colonies. The geography of the Backcountry gave the region its unique appearance and influenced the culture of the people who settled there.

**Geography of the Region** The Backcountry was a region of dense forest and rushing streams in or near the **Appalachian Mountains**. The Appalachians stretch from eastern Canada south to Alabama.

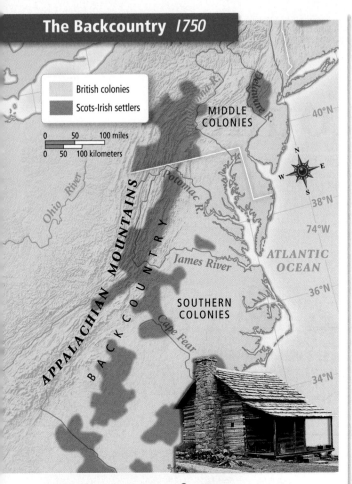

## The Backcountry 1750

British colonies

Scots-Irish settlers

0    50    100 miles

0    50    100 kilometers

OHIO RIVER

APPALACHIAN MOUNTAINS

BACKCOUNTRY

MIDDLE COLONIES

Potomac R.

James River

Cape Fear

SOUTHERN COLONIES

ATLANTIC OCEAN

40°N

38°N

74°W

36°N

34°N

### Connect Geography & History

1. **Region** What geographical feature did the northern and southern areas of the Backcountry have in common?

2. **Make Inferences** Why would geography have helped create an independent spirit in the Backcountry?

In the South, the Backcountry began at the **fall line**, where waterfalls prevent large boats from moving upriver. West of the fall line is the broad plateau known as the **Piedmont**. The Piedmont lies at the foot of the Appalachians.

**Early Settlers** The first Europeans in the Backcountry arrived to trade with the Native Americans. Farmers soon followed but clashed with Native Americans over land. The Backcountry gained a reputation as a wild place, where independent settlers fought with Native Americans and resented government control.

▲ **COMPARE AND CONTRAST** Explain what made Backcountry life unique.

## The Scots-Irish Arrive

▼ **KEY QUESTION** Why did the Scots-Irish emigrate to the colonies?

Most of the Backcountry settlers were forced west because planters had claimed most of the good farmland in the Tidewater, or coastal area. Then, in the 1700s, the **Scots-Irish** arrived.

**A Mass Migration** "Scots-Irish" was the name given to people who came from the borderlands of Scotland and England. Many were Presbyterian Scots who had lived for a time in northern Ireland. Both Northern Ireland and the Scottish borders were troubled regions, torn by warfare. This hostile environment gave the Scots-Irish survival skills that were useful in the American Backcountry.

In the early 1700s, the Scots-Irish suffered drought, rent increases, and persecution by the Anglican church. As a result, the Scots-Irish sailed to America by the thousands.

Like the English Puritans and the German settlers in Pennsylvania, the Scots-Irish traveled in family groups. But Scots-Irish families formed much larger **clans**. Clans are large groups of families that claim a common ancestor. Clan members were fiercely loyal to one another and banded together when danger threatened. The clan system helped families deal with the perils of the Backcountry.

The Scots-Irish came to Pennsylvania because of its religious tolerance. They were settled on the colony's frontier. From there they spread through the frontiers of other colonies until they occupied the entire Backcountry.

**Heritage of the Scots-Irish** In the Backcountry the Scots-Irish developed a unique culture. It was here that the music of Scotland and Ireland slowly changed into Bluegrass and American Country Music. Many sports that are now part of track and field competitions also came from the Scots-Irish.

The Scots-Irish reinforced the desire for democracy and freedom that had already been established in earlier colonies. Their loyalty and warrior ethic also had a long-lasting influence on the American military. Their constant migrations may have helped create that unique sense of restless energy in American life.

**Regionalisms Develop** Between 1700 and 1750, the population of England's colonies in North America doubled and then doubled again. At the start of the century, the colonial population stood at about 251,000. By 1750, they were more than 1,170,000 settlers in North America. These settlers lived in four major regions that were already developing unique characteristics. The chart below describes these different colonial regions and shows how they were able to grow and prosper.

▲ **SUMMARIZE** Explain why the Scots-Irish emigrated to the colonies.

# CONNECT to the Essential Question

## What factors allowed each colonial region to grow and prosper?

|  | Climate | Resources | Economy | Ethnic Background | Social Class | Predominant Religion |
|---|---|---|---|---|---|---|
| **NEW ENGLAND COLONIES** | long winters; short growing season | rocky soil; good fishing grounds | diverse economy small farms, fishing and trade | English, mainly from the eastern counties; few enslaved Africans | middle class | Puritans |
| **MIDDLE COLONIES** | short winters | fertile soil | larger farms and cash crops of grain | Europeans; some Africans in the cities | the poor; the middle class | Quakers (Pennsylvania) |
| **SOUTHERN COLONIES** | warm; nearly year-round growing season | fertile soil | plantation economy; limited number of cash crops | English and other Europeans; many enslaved Africans | rich, noble families; the poor; indentured servants; slaves | Anglicans |
| **THE BACKCOUNTRY** | varied | woods and streams | small farms | Scots-Irish and Native Americans | poor, independent farmers | Presbyterians |

**CRITICAL THINKING** **Compare and Contrast** Which region was least prosperous?

# Beyond the Frontier

 **KEY QUESTION** How did English colonial growth affect other groups?

As Backcountry settlers pushed west they came into contact with various Native American peoples, as well as French and Spanish colonists. As contact increased, so did conflict over land and resources.

**Contact Brings Conflict** Native Americans found themselves caught in between advancing French and English colonists. The French had colonized eastern Canada and the territory along the Mississippi River. French fur traders did not want English settlers interfering with their trade. One Native American told an Englishman, "You and the French are like the two edges of a pair of shears, and we are the cloth that is cut to pieces between them." Tensions over land claims often led to war. In 1753 a young officer named George Washington was sent to ask the French to leave the Ohio River Valley, an act which led to the French and Indian War.

Spain also controlled large western areas of North America. Spanish settlers were farmers, ranchers and priests. Priests, who established missions to convert Native Americans, built forts near the missions. In 1718, Spaniards built Fort San Antonio de Bexar to guard the mission of San Antonio de Valero, later renamed the Alamo.

England's colonies often had to unite against these other groups. As a result, an American identity began to form.

▲ **CAUSES AND EFFECTS** Explain how English colonial growth affected other groups in North America.

---

 **New Jersey Core Curriculum Content Standards** *Review*

**ONLINE QUIZ**
For test practice, go to
**Interactive Review @ ClassZone.com**

**TERMS & NAMES**

1. Explain the importance of
   • Appalachian Mountains  • Scots-Irish

**USING YOUR READING NOTES**

2. **Compare and Contrast** Use the diagram below to contrast Backcountry life with life in the other colonies.

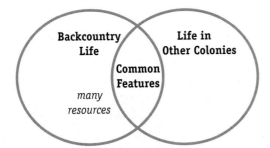

**KEY IDEAS**

3. What were some cultural characteristics of Backcountry settlers?

4. Why did conflict sometimes develop between English colonists and the other peoples of North America?

**CRITICAL THINKING**

5. **Make Inferences** How did the clan system help the Scots-Irish survive?

6. **Analyze Point of View** How might the Native Americans have felt as increasing numbers of colonists and trappers invaded their lands?

7. **Summarize** In what ways did the experiences of the Scots-Irish in the British Isles help prepare them for life on the American frontier?

8. **Art** Research the geography of the Backcountry. Draw a map of the routes that colonists might have taken to settle this region.

## Chapter Summary

**1 Key Idea**
Prosperity and religious diversity brought changes to Puritan New England.

**2 Key Idea**
In the Southern Colonies, the need for cheap labor led to a dependence on slavery.

**3 Key Idea**
Rich farmland and a climate of tolerance helped the Middle Colonies prosper.

**4 Key Idea**
Settlers in the Backcountry developed their own regional traditions and culture.

For detailed Review and Study Notes go to **Interactive Review** @ ClassZone.com

## Name Game

**Complete each sentence online or on your own paper.**

1. I introduced indigo as a successful plantation crop. Eliza Lucas

2. This city on the Delaware River became the fastest growing city in the colonies. _____

3. These mountains stretch from Canada south to Alabama. _____

4. This region was far to the west. _____

5. This 1739 slave rebellion took place in South Carolina. _____

6. These covered wagons were introduced by German immigrants. _____

7. This was a complex system of transatlantic exchange of slaves and goods. _____

8. This was a 1676 rebellion in Virginia. _____

9. This was a Native American uprising against the Puritan colonies. _____

10. The English government passed these acts to profit from colonial trade. _____

A. Backcountry
B. triangular trade
C. Conestoga wagons
D. Eliza Lucas
E. King Philip's War
F. Stono Rebellion
G. Navigation Acts
H. Philadelphia
I. Bacon's Rebellion
J. Appalachian Mountains
K. Scots-Irish
L. mercantilism

## Activities

### CROSSWORD PUZZLE

Complete the online crossword puzzle to show what you know about colonial growth.

**ACROSS**
1. _____ produces a blue dye.

### GEOGAME

Use this online map to reinforce your understanding of the growth and development of the colonies, including economic development of the several colonial regions. Drag and drop the groups and products in the list at the location on the map where they were most common. A score-card helps you keep track of your progress online.

timber

indigo

rice

rum

fur

More items online

## VOCABULARY

**Explain the significance of each of the following.**

1. The Stono Rebellion
2. Conestoga wagons
3. Navigation Acts
4. Scots-Irish
5. Backcountry
6. Appalachian Mountains
7. Bacon's Rebellion
8. triangular trade
9. King Philip's War
10. Philadelphia
11. Eliza Lucas
12. Piedmont

**Identify the word that does not fit in each group and explain why it is out of place.**

13. Appalachian Mountains, Piedmont, Eliza Lucas
14. Backcountry, Scots-Irish, Navigation Acts
15. King Philip's War, Stono Rebellion, indigo
16. cash crops, indigo, Conestoga wagons
17. triangular trade, overseers, fall line

## KEY IDEAS

**① New England: Commerce and Religion (pages 94–101)**

18. What were the Navigation Acts meant to do?
19. How did the resources of New England affect its economy?

**② The Southern Colonies: Plantations and Slavery (pages 102–107)**

20. Why did slavery spread in the South?
21. Which crops were important to the Southern economy?

**③ The Middle Colonies: Farms and Cities (pages 110–115)**

22. What attracted settlers to the Middle Colonies?
23. What effect did religious diversity have on the culture of the Middle Colonies?

**④ The Backcountry (pages 116–120)**

24. How did the geography of the Backcountry foster an independent spirit in the region's settlers?
25. What other groups came into conflict with Backcountry settlers?

## CRITICAL THINKING

26. **Make Inferences** Why did the New England colonists' prosperity threaten England's mercantilist goals?

27. **Summarize** In what ways did settlers in New England take advantage of the Atlantic Ocean?

28. **Compare and Contrast** Create a chart to compare and contrast the Middle Colonies with New England.

| | New England | Middle Colonies |
|---|---|---|
| Religious Groups | | |
| Soil and Climate | | |
| Economy | | |

29. **Causes and Effects** Why did Southern planters pass such harsh slave codes?

30. **Make Inferences** What made Southern plantations self-sufficient?

31. **Causes and Effects** Why did the tolerant culture of the Middle Colonies encourage even greater diversity in the region?

32. **Make Generalizations** Why were Backcountry settlers often in political conflict with the planters and the elite living along the coast?

33. **Interpret Graphs** Which decade saw the largest increase in the number of slaves imported to the colonies?

### Slave Importation Estimates, *1701–1750*

| Years | Number of Persons $\circ$ = 5000 |
|---|---|
| 1701–1710 | o-c  9,000 |
| 1711–1720 | o-o-c 10,800 |
| 1721–1730 | o-c  9,900 |
| 1731–1740 | oooooooo-i 40,500 |
| 1741–1750 | ooooooooooo-c 58,500 |

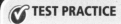
## DOCUMENT-BASED QUESTIONS

### PART 1: Short Answer

Analyze each document and answer the questions that follow.

**DOCUMENT 1:**

**New England Exports 1768–1772**

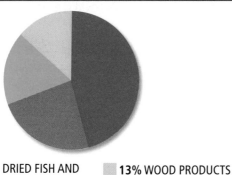

- ■ **44%** DRIED FISH AND WHALE OIL
- ■ **17%** LIVESTOCK
- ■ **13%** WOOD PRODUCTS
- ■ **25%** OTHER

Source: Shepherd and Walton, 1972

**1.** What industry was the most important for New England exports?

**DOCUMENT 2**

**PRIMARY SOURCE**

❝ Of all the American [colonies] his Majesty has, none are so apt for the building of Shipping as New-England. . . and in my poor opinion, there is nothing more. . .dangerous to any Mother-Kingdom, than the increase of Shipping in her Colonies, Plantations, or Provinces. ❞

—Sir Josiah Child, quoted in *American Colonies*

**2.** What is Sir Josiah Child's attitude to the shipping industry of New England?

### Part 2: Essay

**3.** Using information from the documents, your answers to the questions in Part 1, and your knowledge of U.S. history, write two or three paragraphs to describe the economy of colonial New England.

## YOU BE THE HISTORIAN

**34. Compare and Contrast** Why would different cultural attitudes to land ownership have caused conflict between the Native Americans and the colonists?

**35. Synthesize** Why did more large urban centers develop in the North than in the South?

**36. Make Generalizations** How did the South's plantation economy determine who became leaders in the region?

**37. Summarize** Why did changes take place in the population and treatment of African Americans between 1650 and 1750?

**38. Draw Conclusions** Why did regionalisms develop in the colonies?

**39. Connect to Today Citizenship** What modern American values and attitudes can be traced back to the culture of the Middle Colonies?

 Answer the
## ESSENTIAL QUESTION
**What factors allowed each colonial region to grow and prosper?**

**Written Response** Write a four-paragraph response to the Essential Question. Be sure to consider the key ideas of each section. Use the Response Rubric below to guide your thinking and writing.

### Response Rubric
**A strong response will**

- describe the distinct climate and geography of each region
- analyze how climate and geography affected the economy of each region
- compare and contrast the four colonial regions

1. Early American Culture
2. Roots of American Democracy
3. The French and Indian War

# Beginnings of an American Identity

## 1689–1763

 **ESSENTIAL QUESTION**

What traditions, events, and forces helped form an American identity?

Quebec

## CONNECT ↻ Geography & History

**What geographic features helped define colonial borders?**

**Think about:**

**1** the difficulty of travel in the days of few roads and thick forests

**2** how colonial trade tied the colonies to Britain and foreign ports

**3** the Native American nations that occupied the continent's interior

The people of Boston announcing the arrest of Governor Andros

**1735** The Zenger trial

▼

**Effect** Jury's decision helps establish freedom of the press.

## 1689

Massachusetts colonists overthrow royal governor Andros.

**1704** *Boston News Letter* is founded.

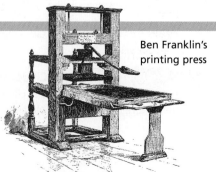

Ben Franklin's printing press

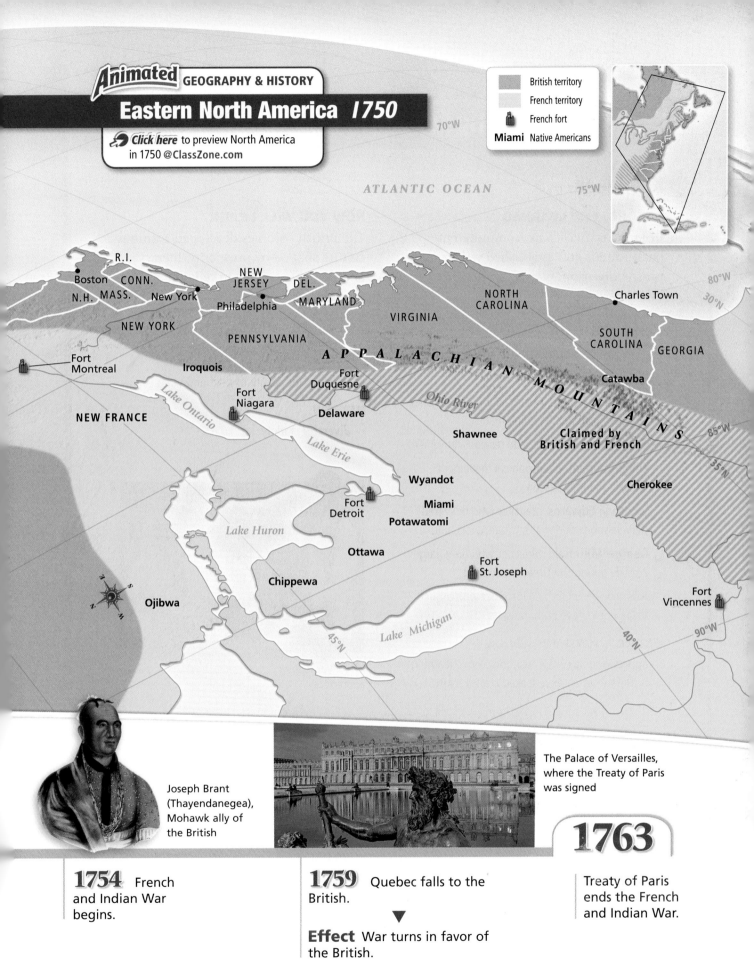

## Eastern North America *1750*

Click here to preview North America in 1750 @ClassZone.com

British territory
French territory
French fort
**Miami** Native Americans

70°W

ATLANTIC OCEAN

75°W

80°W

30°N

R.I.
Boston   CONN.
N.H.   MASS.   New York
NEW JERSEY   DEL.
MARYLAND
NEW YORK
PENNSYLVANIA
Philadelphia

NORTH CAROLINA
VIRGINIA
SOUTH CAROLINA
GEORGIA
Charles Town

Fort Montreal
Iroquois
Fort Niagara
Fort Duquesne
Delaware
Lake Ontario

A P P A L A C H I A N   M O U N T A I N S

Catawba

85°W

NEW FRANCE

Lake Erie

Ohio River
Shawnee

Claimed by British and French

35°N

Wyandot
Fort Detroit
Miami
Potawatomi

Cherokee

Lake Huron

Ottawa

Chippewa

Fort St. Joseph

Fort Vincennes

Ojibwa

45°N   Lake Michigan

40°N   90°W

Joseph Brant (Thayendanegea), Mohawk ally of the British

The Palace of Versailles, where the Treaty of Paris was signed

# 1763

**1754** French and Indian War begins.

**1759** Quebec falls to the British.

▼

**Effect** War turns in favor of the British.

Treaty of Paris ends the French and Indian War.

## ▶ Key Ideas

**BEFORE, YOU LEARNED**

Colonial settlers came from different backgrounds and established varied and prosperous economies.

**NOW YOU WILL LEARN**

The British colonies developed a unique culture shaped by prosperity, literacy, and new movements in religion and thought.

## ▶ Vocabulary

**TERMS & NAMES**

**Benjamin Franklin** American writer, publisher, scientist, inventor, and diplomat

**Great Awakening** Christian religious movement

**Enlightenment** philosophical movement stressing human reason

**Jonathan Edwards** preacher who delivered fiery sermons during the Great Awakening

**George Whitefield** preacher who drew large crowds during the Great Awakening

**John Locke** English philosopher who argued that people have natural rights

**BACKGROUND VOCABULARY**

**apprentice** (a•PREN•tis) one who is learning a trade from an experienced craftsperson

**literacy** the ability to read and write

**REVIEW**

**diversity** variety

Visual Vocabulary
apprentice

## ▶ Reading Strategy

Re-create the diagram shown at right. As you read and respond to the **KEY QUESTIONS**, use the diagram to note important details that support the Main Idea of this section.

 See Skillbuilder Handbook, page R4.

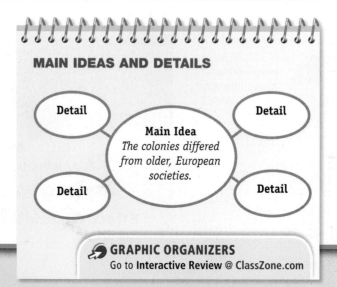

**MAIN IDEAS AND DETAILS**

Detail

Detail

**Main Idea**
*The colonies differed from older, European societies.*

Detail

Detail

**GRAPHIC ORGANIZERS**
Go to **Interactive Review** @ ClassZone.com

# Early American Culture

**6.4.D.1.** Analyze the political, social, and cultural characteristics of the English colonies.
**6.4.D.2** Describe the political, religious, social, and economic institutions that emerged in Colonial America, including New Netherland and colonial New Jersey.

## One American's Story

Colonist Eliza Lucas Pinckney was born in the West Indies. In 1738, she moved to one of her family's South Carolina plantations. Soon after her arrival, her father, a British army officer, was posted to Antigua. When her mother died, Eliza Pinckney was left to manage her family's plantations alone, at the age of 16.

Pinckney enjoyed studying plants. She became interested in one plant in particular.

### PRIMARY SOURCE

❝ Much of my time is spent on my experiments with indigo—the plant which produces such a beautiful blue dye. . . . I have also taken pains to bring the ginger [and] cotton . . . to perfection [but] have greater hopes from indigo. ❞

—Eliza Lucas Pinckney, quoted in *Colonies and Revolution*

Pinckney's experiments were so successful that indigo became South Carolina's second largest export. Pinckney's willingness to experiment was a quality well suited to colonial life. By the early 1700s, the colonists' adventurous energies were helping to create a new kind of society in the Americas.

## A New Kind of Society

🔻 **KEY QUESTION** How did the American colonies differ from older societies?

British culture remained the foundation of all the colonial societies. But life in the "New World" was unlike life in the old. Settlers faced new climates and new living conditions. As colonists adapted their old ways to a new world, an American identity was born.

(*top*) indigo being processed in South Carolina;
(*below*) indigo-dyed dress

**Land, Wealth, and Rights** Cheap farmland and abundant natural resources gave colonists a chance to prosper. There was less opportunity in Europe. In England, less than 5 percent of the population owned land. In fact, land rarely went up for sale. By contrast, in the early colonies, land was plentiful—once Native Americans were forced to give up their claims.

Land ownership gave colonists political rights as well as prosperity. In rural areas, only white male property owners could vote. City dwellers could vote by paying a fee. However, because so many colonists owned land, more Americans had the right to vote than did their British counterparts. In its wider democracy, colonial America was becoming a new kind of society.

**Social Mobility** More widespread land ownership also gave a different shape to the American class system. As in Europe, people were divided into high, middle, and low ranks. Large landholders and their families were high in rank. Owners of small farms were of middle rank. Landless servants or hired workers were low in rank. But America was unique because it had

- no titled aristocracy
- a large middle class
- a huge underclass of slaves

## COMPARING  *Class Systems*

### BRITAIN AND THE AMERICAN COLONIES

Conditions in America created a class system very different from the ancient and rigid class system of Britain. In the diagram below, compare the size of the British and the colonial middle class.

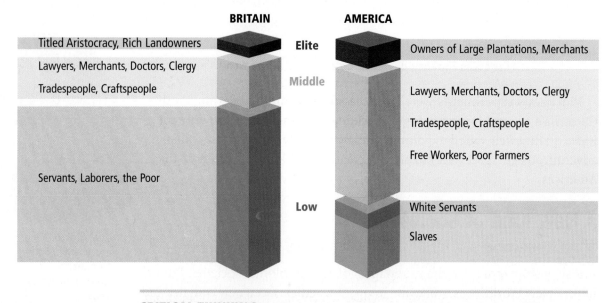

BRITAIN

Titled Aristocracy, Rich Landowners

Lawyers, Merchants, Doctors, Clergy

Tradespeople, Craftspeople

Servants, Laborers, the Poor

**Elite**

**Middle**

**Low**

AMERICA

Owners of Large Plantations, Merchants

Lawyers, Merchants, Doctors, Clergy

Tradespeople, Craftspeople

Free Workers, Poor Farmers

White Servants

Slaves

### CRITICAL THINKING

1. **Compare and Contrast** What differences do you notice between the two diagrams?
2. **Make Inferences** What do the diagrams reveal about social mobility in the colonies?

America had no class of nobles whose titles passed from parent to child. Not even the aristocracy of the South had the right to titles such as "Lord" or "Lady." Another unique feature was America's huge middle class. The greater opportunities in America allowed poor colonists to rise into the middle ranks.

▲ **MAIN IDEAS & DETAILS** Explain how the American colonies differed from older, European societies.

## Colonial Life

▼ **KEY QUESTION** What was life like in the colonies?

Most Americans lived on farms. In this working world, tasks were divided between men and women.

Reenactor churns butter.

**The Working World** Farming women cooked; churned butter; made soap, candles, and clothes, and did many other chores. They tended the garden and looked after farm animals.

Women who lived in towns and cities had similar chores. However, some urban women ran inns or other businesses. A few women, usually the wives or widows of tradespeople, practiced trades themselves.

Although women contributed to the colonial economy, they did not have many rights. Women could not vote. In most churches, with the exception of Quaker meetings, they could not preach. A married woman could not own property without her husband's permission. By law, even the money a woman earned belonged to her husband.

Farming men were expected to work outdoors. They planted, raised, and harvested the crops and took the surplus to market. They cared for the livestock and butchered the meat. In addition to their other chores, they cut trees and chopped wood for the fireplace.

**Life of the Young** American families were large. New England families, for example, had about six to eight children. More children on the farm meant more workers. Even toddlers were expected to help with the chores.

Around age six, boys were "breeched." This meant that they no longer wore the skirts or smocks of all young children, but were given a pair of pants. They then began to help their fathers at work. Sons of craftspeople tended their fathers' shops and learned their fathers' trades.

Around age 13, many boys left their fathers to become **apprentices**. An apprentice learned a trade from an experienced craftsman. The apprentice also received food, clothing, lodging, and a general education. He worked for free, usually for four to seven years, until his contract was fulfilled. Then he could work for wages or start his own business.

Girls rarely were apprenticed. They learned sewing and other household skills from their mothers. In New England, girls of 13 or 14 often were sent away to other households to learn specialized skills such as weaving

Colonial schoolroom

Hornbooks such as these were used to teach children to count and read.

or cheese making. Orphaned girls and boys worked as apprentices for families who housed and fed them until adulthood.

**Education and Literacy** The colonies differed from European societies in level of education. Colonial America had a high rate of **literacy**, or the ability to read and write. In New England, 85 percent of white men were literate, compared with 60 percent of men in England. In the Middle Colonies, 65 percent of white men were literate, and in the South, about 50 percent were.

Most colonists thought that it was more important for males to be educated. In each region, roughly half as many white women as men were literate. Educated African Americans were rare. If they were enslaved, teaching them to read was illegal. If they were free, they were often kept out of schools. Some colonists defied these rules. Eliza Lucas Pinckney educated enslaved children on her plantation.

Children were taught to read so that they could understand the Bible. Education varied according to region. New England had free public schools and a high level of education among the population. Urban areas also provided more free education for the young.

**Colonial Literature** Literacy also helped unite the colonies. In the early 1700s, the colonies had only one local newspaper, the *Boston News Letter*. But over the next 70 years, dozens more newspapers appeared.

Gradually colonists began to publish their own books. Almanacs were very popular. A typical almanac included a calendar, weather predictions, star charts, farming advice, home remedies, recipes, jokes, and proverbs. In 1732, **Benjamin Franklin** began to publish *Poor Richard's Almanac*. It contained sayings that are still repeated today, such as "Haste makes waste."

Colonists also published poetry, regional histories, and autobiographies. A form of literature unique to the Americas was the captivity narrative. In it, a colonist captured by Native Americans described living among them. Mary Rowlandson's 1682 captivity narrative, *The Sovereignty and Goodness of God*, was one of the first colonial bestsellers. It described how Native Americans held Rowlandson hostage for 11 weeks during King Philip's War in 1676.

**A Growing Diversity** The American colonies were notable for the **diversity** of their population. Immigrants came into contact with people of different ethnic groups, races, and nationalities. In some colonies, there was religious diversity as well. Settlers had to learn how to adapt to this new situation. In the Middle Colonies, for example, many settlers adopted Quaker principles of equality, cooperation, and religious tolerance.

▲ **SUMMARIZE** Describe daily life in the colonies.

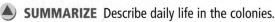

# Religious Revival

▼ **KEY QUESTION** How did the Great Awakening change American society?

As colonists developed a new society in America, they drew inspiration from two cultural movements:

- the **Great Awakening**, a Christian religious revival
- the **Enlightenment**, a movement stressing human reason

While the Great Awakening appealed to faith and emotions, the Enlightenment was based on reason and scientific observation. However, both movements offered people ways of changing themselves and their world—which is exactly what the colonists needed as they created a new society.

**The Great Awakening** In the 1730s and 1740s, a religious movement called the Great Awakening swept through the colonies. Traveling ministers preached that inner religious emotion was more important than outward religious behavior. Huge crowds gathered outdoors to hear famous preachers like **Jonathan Edwards** promise that all could be saved.

**PRIMARY SOURCE**

❝ And now you have an extraordinary opportunity, a day wherein Christ has thrown the door of mercy wide open, and stands in calling and crying with a loud voice to poor sinners. . . . How awful is it to be left behind at such a day! ❞

—Jonathan Edwards, "Sinners in the Hands of an Angry God"

The Great Awakening offered hope that each person could break from the past and begin a spiritual relationship with God. This would happen during a sudden conversion, or rebirth. This is the doctrine, or belief, of Evangelicalism. The evangelical idea of spiritual renewal or rebirth would be very influential in American culture.

The movement led congregations to argue over religious practices. Some left their churches and joined other Protestant groups such as Baptists. As religious diversity increased, it became more difficult for one "established" church to control a colony's religious life. In colonies like Virginia, the established Anglican church was weakened.

Reenactors portray African-American worship in the South.

**Religion and Social Change** In the South, the Great Awakening's focus on spiritual equality threatened the social system. Against the wishes of many plantation owners, the Presbyterian minister Samuel Davies baptized African Americans. Meanwhile Baptist congregations welcomed African Americans and Native Americans. They allowed slaves to preach and women to speak in church.

## History Makers

### Ben Franklin   1706–1790

As an Enlightenment thinker, Benjamin Franklin used reason and scientific methods to improve society. At 42, he retired from business to devote his life to science and public service. He proved that lightning was a form of electricity. Then he invented the lightning rod to protect buildings. The Franklin stove and bifocal eyeglasses were also his inventions. He organized a fire department, a lending library, and a society to discuss philosophy. Later he helped draft the Declaration of Independence.

**CRITICAL THINKING**

 Consider how Franklin's abilities could be useful today. For example, how might Franklin solve environmental problems?

**ONLINE BIOGRAPHY**   For more on Ben Franklin, go to the **Research & Writing Center** @ ClassZone.com

The Great Awakening inspired colonists to help others. **George Whitefield** (HWIT•feeld) drew thousands of people with his sermons and raised funds to start a home for orphans. Other ministers taught Christianity and reading to Native Americans and African Americans.

The Great Awakening helped develop American identity by encouraging a belief in spiritual equality. It also inspired religious debate, which increased religious diversity.

The movement encouraged colonists to challenge authority and question traditional religious practices. Once this had happened, it was easier to challenge other social and political traditions. In this way, the movement laid the groundwork for revolt against British authority.

▲ **EVALUATE** Describe how religion changed society.

## The Enlightenment

▼ **KEY QUESTION** How did the Enlightenment influence the colonists?

Unlike the Great Awakening, which explored religious emotion, the Enlightenment emphasized human reason and science as the paths to knowledge. It encouraged the belief that human beings could use rational thought to improve themselves and their society. Benjamin Franklin was a famous American Enlightenment figure. He conducted scientific experiments to discover the laws of nature.

**Belief in Progress** Writers of the Enlightenment condemned tyranny and superstition and challenged traditional social practices. They valued justice and equality and called for social and political change. Like the Great Awakening, the Enlightenment had far-reaching effects on the colonies.

The Enlightenment began in Europe, as scientists discovered natural laws governing the universe. In the colonies, at first only educated, wealthy people who could afford new books were familiar with Enlightenment ideas. But soon the values of the Enlightenment influenced the wider population.

Other Enlightenment thinkers applied the idea of natural law to human societies. The English philosopher **John Locke** challenged the belief that kings had a God-given right to rule. For many centuries, European kings had claimed that they were divinely appointed by God to rule their kingdoms. Locke challenged this idea. He also claimed that because governments were created by consent of human beings, then human beings had a right to change them. Locke argued that people have natural rights. These are the rights to life, liberty, and property. He insisted that people have the right to change a government that does not protect their natural rights. Locke's ideas would become very influential among American colonists who were dissatisfied with the political relationship with Britain.

Enlightenment writers such as John Locke encouraged a belief in progress—the idea that human beings can improve society and the world. The Enlightenment idea of progress would become one of the fundamental beliefs of American culture. In the following centuries, this optimistic hope for a better future would help Americans through many periods of uncertainty and change.

Enlightenment ideas of progress, natural rights, and government by agreement had a strong impact on colonial leaders. Such ideas encouraged colonists to reexamine their political ties to Britain. They also sparked political debate throughout the colonies. The colonists were beginning to see the British government as a threat to their rights and freedoms.

Ben Franklin experiments with electricity.

 **SUMMARIZE** Explain how the ideas and values of the Enlightenment influenced the colonists.

---

## New Jersey Core Curriculum Content Standards *Review*

 **ONLINE QUIZ**
For test practice, go to
**Interactive Review** @ ClassZone.com

### TERMS & NAMES

**1.** Explain the importance of

- Great Awakening
- George Whitefield
- Enlightenment
- Benjamin Franklin
- Jonathan Edwards
- John Locke

### USING YOUR READING NOTES

**2. Main Ideas and Details** Complete the diagram you started at the beginning of this section.

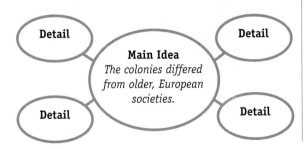

Detail

Detail

**Main Idea**
*The colonies differed from older, European societies.*

Detail

Detail

### KEY IDEAS

**3.** How did the abundance of land in America shape colonial society?

**4.** How did the Great Awakening and the Enlightenment affect the colonies?

### CRITICAL THINKING

**5. Compare and Contrast** How did the colonial class system differ from the class system in Europe?

**6. Make Inferences** Why was the literacy level so high in New England?

**7.** **Connect** *to* **Today** What modern American values can be traced back to the Great Awakening and the Enlightenment?

**8.** **Writing** **Report** Research and write a short report on Benjamin Franklin's contribution to the understanding of electricity.

# Climate and Building Traditions

Regional building styles developed quickly in the colonies. In both the North and the South, the local climate changed the way English settlers built their houses.

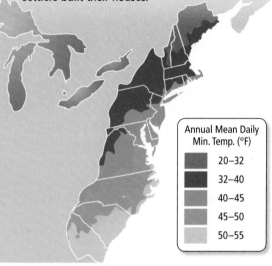

**Annual Mean Daily Min. Temp. (°F)**

- 20–32
- 32–40
- 40–45
- 45–50
- 50–55

See Geography Handbook, pages A10–A11.

**NORTHERN HOME** Several layers of wood protected the house from harsh northern winters. First, planks were fixed to the wood frame. Then a windproof "skin" of clapboards was wrapped tightly over the planks.

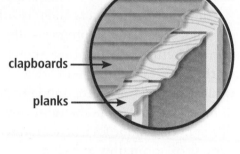

clapboards

planks

The rooms, each with its own fireplace, were grouped around a massive central chimney. The chimney absorbed heat from the fires during the day. At night, when the fires had died, the chimney radiated heat back into the house.

To help hold in the heat from the fires, rooms were small and snug with low ceilings.

Through the long winters, the family stored vegetables in the cellar.

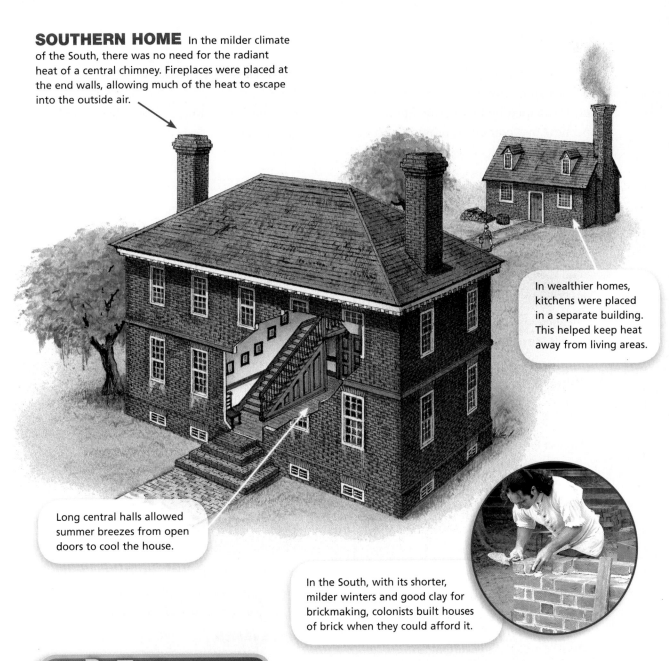

**SOUTHERN HOME** In the milder climate of the South, there was no need for the radiant heat of a central chimney. Fireplaces were placed at the end walls, allowing much of the heat to escape into the outside air.

In wealthier homes, kitchens were placed in a separate building. This helped keep heat away from living areas.

Long central halls allowed summer breezes from open doors to cool the house.

In the South, with its shorter, milder winters and good clay for brickmaking, colonists built houses of brick when they could afford it.

## STRANGE BUT TRUE

By the early 18th century, colonists were using American-made materials to build their houses. However, the first English settlers brought materials such as hinges, nails, and tools with them from England.

## CRITICAL THINKING

1. Study the temperature chart. How much did the Northern and Southern colonies differ in terms of mean daily minimum temperature?

2. What other features do you think builders might have used to cool a Southern house?

## ▶ Key Ideas

**BEFORE, YOU LEARNED**

The British colonies shared a unique culture shaped by prosperity, literacy, and new movements in religion and thought.

**NOW YOU WILL LEARN**

American democracy has its roots in the English tradition of representative government.

## ▶ Vocabulary

**TERMS & NAMES**

**Magna Carta** charter of English political and civil liberties

**Parliament** England's chief lawmaking body

**Edmund Andros** English governor appointed to rule the reorganized northern colonies

**Glorious Revolution** events of 1688–1689, during which the English Parliament invited William and Mary to replace James II as monarchs

**English Bill of Rights** 1689 laws protecting the rights of English subjects and Parliament

**John Peter Zenger** New York publisher who was taken to court for criticizing the governor of New York

**BACKGROUND VOCABULARY**

**prominent** important and well-known

**heritage** tradition

Visual Vocabulary
Magna Carta

## ▶ Reading Strategy

Create a diagram like the one shown at right. As you read and respond to the **KEY QUESTIONS**, use the diagram to describe how each document or event strengthened English rights over the centuries.

 **See Skillbuilder Handbook, page R5.**

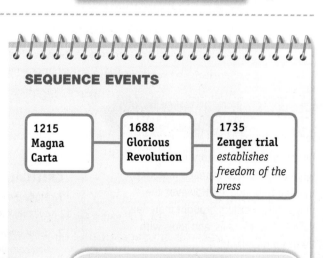

SEQUENCE EVENTS

| 1215 Magna Carta | 1688 Glorious Revolution | 1735 Zenger trial *establishes freedom of the press* |

**GRAPHIC ORGANIZERS**
Go to **Interactive Review** @ ClassZone.com

# Roots of American Democracy

**6.4.D.1.** Analyze the political, social, and cultural characteristics of the English colonies.
**6.4.D.2.** Describe the political, religious, social, and economic institutions that emerged in Colonial America, including New Netherland and colonial New Jersey.

## One American's Story

In 1688, the minister Increase Mather sailed from Massachusetts to England with a complaint. The colonists believed that the new royal governor had trampled their rights as English subjects.

Eventually, Mather came home with a new charter that restored colonists' rights.

**PRIMARY SOURCE**

❝ For all *English* liberties are restored to them: No Persons shall have a Penny of their Estates taken from them; nor any Laws imposed on them, without their own Consent by Representatives chosen by themselves. ❞

—Increase Mather, quoted in *The Last American Puritan*

The English rights guaranteed by the Magna Carta and later documents are the basis for the rights that we enjoy today.

Increase Mather

## The Rights of Englishmen

🔻 **KEY QUESTION** How were English rights strengthened over the centuries?

Throughout the colonies, free Americans enjoyed the rights and liberties of English subjects. England had one of the most advanced political democracies in Europe, and English freedoms were envied throughout the world. The American colonists were fiercely protective of these freedoms, which they called the "rights of Englishmen." The shared belief in certain legal and political principles helped tie the colonies together.

**Justice and Self-Government** English rights had been developing for centuries. The first step toward guaranteeing these rights came in 1215. That year, English nobles forced King John to sign the **Magna Carta** (Great Charter). By signing this document, the king agreed that he was not above the law. Like everyone else, the king had to obey the laws of the land.

The Magna Carta was the document that guaranteed English political and civil liberties. It limited the king's power by guaranteeing rights to nobles and "freemen," or those not bound to a master. Their property could not be seized by the king or his officials. They could not be taxed, unless a council of **prominent**, or important and well-known, men agreed. They could not be put on trial based only on an official's word, without witnesses. They could be punished only by a jury of their peers, people of the same social rank.

### PRIMARY SOURCE

❝ No free man shall be seized or imprisoned, or stripped of his rights or possessions, or exiled . . . nor will we proceed . . . against him . . . except by the lawful judgement of his equals or by the law of the land. ❞

—Magna Carta, translated in *A Documentary History of England*

Over time, the rights promised by the Magna Carta were gradually expanded. One important right was the right to elect representatives to government. The Magna Carta protected the rights of the people and remains the foundation of modern American democracy.

## CONNECT ⟲ *Citizenship and History*

See Citizenship Handbook, page 300.

### TRIAL BY JURY

The Magna Carta promised that no free man would be punished for a crime without being judged by "his equals". By the 1700s, this phrase had helped create a tradition of trial by jury in which jurors listen to the evidence presented in a court and then debate before coming to an agreement.

Jurors are selected from various sources such as voting lists and tax rolls. The Constitution states that jurors in a criminal trial (one that determines the guilt or innocence of a person accused of a crime) must be neutral regarding the case. In addition, a juror must be selected from the community where the crime is supposed to have happened. Every juror is questioned by both defense and prosecuting lawyers, and either lawyer may reject a juror if he/she feels the juror would not serve fairly.

### Activity

#### Set Up a Mock Jury Trial

1 Have one student accuse another of a crime and bring him or her to "trial."

2 Let each student in your class write his or her name on a piece of paper and put the names in a hat.

3 Select twelve jurors.

4 Have the jurors listen to the evidence during the trial.

5 Let the jury discuss the evidence and then vote to determine if the defendant is guilty or innocent.

**Parliament and Colonial Government** **Parliament**, England's lawmaking body, was the colonists' model for representative government. Parliament had two houses. Members of the House of Commons were elected. Members of the House of Lords were nonelected nobles, judges, and clergy.

English colonists in America did not want to give up the right to representative government. Because the king and Parliament were too far away to manage every detail of the colonies, some self-government was allowed. In all the colonies, the colonists formed their own elected assemblies—smaller-scale versions of the House of Commons. Virginia's House of Burgesses was the first of these. The assemblies imposed taxes and managed the colonies.

The relationship between the assemblies and Parliament was awkward. Although Parliament granted the colonists some self-government, it retained ultimate authority. The colonists disliked many of the laws that Parliament passed without their consent. Conflicts also arose when the king appointed royal governors to rule some colonies on his behalf. These conflicts became more intense in the late 1600s.

▲ **SEQUENCE EVENTS** Describe how English rights were strengthened.

**Connecting History**

**Expanding Liberty**
Settlers in all the early colonies had quickly established representative government. See *Chapter 3, pp. 65–73.*

# English Rights Threatened

▼ **KEY QUESTION** How were colonial rights affected by political changes?

The political relationship between the assemblies and the English government caused tension on both sides of the Atlantic. In addition, the policies of some kings of England threatened the rights of Englishmen everywhere.

**Kings Limit Self-Government** In the mid-1600s, Massachusetts and other colonies were smuggling goods and ignoring the Navigation Acts. (See Chapter 4.) When challenged, the people of Massachusetts claimed that England had no right to make laws for them. In response, King Charles II canceled their charter. The charter had given the colony the right of self-government.

When Charles's brother James became king in 1685, he wanted to strengthen royal power. He also changed the way the northern colonies were governed. James combined Massachusetts and the other Northern colonies into one Dominion of New England, ruled by governor **Edmund Andros**. Andros angered the colonists by ending representative assemblies and limiting town meetings.

With their assemblies outlawed, some colonists refused to pay taxes. Andros jailed the loudest protestors. At their trial, they were told, "You have no more privileges left you than not to be Sould [sold] for Slaves."

The colonists sent Increase Mather to England to plead with King James. (See One American's Story on page 137.) However, a revolution in England was underway that changed the situation completely.

Why do you think the colonists resented Governor Andros (*shown below*)?

**BRITISH CROWN**
**King or Queen**

**ROYAL GOVERNOR**

- appointed by the crown
- oversaw colonial trade
- had final approval on laws
- could dismiss colonial assembly

**COUNCIL**

- appointed by governor
- advisory board to governor
- acted as highest court in each colony

**COLONIAL ASSEMBLY**

- elected by eligible colonists
- made laws
- had authority to tax
- paid governor's salary

**CRITICAL THINKING** How were lawmaking powers shared?

**William and Mary Restore English Rights** James II restricted English rights not only in the colonies but in England itself. He severely punished a Protestant rebellion and dismissed Parliament in 1687. Enraged by James's actions, Parliament secretly offered the throne to James's daughter, Mary, and her husband, William of Orange. William was the governor of the Netherlands. With little support in England, James fled the country at the end of 1688. Parliament named William and Mary the new monarchs of England. This change in leadership is called England's **Glorious Revolution**.

William and Mary agreed in 1689 to uphold the **English Bill of Rights**. This was a list of specific rights of English people and of Parliament. The monarch could not cancel laws or impose taxes unless Parliament agreed. Free elections and frequent meetings of Parliament were to be held. Excessive fines and cruel punishments were forbidden. People had the right to complain to the king or queen in Parliament without being arrested.

The English Bill of Rights established an important principle: the government was to be based on laws made by Parliament, not on the desires of a ruler. The rights of English people were strengthened.

**Colonists Claim English Rights** The colonists were quick to claim these rights. When the people of Boston heard of King James's fall, they jailed Governor Andros and asked Parliament to restore their rights. The Massachusetts colonists regained the right to elect representatives to an assembly. However, they had to accept a governor appointed by the crown. This kind of compromise between royal power and colonial self-government took place in other colonies as well.

The diagram on the upper left shows how most colonial governments were organized by 1700. The royal governor, his council, and the assembly shared power. The governor could strike down laws passed by the assembly, but the assembly was responsible for the governor's salary. If he blocked the assembly, the assembly might refuse to pay him.

After the disagreements between the colonists and the king during the late 1600s, the tension between America and the English government eased. During the early 1700s, England interfered very little in colonial affairs. This hands-off policy was called salutary neglect (*salutary* means "helpful" or "beneficial"). Parliament passed many laws regulating trade, the use of money, and even apprenticeships, but governors rarely enforced these laws. The colonists got used to acting independently.

**Zenger and Freedom of the Press** Colonists moved toward gaining a new right, freedom of the press, in 1735. That year, **John Peter Zenger**, publisher of the *New York Weekly Journal*, stood trial for printing criticism of New York's governor. Zenger's paper claimed that the governor accepted bribes. It also said that the governor had removed a judge and tried to fix an election.

### PRIMARY SOURCE

❝ A Governor turns rogue [criminal], does a thousand things for which a small rogue would have deserved a halter [hanging], and because it is difficult . . . to obtain relief against him, . . . it is prudent [wise] to . . . join in the roguery. ❞

— *New York Weekly Journal*, quoted in *Colonial America, 1607–1763*

At that time, it was illegal to criticize the king in print. Because the governor represented the king, some claimed that no one should criticize the governor. Andrew Hamilton defended Zenger at his trial, claiming that people had the right to speak the truth. The jury agreed, and Zenger was released. Freedom of the press became an important new right in America.

English rights were part of the colonial **heritage**, or tradition. Respect for these principles of law continues to unite the American people.

 **CAUSES AND EFFECTS** Explain how colonial rights were affected by political events in England.

---

 **New Jersey Core Curriculum Content Standards** *Review*

📲 **ONLINE QUIZ**
For test practice, go to
**Interactive Review @ ClassZone.com**

### TERMS & NAMES

**1.** Explain the importance of

- Magna Carta
- Parliament
- Edmund Andros
- Glorious Revolution
- English Bill of Rights
- John Peter Zenger

### USING YOUR READING NOTES

**2. Sequence Events** Complete the diagram you started at the beginning of this section.

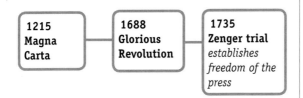

| 1215 Magna Carta | → | 1688 Glorious Revolution | → | 1735 Zenger trial *establishes freedom of the press* |

### KEY IDEAS

**3.** What English political traditions did colonists bring with them to America?

**4.** How did King James II restrict the colonists' rights?

**5.** How did the Zenger trial help expand the colonists' rights?

### CRITICAL THINKING

**6. Make Generalizations** How did England's policies toward the colonies change after the Glorious Revolution?

**7.** **Connect** *to* **Today** What rights enjoyed by modern Americans can be traced back to the Magna Carta of 1215?

**8.** **Writing** Speech Write a speech that Increase Mather might have delivered to the English Parliament, asking for a new charter that would protect the colonists' rights.

## ▶ Key Ideas

**BEFORE, YOU LEARNED**

The French had set up colonies and established a trading relationship with the native peoples of North America.

**NOW YOU WILL LEARN**

Land claims and rivalry among European powers, settlers, and Native Americans led to a war that united the colonies against a common enemy.

## ▶ Vocabulary

**TERMS & NAMES**

**Pontiac's Rebellion** Native American revolt against the British colonies

**French and Indian War** war of 1754–1763 between Britain, France, and their allies for control of North America

**Albany Plan of Union** first formal proposal to unite the colonies

**Battle of Quebec** battle that led to the British victory in the French and Indian War

**Treaty of Paris (1763)** treaty that ended the war between France and Britain

**Proclamation of 1763** British declaration that forbade colonists from settling west of the Appalachians

**BACKGROUND VOCABULARY**

**pact** formal agreement; a bargain

**smallpox** highly infectious and often fatal disease

**Visual Vocabulary**
Battle of Quebec

## ▶ Reading Strategy

Re-create the table shown at right. As you read and respond to the **KEY QUESTIONS**, use the table to show why Native Americans became involved in European conflicts.

 See Skillbuilder Handbook, page R7.

**CAUSES & EFFECTS**

| CAUSE | EFFECT |
|-------|--------|
|       | *Native Americans became involved in conflicts between Europeans.* |

**GRAPHIC ORGANIZERS**
Go to **Interactive Review** @ ClassZone.com

# The French and Indian War

 **6.4.D.4.** Examine the interactions between Native Americans and European settlers, such as agriculture, trade, cultural exchanges, and military alliances and conflicts.
**6.4.D.5.** Describe Native American resistance to colonization, including the Cherokee War against the English, the French and Indian War, and King George's War.

## One American's Story

Chief Pontiac was a leader of the Ottawa, a Native American group. When the British took over French forts in the Great Lakes area, Pontiac led his people in raids against them. This conflict is known as **Pontiac's Rebellion** (1763–1764). Addressing his followers, Pontiac said

**PRIMARY SOURCE**

❝ It is important for us, my brothers, that we exterminate from our lands this nation which seeks only to destroy us. . . . Therefore, my brothers, we must all swear their destruction and wait no longer. ❞

—Pontiac, quoted in *Pontiac and the Indian Uprising*

Pontiac's rebellion followed the **French and Indian War**, in which French forces fought British forces in North America. Each side had Native American allies.

Pontiac

## Europeans in Native American Lands

🔽 **KEY QUESTION** Why were Native Americans involved in conflicts between Europeans?

The English and the French created rival empires in North America. The competition between these two European powers often led to war.

**France Claims Western Lands** The French claimed the Ohio River valley, the Mississippi River valley, and the Great Lakes region. The French territory of Louisiana, claimed by La Salle in 1682, stretched from the Ohio River valley to the Rocky Mountains. They called these lands "New France." Some Europeans in New France were fur traders. Others were Jesuit (JEHZH•oo•iht) priests working to convert Native Americans to Christianity.

❝ Could it not be contrived to send the Small Pox among those disaffected [angry] tribes of Indians? We must on this occasion use every stratagem in our power to reduce them. ❞

—Major General Jeffrey Amherst, quoted in *The Conspiracy of Pontiac*

The officers invited Lenni Lenape war leaders to talk and then gave them **smallpox**-infected blankets as gifts. This started a deadly outbreak of the disease among the Native Americans.

By the fall, the Native Americans had retreated, and three years later a peace treaty was signed. Pontiac's Rebellion showed the British how difficult it was going to be to govern their vast new empire. To avoid further conflicts with Native Americans, the British issued the **Proclamation of 1763**. This forbade colonists from settling west of the Appalachian Mountains.

**A New Colonial Identity** The colonists were angry. They thought they had won the right to settle in the Ohio River valley. In turn, the British government was angry with the colonists, who insisted on settling on Native American lands.

The French and Indian War gave the 13 colonies their first taste of unity as they fought a common enemy. This feeling of unity grew as colonists found themselves in another dispute with Britain. With France no longer a threat, colonial leaders grew more confident in their complaints. The stage was set for the final conflict between the colonies and Britain.

 **MAKE INFERENCES** Explain how the French and Indian War changed the colonial world.

---

 **New Jersey Core Curriculum Content Standards *Review***

**ONLINE QUIZ**
For test practice, go to
**Interactive Review @ ClassZone.com**

**TERMS & NAMES**

1. Explain the importance of
   - Pontiac's Rebellion
   - Battle of Quebec
   - French and Indian War
   - Treaty of Paris (1763)
   - Albany Plan of Union
   - Proclamation of 1763

**USING YOUR READING NOTES**

2. **Causes and Effects** Complete the diagram you started at the beginning of this section.

| CAUSE | EFFECT |
|-------|--------|
|       | *Native Americans became involved in conflicts between Europeans.* |

**KEY IDEAS**

3. Why did Native American tribes form alliances with European powers?

4. What factors caused the French and Indian War?

5. Why were American colonists angry about the Proclamation of 1763?

**CRITICAL THINKING**

6. **Causes and Effects** What were some effects of Pontiac's Rebellion?

7. **Connect** *to* **Today** Many Native American groups were pulled into war because they were trading with the French or British. How do economic alliances continue to pull nations into war?

8. **Art** Imagine you are at the meeting in Albany. Create a poster urging colonial unity.

# Interactive ⟵Review

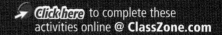 **Click here** to complete these activities online @ **ClassZone.com**

## Chapter Summary

**1 Key Idea**
The British colonies developed a unique culture shaped by prosperity, literacy, and new movements in religion and thought.

**2 Key Idea**
American democracy has its roots in the English tradition of representative government.

**3 Key Idea**
Land claims and rivalry among European powers, settlers, and Native Americans led to a war that united the colonies against a common enemy.

For detailed Review and Study Notes go to **Interactive Review** @ ClassZone.com

## Name Game

Use the Terms & Names list to identify each sentence online or on your own paper.

1. I was a governor who ended representative assemblies. Edmund Andros

2. I was a popular minister who started a home for orphans. _____

3. This was a battle for a French city. _____

4. I experimented with electricity. _____

5. This was a proclamation that restricted westward movement. _____

6. I argued that people have natural rights. _____

7. My sermons promised that all could be saved. _____

8. This was a war fought for North America. _____

9. My court case won freedom of the press. _____

10. This was a Native American revolt. _____

A. John Locke
B. Battle of Quebec
C. French and Indian War
D. George Whitefield
E. John Peter Zenger
F. Jonathan Edwards
G. English Bill of Rights
H. Benjamin Franklin
I. Albany Plan of Union
J. Pontiac's Rebellion
K. Edmund Andros
L. Proclamation of 1763

## Activities

### FLIPCARD

Use the online flipcards to quiz yourself on the terms and names introduced in this chapter.

American writer, publisher, scientist, inventor, and diplomat

**ANSWER** Ben Franklin

### GEOGAME

Use this online map to reinforce your understanding of Eastern North America in 1750, including the location of important forts, Native American groups, and geographic features. Drag and drop each name in the list at its location on the map. A scorecard helps you keep track of your progress online.

Iroquois
Fort Duquesne
Ohio River
Fort Montreal
Lake Erie

Ohio River

## VOCABULARY

**Explain the significance of each of the following.**

1. Benjamin Franklin
2. Pontiac's Rebellion
3. Proclamation of 1763
4. English Bill of Rights
5. Enlightenment
6. John Locke
7. French and Indian War
8. Great Awakening
9. Treaty of Paris (1763)
10. Jonathan Edwards
11. Battle of Quebec
12. George Whitefield
13. Albany Plan of Union
14. Magna Carta
15. John Peter Zenger
16. Edmund Andros

**Explain how the terms and names in each group are related.**

17. Great Awakening, Jonathan Edwards, George Whitefield
18. French and Indian War, Battle of Quebec
19. John Locke, Enlightenment, Benjamin Franklin
20. Parliament, Glorious Revolution

## KEY IDEAS

**1 Early American Culture (pages 126–133)**

21. What made American colonial societies different from European societies?
22. How did the Great Awakening challenge social and political traditions?
23. How did the Enlightenment influence Americans?

**2 Roots of American Democracy (pages 134–139)**

24. Why did the colonists value their rights so highly?
25. How did political changes in England affect colonial rights?

**3 The French and Indian War (page 142–148)**

26. Why did the French and Indian War help unite the colonists?
27. Why did the French and Indian War change the relationship between the colonists and Britain?

## CRITICAL THINKING

28. **Causes and Effects** Why did a new kind of society develop in the colonies?
29. **Make Generalizations** What political values did English colonists share?
30. **Draw Conclusions** How did colonial publishing help shape an American identity?
31. **Compare and Contrast** Create a diagram to compare and contrast the Great Awakening and the Enlightenment. In the space where the circles intersect, record the common features of the two movements.

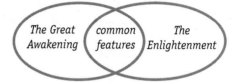

The Great Awakening | common features | The Enlightenment

32. **Problems and Solutions** Why did the relationship between colonial governments and Parliament cause tension?
33. **Causes and Effects** What do you think was the major cause of the French and Indian War?
34. **Draw Conclusions** What role did the Ohio River valley play in the French and Indian War?
35. **Analyze Primary Sources** Benjamin Franklin published this image during the French and Indian War. Each section of the snake represents a colony. What effect was it meant to have on the colonists?

JOIN, or DIE.

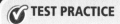
## DOCUMENT-BASED QUESTIONS

### PART 1: Short Answer

**Study each document carefully and answer the questions that follow.**

#### DOCUMENT 1

1. Examine this painting of the Death of Wolfe by Benjamin West. Why does the painter show a Native American at the scene of Wolfe's death?

#### DOCUMENT 2

**PRIMARY SOURCE**

❝ When I go to see the English commander and say to him that some of our comrades are dead, instead of bewailing their death, as our French brothers do, he laughs at me and at you. If I ask anything for our sick, he refuses with the reply that he has no use for us. From all this you can well see that they are seeking our ruin. Therefore, my brothers, we must all swear their destruction and wait no longer. ❞
—Pontiac, 1763

2. What does this quote reveal about Pontiac's Rebellion?

### PART 2: Essay

3. Using information from the documents, your answers to the question in part 1, and your knowledge of U.S. history, write an essay that discusses the relationship between Native Americans and the colonial powers.

## YOU BE THE HISTORIAN

36. **Problems and Solutions** Did the French and Indian War settle one dispute or create another set of problems?

37. **Evaluate** Give an example of bad military or political leadership during the period studied in the chapter. What mistakes were made?

38. **WHAT IF?** Suppose the British had not taken Quebec in 1759. How might this have changed American history?

39. **Make Generalizations** What aspects of modern American culture might be familiar to an 18th-century colonist?

40. **Analyze Point of View** Consider each group's reasons for fighting the French and Indian War. Which group had the most to lose: the British, the French, the Native Americans, or the colonists?

41. **Citizenship** Why is jury duty a requirement of citizenship?

 Answer the
## ESSENTIAL QUESTION
**What traditions, events, and forces helped form an American identity?**

**Written Response** Write a four-paragraph response to the Essential Question. Be sure to consider the key ideas of each section as well as the most significant factors that led to the development of an American identity. Use the Response Rubric below to guide your thinking and writing.

### Response Rubric

**A strong response will**

• discuss the unique conditions governing colonial life

• explain how deeply colonists valued English political traditions

• describe the cultural and political forces that united the colonists

# Creating a New Nation

## 1763–1791

**6** **The Road to Revolution**
1763–1776  pages 154–191

The Declaration of Independence
pages 184–188

**7** **The American Revolution**
1775–1783  pages 192–231

**8** **Confederation to Constitution**
1776–1791  pages 232–259

**Constitution Handbook**

The Living Constitution
pages 260–265

The Constitution of the United States
pages 266–299

Citizenship Handbook
pages 300–307

## Why It Matters Now

America at the beginning of its history was an experiment —a trial to see if democratic and representative government could work. Patriot colonists imperiled "their lives, their fortunes, their sacred honor" for the sake of principle. The values they fought for, and the decisions they wrote into the Constitution, echo through our history and shape our government and our lives to this day.

Is life so dear, or peace so sweet, as to be purchased at the price of chains and slavery? Forbid it, Almighty God! I know not what course others may take; but as for me, give me liberty or give me death!
—Patrick Henry, 1775

## CHAPTER

# 6

1. Tighter British Control
2. Colonial Resistance Grows
3. The Road to Lexington and Concord
4. Declaring Independence

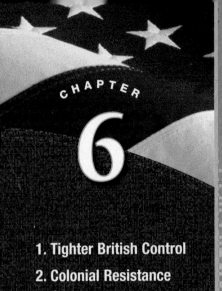

# The Road to Revolution

## 1763–1776

### ESSENTIAL QUESTION

What drove the colonists to declare independence from Great Britain?

**2** To Lexington and Concord

**CONNECT** → **Geography & History**

What role did the geography of 18th-century Boston play in the early days of the Revolution?

**Think about:**

1. why it was so difficult to invade the town
2. the routes from Boston to Lexington and Concord
3. the strategic importance of the surrounding hills

**1** The only road connecting Boston to the mainland

King George III

Teapot decorated to protest Stamp Act, 1766

## 1763

Proclamation of 1763 restricts westward expansion.

**1765** Parliament passes Stamp Act.

▼

**Effect** Colonists organize boycott of British goods.

**1767** Parliament passes Townshend Acts.

▼

**Effect** Boycott is resumed; political activism spreads.

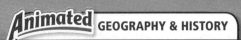
❸

Bunker Hill and Breed's Hill overlook the town.

Charlestown burns during the battle.

*BOSTON*

harbor

British patrols

Massachusetts Minuteman

**1774** Intolerable Acts are passed.

▼

**Effect** Colonists organize First Continental Congress.

**1775** Fighting begins at Lexington and Concord.

**1773** Parliament passes Tea Act.

▼

**Effect** Colonists destroy tea in Boston Tea Party.

Bedford, MA militia flag, 1775

**1776**

Declaration of Independence announces American separation from Britain.

*The Road to Revolution* **155**

## ▶ Key Ideas

**BEFORE, YOU LEARNED**
The British tried to stop colonists from settling on the western frontier.

**NOW YOU WILL LEARN**
Colonists saw British efforts to increase control over the colonies as violations of their rights.

## ▶ Vocabulary

**TERMS & NAMES**

**King George III** British monarch who reigned during the American Revolution

**Quartering Act** act requiring the colonists to quarter, or house, British soldiers and provide them with supplies

**Sugar Act** law placing a tax on sugar, molasses, and other products shipped to the colonies

**Stamp Act** law requiring all legal and commercial documents to carry an official stamp showing that a tax had been paid

**Patrick Henry** member of Virginia's House of Burgesses

**Sons of Liberty** secret society formed to oppose British policies

**BACKGROUND VOCABULARY**

**speculate** to buy as an investment

**boycott** refusal to buy

**REVIEW**

**Proclamation of 1763** British proclamation that forbade the colonists from settling west of the Appalachian Mountains

**Visual Vocabulary**
King George III

## ▶ Reading Strategy

Re-create the diagram shown at right. As you read and respond to the **KEY QUESTIONS**, use the boxes to record the opposing points of view of Parliament and the American colonists.

 See Skillbuilder Handbook, page R8.

**COMPARE AND CONTRAST**

| Parliament | Colonists |
|---|---|
| *Colonies should help pay for their own defense.* | |

 **GRAPHIC ORGANIZERS**
Go to **Interactive Review** @ ClassZone.com

# Tighter British Control

 **6.4.E.1.** Discuss the background and major issues of the American Revolution, including the political and economic causes and consequences of the revolution.

## One American's Story

In 1765 Sally Franklin's father—the famous American diplomat Benjamin Franklin—was in London to protest the Stamp Act. During his stay, Sally Franklin wrote her father long and detailed letters that were filled with news from the colonies. Often she wrote about family and friends, but Sally also had a keen interest in political affairs. In one letter, she vividly described the colonial reaction to the repeal of the Stamp Act:

### PRIMARY SOURCE

**❝** We have heard by a round-about way that the Stamp Act is repealed. . . . The bells rung, we had bonfires and one house was illuminated. Indeed I never heard so much noise in my life; the very children seem distracted. **❞**

—Sally Franklin, quoted in *Founding Mothers*

Sally Franklin (Bache)

Similar celebrations occurred throughout the colonies. Many thought the difficulties between Britain and America had finally come to an end.

## The Colonies and Britain Grow Apart

🔻 **KEY QUESTION** Why were the colonists threatened by Parliament's new laws?

During the French and Indian War, American colonists helped the British defeat the French. The colonists took pride in the British victory, but soon found that their relationship with Britain had soured. In earlier days, the colonies had been allowed, for the most part, to manage their own affairs. In the 1760s, however, Parliament's new laws and restrictions threatened the colonists' freedom.

**Westward Expansion Restricted** After the French and Indian War, **King George III**, the British monarch, issued many reforms to tighten his control of the American colonies. First, he issued the **Proclamation of 1763**, which forbade the colonists from settling beyond the Appalachian Mountains. Although designed to maintain peace between the colonists and Native Americans, this law angered settlers who hoped to **speculate**, or buy as an investment, in western lands. In addition, King George decided to keep 10,000 soldiers in the colonies to enforce the proclamation. But housing the troops proved very expensive. Therefore, Parliament passed the **Quartering Act**, a law that required colonists to house all British soldiers.

These new laws created great anxiety in the colonies. The colonists feared that Parliament intended to use the troops to control their movements and restrict their freedom.

**Parliament Taxes the Colonists** In addition to the cost of keeping troops in the colonies, Britain owed massive debts from the French and Indian War. To pay off these debts, Britain needed more revenue, or income. As a result, Parliament looked to the colonies to pay part of the costs for frontier defense and colonial government.

In 1765, Parliament passed the **Sugar Act**. This law placed a tax on sugar, molasses, and other products shipped to the colonies. Making matters worse, in the following year Parliament passed the **Stamp Act**, a law that required all legal and commercial documents to carry an official stamp showing that a tax had been paid. In addition to wills and contracts, all newspapers and diplomas also had to carry a stamp.

From Parliament's perspective, the Sugar and Stamp Acts were reasonable ways to raise money in the colonies to pay off Britain's debt. From the colonist's perspective, however, these acts were seen as serious threats to their political rights. Their anger focused on two complaints: First, that Parliament had no right to tax the colonies—that was a job for the colonial assembly. And second, that no tax should be created without their consent.

▲ **COMPARE AND CONTRAST** Explain why the colonists disagreed with Parliament.

# Colonists Defy Parliament

▼ **KEY QUESTION** How did the colonists react when Parliament took over the assemblies' power to tax?

The Stamp Act enraged the colonists. Everywhere people took up the cry "No taxation without representation!" to protest the attack on their rights. **Patrick Henry**, a member of Virginia's House of Burgesses, demanded resistance. When another member shouted that resistance was treason, Henry is said to have replied, "If *this* be treason, make the most of it!"

**The Colonists Organize** In 1765, delegates from nine colonies formed the Stamp Act Congress in New York. During this meeting, delegates drafted a petition to the king protesting the Stamp Act and declared that the right to tax the colonists belonged to the colonial assemblies, not to Parliament. This was the first time the colonies had united in opposition to British policy.

Meanwhile, some colonists formed secret societies, such as the **Sons of Liberty**, to oppose British policies. Occasionally they encouraged

Under the Stamp Act of 1765, royal stamps such as these were required on legal documents.

people to attack customs officials and burn the stamps. As a result, many customs officials quit their jobs and returned to England.

**Colonists Threaten British Profits** The colonists' complaints against Parliament were bitter, loud, and sometimes violent. But the most effective protest took the form of a **boycott**, a widespread refusal to buy British goods. By refusing to buy goods from England, the colonists targeted British merchants. The colonists hoped that these merchants, faced with declining sales, would influence Parliament to repeal the Stamp Act. Some British politicians sided with the colonists. Parliamentary leader William Pitt spoke out against the Stamp Act:

(*above*) During the crisis with Great Britian, colonists often met under the Liberty Tree, a symbol of liberty, individuality, and freedom.

**PRIMARY SOURCE**

❝ The Americans have not acted in all things with prudence and [good] temper. They have been driven to madness by injustice. Will you punish them for the madness you have [caused]? . . . . My opinion . . . . is that the Stamp Act be repealed absolutely, totally, and immediately. ❞

—**William Pitt, quoted in** *Patriots*

The colonists' tactic worked, and Parliament finally repealed the Stamp Act in 1766. But at the same time, Parliament passed the Declaratory Act, which stated that Parliament had supreme authority to govern the colonies. Although the colonists celebrated the repeal of the Stamp Act, the great argument between Parliament and the colonies had just begun.

🔺 **CAUSES AND EFFECTS** Explain how the colonists reacted when Parliament took over the assemblies' power to tax.

---

 **New Jersey Core Curriculum Content Standards** *Review*

 **ONLINE QUIZ**
For test practice, go to
**Interactive Review** @ ClassZone.com

**TERMS & NAMES**

1. Explain the importance of
   - King George III
   - Quartering Act
   - Sugar Act
   - Stamp Act
   - Patrick Henry
   - Sons of Liberty

**USING YOUR READING NOTES**

2. **Compare and Contrast** Complete the diagram that you started at the beginning of this section.

| Parliament | Colonists |
|---|---|
| *Colonies should help pay for their own defense.* | |

**KEY IDEAS**

3. Why did Parliament pass new laws governing the colonies?

4. How did the colonists oppose the new acts?

**CRITICAL THINKING**

5. **Analyze Point of View** Why would Britain's new laws have convinced Americans that their freedom was under threat?

6. **Connect Economics & History** Why was boycotting British goods an effective way to protest the Stamp Act?

7. **Writing** Protest Song Imagine that you are one of the Sons of Liberty. Write a song protesting Parliament's new laws.

## ▶ Key Ideas

**BEFORE, YOU LEARNED**

Colonists saw British efforts to increase control over the colonies as violations of their rights.

**NOW YOU WILL LEARN**

Many colonists organized to oppose British policies.

## ▶ Vocabulary

**TERMS & NAMES**

**Crispus Attucks** sailor of African-American and Native American ancestry who died at the Boston Massacre

**Boston Massacre** incident in 1770 in which British troops fired on and killed American colonists

**Townshend Acts** acts passed by Parliament in 1767 to tax imports in the colonies

**writs of assistance** search warrants used to enter homes or businesses to search for smuggled goods

**Daughters of Liberty** organization of colonial women formed to protest British policies

**Samuel Adams** leader of the Boston Sons of Liberty

**committee of correspondence** organization formed to exchange information about British policies and American resistance

**Boston Tea Party** incident in 1773, when colonists protested British policies by boarding British ships and throwing their cargoes of tea overboard

**BACKGROUND VOCABULARY**

**duties** taxes placed on imported goods

**REVIEW**

**John Adams** lawyer who defended British soldiers accused of murder in the Boston Massacre

## ▶ Reading Strategy

Re-create the diagram shown at right. As you read and respond to the **KEY QUESTIONS**, use the boxes to record how each aspect of the Townshend Acts angered the colonists.

 See Skillbuilder Handbook, page R7.

**CAUSES AND EFFECTS**

| Townshend Acts... | anger colonists because... |
|---|---|
| writs of assistance | *customs officials invaded their homes and businesses* |
| duties on imports | |

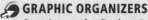

**GRAPHIC ORGANIZERS**
Go to **Interactive Review** @ ClassZone.com

# Colonial Resistance Grows

**6.4.E.1.** Discuss the background and major issues of the American Revolution, including the political and economic causes and consequences of the revolution.
**6.4.E.2.** Discuss the major events . . . and personalities . . . of the American Revolution.

## One American's Story

**Crispus Attucks** was born into slavery in Framingham, Massachusetts, around 1723. It is believed that Attucks was the son of an African-American father and a Native American mother. As a young man, Attucks escaped slavery by running away to sea.

In March 1770, Attucks was in Boston, where feelings against British rule were reaching a fever pitch. He joined a crowd who were protesting British troops. A witness described what happened next.

### PRIMARY SOURCE

❝ [The British officer] is said to have ordered [the troops] to fire, and to have repeated that order. One gun was fired first; then others in succession and with deliberation, till ten or a dozen guns were fired. ❞

—anonymous account of the Boston Massacre

Crispus Attucks

When the smoke cleared Attucks was dead, one of the victims of the **Boston Massacre**. Throughout America, tension between Britain and its colonies was exploding into violence.

## Tightening British Control

🔻 **KEY QUESTION** Why did the Townshend Acts anger the colonists?

After the uproar over the Sugar and Stamp Acts, Britain hoped to avoid further conflict with the colonies. Yet Parliament faced a serious dilemma: how to control the unruly colonists without angering the people with a new set of taxes. The answer, Parliament decided, was the Declaratory Act.

Passed in 1766, the Declaratory Act affirmed Parliament's right to legislate for the colonies "in all cases whatsoever." Importantly, however, no new tax accompanied the act. The purpose of the Declaratory Act was simply to reassert Parliament's control over all colonial affairs.

Most colonists did not feel threatened by the Declaratory Act. Although some politicans did protest the new law in colonial assemblies, most people were not bothered by Parliament's bold political statement. Instead, colonists simply ignored the act and went on with their lives as best they could.

**The Townshend Acts Are Passed** Parliament's new strategy, however, had one major flaw: with the Stamp Act repealed, Britain still needed to raise money in the colonies to pay for troops and other expenses. So Britain's finance minister, Charles Townshend, proposed a new series of **duties**, or taxes on imports, to raise revenue in America.

Approved by Parliament in 1767, the **Townshend Acts** placed duties on numerous imports to the colonies such as glass, paper, paint, lead, and tea. In addition, the acts allowed British officers to issue **writs of assistance**, or search warrants, to enter homes and businesses to search for smuggled or illegal goods.

## Daily Life  *The Colonial Marketplace*

By the 1760s, English merchants were sending hundreds of ships to America with goods for sale to the colonists. Beyond the daily necessities of life—tools, knives, nails, and axes—colonists were eager to buy the latest luxuries and fashions from England, including (**A**) clothing, (**B**) glass and building materials, (**C**) glassware, (**D**) scientific and medical instruments, (**E**) books and periodicals, (**F**) furniture, and (**G**) fine silks.

**BOYCOTT PRESSURES MERCHANTS**

When the colonists boycotted British goods, many English merchants, shippers, and manufacturers lost business as their products went unsold. As a result, in 1765 many merchants pressured Parliament to repeal the acts so their businesses could recover.

**CRITICAL THINKING** Make Generalizations
How did the colonial boycotts affect British merchants?

**Anger Over the Townshend Acts** News of the Townshend Acts sparked immediate protest throughout the colonies. People were furious that Parliament had once again passed a tax without their consent. Colonists felt that only locally elected officials—rather than Parliament—should have the right to create laws and taxes in the colonies. Many people, such as Pennsylvania lawyer John Dickinson, thought the acts were illegal. Dickinson explained his beliefs in a famous pamphlet:

**PRIMARY SOURCE**

❝ We cannot be happy without being free . . . we cannot be free without being secure in our property . . . we cannot be secure in our property, if [taxed] without our consent. ❞

—John Dickinson, *Letters from a Farmer in Pennsylvania*

The colonists were also angry about the writs of assistance. Many believed that the writs went against their natural rights, as defined by English philosopher John Locke. The law of nature, wrote Locke, teaches that "no one ought to harm another in his life, health, liberty, or possessions."

🔺 **CAUSES AND EFFECTS** Explain why the Townshend Acts angered the colonists.

# Colonists Protest

🔻 **KEY QUESTION** In what ways did colonists protest British laws?

In response to the Townshend Acts, merchants in Boston organized another boycott of British goods. By October 1767, other colonies had joined the Massachusetts protests. The colonists were uniting for a common cause.

**Political Activism Spreads** As the boycott spread throughout the colonies, more people became politically active. Many colonists who had not previously participated in politics now had a way of making their voices heard. For example, some women formed their own protest organization called the **Daughters of Liberty**. They urged colonists to weave their own cloth and to use American products instead of British goods.

Meanwhile, colonial leaders urged the people to remain calm and not to protest violently. "No mobs," the *Boston Gazette* suggested, "Constitutional methods are best." Regardless, some colonists continued to protest with anger and threatened to form a mob.

Fearing disorder in the colonies, British officials called for more troops. This angered the colonists—even those who wanted peace. **Samuel Adams**, a leader of the Boston Sons of Liberty, stated, "We will destroy every soldier that dare put his foot on shore. . . . I look upon them as foreign enemies!"

**The Boston Massacre** In the fall of 1768, more than 1,000 additional British soldiers (known as redcoats for their bright red jackets) arrived in Boston under the command of General Thomas Gage. With their arrival, tensions erupted into violence.

**Connecting History**

**Representative Government**
Ever since the House of Burgesses was established in Jamestown in 1619, colonists had the right to raise their own taxes. See *Chapter 3, page 64.*

Paul Revere's etching of the Boston Massacre fueled anger in the colonies.
**Are the soldiers represented fairly in Revere's etching?**

On March 5, 1770, a group of colonists—mostly youths and dockworkers—surrounded some soldiers in front of the State House. Soon, the two groups began trading insults, shouting at each other and even throwing snowballs. As the crowd grew larger, the soldiers began to fear for their safety. Thinking they were about to be attacked, the soldiers fired into the crowd. Five people, including Crispus Attucks, were killed.

The people of Boston were outraged at what came to be known as the Boston Massacre. In the weeks that followed, the colonies were flooded with anti-British propaganda in newspapers, pamphlets, and political posters. Attucks and the four victims were depicted as heroes who had given their lives for the cause of freedom. The British soldiers, on the other hand, were portrayed as evil and menacing villains.

At the same time, the soldiers who had fired the shots were arrested and charged with murder. **John Adams**, a lawyer and cousin of Samuel Adams, agreed to defend the soldiers in court. Many people criticized Adams and some even threatened to harm the lawyer. But Adams believed that everyone—including the British soldiers—was entitled to a fair trial. Although Adams supported the colonists' cause, he wanted to demonstrate that everyone was subject to the rule of law.

Adams argued that the soldiers had acted in self-defense. The jury agreed and acquitted the soldiers. To many colonists, however, the Boston Massacre would stand as a symbol of British tyranny in the colonies.

▲ **SUMMARIZE** Describe how colonists protested British laws.

## Economic Interference

▼ **KEY QUESTION** How did colonists in the port cities react to the Tea Act?

In April 1770, Parliament repealed the Townshend Acts. Once again, the colonial boycott had worked—British trade had been hurt and Parliament had backed down. But Parliament kept the tea tax to show that it still had the right to tax the colonists.

**The Tea Act Increases Anger** To demonstrate their displeasure with the remaining tax on tea, many colonists chose not to purchase luxuries from British merchants. Instead, they drank tea that was smuggled from Holland. As a result, many British tea companies lost money in America as their tea went unsold and rotted in ports.

Attempting to save British tea merchants, Parliament passed the Tea Act in 1773. This law gave one company, the East India Company, the exclusive right to sell tea in the colonies. Although the act lowered the price of tea for colonists, it also restricted colonists from acting as shippers and merchants of the valuable product.

Many colonists—particularly those who had traded in smuggled tea—were enraged by the new tax. Colonists saw the tea act as another attempt by Parliament to interfere in the economic life of the colonies.

**Colonial Unity Expands** By this time, colonial leaders understood the importance of unity among the colonies. Therefore, Samuel Adams urged many towns in Massachusetts to establish **committees of correspondence** to communicate with their neighboring towns and colonial leaders.

In the months that followed, these groups exchanged numerous secret letters on colonial affairs and resistance to British policy. Before long, many other colonies—such as New York, South Carolina, and Rhode Island—had created similar committees of correspondence.

## History Makers *Revolutionary Leaders*

### Samuel Adams  1722–1803

When Parliament levied taxes upon the colonies, no one responded with greater passion and fury than Boston merchant Samuel Adams. A skillful writer, orator, and popular leader of the Sons of Liberty and the Boston Committee of Correspondence, Samuel Adams persuaded many colonists to unite against British policy and taxation. "It does not require a majority to prevail," Samuel Adams wrote, "but rather an irate, tireless minority keen to set brush fires in people's minds."

### John Adams  1735–1826

While his cousin Samuel planned fiery public protests, John Adams used a quieter tactic—the law—to counter British policy. "Facts are stubborn things," Adams wrote, "and whatever may be our wishes, our inclinations, or the dictates of our passions, they cannot alter the state of facts and evidence." Putting this theory into practice, Adams helped draft a legal petition to the king suggesting that Parliament had no right to tax the colonies.

**COMPARING** *Leaders*

**ONLINE BIOGRAPHY** For more information about Samuel and John Adams, go to the **Research & Writing Center** @ ClassZone.com

How did Samuel and John Adams differ in the way they protested British actions?

**The Boston Tea Party** Protests against the Tea Act took place throughout the colonies. In Charlestown, South Carolina, colonists unloaded tea and let it rot on the docks. In New York City and Philadelphia, colonists blocked tea ships from landing. In Boston, the Sons of Liberty organized what came to be known as the **Boston Tea Party**.

On the evening of December 16, 1773, a group of men disguised as Native Americans boarded three tea ships docked in Boston harbor. One of the men, George Hewes, a Boston shoemaker, later recalled the events.

### PRIMARY SOURCE

**❝**We then were ordered by our commander to open the hatches and take out all the chests of tea and throw them overboard. . . . In about three hours from the time we went on board, we had thus broken and thrown overboard every tea chest to be found in the ship; while those in the other ships were disposing of the tea in the same way, at the same time. **❞**

—George Hewes, quoted in *A Retrospect of the Boston Tea-Party*

That night, Hewes and the others destroyed 342 chests of tea to protest the Tea Act. Many colonists rejoiced at the news. British officials, however, were angered by the destructive protest and wanted to punish the culprits.

In the days that followed, some colonial leaders offered to pay for the tea if Parliament agreed to repeal the hated Tea Act. But Britain ruled out any compromise. This decision pushed many Americans into open rebellion.

▲ **CAUSES AND EFFECTS** Describe how colonists reacted to the Tea Act.

---

 **New Jersey Core Curriculum Content Standards *Review***

 **ONLINE QUIZ**
For test practice, go to
**Interactive Review @ ClassZone.com**

### TERMS & NAMES

**1.** Explain the importance of
- Crispus Attucks
- Boston Massacre
- Townshend Acts
- writs of assistance
- Daughters of Liberty
- Samuel Adams
- John Adams
- Boston Tea Party

### USING YOUR READING NOTES

**2. Causes and Effects** Complete the diagram that you started at the beginning of this section.

| Townshend Acts... | anger colonists because... |
|---|---|
| writs of assistance | *customs officials invaded their homes and businesses* |
| duties on imports | |

### KEY IDEAS

**3.** Why did colonists oppose the Townshend Acts?

**4.** How did the colonists express their discontent?

**5.** What prompted the Boston Tea Party?

### CRITICAL THINKING

**6. Draw Conclusions** Why did Parliament keep trying different ways of raising revenue?

**7. Problems and Solutions** Why did the colonists react so violently to the Tea Act?

**8. Summarize** Explain the impact of Paul Revere's etching of the Boston Massacre.

**9. Writing** **Letter** Write a letter to Parliament, urging the British government not to interfere in colonial trade.

# POPULAR RESISTANCE

The colonists found many ways to resist the new laws passed by Parliament. Americans from all walks of life joined in the popular protests.

## PROTESTS IN THE STREETS

Popular protests echoed through the streets of colonial towns. In this illustration, an angry crowd of colonists burns the hated stamps.

## WOMEN BECOME ACTIVISTS

For the first time in American history, large numbers of women became involved in a political cause. Women played a leading role in the boycotts of British goods. They also organized and signed petitions. This British cartoon shows the women of Edenton, North Carolina signing a promise not to buy British products.

## POLITICS IN DAILY LIFE

Protests against the Stamp Act appeared everywhere, from newspapers and periodicals to ordinary household items.

A mock stamp printed by a Pennsylvania journal to protest the Stamp Act

### Join the Boycott

Imagine you have joined the boycott of imported goods. Create a political pamphlet that expresses your opinion about British products.

## ▶ Key Ideas

**BEFORE, YOU LEARNED**
Many Americans organized to oppose
British policies.

**NOW YOU WILL LEARN**
The tensions between Britain and the
colonies led to the outbreak of the
Revolutionary War.

## ▶ Vocabulary

**TERMS & NAMES**

**Minutemen** group of armed civilians, trained
to be ready to fight "at a minute's warning"

**Intolerable Acts** series of laws, known in
Britain as the Coercive Acts, meant to punish
Massachusetts and clamp down on resistance
in other colonies

**First Continental Congress** meeting of
delegates from most of the colonies, called in
reaction to the Intolerable Acts

**Paul Revere** Boston silversmith who rode
into the countryside to spread news of British
troop movement

**Lexington and Concord** first battles of the
Revolutionary War

**Loyalists** Americans who supported the
British

**Patriots** Americans who sided with the rebels

**BACKGROUND VOCABULARY**

**militia** a force of armed civilians pledged to
defend their community

**Visual Vocabulary** Paul Revere

## ▶ Reading Strategy

Re-create the diagram shown at
right. As you read and respond
to the **KEY QUESTIONS**, record
information to support the
generalization.

 See Skillbuilder Handbook, page R11.

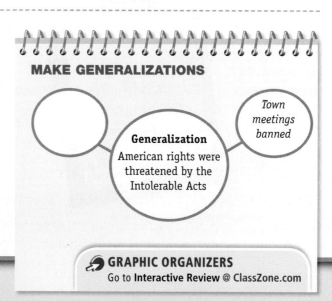

**MAKE GENERALIZATIONS**

**Generalization**
American rights were
threatened by the
Intolerable Acts

*Town
meetings
banned*

**GRAPHIC ORGANIZERS**
Go to **Interactive Review** @ ClassZone.com

# The Road to Lexington and Concord

**6.4.E.2.** Discuss the major events (e.g. Boston Tea Party, Battle of Trenton) and personalities . . . of the American Revolution.

**6.4.E.3.** Identify major British and American leaders and describe their roles in key events, . . . .

## One American's Story

At dawn on April 19, 1775, Captain John Parker and 70 of his men stood on the grassy common at the center of Lexington, a village near Boston. The men under Parker's command belonged to the local **militia**—a force of armed civilians pledged to defend their community. About one-third of the Lexington militia were **Minutemen**, colonists trained to be "ready to act at a minute's warning." A soldier described what happened next:

### PRIMARY SOURCE

❝ There suddenly appeared a Number of King's troops . . . They were . . . on a quick pace Towards us with Three officers in there front on horse back and on full gallop Towards us the foremost of which cryed through down your arms you villains you Rebels." ❞

—John Robbins, quoted in *Redcoats and Rebels*

Colonists battle Redcoats at Lexington, 1775.

Captain Parker was wounded and eight of his men were killed in the first fighting of the War of Independence. Colonial protests had turned into violent revolution.

## The Intolerable Acts

🔻 **KEY QUESTION** What rights were threatened by the Intolerable Acts?

The Boston Tea Party infuriated Parliament. One British official said the people of Boston "ought to be knocked about their ears." King George III declared, "We must master them or totally leave them to themselves and treat them as aliens." Britain chose to "master" the colonies.

**Attacks on Rights and Liberties**  In 1774, Parliament passed a series of laws to punish the Massachusetts colony and to clamp down on resistance in other colonies. The British called these laws the Coercive Acts, but they were so harsh that the colonists called them the **Intolerable Acts**. These acts were a direct attack on colonists' traditional rights and liberties, because they

- closed the port of Boston until colonists paid for the destroyed tea
- altered the Massachusetts charter to ban town meetings
- replaced the elected council with an appointed one
- increased the governor's power over the colonists
- protected British officials accused of crimes in the colonies from being tried by colonists
- allowed British officers to house troops in private dwellings

To enforce the acts, Parliament appointed General Thomas Gage governor of Massachusetts.

## ANALYZING *Political Cartoons*

### HISTORICAL CARTOONS

Historical cartoons show how people viewed the important events of their time. Each cartoon on these pages expresses the point of view of the cartoonist. Notice how the cartoonists use symbols, exaggeration, and humor to get their points across.

### The Bostonians in Distress

This cartoon uses symbols to show the situation in Boston after the Intolerable Acts stopped all ships from entering the town's harbors.

Bostonians are trapped in a cage symbolizing the restrictions of the Intolerable Acts.

Other colonists are shown helping the Bostonians by feeding them fish.

**The First Continental Congress Meets** In 1772, Sam Adams had written, "I wish we could arouse the continent." The Intolerable Acts answered his wish. Other colonies immediately offered Massachusetts their support. They sent food and money to Boston. The committees of correspondence also called for a meeting of colonial delegates to discuss what to do next.

In September 1774, delegates from all the colonies except Georgia met in Philadelphia. At this meeting, called the **First Continental Congress**, delegates voted to ban all trade with Britain until the Intolerable Acts were repealed. They also called on each colony to begin training troops. Georgia agreed to be a part of the actions of the Congress even though it had voted not to send delegates.

The First Continental Congress marked a key step in American history. Although most delegates were not ready to call for independence, they were determined to uphold colonial rights. This meeting planted the seeds of a future independent government. John Adams called it "a nursery of American statesmen." The delegates agreed to meet again in seven months.

### The Bostonians Paying the Excise-Man

This cartoon was published in London in 1774. It shows how Tories (those supporting the King) viewed colonial protests.

A customs informer, who has been tarred and feathered, is being tormented.

The protesters are shown as violent thugs.

### CRITICAL THINKING

1. **Make Inferences** Which cartoon is sympathetic to the colonists?

2. **Synthesize** How would these images have helped unite the colonists against British policies?

 **See Skillbuilder Handbook, page R24.**

## History Makers

### Abigail Adams  1744–1818

Abigail Smith was born on November 11, 1744, in Weymouth, Massachusetts. She married John Adams in 1764, the same year that Britain enacted the Sugar Act. She was often left alone to manage the family farm and raise their children.

During their long separations, Abigail wrote her husband many letters about government and politics. Often she expressed her opinions to her husband and even gave him advice when creating new laws. In one letter, Abigail asked John to give women more rights. "Remember the ladies," she wrote him, "and be more generous and favorable to them than your ancestors." Abigail's views were well ahead of her time, although it was years before women achieved equal rights.

**CRITICAL THINKING Draw Conclusions** What might Abigail Adams think about women's rights today?

**ONLINE BIOGRAPHY** For more on on Abigail Adams, go to the **Research & Writing Center** @ ClassZone.com

**British Control Begins to Slip** The colonists hoped that another trade boycott would force a repeal of the Intolerable Acts. After all, past boycotts had led to the repeal of the Stamp Act and the Townshend Acts. This time, however, Parliament stood firm. It even increased restrictions on colonial trade and sent more troops in the colonies. However, in the countryside, British authorities were already losing control of government. Throughout the colonies, Americans acted forcefully to reestablish the rights that Parliament was taking away. In the summer of 1774 in towns throughout Massachusetts, large crowds gathered to prevent British-appointed judges from holding court. They also forced many unelected officials to resign. In defiance of the royal governor, the people of Massachusetts elected a provincial congress with the power to collect its own taxes and raise its own army.

By the end of 1774, some colonists were preparing to fight. In Massachusetts, John Hancock headed the Committee of Safety, which had the power to call out the militia. In Virginia, House of Burgess member Patrick Henry delivered his most famous speech, calling for war:

### PRIMARY SOURCE

❝ Gentlemen may cry peace, peace—but there is no peace. The war is actually begun! The next gale that sweeps from the north will bring to our ears the clash of resounding arms! Our brethren are already in the field! Why stand we here idle? . . . I know not what course others may take; but as for me, give me liberty or give me death. ❞

—**Patrick Henry, quoted in *Patriots***

But most colonial leaders believed that any fight with Britain would be short. They thought that a public show of force would make the British Parliament change its policies.

▲ **SUMMARIZE** Explain what rights were threatened by the Intolerable Acts.

# The Revolution Begins

▼ **KEY QUESTION** Why did the fighting begin at Lexington?

Since 1770, Sam Adams had been building a network of informants to keep watch over British activities. The British had their spies too. It was from these spies that General Gage learned that the Massachusetts militia was storing arms and ammunition in Concord, about 20 miles northwest of Boston. He also heard that Sam Adams and John Hancock were nearby in Lexington. On the night of April 18, 1775, Gage ordered his troops to arrest Adams and Hancock in Lexington and to destroy the supplies in Concord.

**The Midnight Ride** The Sons of Liberty had prepared for this moment. **Paul Revere**, a Boston silversmith, and a second messenger, William Dawes, were sent to spread the news about British troop movements. Revere would cross the harbor from Boston to Charlestown. From there he would ride to Lexington and Concord. Dawes would take the land route.

Revere had arranged a system of signals to alert colonists across the harbor in Charlestown. One lantern burning in the Old North Church steeple signaled that the British troops were taking the land route out of Boston; two lamps meant that the troops were leaving Boston by water.

## CONNECTING ↻ *History*

### NEW ENGLANDERS OPPOSE THE KING

New Englanders had a long history of fierce opposition to royal authority. During the English Civil War of the 1640s, many New England Puritans returned to England to fight the king. They rejoiced when a republic was set up in England following the king's execution.

Over a century later, in the 1760s and 1770s, descendants of the Puritans were still angered by the same issues that had upset their ancestors:

- the levying of taxes without the people's consent
- the extent of the king's power
- the creation of a standing army that might threaten their freedom

Puritans execute King Charles I in London in 1649.

**CRITICAL THINKING** **Make Generalizations** Why was New England a hotbed of political protest?

# 7

1. The Early Years of the War
2. The War Expands
3. The Path to Victory
4. The Legacy of the War

Battle of Lexington

# The American Revolution

## 1775–1783

### ESSENTIAL QUESTION

How was it possible that American Patriots gained their independence from the powerful British Empire?

---

**CONNECT** 🔄 **Geography & History**

How might the geography of the United States have affected the course of the war?

**Think about:**

**1** how **Saratoga** lies in the Hudson River valley, a major gap through the Appalachian Mountains

**2** how **Yorktown** stands on the Chesapeake Bay, a wide body of water that allowed ships access to ports and plantations

**3** the distance between Britain and America, roughly 3,400 miles

Travel time: 4 weeks to 4 months

---

# 1775

Revolution begins at **Lexington** and **Concord.**

**1776** Declaration of Independence

After their victory at the **Battle of Long Island,** the British make New York their base of operations.

**1777** The American victory at **Saratoga** convinces foreign powers that America can win.

▼

**Effect** France enters the war on the American side.

**1778** The British capture **Savannah,** Georgia—their first major victory in their new Southern campaign.

192 Chapter 7

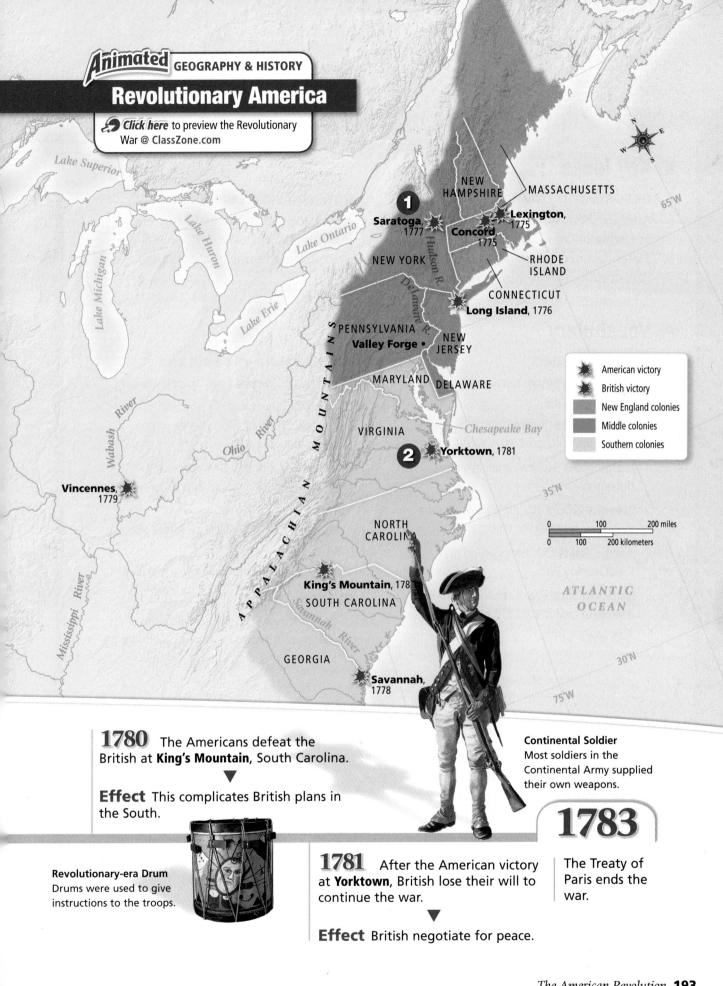

# Revolutionary America

*Click here* to preview the Revolutionary War @ ClassZone.com

**1** Saratoga, 1777

Lexington, 1775

Concord, 1775

NEW HAMPSHIRE

MASSACHUSETTS

RHODE ISLAND

CONNECTICUT

NEW YORK

Long Island, 1776

PENNSYLVANIA

Valley Forge •

NEW JERSEY

MARYLAND

DELAWARE

VIRGINIA

**2** Yorktown, 1781

*Chesapeake Bay*

Vincennes, 1779

NORTH CAROLINA

King's Mountain, 178

SOUTH CAROLINA

*Savannah River*

GEORGIA

Savannah, 1778

ATLANTIC OCEAN

Lake Superior

Lake Michigan

Lake Huron

Lake Erie

Lake Ontario

*Hudson R.*

*Delaware R.*

*Wabash River*

*Ohio River*

*Mississippi River*

A P P A L A C H I A N   M O U N T A I N S

65°W

35°N

30°N

75°W

| | American victory |
| | British victory |
| | New England colonies |
| | Middle colonies |
| | Southern colonies |

0   100   200 miles

0   100   200 kilometers

**1780** The Americans defeat the British at **King's Mountain**, South Carolina.

▼

**Effect** This complicates British plans in the South.

**Continental Soldier**
Most soldiers in the Continental Army supplied their own weapons.

**1783**

**Revolutionary-era Drum**
Drums were used to give instructions to the troops.

**1781** After the American victory at **Yorktown**, British lose their will to continue the war.

The Treaty of Paris ends the war.

▼

**Effect** British negotiate for peace.

## ▶ Key Ideas

**BEFORE, YOU LEARNED**

After the Revolutionary War broke out at Lexington and Concord, the United States declared independence from British rule.

**NOW YOU WILL LEARN**

Although the Continental Army had difficulty fighting in a divided America, the Patriots triumphed at Saratoga.

## ▶ Vocabulary

**TERMS & NAMES**

**George Washington**  commander of the Continental Army

**John Burgoyne**  (buhr•GOIN) British army general in the Revolutionary War

**Joseph Brant**  Mohawk chief allied with the British

**Benedict Arnold**  U.S. army general in the Revolutionary War who later turned traitor

**Horatio Gates**  U.S. army general in the Revolutionary War

**Battles of Saratoga**  (sair•uh•TOH•guh) a series of conflicts in 1777 near Albany, New York

**BACKGROUND VOCABULARY**

**neutral**  (NEW•truhl) not favoring any one side

**pacifist**  (PAS•uh•fist) someone who is opposed to all war

**mercenary**  (MUR•suh•NAIR•ee) a professional soldier hired to fight for a foreign country

**strategy**  (STRA•tuh•jee) an overall plan of action

**rendezvous**  (RAHN•day•voo) a meeting

**REVIEW**

**guerrillas**  (guh•RIL•uhz) small bands of fighters who weaken the enemy with surprise raids and hit-and-run attacks

## ▶ Reading Strategy

Re-create the diagram shown at right. As you read and respond to the **KEY QUESTIONS**, use the diagram to note important events and their effects. Add boxes or start a new diagram as needed.

 **See Skillbuilder Handbook, page R3.**

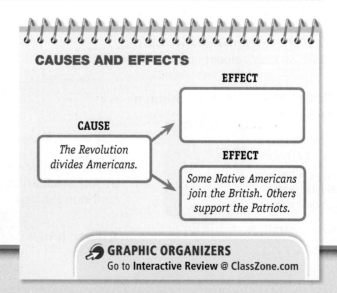

**CAUSES AND EFFECTS**

**CAUSE**

*The Revolution divides Americans.*

**EFFECT**

**EFFECT**

*Some Native Americans join the British. Others support the Patriots.*

**GRAPHIC ORGANIZERS**
Go to **Interactive Review** @ ClassZone.com

# The Early Years of the War

**6.4.E.2.** Discuss the major events . . . and personalities . . . of the American Revolution.
**6.4.E.4.** Explain New Jersey's critical role in the American Revolution, including major battles, . . . .

## One American's Story

When John Singleton Copley painted this portrait of his own Loyalist family, the Copleys had only recently escaped the violence of the Revolution. Copley's father-in-law (shown seated) lost his investments during the Boston Tea Party. Copley's wife (in the blue dress) lost her infant son during the siege of Boston. In the background stands Copley himself—an American who became one of the greatest painters in the British Empire.

Copley was born and raised in Boston. Before the war, he left Boston to study overseas. When he received news of the fighting in America, he wrote to his half-brother.

### PRIMARY SOURCE

❝ Could anything be more fortunate than the time of my leaving Boston? Poor America. I hope for the best, but I fear the worst. Yet certain I am she will finally emerge from her present calamity and become a mighty empire. ❞

—John Singleton Copley, letter to Henry Pelham

*The Copley Family*, by John Singleton Copley

Copley worried about his family as he traveled through Europe. Eventually, he found them safe in London. They had arrived with the first wave of Loyalist refugees. Copley painted this portrait after their reunion.

## Americans Divided

🔻 **KEY QUESTION** In what ways was the Revolution like a civil war?

The issue of separating from Britain divided American society. Historians estimate that 20 to 30 percent of Americans were Loyalists, 40 to 45 percent were Patriots, and the rest were **neutral**, or not favoring any one side.

**Americans Choose Sides** The conflict divided Americans along social, religious, and ethnic lines. New England and Virginia had many Patriots. Loyalists were numerous in cities, New York State, and the South. Judges, councilors, and governors tended to be Loyalists. Many Loyalists were clergy or members of the Church of England. Some Quakers were active Loyalists, although many were **pacifists**—people opposed to all war. The Patriots drew support from Congregationalists, Presbyterians, and Baptists.

Most Southern states did not allow African Americans to enlist. They feared that armed African Americans might lead slave revolts. In contrast, the British offered enslaved persons their freedom if they joined British forces. Many slaves ran away to fight for the British. In the North, however, about 5,000 African Americans served in the Continental Army.

The American Revolution was the largest Indian war in American history. All Native American nations east of the Mississippi were caught up in the fighting. Some Native Americans, like the Mohawks, joined the British because they feared Americans would take Native American land. Others, who lived within areas settled by the colonists, sided with the Americans.

▲ **CAUSES AND EFFECTS** Explain how the Revolution caused divisions among the population.

## Connecting History

**Dissent and Rebellion**
The oldest English settlements were in New England and Virginia. They both had a tradition of dissent and rebellion. *See Chapter 3, p. 72, Chapter 4, p. 104.*

**ONLINE PRIMARY SOURCE**

Hear the debate at the **Research & Writing Center** @ ClassZone.com

## COMPARING Perspectives

Patriots and Loyalists (or "Tories") viewed the political situation from radically different perspectives. These were some of the arguments heard as debate gave way to bloodshed.

### ◄)) Patriots Speak

❝ [Shall] a body of men in Great Britain, who . . . know nothing of us . . . invest themselves with a power to command our lives and properties . . . ?
—*a lady from Philadelphia*

If our Trade be taxed, why not our Lands, or Produce . . . in short, everything we possess? They tax us without having legal representation. ❞
—*Samuel Adams*

### ◄)) Loyalists Speak

❝ They call me a brainless Tory; but tell me, which is better—to be ruled by one tyrant three thousand miles away, or by three thousand tyrants not one mile away?
—*Mather Byles*

Whenever a . . . people . . . prevent the execution of laws, or destroy the property of individuals . . . there is an end of all order and government. . . ❞
—*Massachusetts Gazette, and Boston News-Letter*

### CRITICAL THINKING

1. **Analyze Primary Sources** What were the Loyalists' greatest fears? What angered the Patriots most?

2. **Analyze Point of View** What would you have said to oppose each argument listed above?

# Preparing for War

🔻 **KEY QUESTION** Why did both America and Britain have trouble raising an army?

In June 1775, Congress named **George Washington** commander of the Continental Army. This army faced many problems.

**Problems of the Army** At first, this new national army was formed from state militias, made up of untrained and undisciplined volunteers. The militia were part-time, emergency fighters who were not prepared for the hardship of a long war.

Washington's main goal was to keep the Revolution alive. To do so, he needed to keep an army in the field, win some battles—no matter how small—and avoid a crushing defeat. He knew he could not win a major battle until he had a large, well-trained army.

At the start of the war, Congress asked men to enlist only for one year. When the soldiers' time was up, they went home. As a result, Washington's army never numbered more than 17,000 men. In the early years of the war, Washington always worried about losing men whose enlistments had expired.

Congress's inability to supply the army also frustrated Washington. The soldiers lacked blankets, shoes, food, and even guns and ammunition.

Fortunately, many women helped the army. George Washington's wife Martha and other wives followed their husbands to camp. The women cooked, did laundry, and nursed sick or wounded soldiers. Some women even disguised themselves to help fight. Twenty-two-year-old Deborah Sampson dressed as a man, enlisted, and fought in several battles. But many women who never ventured near a battlefield also helped the nation by managing farms and businesses while their husbands were away fighting. In the days when women had few civil rights and freedoms, the war brought them greater responsibilities.

## History Makers

### George Washington  1732–1799

When Washington saw the army he was asked to lead, he was shocked by its disunity. Soldiers shared a common enemy but had no sense of national unity. Officers from different regions refused to co-operate with each other. Troops would only obey officers from their own province. Angrily, Washington wrote, "Could I have foreseen what I have experienced, and am likely to experience, no consideration upon earth would have induced me to accept this command." But Washington was determined to hold the army together. His efforts helped create a model of unity for the nation.

 **COMPARING** *Leaders*

As you read through the chapter, look for other examples of Washington's leadership. Compare his leadership qualities to those of British generals described in this chapter.

🔊 **ONLINE BIOGRAPHY**  For more on the life of George Washington, go to the **Research & Writing Center** @ ClassZone.com

**Britain Prepares** Many British viewed the Americans as disorganized, inexperienced rebels who would be easily defeated. In contrast to Washington's troops, the British army was experienced and professional. But the British military faced problems of its own. For personal and political reasons, many British officers refused to fight the Americans. Many British people were not enthusiastic about the war, so the king had trouble recruiting soldiers in

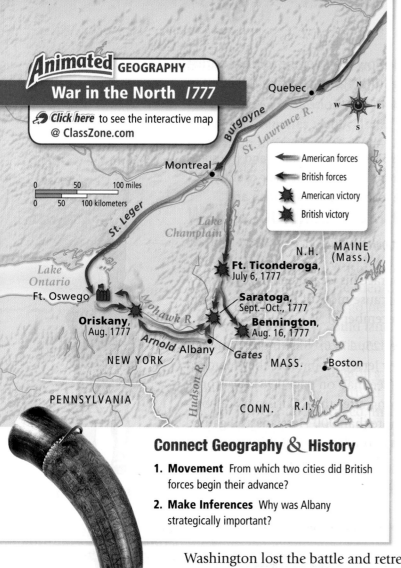

**Animated** GEOGRAPHY

**War in the North** *1777*

**Click here** to see the interactive map
@ ClassZone.com

Quebec

Burgoyne

St. Lawrence R.

Montreal

0    50    100 miles
0    50    100 kilometers

St. Leger

Lake
Champlain

Lake
Ontario

Ft. Oswego

St. Leger

N.H.    MAINE
(Mass.)

**Ft. Ticonderoga**,
July 6, 1777

**Saratoga**,
Sept.–Oct., 1777

Mohawk R.

**Oriskany**,
Aug. 1777

**Bennington**,
Aug. 16, 1777

Arnold   Albany   Gates

NEW YORK

MASS.   Boston

Hudson R.

PENNSYLVANIA

CONN.   R.I.

American forces
British forces
American victory
British victory

### Connect Geography & History

1. **Movement** From which two cities did British forces begin their advance?

2. **Make Inferences** Why was Albany strategically important?

**Powder Horn**
Revolutionary-era soldiers used horns like this to carry gunpowder.
**Why was horn a good material in which to store gunpowder?**

for the British. Burgoyne realized that the countryside was rising up against him. It was a lesson that other British generals would soon learn: they were not simply fighting an enemy army, they were fighting an entire people.

**Britain's Strategy Unravels** Burgoyne still looked forward to the **rendezvous**, or meeting, with St. Leger and Howe in Albany. But on August 4, Burgoyne received a message that Howe would not be coming north; instead, he had decided to try to capture Philadelphia—where the Continental Congress met. "Success be ever with you," wrote Howe. Yet Burgoyne needed Howe's soldiers, not his good wishes.

When Washington heard that Howe was heading south, he rushed to protect Philadelphia. However, in September 1777, Howe defeated Washington at Brandywine. (See map on page 198.) Howe then occupied Philadelphia. In October, Washington attacked Howe at Germantown. Again, Washington lost the battle and retreated to winter camp.

As Burgoyne received Howe's message, St. Leger faced his own obstacle in reaching Albany. In the summer of 1777, he was trying to defeat a small American force at Fort Stanwix, near Oriskany in the Mohawk River valley of New York. St. Leger's forces included Iroquois led by Mohawk chief **Joseph Brant**, also called Thayendanegea (thi•ehn•DAH•nah•gee•ah). Brant had been promised that the British would protect Iroquois land.

During August 1777, American general **Benedict Arnold** led an army up the Mohawk River. He wanted to chase the British away from Fort Stanwix. Arnold sent a captured Loyalist and some Iroquois to spread the rumor that he had a large army. The trick worked, and the British retreated to Fort Oswego. Now no one was left to rendezvous with Burgoyne.

🔺 **MAIN IDEAS & DETAILS** Explain Britain's northern strategy—and why it failed.

## Saratoga: A Turning Point

🔻 **KEY QUESTION** Why has Saratoga been called a "turning point"?

Burgoyne's army was running out of supplies. A raiding party was sent into Vermont where it was defeated by New England militia at the Battle of Bennington on August 16, 1777.

**British Advance on Albany** Despite these setbacks, Burgoyne's army continued south. But an American force led by General **Horatio Gates** blocked their way on a ridge called Bemis Heights, near Saratoga, New York. There the Polish engineer Tadeusz Kosciuszko (TAH•deh•oosh KAWSH•choosh•kaw) had helped the Americans create fortifications, or built-up earthen walls.

Starting on September 19, Burgoyne attacked the fortifications. While Gates commanded the Americans on the ridge, Benedict Arnold led an attack on nearby Freeman's Farm. His men repeatedly charged the British, with Arnold galloping through the battlefield "like a madman." Despite heavy casualties, the British held their position, but on October 7, Burgoyne was forced to retreat.

**Burgoyne Surrenders** Burgoyne's army moved slowly through heavy rain to a former army camp at Saratoga. By the time they arrived, the men were exhausted. The Continental Army then surrounded Burgoyne's army and fired on it day and night until Burgoyne surrendered. The series of conflicts that led to this surrender is known as the **Battles of Saratoga**.

The victory at Saratoga was a turning point. It prevented the British from dividing the States and isolating New England. It also showed Europeans that the Americans might win their war for independence. Because of this, some European nations hostile to Great Britain decided to help.

 **CAUSES AND EFFECTS** Explain why Saratoga has been called "a turning point."

**Connect** *to the* **World**

In London, after hearing the news of Burgoyne's surrender, William Pitt (Lord Chatham) warns Parliament: "You cannot conquer America."

---

**New Jersey Core Curriculum Content Standards *Review***

 **ONLINE QUIZ**
For test practice, go to
**Interactive Review @ ClassZone.com**

**TERMS & NAMES**

**1.** Explain the importance of

- George Washington
- John Burgoyne
- Joseph Brant
- Benedict Arnold
- Horatio Gates
- Battles of Saratoga

**USING YOUR READING NOTES**

**2. Analyze Causes and Effects** Complete the diagram you started at the beginning of this section. Then create a diagram for each of the other main events in this section.

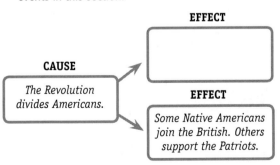

EFFECT

CAUSE

*The Revolution divides Americans.*

EFFECT

*Some Native Americans join the British. Others support the Patriots.*

**KEY IDEAS**

**3.** Why did the British want to control the Hudson River valley?

**4.** Why were the Battles of Saratoga important?

**CRITICAL THINKING**

**5. Analyze Graphs** The graph shows how colonists were divided in 1776. Why is it surprising that the Patriots won?

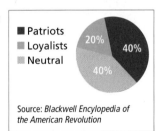

- ■ Patriots
- ▨ Loyalists
- ▦ Neutral

20%
40%
40%

Source: *Blackwell Encylopedia of the American Revolution*

**6. Connect *to* Today** Use of mercenaries was banned by a United Nations agreement in 1989. Why do you think this was?

**7. Writing Letter** Write a one-page letter from Burgoyne to General Howe. Respond to Howe's letter in which he says he will head to Pennsylvania. Describe how this news affects your strategy.

# Animated HISTORY

## BATTLE TACTICS

Click here to enter a Revolutionary War battlefield @ ClassZone.com

### Formal Battle

The majority of Revolutionary War battles followed a standard sequence. A battle would begin after the armies formed rows, or lines, facing each other. Americans used lines of both "regulars" (members of the Continental Army) and militia.

Click here First, field artillery (cannon) blast the enemy's lines.

Click here Next, front line soldiers advance to 50–100 yards of the enemy and fire muskets.

Click here Finally, soldiers attack with bayonets (knives attached to the end of a gun), while cavalry (soldiers on horseback) charge.

## Formal Battle and Guerrilla War

The militia's expert marksmanship played an important role in formal battles. However, the militia often practiced more informal guerrilla fighting. As part-time soldiers, they operated locally to disrupt supplies and communication and ambush enemy units. The militia ensured that the British could not depend on the countryside for supplies or support.

## Activity

### Take to the Battlefield!

1. Divide into two armies, one on each side of the room.

2. Each group then selects a "general," who divides them into these groups:
   • artillery  • infantry (front & second lines)  • cavalry

3. The two "generals" command their "troops" to move forward as they would in a formal battle.

## ▶ Key Ideas

**BEFORE, YOU LEARNED**

Despite the Continental Army's difficulties, the Patriots triumphed at Saratoga.

**NOW YOU WILL LEARN**

The expansion of the war weakened the British by forcing them to spread their military resources around the world.

## ▶ Vocabulary

**TERMS & NAMES**

**Marquis de Lafayette** (mahr•KEE•deh laf•eye•EHT) French aristocrat who volunteered to serve in Washington's army

**Valley Forge** site in southeast Pennsylvania where Washington and his army camped in the winter of 1777–1778

**George Rogers Clark** frontiersman who helped defend the Western frontier

**John Paul Jones** sea commander who attacked British ships near the British coast

**Wilderness Road** a trail into Kentucky

**BACKGROUND VOCABULARY**

**ally** (AL•eye) a country that agrees to help another country achieve a common goal

**desert** (duh•ZERT) to leave military duty without permission

**privateer** (pry•vuh•TEER) a privately owned ship that has been granted permission by a wartime government to attack an enemy's merchant ships

**Visual Vocabulary**
privateer

photograph courtesy of Peabody Essex Museum

## ▶ Reading Strategy

Recreate the diagram shown at right. As you read and respond to the **KEY QUESTIONS**, use the center box to record the main idea; use the outer ovals to note important details. Add ovals or start a new diagram as needed.

 **See Skillbuilder Handbook, page R2.**

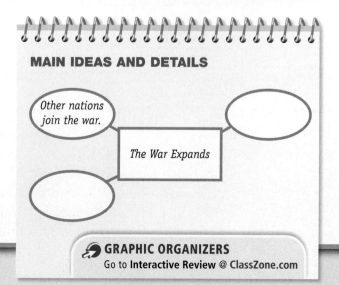

**MAIN IDEAS AND DETAILS**

*Other nations join the war.*

*The War Expands*

**GRAPHIC ORGANIZERS**
Go to **Interactive Review** @ ClassZone.com

# The War Expands

**6.4.E.2.** Discuss the major events . . . and personalities . . . of the American Revolution.
**6.4.E.3.** Identify major British and American leaders and describe their roles in key events, . . . .

## One American's Story

In 1778, General Washington hoped to take Newport, Rhode Island, from the British. The French had just entered the war, and their fleet had arrived to help the Americans. But a storm damaged the ships, and the Americans retreated, pursued by the British. A regiment of African Americans saved the day by holding the enemy at bay. An eyewitness described the bravery of the all-black First Rhode Island Regiment.

*The First Rhode Island Regiment*, by David R. Wagner

© David Wagner
http://davidrwagner.com

### PRIMARY SOURCE

❝ There was a black regiment in the same situation. Yes, a regiment of negroes, fighting for our liberty and independence,—not a white man among them but the officers. . . . Had they been unfaithful, or given way before the enemy, all would have been lost. Three times in succession were they attacked . . . and three times did they successfully repel the assault, and thus preserve our army from capture. ❞

—Dr. Harris, a veteran of the Battle of Rhode Island

In 1778 the war was expanding on many fronts. Not only were some states allowing African Americans to enlist, but foreign soldiers began arriving to help the American cause.

## Help from Abroad

🔻 **KEY QUESTION** Why did France and Spain enter the war?

The French were still bitter over their defeat by Britain in the French and Indian War, in which France lost its North American colonies. The French hoped to weaken the British by helping Britain's American colonies break free. In 1776, France began to give secret aid to the Americans. However, the French didn't become an overt American **ally** until the Americans had proved they could win a conventional battle against British forces. An ally is a country that helps another country achieve a common goal.

**France and Spain Enter the War** After hearing of the American victory at Saratoga, King Louis XVI of France publicly recognized U.S. independence. In 1778, France signed two treaties of alliance with the United States. By doing so, France went to war with Britain. As part of its new alliance, France promised to send badly needed funds, supplies, and troops to America.

In 1779, France persuaded its ally Spain to help the Americans, too. Spain was also Britain's rival. The Spanish governor of Louisiana, General Bernardo de Gálvez, acted quickly. He captured the British strongholds of Natchez and Baton Rouge in the lower Mississippi Valley. From there, his small army went on to take Mobile and, in 1781, Pensacola, in West Florida. These victories prevented the British from attacking the United States from the southwest. However, like France, Spain wanted more than just to help the United States. Gálvez's victories helped extend Spain's empire.

By entering the war against Britain, France and Spain forced the British to fight a number of enemies on land and sea. For instance, the British expected to have to fight the French in the West Indies, so they sent troops there. And thousands of British troops were busy fighting Gálvez in the west. The British now had to spread their military resources over many fronts.

## ANALYZE *Political Cartoons*

This cartoon was published in London in 1779, a year after France had formed an alliance with the United States. In political cartoons, sometimes a nation is represented by a figure wearing clothes associated with that nation. For example, in 18th-century cartoons, a Native American symbolized America. Here, figures representing different nations surround a sleeping figure representing Great Britain.

France is on the attack.

Scotland defends Britain.

Britain sleeps through the war.

America steals the cap of liberty.

Holland (whose merchants were trading with the Americans) picks Britain's pocket.

THE PRESENT STATE OF GREAT BRITAIN.

 **Skillbuilder Handbook, page R18.**

**CRITICAL THINKING**

1. **Analyze Point of View** Why would the cartoonist have shown Britain as sleeping?

2. **Make Inferences** Why is Holland shown picking Britain's pocket?

3. **Synthesize** What is the basic meaning of the cartoon?

**Foreign Officers Arrive** European military officers from France, Poland, and the German states came to Washington's aid. One of these was the **Marquis de Lafayette** (laf•eye•EHT), a 19-year-old French aristocrat who volunteered to serve in Washington's army. He wanted a military career, and he believed in the American cause. Soon after Lafayette arrived in June 1777, he was given the command of an army division and quickly gained Washington's confidence. Lafayette won his men's respect and love by sharing their hardships. Called "the soldier's friend," he used his own money to buy warm clothing for his ragged troops. Washington regarded him as a son.

Lafayette fought in many battles and also persuaded the French king to send a 6,000-man army to America. He became a hero in both France and the United States. Later he took part in France's own revolution.

Along with Lafayette came the Baron de Kalb, a German officer who had served in the French army. He became one of Washington's generals with a reputation for bravery.

🔺 **MAIN IDEAS & DETAILS** Tell why France and Spain entered the war.

## Winter at Valley Forge

🔻 **KEY QUESTION** How did Valley Forge transform the American army?

Help from France and Spain came when the Americans desperately needed it. As you have read, in late 1777 Britain's General Howe had forced Washington to retreat from Philadelphia. In the winter of 1777–1778, Washington and his army camped at **Valley Forge** in southeast Pennsylvania.

Marquis de Lafayette

**Hardship at Valley Forge** On the march to Valley Forge, Washington's army lacked supplies. Many soldiers had only blankets to cover themselves. They also lacked shoes. The barefoot men left tracks of blood on the frozen ground as they marched.

The soldiers' condition did not improve at camp. Over the winter, the soldiers at Valley Forge grew weak from not having enough food or warm clothing. Roughly a quarter of them died from malnutrition, exposure, or diseases such as smallpox and typhoid fever. Because of this suffering, the name Valley Forge came to stand for the great hardships that Americans endured in the Revolutionary War.

Washington appealed to Congress for supplies, but it was slow in responding. Luckily, private citizens sometimes helped the soldiers. On New Year's Day 1778, a group of Philadelphia women drove ten teams of oxen into camp. The oxen were pulling wagons full of supplies and 2,000 shirts. The women had the oxen killed to provide food for the troops.

**Patriotism Unites the Army** Despite the hardships, American soldiers showed amazing endurance. Under such circumstances, soldiers often **desert**, or leave military duty without permission. Soldiers did desert, but Lieutenant

## A Deadly Winter

Due to poor planning, thievery, and muddy roads, supplies were lacking during the army's winter camp at Valley Forge. An estimated 2,500 to 3,000 men died from exposure, disease, or malnutrition. According to the Marquis de Lafayette,

> The unfortunate soldiers were in want of everything; they had neither coats nor hats, nor shirts, nor shoes. Their feet and their legs froze until they were black, and it was often necessary to amputate them.

◀ The **amputation saw** was an important piece of the surgeon's kit.

### STRANGE BUT TRUE

A soldier in pain hated to see a surgeon approaching with this tool.

## What is it?

ANSWER: A tooth extractor

## Data File

**WHO** approx. 12,000 regulars, officers, and advisers

**WHAT** 14' x 16' log huts housed 12 privates each; officers had more space, depending on rank

**WHERE** 25 miles NW of Philadelphia

**WHEN** Dec. 19, 1777, to June 19, 1778

**WHY** near major crossroads, with plenty of wood and water

### HARDSHIPS AT VALLEY FORGE

- In February, almost 5,000 soldiers were too sick to fight; another 3,700 lacked either shoes or clothes.

- Shipments intended for troops were often stolen by government employees.

- Many local farmers were Loyalist and refused to sell food to the army. Others would not sell food because American currency was worthless.

- Common ailments included typhus and dysentery.

- Desertions exceeded 2,000. By February, 8–10 men were deserting each day.

- When frostbitten flesh dies, it turns black. The condition, called gangrene, can spread through the body and can be fatal. Amputations were performed without anesthetics or antiseptics, so amputees often died from infections anyway.

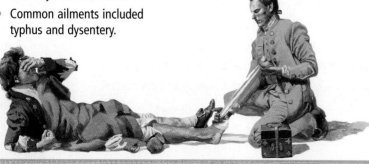

Colonel John Brooks wrote that the army stayed together because of the "Love of our Country." Once again, Washington's determination and patriotic vision inspired the troops to keep fighting.

**The Army Grows Stronger** Thanks to a German officer, the Baron von Steuben, the inexperienced American army was transformed into a skilled fighting force. Von Steuben began by forming a model company of 100 men. He taught them how to handle weapons properly. He also showed them how to fight the kind of formal battles favored by the British. (See Battle Tactics on page 202.) Within a month, the troops were executing drills with speed and precision. Because of this, the American army emerged from Valley Forge as a more efficient and stronger fighting machine.

▲ **SUMMARIZE** Describe how Valley Forge transformed the American army.

# Frontier Fighting

▼ **KEY QUESTION** Why did the war spread to the frontier?

In the late 18th century, the region between the Appalachian Mountains and the Mississippi River was known as the frontier; colonists had only just begun to settle there. In 1763, the British had tried to restrict settlement in this area and had built forts in the region. But some believed that the frontier should be open to settlement. In 1775 Daniel Boone helped build the **Wilderness Road**, a trail into Kentucky. Because Kentucky was claimed by Virginia in 1777, 24-year-old Kentuckian **George Rogers Clark** persuaded Virginia's governor, Patrick Henry, to allow him to raise an army to capture British outposts on the Western frontier. Clark wanted to expand the war into the frontier by attacking the British and their Native American allies in what is now Indiana and Illinois.

**Clark's Army** In May 1778, Clark led a group of frontiersmen to Kaskaskia, a British fort guarding the Mississippi River. They captured Kaskaskia without a fight.

Then they moved east to take Fort Sackville at Vincennes, in present-day Indiana. Earlier, a small force sent by Clark had taken Vincennes, but British forces under Henry Hamilton had recaptured it. Settlers called Hamilton the "Hair Buyer" because he supposedly paid rewards for American scalps.

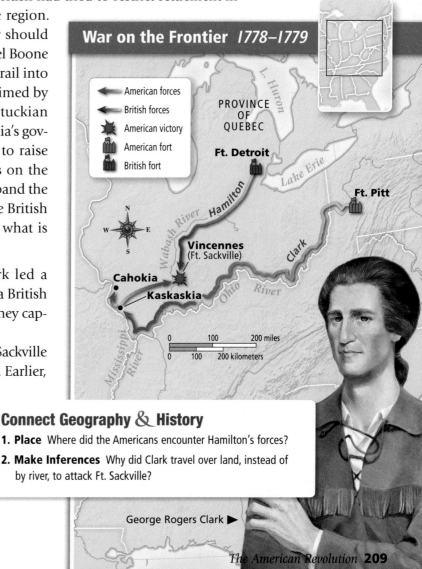

**War on the Frontier** *1778–1779*

- American forces
- British forces
- American victory
- American fort
- British fort

PROVINCE OF QUEBEC

L. Huron

Lake Erie

Ft. Detroit

Ft. Pitt

Hamilton

Wabash River

Vincennes (Ft. Sackville)

Cahokia

Kaskaskia

Clark

Ohio River

Mississippi River

0    100    200 miles
0    100    200 kilometers

**Connect Geography & History**
1. **Place** Where did the Americans encounter Hamilton's forces?
2. **Make Inferences** Why did Clark travel over land, instead of by river, to attack Ft. Sackville?

George Rogers Clark ▶

**Americans Seize the Frontier** Determined to retake Fort Sackville, Clark and his men set out for Vincennes from Kaskaskia in February 1779. Hamilton wasn't expecting an attack because the rivers were flooding the woods. But Clark's men slogged through miles of icy swamps and waded through chest-deep water. They caught the British at Vincennes by surprise.

When Hamilton and his troops tried to remain in the fort, Clark pretended to have a larger force than he really had. Clark also executed some Native American allies of the British in plain view of the fort. He threatened to do the same to the British unless they surrendered. Frightened, the British gave up.

Clark's victory gave the Americans a hold on the vast region between the Great Lakes and the Ohio River (even though Fort Detroit on Lake Erie remained in the hands of the British). This area was more than half the total size of the original 13 states. The expansion of the war into the frontier also had another consequence: it forced the British again to spread their troops over a larger area and further weakened the British war effort.

▲ **CAUSES AND EFFECTS** Explain why the war spread to the frontier.

## War on the Waves

▼ **KEY QUESTION** How did Americans expand the naval war?

The war expanded not only west into the frontier but also eastward to the high seas. By 1777, Britain had over 200 warships off the American coast. This allowed Britain to control the Atlantic trade routes to European markets.

James Forten, who later became famous for his efforts to end slavery, joined a privateer at the age of 14.

**British Trade Disrupted** Because the American navy was small and weak, Congress encouraged American **privateers** to attack British merchant ships. A privateer is a privately owned ship that has been granted permission by a wartime government to attack an enemy's merchant ships. After capturing a ship, the crew of a privateer sold its cargo and shared the money. America commissioned more than 1,000 privateers to prey on the British. They captured hundreds of ships, causing British merchants to call on their government to end the war.

Though outnumbered, the Continental Navy scored several victories. A daring officer named **John Paul Jones** inspired Americans by sailing across the Atlantic to attack British ships along the coast of Britain itself.

**"I Have Not Yet Begun to Fight"** In 1779, Jones became the commander of a ship named *Bonhomme Richard*. With four other ships, he patrolled the English coast. In September, Jones's vessels approached a convoy in which two British warships were guarding a number of supply ships.

Jones closed in on the *Serapis*, the larger of the two warships. At one point, the *Bonhomme Richard* rammed the better-armed British vessel. As the two ships locked together, the confident British captain demanded that Jones surrender. In words that have become a famous U.S. Navy slogan, Jones is said to have replied, "I have not yet begun to fight!"

The two warships were virtually locked together; the muzzles of their guns almost touched. They blasted away, each seriously damaging the other. On the shore, crowds of Britons gathered under a full moon to watch the fighting. After a fierce three-and-a-half-hour battle, the main mast of the *Serapis* cracked and fell. The ship's captain then surrendered. The *Bonhomme Richard* was so full of holes that it eventually sank, so Jones and his crew had to sail away in the *Serapis*!

Jones's success angered the British and inspired the Americans. Even so, the Americans knew that the war had to be won on land. The next section discusses the major land battles in the closing years of the war.

▲ **SUMMARIZE** Explain how Americans expanded the naval war.

*John Paul Jones,*
*by N. C. Wyeth*

---

 **New Jersey Core Curriculum Content Standards *Review***

🔍 **ONLINE QUIZ**
For test practice, go to
**Interactive Review @ ClassZone.com**

### TERMS & NAMES

**1.** Explain the importance of
- Marquis de Lafayette • John Paul Jones
- Valley Forge • Wilderness Road
- George Rogers Clark

### USING YOUR READING NOTES

**2. Main Ideas & Details** List the ways in which the war expanded from 1776–1779. For each, identify one key event and explain its importance.

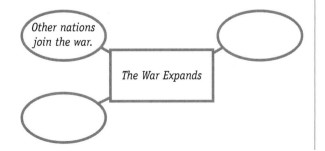

*Other nations join the war.*

The War Expands

### KEY IDEAS

**3.** List reasons why France decided to help America. Were Spain's reasons the same or different? Explain.

**4.** How did foreign officers help General Washington?

### CRITICAL THINKING

**5. Connect Economics & History** How did the alliance with France alter America's financial situation?

**6. Analyze Point of View** Why do you think so many Native Americans on the frontier supported the British?

**7.** **Connect** *to* **Today** Why has Valley Forge remained an important symbol of America's heritage?

**8.** **Math** Research to find out how many soldiers fought in Washington's army during each year of the Revolution. Then calculate the average size of the army throughout the war.

## ▶ Key Ideas

**BEFORE, YOU LEARNED**

The expansion of the war forced the British to spread their military resources over a wide area.

**NOW YOU WILL LEARN**

The Continental Army, their allies, and the American people brought about an American victory.

## ▶ Vocabulary

**TERMS & NAMES**

**Battle of Charles Town** British siege of Charles Town (Charleston), South Carolina, in May 1780, in which the Americans suffered their worst defeat of the war

**Lord Cornwallis** (korn•WAHL•ihs) British general whose campaigns in the South led to his defeat at Yorktown

**Battle of Yorktown** final battle of the war, in which French and American forces led by George Washington defeated British General Cornwallis

**BACKGROUND VOCABULARY**

**redoubt** (re•DOWT) a small fort

Visual Vocabulary
redoubt at Yorktown

## ▶ Reading Strategy

Re-create the diagram shown at right. As you read and respond to the **KEY QUESTIONS**, use the diagram to record important events in the order in which they occurred.

 **See Skillbuilder Handbook, page R5.**

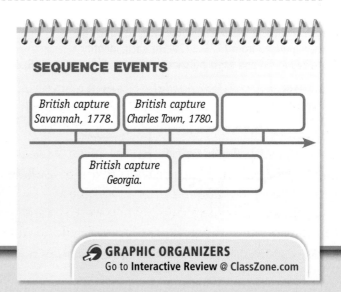

**SEQUENCE EVENTS**

British capture Savannah, 1778. → British capture Charles Town, 1780. →

British capture Georgia.

**GRAPHIC ORGANIZERS**
Go to **Interactive Review** @ ClassZone.com

# The Path to Victory

**6.4.E.2.** Discuss the major events . . . and personalities . . . of the American Revolution.
**6.4.E.3.** Identify major British and American leaders and describe their roles in key events, . . . .

## One American's Story

James P. Collins, a 16-year-old American, found himself in the midst of a civil war as the Revolution raged in the South. He watched as both sides committed war crimes. At the Battle of King's Mountain, fought on the border of North and South Carolina in October 1780, he saw American Patriots surround and slaughter about 1,000 American Loyalist militia, led by Major General Patrick Ferguson. Collins described the scene.

**PRIMARY SOURCE**

**❝** The dead lay in heaps on all sides, while the groans of the wounded were heard in every direction. I could not help turning away from the scene before me with horror and, though exulting in victory, could not refrain from shedding tears. **❞**

—James P. Collins, quoted in *The Spirit of Seventy-Six*

The Battle of King's Mountain

As James Collins's story demonstrates, fighting in the South was vicious.

## The War Moves South

🔻 **KEY QUESTION** What happened when the British shifted the war to the South?

After three years of fighting in the North, the British were no closer to victory. Although they had captured many important Northern coastal cities, they didn't have enough troops to control the countryside.

**The British Change Their Strategy** In 1778 the British decided to move the war to the South. They believed that most Southerners were Loyalists, who would support an invading British army.

The British also expected Southern slaves to escape and join them because they had promised to grant the slaves freedom. Although thousands of African Americans did join the British, not all were set free.

**Savannah and Charles Town Fall** In December 1778, the British captured the port of Savannah, Georgia. (See Map Ⓐ on p. 215.) They then conquered most of Georgia. In 1780, a British army led by General Henry Clinton landed in South Carolina. They trapped American forces in Charles Town (now Charleston), the largest Southern city. **The Battle of Charles Town** ended when the city surrendered. The Americans lost almost their entire Southern army. It was the worst American defeat of the war.

After that loss, Congress assigned General Horatio Gates—the victor at Saratoga—to form a new Southern army. Continental soldiers led by Baron de Kalb formed the army's core. Gates added about 2,000 new and untrained militia. He then headed for Camden, South Carolina, to challenge the army led by the British general **Lord Cornwallis**. (Cornwallis had assumed control of British forces after Clinton returned to New York.)

In August 1780, Gates's army ran into British troops outside Camden. (See Map Ⓐ on p. 215.) The Americans were in no condition to fight. They were out of supplies and half-starved. Even worse, Gates put the inexperienced militia along part of the frontline instead of behind the veterans. When the British attacked, the militia panicked and ran. Gates also fled,

## CONNECT ⟳ *To Today*

### MILITARY COMMUNICATION

In the 18th century, military communications were painfully slow. Ships from London might take up to four months to bring orders to British generals.

Mail did not travel much faster within America itself. British General Cornwallis was frustrated by the "delay and difficulty of conveying letters" and "the impossibility of waiting for answers." Not only were journeys long, but bands of Patriots made sure that British lines of communication were constantly disrupted.

Today, wars are fought with the help of technology that provides instant communication. Computers and satellites relay information quickly between sea, air, and ground forces. For example, a video of an attack on enemy forces in Afghanistan can be sent via satellite to the Florida command center and then relayed live to the White House.

A woman gives a message to an officer of the Continental Army.

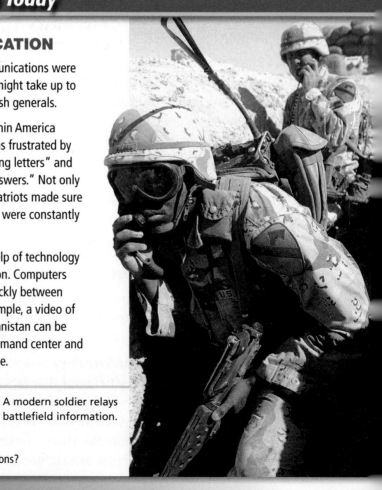

A modern soldier relays battlefield information.

### CRITICAL THINKING

1. **Draw Conclusions** Which side in the Revolutionary War would have suffered most from slow communications? Why?

2. **Evaluate** What are the advantages of today's faster communications?

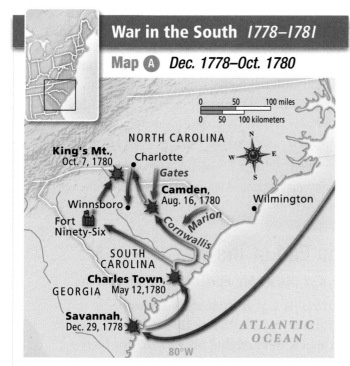

## War in the South *1778–1781*

**Map A** *Dec. 1778–Oct. 1780*

NORTH CAROLINA

King's Mt.,
Oct. 7, 1780  Charlotte
*Gates*
Camden,
Aug. 16, 1780
Winnsboro  Wilmington
Fort
Ninety-Six  *Marion*
SOUTH  *Cornwallis*
CAROLINA
Charles Town,
GEORGIA  May 12, 1780
Savannah,
Dec. 29, 1778  ATLANTIC
OCEAN
80°W

0   50   100 miles
0   50   100 kilometers

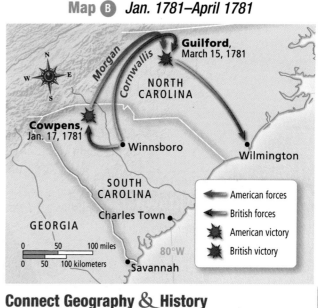

**Map B** *Jan. 1781–April 1781*

*Morgan*  *Cornwallis*  Guilford,
March 15, 1781
NORTH
CAROLINA
Cowpens,
Jan. 17, 1781
Winnsboro  Wilmington
SOUTH
CAROLINA
Charles Town
GEORGIA
80°W
Savannah

← American forces
← British forces
✦ American victory
✦ British victory

0   50   100 miles
0   50   100 kilometers

### Connect Geography & History

1. **Place** Where did the British begin their attacks in the South?

2. **Identify Problems and Solutions** Why do you think Cornwallis headed for the coast after the Battle of Guilford?

but de Kalb remained with his soldiers and received fatal wounds. This second defeat in the South ended Gates's term as head of an army. American spirits fell to a new low.

**Guerrilla War** Although the Americans had been defeated at Camden, the British were having difficulty controlling the South. The countryside was hostile and filled with more rebel sympathizers than Loyalists. Rebel guerrillas repeatedly attacked British messengers. This made it difficult for British forces moving inland to keep in touch with their bases on the coast. British commanders in the South were discovering what General Burgoyne had realized in the North: the countryside was a dangerous place for the British army.

One of the most famous rebel guerrilla leaders was Francis Marion, called the "Swamp Fox" because he led cunning attacks from his base in the swamps. An American officer described Marion's guerrilla band: "Their number did not exceed 20 men and boys, some white, some black, and all mounted, but most of them miserably equipped." Despite their poor equipment, Marion's men were able to cut the British supply line that led inland from Charles Town.

**General Greene Takes Charge** After Gates's defeat at Camden, Washington put Nathanael Greene in charge of the Southern army. Greene was one of Washington's best generals. In January 1781, he sent part of his army south to confront Cornwallis. In a formal, linear battle, the Americans won a spectacular victory at Cowpens. (See Map B above.) The victory proved that Americans had mastered the formal battle tactics of the British.

Cornwallis's main army now pursued Greene up into North Carolina. The British still had the advantage in a full-scale battle due to their greater firepower. However, the Americans used their knowledge of the landscape to keep one step ahead of the advancing British. Greene's strategy was to let the British wear themselves out. When the Americans did fight, they did their best to make sure the British suffered heavy losses. In fact, Cornwallis lost so many men at the Battle of Guilford Court House that he decided to retreat to Wilmington, on the coast. With his army exhausted, Cornwallis had to face a bitter truth: there were more active Patriots than Loyalists in the South. Britain's southern strategy had failed.

▲ **CAUSES AND EFFECTS** Explain what happened when the British shifted the war to the South.

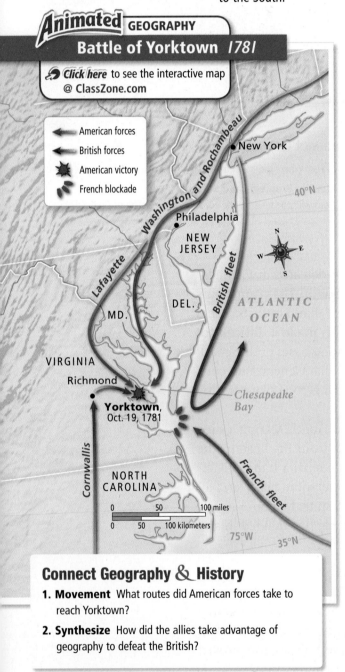

**Animated GEOGRAPHY**

**Battle of Yorktown** *1781*

🖱 *Click here* to see the interactive map @ ClassZone.com

American forces
British forces
American victory
French blockade

Washington and Rochambeau

New York

40°N

Philadelphia

NEW JERSEY

Lafayette

DEL.

British fleet

ATLANTIC OCEAN

MD.

VIRGINIA

Richmond

**Yorktown,** Oct. 19, 1781

Chesapeake Bay

Cornwallis

NORTH CAROLINA

French fleet

0       50      100 miles
0    50    100 kilometers

75°W

35°N

**Connect Geography & History**

1. **Movement** What routes did American forces take to reach Yorktown?

2. **Synthesize** How did the allies take advantage of geography to defeat the British?

## The End of the War

🔻 **KEY QUESTION** How was Cornwallis trapped?

Cornwallis was frustrated by his setbacks in the Carolinas. He had come to believe that Southern rebels were relying on Virginia for their supplies. So, in 1781, without waiting for orders, he marched north into Virginia. In August Cornwallis set up his base at Yorktown, located on a peninsula in Chesapeake Bay. From there, his army could receive supplies by ship from New York. It was a fatal mistake.

**Setting the Trap** Cornwallis's decision gave Washington a golden opportunity to trap the British on the peninsula. Washington first joined forces with General Jean Rochambeau's French army in New York and headed south. In August 1781, as these armies came south, a large French fleet arrived from the West Indies and blocked Chesapeake Bay. (See map at left.) The French fleet prevented the British ships from reaching Yorktown and delivering supplies—and prevented the British in Yorktown from escaping.

Meanwhile, the **Battle of Yorktown** had begun. The British tried to protect themselves by encircling the town with numerous **redoubts**, or small forts. These forts were meant to keep the allies' artillery at a distance from the town. But as the allies captured British redoubts, they brought their artillery closer to the town's defenses. The American and French cannon bombarded Yorktown, turning its buildings to rubble. Cornwallis had no way out. On October 19, 1781, he surrendered his force of about 8,000.

History *through* Art

Although fighting continued in the South and on the frontier, Yorktown was the last major battle of the war. When the British prime minister, Lord North, heard the news, he gasped, "It is all over!" Indeed, he and other British leaders were soon forced to resign. Britain's new leaders began to negotiate a peace treaty, which is discussed in the next section.

🔺 **SUMMARIZE** Describe how Cornwallis was trapped.

*The Surrender of Lord Cornwallis* by John Trumbull shows a British officer surrendering to a mounted American officer, with French troops on the left and Americans on the right. Unwilling to face public humiliation, Cornwallis pretended to be ill, sending General Charles O'Hara to offer his sword to the French. The French sent O'Hara to General Washington, who allowed General Benjamin Lincoln to accept the sword of surrender.

**CRITICAL VIEWING** How does the positioning of the troops symbolize the British defeat?

## Why the Americans Won

🔻 **KEY QUESTION** How were the Americans able to defeat the British?

By their persistence, the Americans won independence even though they faced many obstacles. As you have read, the American army lacked training and experience. American soldiers served only for short periods of time. They often lacked proper supplies and weapons. In contrast, the British forces ranked among the best trained in the world. Yet the Americans had advantages that had not been obvious at first; only as the war progressed did American strengths become apparent. The chart on the next page sets these American strengths against the weaknesses of the British.

The British were defeated not only by the American army, but by civilians who kept the resistance alive. The British were not prepared for a popular uprising. In Europe, only armies fought the wars, and civilians either fled or hid before advancing forces. In America, however, the British discovered that

# American Spirit

# RALLYING TO THE CAUSE

During the Revolution, American Patriots supported the war effort in a variety of ways. Why was popular support so important for the American victory?

## Teens in History

### RAISING THE LIBERTY POLE

Americans imagined liberty as a tree grown from a seed planted by the early colonists. Many American communities had a liberty tree (or pole) in the center of town that served as a meeting spot where Patriots rallied supporters and exchanged news.

### THE YOUNG ENLIST

Although the Continental Army was not supposed to enlist boys younger than sixteen, recruiters did not usually ask for proof of age. In fact, teenage boys made up a large proportion of the army. Posters like this one were designed to persuade young men to enlist.

TO ALL BRAVE, HEALTHY, ABLE BODIED, AND WELL DISPOSED YOUNG MEN, IN THIS NEIGHBOURHOOD, WHO HAVE ANY INCLINATION TO JOIN THE TROOPS, NOW RAISING UNDER GENERAL WASHINGTON, FOR THE DEFENCE OF THE LIBERTIES AND INDEPENDENCE OF THE UNITED STATES,

**TAKE NOTICE,**

> "To the enemies of our country! May they have cobweb breeches, a *porcupine saddle*, a hard-trotting horse, and an eternal journey!"

> "May the enemies of America be destitute of (lacking in) beef and claret (wine)"

### PATRIOTIC CURSES

Patriots raised their spirits by laughing at the enemy.

## PATRIOT POET

Phillis Wheatley, the first African-American writer to achieve fame, was a poet who supported the Patriot cause. During the war, Washington invited her to his headquarters after she sent him a poem that ended with this verse:

*"Proceed, great chief,
with virtue on thy side,
Thy ev'ry action
let the goddess guide.
A crown, a mansion,
and a throne that shine,
With gold unfading,
Washington be thine."*

## SECRET CODES

Information was often coded, in case letters fell into enemy hands. One kind of secret message did not look like a code at all, but lay hidden in an innocent-looking letter like the one shown here. By cutting the right shape out of another piece of paper and laying it on top of the letter, the secret message would be revealed.

## SPYING FOR THE CAUSE

Many women spied for the Patriots. The American-born Patience Wright worked in London as a sculptor. Some historians believe that she coaxed military information out of her subjects as she sculpted their likenesses. Then she apparently passed on the information to Patriot agents in London.

## Activity

### Decode a secret message!

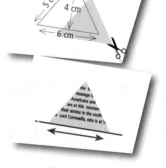

**1** In the middle of a sheet of paper, cut out a triangle with these dimensions:
Base: 6 cm; Height: 4 cm; Sides: 5 cm.

**2** Place the sheet over the message below. Align the base of the triangle with the blue line below the message. Then slide the sheet slowly from left to right until you find the secret message.

M. may have told you the secret news by this time. But, if you have not heard, the message is that the city of New York will be attacked by some Americans and French, who are growing bolder day by day and are at this moment moving their armies there. They will not take their armies to the south to attack British forces there because my Lord Cornwallis, who is at Yorktown, is not a threat.

## ▶ Key Ideas

**BEFORE, YOU LEARNED**
A combination of factors brought about an American victory.

**NOW YOU WILL LEARN**
Americans emerged from the Revolution as citizens of a unified nation that valued the ideal of liberty.

## ▶ Vocabulary

**TERMS & NAMES**

**Treaty of Paris** the 1783 treaty that ended the Revolutionary War

**Elizabeth Freeman** enslaved African American who won her freedom in court

**Richard Allen** African-American preacher who helped start the Free African Society

**Virginia Statute for Religious Freedom** statement of religious liberty, written by Thomas Jefferson

**BACKGROUND VOCABULARY**

**disputes** (dis•PYOOTS) disagreements

**outposts** (OWT•posts) military bases, usually located on the frontier

**nondenominational** not favoring any particular religion

Visual Vocabulary
outpost

## ▶ Reading Strategy

Re-create the spider diagram shown at right. As you read and respond to the **KEY QUESTIONS**, use the main branches to note categories of facts about results of the war. Add stems to record important details in each category.

 **See Skillbuilder Handbook, page R6.**

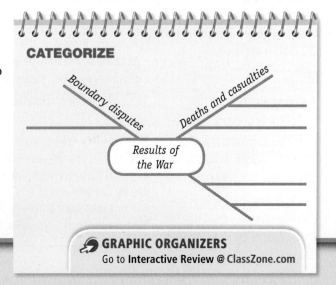

CATEGORIZE

Boundary disputes

Deaths and casualties

Results of the War

**GRAPHIC ORGANIZERS**
Go to **Interactive Review** @ ClassZone.com

# The Legacy of the War

**6.4.E.1.** Discuss the background and major issues of the American Revolution, including the political and economic causes and consequences of the revolution.
**6.4.E.3.** Identify major British and American leaders and describe their roles in key events, . . . .

## One American's Story

Haym Salomon, a Jew living in Poland, moved to New York before the Revolution in search of liberty. He soon became a successful merchant and banker. During the war, Salomon supported the Patriot cause.

When the British captured New York in 1776, Salomon was arrested. Because he spoke many languages, the British thought he could help them deal with foreign merchants, so they let him out of prison. Unfortunately, prison had permanently damaged his health.

In 1778, Salomon fled to Philadelphia. He loaned the new government more than $600,000, which was never repaid. Like many other Americans, Salomon had sacrificed his health and fortune to help his country survive.

A 1975 U.S. postage stamp honors Haym Salomon.

## Costs of the War

▼ **KEY QUESTION** What were the costs of the war?

No one knows exactly how many people died in the war, but eight years of fighting took a terrible toll. An estimated 25,700 Americans died in the war, and 1,400 remained missing. Over 8,200 Americans were wounded. Some were left with permanent disabilities, such as amputated limbs. The British military suffered about 10,000 deaths.

**Debts and Losses** Many soldiers who survived the war left the army with no money. They had received little or no pay. Instead of back pay, the government gave some soldiers certificates for land in the West. Many men sold that land to get money for food and other basic needs.

Both the Congress and the states had borrowed money to finance the conflict. The war left the nation with a debt of about $27 million—a debt that would prove difficult to pay off.

Those who supported the losing side in the war also suffered. Thousands of Loyalists lost their property. Between 60,000 and 100,000 Loyalists

## PAYING FOR THE WAR

The Continental Congress—our first national government—did not have the power to tax; it asked for funds and then hoped that the states would pay. It did have the power to borrow, however. Fighting the Revolutionary War cost America around $100 million, and by 1782, the new U.S. government was approximately $30 million in debt. To fund the Continental Army, the United States borrowed money in several ways.

| TREASURY NOTES | CERTIFICATES | PERSONAL NOTES |
|---|---|---|
| A treasury note states the government's promise to repay a specified amount at a specified date. Notes were sold to **patriotic investors** and to **foreign countries** such as France. | Printed money, known as "certificates," could be exchanged for an amount of silver—*if* the government had enough. This is how many **"regulars"** (soldiers), **farmers**, and **tradespeople** were paid. | **Wealthy individuals**, such as Haym Salomon and Robert Morris—the country's first superintendent of finance—issued personal notes (or loans) to pay government expenses. |
|  |  |  |

**Connect** *to* **Today** Do you think it's a good idea for a modern government to borrow money? Why or why not?

left the United States during and after the war. Among them were several thousand African Americans and Native Americans, including Mohawk chief Joseph Brant. Most of the Loyalists went to Canada. There they settled new towns and provinces. They also brought English traditions to areas that the French had settled. To this day, Canada has both French and English as official languages.

The Revolution had been a civil war that left both Patriots and Loyalists with bitter memories. Patriots found it especially difficult to forgive the former American general Benedict Arnold. In 1780 Arnold had betrayed his country by trying to turn over an American fort to the British. Throughout American history, the name Benedict Arnold is used to mean traitor.

▲ **SUMMARIZE** List some of the costs of the war.

## The Treaty of Paris

▼ **KEY QUESTION** What did America gain most from the Treaty of Paris?

Benjamin Franklin, John Adams, and John Jay began formal peace negotiations with the British on September 27, 1782. The final **Treaty of Paris**, which ended the Revolutionary War, was signed on September 3, 1783.

**Favorable Terms** The Americans won favorable terms in the peace treaty:

- The United States was independent.
- Its boundaries would be the Mississippi River on the west, Canada on the north, and Spanish Florida on the south.
- The United States would receive the right to fish off Canada's Atlantic Coast, near Newfoundland and Nova Scotia.
- Each side would repay debts it owed the other.
- The British would return any enslaved persons they had captured.
- Congress would recommend that the states return any property they had seized from Loyalists.

Neither Britain nor the United States fully lived up to the treaty's terms. Americans did not repay the prewar debts they owed British merchants or return Loyalist property. The British did not return runaway slaves.

**Boundary Disputes** The Treaty of Paris led to boundary **disputes**, or disagreements, with Spain, who could now claim control of both banks of the Mississippi river for over 100 miles north of the Gulf of Mexico. This Spanish control threatened American shipping. In the northwest, the British refused to give up military **outposts**, or bases, in the Great Lakes area, such as Fort Detroit.

## COMPARING  *Prewar and Postwar Boundaries*

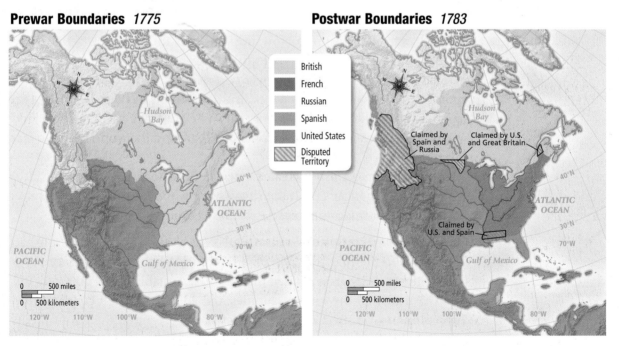

**Prewar Boundaries** *1775*

**Postwar Boundaries** *1783*

British
French
Russian
Spanish
United States
Disputed Territory

Claimed by Spain and Russia

Claimed by U.S. and Great Britain

Claimed by U.S. and Spain

### Connect Geography & History

1. **Place** What was the southern limit of British territory in 1775?

2. **Evaluate** Which foreign nation benefited most from the Treaty of Paris?

**The Threat to Native American Lands** The Treaty of Paris redrew the national boundaries with little concern for Native American interests. In Chapter 5, you learned that the British had attempted to keep white settlers away from Native American territory by establishing the Proclamation Line of 1763. Because of this, many tribes had supported the British in the war. But in the treaty, the British handed over Native American lands without even consulting their former allies. When Mohawk chief Joseph Brant heard the news, he was horrified by the betrayal.

**PRIMARY SOURCE**

❝ When I joined the English in the beginning of the War, it was purely on account of my forefathers' engagements with the King. I always looked upon these engagements, or covenants between the King and the Indian nation, as a sacred thing. ❞

—Joseph Brant, 1783

Joseph Brant, or Thayendanegea, was not born to be a chief but earned the esteem of his people by his leadership. The giant shell he wears is a symbol of wealth and status.

Native Americans who lived east of the Mississippi found themselves living within the boundaries of a new nation that was intent on westward expansion. Their lands were now at risk.

▲ **MAIN IDEAS & DETAILS** Identify what America gained from the Treaty of Paris.

## Creating a New Nation

▼ **KEY QUESTION** What ideals emerged from the Revolution?

"Liberty" had been the rallying cry of the Revolution as Americans freed themselves from British rule. Now, the success of the Revolution challenged the existing world order. For the first time in the Americas, a colonial rebellion against an imperial power had succeeded. By destroying British authority, the Revolution offered political reformers a chance to prove that republicanism, the idea that a country can be governed by the people, and without a king, could work. Imperial powers around the world began to fear this new threat.

At the same time, the war created a new nation—one that valued the ideal of liberty. As Americans built their new society, the ideal of liberty became one of the most important legacies of the Revolution.

**New State and National Governments** As early as 1775 British rule had become ineffective in many areas of the colonies. Eventually, in May of 1776, the Continental Congress advised the colonies to establish new governments. By 1777 nearly all the former colonies had adopted written constitutions. Two colonies—Connecticut and Rhode Island—retained the governments established by their royal charters.

All the new state constitutions contained some enumeration of individual rights and liberties. For instance, Virginia's new Constitution of 1776 was based on the Virginia Declaration of Rights. It protected many rights and guaranteed freedom of the press and freedom of religion. Some states, including Delaware, prohibited slavery and a state-supported religion. Georgia's constitution established public schools.

The states also realized early on that they needed a national government, if only to conduct the war. By 1777, the Continental Congress had drafted a plan: the Articles of Confederation. (The new government finally took charge in 1781.) The Articles gave very limited powers to the central government—little more than waging war and signing treaties. (See Chapter 8.)

**Freedom and Slavery** During the Revolution, some people began to see a conflict between slavery and the ideal of liberty. In response, Vermont outlawed slavery, and Pennsylvania passed a law to free slaves gradually. Individual African Americans also fought to end slavery, sometimes suing for freedom in the courts. For example, **Elizabeth Freeman** sued for her freedom in a Massachusetts court and won. Her victory in 1781 and other similar cases ended slavery in that state.

Freed African Americans formed their own institutions. For example, in Philadelphia **Richard Allen** helped start the Free African Society, a **nondenominational** group that encouraged people to help each other. (*Nondenominational* means not favoring any particular religion.) Richard Allen had earned the money to buy his freedom by working for the Revolutionary forces. As a preacher, Allen's leadership was shaped by his belief that he had a special duty to teach and help people, of all backgrounds, who had suffered from discrimination. Allen also founded the African Methodist Episcopal Church, the first African-American church in the United States.

Despite the efforts to end slavery in the North, in the South slavery continued. However, many people, including Southern plantation owners, were troubled by the new nation's dependence on slavery. In 1784, Thomas Jefferson, a slave owner himself, wrote of his fears for America if slavery were allowed to continue: "I tremble for my country when I reflect that God is just; that his justice cannot sleep forever."

**Connecting History**

**Regionalism**
The South's dependence on slavery would lead to a terrible civil war that threatened to tear apart the United States itself. You will see this theme emerge as you study events leading to the Civil War.

Richard Allen

**Defining Religious Freedom** For many Americans, central to the ideal of liberty was the idea that religion is a private matter and that people should have the right to choose and practice their personal religious beliefs. People such as James Madison and Thomas Jefferson called for a "separation of church and state," meaning that the state should not be involved in religious affairs.

In 1777 Thomas Jefferson proposed his **Virginia Statute for Religious Freedom**. In it, he claimed that people have a "natural right" to freedom of opinion, including religious opinion. Jefferson opposed state laws that prohibited Jews or Catholics from holding public office. He also opposed the practice of using tax money to support churches, because, he wrote, "to compel a man to furnish contributions of money for the propagation of opinions which he disbelieves, is sinful and tyrannical."

Jefferson's statute was eventually adopted as law in Virginia. Later, it became the basis of the religious rights guaranteed by the Bill of Rights in the U.S. Constitution.

**Uniting the States** For almost two centuries each colony had been governed independently of its neighbors. The colonies had been quarrelsome and often uncooperative. However, as the war turned colonies into states, Americans saw how important it was for these states to work together as a nation. The great challenge that lay ahead was how to remain united as a nation of independent states, despite regional and religious differences.

 **SUMMARIZE** Describe the ideals that emerged from the Revolution.

---

 **New Jersey Core Curriculum Content Standards** *Review*

**ONLINE QUIZ**
For test practice, go to
**Interactive Review @ ClassZone.com**

### TERMS & NAMES

**1.** Explain the importance of

- Treaty of Paris
- Elizabeth Freeman
- Richard Allen
- Virginia Statute for Religious Freedom

### USING YOUR READING NOTES

**2. Categorize** List and categorize the major results of the Revolutionary War.

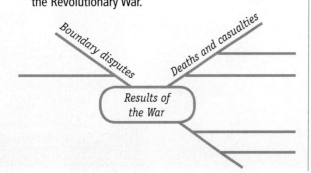

Boundary disputes

Deaths and casualties

Results of the War

### KEY IDEAS

**3.** What groups gained least from the Treaty of Paris?

**4.** How did the goals of the Revolution guide Americans toward a more just society after the war?

### CRITICAL THINKING

**5. Connect Economics & History** How did the Treaty of Paris protect America's economic interests?

**6. Causes and Effects** How did the Patriot victory affect Native Americans?

**7. Historical Perspective** What might have happened if, during the peace negotiations, each state had tried to negotiate independently?

**8.** **Writing** **Citizenship Report** Use the Internet to research Elizabeth Freeman and Richard Allen. Write a brief report explaining how their efforts helped improve their communities.

## Chapter Summary

**1** **Key Idea**
Although the Continental Army had difficulty fighting in a divided America, the Patriots triumphed at Saratoga.

**2** **Key Idea**
The expansion of the war weakened the British by forcing them to spread their military resources around the world.

**3** **Key Idea**
The Continental Army, their allies, and the American people brought about an American victory.

**4** **Key Idea**
Americans emerged from the Revolution as citizens of a unified nation that valued the ideal of liberty.

 To create **Review and Study Notes** go to **Interactive Review** @ ClassZone.com

## Name Game

**Use the Terms & Names list to complete each sentence online or on your own paper.**

1. I carried the war to the western frontier. George Rogers Clark 🖑

2. I led my troops to defeat at Saratoga. ____

3. I was a French officer who fought for America. ____

4. My leadership unified a nation. ____

5. I was trapped between allied forces and the French fleet. ____

6. I brought the war to the coasts of Britain. ____

7. The ideal of liberty helped me win my freedom in court. ____

8. I lost my lands when my ally betrayed me. ___

9. Here the Patriots first proved that they might win the war. ____

10. Here the Continental Army endured a difficult winter. ____

A. Joseph Brant
B. John Paul Jones
C. George Rogers Clark
D. Benedict Arnold
E. Valley Forge
F. Richard Allen
G. John Burgoyne
H. Marquis de Lafayette
I. Treaty of Paris
J. George Washington
K. Horatio Gates
L. Lord Cornwallis
M. Elizabeth Freeman
N. Yorktown
O. Saratoga

## Activities

### CROSSWORD PUZZLE

Complete the online crossword puzzle to show what you know about the American Revolution.

**ACROSS**
**1.** _____ captured the British warship *Serapis*.

### GEOGAME

Use this online map to reinforce your understanding of the Revolutionary War, including the locations of important battles and geographic features. Drag and drop each place name in the list at its location on the map. A scorecard helps you keep track of your progress online.

Trenton

Saratoga

Lake Ontario

Valley Forge

Hudson River

More place names online

## VOCABULARY

**Explain the significance of each of the following:**

1. Joseph Brant
2. Treaty of Paris
3. Battles of Saratoga
4. privateer
5. Battle of Yorktown
6. neutral
7. Richard Allen
8. Valley Forge
9. guerrilla
10. George Washington

**Explain how the terms and names in each group are related.**

11. George Washington, Marquis de Lafayette, Valley Forge, mercenary

12. John Burgoyne, Horatio Gates, Benedict Arnold

13. Lord Cornwallis, Battle of Yorktown, redoubt

Marquis de Lafayette

## KEY IDEAS

**① The Early Years of the War (pages 194–201)**

14. What difficulties did the Americans have in readying a military force to fight the Revolutionary War?

15. What events led to British defeat at Saratoga?

**② The War Expands (pages 204–211)**

16. Explain the importance of George Rogers Clark and John Paul Jones in expanding the war.

17. Explain three effects of America's alliances with France and Spain.

**③ The Path to Victory (pages 212–219)**

18. Why did the British decide to attack the South?

19. Describe the tactics and technologies used during the fighting in the Southern colonies.

**④ The Legacy of the War (pages 222–228)**

20. In what ways did the Treaty of Paris of 1783 favor America?

21. Describe three challenges America faced after defeating Britain.

## CRITICAL THINKING

22. **Causes and Effects** How did shortages of soldiers and supplies affect Washington's plans at the start of the war?

23. **Summarize** Summarize the role of Britain's navy in the war.

24. **Compare** Create a table to compare and contrast the battles of Saratoga and Yorktown. After you complete your table, explain the significance of each battle.

| Battles of Saratoga | Battle of Yorktown |
|---|---|
| *mountainous* | *town* |
| *wooded terrain* | *flat land* |

25. **Synthesize** Why did the war last such a long time?

26. **Evaluate** Refer to the "American Strengths/British Weaknesses" chart on page 218. Which British weakness do you think proved most important in the Patriot victory? Explain your choice.

27. **Draw Conclusions** How was America able to overcome its lack of resources and soldiers?

28. **Interpret Graphs** Study the graph below. How do you explain the change in data from 1779 to 1780?

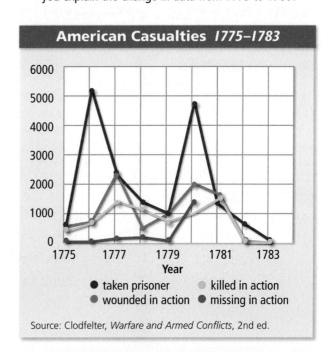

Source: Clodfelter, *Warfare and Armed Conflicts*, 2nd ed.

☑ **TEST PRACTICE**

• **Online Test Practice @ ClassZone.com**
• **Test-Taking Strategies & Practice** at the front of this book

## DOCUMENT-BASED QUESTIONS

### PART 1: Short Answer

**Analyze each document, and answer the questions that follow.**

### DOCUMENT 1

1. This artwork shows Catherine Van Rensselaer Schuyler, the wife of American general Philip Schuyler, setting fire to her own family's fields near Saratoga, New York, in 1777. Why is Mrs. Schuyler burning her fields?

### DOCUMENT 2

#### PRIMARY SOURCE

**❝** When ... it [became] impossible for any but the wealthiest to import anything to eat or wear, and all had to be raised and manufactured at home, from bread stuffs, sugar, and rum to the linen and woollen for our clothes and bedding, you may well imagine that my duties were not light. **❞**

—Temperance Smith

2. Temperance Smith wrote this while her husband was serving at Fort Ticonderoga during the American Revolution. How did Temperance Smith's life change during the war?

### Part 2: Essay

3. In two or three short paragraphs, explain how civilians contributed to the Patriot victory in the Revolutionary War. Use information from your answers to Part 1 and your knowledge of U.S. history.

## YOU BE THE HISTORIAN

29. **Make Judgments** Do you think America was stronger before or after the war? Explain and justify your opinion.

30. **Causes and Effects** How did the war change the daily life of an average merchant or farm family?

31. **WHAT IF?** Suppose France had not come to America's aid. In what ways would this have affected Washington's ability to defeat the British?

32. **Analyze Motives** Why do you think most Patriots who fought the Revolutionary War to protect liberty did not try to banish slavery?

33. **Citizenship** How did independence change Americans' responsibilities as citizens?

    **Connect** *to* **Today** Give some examples of how people in your community fulfill these responsibilities today.

Answer the

## ESSENTIAL QUESTION

**How was it possible that American Patriots gained their independence from the powerful British Empire?**

**Written Response** Write a four-paragraph response to the Essential Question. Be sure to consider the key ideas of each section as well as the most significant factors that led to the American victory. Use the Response Rubric below to guide your thinking and writing.

### Response Rubric

**A strong response will**

• discuss major events that led to the American victory
• analyze American strengths and British weaknesses
• explain the importance of strong leadership
• describe the role of allies in the war.

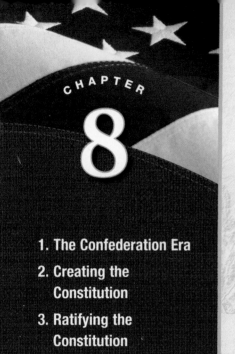

# CHAPTER 8

# Confederation to Constitution

## 1776–1791

1. The Confederation Era
2. Creating the Constitution
3. Ratifying the Constitution

 **ESSENTIAL QUESTION**

How did Americans create a national government that respected both the independence of states and the rights of individuals?

---

**CONNECT** ⟳ **Geography & History**

**How might the geography of the United States have affected the policies of the new national government?**

**Think about:**

**1** the newly acquired territory between the Appalachian Mountains and the Mississippi River

**2** the regions with the densest population concentration

**3** the distance between Maine and Georgia, about 1,300 miles

---

Independence Hall as it appeared in 1776.

## 1776

American independence

**1777** Continental Congress passes the Articles of Confederation.

**1781** Articles of Confederation passed.

▼

**Effect** The United States has its first national government.

This early flag has 13 stars representing the original 13 colonies.

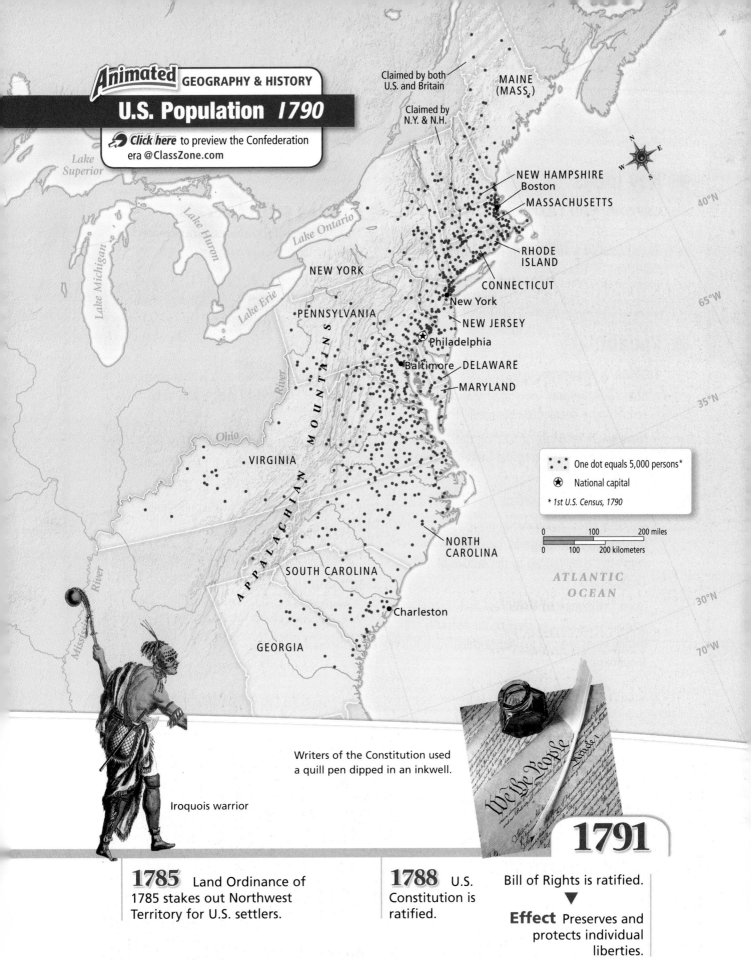

Lake Superior

Lake Michigan

Lake Huron

Lake Ontario

Lake Erie

Claimed by both U.S. and Britain

MAINE (MASS.)

Claimed by N.Y. & N.H.

NEW HAMPSHIRE
Boston
MASSACHUSETTS

RHODE ISLAND

CONNECTICUT

40°N

NEW YORK

PENNSYLVANIA

New York

NEW JERSEY

Philadelphia

65°W

Baltimore    DELAWARE

MARYLAND

35°N

River

Ohio

A P P A L A C H I A N   M O U N T A I N S

VIRGINIA

· · · One dot equals 5,000 persons*

★ National capital

* *1st U.S. Census, 1790*

NORTH CAROLINA

SOUTH CAROLINA

0    100    200 miles
0    100    200 kilometers

ATLANTIC OCEAN

30°N

Mississippi River

Charleston

GEORGIA

70°W

Writers of the Constitution used a quill pen dipped in an inkwell.

We the People

Iroquois warrior

**1791**

**1785** Land Ordinance of 1785 stakes out Northwest Territory for U.S. settlers.

**1788** U.S. Constitution is ratified.

Bill of Rights is ratified.
▼
**Effect** Preserves and protects individual liberties.

## ▶ Key Ideas

**BEFORE, YOU LEARNED**
Americans emerged from the Revolution as citizens of a unified nation that valued the ideal of liberty.

**NOW YOU WILL LEARN**
The Articles of Confederation created a weak national government.

## ▶ Vocabulary

**TERMS & NAMES**

**Shays's Rebellion** uprising of Massachusetts farmers who demanded debt relief

**Northwest Territory** lands northwest of the Appalachians, covered by the Land Ordinance of 1785

**Articles of Confederation** plan for national government ratified in 1781

**Confederation Congress** national legislative body formed by the Articles of Confederation

**Land Ordinance of 1785** law that established a plan for dividing the federally owned lands west of the Appalachian Mountains

**Northwest Ordinance** law that described how the Northwest Territory was to be governed

**BACKGROUND VOCABULARY**

**republic** state, country or nation in which people elect representatives to govern.

**ratification** act of official confirmation

**levy** impose or raise a tax

**arsenal** place where weapons are stored

**REVIEW**

**neutral** not siding with one country or another

## ▶ Reading Strategy

Create an outline like the one shown at right. As you read and respond to the **KEY QUESTIONS**, note the main ideas and supporting details about the Articles of Confederation.

 **See Skillbuilder Handbook, page R9.**

**MAIN IDEAS & DETAILS**

**The Articles of Confederation**

I. Features of the A. of C.
   —
   —
II. Needs addressed by the A. of C.
   —
   —

 **GRAPHIC ORGANIZERS**
Go to **Interactive Review** @ ClassZone.com

# The Confederation Era

**6.4.E.1. Discuss** the background and major issues of the American Revolution, including the political and economic causes and consequences of the revolution.
**6.4.E.3.** Identify major British and American leaders and describe their roles in key events, . . . .

## One American's Story

After the Revolutionary War, the nation faced hard economic times. People had little money, but the states continued to levy high taxes. In Massachusetts, many farmers fell deeply into debt.

### PRIMARY SOURCE

❝ I have been obliged to pay and nobody will pay me. I have lost a great deal by this man and that man . . . and the great men are going to get all we have, and I think it is time for us to rise and put a stop to it. . . . ❞

—Plough Jogger, quoted in *The People Speak: American Voices, Some Famous, Some Little Known*

Shays's rebels take over a Massachusetts courthouse. Today a stone marker rests on the spot of the rebellion.

From August 1786 to February 1787, Daniel Shays, a Revolutionary War veteran, led Jogger and other farmers in an armed uprising. To protest what the farmers viewed as unfair taxation, they attacked county courts in Massachusetts. At first, using force, they succeeded in stopping the courts from selling farmers' possessions and jailing people who couldn't pay their debts.

The state militia put down **Shays's Rebellion**, as the uprising came to be known. But many people sided with the farmers. America's leaders realized that a popular armed uprising spelled danger to the new nation. It was clearly time to talk about a stronger national government.

## Forming a New Government

🔻 **KEY QUESTION** What did the states want from a national government?

Ten years before Shays's Rebellion, the colonists had resisted the harsh rule of a distant government. As Americans planned their first national government, in 1776-1777, their main goal was to prevent governmental tyranny from reappearing in the new nation.

**Republicanism and Citizenship** American leaders felt strongly that the people needed to exercise control over their government. It was decided that the new nation would be a **republic**, a country in which the people choose representatives to govern them. But not everyone in the United States would be allowed to help select these representatives. Most states had fairly high property qualifications, and only property owners, who were considered citizens, would be allowed to vote. African Americans were generally not allowed to vote. Some states granted voting rights to all white males. All states, except Pennsylvania and Georgia, made property ownership a requirement for voting. Women were also denied the right to vote in most states.

**State Constitutions Lead the Way** Once the American colonies declared independence in 1776, each of the states set out to create its own government. The framers, or creators, of the state constitutions did not want to destroy the political systems that they had had as colonies. They simply wanted to make those systems more representative.

Some states experimented with giving different powers to different parts of government. By creating separate branches of government, Americans hoped to prevent any one part of the government from becoming too powerful. All state governments limited the powers of their governors because of the colonists' unpleasant experience with the British king.

Some states included a Bill of Rights in their constitutions. Based on the English Bill of Rights of 1689, these bills were lists of freedoms that Americans were most eager to protect. The first constitutional document in the United States was Virginia's constitution of 1776. It protected freedom of the press and freedom of religion.

As citizens set up their state governments, they discussed how to form a national government. During the Revolutionary War, Americans realized that they had to unite to win the war against Britain. Forming a national government was key to national unity. And diplomat John Dickinson's words, "By uniting we stand, by dividing we fall," became a popular slogan.

**The Articles of Confederation** In 1776, the Continental Congress began to plan for a national government. Congress agreed that the government should be a republic. But the delegates disagreed about whether each state should have one vote or voting should be based on population.

They also disagreed about who should control the **Northwest Territory**, or the lands west of the Appalachians. The Continental Congress eventually arrived at a plan called the **Articles of Confederation**. In the Articles, the national government would be run by a legislative body to be called the **Confederation Congress**. Congress had the power to wage war, make peace, sign treaties, run Indian affairs, and issue money. Each state had only one vote in the Congress.

## Powers Granted and Denied Congress

| GRANTED CONGRESS | DENIED CONGRESS |
|---|---|
| • Conduct foreign affairs | • Establish executive branch |
| • Declare war and make peace | • Enforce national laws |
| • Issue or borrow money | • Enact and collect taxes |
| • Control Western territories | • Regulate interstate or foreign trade |
| • Control Indian affairs | • Establish federal courts |
| • Run postal service | • Amend the Articles |

**CRITICAL THINKING** **Evaluate** Why did the powers denied Congress lead to a weak government?

But the Articles left most important powers to the states. These powers included the authority to set taxes and enforce national laws. The proposed Articles left the individual states in control of the lands west of the Appalachian Mountains.

**The Articles Are Ratified** The Continental Congress passed the Articles of Confederation in November 1777. It then sent the Articles to the states for **ratification,** or approval. By July 1778, eight states had ratified the Articles. But some of the small states that did not have Western land claims refused to sign. These states worried that they would be at a disadvantage unless the Western lands were placed under the control of the national government. The states with Western lands could sell them to pay off debts left from the Revolution and possibly become overwhelmingly powerful. But states without lands would have difficulty paying off the high war debts.

Gradually, all the states gave up their claims to Western lands. This led the small states to ratify the Articles. In 1781, Maryland became the 13th state to accept the Articles. As a result, the United States finally had an official government.

▲ **SUMMARIZE** Discuss the powers of the states under the Articles of Confederation.

**Western Land Claims** *1789*

**Connect Geography & History**

1. **Location** How far west did the Western land claims extend?

2. **Draw Conclusions** The western lands were vast. What might be some of the challenges of governing such a large territory?

# Strengths and Weaknesses of the Articles

▼ **KEY QUESTION** What were the weaknesses of the national government?

The Confederation Congress had run the country during the Revolutionary War and had some success in handling land issues. But Americans began to realize the Confederation Congress was too weak to deal with most other national issues.

**The Land Ordinance of 1785** One issue the Confederation Congress successfully handled was what to do with the Western lands that it now controlled. Starting in 1785, the Congress passed important laws on how to divide and govern these lands.

The **Land Ordinance of 1785** called for surveyors to stake out six-mile-square plots, called townships, in the Western lands. These lands later became known as the Northwest Territory. The Northwest Territory included land that formed the states of Ohio, Indiana, Michigan, Illinois, Wisconsin, and part of Minnesota.

**Governing the Northwest Territory** The **Northwest Ordinance** of 1787 outlined how the Northwest Territory was to be governed. The bill had many democratic features. As the territory grew in population, it would gain rights to self-government. When there were 5,000 free adult males in an area, men who owned at least 50 acres of land could elect an assembly. When there were 60,000 people, they could apply to become a new state. Slavery was outlawed. Rivers were to be open to navigation for all. Freedom of religion and trial by jury were guaranteed.

The Northwest Ordinance was a big success for the Confederation Congress. The bill created a model for the orderly growth of the United States well into the 19th century. But the Northwest Ordinance was bad for the lands' original inhabitants. The Ordinance promised Native Americans fair treatment, and Native American lands were not to be taken from them. However, the increased contact between settlers and natives led to territorial conflicts that were not easily resolved.

**Problems with Britain and Spain** To fight the Revolutionary War, Congress had borrowed large sums of money. With the war over, it was now time to pay back the loans. Yet the Confederation Congress did not have the money to do so. Congress also found that it did not have the power to deal on an equal basis with other nations. Some of the challenges Congress faced with other nations were:

- Britain competed against the American fur trade by refusing to evacuate its military forts south of the Great Lakes.
- Britain barred American-owned ships from British waters in the Caribbean.
- Spain also put up barriers to American shipping in the Caribbean.
- Spain refused to allow Americans to use the Mississippi River or to deposit goods in New Orleans.
- Spain and Congress argued over the boundary of Florida.

In the late 1700s, Spain held the crucial port of New Orleans. **Why did this have an impact on American traders?**

The problems the Confederation faced in foreign relations revealed the basic weaknesses of the national government. The United States did not have the strength to face up to the superior forces of the British or the Spanish.

**Economic Problems and Shays's Rebellion** With American trade weakened, the nation was facing a serious economic crisis. Much of the Confederation's debt was owed to soldiers of the Revolutionary army. Upset at not being paid, approximately 300 soldiers demonstrated before the Pennsylvania State House where Congress was meeting in June 1783. The delegates were forced to flee the city. The event was another clear sign of Congress's weakness.

One reason Congress was unable to raise money to pay the soldiers was that it did not have the power to **levy**, or collect, taxes. The national government depended on the states to send money. The states, who also owed money because of the war, tried to raise money through taxes. However, few ordinary Americans could afford to pay them. Taxes on imported goods raised the cost of everyday necessities, further hurting average Americans.

Taxes in Massachusetts were some of the highest in the nation. The government's refusal to grant debt relief led to an uprising known as Shays's Rebellion. In January 1787, Shays led a march on a federal **arsenal**, a place where weapons are stored. Around one thousand soldiers from the state militia quickly defeated Shays's men.

America's leaders realized that an armed uprising of common farmers spelled danger for the nation. Some leaders hoped that the nation's ills could be solved by giving more power to the national government.

 **PROBLEMS AND SOLUTIONS** Identify the reasons why the national government was not strong enough.

---

**New Jersey Core Curriculum Content Standards *Review***

 **ONLINE QUIZ**
For test practice, go to
**Interactive Review @ ClassZone.com**

**TERMS & NAMES**

**1.** Explain the importance of
- Shays's Rebellion
- Confederation Congress
- Northwest Territory
- Land Ordinance of 1785
- Articles of Confederation
- Northwest Ordinance

**USING YOUR READING NOTES**

**2. Problems and Solutions** Complete the outline you started at the beginning of this section.

> **The Articles of Confederation**
>
> I. *Features of the A. of C.*
> —
> —
>
> II. *Needs addressed by the A. of C.*
> —
> —

**KEY IDEAS**

**3.** How did the Articles of Confederation prevent the national government from becoming too powerful?

**4.** Why was the Confederation Congress unable to resolve problems with Britain and Spain?

**CRITICAL THINKING**

**5. Connect Economics and History** Which side would you have supported in Shays's Rebellion— the farmers or the officials who called out the militia? Why?

**6. Analyze** Why were the states afraid of centralized authority and a strong national government?

**7.** **Writing** **Letter** Write a one-page letter from Daniel Shays to the governor of Massachusetts. In your letter, ask the governor to pardon, or forgive, your rebellion against the government.

# The Northwest Territory

In the mid-1780s, Congress decided to sell the land known as "the Territory Northwest of the river Ohio" to settlers—although this policy was often fiercely resisted by the Native Americans living in the region. The sale of land solved two problems. First, it provided cash for the government. Second, it increased American control over the land. The first organized American settlement in the Northwest Territory was Marietta, Ohio, founded in 1788.

The Land Ordinance of 1785 outlined how the land in the Northwest Territory would be divided. Congress created townships that could be divided into sections, as shown on the map below. Each township was six miles by six miles. This was an improvement over earlier methods of setting boundaries. Previously people had used rocks, trees, or other landmarks to set boundaries.

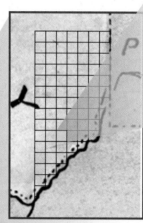

**Township 1785**

| 36 | 30 | 24 | 18 | 12 | 6 |
|----|----|----|----|----|----|
| 35 | 29 | 23 | 17 | 11 | 5 |
| 34 | 28 | 22 | 16 | 10 | 4 |
| 33 | 27 | 21 | 15 | 9 | 3 |
| 32 | 26 | 20 | 14 | 8 | 2 |
| 31 | 25 | 19 | 13 | 7 | 1 |

Each township contained 36 sections. Each section was one square mile.

## NATIVE AMERICANS

This area that became the Northwest Territory was the homeland of many Native American tribes — such as the Miami and Shawnee. The tribes grew crops and supplemented their diet with hunting and fishing. Some built bark houses. Besides trading with European fur traders, Native Americans traded with other tribes. Miami corn, for example, was valued for its high quality and the ease with which it could be turned into fine flour.

Shawnee fishing

one square mile

## GOVERNMENT SURVEYORS

Congress provided for official surveys of the Territory. Basic surveying tools included a compass, chain and stakes, a jacob staff (a long, straight wooden rod used as a base for instruments), and a theodolite. (See photo.) A theodolite consists of a telescope that can be moved from side to side and up and down. It measures angles and determines alignment.

## Connect Geography & History

1. **Summarize** What was the land in the Northwest Territory like before American settlers moved there?

2. **Problems and Solutions** How did American settlers affect the landscape in the territory?

3. **Make Inferences** Why would geography have helped create an independent spirit in the territory?

See Geography Handbook, page A2.

## ▶ Key Ideas

**BEFORE, YOU LEARNED**
The Articles of Confederation created a weak national government.

**NOW YOU WILL LEARN**
The Constitution created a new, stronger government that replaced the Confederation.

## ▶ Vocabulary

**TERMS & NAMES**

**Constitutional Convention** 1787 meeting at which the U.S. Constitution was created

**Founders** people who helped create the U.S. Constitution

**James Madison** prominent adviser to the Constitutional Convention

**Virginia Plan** proposal for a two-house legislature with representation according to each state's population or wealth

**New Jersey Plan** proposal for a legislature in which each state would have one vote

**Great Compromise** agreement to establish a two-house national legislature, with all states having equal representation in one

house and each state having representation based on its population in the other house.

**Three-Fifths Compromise** agreement that three-fifths of a state's slave population would be counted for representation and taxation

**executive branch** government department that enforces laws

**judicial branch** government department that interprets laws

**legislative branch** government department that makes laws

**checks and balances** the ability of each branch of government to exercise checks, or controls, over the other branches

## ▶ Reading Strategy

Re-create the diagram shown at right. As you read and respond to the **KEY QUESTIONS**, use the ovals to show why there was a need for a Constitutional Convention.

 **See Skillbuilder Handbook, page R3.**

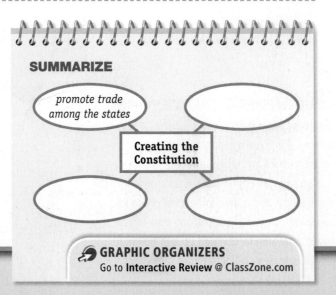

SUMMARIZE

*promote trade among the states*

**Creating the Constitution**

**GRAPHIC ORGANIZERS**
Go to **Interactive Review** @ ClassZone.com

# Creating the Constitution

 **6.4.E.1.** Discuss the background and major issues of the American Revolution, including the political and economic causes and consequences of the revolution.
**6.4.E.5.** Discuss the political and philosophical origins of the United States Constitution and its implementation in the 1790s.

## One American's Story

On May 15, 1787, Virginia Governor Edmund Randolph arrived in Philadelphia. The young nation faced conflict, as Shays's Rebellion had shown. Now delegates from throughout the states were coming to Philadelphia to discuss reforming the government.

Early in the convention Randolph spoke.

### PRIMARY SOURCE

❝ Let us not be afraid to view with a steady eye the [dangers] with which we are surrounded. . . . Are we not on the eve of [a civil] war, which is only to be prevented by the hopes from this convention? ❞

—Edmund Randolph, quoted in *Edmund Randolph: A Biography*

The Pennsylvania State House is where (*inset*) Edmund Randolph attended the Constitutional Convention.

At first, many Americans doubted that the national government needed strengthening. But fear of rebellion and lawlessness had changed people's minds. For over four months, Congress debated how best to keep the United States from falling apart.

## The Call for a Constitutional Convention

🔻 **KEY QUESTION** Why was there a call for a Constitutional Convention?

In September 1786, delegates from five states met in Annapolis, Maryland, to discuss ways to promote trade among the states. At the time, most states charged high taxes on goods imported from other states. The Annapolis delegates believed that creating national trade laws would help the economies of all the states. However, making such changes required amending the Articles of Confederation, because the national government had been granted no

## History Makers

### James Madison 1751–1836

James Madison was a soft-spoken, scholarly man. In the months before the convention, Madison studied the history of other confederacies that had failed. He saw that without a strong central government, states tended to concentrate too much on their individual interests and not enough on the common good. He came to believe that simply revising the Articles of Confederation would not be enough. Out of this research emerged the Virginia Plan, which provided the basic structure of the new government.

Madison may have made the greatest contribution of any of the Founders at the Constitutional Convention. His contributions were so important that he earned the title "Father of the Constitution."

**COMPARING** *Leaders*

As you read through the chapter, look for other examples of Madison's leadership. Compare his leadership qualities to those of American statesmen described in previous chapters.

 **ONLINE BIOGRAPHY** For more on James Madison, go to the **Research & Writing Center** @ ClassZone.com

power to regulate trade among the states. Some delegates, led by Alexander Hamilton, called for a convention in Philadelphia the following May. Twelve states sent delegates to the Convention. Only Rhode Island declined.

**Constitutional Convention** The convention opened on May 25, 1787. The first order of business was to nominate a president for the convention. Every delegate voted for the hero of the Revolution, George Washington. Washington's quiet and dignified leadership set the tone for the convention.

The delegates did not want to be pressured by the politics of the day. For this reason, they decided their discussions would remain secret. Much of what we know today about the debates and drama of the Constitutional Convention is thanks to Virginia delegate **James Madison**. In addition to contributing many ideas that shaped the Constitution, Madison took detailed notes on the proceedings.

**Who Was There?** The 55 delegates to the **Constitutional Convention**, as the Philadelphia meeting became known, were a very impressive group. Many had been members of their state legislatures and had helped write their state constitutions. Along with other leaders of the time, these delegates are called the **Founders**, or Founding Fathers, of the United States. Many of the delegates who helped draft the proposals presented at the Convention were already well known. Roger Sherman, a Connecticut delegate, was a signer of The Declaration of Independence and the Articles of Confederation. Pennsylvania's Gouverneur Morris had also signed the Articles of Confederation. Morris and Washington were friends.

Another prominent Pennsylvania delegate, Scots-born James Wilson, was known for his brilliant legal mind. Wilson worked with James Madison in pushing for a system of **popular sovereignty**, which is a government system in which the people rule. He backed the election of a national legislature by the people to be "not only the cornerstone, but the foundation of the fabric."

**Who Was Missing?** A number of key people were unable to attend. Thomas Jefferson and John Adams were overseas at their diplomatic posts. But they wrote home to encourage the delegates. Others had a less positive outlook. For example, Patrick Henry, who had been elected as a delegate from Virginia, refused to go. He said he "smelled a rat . . . tending toward monarchy."

Also, the convention did not reflect the diverse U.S. population of the 1780s. There were no Native Americans, African Americans, or women among the delegates. These groups of people were not recognized as citizens and were not invited to attend. However, the framework of government the Founders established at the Constitutional Convention is the very one that would eventually provide full rights and responsibilities to all Americans.

▲ **SUMMARIZE** Explain why the United States needed a constitutional convention.

## Some Challenges of the Convention

▼ **KEY QUESTION** What were some of the major challenges facing the Convention?

By 1787, many Americans realized that people and states often came into conflict and needed a government that could keep order. They wanted a government that was strong enough to protect people's rights but not so strong that it would oppress them.

**Disagreements over Representation** As the Convention began, the delegates disagreed about what form the new government would take. Two plans emerged. James Madison and the other Virginia delegates had drawn up their plan while they waited for the convention to open. Edmund Randolph presented the plan. The **Virginia Plan** proposed a government with three branches. The **executive branch** would enforce the laws. The **judicial branch** would interpret the laws. The third branch, the **legislative branch,** would create the laws.

The Virginia Plan wanted the legislature to have two sections: an Upper House and a Lower House. In both houses, the number of representatives

## COMPARING *Plans for Government*

| | VIRGINIA PLAN | NEW JERSEY PLAN |
|---|---|---|
| **Legislative branch** | Two (branches) houses: representation determined by state population or wealth | One house: one vote for each state, regardless of size |
| | Lower House: elected by the people Upper House: elected by lower house | Elected by state legislatures |
| **Executive branch** | Appointed by Legislature | Appointed by Legislature |
| **Judicial branch** | Appointed by Legislature | Appointed by Executive |

**CRITICAL THINKING Analyze** Which plan appealed more to the smaller states?

from each state would be based on the state's population or its wealth. The legislature would have the power to make laws "in all cases to which the separate states are incompetent [unable]."

As well as having its own distinct powers, each branch could check the powers of the other branches in certain circumstances. This system of "**checks and balances**" is a way of controlling the power of government. As James Madison said, "All power in human hands is liable to be abused." The Founders designed the new government to limit that abuse.

Delegates from the small states strongly objected to the Virginia Plan because it gave more power to states with larger populations. In response to the Virginia Plan, New Jersey delegate William Paterson presented an alternative. Like the Articles, the **New Jersey Plan** called for a single-house congress in which each state had an equal vote. Small states supported the New Jersey Plan.

**The Great Compromise** Emotions ran high as the delegates struggled to solve the problem of representation in the legislature. In early July, a committee led by Roger Sherman and other delegates from Connecticut offered a deal known as the **Great Compromise**. Sherman proposed:

**PRIMARY SOURCE**

❝ That the proportion of suffrage in the first branch should be according to the respective numbers of free inhabitants, and that in the second branch or Senate, each State should have one vote and no more. ❞

—Roger Sherman, June 11, 1787

In other words, to satisfy the smaller states, each state would have an equal number of votes in the Senate. To satisfy the larger states, representation in the House of Representatives was set according to state populations. On July 16, 1787, the convention passed the plan.

▲ **PROBLEMS AND SOLUTIONS** Describe the major challenges of the Convention in creating a stronger national government.

# Challenges Over Slavery

▼ **KEY QUESTION** How did the Constitutional Convention compromise over slavery?

Because representation in the House of Representatives would be based on the population of each state, the delegates had to decide who would be counted in that population. For example, were slaves to be counted as part of the population?

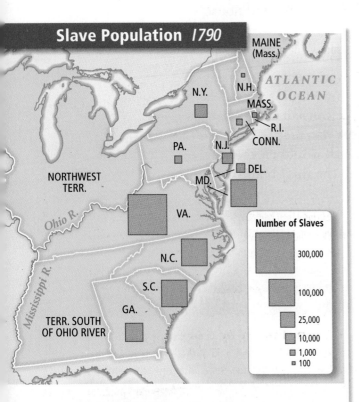

**Slave Population 1790**

Number of Slaves

300,000

100,000

25,000

10,000

1,000

100

## Connect Geography & History

1. **Place** Which state would have the greatest interest in having slaves counted as part of their population for purposes of representation?

2. **Clarify** Why did the North and the South have differing opinions on whether or not slaves should be counted as part of a state's population?

**The Three-Fifths Compromise** Representation based on population raised the question of whether slaves should be counted as people. The Southern states had many more slaves than the Northern states. Southerners wanted the slaves to be counted as part of the population for representation but not for taxation. Northerners, whose states had few slaves, argued that slaves were not citizens and should not be counted for representation but should be counted for taxation.

The delegates reached an agreement, known as the **Three-Fifths Compromise**. Three-fifths of the slave population would be counted for both purposes: representation in the legislature and taxation.

The delegates had another point of disagreement. Slavery had already been outlawed in several Northern states. Many Northerners wanted to see this ban extended to the rest of the nation. But Southern slaveholders disagreed. The delegates from South Carolina and Georgia stated that they would never accept any plan "unless their right to import slaves be untouched." Again, the delegates settled on a compromise. On August 29, they agreed that Congress could not ban the slave trade until 1808.

On September 17, 1787, the delegates passed the Constitution. All but three of the 42 delegates present signed the Constitution. It was then sent to each state for approval.

 **ANALYZE POINT OF VIEW** Explain how the Constitutional Convention compromised on the issue of slavery.

---

**New Jersey Core Curriculum Content Standards *Review***

 **ONLINE QUIZ**
For test practice, go to
**Interactive Review @ ClassZone.com**

**TERMS & NAMES**

**1.** Explain the importance of

- Constitutional Convention
- checks and balances
- New Jersey Plan
- Founders
- Great Compromise
- James Madison
- executive branch
- legislative branch
- judicial branch
- Virginia Plan
- Three-Fifths Compromise

**USING YOUR READING NOTES**

**2. Summarize** Summarize the important achievements of the Constitution.

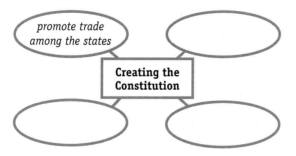

**KEY IDEAS**

**3.** What was the relationship between the Annapolis Convention and the Constitutional Convention?

**4.** Why did the Virginia delegates insist that the new government have three branches?

**5.** Under the Three-Fifths Compromise, how would each state's population be decided?

**CRITICAL THINKING**

**6. Analyze Point of View** Why did supporters of the Virginia Plan believe their plan was the best way to create a new government?

**7. Connect *to* Today** What American political traditions can be traced back to the Constitutional Convention?

**8. Art** Think about the Three-Fifths Compromise. Draw a political cartoon that expresses your views on the issue.

## ▶ Key Ideas

**BEFORE, YOU LEARNED**
The Constitution created a new, stronger government that replaced the Confederation.

**NOW YOU WILL LEARN**
American liberties are protected by the U.S. Constitution and a Bill of Rights.

## ▶ Vocabulary

**TERMS & NAMES**

**Antifederalists** people who opposed ratification of the Constitution

**federalism** system of government in which power is shared between the national (or federal) government and the states

**Federalists** people who supported ratification of the Constitution

**The Federalist papers** ratification essays published in New York newspapers

**Bill of Rights** first ten amendments to the U.S. Constitution

**BACKGROUND VOCABULARY**

**majority rule** a system in which more than one half of a group holds the power to make decisions binding the entire group

**amendment** addition to a document

**REVIEW**

**Parliament** Britain's chief lawmaking body

**Enlightenment** 18th-century movement that emphasized the use of reason and the scientific method to obtain knowledge

## ▶ Reading Strategy

Re-create the diagram shown at right. As you read and respond to the **KEY QUESTIONS,** use the circles to compare the positions of Federalists and Antifederalists.

 See Skillbuilder Handbook, page R8.

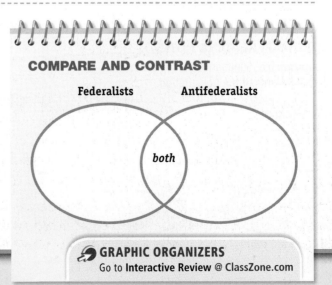

**COMPARE AND CONTRAST**

Federalists      Antifederalists

*both*

**GRAPHIC ORGANIZERS**
Go to **Interactive Review** @ ClassZone.com

# Ratification and the Bill of Rights

**6.4.E.3.** Identify major British and American leaders and describe their roles in key events, . . . .

**6.4.E.5.** Discuss the political and philosophical origins of the United States Constitution and its implementation in the 1790s.

## One American's Story

In February of 1788, **Antifederalists**, people who opposed the Constitution, sent out a pamphlet voicing their concerns over the form of the new government. The title of the essay was "Observations on the New Constitution, and on the Federal and State Conventions." To the surprise of many people, a woman, Mercy Otis Warren, was responsible for the pamphlet. The pamphlet stressed the importance of a democratic nation ruled by the people.

### PRIMARY SOURCE

❝ Government is instituted for the protection, safety and happiness of the people. . . . That the origin of all power is in the people, and that they have an [incontestable] right to check the creatures of their own creation, vested with certain powers to guard the life, liberty and property of the community. ❞

—Mercy Otis Warren, quoted in *Mercy Otis Warren*

Mercy Otis Warren was an Antifederalist and a respected historian of the American Revolution.

Warren's essay became an important part of the debate between supporters and opposers of the Constitution.

## Federalists and Antifederalists

🔻 **KEY QUESTION** What key issues divided Federalists and Antifederalists?

By the time Warren's essay was published, Americans had already been debating the new Constitution for months. The document had been widely distributed in newspapers and pamphlets across the country. The framers of the Constitution knew that the document would cause controversy. At once they began to campaign for ratification, or approval, of the Constitution.

**Concerns of the Federalists** The framers suspected that people might be afraid the Constitution would take too much power away from the states. To address this fear, the framers explained that the Constitution was based on federalism. **Federalism** is a system of government in which power is shared between the central (or federal) government and the states. Linking themselves to the idea of federalism, the people who supported the Constitution took the name **Federalists**.

The Federalists promoted their views and answered their critics in a series of essays, known as *The Federalist* **papers**. Three well-known politicians wrote *The Federalist* papers—James Madison, Alexander Hamilton, and John Jay. These essays first appeared as letters in New York newspapers. Calling for ratification of the Constitution, *The Federalist* papers appealed both to reason and emotion. In *The Federalist* papers, Hamilton described why people should support ratification.

**PRIMARY SOURCE**

❝ Yes, my countrymen, . . . I am clearly of opinion it is your interest to adopt it [the Constitution]. I am convinced that this is the safest course for your liberty, your dignity, and your happiness. ❞

—**Alexander Hamilton**, *The Federalist* "Number 1"

🔊 **ONLINE PRIMARY SOURCE**

Hear the debate at the **Research & Writing Center** @ ClassZone.com

## COMPARING *Perspectives*

Federalists and Antifederalists had very different ideas about how the United States should be governed. These were some of the arguments made as Americans passionately debated ratification of the Constitution.

Patrick Henry

### 🔊 Antifederalists

❝ Your president may easily become king: Your Senate is so imperfectly constructed that your dearest rights may be sacrificed by what may be a small minority; and a very small minority may continue for ever unchangeably this government, although horridly defective. Where are your checks in this government?

—*Patrick Henry*

The mode of levying taxes is of the utmost consequence; and yet here it is to be determined by those who have neither knowledge of our situation, nor a common interest with us. ❞

—*George Mason*

### 🔊 Federalists

❝ I am persuaded that a firm union is as necessary to perpetuate our liberties as it is to make us respectable; and experience will probably prove that the national government will be as natural a guardian of our freedom as the state legislature[s] themselves.

—*Alexander Hamilton*

As all the States are equally represented in the Senate, and by men the most able and the most willing to promote the interests of their constituents, they will all have an equal degree of influence in that body. ❞

—*John Jay*

John Jay

**CRITICAL THINKING** Analyze What was it about a strong federal government that frightened the Antifederalists?

**Concerns of the Antifederalists** The Antifederalists thought the Constitution took too much power away from the states and did not guarantee rights for the people. Some feared that a strong president might be declared king. Others feared the Senate might become a powerful ruling class. In either case, they thought, the liberties fiercely won during the Revolution might be lost.

Antifederalists received support from rural areas, where people feared a strong government that might add to their tax burden. Large states and those with strong economies, such as New York, which had greater freedom under the Articles of Confederation, also were unsupportive of the Constitution at first.

New Yorkers cheer a "Ship of State" float in honor of the new Constitution of 1798. **Why did Alexander Hamilton deserve a float in his honor?**

▲ **COMPARE AND CONTRAST** Describe the disagreements between Federalists and Antifederalists.

## The Battle for Ratification

▼ **KEY QUESTION** How did the lack of a bill of rights endanger the Constitution?

The proposed U.S. Constitution contained no guarantee that the government would protect the rights of the people, or of the states. Some supporters of the Constitution, including Thomas Jefferson, wanted to add a bill of rights—a formal summary of citizens' rights and freedoms, as a set of amendments to the Constitution.

**The Call for a Bill of Rights** Virginia's convention opened in June of 1788. Antifederalist Patrick Henry fought against ratification, or approval, of the Constitution. George Mason, who had been a delegate to the Constitutional Convention in Philadelphia, also was opposed to it.

Antifederalists wanted written guarantees that the people would have freedom of speech, of the press, and of religion. They demanded assurance of the right to trial by jury and the right to bear arms.

Federalists insisted that the Constitution granted only limited powers to the national government so that it could not violate the rights of the states or of the people. They also pointed out that the Constitution gave the people the power to protect their rights through the election of trustworthy leaders. In the end, Federalists yielded to the people's demands and promised to add a bill of rights if the states ratified the Constitution.

**Final Ratification** In December 1787, Delaware, New Jersey, and Pennsylvania voted for ratification. In January 1788, Georgia and Connecticut ratified the Constitution, followed by Massachusetts in early February. By late June, nine states had ratified. The Constitution was officially ratified with nine votes. It was vital, however, to get the support of Virginia, the largest state, and New York. Without New York, the nation would be split geographically into two parts. James Madison recommended that Virginia ratify the Constitution, with the addition of a bill of rights.

As other states ratified, however, the Virginia Antifederalists played on Southern fear of Northern domination. Under the Articles of Confederation, each state had one vote, and major decisions required the approval of nine of the 13 states. The Constitution, however, provided for **majority rule**, which means that more than one half of a group holds the power to make decisions binding on the entire group. The North, Virginia Antifederalists warned, would then dictate policy in trade, slavery, and other important issues bearing on the southern economy.

After bitter debate, at the end of June, Virginia narrowly ratified the Constitution with 89 in favor and 79 opposed. The news of Virginia's vote arrived while the New York convention was in debate. Until then, the Antifederalists had outnumbered the Federalists. But with Virginia's ratification, New Yorkers decided to join the Union. New York also called for a bill of rights.

It would be another year before North Carolina ratified the Constitution, followed by Rhode Island in 1790. By then, the new Congress had already written a bill of rights and submitted it to the states for approval.

▲ **EVALUATE** Explain how the lack of a bill of rights made ratification of the Constitution more difficult.

## CONNECT  *Citizenship and History*

### DEBATE AND FREE SPEECH

To debate is to engage in argument by discussing opposing points of view. Debate has long been an important method of exploring public issues. The Founding Fathers engaged in intense debate before the ratification of the U.S. Constitution.

Today, many students learn about the ideas of democracy through programs like the YMCA Youth in Government program. Most of these programs consist of a model legislature composed of high school students writing legislation. Participants then meet to debate their proposed laws in their actual state capitol building.

### Activity

#### Organize a Debate!

1 Choose a debate opponent and an issue to debate. Research the topic you chose.

2 Agree on a format for your debate—presentation, rebuttal, and closing.

3 Debate your opponent in front of the class. Ask the audience to cast their votes; then report the result to the class.

See Citizenship Handbook, page 300.

How did Americans create a national government that respected both the independence of states and the rights of individuals?

| | CONFEDERATION WEAKNESSES | NEW GOVERNMENT STRENGTHS |
| --- | --- | --- |
| Taxes | Congress could not levy or collect taxes. | Congress empowered to levy and collect taxes |
| Trade | Congress could not regulate trade carried on between states or with foreign nations. | Congress empowered to regulate interstate and foreign commerce |
| Courts | No regular Confederation courts; Congress depended on state courts to settle legal disputes arising from its laws. | A national system of courts set up with district and circuit courts and a supreme court |
| Executive | No national executive branch; enforcement of acts of Congress left to the states. | National government had the power to enforce federal laws. |
| States' Rights | Equality of states in voting, regardless of size or population | Proportional representation in the House; equality of states in the Senate. |
| Amendments | Unanimous vote required to amend Articles | Two-thirds vote in each House of Congress |
| Laws | Nine states had to approve an ordinary bill. | A majority required to pass a bill |

**CRITICAL THINKING Evaluate** How were states' rights protected under the new government?

# The Bill of Rights and the Constitution

🔻 **KEY QUESTION** How does the Bill of Rights protect people's rights?

Madison, who took office in the first Congress in the winter of 1789, took up the cause of the bill of rights. Madison submitted ten **amendments**, or additions to a document, to the Constitution. Congress proposed that they be placed at the end of the Constitution in a separate section. These ten amendments to the U.S. Constitution became known as the **Bill of Rights.**

**The Bill of Rights** Of these amendments to the Constitution, the first nine guarantee basic individual freedoms. Jefferson and Madison believed that government enforcement of religious laws was the source of much social conflict. They supported freedom of religion as a way to prevent such conflict. Even before Madison wrote the Bill of Rights, he worked to ensure religious liberty in Virginia. (In 1786, Madison had helped pass the Virginia Statute for Religious Freedom, originally written by Jefferson in 1779.)

# Objections to the Constitution

**SETTING THE STAGE** George Mason was one of the leading Antifederalists. In "Objections to the Constitution of Government Formed by the Convention," he listed his reasons for opposing ratification. Above all, he feared that the Constitution created a government that would destroy democracy in the young nation.

## Declaration Of Rights

At the time of the ratification debate, Americans across the nation complained that the Constitution did not include a bill of rights.

**3. What arguments does Mason make about the lack of a Declaration of Rights?**

## Abuse Of Power

Mason believed that presidents might abuse the power to grant pardons for treason in order to protect the guilty.

**4. What reasons might favor a presidential power to pardon?**

There is no Declaration of Rights; and the Laws of the general Government being **paramount**[1] to the Laws and Constitutions of the several States, the Declaration of Rights in the separate states are no Security. Nor are the people secured even in the Enjoyment of the Benefits of the common-Law. . . .

In the House of Representatives, there is not the Substance, but the Shadow only of Representation; which can never produce proper Information in the Legislature, or inspire Confidence in the People; the Laws will therefore be generally made by Men little concern'd in, and **unacquainted**[2] with their Effects and Consequences.

The Senate have the Power of altering all Money-Bills and of originating Appropriations of Money and the **Sallerys**'[3] of the Officers of their own Appointment in **Conjunction**[4] with the President of the United States; altho' they are not the Representatives of the People, or **amenable**[5] to them. . . .

The President of the United States has the unrestrained Power of granting Pardon for Treason; which may be sometimes exercised to screen from Punishment those whom he had secretly **instigated**[6] to commit the Crime, and thereby prevent a Discovery of his own Guilt.

This government will **commence**[7] in a moderate **Aristocracy**;[8] it is at present impossible to foresee whether it will, in (its) Operation, produce a **Monarchy**[9] or a corrupt oppressive Aristocracy; it will most probably vibrate some Years between the two, and then terminate in the one or the other.

—George Mason

---

1. **paramount:** most important.
2. **unacquainted:** unfamiliar.
3. **sallerys:** salaries.
4. **conjunction:** joining.
5. **amenable:** agreeable.
6. **instigated:** caused.
7. **commence:** begin.
8. **aristocracy:** rule by a few, usually nobles.
9. **monarchy:** rule by one, usually a king.

## DOCUMENT-BASED QUESTIONS

**Short Answer**

1. Why does Madison believe that a fragmented society will not endanger minority rights?

2. What does Mason argue might happen if the president had the power to pardon people?

**Extended Answer**

3. Compare how each writer supports his opinions with facts.

## Chapter Summary

**1** **Key Idea**
The Articles of Confederation created a weak national government.

**2** **Key Idea**
The Constitution created a new, stronger government that replaced the Confederation.

**3** **Key Idea**
American liberties are protected by the U.S. Constitution and a Bill of Rights.

For detailed Review and Study Notes go to **Interactive Review** @ **ClassZone.com**

## Name Game

**Use the Terms & Names list to complete each sentence online or on your own paper.**

1. The first government of the United States was established by the Articles of Confederation

2. A group known as ____ opposed ratification of the Constitution.

3. Angered by new taxes, farmers attacked the courts in Massachusetts during ____

4. In a ____, the people elect representatives to govern them.

5. State representation in the House and Congress was determined by the ____

6. The ____ established law in the Northwest Territory.

7. ____ was the primary author of the Virginia Plan.

8. The Constitution was created at the ____ in 1787.

9. The ____ interprets the law.

10. The first ten amendments of the Constitution are known as the ____

A. New Jersey Plan

B. Constitutional Convention

C. Republic

D. Articles of Confederation

E. Legislative Branch

F. Shays's Rebellion

G. Antifederalists

H. James Madison

I. Northwest Ordinance

J. Judicial Branch

L. Land Ordinance of 1785

M. Founders

N. Bill of Rights

O. Great Compromise

P. Federalist Papers

## Activities

### CROSSWORD PUZZLE

Complete the online crossword puzzle to show what you know about the Constitution.

**ACROSS**
**1.** _____ is known as "Father of the Constitution."

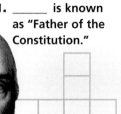

### GEOGAME

Use this online map to reinforce your knowledge of the Confederation Era, including the locations of important cities and events. Drag and drop each name in the list at its location on the map. A scorecard helps you keep track online.

Constitutional Convention

Shays's Rebellion

Northwest Territory

Confederation Congress

*The Federalist* papers published here

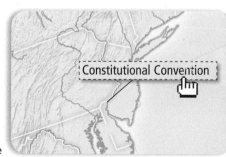

Constitutional Convention

More items online

## VOCABULARY

**Explain the significance of each of the following.**

1. Shays's Rebellion
2. Great Compromise
3. Constitutional Convention
4. Bill of Rights
5. James Madison
6. Northwest Ordinance
7. Founders
8. Three-Fifths Compromise
9. Articles of Confederation
10. Confederation Congress

**Explain how the terms and names in each group are related.**

11. ratification, amendment
12. Virginia Plan, New Jersey Plan
13. Confederation Congress, Land Ordinance of 1785
14. Federalists, Antifederalists

## KEY IDEAS

**1 The Confederation Era (pages 234–239)**

15. What problems did the Continental Congress successfully address?
16. How did Shays's Rebellion affect people's views on the Articles of Confederation?

**2 Creating the Constitution (pages 242–247)**

17. What groups of people were not represented at the Constitutional Convention?
18. What compromises did the delegates make during the convention?

**3 Ratifying the Constitution (pages 248–254)**

19. Why were Virginia and New York important in the battle for ratification of the Constitution?
20. Why did some states think that it was necessary to add a bill of rights to the Constitution?

## CRITICAL THINKING

21. **Causes and Effects** How did America's history as a British colony cause the Confederation to fail?
22. **Evaluate** Why is the Northwest Ordinance sometimes called the Confederation Congress's only success?
23. **Problems & Solutions** Create a chart to identify the specific problems faced by the new nation, and the solutions it tried.

| Problem | Solution |
|---|---|
| Western lands | Northwest Ordinance, 1787 |
| Postwar depression | |
| Representation in the new government | |

24. **Compare and Contrast** How do the Articles of Confederation and the Constitution each carry out democratic ideals?
25. **Evaluate** How did the Antifederalists have an impact on the Constitution?
26. **Interpret Maps** In which states did the Federalists have statewide majorities?

### Ratification in Middle States 1790

Federalist majority
Anti-federalist majority
Evenly divided
Sparsely populated

NEW YORK

PENNSYLVANIA

NEW JERSEY

DELAWARE

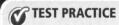 
## DOCUMENT-BASED QUESTIONS

### PART 1: Short Answer
**Study each document carefully and answer the questions that follow.**

#### DOCUMENT 1

THE CONSTITUTIONAL CONVENTION · 1787

**1.** Examine the mural that shows (left to right) Hamilton, James Wilson, Madison, and Franklin at the Constitutional Convention. What does the art tell you about the type of delegates who attended?

#### DOCUMENT 2

**PRIMARY SOURCE**

❝ I like much the general idea of framing a government which should go on of itself . . . [but] I do not like. . . . First, the omission of a bill of rights. . . . Let me add that a bill of rights is what the people are entitled to against every government on earth, general or particular; and what no just government should refuse. . . ❞

—Thomas Jefferson, December 20, 1787

**2.** Is Jefferson stating the Federalist or Antifederalist point of view?

### PART 2: Essay

**3.** Using information from the documents, your answers to the questions in Part 1, and your knowledge of U.S. history, write an essay that explains the events leading to the ratification of the Bill of Rights.

## YOU BE THE HISTORIAN

**27. Make Decisions** How might the United States have developed if the Articles of Confederation had continued to provide the basis for government?

**28. Draw Conclusions** In what ways was the land of the Northwest Territory distributed democratically?

**29. Connect Economics & History** How did the Three-Fifths Compromise satisfy both North and South?

**30. Compare & Contrast** Consider the two groups that rebelled against the government: farmers and Revolutionary War veterans. Compare what life was probably like for these people as opposed to what life might have been like for the Founders.

**31.** **Connect** *to* **Today** How does the Constitution give Americans a voice in their national government?

 Answer the
## ESSENTIAL QUESTION
**How did Americans create a strong national government that respected both the rights of states and the rights of individuals?**

**Written Response** Write a two-to-three-paragraph response to the Essential Question. Be sure to consider the key ideas of each section as well as the ideals that Americans value today. Use the Response rubric to guide your thinking and writing.

### Response Rubric
**A strong response will**

- discuss the values and ideals of modern America
- analyze the post-revolutionary events and conflicts out of which these ideals emerged
- explain the unique nature of the American constitution

# Constitution Handbook

## The Living Constitution

The Framers of the Constitution created a flexible plan for governing the United States far into the future. They also described ways to allow changes in the Constitution. For over 200 years, the Constitution has guided the American people. It remains a "living document." The Constitution still thrives, in part, because it echoes the principles the delegates valued. Each generation of Americans renews the meaning of the Constitution's timeless ideas. These two pages show you some ways in which the Constitution has shaped events in American history.

> ❝ In framing a system which we wish to last for ages, we should not lose sight of the changes which ages will produce. ❞
>
> —James Madison, Constitutional Convention

### Table of Contents

Seven Principles
   of the Constitution . . . . . . 262

The Constitution
   of the United States . . . . . 266
Preamble . . . . . . . . . . . . . . 266
Article 1 . . . . . . . . . . . . . . 267
Article 2 . . . . . . . . . . . . . . 276
Article 3 . . . . . . . . . . . . . . 280
Article 4 . . . . . . . . . . . . . . 282
Article 5 . . . . . . . . . . . . . . 283
Article 6 . . . . . . . . . . . . . . 284
Article 7 . . . . . . . . . . . . . . 285
Amendments 1–10
   (Bill of Rights) . . . . . . . . 286
Amendments 11–27 . . . . . . 289

Constitution Assessment . . . 298

**1963**
Reverend Dr. Martin Luther King, Jr. addresses demonstrators at the civil rights march on Washington in August 1963.

**1787**
Delegates in Philadelphia sign the Constitution.

## 1971

The 26th Amendment to the Constitution gives young people "18 years of age or older" the right to vote. Here, the Voters Project encourages young people to register and vote.

## 1981

A Supreme Court decision rules that Congress can exclude women from the draft. In the early 2000s, there were 215,243 women in the U.S. military.

## 2002

Attorney General John Ashcroft's positions on privacy and civil liberties issues made him a controversial figure in the George W. Bush cabinet. Ashcroft was a key supporter of the passage of the USA Patriot act. The act, which was dubbed the "anti-terrorism" act, drew fire from both liberals and conservatives. Critics of the act said it endangered the basic freedoms guaranteed under the U.S. Constitution.

## ④ Separation of Powers
### *How Is Power Divided?*

The Framers were concerned that too much power might fall into the hands of a single group. To avoid this problem, they built the idea of **separation of powers** into the Constitution. This principle means the division of basic government roles into branches. No one branch is given all the power. Articles 1, 2, and 3 of the Constitution detail how powers are split among the three branches.

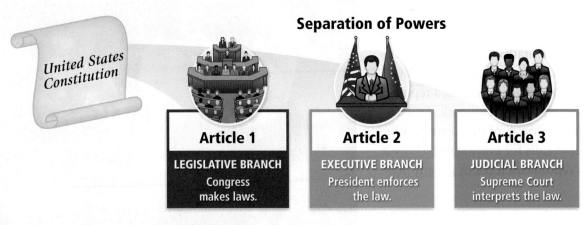

**Separation of Powers**

*United States Constitution*

**Article 1**
LEGISLATIVE BRANCH
Congress makes laws.

**Article 2**
EXECUTIVE BRANCH
President enforces the law.

**Article 3**
JUDICIAL BRANCH
Supreme Court interprets the law.

## ⑤ Checks and Balances
### *How Is Power Evenly Distributed?*

Baron de Montesquieu, an 18th-century French thinker, wrote, "power should be a check to power." His comment refers to the principle of **checks and balances**. Each branch of government can exercise checks, or controls, over the other branches. Though the branches of government are separate, they rely on one another to perform the work of government.

The Framers included a system of checks and balances in the Constitution to help make sure that the branches work together fairly. For example, only Congress can pass laws. Yet the president can check this power by refusing to sign a law into action. In turn, the Supreme Court can declare that a law, passed by Congress and signed by the president, violates the Constitution.

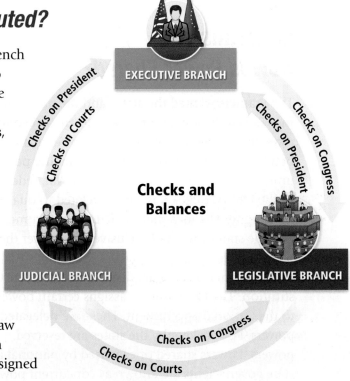

EXECUTIVE BRANCH

Checks on President
Checks on Courts
Checks on President
Checks on Congress

**Checks and Balances**

JUDICIAL BRANCH

LEGISLATIVE BRANCH

Checks on Congress
Checks on Courts

## 6 Limited Government
### *How Is Abuse of Power Prevented?*

The Framers restricted the power of government. Article 1, Section 9, of the Constitution lists the powers denied to the Congress. Article 1, Section 10, forbids the states to take certain actions.

The principle of **limited government** is also closely related to the "rule of law": In the American government everyone, citizens and powerful leaders alike, must obey the law. Individuals or groups cannot twist or bypass the law to serve their own interests.

In mid-1987, Congress conducted a dramatic inquiry into the Iran-Contra affair. (*above*) Lieutenant Colonel Oliver North testifies before the hearings. North was found guilty of taking part in a cover-up.

## 7 Individual Rights
### *How Are Personal Freedoms Protected?*

The first ten amendments to the Constitution shield people from an overly powerful government. These amendments are called the Bill of Rights. The Bill of Rights guarantees certain **individual rights**, or personal liberties and privileges. For example, government cannot control what people write or say. People also have the right to meet peacefully and to ask the government to correct a problem. Later amendments to the Constitution also advanced the cause of individual rights.

Students and teachers in Oakland, California, protest measures proposed in the 2005 election.

### Seven Principles of the Constitution **Assessment**

**MAIN IDEAS**

1. What are the seven principles of government?
2. How does the Constitution reflect the principle of separation of powers?
3. Why did the Framers include a system of checks and balances in the Constitution?

**CRITICAL THINKING**

4. **Form Opinions** How do the rights and responsibilities of U.S. citizenship reflect American national identity?

   **Think about**
   - what it means to be an American
   - the rights and responsibilities of U.S. citizens

# The Constitution of the United States

**ESSENTIAL QUESTION**

How has our 220-year-old Constitution remained a living document?

## How to Read the Constitution

- The main column has the actual text.
- Notes in the side column point out or explain important aspects of the document.
- Some of the spellings and punctuation have been updated for easier reading.
- Headings and subheadings have been added to help you find specific topics.
- Those parts of the Constitution that are no longer in use have been crossed out.

Visitors hear a lecture on the Constitution at the National Archives Building, which also houses the Declaration of Independence and the Bill of Rights.

## PREAMBLE. Purpose of the Constitution

We the people of the United States, in order to form a more perfect Union, establish justice, insure domestic tranquility, provide for the common defense, promote the general welfare, and secure the blessings of liberty to ourselves and our posterity, do ordain and establish this Constitution for the United States of America.

### Goals of the Preamble

| Preamble | Explanation | Examples |
|---|---|---|
| "Form a more perfect Union" | Create a nation in which states work together | • Interstate road network<br>• U.S. coins, paper money |
| "Establish justice" | Make laws and set up courts that are fair | • Court system<br>• Jury system |
| "Insure domestic tranquility" | Keep peace within the country | • National Guard<br>• Federal marshals |
| "Provide for the common defense" | Safeguard the country against attack | • Army<br>• Navy |
| "Promote the general welfare" | Contribute to the happiness and well-being of all the people | • Safety in the workplace<br>• Aid to the poor |
| "Secure the blessings of liberty to ourselves and our posterity" | Make sure future citizens remain free | • Commission on Civil Rights<br>• Federal Election Commission |

### CRITICAL THINKING

1. Which goal of the preamble do you think is most important? Why?
2. How does the preamble reflect the principle of popular sovereignty?

# ARTICLE 1. The Legislature

▼ **KEY QUESTION** What is the main role of the legislative branch?

## SECTION 1. Congress

All legislative powers herein granted shall be vested in a Congress of the United States, which shall consist of a Senate and House of Representatives.

## SECTION 2. The House of Representatives

**1. Elections** The House of Representatives shall be composed of members chosen every second year by the people of the several states, and the **electors** in each state shall have the qualifications requisite for electors of the most numerous branch of the state legislature.

**2. Qualifications** No person shall be a Representative who shall not have attained to the age of twenty-five years, and been seven years a citizen of the United States, and who shall not, when elected, be an inhabitant of that state in which he shall be chosen.

**3. Number of Representatives** Representatives and direct taxes shall be apportioned among the several states which may be included within this Union, according to their respective numbers, which shall be determined by adding to the whole number of free persons, including those bound to service for a term of years, and excluding Indians not taxed, three-fifths of all other Persons. The actual **enumeration** shall be made within three years after the first meeting of the Congress of the United States, and within every subsequent term of ten years, in such manner as they shall by law direct. The number of Representatives shall not exceed one for every thirty thousand, but each state shall have at least one Representative; and until such enumeration shall be made, the state of New Hampshire shall be entitled to choose three, Massachusetts eight, Rhode Island and Providence Plantations one, Connecticut five, New York six, New Jersey four, Pennsylvania eight, Delaware one, Maryland six, Virginia ten, North Carolina five, South Carolina five, and Georgia three.

**4. Vacancies** When vacancies happen in the representation from any state, the executive authority thereof shall issue writs of election to fill such vacancies.

**5. Officers and Impeachment** The House of Representatives shall choose their Speaker and other officers; and shall have the sole power of **impeachment**.

## SECTION 3. Congress

**1. Numbers** The Senate of the United States shall be composed of two Senators from each state, chosen by the legislature thereof, for six years; and each Senator shall have one vote.

---

**BACKGROUND VOCABULARY**

**electors** voters

**enumeration** an official count, such as a census

**impeachment** the process of accusing a public official of wrongdoing

### Elections

Representatives are elected every two years. There are no limits on the number of terms a person can serve.

**1. What do you think are the advantages of holding frequent elections of representatives?**

### Representation

Some delegates, such as Gouverneur Morris (*above*), thought that representation should be based on wealth as well as population. Others, such as James Wilson, thought representation should be based on population only. Ultimately, the delegates voted against including wealth as a basis for apportioning representatives.

**2. How do you think the United States would be different today if representation were based on wealth?**

**2. Classifying Terms** Immediately after they shall be assembled in consequence of the first election, they shall be divided as equally as may be into three classes. The seats of the Senators of the first class shall be vacated at the expiration of the second year, of the second class at the expiration of the fourth year, and of the third class at the expiration of the sixth year, so that one-third may be chosen every second year; ~~and if vacancies happen by resignation, or otherwise, during the recess of the legislature of any state, the executive thereof may make temporary appointments until the next meeting of the legislature, which shall then fill such vacancies.~~

**3. Qualifications** No person shall be a Senator who shall not have attained to the age of thirty years, and been nine years a citizen of the United States, and who shall not, when elected, be an inhabitant of that state for which he shall be chosen.

## COMPARING  *Federal Office Terms and Requirements*

| Position | Term | Minimum Age | Residency | Citizenship |
|---|---|---|---|---|
| Representative | 2 years | 25 | state in which elected | 7 years |
| Senator | 6 years | 30 | state in which elected | 9 years |
| President | 4 years | 35 | 14 years in the U.S. | natural-born |
| Supreme Court Justice | unlimited | none | none | none |

**CRITICAL THINKING**  Why do you think the term and qualifications for a senator are more demanding than for a representative?

**Impeachment**

The House brings charges against the president. The Senate acts as the jury. The Chief Justice of the Supreme Court presides over the hearings.

**3. How many presidents have been impeached?**

**4. Role of Vice President** The Vice President of the United States shall be President of the Senate, but shall have no vote, unless they be equally divided.

**5. Officers** The Senate shall choose their other officers, and also a President **pro tempore**, in the absence of the Vice President, or when he shall exercise the office of President of the United States.

**6. Impeachment Trials** The Senate shall have the sole power to try all impeachments. When sitting for that purpose, they shall be on oath or affirmation. When the President of the United States is tried, the Chief Justice shall preside: and no person shall be convicted without the concurrence of two-thirds of the members present.

**7. Punishment for Impeachment** Judgment in cases of impeachment shall not extend further than to removal from office, and disqualification to hold and enjoy any office of honor, trust or profit under the United States; but the party convicted shall nevertheless be liable and subject to **indictment**, trial, judgment and punishment, according to law.

## SECTION 4. **Congressional Elections**

**1. Regulations** The times, places and manner of holding elections for Senators and Representatives shall be prescribed in each state by the legislature thereof; but the Congress may at any time by law make or alter such regulations, except as to the places of choosing Senators.

**2. Sessions** The Congress shall assemble at least once in every year, ~~and such meeting shall be on the first Monday in December, unless they shall by law appoint a different day.~~

## SECTION 5. **Rules and Procedures**

**1. Quorum** Each house shall be the judge of the elections, returns and qualifications of its own members, and a majority of each shall constitute a **quorum** to do business; but a smaller number may adjourn from day to day, and may be authorized to compel the attendance of absent members, in such manner, and under such penalties as each house may provide.

**2. Rules and Conduct** Each house may determine the rules of its proceedings, punish its members for disorderly behavior, and, with the concurrence of two-thirds, expel a member.

**3. Congressional Records** Each house shall keep a journal of its proceedings, and from time to time publish the same, excepting such parts as may in their judgment require secrecy; and the yeas and nays of the members of either house on any question shall, at the desire of one-fifth of those present, be entered on the journal.

**4. Adjournment** Neither house, during the session of Congress, shall, without the consent of the other, adjourn for more than three days, nor to any other place than that in which the two houses shall be sitting

## SECTION 6. **Payment and Privileges**

**1. Salary** The Senators and Representatives shall receive a compensation for their services, to be ascertained by law, and paid out of the treasury of the United States. They shall in all cases, except treason, felony and breach of the peace, be privileged from arrest during their attendance at the session of their respective houses, and in going to and returning from the same; and for any speech or debate in either house, they shall not be questioned in any other place.

**2. Restrictions** No Senator or Representative shall, during the time for which he was elected, be appointed to any civil office under the authority of the United States, which shall have been created, or the emoluments whereof shall have been increased during such time; and no person holding any office under the United States, shall be a member of either house during his continuance in office.

### Senate Rules

Senate rules allow for debate on the floor. Using a tactic called filibustering, senators give long speeches to block the passage of a bill. (*above*) Senator Strom Thurmond holds the filibustering record—24 hours, 18 minutes.

**4. Why might a senator choose filibustering as a tactic to block a bill?**

### Connect *to* Today

**Salaries** Senators and representatives are paid $165,200 a year. The Speaker of the House is paid $212,100—the same as the vice president.

**5. How do the salaries of members of Congress compare to those of adults—like teachers or famous sports figures?**

**SECTION 7. How a Bill Becomes a Law**

**1. Tax Bills** All bills for raising **revenue** shall originate in the House of Representatives; but the Senate may propose or concur with amendments as on other Bills.

**2. Lawmaking Process** Every bill which shall have passed the House of Representatives and the Senate, shall, before it become a law, be presented to the President of the United States; if he approves he shall sign it, but if not he shall return it, with his objections to that house in which it shall have originated, who shall enter the objections at large on their journal, and proceed to reconsider it. If after such reconsideration two-thirds of that house shall agree to pass the bill, it shall be sent, together with the objections, to the other house, by which it shall likewise be reconsidered, and if approved by two-thirds of that house, it shall become a law. But in all such cases the votes of both houses shall be determined by yeas and nays, and the names of the persons voting for and against the bill shall be entered on the journal of each house respectively. If any bill shall not be returned by the President within ten days (Sundays excepted) after it shall have been presented to him, the same shall be a law, in like manner as if he had signed it, unless the Congress by their adjournment prevent its return, in which case it shall not be a law.

## CONNECT TO GOVERNMENT  *How a Bill Becomes a Law*

| INTRODUCTION | COMMITTEE ACTION | FLOOR ACTION | |
|---|---|---|---|

**1**

**The House** introduces a bill and refers it to a committee.

**The Senate** introduces a bill and refers it to a committee.

**2**

**The House** committee may approve, rewrite, or kill the bill.

**The Senate** committee may approve, rewrite, or kill the bill.

**3**

**The House** debates and votes on its version of the bill.

**The Senate** debates and votes on its version of the bill.

**4**

**The House and Senate** committee members work out the differences between the two versions.

**3. Role of the President** Every order, resolution, or vote to which the concurrence of the Senate and House of Representatives may be necessary (except on a question of adjournment) shall be presented to the President of the United States; and before the same shall take effect, shall be approved by him, or being disapproved by him, shall be repassed by two-thirds of the Senate and House of Representatives, according to the rules and limitations prescribed in the case of a bill.

 **Activity**

★ **How a Bill Becomes a Law** ★

**Creating a Play**

**1** Study the diagram below.

**2** Work with a small group to create a presentation to teach an audience of younger students how a bill becomes a law.

- Assign the tasks of actor, illustrator, narrator, and scriptwriter.
- Develop a script.
- Gather props and rehearse your presentations.

**3** Present the drama to a class of younger students.

**FINAL APPROVAL**　　　　　　　　　　　　　　**ENACTMENT**

**5**
Both houses of
Congress pass
the revised bill.

**6**
President vetoes the bill.
**OR**
President signs the bill.

**7**
Two-thirds majority vote
of Congress is needed
to approve a vetoed bill.

**8**
**Bill
becomes
law.**

### SECTION 8. Powers Granted to Congress

**1. Taxation** The Congress shall have power to lay and collect taxes, duties, imposts and excises, to pay the debts and provide for the common defense and general welfare of the United States; but all duties, imposts and excises shall be uniform throughout the United States;

**2. Credit** To borrow money on the credit of the United States;

**3. Commerce** To regulate commerce with foreign nations, and among the several states, and with the Indian tribes;

**4. Naturalization, Bankruptcy** To establish a uniform rule of naturalization, and uniform laws on the subject of bankruptcies throughout the United States;

**5. Money** To coin money, regulate the value thereof, and of foreign coin, and fix the standard of weights and measures;

**6. Counterfeiting** To provide for the punishment of counterfeiting the securities and current coin of the United States;

**7. Post Office** To establish post offices and post roads;

**8. Patents, Copyrights** To promote the progress of science and useful arts, by securing for limited times to authors and inventors the exclusive right to their respective writings and discoveries;

## COMPARING *Military Responsibilities*

The president is the Commander-in-Chief of the U.S. Armed Forces. There are five military branches—the Army, Marine Corps (USMC), Navy (USN), and Air Force (USAF), and the Coast Guard (USCG). The National Guard is the home based militia.

**United States Army** The largest branch of the U.S. armed forces, the U.S. Army has its roots in the Continental Army which was formed in June 1775. The army is responsible for land-based military operations. Motto: "Call to Duty."

**U.S. Navy (USN)** The branch of the U.S. armed forces responsible for naval operations. Unofficial motto: *"Non sibi sed patriae"* meaning "Not self but country."

**U.S. Air Force (USAF)** The largest and most technologically advanced air force in the world, USAF is trained for "offensive and defensive air operations." Unofficial motto: "No One Comes Close."

**9. Federal Courts** To constitute **tribunals** inferior to the Supreme Court;

**10. International Law** To define and punish piracies and **felonies** committed on the high seas, and offenses against the law of nations;

**11. War** To declare war, grant letters of marque and reprisal, and make rules concerning captures on land and water;

**12. Army** To raise and support armies, but no **appropriation** of money to that use shall be for a longer term than two years;

**13. Navy** To provide and maintain a navy;

**14. Regulation of Armed Forces** To make rules for the government and regulation of the land and naval forces;

**15. Militia** To provide for calling forth the **militia** to execute the laws of the Union, suppress insurrections and repel invasions;

**16. Regulations for Militia** To provide for organizing, arming, and disciplining the militia, and for governing such part of them as may be employed in the service of the United States, reserving to the states respectively the appointment of the officers, and the authority of training the militia according to the discipline prescribed by Congress;

### Connect *to* Today

**Declaring War** Only Congress can declare war. Yet in the following "undeclared" wars, Congress bowed to the president's power to take military action and send troops overseas: Korean War (1950–1953), Vietnam War (1957–1975), Persian Gulf War (1991), and Kosovo crisis (1999).

**6. Why do you think the Constitution sets limits on the president's power to make war?**

**U.S. Marine Corps (USMC)** The marines have a multi-purpose role, including providing presidential protection and helicopter service. Marines also provide security for American embassies and consulates overseas. Motto: "*Semper Fidelis*" meaning "Always Faithful."

## U.S. National Guard

The National Guard is a component of the U.S. Army and USAF. National Guard units can be mobilized at any time to supplement regular armed forces.

### CRITICAL THINKING

**1. Form and Support Opinions** Women now serve in combat roles in the U.S. Armed Forces? Do you agree or disagree with this policy?

**2.** Connect *to* Today Under what circumstances do you think the president should call out the National Guard?

**natural-born citizen** a citizen born in the United States or a U.S. commonwealth, or to parents who are U.S. citizens living outside the country

**affirmation** a statement declaring that something is true

# ARTICLE 2. The Executive

**KEY QUESTION** What is the chief purpose of the executive branch?

## SECTION 1. The Presidency

**1. Terms of Office** The executive power shall be vested in a President of the United States of America. He shall hold his office during the term of four years, and, together with the Vice President, chosen for the same term, be elected, as follows:

**2. Electoral College** Each state shall appoint, in such manner as the Legislature thereof may direct, a number of electors, equal to the whole number of Senators and Representatives to which the State may be entitled in the Congress; but no Senator or Representative, or person holding an office of trust or profit under the United States, shall be appointed an elector.

## CONNECT TO GOVERNMENT — *Electoral College*

American voters do not choose their president directly. Members of a group called the Electoral College actually elect the president. Each state has electors. Together they form the Electoral College. In most states, the winner takes all. Except for Maine and Nebraska, all the electoral votes of a state go to one set of candidates.

**CRITICAL THINKING**

**1. Place** How many electoral votes does your state have?

**2. Draw Conclusions** In which states would a presidential candidate campaign most heavily? Why?

Number of electors for each state = total number of its senators and representatives

**3. Former Method of Electing President** The electors shall meet in their respective states, and vote by ballot for two persons, of whom one at least shall not be an inhabitant of the same state with themselves. And they shall make a list of all the persons voted for, and of the number of votes for each; which list they shall sign and certify, and transmit sealed to the seat of the government of the United States, directed to the President of the Senate. The President of the Senate shall, in the presence of the Senate and House of Representatives, open all the certificates, and the votes shall then be counted. The person having the greatest number of votes shall be the President, if such number be a majority of the whole number of electors appointed; and if there be more than one who have such majority, and have an equal number of votes, then the House of Representatives shall immediately choose by ballot one of them for President; and if no person have a majority, then from the five highest on the list the said House shall in like manner choose the President. But in choosing the President, the votes shall be taken by States, the representation from each state having one vote; a quorum for this purpose shall consist of a member or members from two-thirds of the states, and a majority of all the states shall be necessary to a choice. In every case, after the choice of the President, the person having the greatest number of votes of the electors shall be the Vice President. But if there should remain two or more who have equal votes, the Senate shall choose from them by ballot the Vice President.

**4. Election Day** The Congress may determine the time of choosing the electors, and the day on which they shall give their votes, which day shall be the same throughout the United States.

**5. Qualifications** No person except a **natural-born citizen**, or a citizen of the United States at the time of the adoption of this Constitution, shall be eligible to the office of President; neither shall any person be eligible to that office who shall not have attained to the age of thirty-five years, and been fourteen years a resident within the United States.

**6. Succession** In case of the removal of the President from office, or of his death, resignation, or inability to discharge the powers and duties of the said office, the same shall devolve on the Vice President, and the Congress may by law provide for the case of removal, death, resignation or inability, both of the President and Vice President, declaring what officer shall then act as President, and such officer shall act accordingly, until the disability be removed, or a President shall be elected.

**7. Salary** The President shall, at stated times, receive for his services, a compensation, which shall neither be increased nor diminished during the period for which he shall have been elected, and he shall not receive within that period any other emolument from the United States, or any of them.

**8. Oath of Office** Before he enter on the execution of his office, he shall take the following oath or **affirmation**: I do solemnly swear (or affirm) that I will faithfully execute the office of President of the United States, and will to the best of my ability, preserve, protect and defend the Constitution of the United States.

## SECTION 2. Powers of the President

**1. Military Powers** The President shall be commander in chief of the Army and Navy of the United States, and of the militia of the several states, when called into the actual service of the United States; he may require the

### Succession

Vice President Gerald Ford (*left*), next in the line of succession, takes the oath of office after the resignation of President Richard Nixon on August 9, 1974. Ford, like every U.S. president, promises to uphold the Constitution. The 25th Amendment sets up clearer procedures for presidential succession.

### President's Salary

The president's yearly salary is $400,000. The president also gets special allowances, such as funds for travel expenses. Benefits include:

- living in a mansion, the White House
- vacationing at Camp David, an estate in Maryland
- using *Air Force One*, a personal jet plane

**10. Why do you think the president needs to have a plane and a vacation spot?**

### Chief Executive
Like a business executive, the president solves problems and makes key decisions. President George W. Bush is shown in the oval office in 2006.

### Commander in Chief
As a military leader, President Abraham Lincoln meets with General McClellan during the Civil War.

### Head of a Political Party
President Andrew Jackson on his way to Washington, D.C. for his inauguration in 1829. Jackson was a leader of the Democratic-Republican Party—the forerunner of today's Democratic Party.

### Chief Diplomat and Chief of State
As a foreign policy maker, President Ronald Reagan visits British Prime Minister Margaret Thatcher in 1984.

### Legislative Leader
President Franklin D. Roosevelt signs the Social Security Act of 1935. All modern presidents have legislative programs they want Congress to pass.

#### CRITICAL THINKING

1. **Make Inferences** Why is it important that the commander in chief of the armed forces of the United States be a civilian (the president) rather than a military commander?

2. **Connect to Today** Why do you think the United States enjoys close relations with Britain?

opinion, in writing, of the principal officer in each of the executive departments, upon any subject relating to the duties of their respective offices, and he shall have power to grant **reprieves** and pardons for offenses against the United States, except in cases of impeachment.

**2. Treaties, Appointments** He shall have power, by and with the advice and consent of the Senate, to make treaties, provided two-thirds of the Senators present concur; and he shall nominate, and by and with the advice and consent of the Senate, shall appoint ambassadors, other public ministers and consuls, judges of the Supreme Court, and all other officers of the United States, whose appointments are not herein otherwise provided for, and which shall be established by law; but the Congress may by law vest the appointment of such inferior officers, as they think proper, in the President alone, in the courts of law, or in the heads of departments.

**3. Vacancies** The President shall have power to fill up all vacancies that may happen during the recess of the Senate, by granting commissions which shall expire at the end of their next session.

## SECTION 3. Presidential Duties

He shall from time to time give to the Congress information of the State of the Union, and recommend to their consideration such measures as he shall judge necessary and expedient; he may, on extraordinary occasions, **convene** both houses, or either of them, and in case of disagreement between them, with respect to the time of adjournment, he may adjourn them to such time as he shall think proper; he shall receive ambassadors and other public ministers; he shall take care that the laws be faithfully executed, and shall commission all the officers of the United States.

## SECTION 4. Impeachment

The President, Vice President and all civil officers of the United States shall be removed from office on impeachment for, and conviction of, treason, bribery, or other high crimes and **misdemeanors**.

### BACKGROUND VOCABULARY

**reprieves** delays or cancellations of punishment

**convene** call together

**misdemeanors** violations of the law

### Appointments

Recent presidents have used their power of appointment to add minorities and women to the Supreme Court. In 1967, President Lyndon Johnson appointed the first African-American justice, Thurgood Marshall. In 1981, President Ronald Reagan appointed the first woman, Sandra Day O'Connor.

**11. What do you think influences a president's choice for a Supreme Court justice?**

### Connect *to* Today

**State of the Union** Major TV networks broadcast the State of the Union address to the whole nation. In this yearly message, the president urges Congress to achieve certain lawmaking goals. The president's speech also must gain the attention of TV viewers.

**12. Why is the president's power to persuade an important political skill?**

## Article ❷ Assessment

### MAIN IDEAS

**1.** What is the chief purpose of the executive branch?

**2.** What are the requirements for becoming president?

**3.** How does the Constitution limit the president's power to make appointments and treaties?

### CRITICAL THINKING

**4. Analyze Issues** Why do you think the Constitution states that the president must seek approval from the Senate for most political appointments and treaties?

### Think about

• the abuse of power   • the will of the voters

BACKGROUND
VOCABULARY

**inferior courts** courts
with less authority than the
Supreme Court

**appellate** having power to
review court decisions

### Federal Courts

The Judiciary Act of 1789, passed
by the first Congress, included
establishing a Supreme Court
with a chief justice and five
associate justices and other lower
federal courts.

**13. How many Supreme
Court justices are there
today?**

### Judicial Power

Judicial power gives the Supreme
Court and other federal courts the
authority to hear certain kinds
of cases. These courts have the
power to rule in cases involving
the Constitution, national laws,
treaties, and states' conflicts.

**14. What federal cases have
you seen reported on TV?**

# ARTICLE 3. The Judiciary

▼ **KEY QUESTION** What is the main purpose of the judicial branch?

## SECTION 1. Federal Courts and Judges

The judicial power of the United States shall be vested in one Supreme
Court, and in such **inferior courts** as the Congress may from time to time
ordain and establish. The judges, both of the Supreme and inferior courts,
shall hold their offices during good behavior, and shall, at stated times,
receive for their services a compensation, which shall not be diminished
during their continuance in office.

## SECTION 2. The Courts Authority

**1. General Authority** The judicial power shall extend to all cases, in law
and equity, arising under this Constitution, the laws of the United States,
and treaties made, or which shall be made, under their authority;—to all
cases affecting ambassadors, other public ministers and consuls;—to all
cases of admiralty and maritime jurisdiction;—to controversies to which
the United States shall be a party;—to controversies between two or more
states;—between a state and citizens of another state;—between citizens of
different states;—between citizens of the same state claiming lands under
grants of different states, and between a state, or the citizens thereof, and
foreign states, citizens or subjects.

**2. Supreme Court** In all cases affecting ambassadors, other public ministers
and consuls, and those in which a state shall be party, the Supreme Court
shall have original jurisdiction. In all the other cases before mentioned, the
Supreme Court shall have **appellate** jurisdiction, both as to law and fact, with
such exceptions, and under such regulations, as the Congress shall make.

**3. Trial by Jury** The trial of all crimes, except in cases of impeachment, shall
be by jury; and such trial shall be held in the state where the said crimes shall
have been committed; but when not committed within any state, the trial
shall be at such place or places as the Congress may by law have directed.

The Constitution actually
creates only one court—
the U.S. Supreme Court.
(*right*) The members of the
Supreme Court in 2006.

## COMPARING  *Checks and Balances*

### EXECUTIVE BRANCH (President)

| CHECKS ON COURTS | CHECKS ON CONGRESS |
|---|---|
| • Appoints federal judges<br>• Can grant reprieves and pardons for federal crimes | • Can veto acts of Congress<br>• Can call special sessions of Congress<br>• Can suggest laws and send messages to Congress |

### JUDICIAL BRANCH (Supreme Court)

| CHECKS ON PRESIDENT | CHECKS ON CONGRESS |
|---|---|
| • Can declare executive acts unconstitutional<br>• Judges, appointed for life, are free from executive control | • Judicial review—Can declare acts of Congress unconstitutional |

### LEGISLATIVE BRANCH (Congress)

| CHECKS ON COURT | CHECKS ON PRESIDENT |
|---|---|
| • Can impeach and remove federal judges<br>• Establishes lower federal courts<br>• Can refuse to confirm judicial appointments | • Can impeach and remove the president<br>• Can override veto<br>• Controls spending of money<br>• Senate can refuse to confirm presidential appointments and to ratify treaties |

### CRITICAL THINKING

1. Why is judicial review an important action of the Supreme Court?
2. Which check do you think is the most powerful? Why?

---

SECTION 3. **Treason**

**1. Definition**  Treason against the United States shall consist only in levying war against them, or in adhering to their enemies, giving them aid and comfort. No person shall be convicted of treason unless on the testimony of two witnesses to the same overt act, or on confession in open court.

**2. Punishment**  The Congress shall have power to declare the punishment of treason, but no attainder of treason shall work corruption of blood, or forfeiture except during the life of the person attained.

---

## Article 3 Assessment

### MAIN IDEAS

1. What is the main purpose of the judicial branch?
2. What is judicial review?
3. What are two kinds of cases that can begin in the Supreme Court?

### CRITICAL THINKING

4. **Draw Conclusions**  Why might the Supreme Court feel less political pressure than Congress in making judgments about the Constitution?

**Think about**
- the appointment of Supreme Court justices
- Congress members' obligation to voters

**BACKGROUND VOCABULARY**

**immunities** legal protections

**suffrage** right to vote

# ARTICLE 4. Relations Among States

## SECTION 1. State Acts and Records

Full faith and credit shall be given in each state to the public acts, records, and judicial proceedings of every other state. And the Congress may by general laws prescribe the manner in which such acts, records and proceedings shall be proved, and the effect thereof.

## SECTION 2. Rights of Citizens

**1. Citizenship** The citizens of each state shall be entitled to all privileges and **immunities** of citizens in the several states.

**2. Extradition** A person charged in any state with treason, felony, or other crime, who shall flee from justice, and be found in another state, shall on demand of the executive authority of the state from which he fled, be delivered up, to be removed to the state having jurisdiction of the crime.

3. Fugitive Slaves  No person held to service or labor in one state, under the laws thereof, escaping into another, shall, in consequence of any law or regulation therein, be discharged from such service or labor, but shall be delivered up on claim of the party to whom such service or labor may be due.

### Extradition

Persons charged with serious crimes cannot escape punishment by fleeing to another state. They must be returned to the first state and stand trial there.

**15. Why do you think the Framers included the power of extradition?**

1 Form small groups to illustrate a chart showing the national, shared, and state powers.

2 Display the chart in your classroom.

---

## COMPARING  *Federal and State Powers*

### Americans live under both national and state governments.

**NATIONAL POWERS**
- Maintain military
- Declare war
- Establish postal system
- Set standards for weights and measures
- Protect copyrights and patents

**SHARED POWERS**
- Collect taxes
- Establish courts
- Regulate interstate commerce
- Regulate banks
- Borrow money
- Provide for the general welfare
- Punish criminals

**STATE POWERS**
- Establish local governments
- Set up schools
- Regulate state commerce
- Make regulations for marriage
- Establish and regulate corporations

**CRITICAL THINKING  Evaluate**  What do you think is the purpose of dividing the powers between national and state governments?

### SECTION 3. **New States**

**1. Admission** New states may be admitted by the Congress into this Union; but no new state shall be formed or erected within the jurisdiction of any other state; nor any state be formed by the junction of two or more states, or parts of states, without the consent of the legislatures of the states concerned as well as of the Congress.

**2. Congressional Authority** The Congress shall have power to dispose of and make all needful rules and regulations respecting the territory or other property belonging to the United States; and nothing in this Constitution shall be so construed as to prejudice any claims of the United States, or of any particular state.

### SECTION 4. **Guarantees to the States**

The United States shall guarantee to every state in this Union a republican form of government, and shall protect each of them against invasion; and on application of the legislature, or of the executive (when the legislature cannot be convened) against domestic violence.

## ARTICLE 5. **Amending the Constitution**

The Congress, whenever two-thirds of both houses shall deem it necessary, shall propose amendments to this Constitution, or, on the application of the legislatures of two-thirds of the several states, shall call a convention for proposing amendments, which, in either case, shall be valid to all intents and purposes, as part of this Constitution, when ratified by the legislatures of three-fourths of the several states, or by conventions in three- fourths thereof, as the one or the other mode of ratification may be proposed by the Congress; ~~provided that no amendment which may be made prior to the year one thousand eight hundred and eight shall in any manner affect the first and fourth clauses in the ninth section of the first article;~~ and that no state, without its consent, shall be deprived of its equal **suffrage** in the Senate.

---

### Admission to Statehood

In 1998, Puerto Ricans voted against their island becoming the 51st state. A lawyer in Puerto Rico summed up a main reason: "Puerto Ricans want to have ties to the U.S., but they want to protect their culture and language." Also, as a U.S. commonwealth, Puerto Rico makes its own laws and handles its own finances

**16. Do you think Puerto Rico should become a state? Why or why not?**

---

### Amending the Constitution

**There are two ways to propose an amendment:**

| **2/3** of each house of **Congress** vote to amend the Constitution* | **2/3** of **state legislatures** call for a national convention to amend the Constitution |
|---|---|

*All 27 amendments have been proposed by this method.

**There are also two ways to ratify an amendment:**

| **3/4** of state legislatures approve the amendment | **3/4** of states approve the amendment at state conventions |
|---|---|

**CRITICAL THINKING** Why do you think more votes are needed to ratify an amendment than to propose one?

## BACKGROUND VOCABULARY

**ratification** official approval

**unanimous consent** complete agreement

### Federal Supremacy

In 1957, the "supreme law of the land" was put to a test. The governor of Arkansas defied a Supreme Court order. The Court ruled that African-American students could go to all-white public schools. President Dwight D. Eisenhower then sent federal troops to protect the first African-American students to enroll in Central High School in Little Rock, Arkansas.

# ARTICLE 6. Supremacy of the National Government

## SECTION 1. Valid Debts

All debts contracted and engagements entered into, before the adoption of this Constitution, shall be as valid against the United States under this Constitution, as under the Confederation.

## SECTION 2. Supreme Law

This Constitution, and the laws of the United States which shall be made in pursuance thereof; and all treaties made, or which shall be made, under the authority of the United States, shall be the supreme law of the land; and the judges in every state shall be bound thereby, anything in the constitution or laws of any state to the contrary notwithstanding.

## SECTION 3. Loyalty to Constitution

The Senators and Representatives before mentioned, and the members of the several state legislatures, and all executive and judicial officers, both of the United States and of the several states, shall be bound by oath or affirmation to support this Constitution; but no religious test shall ever be required as a qualification to any office or public trust under the United States.

Members of the House of Representatives swear to support and defend the U.S. Constitution at the opening of the 109th Congress in 2005.

# ARTICLE 7. **Ratification**

The **ratification** of the conventions of nine states shall be sufficient for the establishment of this Constitution between the states so ratifying the same. Done in convention by the **unanimous consent** of the states present, the seventeenth day of September in the year of our Lord one thousand seven hundred and eighty-seven and of the independence of the United States of America the twelfth. In witness whereof we have hereunto subscribed our names.

*George Washington*
President and deputy from Virginia

**New Hampshire:** *John Langdon, Nicholas Gilman*

**Massachusetts:** *Nathaniel Gorham, Rufus King*

**Connecticut:** *William Samuel Johnson, Roger Sherman*

**New York:** *Alexander Hamilton*

**New Jersey:** *William Livingston, David Brearley, William Paterson, Jonathan Dayton*

**Pennsylvania:** *Benjamin Franklin, Thomas Mifflin, Robert Morris, George Clymer, Thomas FitzSimons, Jared Ingersoll, James Wilson, Gouverneur Morris*

**Delaware:** *George Read, Gunning Bedford, Jr., John Dickinson, Richard Bassett, Jacob Broom*

**Maryland:** *James McHenry, Dan of St. Thomas Jenifer, Daniel Carroll*

**Virginia:** *John Blair, James Madison, Jr.*

**North Carolina:** *William Blount, Richard Dobbs Spaight, Hugh Williamson*

**South Carolina:** *John Rutledge, Charles Cotesworth Pinckney, Charles Pinckney, Pierce Butler*

**Georgia:** *William Few, Abraham Baldwin*

## The Signers

The 39 men who signed the Constitution were wealthy and well educated. About half of them were trained in law. Others were doctors, merchants, bankers, and slaveholding planters. Missing from the list of signatures are the names of African Americans, Native Americans, and women. These groups reflected the varied population of the United States in the 1780s.

**17. How do you think the absence of these groups affected the decisions made in creating the Constitution?**

## Articles 4–7 **Assessment**

### MAIN IDEAS

1. What rights does Article 4 guarantee to citizens if they go to other states in the nation?
2. What are two ways of proposing an amendment to the Constitution?
3. What makes up "the supreme law of the land"?

### CRITICAL THINKING

4. **Form and Support Opinions** Should the Framers of the Constitution have allowed the people to vote directly for ratification of the Constitution? Why or why not?

### Think about

• the idea that the government belongs to the people
• the general public's ability to make sound political decisions

**285**

# The Bill of Rights and Amendments 11–27

In 1787, Thomas Jefferson sent James Madison a letter about the Constitution. Jefferson wrote, "I will now add what I do not like . . . [there is no] bill of rights." He explained his reasons: "A bill of rights is what the people are entitled to against every government on earth . . . and what no just government should refuse." Jefferson's disapproval is not surprising. In writing the Declaration of Independence, he spelled out basic individual rights that cannot be taken way. These are "life, liberty, and the pursuit of happiness." The Declaration states that governments are formed to protect these rights.

Several states approved the Constitution only if a list of guaranteed freedoms was added. While serving in the nation's first Congress, James Madison helped draft the Bill of Rights. In 1791, these first ten amendments became part of the Constitution.

James Madison played a leading role in the creation of the U.S. Constitution.

## AMENDMENTS 1–10. The Bill of Rights

▼ **KEY QUESTION** Why do some individual rights need special protection in the Constitution?

### AMENDMENT 1. Religious and Political Freedom 1791

Congress shall make no law respecting an establishment of religion, or prohibiting the free exercise thereof; or **abridging** the freedom of speech, or of the press; or the right of the people peaceably to assemble, and to petition the Government for a redress of grievances.

**The Five Freedoms**

1. Freedom of Religion
2. Freedom of Speech
3. Freedom of the Press
4. Freedom of Assembly
5. Freedom to Petition

**AMENDMENT 2. Right to Bear Arms** 1791 A well-regulated militia, being necessary to the security of a free state, the right of the people to keep and bear arms, shall not be infringed.

**AMENDMENT 3. Quartering Troops** 1791 No soldier shall, in time of peace be quartered in any house, without the consent of the owner, nor in time of war, but in a manner to be prescribed by law.

**AMENDMENT 4. Search and Seizure** 1791 The right of the people to be secure in their persons, houses, papers, and effects, against unreasonable searches and seizures, shall not be violated, and no warrants shall issue, but upon probable cause, supported by oath or affirmation, and particularly describing the place to be searched, and the persons or things to be seized.

**AMENDMENT 5. Rights of Accused Persons** 1791 No person shall be held to answer for a capital, or otherwise infamous crime, unless on a presentment or indictment of a Grand Jury, except in cases arising in the land or naval forces, or in the militia, when in actual service in time of war or public danger; nor shall any person be subject for the same offense to be twice put in jeopardy of life or limb; nor shall be compelled in any criminal case to be a witness against himself, nor be deprived of life, liberty, or property, without **due process of law**; nor shall private property be taken for public use, without just compensation.

**AMENDMENT 6. Right to a Speedy, Public Trial** 1791 In all criminal prosecutions, the accused shall enjoy the right to a speedy and public trial, by an impartial jury of the State and district wherein the crime shall have been committed, which district shall have been previously ascertained by law, and to be informed of the nature and cause of the accusation; to be confronted with the witnesses against him; to have **compulsory process** for obtaining witnesses in his favor, and to have the assistance of **counsel** for his defense.

**BACKGROUND VOCABULARY**

**abridging** reducing

**quartered** given a place to stay

**due process of law** fair treatment under the law

**compulsory process** required procedure

**counsel** a lawyer

### Legal Rights

In 1966, the Supreme Court made a decision based on the 5th and 6th Amendments. The outcome of this ruling is called "Miranda rights." Miranda rights protect suspects from giving forced confessions. Police must read these rights to a suspect they are questioning. For example:

- "You have the right to remain silent."
- "Anything that you say can and will be used against you in a court of law."
- "You have the right to an attorney."

(*left*) Demonstrators exercise their First Amendment rights of freedom of assembly and of speech at a rally in favor of immigration reform in 2006. (*above*) A journalist, utilizing freedom of the press, interviews a Hispanic family rallying for the same cause.

**common law** a system of law developed in England, based on customs and previous court decisions

**bail** money paid by arrested persons to guarantee they will return for trial

**equity** a system of justice not covered under common law

Members of the jury are expected to determine the guilt or innocence of a defendant in a court proceeding.

### States Powers

The 10th Amendment gives the states reserved powers. Any powers not clearly given to the national government by the U.S. Constitution or denied to the states in Article I, Section 10, belong to the states. State constitutions sometimes assume authority in unexpected areas. For example, California's constitution sets rules for governing the use of fishing nets.

**18. What are some common areas in which states have authority?**

**AMENDMENT 7. Trial by Jury in Civil Cases** 1791 In suits at common law, where the value in controversy shall exceed twenty dollars, the right of trial by jury shall be preserved, and no fact tried by a jury, shall be otherwise reexamined in any court of the United States, than according to the rules of the common law.

**AMENDMENT 8. Limits of Fines and Punishments** 1791 Excessive bail shall not be required, nor excessive fines imposed, nor cruel and unusual punishments inflicted.

**AMENDMENT 9. Rights of People** 1791 The enumeration in the Constitution of certain rights shall not be construed to deny or disparage others retained by the people.

**AMENDMENT 10. Powers of States and People** 1791 The powers not delegated to the United States by the Constitution, nor prohibited by it to the States, are reserved to the States respectively, or to the people.

## Bill of Rights Assessment

### MAIN IDEAS

1. Why do some individual rights need special protection in the Constitution?

2. Which amendment protects your privacy?

3. Which amendments guarantee fair legal treatment?

4. Which amendment prevents the federal government from taking powers away from the states and the people?

### CRITICAL THINKING

5. **Form and Support Opinions** The 4th, 5th, 6th, 7th, and 8th Amendments protect innocent people accused of crimes. Do you think these five amendments also favor the rights of actual criminals?

**Think about**

- criminals who go free if valuable evidence is found after their trials

- criminals released on bail

# Amendments 11–27

▼ **KEY QUESTION** How has the Constitution adapted to social changes and trends?

## AMENDMENT 11. **Lawsuits Against States** 1795

**Passed by Congress March 4, 1794. Ratified February 7, 1795. Proclaimed 1798.**
**Note: Article 3, Section 2, of the Constitution was modified by Amendment 11.**

The Judicial power of the United States shall not be construed to extend to any suit in law or **equity**, commenced or prosecuted against one of the United States by citizens of another state, or by citizens or subjects of any foreign state.

## AMENDMENT 12. **Election of Executives** 1804

**Passed by Congress December 9, 1803. Ratified June 15, 1804.**
**Note: Part of Article 2, Section 1, of the Constitution was replaced by the 12th Amendment.**

The electors shall meet in their respective states and vote by ballot for President and Vice-President, one of whom, at least, shall not be an inhabitant of the same state with themselves; they shall name in their ballots the person voted for as President, and in distinct ballots the person voted for as Vice-President, and they shall make distinct lists of all persons voted for as President, and of all persons voted for as Vice-President, and of the number of votes for each, which lists they shall sign and certify, and transmit sealed to the seat of the government of the United States, directed to the President of the Senate;—the President of the Senate shall, in the presence of the Senate and House of Representatives, open all the certificates and the votes shall then be counted;—the person having the greatest number of votes for President, shall be the President, if such number be a majority of the whole number of electors appointed; and if no person have such majority, then from the persons having the highest numbers not exceeding three on the list of those voted for as President, the House of Representatives shall choose immediately, by ballot, the President. But in choosing the President, the votes shall be taken by states, the representation from each state having one vote; a quorum for this purpose shall consist of a member or members from two-thirds of the states, and a majority of all the states shall be necessary to a choice. And if the House of Representatives shall not choose a President whenever the right of choice shall devolve upon them, ~~before the fourth day of March next following~~, then the Vice-President shall act as President, as in the case of the death or other constitutional disability of the President. The person having the greatest number of votes as Vice-President, shall be the Vice-President, if such number be a majority of the whole number of Electors appointed, and if no person have a majority, then from the two highest numbers on the list, the Senate shall choose the Vice-President; a quorum for the purpose shall consist of two-thirds of the whole number of Senators, and a majority of the whole number shall be necessary to a choice. But no

**Separate Ballots**

The presidential election of 1800 ended in a tie between Thomas Jefferson and (*above*) Aaron Burr. At this time, the candidate with the most votes became president. The runner-up became vice-president. The 12th Amendment calls for separate ballots for the president and vice president. The vice president is specifically elected to the office, rather than being the presidential candidate with the second-most votes.

### Civil Rights Laws

The 14th Amendment laid the groundwork for many civil rights laws, such as the Americans with Disabilities Act (1990). This act gave people with mental or physical disabilities "equal protection of the laws." For example, public places had to be designed for wheelchair use. Wider doors and ramps allow people with disabilities to go in and out of buildings, and wheelchair lifts make public buses accessible to people with disabilities.

person constitutionally ineligible to the office of President shall be eligible to that of Vice-President of the United States.

### AMENDMENT 13. **Slavery Abolished** 1865

**Passed by Congress January 31, 1865. Ratified December 6, 1865.**

**Note: A portion of Article 4, Section 2, of the Constitution was superseded by the 13th Amendment.**

**Section 1.** Neither slavery nor involuntary **servitude**, except as a punishment for crime whereof the party shall have been duly convicted, shall exist within the United States, or any place subject to their jurisdiction.

**Section 2.** Congress shall have power to enforce this article by appropriate legislation.

### AMENDMENT 14. **Civil Rights** 1868

**Passed by Congress June 13, 1866. Ratified July 9, 1868.**

**Note: Article 1, Section 2, of the Constitution was modified by Section 2 of the 14th Amendment.**

**Section 1.** All persons born or **naturalized** in the United States, and subject to the jurisdiction thereof, are citizens of the United States and of the state wherein they reside. No state shall make or enforce any law which shall abridge the privileges or immunities of citizens of the United States; nor shall any state deprive any person of life, liberty, or property, without due process of law; nor deny to any person within its jurisdiction the equal protection of the laws.

**Section 2.** Representatives shall be apportioned among the several states according to their respective numbers, counting the whole number of persons in each state, excluding Indians not taxed. But when the right to vote at any election for the choice of electors for President and Vice-President of the United States, Representatives in Congress, the executive and judicial officers of a state, or the members of the legislature thereof, is denied to any of the male inhabitants of such state, being twenty-one years of age, and citizens of the United States, or in any way abridged, except for participation in rebellion, or other crime, the basis of representation therein shall be reduced in the proportion which the number of such male citizens shall bear to the whole number of male citizens twenty-one years of age in such state.

**Section 3.** No person shall be a Senator or Representative in Congress, or elector of President and Vice-President, or hold any office, civil or military, under the United States, or under any state, who, having previously taken an oath, as a member of Congress, or as an officer of the United States, or as a member of any state legislature, or as an executive or judicial officer of any state, to support the Constitution of the United States, shall have engaged in **insurrection** or rebellion against the same, or given aid or comfort to the enemies thereof. But Congress may, by a vote of two-thirds of each house, remove such disability.

**Section 4.** The validity of the public debt of the United States, authorized by law, including debts incurred for payment of pensions and **bounties** for services in suppressing insurrection or rebellion, shall not be questioned. But neither the United States nor any state shall assume or pay any debt or obligation incurred in aid of insurrection or rebellion against the United States, or any claim for the loss or emancipation of any slave; but all such debts, obligations and claims shall be held illegal and void.

**Section 5.** The Congress shall have power to enforce, by appropriate legislation, the provisions of this article.

**AMENDMENT 15. Right to Vote** 1870

**Passed by Congress February 26, 1869. Ratified February 3, 1870.**

**Section 1.** The right of citizens of the United States to vote shall not be denied or abridged by the United States or by any state on account of race, color, or previous condition of servitude.

**Section 2.** The Congress shall have power to enforce this article by appropriate legislation.

**Voting Rights**

The Voting Rights Act of 1965 extended the 15th Amendment. To qualify as voters, African Americans were no longer required to take tests proving that they could read and write. Also, federal examiners could help register voters. As a result, the number of African-American voters rose sharply. (*above*) Federal voter registrars enforce the Voting Rights Act in Canton, Miss. in 1965.

**19. What effect do you think the Voting Rights Act had on candidates running for office?**

**COMPARING** *Reconstruction Amendments*

The 13th, 14th, and 15th Amendments are often called the Reconstruction Amendments. They were passed after the Civil War during the government's attempt to rebuild the Union and to grant rights to recently freed African Americans.

EQUALITY

YES NO

BALLOTS

**13th Amendment** 1865
• Ended slavery in the United States

**14th Amendment** 1868
• Defined national and state citizenship
• Protected citizens' rights
• Promised equal protection of the laws

**15th Amendment** 1870
• Designed to protect African Americans' voting rights

**CRITICAL THINKING** What problems did these amendments try to solve?

## AMENDMENT 16. Income Tax 1913

**Passed by Congress July 12, 1909. Ratified February 3, 1913.**

**Note: Article 1, Section 9, of the Constitution was modified by the 16th Amendment.**

The Congress shall have power to lay and collect taxes on incomes, from whatever source derived, without apportionment among the several states, and without regard to any census or enumeration.

## AMENDMENT 17. Direct Election of Senators 1913

**Passed by Congress May 13, 1912. Ratified April 8, 1913.**

**Note: Article 1, Section 3, of the Constitution was modified by the 17th Amendment.**

**Section 1.** The Senate of the United States shall be composed of two Senators from each state, elected by the people thereof, for six years; and each Senator shall have one vote. The electors in each state shall have the qualifications requisite for electors of the most numerous branch of the state legislatures.

**Section 2.** When vacancies happen in the representation of any state in the Senate, the executive authority of such state shall issue writs of election to fill such vacancies: Provided, that the legislature of any state may empower the executive thereof to make temporary appointments until the people fill the vacancies by election as the legislature may direct.

**Section 3.** This amendment shall not be so construed as to affect the election or term of any Senator chosen before it becomes valid as part of the Constitution.

## AMENDMENT 18. Prohibition 1919

**Passed by Congress December 18, 1917. Ratified January 16, 1919. Repealed by the 21st Amendment.**

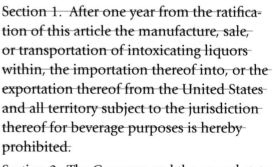

Section 1. After one year from the ratification of this article the manufacture, sale, or transportation of intoxicating liquors within, the importation thereof into, or the exportation thereof from the United States and all territory subject to the jurisdiction thereof for beverage purposes is hereby prohibited.

Section 2. The Congress and the several states shall have concurrent power to enforce this article by appropriate legislation.

Section 3. This article shall be inoperative unless it shall have been ratified as an amendment to the Constitution by the legislatures of the several states, as provided in the Constitution, within seven years from the date of the submission hereof to the states by the Congress.

---

**Income Tax**

People below the poverty level, as defined by the federal government, do not have to pay income tax. In 2004, the poverty level for a family of four was $19,307 per year. About 12.7 percent of all Americans were considered poor in 2004.

**20. Why do you think people below the poverty level do not pay any income tax?**

**Prohibition**

Under Prohibition, people broke the law if they made, sold, or shipped alcoholic beverages. Powerful crime gangs turned selling illegal liquor into a big business. This photo shows a federal agent enforcing the 18th Amendment by destroying kegs of illegal beer.

(*left*) These women are campaigning in favor of the 19th Amendment—woman suffrage. Since winning the right to vote in 1920, women have slowly gained political power.

## AMENDMENT 19. **Woman Suffrage** 1920

**Passed by Congress June 4, 1919. Ratified August 18, 1920.**

**Section 1.** The right of citizens of the United States to vote shall not be denied or abridged by the United States or by any state on account of sex.

**Section 2.** Congress shall have power to enforce this article by appropriate legislation.

## AMENDMENT 20. **"Lame Duck" Sessions** 1933

**Passed by Congress March 2, 1932. Ratified January 23, 1933.**

Note: Article 1, Section 4, of the Constitution was modified by Section 2 of this amendment. In addition, a portion of the 12th Amendment was superseded by Section 3.

**Section 1.** The terms of the President and Vice-President shall end at noon on the 20th day of January, and the terms of Senators and Representatives at noon on the 3rd day of January, of the years in which such terms would have ended if this article had not been ratified; and the terms of their successors shall then begin.

**Section 2.** The Congress shall assemble at least once in every year, and such meeting shall begin at noon on the 3rd day of January, unless they shall by law appoint a different day.

**Section 3.** If, at the time fixed for the beginning of the term of the President, the President elect shall have died, the Vice-President elect shall become President. If a President shall not have been chosen before the time fixed for the beginning of his term, or if the President elect shall have failed to qualify, then the Vice-President elect shall act as President until a President shall have qualified; and the Congress may by law provide for the case wherein neither a President elect nor a Vice-President elect shall have qualified, declaring who shall then act as President, or the manner in which one who is to act shall be selected, and such person shall act accordingly until a President or Vice-President shall have qualified.

### Connect *to* Today

**The Equal Rights Amendment (ERA)** In 1920, the 19th Amendment took effect, guaranteeing women the right to vote. Nevertheless, many women have continued to face discrimination in the United States. In 1923, the National Women's Party supported the passage of an equal rights amendment to protect women. Congress did not pass such an amendment until 1972. In 1982, however, the amendment died after it failed to be ratified by enough states to be added to the Constitution. As of the mid-2000s, the ERA was still not part of the U.S. Constitution.

**21. Why do you think the 19th Amendment failed to create equality for women?**

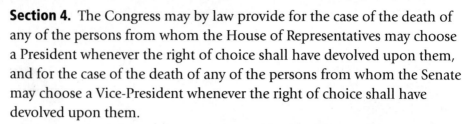

**Section 4.** The Congress may by law provide for the case of the death of any of the persons from whom the House of Representatives may choose a President whenever the right of choice shall have devolved upon them, and for the case of the death of any of the persons from whom the Senate may choose a Vice-President whenever the right of choice shall have devolved upon them.

**Section 5.** Sections 1 and 2 shall take effect on the 15th day of October following the ratification of this article.

**Section 6.** This article shall be **inoperative** unless it shall have been ratified as an amendment to the Constitution by the legislatures of three-fourths of the several states within seven years from the date of its submission.

### AMENDMENT 21. Repeal of Prohibition 1933
**Passed by Congress February 20, 1933. Ratified December 5, 1933.**

**Section 1.** The eighteenth article of amendment to the Constitution of the United States is hereby repealed.

**Section 2.** The transportation or importation into any state, territory, or possession of the United States for delivery or use therein of intoxicating liquors, in violation of the laws thereof, is hereby prohibited.

**Section 3.** This article shall be inoperative unless it shall have been ratified as an amendment to the Constitution by conventions in the several states, as provided in the Constitution, within seven years from the date of the submission hereof to the states by the Congress.

### AMENDMENT 22. Limit on Presidential Terms 1951
**Passed by Congress March 21, 1947. Ratified February 27, 1951.**

**Section 1.** No person shall be elected to the office of the President more than twice, and no person who has held the office of President, or acted as President, for more than two years of a term to which some other person was elected President shall be elected to the office of the President more than once. But this article shall not apply to any person holding the office of President when this article was proposed by the Congress, and shall not prevent any person who may be holding the office of President, or acting as President, during the term within which this article becomes operative from holding the office of President or acting as President during the remainder of such term.

**Term Limits**

George Washington set the tradition of limiting the presidency to two terms. Franklin Roosevelt broke this custom when he was elected president four terms in a row—1932, 1936, 1940, and 1944. His record-long presidency led to the 22nd Amendment. A two-term limit, written into the Constitution, checks the president's power.

President Roosevelt (*far right*) campaigns with farmers in Atlanta, Ga. before the 1932 election.

**Section 2.** This article shall be inoperative unless it shall have been ratified as an amendment to the Constitution by the legislatures of three-fourths of the several states within seven years from the date of its submission to the states by the Congress.

### AMENDMENT 23. **Voting in District of Columbia** 1961
**Passed by Congress June 16, 1960. Ratified March 29, 1961.**

**Section 1.** The district constituting the seat of government of the United States shall appoint in such manner as Congress may direct: a number of electors of President and Vice-President equal to the whole number of Senators and Representatives in Congress to which the district would be entitled if it were a state, but in no event more than the least populous state; they shall be in addition to those appointed by the states, but they shall be considered, for the purposes of the election of President and Vice-President, to be electors appointed by a state; and they shall meet in the district and perform such duties as provided by the twelfth article of amendment.

**Section 2.** The Congress shall have power to enforce this article by appropriate legislation.

### AMENDMENT 24. **Abolition of Poll Taxes** 1964
**Passed by Congress August 27, 1962. Ratified January 23, 1964.**

**Section 1.** The right of citizens of the United States to vote in any **primary** or other election for President or Vice-President, for electors for President or Vice-President, or for Senator or Representative in Congress, shall not be denied or abridged by the United States or any state by reason of failure to pay any poll tax or other tax.

**Section 2.** The Congress shall have power to enforce this article by appropriate legislation.

### AMENDMENT 25. **Presidential Disability, Succession** 1967
**Passed by Congress July 6, 1965. Ratified February 10, 1967.**
**Note: Article 2, Section 1, of the Constitution was affected by the 25th Amendment.**

**Section 1.** In case of the removal of the President from office or of his death or resignation, the Vice-President shall become President.

**Section 2.** Whenever there is a vacancy in the office of the Vice-President, the President shall nominate a Vice-President who shall take office upon confirmation by a majority vote of both houses of Congress.

**Section 3.** Whenever the President transmits to the President pro tempore of the Senate and the Speaker of the House of Representatives his written declaration that he is unable to discharge the powers and duties of his office, and until he transmits to them a written declaration to the contrary, such powers and duties shall be discharged by the Vice-President as Acting President.

**Poll Tax**

The poll tax was aimed at preventing African Americans from exercising their rights. Many could not afford to pay this fee required for voting.

**22. How do you think the 24th Amendment affected elections?**

**Line of Succession**

On June 29, 2002, President George W. Bush underwent a medical procedure which required sedation. Bush declared himself temporarily unable to perform the duties of the presidency. Vice-President Dick Cheney acted as President for about two hours that day—until Bush notified in writing that he was resuming the powers and duties of the office.

**23. What do you think can happen in a country where the rules for succession are not clear?**

## Succession

Who takes over if a president dies in office or is unable to serve? The top five in the line of succession follow:

- vice-president
- speaker of the house
- president pro tempore of the Senate
- secretary of state
- secretary of the treasury

**24. Why should voters know the views of the vice-president?**

**Section 4.** Whenever the Vice-President and a majority of either the principal officers of the executive departments or of such other body as Congress may by law provide, transmit to the President pro tempore of the Senate and the Speaker of the House of Representatives their written declaration that the President is unable to discharge the powers and duties of his office, the Vice-President shall immediately assume the powers and duties of the office as Acting President. Thereafter, when the President transmits to the President pro tempore of the Senate and the Speaker of the House of Representatives his written declaration that no inability exists, he shall resume the powers and duties of his office unless the Vice-President and a majority of either the principal officers of the executive department[s] or of such other body as Congress may by law provide, transmit within four days to the President pro tempore of the Senate and the Speaker of the House of Representatives their written declaration that the President is unable to discharge the powers and duties of his office. Thereupon Congress shall decide the issue, assembling within forty-eight hours for that purpose if not in session. If the Congress, within twenty-one days after receipt of the latter written declaration, or, if Congress is not in session, within twenty-one days after Congress is required to assemble, determines by two thirds vote of both houses that the President is unable to discharge the powers and duties of his office, the Vice-President shall continue to discharge the same as Acting President; otherwise, the President shall resume the powers and duties of his office.

## Amendments Timeline

**Use the key below to help you categorize the amendments.**

- ■ **Voting Rights**
- ■ **Overturned Supreme Court Decisions**
- ■ **Social Changes**
- ■ **Election Procedures and Conditions of Office**

**1791**
**Bill of Rights**
Amendments 1–10

**1868**
**Amendment 14**
Defines American citizenship and citizens' rights.

**1870**
**Amendment 15**
Stops national and state governments from denying the vote based on race.

**1791** **1800** **1850**

**1798**
**Amendment 11**
Protects state from lawsuits filed by citizens of other states or countries.

**1804**
**Amendment 12**
Requires separate electoral ballots for president and vice-president.

**1865**
**Amendment 13**
Bans slavery.

## AMENDMENT 26. 18-year-old Vote 1971

**Passed by Congress March 23, 1971. Ratified July 1, 1971.**

Note: Amendment 14, Section 2, of the Constitution was modified by Section 1 of the 26th Amendment.

**Section 1.** The right of citizens of the United States, who are eighteen years of age or older, to vote shall not be denied or abridged by the United States or by any state on account of age.

**Section 2.** The Congress shall have power to enforce this article by appropriate legislation.

## AMENDMENT 27. Congressional Pay 1992

**Passed by Congress September 25, 1789. Ratified May 7, 1992.**

No law, varying the compensation for the services of the Senators and Representatives, shall take effect, until an election of Representatives shall have intervened.

### The Youth Vote

Members of the recording industry founded Rock the Vote. They urge young people to vote in elections.

## Amendments 11–27 Assessment

### MAIN IDEAS

1. How has the Constitution adapted to social changes and trends?
2. Which amendments affected the office of president?
3. Which pair of amendments shows the failure of laws to solve a social problem?
4. Which amendments corrected unfair treatment toward African Americans and women?

### CRITICAL THINKING

5. **Summarize** What is the purpose of amending the Constitution?

**Think about**

- the purpose of the Constitution
- problems and issues that Americans have faced throughout U.S. history

**1961**
**Amendment 23**
Gives citizens of Washington, D.C., right to vote in presidential elections.

**1964**
**Amendment 24**
Bans poll taxes.

**1920**
**Amendment 19**
Extends the vote to women.

**1919**
Amendment 18
Prohibits making, selling, and shipping alcoholic beverages.

**1933**
Amendment 21
Repeals Amendment 18.

**1971**
**Amendment 26**
Gives 18-year-olds right to vote in federal and state elections.

**1900**        **1950**        **2000**

**1913**
Amendment 16
Allows Congress to tax incomes.

**Amendment 17**
Establishes direct election of U.S. senators.

**1933**
**Amendment 20**
Changes date for starting new Congress and inaugurating new president.

**1951**
**Amendment 22**
Limits terms president can serve to two.

**1967**
**Amendment 25**
Sets procedures for presidential succession.

**1992**
**Amendment 27**
Limits ability of Congress to increase its pay.

I'M AGAINST THE 3rd TERM
WASHINGTON WOULDN'T
GRANT COULDN'T
ROOSEVELT SHOULDN'T

# The Role of the Citizen

Citizens of the United States enjoy many basic rights and freedoms. Freedom of speech and religion are examples. These rights are guaranteed by the Constitution, the Bill of Rights, and other amendments to the Constitution. Along with these rights, however, come **responsibilities**. Obeying rules and laws, voting, and serving on juries are some examples.

**Reason** and **respect** are also important aspects of citizenship. Reason—considering perspectives, applying logical and analytical thought, and exercising good judgment—is an important part of developing positive character qualities. Respect—for one's self, for other people, and for the community—plays a key role in how you participate in society. These Three R's of Democratic Citizenship are listed below. As you read through this handbook, note how the Three R's impact all aspects of citizenship.

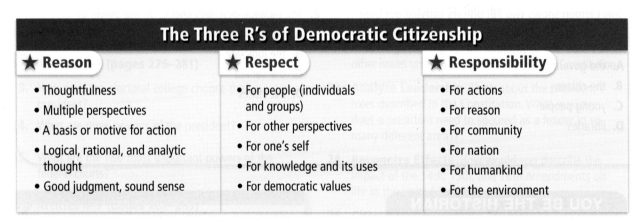

## The Three R's of Democratic Citizenship

| ★ Reason | ★ Respect | ★ Responsibility |
|---|---|---|
| • Thoughtfulness | • For people (individuals and groups) | • For actions |
| • Multiple perspectives | • For other perspectives | • For reason |
| • A basis or motive for action | • For one's self | • For community |
| • Logical, rational, and analytic thought | • For knowledge and its uses | • For nation |
| • Good judgment, sound sense | • For democratic values | • For humankind |
| | | • For the environment |

## Active Citizenship

Active citizenship is not limited to adults. Younger citizens can help their communities become better places. The following pages will help you to learn about your rights and responsibilities. Knowing them will help you to become an active and involved citizen of your community.

The chart below lists five important ways *you* can be a model citizen. The examples in the pages that follow provide details about the five aspects of citizenship listed here.

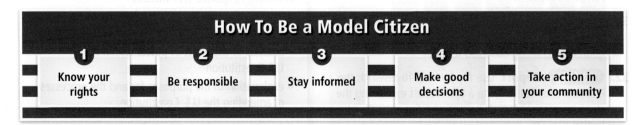

## How To Be a Model Citizen

| 1 | 2 | 3 | 4 | 5 |
|---|---|---|---|---|
| Know your rights | Be responsible | Stay informed | Make good decisions | Take action in your community |

The weather was sunny but cold on January 20, 1961—the day that John F. Kennedy became the 35th president of the United States. In his first speech as president, he urged all Americans to serve their country. Since then, Kennedy's words have inspired millions of Americans to become more active citizens.

> 66 Ask not what your country can do for you—ask what you can do for your country! 99
>
> —John F. Kennedy

President John F. Kennedy urged all Americans to become active citizens and work to improve their communities.

## What Is a Citizen?

A citizen is a legal member of a nation and pledges loyalty to that nation. A citizen has certain guaranteed rights, protections, and responsibilities. A citizen is a member of a community and wants to make it a good place to live.

Today in the United States there are a number of ways to become a citizen. The most familiar are citizenship by birth and citizenship by naturalization. All citizens have the right to equal protection under the law.

**Citizenship by Birth** A child born in the United States is a citizen by birth. Children born to U.S. citizens traveling or living outside the country are citizens. Even children born in the United States to parents who are not citizens of the United States are considered U.S. citizens. These children have dual citizenship. This means they are citizens of two countries—both the United States and the country of their parents' citizenship. At the age of 18, the child may choose one of the countries for permanent citizenship.

New U.S. citizens being sworn in on Ellis Island.

**Citizenship by Naturalization** A person who is not a citizen of the United States may become one through a process called naturalization. To become a naturalized citizen, a person must meet certain requirements.

- Be at least 18 years old. Children under the age of 18 automatically become naturalized citizens when their parents do.
- Enter the United States legally.
- Live in the United States for five years as a permanent resident prior to application.
- Read, write, and speak English.
- Show knowledge of American history and government.

## The Naturalization Process

1. File an application.
2. Get fingerprints taken.
3. Be interviewed and take an examination.
4. Take an oath of allegiance.

# What Are Your Rights?

Citizens of the United States are guaranteed rights by the U.S. Constitution, state constitutions, and state and federal laws. All citizens have three kinds of rights:

**1** **Basic Freedoms** Citizens' basic rights and freedoms are sometimes called **civil rights**. Some of these rights are personal, and others are political.

**2** **Protection From Unfair Government Actions** The second category of rights is intended to protect citizens from unfair government actions.

**3** **Equal Treatment Under the Law** The third category is the right to equal treatment under the law. The government cannot treat one individual or group differently from another.

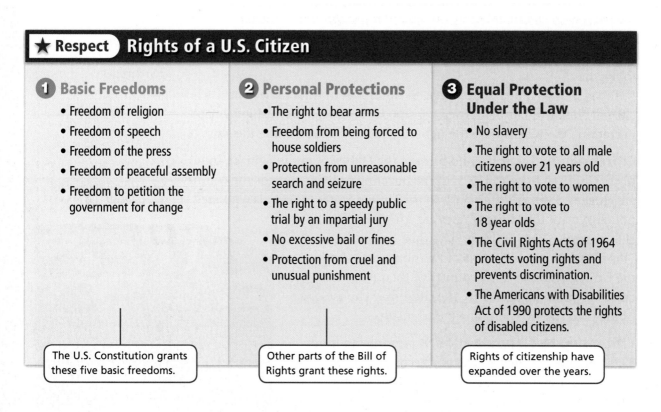

**★ Respect  Rights of a U.S. Citizen**

**1 Basic Freedoms**
- Freedom of religion
- Freedom of speech
- Freedom of the press
- Freedom of peaceful assembly
- Freedom to petition the government for change

The U.S. Constitution grants these five basic freedoms.

**2 Personal Protections**
- The right to bear arms
- Freedom from being forced to house soldiers
- Protection from unreasonable search and seizure
- The right to a speedy public trial by an impartial jury
- No excessive bail or fines
- Protection from cruel and unusual punishment

Other parts of the Bill of Rights grant these rights.

**3 Equal Protection Under the Law**
- No slavery
- The right to vote to all male citizens over 21 years old
- The right to vote to women
- The right to vote to 18 year olds
- The Civil Rights Acts of 1964 protects voting rights and prevents discrimination.
- The Americans with Disabilities Act of 1990 protects the rights of disabled citizens.

Rights of citizenship have expanded over the years.

**Limits to Rights** The rights guaranteed to citizens have sensible limits. For example, the right to free speech does not allow a person to falsely shout, "Fire!" at a crowded concert. The government may place limits on certain rights to protect national security or to provide equal opportunities for all citizens. And rights come with responsibilities.

# What Are Your Responsibilities?

For American democracy to work, citizens must carry out important responsibilities. There are two kinds of responsibilities—personal and civic. Personal responsibilities include taking care of yourself, helping your family, knowing right from wrong, and behaving in a respectful way.

Civic responsibilities are those that involve your government and community. They include obeying rules and laws, serving on juries, paying taxes, and defending your country when called upon. One of the most important responsibilities is voting. When you turn 18, you will have that right.

As a young person, you can be a good citizen in a number of ways. You might work with other people in your community to make it a fair and just place to live. Working for a political party or writing to your elected officials about issues that concern you are some other examples.

The chart below shows how responsibilities change with a citizen's age. Notice that all citizens share the responsibility to obey the laws of their communities.

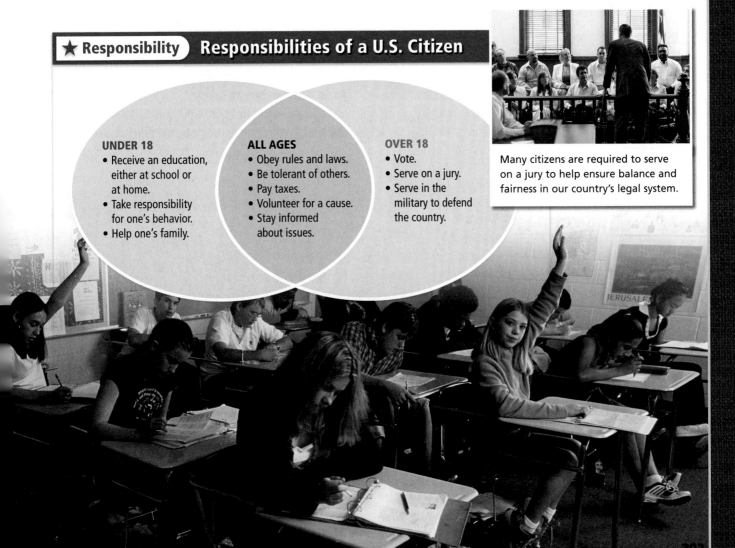

★ **Responsibility** **Responsibilities of a U.S. Citizen**

**UNDER 18**
- Receive an education, either at school or at home.
- Take responsibility for one's behavior.
- Help one's family.

**ALL AGES**
- Obey rules and laws.
- Be tolerant of others.
- Pay taxes.
- Volunteer for a cause.
- Stay informed about issues.

**OVER 18**
- Vote.
- Serve on a jury.
- Serve in the military to defend the country.

Many citizens are required to serve on a jury to help ensure balance and fairness in our country's legal system.

# Building Citizenship Skills

Good citizenship skills include staying informed, solving problems or making decisions, and taking action. Every citizen can find ways to build citizenship skills. By showing respect for the law and for the rights of others in your daily life, you promote democracy. You can also work to change conditions in your community to make sure all citizens experience freedom and justice.

## How Do You Stay Informed?

Americans can sometimes feel that they have access to too much information. It may seem overwhelming. Even so, you should stay informed on issues that affect your life. Staying informed gives you the information you need to make wise decisions and helps you find ways to solve problems.

---

### ★ Responsibility   Staying Informed

**1 Watch, Listen, and Read**

The first step in practicing good citizenship is to know how to find information that you need.

Sources of information include broadcast and print media and the Internet. Public officials and civic organizations are also good sources for additional information. Remember as you are reading to evaluate your sources.

**2 Evaluate**

As you become informed, you will need to make judgments about the accuracy of your news sources. You must also be aware of those sources' points of view and biases. (Bias is a one-sided presentation of an issue.)

You should determine if you need more information, and if so, where to find it. After gathering information, you may be ready to form an opinion or a plan of action to solve a problem.

**3 Communicate**

To bring about change in their communities, active citizens may need to contact public officials. In today's world, making contact is easy.

You can reach most public officials by telephone, voice mail, fax, or letter. Many public officials also have Internet pages or e-mail that encourages input from the public.

Teens from Stand, an Ohio youth group, with Ohio Governor Bob Taft and first lady Hope Taft.

# How Do You Make Good Decisions?

Civic life involves making important decisions. As a voter, whom should you vote for? As a juror, should you find the defendant guilty or not guilty? As an informed citizen, should you support or oppose a proposed government action? Unlike decisions about which video to rent, civic decisions cannot be made by a process as easy as tossing a coin. Instead, you should use a problem-solving approach like the one shown in the chart below. Decision making won't always proceed directly from step to step. Sometimes it's necessary to backtrack a little. For example, you may get to the "Analyze the Information" step and realize that you don't have enough information to analyze. Then you can go back a step and gather more information.

## ★ Reason   Making Good Decisions

Problem-solving and decision-making involves many steps. This chart shows you how to take those steps. Notice that you may have to repeat some steps depending on the information you gather.

**1 Identify the Problem**
Decide what the main issues are and what your goal is.

**2 Gather Information**
Get to know the basics of the problem. Find out as much as possible about the issues.

**3 Analyze the Information**
Look at the information and determine what it reveals about solving the problem.

**4 Consider Options**
Think of as many ways as possible to solve the problem. Don't be afraid to include ideas that others might think of as unacceptable.

**5 Choose a Solution**
Choose the solution you believe will best solve the problem and help you reach your goal.

**6 Implement the Solution**
Take action or plan to take action on a chosen solution.

**7 Evaluate the Solution**
Review the results of putting your solution into action. Did the solution work? Do you need to adjust the solution in some way?

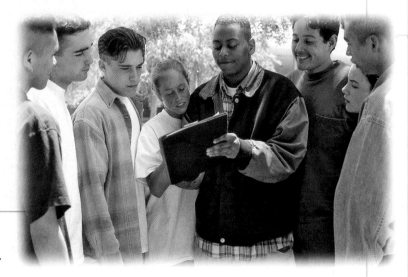

Conducting a survey is one way to gather information.

# How Do You Take Action in Your Community?

Across the country many young people have come up with ways to make their communities better places to live. Thirteen-year-old Aubyn Burnside of Hickory, North Carolina, is just one example. Aubyn felt sorry for foster children she saw moving their belongings in plastic trash bags. She founded Suitcases for Kids. This program provides used luggage for foster children who are moving from one home to another. Her program has been adopted by other young people in several states. Below are some ways in which you can participate in your community.

## ★ Respect ) Taking Action

### 1 Find a Cause
How can you become involved in your community? First, select a community problem or issue that interests you. Some ideas from other young people include starting a support group for children with cancer, publishing a neighborhood newspaper with children's stories and art, and putting on performances to entertain people in shelters and hospitals.

### 2 Develop Solutions
Once you have found a cause on which you want to work, develop a plan for solving the problem. Use the decision-making or problem-solving skills you have learned to find ways to approach the problem. You may want to involve other people in your activities.

### 3 Follow Through
Solving problems takes time. You'll need to be patient in developing a plan. You can show leadership in working with your group by following through on meetings you set up and plans you make. When you finally solve the problem, you will feel proud of your accomplishments.

Members of Clean & Green, a Los Angeles Conservation Corps program, help to renovate a city building.

# Practicing Citizenship Skills

You have learned that good citizenship involves three skills: staying informed, making good decisions, and taking action. Below are some activities to help you improve your citizenship skills. By practicing these skills you can work to make a difference in your own life and in the lives of those in your community.

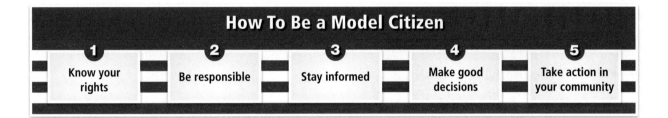

**How To Be a Model Citizen**

| 1 | 2 | 3 | 4 | 5 |
|---|---|---|---|---|
| Know your rights | Be responsible | Stay informed | Make good decisions | Take action in your community |

## Stay Informed

▷ *Create a pamphlet or recruiting commercial*

Ask your school counselors or write to your state department of education to get information on state-run colleges, universities, or technical schools. Use this information to create a brochure or recruiting commercial showing these schools and the different programs and degrees they offer.

**Keep in mInd**

**What's there for me?**
It may help you to think about what areas students are interested in and may want to pursue after graduation.

**Where is it?**
You may want to have a map showing where the schools are located in your state.

**How can I afford it?**
Students might want to know if financial aid is available to attend the schools you have featured.

## Make Good Decisions

▷ *Create a game board or skit*

Study the steps on page 305. With a small group, develop a skit that explains the steps in problem solving. Present your skit to younger students in your school. As an alternative, create a game board that would help younger students understand the steps in making a decision.

**Keep in mind**

**What do children this age understand?**
Be sure to create a skit or game at an age-appropriate level.

**What kinds of decisions do younger students make?**
Think about the kinds of decisions that the viewers of your skit or players of the game might make.

**How can I make it interesting?**
Use visual aids to help students understand the steps in decision making.

## Take Action

▷ *Create a bulletin board for your class*

Do some research on the Internet or consult the yellow pages under "Social Services" to find the names of organizations that have volunteer opportunities for young people. Call or write for more information. Then create a bulletin board for your class showing groups that need volunteer help.

**Keep in mind**

**What kinds of jobs are they?**
You may want to list the types of skills or jobs that volunteer groups are looking for.

**How old do I have to be?**
Some groups may be looking for younger volunteers; others may need older volunteers.

**How do I get there?**
How easy is it to get to the volunteer group's location?

9 Launching a New Republic
1789–1800 pages 310–335

10 The Jefferson Era
1800–1816 pages 336–361

11 National and
Regional Growth
1800–1844 pages 362–389

# Why It Matters Now

It was one thing for the founders to write a
Constitution, another to make it work. Every
decision made by the president and the Congress
in the first 25 years of the Republic established
a tradition of governance that continues to
influence how we live today.

The history of liberty is a history of resistance.
The history of liberty is a history of limitations
of governmental power, not the increase of it.
—Woodrow Wilson

# Launching a New Republic

## 1789–1800

1. Washington's Presidency

2. Challenges to the New Government

3. The Federalists in Charge

**ESSENTIAL QUESTION**

What political traditions and tensions first appeared in the early years of the new republic?

---

**CONNECT** ↻ **Geography & History**

How might the politics and geography of the United States have affected the choice of a capital?

**Think about:**

**1** why two capitals preceded the final choice of Washington, D.C.

**2** why the land forming the District of Columbia came from the states of Virginia and Maryland.

**3** the geographic location of early settlement.

Washington's inaugural

Washington's medicine chest

**1789**

George Washington becomes the first president of the United States.

French Revolution in progress

**1795** Pinckney's Treaty ratified.

▼

**Effect** U.S. southern border set at 31st parallel

**1794** Battle of Fallen Timbers takes place.

▼

**Effect** Treaty of Greenville (1795) is signed.

# Washington's Presidency

 **6.4.E.5.** Discuss the political and philosophical origins of the United States Constitution and its implementation in the 1790s.

## One American's Story

Charles Thomson had served as secretary of the Continental Congress in 1774. Now, on April 14, 1789, he came to Mount Vernon in Virginia with a letter for George Washington. Washington knew the reason for the visit. Thomson's letter was to tell him that he had been elected the nation's first president. Before giving Washington the letter, Thomson made a short speech.

**PRIMARY SOURCE**

❝ I have now Sir to inform you that . . . your patriotism and your readiness to sacrifice . . . private enjoyments to preserve the happiness of your Country [convinced the Congress that you would accept] this great and important Office to which you are called not only by the unanimous votes of the Electors but by the voice of America. ❞

—Charles Thomson, quoted in *George Washington's Papers, at the Library of Congress 1741–1799*

George Washington— shown in a wax likeness—was a popular choice for first president of the new nation.

Washington accepted the honor and the burden of his new office. He would soon guide the nation through its early years.

## Washington's New Government

▼ **KEY QUESTION** How did Washington's presidency shape new political traditions?

Under the new Constitution, the first presidential election was held in 1789. Washington won, and traveled to New York City, the nation's capital, to be **inaugurated**, or formally sworn in, as president. On April 30, 1789 at Federal Hall, the inauguration took place. The runner-up, John Adams of Massachusetts, became Washington's vice-president. As the nation's first president, Washington knew that his every action would set a **precedent** —an example that becomes standard practice. Under the first president, many political institutions and traditions were established.

**Congressional Decisions** Washington took charge of a political system that was a bold experiment. No one knew if a government based on the will of the people could really work. The new government began to take shape in the summer of 1789. First, people argued over what to call Washington. Some suggested "His Excellency," but others argued that made the president sound as if he was a king. Finally, in keeping with the simplicity of a republic, Washington agreed to "Mr. President."

The writers of the Constitution had left many matters to be decided by Congress. For example, the Constitution created a Supreme Court but left it to Congress to decide on the details. What type of additional courts should there be and how many? What would happen if federal court decisions conflicted with state laws?

To help answer these questions, Congress passed a federal court system under the **Federal Judiciary** (joo•DISH•ee•AIR•ee) **Act** of 1789. This act gave the Supreme Court six members: a chief justice, or judge, and five associate justices. Over time, that number has grown to nine. The law also provided for less powerful federal courts. Washington appointed **John Jay**, the prominent lawyer and diplomat, as the first chief justice of the Supreme Court.

**Assembling a Cabinet** The Constitution also gave Congress the task of creating departments to help the president lead the nation. The president had the power to appoint the heads of these departments.

Congress created the departments: state, war, treasury, justice and postal service. The State Department dealt with relations with other countries. The War Department was in charge of the nation's defense. The Treasury Department was in charge of the nation's economy, or financial security.

George Washington's first cabinet

Washington chose talented people to run the departments. For secretary of war, he picked Henry Knox, a trusted general during the Revolution. For secretary of state, Washington chose Thomas Jefferson. He had been serving as U.S. minister to France. Washington chose the brilliant Alexander Hamilton to be secretary of the treasury. Hamilton was to manage the government's money. The secretary's ties to the president began during the war when he had served as one of Washington's aides. To advise the government on legal matters, Washington picked Edmund Randolph as **attorney general**.

These department heads and the attorney general made up Washington's **cabinet**. The Constitution made no mention of a cabinet, but Washington began the practice of calling his cabinet to advise him on official matters. Another high office, that of postmaster general, was not elevated to cabinet status until 1829.

🔺 **EVALUATE** Explain how the decisions made by the first Congress created political traditions.

## The Nation's Finances

🔻 **KEY QUESTION** What financial problems faced the new nation?

Washington assigned his secretary of the treasury, Alexander Hamilton, the task of straightening out the nation's finances. The most urgent money issue was the U.S. government's war debts.

**War Debts** During the Revolution, the United States had borrowed millions of dollars from France, Spain, and the Netherlands. The new nation was also in debt to private citizens, including soldiers who had received bonds—certificates that promised payment plus interest—as compensation for their services during the war. State governments also had wartime debts. By 1789, the national debt—foreign and domestic—totaled more than $52 million.

Most government leaders agreed that the nation must pay its debts to win the respect of both foreign nations and its own citizens. Hamilton saw that the new nation must assure other countries that it was responsible about money. These nations would do business with the United States if they saw that the country would pay its debts.

**Hamilton's Political Views** Hamilton believed in a strong central government. He thought the power of the national government should be stronger than that of the state governments. Hamilton also believed that government should encourage business and industry and that the nation's prosperity depended on the support of the nation's wealthy merchants and manufacturers. The government owed money to many of these rich men. By paying them back, Hamilton hoped to win their support for the new government.

**Hamilton's Proposals** In 1790, Hamilton presented his plan to Congress. He proposed three steps to improve the nation's finances and to strengthen the national government: 1) paying off all war debts, 2) raising government revenues, and 3) creating a national bank.

Hamilton also wanted the federal government to pay off the war debts of the states. However, sectional differences arose over repayment of state debts. Many Southern states resisted because they had already gone further

## History Makers

### Alexander Hamilton    1755–1804

Hamilton was one of the giants of American history. In his early twenties, he was a personal aide to General George Washington during the American Revolution. In the 1780s, he was a signer of the U.S. Constitution. He was one of the authors of a set of essays called *The Federalist* papers that persuaded Americans to ratify the Constitution.

As the first secretary of the treasury, Hamilton helped ensure the economic health of the new republic. His actions helped support his belief in a strong government and helped establish the executive branch as the most powerful branch of the government.

**COMPARING** *Leaders*

Compare Hamilton's leadership qualities to those of other American leaders mentioned in the chapter.

🔌 **ONLINE BIOGRAPHY**    For more on Alexander Hamilton, go to the **Research & Writing Center** @ ClassZone.com

## HOW BANKS WORK

**Hamilton believed that a national bank could help the economy of the new nation. It would be funded by a partnership between the federal government and wealthy private investors. In that way, private money would be tied to the country's welfare.**

DEPOSITS

LOANS

LOANS

DEPOSITS

If people want to buy something, like a house or a car, they ask the bank to lend them the money. But they have to pay back the money they borrow, plus interest. The interest rate is higher than the interest rate they get when they make a deposit.

Savers are loaning their money to the bank when they put it in a savings account. The bank pays them interest for using their money. The bank uses their money to make more money.

Businesses use loans to create new products and services. As they sell more, they hire more workers and raise wages.

PURCHASES

### CRITICAL THINKING

1. **Analyze Point of View** Do you think that the people who feared a strong central government supported Hamilton's idea of a national bank? Why or why not?

2. **Make Inferences** What are some ways that banks make money?

towards paying off their debts. Hamilton asked Thomas Jefferson of Virginia to help him gain Southern support. They reached a compromise by agreeing that the southern states would support Hamilton's plan and back payment of state debts. In return, northerners would support locating the capital in the South. The location chosen was on the banks of the Potomac River.

**Building a Strong Government** To raise revenue, the secretary of the treasury favored **tariffs**, which are taxes on imported goods. Tariffs serve two purposes: raising money for the government and encouraging the growth of national business. Americans bought goods from overseas in large quantities, including hemp, steel, and molasses. Tariffs on these goods kept a steady income flowing to the government. Since tariffs made foreign goods more expensive, they encouraged people to buy American goods.

Hamilton also called for the creation of a national bank. It would give the government a safe place to keep money. It would also make loans to businesses and government. Most important, it would issue bank notes—paper money that could be used as currency.

**Hamilton's Opponents** Overall, Hamilton's plan was to strengthen the national government. Opponents of a national bank, including Jefferson and Madison, claimed that the bank would encourage an unhealthy partnership between the government and wealthy business interests. This angered Jefferson in particular. Those against the bank also argued that, since the Constitution does not mention a national bank, the government cannot create a national bank. They believed in the narrow or "strict" interpretation of the Constitution.

These differences began the debate among those who favored a "strict" interpretation of the Constitution, one in which the federal government has very limited powers, and a "loose" interpretation, which favors greater federal powers. Jefferson favored a strict interpretation, and Hamilton favored a broad or loose interpretation of the Constitution.

Hamilton's group used the so-called "Elastic Clause" of the Constitution (Article 1, Section 8, Number 18) to argue their case. This clause gives Congress the authority to do whatever is "necessary and proper" to carry out its specific powers, such as regulating commerce.

Washington backed Hamilton, and the Bank of the United States was established in 1791. Washington mostly tried to remain above the conflict between Hamilton and Jefferson and to encourage them to work together despite their basic differences. However, the formation of the two political factions, based on Hamilton's and Jefferson's opposing philosophies, laid the foundation for the American political factions that followed.

▲ **CATEGORIZE** List Hamilton's solutions for the nation's finances.

---

**New Jersey Core Curriculum Content Standards *Review***

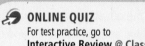

**ONLINE QUIZ**
For test practice, go to
**Interactive Review @ ClassZone.com**

**TERMS & NAMES**

**1.** Explain the importance of
- Federal Judiciary Act
- John Jay
- attorney general
- cabinet

**USING YOUR READING NOTES**

**2. Categorize** Complete the diagram you started at the beginning of the section.

| Cabinet Member | Responsibilities |
|---|---|
| Hamilton | managed the nation's money |
| Jefferson | oversaw foreign relations |
| | |
| | |

**KEY IDEAS**

**3.** What was the purpose of Washington's cabinet?

**4.** What were the three steps proposed by Hamilton for helping the nation's finances?

**CRITICAL THINKING**

**5. Compare and Contrast** How did Hamilton and Jefferson differ in their interpretation of the Constitution?

**6. Make Inferences** Why might merchants and manufacturers support a strong central government?

**7. Connect *to* Today** What organizational decisions made by the first Congress are still in effect today?

**8. Writing Letter** Imagine it's the 1790s. Write a letter to the editor that either supports or opposes Hamilton's plan for a national bank.

# Reading for Understanding

## ▶ Key Ideas

**BEFORE, YOU LEARNED**
George Washington faced many challenges during his presidency.

**NOW YOU WILL LEARN**
Washington established central authority at home and avoided war abroad

## ▶ Vocabulary

### TERMS & NAMES

**Battle of Fallen Timbers** 1794 battle between Native Americans and American forces

**Treaty of Greenville** 1795 treaty in which 12 Native American tribes ceded control of much of Ohio and Indiana to the U.S. government

**Whiskey Rebellion** 1794 protest against the government's tax on whiskey by backcountry farmers

**French Revolution** revolution overthrowing the government in France that began in 1787 and ended in violence and mass executions

**Jay's Treaty** agreement that ended the dispute with Britain over American shipping during the French Revolution

**Pinckney's** (PINK•neez) **Treaty** 1795 treaty with Spain allowing U.S. commercial use of the Mississippi River

### BACKGROUND VOCABULARY

**cede** surrender, or give up

### REVIEW

**Northwest Territory** area bounded by the Ohio and Mississippi Rivers and the Great Lakes

**neutral** (NOO•truhl) not siding with any other country in dispute

## ▶ Reading Strategy

Re-create the diagram shown at right. As you read and respond to the **KEY QUESTIONS**, use the table to note important challenges and responses of the first U.S. government.

 **See Skillbuilder Handbook, page R3.**

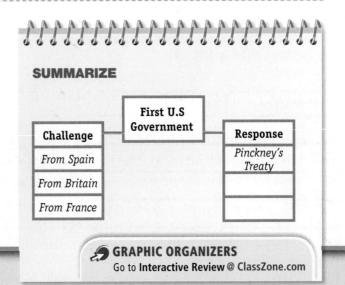

**SUMMARIZE**

**First U.S Government**

| Challenge | | Response |
|---|---|---|
| From Spain | | Pinckney's Treaty |
| From Britain | | |
| From France | | |

**GRAPHIC ORGANIZERS**
Go to **Interactive Review** @ ClassZone.com

# Challenges to the New Government

 **6.4.E.6.** Describe and map American territorial expansions and the settlement of the frontier during this period.
**6.4.E.7.** Analyze the causes and consequences of continuing conflict between Native American tribes and colonists (e.g., Tecumseh's rebellion).

## One American's Story

Settlers moving west often met fierce resistance from Native Americans. In 1790 and 1791, for example, Chief Little Turtle of the Miami tribe of Ohio had won decisive victories against U.S. troops.

In 1794, the Miami again faced attack by American forces. Little Turtle warned his people about the troops led by General "Mad Anthony" Wayne.

**PRIMARY SOURCE**

❝ We have beaten the enemy twice under separate commanders. . . . The Americans are now led by a chief [Wayne] who never sleeps. . . . We have never been able to surprise him. . . . It would be prudent [wise] to listen to his offers of peace. ❞

—Little Turtle, quoted in *The Life and Times of Little Turtle*

Chief Little Turtle was willing to negotiate with U.S. leaders, but his tribal council voted for war.

While the council members weighed Little Turtle's warning, President Washington was making plans to secure, or to guard or protect, the western borders of the new nation.

## Problems at Home

🔻 **KEY QUESTION** How did two crises reveal the power of the national government?

Washington had always supported the idea of a strong national government. During his presidency, the government revealed its strength when dealing with a number of threatening situations.

**Competing Claims to Territory** Washington knew the nation needed peace to prosper. But trouble brewed in the Trans-Appalachian West, the land between the Appalachian Mountains and the Mississippi River. The source of conflict was competing claims for these lands. The 1783 Treaty of Paris had tried to resolve the claims. And some years later, Spain, Britain, the United States, and Native Americans all claimed parts of the area.

The strongest resistance to white settlement came from Native Americans in the **Northwest Territory**. This territory was bordered by the Ohio River to the south and Canada to the north. Native Americans in that territory hoped to unite to form an independent Native American nation. The British, who still held forts north of the Ohio River, supported Native Americans because they did not want to lose their access to trade in these territories.

Washington sent troops to the Northwest Territory to defend American interests. In 1790 this first federal army was no match for warriors led by Little Turtle. A second American force was defeated in 1791. Washington then formed another army and gave command to Revolutionary hero General Anthony ("Mad Anthony") Wayne.

**Native Americans are Defeated** On August 20, 1794, a force of around 2,000 Native Americans met Wayne's 1,000 troops near the future site of Toledo, Ohio. The Native Americans were easily defeated. The battlefield was covered with trees that had been struck down in a storm so the Americans called it the **Battle of Fallen Timbers**.

Native Americans were defeated by U.S. troops at the Battle of Fallen Timbers. They were disappointed when the British did not come to their aid.

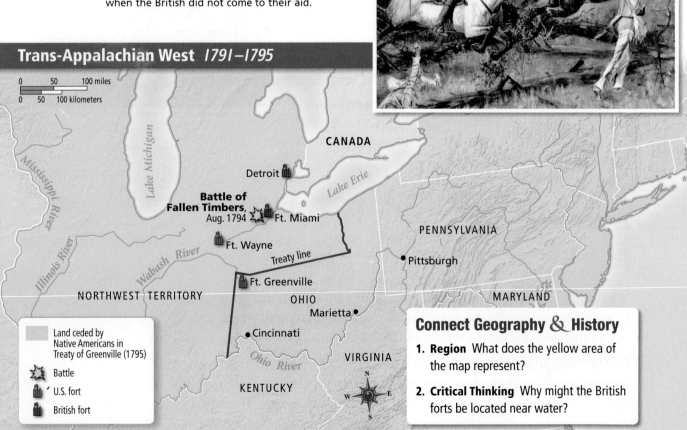

## Trans-Appalachian West *1791–1795*

0    50    100 miles
0    50    100 kilometers

CANADA

Detroit

Battle of
**Fallen Timbers**,
Aug. 1794    Ft. Miami

Ft. Wayne

Treaty line

PENNSYLVANIA

Pittsburgh

Ft. Greenville

NORTHWEST TERRITORY

OHIO

MARYLAND

Marietta

Mississippi River

Lake Michigan

Lake Erie

Illinois River

Wabash River

Ohio River

Cincinnati

VIRGINIA

KENTUCKY

Land ceded by
Native Americans in
Treaty of Greenville (1795)

Battle

U.S. fort

British fort

### Connect Geography & History

1. **Region** What does the yellow area of the map represent?

2. **Critical Thinking** Why might the British forts be located near water?

The Native Americans withdrew. The British, not wanting war with the United States, refused to help them. The Battle of Fallen Timbers crushed Native American hopes of keeping their land in the Northwest Territory. Twelve tribes signed the **Treaty of Greenville** in 1795. They agreed to **cede**, or surrender, much of present-day Ohio as well as numerous ports and outposts in Illinois, Michigan, and Indiana to the U.S. government.

**Trouble in the Backcountry** In spite of the United States' success at the Battle of Fallen Timbers, Washington soon found it necessary to put another army into the field. This was in response to a conflict over a new tax.

To raise revenue, Treasury Secretary Hamilton had pushed through Congress a tax to be levied specifically on the manufacture of whiskey. The tax hit small, backcountry farmers the hardest. One of their major crops was corn. But whiskey made from corn was more profitable than raw grain, so whiskey became central to the Backcountry economy. Having little money with which to buy goods, small farmers used whiskey like money to trade for other goods. As well, whiskey was one of the few local products suitable for transport to markets across the Appalachians. When the whiskey tax was enacted, outraged farmers from Pennsylvania to Georgia resisted.

**Farmers Revolt** In the summer of 1794, a group of farmers in western Pennsylvania staged the **Whiskey Rebellion** against the tax. One armed group attacked and burned the home of the regional tax collector. Others threatened an armed attack on Pittsburgh.

Most backcountry farmers had a long tradition of independent living and resistance to authority. And backcountry rebelliousness had helped defeat the British. That same rebelliousness was now seen as a threat to the new republic, and Washington and Hamilton needed to keep order. They looked upon the Whiskey Rebellion as an opportunity for the federal government to show it could enforce the law along the western frontier. Hamilton scolded the rebels for resisting the law.

PRIMARY SOURCE

❝ Such a resistance is treason against society, against liberty, against everything that ought to be dear to a free, enlightened, and prudent people. To tolerate it were to abandon your most precious interests. Not to subdue it were to tolerate it. ❞

—Alexander Hamilton, *The Works of Alexander Hamilton*

In October 1794, General Henry Lee, with Hamilton at his side, led an army of 13,000 soldiers into western Pennsylvania to put down the uprising. As news of the army's approach spread, the rebels fled. After much effort, federal troops rounded up a group of about 20 accused leaders. Washington had proved his point. He had shown that the government had the power and the will to enforce its laws. Meanwhile, events in Europe gave Washington a different kind of challenge.

▲ **SUMMARIZE** Describe how Washington dealt with two early crises.

**Connecting History**

**Individual Rights vs. Majority Rule**
The Whiskey Rebellion marked the first major challenge to the authority of the federal government. When the armed rebels gathered in Pittsburgh in 1794, they were angry not only about the whiskey tax but also about their under-representation in the state legislatures.

▼ **KEY QUESTION** Why did events in Europe create problems for America?

The United States was now independent, but it remained tied to European nations by treaty and through trade. Britain was still the United States's biggest trading partner. France was allied with the United States by a treaty of 1778. When European nations went to war, Americans feared being dragged into the conflict.

**Trouble in France** In 1789, a financial crisis led the French people to rebel against their government. As in the American Revolution, the French revolutionaries demanded liberty and equality. At first, Americans supported the **French Revolution**. By 1792, however, the revolution had become very violent. Thousands were killed. Then, in 1793, the revolutionaries executed both the king and queen of France.

Other European monarchs believed the revolution threatened their own thrones by spreading outside of France. They joined in opposition to the revolution. France soon declared war on Britain, Holland, and Spain. Britain took the lead in the fight against France.

**France and Britain at War** War between France and Britain put the United States in an awkward position. France had backed America in the Revolution against the British. Also, many ordinary Americans saw France's revolution as proof that the American cause had been just.

Jefferson felt that a move to crush the French Revolution was an attack on liberty everywhere. But Hamilton argued that Britain was the United States' primary trading partner, and British trade was too vital to risk war. In April 1793, Washington declared that the United States would remain **neutral**, meaning it would not take sides. Congress then passed a law forbidding the United States to help either Britain or France.

Hamilton and Jefferson came to agree that entering a war was not in the new nation's interest. But Federalists attacked Jefferson for his support of France anyway. Jefferson was also tired of Washington's support of Hamilton's ideas. In 1793, Jefferson resigned as secretary of state.

Britain made it hard for the United States to remain neutral. The British were seizing the cargoes of American ships carrying goods from the French West Indies. Chief Justice John Jay went to England for talks about the seizure of U.S. ships. Jay also hoped to persuade the British to give up their forts on the northwest frontier.

## History *through* Art

### The Women of Les Halles Marching to Versailles, 5th October 1789
#### by Jean-Francois Janinet

The work shows hungry, angry French women marching in support of the revolution. They are out to confront the French royal family who live in the palace of Versailles, about 15 miles (24 km) southwest of Paris, the capital of France.

**CRITICAL VIEWING** Why did the artist choose to portray some ordinary people of the revolution?

**Jay's Treaty** During the talks in 1794, news came of the U.S. victory at the Battle of Fallen Timbers. Fearing another entanglement, the British agreed to leave the Ohio Valley by 1796. In what is called **Jay's Treaty**, the British also agreed to pay damages for U.S. vessels they had seized. Jay failed, however, to open up the profitable British Caribbean trade to Americans. Because of this, Jay's Treaty got through the House and Senate with great difficulty. Western settlers, for example, were angry that the British were still allowed to continue their fur trade on the American side of the U.S.-Canadian border. In spite of criticism, Jay's Treaty did help to reduce frontier tensions.

Like Jay, U.S. diplomat Thomas Pinckney helped reduce tensions along the frontier with the signing of **Pinckney's** (PINK•neez) **Treaty** of 1795. The United States won favorable terms with Spain in the peace treaty.

- Americans had the right to travel freely on the Mississippi River,
- U.S. goods could be stored at the port of New Orleans free of customs duties.
- Spain accepted the 31st parallel as the northern boundary of Florida and the southern boundary of the United States.

Together, Jay's Treaty and Pinckney's Treaty gave Americans a greater sense of security. With far less fear of European hostility, more Americans were moving west. But when Washington announced he would not run again for president, Americans were deeply divided over how the nation should be governed.

 **ANALYZE** Describe how crises in Europe created challenges for the new American government.

---

 **New Jersey Core Curriculum Content Standards** *Review*

🔁 **ONLINE QUIZ**
For test practice, go to
**Interactive Review @ ClassZone.com**

**TERMS & NAMES**

**1.** Explain the importance of:

- Battle of Fallen Timbers
- Treaty of Greenville
- Whiskey Rebellion
- French Revolution
- Jay's Treaty
- Pinckney's Treaty

**USING YOUR READING NOTES**

**2. Summarize** Complete the diagram you started at the beginning of the section.

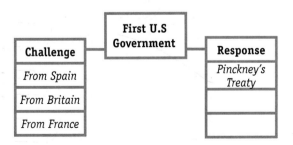

**KEY IDEAS**

**3.** Why did Washington consider it important to put down the Whiskey Rebellion?

**4.** How did the French Revolution create problems for the United States?

**CRITICAL THINKING**

**5. Evaluate** What were some of the advantages of the new nation remaining neutral?

**6.** **Connect** *to* **Today** The Whiskey Rebellion threatened civil order. What are some more current example of citizens threatening civil order in the belief that their cause is just?

**7.** **Connect Economics & History** How did Pinckney's Treaty protect American interests?

**8.** **Geography/Art** **Map** Make a map that shows a plan of the Battle of Fallen Timbers, or draw a scene from that battle.

# NEW STYLES FOR A NEW NATION

The decade of the 1790s is often called the Federal period in the arts. During this time, Americans created art that expressed the attitudes, ideals, and hopes of their new nation.

## A REVOLUTION IN FASHION

Clothing styles reflected the revolutionary political changes underway in America and France. Here, the old-style couple on the right is startled by the new fashions of youth. The ornate clothing and wigs of the aristocracy were on their way out, and a more relaxed, plainer style was on its way in.

## ACHIEVEMENTS IN ART

Charles Willson Peale was America's greatest artist at this time. His work captured the informality and good humor of American culture. This painting of Peale's sons fooled even George Washington into thinking the stairs were real.

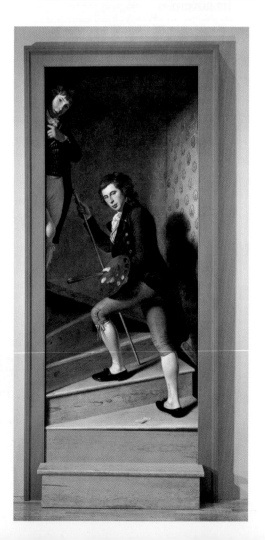

## THE MODEL OF LIBERTY

The goddess of Liberty, who appeared on U.S. coins in 1795, was modeled on a famous woman of the Federal period—Anne Willing Bingham. Brilliant and highly educated, Bingham was a friend of Thomas Jefferson. Her world-famous intelligence, independent spirit, and beauty made her the perfect choice to represent liberty on America's new coins.

## ABOLISHING SLAVERY

Many Americans in the early republic wanted to make America a place where "All men are created equal." Throughout the 1780s and '90s the Northern states slowly began abolishing slavery. The image shown here became an important symbol for the antislavery movement in America.

## BACK TO THE FUTURE

Americans saw a link between their new republic and the ancient republic of Rome. Like the Romans, Americans had rebelled against a king and established a democracy. Architects began designing buildings for their new government using Roman forms to represent the nation's ideals of democracy and justice.

Massachusetts State House 1797

Virginia State Capitol 1789

Now look for pictures of other state capitols and identify the Roman forms you see.

## Activity

### Reveal the Romans!

Study the architectural forms below. Then identify Roman elements that you find in the American buildings on the left. (Some buildings might combine several Roman forms.)

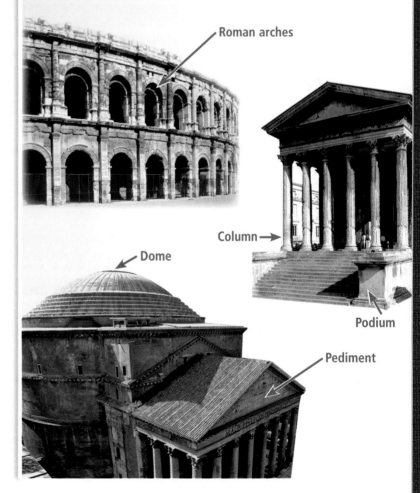

Roman arches

Column →

Dome

Podium

Pediment

## ▶ Key Ideas

**BEFORE, YOU LEARNED**
Washington established central authority at home and avoided war overseas.

**NOW YOU WILL LEARN**
The Federalists dominated politics under the presidency of John Adams.

## ▶ Vocabulary

**TERMS & NAMES**

**John Adams** Second President of the United States

**XYZ Affair** 1797 incident in which French officials demanded a bribe from U.S. diplomats

**Alien and Sedition Acts** series of four laws enacted in 1798 to reduce the political power of recent immigrants

**states' rights** idea that the states have certain rights that the federal government cannot overrule

**nullification** idea that a state could cancel a federal law within the state

**Kentucky and Virginia Resolutions**
Resolutions passed by Kentucky and Virginia in 1798 giving the states the right to declare acts of Congress null and void

**BACKGROUND VOCABULARY**

**foreign policy** relations with the governments of other nations

**political party** group of people that tries to promote its ideas and influence government

**aliens** immigrants who are not yet citizens

**sedition** stirring up rebellion against a government

**REVIEW**

**Federalists** people who supported a strong national government; and heirs to the supporters of the ratification of the Constitution

## ▶ Reading Strategy

Re-create the diagram shown at right. As you read and respond to the **KEY QUESTIONS**, use the diagram to record important events in the new nation.

 See Skillbuilder Handbook, page R4.

**MAIN IDEAS AND DETAILS**

rise of political parties

**Federalist concerns**

states' rights

**GRAPHIC ORGANIZERS**
Go to **Interactive Review** @ ClassZone.com

# The Federalists in Charge

 **6.2.C.3.** Discuss the role of political parties in the American democratic system including candidates, campaigns, financing, primary elections, and voting systems.

## One American's Story

Benjamin Banneker was born a free man at a time when most African Americans were enslaved. Largely self-educated, he became a surveyor, astronomer, and mathematician, and he published a yearly almanac. In 1790 Washington appointed him to the commission planning the new nation's capital.

Banneker was an exceptional example of what African Americans could achieve if released from the bondage of slavery and racism. In a letter to Jefferson, Banneker reminded him that "all men are created equal."

**PRIMARY SOURCE**

❝ [God] hath not only made us all of one flesh, but that he hath also, without partiality, afforded us all the same sensations and endowed us all with the same faculties; and that however variable we may be in society or religion, however diversified in situation or color, we are all of the same family, and stand in the same relation to him. ❞

—Benjamin Banneker, *letter to Thomas Jefferson 1791*

(*above*) Benjamin Banneker helped to survey the new capital of Washington, D.C.

Despite his efforts, Banneker was unable to change attitudes to slavery. However, Banneker will always be remembered as one of the outstanding Americans who helped launch the new republic.

## Washington Retires

🔽 **KEY QUESTION** What dangers did President Washington warn against?

In 1796, President George Washington decided that two terms in office was enough. He wanted to return to Mount Vernon, his estate in Virginia. Throughout his eight years in office (1789–1797), he had tried to serve as a symbol of national unity. In large part, he succeeded.

**Washington's Final Concerns** During Washington's second term, opponents of Jay's Treaty, and other critics, led attacks on the president's policies. Thomas Paine, for example, called Washington "treacherous in private friendship . . . and a hypocrite in public life" because he failed to support the French Revolution. Washington saw such attacks as the outcome of political disagreements. In his farewell address, he warned that such differences could weaken the nation. Despite this advice, political differences became a part of American politics.

Americans listened more closely to Washington's parting words on **foreign policy**, or relations with the governments of other countries. He urged the nation's leaders to remain neutral and "steer clear of permanent alliances with any portion of the foreign world." He warned that agreements with foreign nations might work against U.S. interests.

**Political Differences Continue** Despite Washington's warnings against political differences, Americans were deeply divided over how the nation should be run. Hamilton and Jefferson had hotly debated the direction the new nation should take. But, after his frustrated resignation from public office in 1793, Jefferson returned to Virginia. During Washington's second term, Madison replaced Jefferson in the debates with Hamilton.

The two sides disagreed notably on how to interpret the Constitution and on economic policy. Hamilton favored the British and wanted to preserve good relations with them. He opposed the French Revolution. Jefferson and Madison supported it. Hamilton believed in a strong central government. Jefferson and Madison feared such a government might lead to tyranny. Hamilton wanted a United States in which trade, manufacturing, and cities grew. Jefferson and Madison pictured a rural nation of farmers.

**Growth of Political Parties** These differences on foreign and domestic policy led to the nation's first political parties. A **political party** is a group of people that tries to promote its ideas and influence government. It also backs candidates for office.

Together, Jefferson and Madison founded the Democratic-Republican Party. The party name reflected their strong belief in democracy and the republican system. Their ideas drew farmers' and workers' support to the new political party.

Jefferson and Madison's Democratic-Republican party eventually turned into the Democratic Party that is still active today. Hamilton and his friends formed the Federalist Party which reflected their belief in a strong national government. Many Northern merchants and manufacturers became **Federalists**, following the supporters of the ratification of the U.S. Constitution.

▲ **SUMMARIZE** List the dangers Washington warned about.

**Connecting History**

**Isolationism**
Washington's advice laid the ground for America's policy of isolationism, or steering clear of foreign affairs. This policy lasted through most of the country's history before World War II.

Terence Kennedy's 1847 *Political Banner* combined several symbols of the young nation. **Would the banner have had greater appeal to Jefferson or Hamilton?**

Events in France not only affected politics in the United States, they influenced styles of clothing as well. Political differences could often be detected by observing different styles of dress and appearance.

**FEDERALISTS**

**LEADERS:**
Hamilton, Adams

**SUPPORTERS:**
lawyers, merchants, manufacturers, clergy

**BELIEFS:**
• strong national government
• loose construction of the Constitution
• favored national bank
• economy based on trade

**DEMOCRATIC-REBUBLICANS**

**LEADERS:**
Jefferson, Madison

**SUPPORTERS:**
farmers, urban workers

**BELIEFS:**
• limited national government
• strict construction of the Constitution
• opposed national bank
• agricultural economy

powdered hair or wig

loose hair

bow tie

neckerchief

broad coattails

narrow coattails

breeches & stockings

trousers

buckles

laces

**CRITICAL THINKING** **Compare and Contrast** Why might the Federalists be considered more supportive of business than the Democratic-Republicans?

# John Adams's Administration

🔻 **KEY QUESTION** What issues divided Americans during Adams' presidency?

In 1796, the United States held its first elections in which political parties competed. The Federalists picked vice-president **John Adams** as their candidate for president. The Democratic-Republicans chose Jefferson.

In the Electoral College, Adams received 71 votes and Jefferson 68. The Constitution stated that the runner-up should become vice-president. Therefore, the country had a Federalist president and a Democratic-Republican vice-president. Adams became president in 1797. His chief rival, Jefferson, was his vice-president.

**Problems with France** When Washington left office in 1797, relations between France and the United States were tense. With Britain and France still at war, the French began seizing and harassing U.S. ships. Within the year, France had looted more than 300 U.S. ships.

Some Federalists called for war with France, but Adams hoped talks would restore calm. He sent Charles Pinckney, Elbridge Gerry, and John

The Kentucky Resolution, in particular, insisted on the principle of **nullification**, or the idea that a state could nullify, or cancel, any act of Congress that it considered unconstitutional. The **Kentucky and Virginia Resolutions** warned of the dangers that the Alien and Sedition Acts posed to a government of checks and balances as these checks and balances were guaranteed by the Constitution. Jefferson and Madison were not successful in overturning the acts while Adams was President. However, within two years the Democratic-Republicans won control of Congress, and they either reversed the acts or let them expire between 1800 and 1802.

**Peace with France** While Federalists and Democratic-Republicans battled at home, the United States made peace with France. Although war fever was high, Adams reopened talks with France. This time the two sides quickly signed the Convention of 1800, an agreement to stop all naval attacks. This treaty cleared the way for U.S. and French ships to sail the ocean in peace.

Adams's actions made him enemies among the Federalists. Despite this, he was proud of having saved the nation from bloodshed. In 1800, Adams became the first president to govern from the nation's new capital city, Washington, D.C. In 1800, however, he lost the presidential election to Thomas Jefferson.

 **MAIN IDEAS & DETAILS** Explain the issues that divided Americans during Adams' presidency.

---

 **New Jersey Core Curriculum Content Standards** *Review*

**ONLINE QUIZ**
For test practice, go to
**Interactive Review** @ ClassZone.com

### TERMS & NAMES

**1.** Explain the importance of:

- John Adams
- XYZ Affair
- Alien and Sedition Acts
- states' rights
- nullification
- Kentucky & Virginia Resolutions

### USING YOUR READING NOTES

**2. Main Ideas and Details** Complete the diagram you started at the beginning of the section.

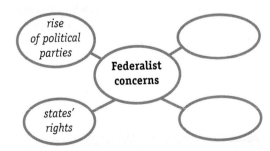

### KEY IDEAS

**3.** What did Washington warn against before he left office?

**4.** What led to the rise of political parties?

**5.** Why did Congress pass the Alien and Sedition Acts?

### CRITICAL THINKING

**6. Evaluate** Why was Washington's warning about political parties not heeded?

**7. Make Inferences** Why do you think so many merchants and manufacturers were Federalists?

**8. Draw Conclusions** How did the XYZ Affair show the young nation's growing confidence?

**9. Synthesize** How might the theory of states' rights undermine the federal government?

**10.** **Connect** *to* **Today** What are some issues that the two leading American political parties disagree on today?

**11.** **Writing** **Editorial** Imagine you are a newspaper editor in 1798. Write an editorial in favor of, or opposed to, the Alien and Sedition Acts.

## Chapter Summary

**1** **Key Idea**
George Washington and his
advisers faced many challenges
during his presidency.

**2** **Key Idea**
Washington established central
authority at home and avoided
war abroad.

**3** **Key Idea**
The Federalists dominated
politics under the presidency of
John Adams.

For detailed Review and Study Notes
go to **Interactive Review**
@ ClassZone.com

## Name Game

**Use the Terms & Names list to complete each
sentence online or on your own paper.**

1. In 1789, Congress passed the _____ to set up
America's new court system.
Federal Judiciary Act

2. Fighting over western territory in 1794, American
troops clashed with Native Americans at the _____.

3. America's _____ dictates its relations and interactions
with other countries.

4. _____ was the first chief justice of the United States
Supreme Court.

5. The treaty that allowed Americans to use the
Mississippi River was _____.

6. An exact or literal interpretation of the Constitution
is called a _____.

7. Angry Pennsylvania farmers clashed with the
American government during the _____.

8. The _____ in 1789 ended the monarchy in France.

9. The _____ restricted the political power of immigrants.

10. During the _____, French officials tried to bribe
U.S. diplomats.

A. loose construction
B. Federal Judiciary
   Act
C. attorney general
D. strict construction
E. Battle of Fallen
   Timbers
F. Alien and Sedition
   Acts
G. foreign policy
H. John Jay
I. Whiskey Rebellion
J. Kentucky
   and Virginia
   Resolutions
K. French Revolution
L. Pinckney's Treaty
M. XYZ Affair
N. Treaty of Greenville
O. states' rights
P. nullification

## Activities

### CROSSWORD PUZZLE

Complete the online crossword to show what
you know about the new republic.

**ACROSS**
1. _____ was the second
American president.

### GEOGAME

Use this online map to reinforce your understanding of
early America, incuding the locations of important cities
and geographic features. Drag and drop each place name
in the list at its location on the map. A scorecard helps you
keep track of your progress online.

Philadelphia

New York

District of Columbia

Ohio River

St. Augustine

District of Columbia

## VOCABULARY

**Explain the significance of each of the following.**

1. Federal Judiciary Act
2. cabinet
3. nullification
4. Alien and Sedition Acts
5. French Revolution
6. John Jay
7. Attorney General
8. Whiskey rebellion
9. states' rights
10. Treaty of Greenville.

**Choose the best answer from each pair.**

11. This agreement ended the dispute with Britain over American shipping during the French Revolution. (Jay's Treaty / Pinckney's Treaty)

12. Which treaty ended a war with Native Americans? (Jay's Treaty / Treaty of Greenville)

13. Which law was passed in 1798 to reduce criticism of the government and limit the political activities of recent immigrants? (Alien and Sedition Acts / Federal Judiciary Act)

## KEY IDEAS

**1 Washington's Presidency (pages 312–317)**

14. What questions about the judiciary were left open by the Constitution? How were they answered?

15. What financial problems did the new nation face?

16. How did Hamilton and Jefferson interpret the Constitution differently?

**2 Challenges to the New Government (pages 318–323)**

17. What did Washington do to secure the West?

18. What were the major arguments regarding taxation under the new government?

19. Why did Washington favor neutrality in the conflict between France and Britain?

**3 The Federalists in Charge (pages 326–332)**

20. Why did Washington oppose political parties?

21. Why did the Federalists pass the Alien and Sedition Acts?

## CRITICAL THINKING

22. **Draw Conclusions** Why did Washington want both Thomas Jefferson and Alexander Hamilton to be among his closest advisers?

23. **Evaluate** Why did the federal government demonstrate its authority during the Whiskey Rebellion?

24. **Problems & Solutions** Create a chart to record the major problems and solutions faced by the leaders of the new nation.

| Problems | Solutions |
|---|---|
| *Need for executive aid and advice* | *Cabinet appointments* |
| *Government source of income* | |
| *Disputes with foreign nations* | |

25. **Draw Conclusions** Why do you think John Adams lost the presidential election of 1800?

26. **Causes and Effects** How did the French Revolution affect American politics?

27. **Citizenship** How did Washington's efforts to serve as a symbol of national unity help the new nation?

28. **Interpret Graphs** How much money did the government owe between 1789–1791?

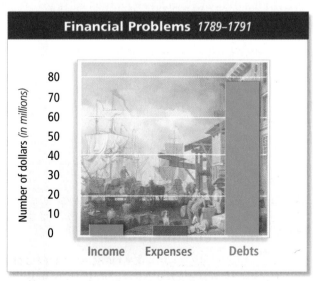

**Financial Problems** *1789–1791*

Number of dollars (*in millions*)

80
70
60
50
40
30
20
10
0

Income     Expenses     Debts

Source: *Historical Statistics of the United States*

## DOCUMENT-BASED QUESTIONS

### Part 1: Short Answer
Analyze each document and answer the questions that follow.

### DOCUMENT 1

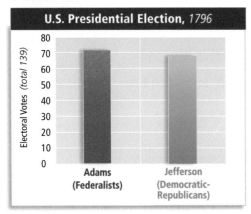

**U.S. Presidential Election,** *1796*

Electoral Votes (total 139)

Adams (Federalists)
Jefferson (Democratic-Republicans)

**1.** How do the election results shown in the graph reflect the political divisions in the new nation?

### DOCUMENT 2

**PRIMARY SOURCE**

" Let me now . . . warn you . . . against the harmful effects of the spirit of party. . . . This spirit, unfortunately . . . exists in different shapes in all governments . . . but in those of the popular form, it is seen in its greatest rankness and is truly their worst enemy. "

—George Washington, Farewell Address

**2.** Why might Washington's advice to avoid political parties be difficult to follow?

### Part 2: Essay

**3.** Using information from the documents, your answers to the questions in Part 1 and your knowledge of U.S. history, write an essay that discusses the progression of the American two-party system.

## YOU BE THE HISTORIAN

**29. Problems and Solutions** How might the farmers in the Whiskey Rebellion have expressed their disapproval of the whiskey tax while staying within the law?

**30. Compare and Contrast** What are some of the similarities and differences between the American Revolution and the French Revolution?

**31. Evaluate** How did the Virginia and Kentucky Resolutions challenge the authority of the federal government?

**32. WHAT IF?** What might have happened to immigrants and members of the press if the Alien and Sedition Acts had remained in effect?

**33. Draw Conclusions** Why did Native Americans demand negotiations with the United States over the Northwest Territory?

**34.** **Connect** *to* **Today** What are some examples of how people exercise their rights of free speech today?

**Answer the**
## ESSENTIAL QUESTION
**What political traditions and tensions first appeared in the early years of the new republic?**

**Written Response** Write a two or three paragraph response to the Essential Question. Be sure to consider the key ideas of each section, as well significant events that formed the political life of the new nation. Use the Rubric Response below to guide your thinking and writing.

### Response Rubric
**A strong response will**

• discuss the precedents and challenges faced by Washington and Adams
• analyze the differences between Hamilton and Jefferson
• compare and contrast the Federalists and Democratic-Republicans

1. Jeffersonian Democracy

2. The Louisiana Purchase and Exploration

3. The War of 1812

# The Jefferson Era

## 1800–1816

 **ESSENTIAL QUESTION**

How did the events of the Jefferson Era strengthen the nation?

---

**CONNECT** ↻ **Geography & History**

How might the United States have been changed by the purchase and exploration of western land?

**Think about:**

**1** the amount of information about **physical features,** such as hills and lakes, in the West

**2** how many **settlements** there were in the East

**3** what **challenges** a nation might face in expanding its territory

---

George Catlin, *Buffalo Chase*

**1800**

Thomas Jefferson is elected president.

**1804** Lewis and Clark explore the Louisiana Territory.

▼

**Effect** Expands knowledge of the American West.

A page from Lewis's journal

**1803** The United States purchases the Louisiana Territory.

*Marbury* v. *Madison* affirms the Supreme Court's power of judicial review.

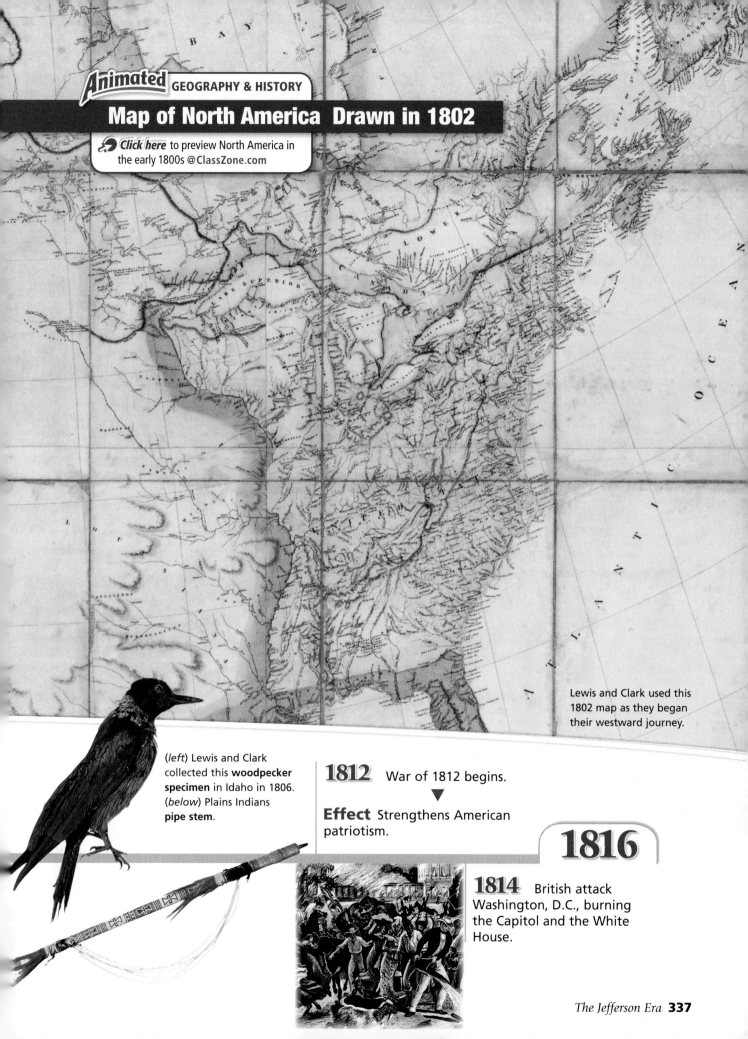

## Map of North America Drawn in 1802

**Click here** to preview North America in the early 1800s @ClassZone.com

Lewis and Clark used this 1802 map as they began their westward journey.

(*left*) Lewis and Clark collected this **woodpecker specimen** in Idaho in 1806. (*below*) Plains Indians **pipe stem**.

**1812** War of 1812 begins.

▼

**Effect** Strengthens American patriotism.

**1816**

**1814** British attack Washington, D.C., burning the Capitol and the White House.

*The Jefferson Era* **337**

## ▶ Key Ideas

**BEFORE, YOU LEARNED**

The Federalists dominated politics under the presidency of John Adams.

**NOW YOU WILL LEARN**

After a tied election, Jefferson became president and the Democratic-Republicans reduced the power of the federal government.

## ▶ Vocabulary

**TERMS & NAMES**

**Thomas Jefferson** third president of the United States, elected in 1801

**Judiciary Act of 1801** law that let President John Adams fill federal judgeships with Federalists

**John Marshall** chief justice of the Supreme Court appointed by President John Adams

**judicial review** principle that states that the Supreme Court has the final say in interpreting the Constitution

**BACKGROUND VOCABULARY**

**radical** person who takes extreme political positions

**REVIEW**

**Federalist** political party of Hamilton and Adams; supported a strong central government

**Democratic-Republican** Jefferson's political party; feared a strong central government

## ▶ Reading Strategy

Re-create the diagram shown at right. As you read and respond to the **KEY QUESTIONS**, use the boxes to show some of the changes made by Jefferson and his party.

 See Skillbuilder Handbook, page R4.

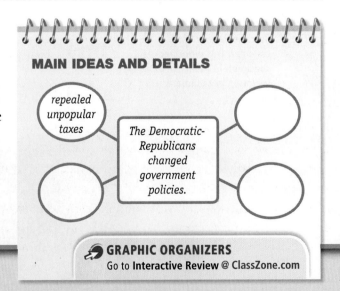

**MAIN IDEAS AND DETAILS**

*repealed unpopular taxes*

*The Democratic-Republicans changed government policies.*

🔁 **GRAPHIC ORGANIZERS**
Go to **Interactive Review** @ ClassZone.com

# Jeffersonian Democracy

**6.2.C.3.** Discuss the role of political parties in the American democratic system including candidates, campaigns, financing, primary elections, and voting systems.

## One American's Story

During the election of 1800, supporters of President John Adams and challenger **Thomas Jefferson** fought for their candidates with nasty personal attacks. For instance, journalist James Callender published pamphlets that warned voters not to re-elect Adams.

**PRIMARY SOURCE**

❝ In the fall of 1796 . . . the country fell into a more dangerous juncture than almost any the old confederation ever endured. The tardiness and timidity of Mr. Washington were succeeded by the rancour [bitterness] and insolence [arrogance] of Mr. Adams. . . . Think what you have been, what you are, and what, under [Adams], you are likely to become. ❞

—James Callender, quoted in *American Aurora*

This campaign banner declared: "T. Jefferson President of the United States of America—John Adams no more."

Adams's defenders were just as vicious. Yet, in spite of the campaign's nastiness, the election ended with a peaceful transfer of power from one party to another.

## A New Party Comes to Power

🔻 **KEY QUESTION** How was the presidential election of 1800 resolved?

The 1800 election was a contest between two parties with different ideas about the role of government.

**Election of 1800** The two parties contesting the election of 1800 were the **Federalists**, led by President John Adams, and the **Democratic-Republicans**, represented by Thomas Jefferson. Each party believed that the other was a threat to the Constitution and the American republic.

The Democratic-Republicans thought they were saving the nation from monarchy and oppression. They argued that the Alien and Sedition Acts passed by the Federalist congress in 1798 violated the Bill of Rights.

Meanwhile, the Federalists thought that the nation was about to be ruined by **radicals**—people who take extreme political positions. The Federalists remembered the violence of the French Revolution, in which radicals executed thousands in the name of liberty.

When election day came, the Democratic-Republicans won the presidency. Jefferson received 73 votes in the electoral college, and Adams earned 65. But there was a problem. Aaron Burr, whom the Democratic-Republicans wanted as vice president, also received 73 votes.

**Breaking the Tie** According to the Constitution, the House of Representatives had to choose between Burr and Jefferson. The Democratic-Republicans clearly wanted Jefferson to be president. However, the new House of Representatives, dominated by Jefferson's party, was not yet in office. Federalists still had a House majority, and their votes would decide the winner.

The Federalists were divided. Some feared Jefferson so much that they decided to back Burr. Others, such as Alexander Hamilton, considered Burr an unreliable man and urged the election of Jefferson.

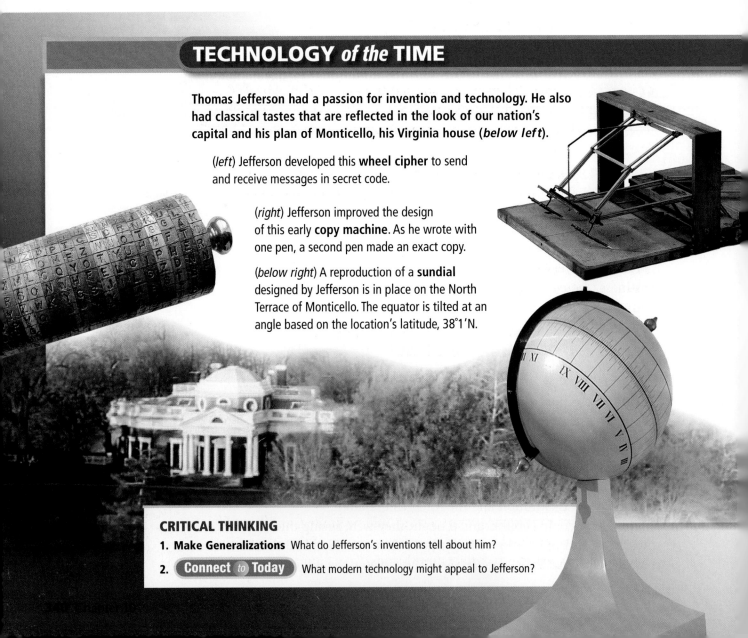

# TECHNOLOGY *of the* TIME

**Thomas Jefferson had a passion for invention and technology. He also had classical tastes that are reflected in the look of our nation's capital and his plan of Monticello, his Virginia house (*below left*).**

(*left*) Jefferson developed this **wheel cipher** to send and receive messages in secret code.

(*right*) Jefferson improved the design of this early **copy machine**. As he wrote with one pen, a second pen made an exact copy.

(*below right*) A reproduction of a **sundial** designed by Jefferson is in place on the North Terrace of Monticello. The equator is tilted at an angle based on the location's latitude, 38°1′N.

**CRITICAL THINKING**

1. **Make Generalizations** What do Jefferson's inventions tell about him?

2. **Connect** *to* **Today** What modern technology might appeal to Jefferson?

Hamilton did not like Jefferson, but he believed that Jefferson would do more for the good of the nation than Burr. "If there be a man in the world I ought to hate," he said, "it is Jefferson. . . . But the public good must be [more important than] every private consideration."

From February 11 to February 17, the House voted 35 times without a winner. Finally, Alexander Hamilton's friend James A. Bayard persuaded several Federalists not to vote for Burr. On the thirty-sixth ballot, Jefferson was elected president. Aaron Burr became vice president.

People were overjoyed by Jefferson's election. His many achievements and talents went beyond politics. He was a skilled violinist, amateur scientist, and devoted reader. His book collection later became the core of the Library of Congress. In addition, Jefferson's deep interest in the architecture of ancient Greece and Rome is reflected in the architecture of the nation's capital.

▲ **SUMMARIZE** Explain how the election of 1800 was resolved.

# Jefferson and Democracy

▼ **KEY QUESTION** How did Jefferson's policies differ from those of the Federalists?

On inauguration day, no guards, no coach, not even a horse waited at the door for Thomas Jefferson. He strolled through Washington, D.C., accompanied by a few friends. As Americans would learn in the months to come, Jefferson's humble behavior on inauguration day reflected his ideas about government.

**Jefferson's View of Government** The new president's first order of business was to heal political wounds. He urged political enemies to unite as Americans.

**PRIMARY SOURCE**

❝ Let us, then, fellow-citizens, unite with one heart and one mind. . . . Every difference of opinion is not a difference of principle. . . . We are all Republicans, we are all Federalists. ❞

—Thomas Jefferson, First Inaugural Address

**Connecting History**

**Change & Continuity**
Americans' concerns about overcrowding grew during the first half of the eighteenth century. You will see this theme develop in later chapters when you study the emergence of industry and the effects of immigration.

One way Jefferson sought to unify Americans was by promoting a common way of life. He wanted the United States to remain a nation of small independent farmers. Such a nation, he believed, would uphold the strong morals and democratic ideals he associated with country living. Jefferson also hoped that the enormous amount of land available in the United States would prevent Americans from crowding into cities, as so many people had in Europe.

Jefferson wanted to avoid having too much government. He believed that the power of the central government should be limited, and that the people should be enabled to govern themselves. Some of the changes he made during his presidency reflect these beliefs.

# Marbury v. Madison (1803)

KEY ISSUE    Judicial review

KEY PEOPLE

| | |
|---|---|
| John Adams | president 1797–1801; appointed Federalists as judges |
| Thomas Jefferson | president 1801–1809; Democratic-Republican |
| James Madison | secretary of state to President Jefferson |
| William Marbury | Federalist financier; appointed as justice by President Adams |

## History Makers

### John Marshall
### 1755–1835

John Marshall was the fourth chief justice of the U.S. Supreme Court. Marshall set out to make the judiciary a force to be reckoned with.

In 1803, in the case of *Marbury* v. *Madison*, Marshall upheld the power of judicial review. Many other rulings during Marshall's tenure as chief justice also strengthened federal power over the states.

Jefferson and Madison were angry when Marshall claimed this power for the Court, but they could hardly fight his decision. After all, *Marbury* v. *Madison* was decided in their favor.

**ONLINE BIOGRAPHY**

For more on John Marshall, go to the **Research & Writing Center** @ ClassZone.com

## The Case

President John Adams appointed William Marbury to be a justice of the peace. However, Adams's term as president ended before the appointment papers were delivered to Marbury. After Thomas Jefferson took office, he named James Madison as secretary of state. Normally it would have been Madison's job to deliver appointment papers, but Jefferson ordered Madison not to deliver Marbury's papers.

Marbury then sued. He asked the Supreme Court to order Madison to deliver the papers.

**The Court's Decision**   Marbury based his demand on two sections of the Judiciary Act of 1789. One section of that law created federal judgeships. Another section named the Supreme Court to settle disputes about certain judicial appointments.

The Supreme Court decided that the Judiciary Act was an invalid law. When Congress passed the Judiciary Act it gave a new power to the Supreme Court. But the Constitution does not allow Congress to do that. As Chief Justice John Marshall wrote, if the Constitution is to be the supreme law of the land, then any law contrary to the Constitution "is not law."

**Historical Impact**   This was the first time the Supreme Court exercised the power of judicial review by overruling a law passed by Congress. Until this time, the Supreme Court was thought of as virtually powerless. That changed after Marshall proclaimed, "It is, emphatically, the province and the duty of the judicial department to say what the law is." Marshall's decision strengthened the Constitution's system of checks and balances by affirming an important power of the courts.

By upholding judicial review, Marshall helped to create a lasting balance among the three branches of government. The strength of this balance would be tested as the United States grew.

**CRITICAL THINKING**   **Summarize**   Explain how John Marshall strengthened the Supreme Court.

**Jefferson and the Federalists** Jefferson wanted the government to have less power than it had under the Federalists. He reduced the number of federal employees and the size of the military, and sought to end Federalist programs. Congress, now controlled by Democratic-Republicans, let the Alien and Sedition Acts end. Jefferson released prisoners convicted under the acts. Congress also ended many taxes, such as the unpopular whiskey tax.

Next, Jefferson made changes to Federalist financial policies. Alexander Hamilton had created a system that depended on a certain amount of public debt. Hamilton believed that people who were owed money by their government would make sure the government was run properly. But Jefferson opposed public debt. He used revenues from tariffs and land sales to reduce the amount of money owed by the government.

**Conflict with the Courts** Although Jefferson ended many Federalist programs, he had little power over the courts. Under the **Judiciary Act of 1801**, Adams had appointed as many Federalist judges as he could between the election of 1800 and Jefferson's inauguration. Because judges were appointed for life, Jefferson could do little about Federalist control of the courts.

Under Chief Justice **John Marshall**, the Supreme Court upheld federal authority and strengthened federal courts. In 1803, in *Marbury* v. *Madison*, Marshall affirmed the principle of **judicial review**—the final authority of the Supreme Court on the meaning of the Constitution. (See page 342.)

 **COMPARE AND CONTRAST** Explain how Jefferson's policies differed from those of the Federalists.

---

**New Jersey Core Curriculum Content Standards *Review***

 **ONLINE QUIZ**
For test practice, go to
**Interactive Review @ ClassZone.com**

### TERMS & NAMES

**1.** Explain the significance of
- Thomas Jefferson
- John Marshall
- Judiciary Act of 1801
- judicial review

### USING YOUR READING NOTES

**2. Main Ideas and Details** Complete the chart you started at the beginning of this section.

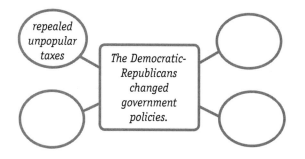

repealed unpopular taxes

The Democratic-Republicans changed government policies.

### KEY IDEAS

**3.** What was unusual about the election of 1800?

**4.** Why did Jefferson seek unity between political parties?

**5.** What is the lasting importance of *Marbury* v. *Madison*?

### CRITICAL THINKING

**6. Compare and Contrast** In what ways did the Federalists and Democratic-Republicans differ?

**7. Analyze Point of View** Why do you think Jefferson wished to promote a modest lifestyle?

**8. Causes and Effects** How did Adams's last-minute appointments affect the new president?

**9.** **Technology** Research Thomas Jefferson's interests. Design an Internet page about Jefferson that shows his inventions or a building he designed.

## ▶ Key Ideas

**BEFORE, YOU LEARNED**

After a tied election, Jefferson became president and the Democratic-Republicans reduced the power of the federal government.

**NOW YOU WILL LEARN**

The nation doubled in size when Jefferson acquired the Louisiana Purchase.

## ▶ Vocabulary

**TERMS & NAMES**

**Meriwether Lewis** army captain appointed by President Jefferson to explore the Louisiana Territory and lands west to the Pacific Ocean

**William Clark** co-leader of the Lewis and Clark expedition

**Sacagawea** (sak•uh•juh•WEE•uh) Shoshone woman who assisted the Lewis and Clark expedition

**Louisiana Purchase** American purchase of the Louisiana Territory from France in 1803

**Lewis and Clark expedition** group that explored the Louisiana Territory and lands west; also known as the Corps of Discovery

**Zebulon Pike** leader of a southern expedition in the Louisiana Territory

**BACKGROUND VOCABULARY**

**corps** (kor) a number of people acting together for a similar purpose

**Visual Vocabulary**
William Clark (*left*) and Meriwether Lewis

## ▶ Reading Strategy

Re-create the diagram shown at right. As you read and respond to the **KEY QUESTIONS**, use the diagram to record important events and their effects. Add more boxes or start a new diagram as needed.

 See Skillbuilder Handbook, page R7.

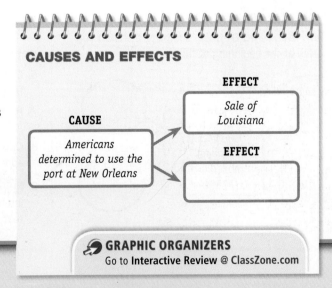

**CAUSES AND EFFECTS**

**CAUSE**

Americans determined to use the port at New Orleans

**EFFECT**

Sale of Louisiana

**EFFECT**

🖱 **GRAPHIC ORGANIZERS**
Go to **Interactive Review** @ ClassZone.com

# The Louisiana Purchase and Exploration

**6.4.E.6.** Describe and map American territorial expansions and the settlement of the frontier during this period.
**6.4.F.9.** Describe and map the continuing territorial expansion and settlement of the frontier, including the acquisition of new territories and conflicts with Native Americans, the Louisiana Purchase, . . . .

## One American's Story

In 1803, an expedition led by explorers **Meriwether Lewis** and **William Clark** set out to explore the American West. As they neared the Rocky Mountains, Lewis and Clark hired a French trapper to act as an interpreter with the Native Americans. He brought along his young wife, **Sacagawea**, a Shoshone Indian. Her knowledge of Native American languages and the land played an essential role in the expedition.

### PRIMARY SOURCE

❝ *The sight* of this Indian woman . . . [assured the Native Americans] of our friendly intentions. . . . No woman ever accompanied a war party in this quarter. ❞

—William Clark, journal entry, October 19, 1805

This detail from *Lewis and Clark* by N. C. Wyeth shows Sacagawea with Meriwether Lewis.

Sacagawea did more than enable conversation and trade. Her presence led many tribes to believe that the explorers came in peace.

## The Louisiana Purchase

🔻 **KEY QUESTION** How did the United States acquire the Louisiana Purchase?

When Americans talked about the West in 1800, they meant the area between the Appalachian Mountains and the Mississippi River.

**The West in 1800** By 1800, thousands of settlers were moving westward across the Appalachians. Many settled on land inhabited by Native Americans. Even so, several U.S. territories soon declared statehood. Kentucky and Tennessee became states by 1800, and Ohio entered the union in 1803.

Although the Mississippi River was then the western border of the United States, there was much activity farther west. France and Spain were negotiating for ownership of the Louisiana Territory—the vast region between the Mississippi River and the Rocky Mountains.

**The Mississippi River and New Orleans** As the number of westerners grew, so did their political influence. A vital issue for many farmers and merchants was the use of the Mississippi River. They used this highway of commerce to transport their products through the New Orleans port, across the Gulf of Mexico, and then to East Coast markets.

Although originally claimed by France, the port was turned over to Spain after the French and Indian War. In a secret treaty in 1800, Spain returned the port to France's powerful leader, Napoleon. Now Napoleon planned to colonize the American territory. This brought America close to war.

**The United States Expands** In 1802, before turning Louisiana over to France, Spain closed New Orleans to American shipping. Angry westerners called for war against both Spain and France. To avoid hostilities, Jefferson offered to buy New Orleans from France. He received a surprising answer. The French asked if the United States wanted to buy all of the Louisiana Territory—a tract of land even larger than the entire United States at that time.

A number of factors may have influenced Napoleon's offer. He was probably alarmed by America's determination to keep the port of New Orleans open. Also, his enthusiasm for a colony in America may have been lessened by events in Haiti, a French colony in the West Indies. There, a revolt led by Toussaint L'Ouverture (too•SAN loo•vehr•TOOR) had resulted in disastrous losses for the French. Another factor was France's costly war against Britain. America's money may have been more valuable to Napoleon than land.

Jefferson was thrilled by Napoleon's offer. However, the Constitution said nothing about the president's right to buy land. This troubled Jefferson, who believed in the strict interpretation of the Constitution. But he also believed in a republic of small farmers, and that required land. So, on April 30, 1803, the **Louisiana Purchase** was approved for $15 million—about three cents per acre. The size of the United States doubled. At the time, most Americans knew little about this territory. But that would soon change.

🔺 **SUMMARIZE** Explain how the United States acquired the Louisiana Territory.

**Connect** *to the* **World**

**Dissent and Rebellion**
Haiti had been a highly profitable French colony that used slave labor. Toussaint L'Ouverture, a former slave, led a 1791 rebellion against French rule. Thirteen bloody years later, Haiti became the first independent black republic in the world.

# Exploring the Louisiana Territory

🔻 **KEY QUESTION** What were some effects of exploring the Louisiana Territory?

Since 1802, Thomas Jefferson had planned an expedition to the Louisiana country. Now that the Louisiana Purchase had been made, learning about the territory became more important than ever.

**The Lewis and Clark Expedition** Jefferson chose a young officer, Captain Meriwether Lewis, to lead an exploration of the Louisiana country. Lewis asked Lieutenant William Clark, a mapmaker and outdoorsman, to help him oversee a volunteer force, or **corps**. They called it the Corps of Discovery, but it soon became known as the **Lewis and Clark expedition**.

Clark was accompanied by York, his African-American slave. York's hunting skills won him many admirers. The first black man that many Native Americans had seen, he became something of a celebrity among them.

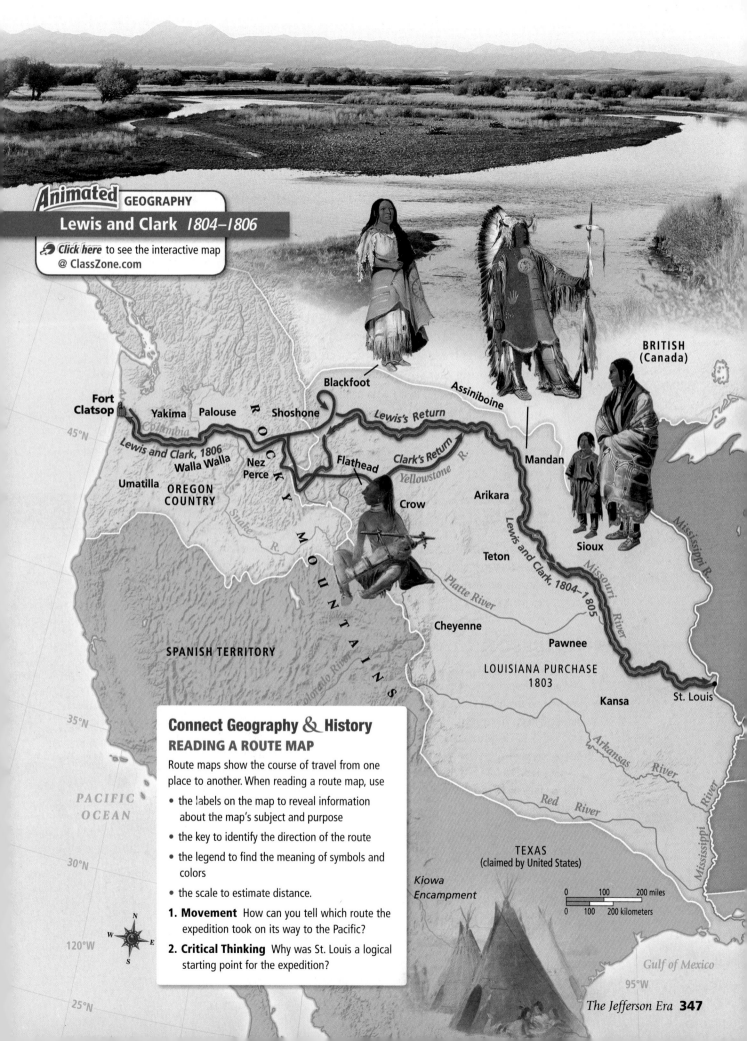

## Lewis and Clark 1804–1806

*Click here* to see the interactive map
@ ClassZone.com

BRITISH
(Canada)

Blackfoot

Assiniboine

Fort
Clatsop

Yakima   Palouse      Shoshone         Lewis's Return

*Columbia*

Lewis and Clark, 1806

Walla Walla

Nez
Perce      Flathead      Clark's Return      Mandan

Umatilla   OREGON
COUNTRY

*Yellowstone R.*

Crow         Arikara

*Snake R.*

R

O

C

K

Y

M

O

U

N

T

A

I

N

S

Teton       Sioux

*Platte River*

Lewis and Clark, 1804–1805

*Missouri River*

*Mississippi R.*

Cheyenne

Pawnee

SPANISH TERRITORY

*Colorado River*

LOUISIANA PURCHASE
1803

Kansa        St. Louis

35°N

*Arkansas*

*River*

PACIFIC
OCEAN

*Red*   *River*

*Mississippi River*

### Connect Geography & History
#### READING A ROUTE MAP

Route maps show the course of travel from one
place to another. When reading a route map, use

- the labels on the map to reveal information
  about the map's subject and purpose

- the key to identify the direction of the route

- the legend to find the meaning of symbols and
  colors

- the scale to estimate distance.

1. **Movement** How can you tell which route the
   expedition took on its way to the Pacific?

2. **Critical Thinking** Why was St. Louis a logical
   starting point for the expedition?

TEXAS
(claimed by United States)

Kiowa
Encampment

| 0 | 100 | 200 miles |
| 0 | 100 | 200 kilometers |

30°N

120°W

*Gulf of Mexico*

N
W        E
S

25°N                                                95°W

**The Journey Begins** Lewis and Clark set out in the summer of 1803. By winter, they reached St. Louis. Located on the western bank of the Mississippi River, St. Louis would soon become the gateway to the West. But in 1803 it was a sleepy town. Lewis and Clark spent the winter there, waiting for the official transfer of Louisiana to the United States. In March 1804, the American flag flew over St. Louis for the first time.

**West to the Ocean** The expedition, which numbered about 40, left St. Louis in May of 1804. Jefferson had instructed them to explore the Missouri River in hopes of finding a water route across the continent. He also told them to establish good relations with Native Americans and to describe the landscape, plants, and animals they saw.

After reaching what is now North Dakota, the explorers spent the winter with the Mandan people. They also met British and Canadian trappers and traders, who were not happy to see them. The traders feared American competition in the trade in beaver fur—and they would be proved right.

In the spring of 1805, the expedition set out again. This time they were joined by Sacagawea, who was a Shoshone Indian. Her language skills—she knew sign language and several Native American languages—and her knowledge of geography would be of great value to Lewis and Clark.

🔊 **ONLINE PRIMARY SOURCE**

Hear the perspectives at the **Research & Writing Center** @ ClassZone.com

## COMPARING *Perspectives*

President Thomas Jefferson sponsored Lewis and Clark's expedition to the West, where they met almost 50 tribes. In an 1806 speech, Jefferson described his goals for relations between the United States and Native Americans. From the Native American perspective, Kiowa Chief Satanta (c. 1830–1878) later described the impact of Jefferson's policies.

### 🔊 Jefferson Speaks

“ My friends and children. We are descended from the old nations which live beyond the great water: but we and our forefathers have been so long here that we seem like you to have grown out of this land . . . you are all my children . . . we wish as a true father should do, that we may all live together as one household. ”

—Thomas Jefferson, Speech to a Delegation of Indian Chiefs, January 4, 1806

### 🔊 Satanta Speaks

“ I hear a great deal of good talk from the gentlemen the Great Father sends us . . . I have heard you intend to settle us on a reservation near the mountains. I don't want to settle. . . . A long time ago this land belonged to our fathers, but when I go up to the river I see camps of soldiers on its banks. These soldiers cut down my timber, they kill my buffalo and when I see that, my heart feels like bursting. ”

—Satanta, Kiowa Chief, September 1876

#### CRITICAL THINKING

1. **Make Inferences** What did Jefferson want for Native Americans?
2. **Analyze** Why were the Native Americans resentful of the soldiers?

As they approached the Rocky Mountains, Sacagawea pointed out Shoshone lands. Lewis and a small party made their way overland. The chief recognized Sacagawea as his sister and traded horses to Lewis and Clark. This enabled the explorers to cross the mountains. The expedition continued on to the Columbia River, which leads to the Pacific Ocean. The group arrived at the Pacific Coast in November 1805 and returned to St. Louis in 1806.

Lewis and Clark brought back a wealth of valuable information. Though they learned that an all-water route across the continent did not exist, Americans received an exciting report of what lay to the west. More importantly, the expedition produced the first good maps of the Louisiana Territory.

### Zebulon Pike and the Southern Route
In 1806, an expedition led by explorer **Zebulon Pike** left St. Louis on a southerly route to find the sources of the Arkansas and Red rivers. The group entered Spanish territory and was arrested. The explorers were released in 1807 and returned to the United States.

Pike's group brought back valuable descriptions of the land it explored. Not all these descriptions were accurate, however. For example, Pike described the treeless Great Plains as a desert. This led many Americans to believe, mistakenly, that the Plains region was useless for farming.

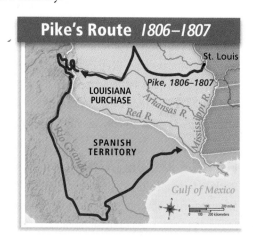

Pike's Route 1806–1807

 **CAUSES AND EFFECTS** Describe some effects of exploring the Louisiana Territory.

---

 New Jersey Core Curriculum Content Standards *Review*

**ONLINE QUIZ**
For test practice, go to
**Interactive Review @ ClassZone.com**

### TERMS & NAMES

**1.** Explain the importance of
- Louisiana Purchase
- Sacagawea
- Meriwether Lewis
- Zebulon Pike
- William Clark

### USING YOUR READING NOTES

**2. Causes and Effects** Complete the diagram you started at the beginning of this section. Then create a diagram for each of the other main events in this section.

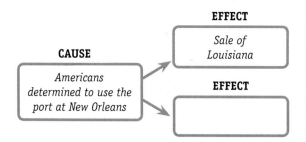

CAUSE

Americans determined to use the port at New Orleans

EFFECT

Sale of Louisiana

EFFECT

### KEY IDEAS

**3.** Why was the Louisiana Purchase important to Jefferson?

**4.** Why were Lewis and Clark instructed to document the natural resources they found in their travels?

### CRITICAL THINKING

**5. Evaluate** How did the Louisiana Purchase change the United States?

**6. Make Inferences** How might the information gathered by the explorers be useful to Jefferson?

**7. Recognize Bias and Propaganda** Read the quote by Jefferson on page 348. Is it propaganda? Explain.

**8. Connect** *to* **Today** Explorers still seek government funding for new expeditions. Where might today's explorers want to study?

**9. Writing Letter** Write a one-page letter from Jefferson to Lewis in which you describe your goals for the exploration of the Louisiana Territory.

# American Landscapes

**PACIFIC NORTHWEST** Damp ocean winds help keep the coastal region green. East of the Cascades lie relatively dry highlands. The mountains of the region include more than a dozen major volcanoes.

**SOUTHWEST** For thousands of years, Native Americans have lived in the desert Southwest. Spanish settlement began here in 1598 and lasted to the 1840s. Explorer Zebulon Pike was arrested by Spanish authorities in the region in 1807.

**ROCKY MOUNTAINS** The majestic Rockies form the Continental Divide, which separates east-flowing and west-flowing rivers. Lewis and Clark crossed these mountains with the aid of Sacagawea, who obtained horses for them.

**GREAT PLAINS** The Plains region stretches from the foothills of the Rocky Mountains to the humid grasslands that lie west of the Mississippi River. It is mostly flat. At the time of the Lewis and Clark expedition, it was home to millions of bison.

**GULF COAST** The low, marshy region bordering the Gulf of Mexico is known as the Gulf Coast. Riverways and natural ports have long made commerce important here. The United States gained the valuable Lower Mississippi Valley in the 1803 Louisiana Purchase.

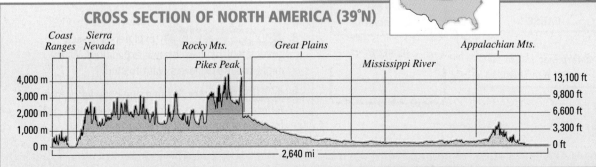

**CROSS SECTION OF NORTH AMERICA (39°N)**

Rocky Mountains

ROCKY MOUNTAINS

GREAT PLAINS

Great Plains

## History Makers

### Sacagawea    c. 1786–1812

A Shoshone Indian, Sacagawea was born in what is now Idaho. When she was about 12 years old she was kidnapped by the Hidatsa Sioux and taken to what is now North Dakota. About four years later she married a French trader, Toussaint Charbonneau. Sacagawea and her husband traveled with Lewis and Clark from 1804 to 1806. Their son Jean Baptiste was born during the journey. When the expedition reached Shoshone territory in the Rocky Mountains, Sacagawea met her brother, Chief Cameahwait. He agreed to trade the horses that the explorers needed to cross the mountains.

**CRITICAL THINKING  Make Inferences** How might living in different cultures have helped Sacagawea as a guide?

**ONLINE BIOGRAPHY**   For more on Sacagawea, go to the **Research & Writing Center** @ ClassZone.com

### Connect Geography & History

**1. Region** Where are regions connected by water routes?

**2. Make Inferences** Which region would you expect to be the hardest to cross on foot? Why?

 See Geography Handbook, pages A8–A11.

Gulf Coast

Gulf of Mexico

## ▶ Key Ideas

**BEFORE, YOU LEARNED**
After Jefferson acquired the Louisiana Purchase, the nation doubled in size.

**NOW YOU WILL LEARN**
The nation gained confidence and worldwide respect as a result of the War of 1812.

## ▶ Vocabulary

**TERMS & NAMES**

**Embargo Act of 1807** law that forbade American ships from sailing to foreign ports and closed American ports to British ships

**Tecumseh** (tih•KUM•seh) Shawnee chief who sought to stop the loss of Native American land to white settlers

**war hawk** westerner who supported the War of 1812

**Oliver Hazard Perry** naval officer who led the U.S. victory over the British on Lake Erie in 1813

**BACKGROUND VOCABULARY**

**tribute** (TRIHB•yoot) payment in exchange for protection

**impressment** the act of seizing by force; between 1803 and 1812, the British impressed, or kidnapped, about 6,000 American sailors to work on British ships

**coercion** (ko•ER•shun) practice of forcing someone to act in a certain way by use of pressure or threats

Visual Vocabulary
impressment

## ▶ Reading Strategy

Re-create the diagram shown at right. As you read and respond to the **KEY QUESTIONS**, use the diagram to record important events in the order in which they occurred.

 **See Skillbuilder Handbook, page R5.**

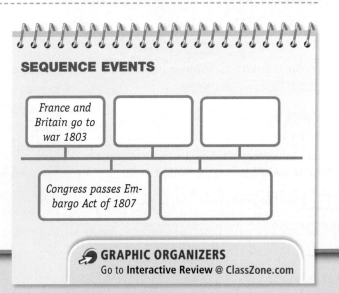

**SEQUENCE EVENTS**

France and Britain go to war 1803

Congress passes Embargo Act of 1807

**GRAPHIC ORGANIZERS**
Go to **Interactive Review** @ ClassZone.com

# The War of 1812

**6.4.E.8.** Discuss the background and major issues of the War of 1812 (e.g., sectional issues, role of Native Americans).

**6.4.F.7.** Compare political interests and views regarding the War of 1812 (e.g., US responses to shipping harassment, interests of Native Americans and white settlers in the Northwest Territory).

## One American's Story

From 1801 to 1805, the United States was at war with Tripoli, a state on the Barbary coast of North Africa. The war began because of attacks on American merchant ships by Barbary pirates. The United States had been paying protection money, or **tribute**, but the pasha (ruler) of Tripoli wanted more money.

In February 1804, President Thomas Jefferson sent U.S. Navy Lieutenant Stephen Decatur to destroy the U.S. ship *Philadelphia*, which was in the hands of Barbary pirates. Decatur set fire to the *Philadelphia* and then escaped under enemy fire. Later, he issued this rallying cry.

**PRIMARY SOURCE**

❝ Our country! In her [relationships] with foreign nations may she always be in the right; but our country, right or wrong. ❞

—Stephen Decatur, 1816

Stephen Decatur was a hero of the war between the United States and the North African state of Tripoli.

The conflict with Tripoli showed how hard it was for the United States to stay out of foreign affairs while its citizens were involved in overseas trade.

## The Path to War

▼ **KEY QUESTION** What conflicts with other nations did the United States have in the early 1800s?

Jefferson wanted the United States to seek the friendship of all nations but have "entangling alliances with none." However, his desire to keep the United States out of conflict with other nations was doomed from the start. American merchants were engaged in trade all over the world. Besides, the United States had little control over the actions of foreign powers.

**Problems with France and England** War broke out between France and Great Britain in 1803. The United States tried to stay out of the war. But many American trading ships made stops in Europe. The British captured any ship bound for France, and the French stopped all ships bound for Britain.

Another conflict grew out of Britain's shortage of sailors. Life in the British navy was so bad at the time that few British citizens chose to join—and many deserted. To fill its need for sailors, Britain used the policy of **impressment**, or kidnapping, of American merchant sailors. Between 1803 and 1812, the British impressed about 6,000 Americans to work on British ships.

**No More Trade** Instead of declaring war, Jefferson asked Congress to pass legislation that would stop all foreign trade. The president described his policy as "peaceable **coercion**." Coercion means forcing someone to act in a certain way by pressure or threats. Jefferson believed that the legislation would prevent further bloodshed.

In December, Congress passed the **Embargo Act of 1807**, which forbade American ships from sailing to foreign ports. The act also closed American ports to British ships. The policy harmed the United States more than it harmed France or Britain. American farmers lost key markets for their products. Shippers lost income, and many chose to violate the embargo by making false claims about where they were going.

The embargo became an issue in the election of 1808, which James Madison won. By then, Congress had repealed the act. Madison's solution to the problem was a law that allowed merchants to trade with any country except France and Britain. Trade with them would resume when they agreed to respect U.S. ships. This law was no more effective than the embargo.

**Tecumseh and Native American Unity** British interference with American shipping and impressment of U.S. citizens made Americans angry. Many also believed the British were trying to stop American expansion in the Northwest by stirring up Native American resistance to frontier settlements.

Since the Battle of Fallen Timbers in 1794, Native Americans had continued to lose their land to white settlers. **Tecumseh**, a Shawnee chief, vowed to stop this. He believed that Native American tribes had to unite in order to protect their land. Events in 1809 proved him right. That September, William Henry Harrison, governor of the Indiana Territory, signed the Treaty of Fort Wayne with chiefs of the Miami, Delaware, and Potawatomi tribes. They agreed to sell more than three million acres of land. But Tecumseh declared the treaty void. He believed that the sale could go through only with the agreement of all tribes, not just some.

(*below right*) The Shawnee were defeated at the Battle of Tippecanoe. **How did the Battle of Tippecanoe affect Tecumseh's hopes for unity?**

Chief Tecumseh

Many Native Americans did answer Tecumseh's call for unity. But he was too late. In late 1811, while Tecumseh was away recruiting for his alliance, Harrison's forces defeated the Shawnee at the Battle of Tippecanoe. Following this defeat, Tecumseh sided with the British in Canada. Tecumseh's welcome in Canada increased anti-British feelings in the West.

▲ **SUMMARIZE** Explain what conflicts with other nations the United States had in the early 1800s.

## The War of 1812

▼ **KEY QUESTION** What were the effects of the War of 1812?

By 1812, more and more Americans were calling for war against Britain for its role in helping Native Americans and its policy on the high seas. Those who supported war were called **war hawks**. Many of them came from the western part of the country. Those in the Northeast, which had business ties with Britain, were less eager for war. The American government wanted all Americans to feel that their country could protect them. Finally on June 18, 1812, President James Madison asked Congress to declare war on Britain.

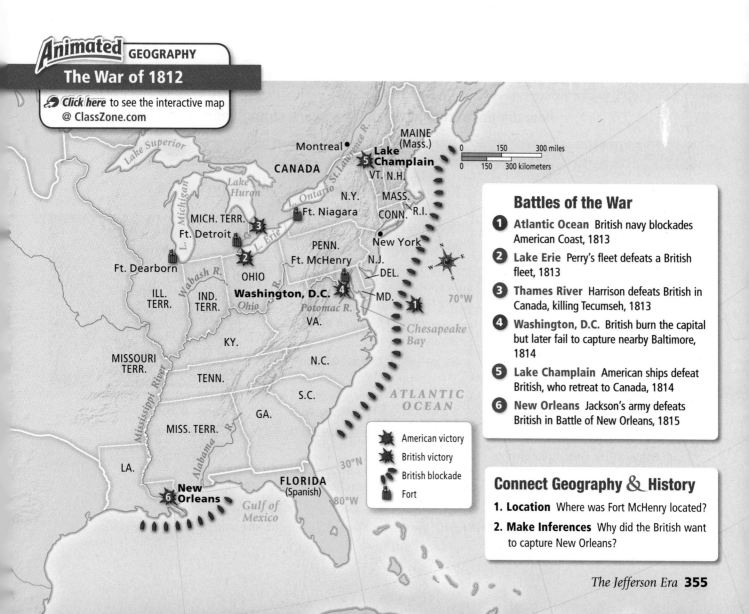

**Animated GEOGRAPHY**

**The War of 1812**

Click here to see the interactive map @ ClassZone.com

**Battles of the War**

1. **Atlantic Ocean** British navy blockades American Coast, 1813

2. **Lake Erie** Perry's fleet defeats a British fleet, 1813

3. **Thames River** Harrison defeats British in Canada, killing Tecumseh, 1813

4. **Washington, D.C.** British burn the capital but later fail to capture nearby Baltimore, 1814

5. **Lake Champlain** American ships defeat British, who retreat to Canada, 1814

6. **New Orleans** Jackson's army defeats British in Battle of New Orleans, 1815

American victory
British victory
British blockade
Fort

**Connect Geography & History**

1. **Location** Where was Fort McHenry located?

2. **Make Inferences** Why did the British want to capture New Orleans?

**The First Phase of the War** The War of 1812 had two main phases. From 1812 to 1814, Britain concentrated on its war with France. It spent little energy on its conflict in North America, although it did send ships to blockade the American coast.

The American military was weak at the beginning of the war. Democratic-Republicans had reduced the size of the American armed forces. The U.S. Navy had only 16 warships. In spite of its small size, the U.S. Navy rose to the challenge. Ships such as the *Constitution* and the *United States* won stirring victories that boosted American confidence.

**Triumph on Lake Erie** The most important U.S. naval victory took place on Lake Erie. In September 1813, a small British force on the lake set out to attack a new fleet of American ships. Commodore **Oliver Hazard Perry**, who had taken charge of the fleet, sailed out to meet the enemy. Perry's ship, the *Lawrence*, flew a banner reading, "Don't give up the ship."

For two hours, the British and Americans exchanged cannon shots. Perry's ship was demolished and the guns put out of action. Under British fire, Perry grabbed the banner as he and four companions escaped and rowed to another ship. Commanding the second ship, Perry soon forced the British to surrender. In a message to General William Henry Harrison, commander

# CONNECT to the Essential Question

## How did the events of the Jefferson Era strengthen the nation?

| EVENT | EFFECTS |
|---|---|
| **1801–1804** Jefferson takes office; Democratic-Republicans in power | Many Federalist policies end, though Federalists retain control of Judiciary |
| Jefferson purchases Louisiana Territory | Doubles size of the United States |
| Lewis and Clark expedition charts important information about the West | Western settlement fever begins |
| **1807–1812** Congress passes Embargo Act of 1807 | American shipping and trade suffer |
| Shawnee defeated at the Battle of Tippecanoe | Shawnee chief Tecumseh sides with British in Canada |
| Congress declares war on Britain | Britain and the United States are at war |
| **1814–1815** British defeat Napoleon, turn focus to war with the United States | British burn Capitol building, White House; attack Fort McHenry |
| Treaty of Ghent is signed | War ends, but news reaches the United States too late to prevent further hostilities |
| At Battle of New Orleans, Jackson's forces defeat British | Increases American patriotism; weakens Native American resistance; strengthens American manufacturing |

**CRITICAL THINKING** **Synthesize** How would you describe the characteristics of the Jefferson Era?

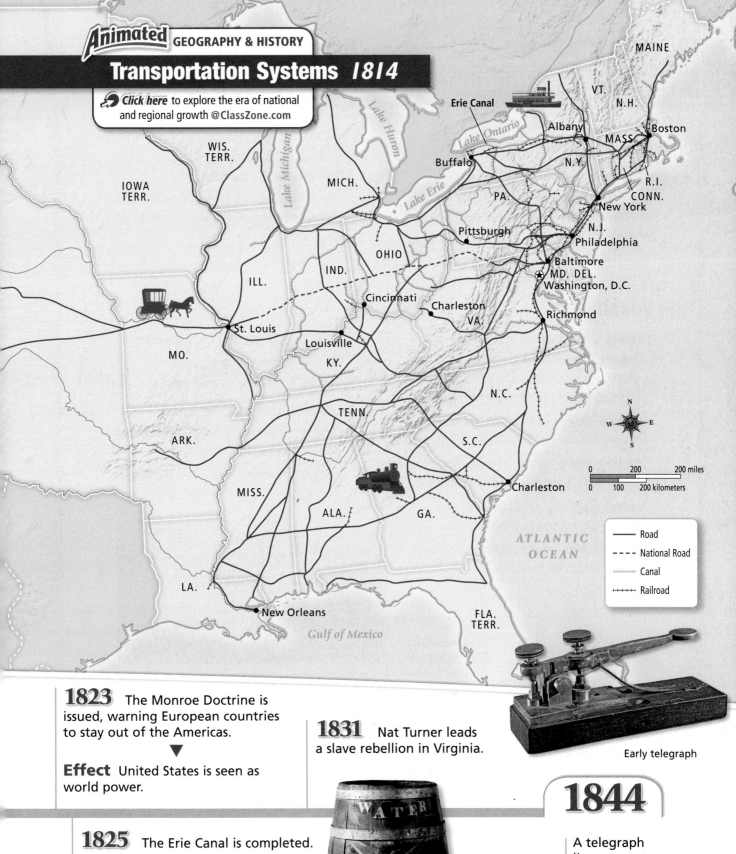

# Transportation Systems 1814

Click here to explore the era of national and regional growth @ClassZone.com

Erie Canal

MAINE

VT.

N.H.

Lake Ontario

Albany

Boston

MASS.

Lake Huron

Buffalo

N.Y.

R.I.

CONN.

New York

N.J.

Philadelphia

Pittsburgh

WIS. TERR.

Lake Michigan

MICH.

Lake Erie

PA.

IOWA TERR.

OHIO

IND.

Baltimore

MD. DEL.

Washington, D.C.

ILL.

Cincinnati

Charleston

VA.

Richmond

St. Louis

Louisville

KY.

MO.

N.C.

TENN.

S.C.

ARK.

Charleston

MISS.

ALA.

GA.

ATLANTIC OCEAN

| 0 | 200 | 200 miles |
| 0 | 100 | 200 kilometers |

LA.

New Orleans

FLA. TERR.

Gulf of Mexico

| — | Road |
| - - - | National Road |
| ......... | Canal |
| +++++ | Railroad |

**1823** The Monroe Doctrine is issued, warning European countries to stay out of the Americas.

▼

**Effect** United States is seen as world power.

**1831** Nat Turner leads a slave rebellion in Virginia.

Early telegraph

**1825** The Erie Canal is completed.

▼

**Effect** The canal creates a water route between New York City and the Great Lakes.

Barrel used on the Erie Canal

**1844**

A telegraph line connects Washington, D.C., and Baltimore.

## ▶ Key Ideas

**BEFORE, YOU LEARNED**

The nation gained confidence and worldwide respect as a result of the War of 1812.

**NOW YOU WILL LEARN**

New industries and inventions changed the way people lived and worked in the early 1800s.

## ▶ Vocabulary

**TERMS & NAMES**

**Industrial Revolution** the economic changes of the late 1700s, when manufacturing replaced farming as the main form of work

**Samuel Slater** builder of the first water-powered textile mill in America

**factory system** method of production using many workers and machines in one building

**Lowell mills** textile mills located in the factory town of Lowell, Massachusetts

**Robert Fulton** inventor of America's first widely successful steamboat

**Peter Cooper** builder of America's first successful steam-powered locomotive

**Samuel F. B. Morse** inventor of the telegraph

**BACKGROUND VOCABULARY**

**threshing machine** a device that separates kernels of wheat from their husks

**mechanical reaper** a device that cuts grain

**Visual Vocabulary**
threshing machine

## ▶ Reading Strategy

As you read and respond to the **KEY QUESTIONS**, use a graphic organizer like the one shown to record important events in the order in which they occurred.

 See Skillbuilder Handbook, page R5.

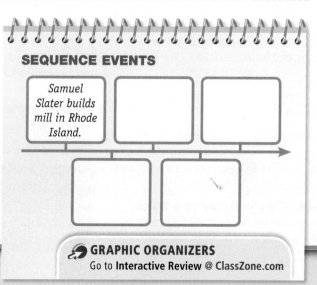

**SEQUENCE EVENTS**

| Samuel Slater builds mill in Rhode Island. | | |

**🔁 GRAPHIC ORGANIZERS**
Go to **Interactive Review** @ ClassZone.com

# Early Industry and Inventions

**6.4.F.1.** Describe the political, economic, and social changes in New Jersey and American society preceding the Civil War, including the early stages of industrialization, the growth of cities, and the political, legal, and social controversies surrounding the expansion of slavery.

## One American's Story

Harriet Hanson Robinson began working in the textile mills in Lowell, Massachusetts, in 1835, when she was ten years old. At the time, there were few opportunities for girls and women to work outside the home, and Harriet was proud to earn a good wage. As an adult, Harriet described the life of the mill girls.

### PRIMARY SOURCE

❝ Though the hours of labor were long, they were not overworked; they were obliged to tend no more looms and frames than they could easily take care of, and they had plenty of time to sit and rest. . . . They were treated with consideration by their employers, and there was a feeling of respectful equality between them. . . . In those days, there was no need of advocating the doctrine of the proper relation between employer and employed. *Help was too valuable to be ill-treated.* ❞

—Harriet Hanson Robinson, from *Loom and Spindle; or, Life Among the Early Mill Girls*

The textile industry employed young workers such as this unidentified mill girl, photographed holding a spindle (for spinning fibers).

Later, when laborers were more plentiful, the mill owners were able to cut wages, and life in the mills became much more difficult.

## The Industrial Revolution

🔻 **KEY QUESTION** How did the Industrial Revolution change the way Americans lived and worked?

After the War of 1812, Americans experienced a new kind of revolution. This was not a political revolution, but a change in the way that goods were produced. For centuries, people had made clothing, furniture, and other goods at home. Then, in late-18th-century Britain, factory machines started replacing hand tools. Soon large-scale manufacturing was producing huge quantities of goods. These changes are called the **Industrial Revolution**.

**Child Labor**

In the late 1700s, a great many workers in British textile factories were children. Their small, agile fingers were considered well-suited to textile work. Children as young as five years old might work 12 to 16 hours a day.

 **ONLINE PRIMARY SOURCE**

Hear the perspectives at the **Research & Writing Center** @ ClassZone.com

**Factories Rise in New England** In America, the Industrial Revolution began in 1793, when the Englishman **Samuel Slater** built the first spinning mill in Pawtucket, Rhode Island. The year before, he had sailed to the United States, perhaps under a false name—it was illegal for British textile workers to leave the country. Britain did not want another nation to copy its machines for making thread and cloth. But Slater brought the secrets to America.

At first, Slater hired a small group of children and paid them a low wage. Later, he built a larger mill and employed whole families. As Slater influenced others to start mills, his family system of employment spread through Rhode Island, Connecticut, and southern Massachusetts.

New England was a good place to build factories. The mills needed water power, and New England had many fast-moving rivers. For transportation, it had ships and access to the ocean. The region also had a ready labor force of farmers who were tired of scraping together a living from stony fields.

The **factory system** brought many workers and machines together under one roof. People left their family farms and crowded into cities to take jobs in factories. They worked for wages on a set schedule. Their way of life changed—and not always for the better.

## COMPARING Perspectives

### LIFE IN THE MILLS

The Industrial Revolution swept England in the mid-1700s. Half a century later, America, too, began to be transformed from a land of small farmers to an industrial nation. In these excerpts, observers from America and England described what they saw on visits to America's then-new Lowell mills.

### An American Speaks

❝ The din and clatter of these five hundred looms under full operation, struck us . . . as something frightful and infernal . . . The atmosphere of such a room . . . is charged with cotton filaments and dust, which, we were told, are very injurious to the lungs. On entering the room, although the day was warm, we remarked that the windows were down . . . [W]e found ourselves . . . in quite a perspiration. ❞

—*A Description of Factory Life by an Associationist*, 1846

### An Englishman Speaks

❝ The rooms in which [the girls] worked were as well ordered as themselves. In the windows of some, there were green plants, which were trained to shade the glass; in all, there was as much fresh air, cleanliness, and comfort, as the nature of the occupation would possibly admit of. . . . I solemnly declare, that from all the crowd I saw . . . I cannot recall . . . one young face that gave me a painful impression . . . ❞

—Charles Dickens, *American Notes*, 1842

### CRITICAL THINKING

1. **Make Inferences** What do you think working conditions were like in the mills in England?

2. **Recognizing Bias and Propaganda** Why might the two writers describe the same working conditions in such different ways?

Many Americans, such as Thomas Jefferson, did not want the United States to industrialize. But the War of 1812 brought growth to American industry. Because the British naval blockade kept imported goods from reaching U.S. shores, Americans had to manufacture their own goods. The blockade also stopped investors from spending money on shipping and trade. Instead, they invested in new American industries. Entrepreneurs built factories, starting in New England. These entrepreneurs and their region grew wealthier.

**The Lowell Mills Hire Women** In 1814, the U.S. textile industry took a leap forward when Francis Cabot Lowell built a factory in eastern Massachusetts. This factory spun raw cotton into yarn, and then wove the yarn into cloth on power looms. Lowell had seen power looms in English mills and had figured out how to build them.

The factory was so successful that Lowell's associates built a new factory town, Lowell, near the Merrimack and Concord rivers. The **Lowell mills**, textile mills in the town, brought another significant change as large numbers of women entered the workforce. Many were farm girls who lived in company-owned boardinghouses. In the early years, the Lowell girls' wages were high—between two and four dollars a week. Older women supervised the girls. Later, falling profits meant that wages dropped and working conditions worsened at the Lowell mills.

The Lowell mills and other early factories ran on water power. Factories built after the 1830s were run by more powerful steam engines. Because steam engines used coal and wood, not fast-moving water, these newer factories could be built away from rivers and beyond New England.

**New Manufacturing Methods Spread** New manufacturing methods changed work in other industries as well. In 1797, the U.S. government hired the inventor Eli Whitney to make 10,000 muskets for the army. Before this time, guns were made one at a time by a gunsmith. Each gun differed slightly. If a part broke, a new part had to be created to match the broken one.

Whitney sought a better way to make guns. In 1801, he went to Washington and laid out several piles of musket parts. He took a part from each pile and quickly assembled a musket. He had just demonstrated the use of interchangeable parts—parts that are exactly alike.

Machines that produced identical parts soon became standard. Interchangeable parts speeded up production, made repairs easy, and allowed the use of less-skilled workers.

▲ **SYNTHESIZE** Describe how the Industrial Revolution changed the way Americans lived and worked.

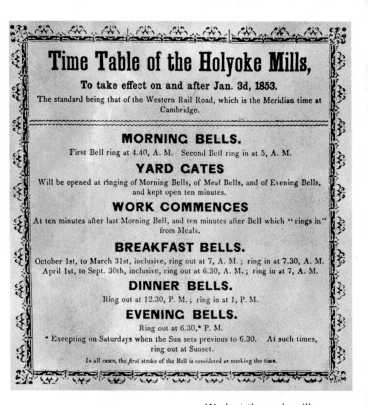

Work at the early mills was guided by a bell schedule such as this one, which begins with a wake-up bell at 4:40 in the morning. **What does this schedule tell you about the workers' daily lives?**

**1765**

▶ **1769**
**Improved
Steam engine,**
James Watt

**c. 1786**
**Threshing machine,** Andrew Meikle

**1793**
**Cotton gin,** Eli Whitney

▲ **c. 1803**
**Locomotive,**
Richard Trevithick

**1807**
**Steamboat,**
◀ Robert Fulton

**1834 Reaper,** Cyrus McCormick

**1837 Telegraph,** Samuel F. B. Morse
**Steel plow,** John Deere

**1839**
**Photography,** ▶
Louis Daguerre

**1845**

**CRITICAL THINKING Evaluate** Which of these inventions do you think had the greatest impact on life in the middle of the 19th century?

# New Inventions Improve Life

▼ **KEY QUESTION** How did new inventions improve American life?

New inventions improved transportation, communication, and production. They also quickened the pace of life.

**Transportation and Communication** Inventor **Robert Fulton** developed a steamboat that could move against the current or a strong wind. He launched the *Clermont* on the Hudson River in 1807. Its steam engine turned two side paddle wheels, which pulled the boat through the water. Many thought it looked silly and nicknamed it "Fulton's Folly," but it made the 300-mile round-trip from New York to Albany and back in a record 62 hours.

In 1811, a steamship first traveled down the Ohio and Mississippi rivers. However, its engine was not powerful enough to return upriver against the current. Henry Miller Shreve, a trader on the Mississippi, designed a steamship that could be powered up the Mississippi, against the current. In 1816, his boat launched a new era of transportation on the river.

Some cities, however, were not on rivers that could be navigated by steamship. Traders in these cities needed a way to ship goods. Steam-powered trains were the answer. English engineer Richard Trevithick had introduced the locomotive around 1803. In 1830, **Peter Cooper** built America's first successful steam-powered locomotive, called the *Tom Thumb*. By 1833, the 136-mile railroad track connecting Charleston and Hamburg, South Carolina, was the longest in the world.

Around 1837, **Samuel F. B. Morse** first demonstrated his telegraph. This machine sent long and short pulses of electricity along a wire. These pulses could be translated into letters spelling out messages. With the telegraph, it took only seconds to communicate with someone in another city. In 1844, the first long-distance telegraph line carried news from Baltimore to Washington, D.C., about who had been nominated for president. Telegraph lines spanned the country by 1861, bringing people closer as a nation.

**Technology Improves Farming** Other new inventions increased farm production. In 1837, blacksmith John Deere invented a lightweight plow with a steel cutting edge. Older cast-iron plows were designed for the relatively light and sandy soil of New England. But rich, heavy Midwestern soil clung to the bottom of these plows and slowed down farm work. Deere's new plow made preparing ground to plant crops much less work. As a result, more farmers began to move to the Midwest.

The **threshing machine** and the **mechanical reaper** were other inventions that improved agricultural production by making farm work quicker and more efficient. The threshing machine, which was invented around 1786 by Andrew Meikle of Scotland, mechanically separated kernels of wheat from husks. In 1831, Cyrus McCormick developed a reaper that cut ripe grain quickly and efficiently. McCormick patented his invention in 1834 and brought it to Europe in the 1850s.

New technologies linked regions and contributed to a feeling of national unity. With new farm equipment, Midwestern farmers grew food to feed Northeastern factory workers. In turn, Midwestern farmers became a market for Northeastern manufactured goods. The growth of Northeastern textile mills increased demand for Southern cotton, which, unfortunately, led to the expansion of slavery in the South.

 **MAIN IDEAS & DETAILS** Explain how new inventions improved American life.

---

 **ONLINE QUIZ**
For test practice, go to
**Interactive Review @ ClassZone.com**

**New Jersey Core Curriculum Content Standards** *Review*

**TERMS & NAMES**

1. Explain the importance of
   - Industrial Revolution
   - Robert Fulton
   - Samuel Slater
   - Peter Cooper
   - factory system
   - Samuel F. B. Morse
   - Lowell mills

**USING YOUR READING NOTES**

2. **Sequence Events** Complete the diagram you started at the beginning of this section.

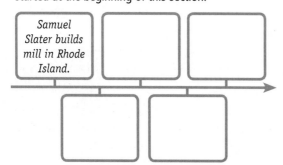

Samuel Slater builds mill in Rhode Island.

**KEY IDEAS**

3. Why was New England a good place to set up factories?

4. How were different regions of the United States linked economically?

**CRITICAL THINKING**

5. **Summarize** Explain how the use of interchangeable parts improved the manufacturing process.

6. **Form and Support Opinions** Samuel Slater and Francis Lowell both illegally brought industrial secrets to the United States. Do you think they were wrong to do this? Explain.

7. **Art** Use the library to find an image of one of the early inventions mentioned in this section. Draw a detailed picture of it. Then write a paragraph explaining how the invention worked.

# AMERICAN TEXTILE MILL

**Click here** to see an American textile mill in operation
...ssZone.com

...st textile mills in America ran on
...r power. Falling or flowing water
...owered the machinery through a system of
gears and belts. Eventually, however, steam
engines replaced water as the source of
power for the mills.

*Click here* Early mills were built on
deep, fast-moving rivers in the Northeast.

*Click here* The mills changed working
life by bringing together many workers and
machines in the same building.

*Click here* Many children worked at the
early textile mills.

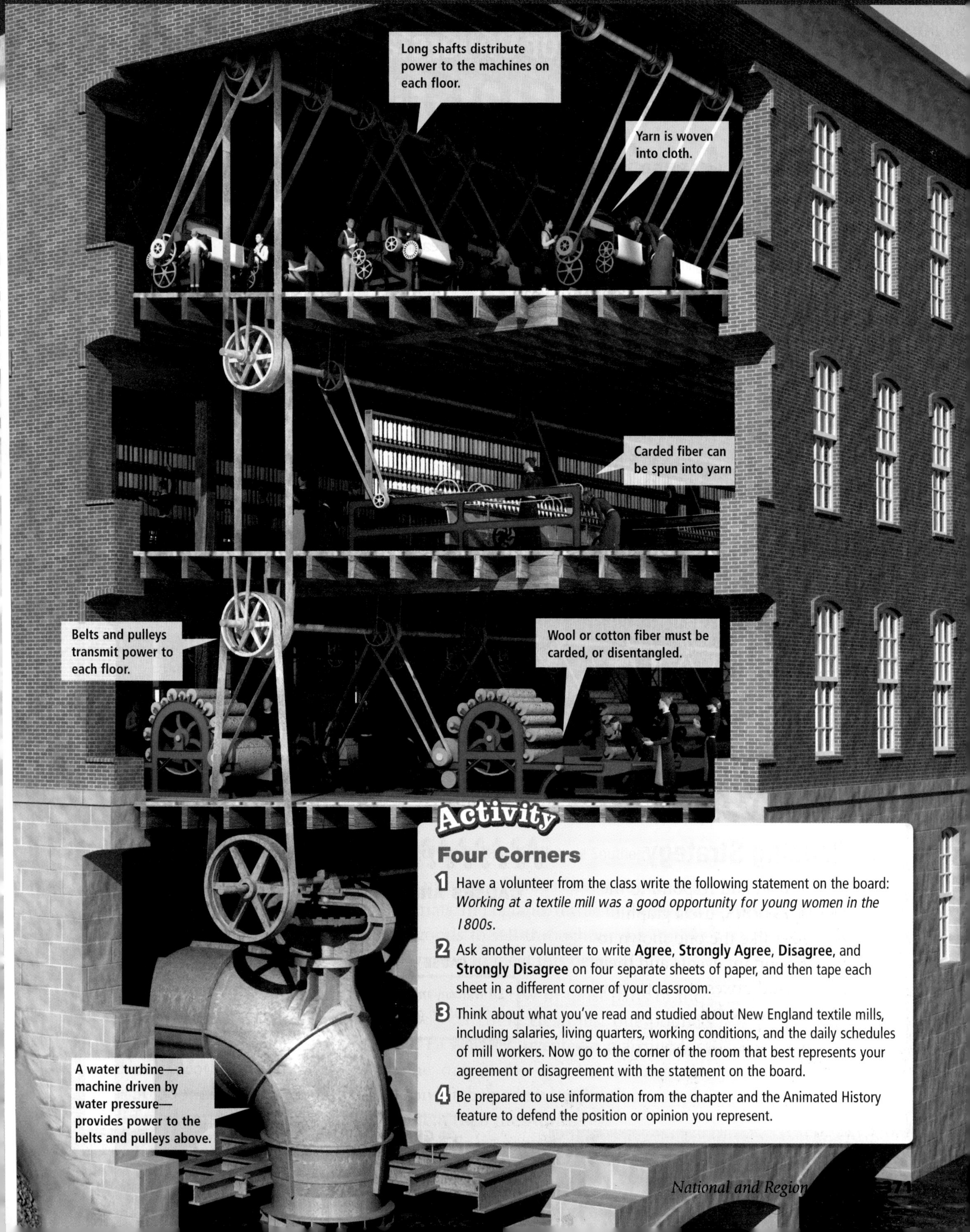

Long shafts distribute power to the machines on each floor.

Yarn is woven into cloth.

Carded fiber can be spun into yarn

Belts and pulleys transmit power to each floor.

Wool or cotton fiber must be carded, or disentangled.

A water turbine—a machine driven by water pressure—provides power to the belts and pulleys above.

## Activity

### Four Corners

1. Have a volunteer from the class write the following statement on the board: *Working at a textile mill was a good opportunity for young women in the 1800s.*

2. Ask another volunteer to write **Agree**, **Strongly Agree**, **Disagree**, and **Strongly Disagree** on four separate sheets of paper, and then tape each sheet in a different corner of your classroom.

3. Think about what you've read and studied about New England textile mills, including salaries, living quarters, working conditions, and the daily schedules of mill workers. Now go to the corner of the room that best represents your agreement or disagreement with the statement on the board.

4. Be prepared to use information from the chapter and the Animated History feature to defend the position or opinion you represent.

## History Makers

### Nat Turner   1800–1831

Nat Turner (above left) was born into slavery in Virginia. He learned to read as a child and became an enthusiastic reader of the Bible. Enslaved people gathered in forest clearings to listen to Turner's powerful sermons.

In 1831, Turner led a group of followers in killing about 55 white Virginians, starting with the family of his former owner. It was the bloodiest slave rebellion in American history. In an account of events that he dictated to Thomas R. Gray before his execution, Turner called himself a "prophet" and said that God had called him to commit his violent acts.

**CRITICAL THINKING** **Analyze Point of View** How did Turner justify his use of violence?

 **ONLINE BIOGRAPHY**   For more on Nat Turner, go to the **Research & Writing Center** @ ClassZone.com

**Families Under Slavery** Perhaps the cruelest part of slavery was the sale of family members away from one another. Although some slaveholders would not part mothers from children, many did, causing unforgettable grief.

When enslaved families could manage to be together, they took comfort in family life. Enslaved people did marry each other, although their marriages were not legally recognized. They tried to raise children, while knowing that their children could be taken from them and sold at any time. Abolitionist Frederick Douglass, who was born into slavery, recalled visits from his mother, who lived 12 miles away.

### PRIMARY SOURCE

❝ I do not recollect [remember] ever seeing my mother by the light of day. She was with me in the night. She would lie down with me, and get me to sleep, but long before I waked she was gone. ❞

—Frederick Douglass, *Narrative of the Life of Frederick Douglass*

Douglass's mother resisted slavery by the simple act of visiting her child. Douglass later rebelled by escaping to the North. A small number of enslaved people rebelled in violent ways.

**Slave Rebellions** Armed rebellion by enslaved persons was an extreme form of resistance to slavery. Gabriel Prosser planned an attack on Richmond, Virginia, in 1800. In 1822, Denmark Vesey planned a revolt in Charleston, South Carolina. Both plots were betrayed and the leaders, as well as numerous followers, were hanged.

The most famous rebellion was led by **Nat Turner** in Southampton County, Virginia, in 1831. Beginning on August 21, Turner and 70 followers killed about 55 white men, women, and children. Most of Turner's men were captured when their ammunition ran out, and some were killed. After Turner was caught, he was tried and hanged.

Turner's rebellion spread fear in the South. Whites killed more than 200 African Americans in revenge. The state of Virginia considered ending slavery because of the upheaval, but the proposal was narrowly defeated. Some state legislatures, however, passed harsh laws that further limited the freedom of both free and enslaved African Americans. For African Americans in the South, the grip of slavery grew even tighter.

## Chapter Summary

**1** **Key Idea**
New industries and inventions changed the way people lived and worked in the early 1800s.

**2** **Key Idea**
The invention of the cotton gin and the demand for cotton caused slavery to spread in the South.

**3** **Key Idea**
While patriotic pride increased national unity, tensions grew between the North and the South.

For detailed Review and Study Notes go to **Interactive Review** @ ClassZone.com

## Name Game

**Use the list of terms and names to identify each sentence online or on your own paper.**

1. I led a rebellion against slavery in Virginia in 1831. Nat Turner 🖑

2. I built a water-powered textile mill. ____

3. This connected New York City with Buffalo, New York, by water. ____

4. This policy opposed European interference in the Western Hemisphere. ____

5. The invention of this led to the expansion of slavery. ____

6. This was enacted in 1820 to keep a balance of power between slave states and free states. ____

7. I promoted the American System. ____

8. This is a feeling of pride, loyalty, and protectiveness toward one's country. ____

9. The telegraph is my invention. ____

10. I built America's first successful steam-powered locomotive. ____

A. Missouri Compromise

B. Erie Canal

C. Peter Cooper

D. Nat Turner

E. sectionalism

F. Monroe Doctrine

G. Henry Clay

H. nationalism

I. steamboat

J. Samuel F. B. Morse

K. Eli Whitney

L. Samuel Slater

M. cotton gin

## Activities

### CROSSWORD PUZZLE

Complete the online crossword puzzle to show what you know about the Industrial Revolution.

**DOWN**
1. The ____ made cleaning cotton faster

### FLIPCARD

Use the online flipcards to quiz yourself on the terms and names introduced in this chapter.

Method of production that brought workers and machines together in one building.

ANSWER
factory system

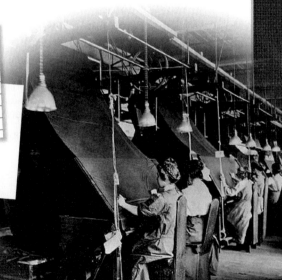

## VOCABULARY

**Explain the significance of each of the following.**

1. Samuel Slater
2. Industrial Revolution
3. Missouri Compromise
4. spirituals
5. cotton gin
6. Nat Turner
7. nationalism
8. sectionalism

**Explain how the terms and names in each group are related.**

9. Samuel F. B. Morse, Eli Whitney, interchangeable part
10. Monroe Doctrine, James Monroe, nationalism
11. mechanical reaper, threshing machine, cotton gin
12. Robert Fulton, Peter Cooper, Erie Canal
13. Henry Clay, protective tariff, American System
14. factory system, Industrial Revolution, Lowell mills

Robert Fulton

## KEY IDEAS

**1 Early Industry and Inventions (pages 364–369)**

15. How did the War of 1812 cause economic changes in the United States?

16. How did interchangeable parts transform the manufacturing process?

**2 Plantations and Slavery Spread (pages 372–377)**

17. How did the rise in cotton production affect slavery?

18. What was family life like for enslaved people?

**3 Nationalism and Sectionalism (pages 378–384)**

19. How did the Erie Canal help the nation to grow?

20. How did the Missouri Compromise attempt to resolve a conflict between the North and the South?

## CRITICAL THINKING

21. **Summarize** How did the Industrial Revolution change the way Americans worked?

22. **Causes and Effects** In a chart like the one shown, note new inventions discussed in the chapter and their effects on the United States. Then explain which inventions helped to link the nation, and how.

| Invention | Effects |
|---|---|
| *threshing machine* | |
| | |

23. **Form and Support Opinions** In your opinion, were free African Americans in the South truly free? Explain.

24. **Make Generalizations** What role did religion play in the system of slavery?

25. **Analyze Point of View** Why was it so important to Southerners to admit Missouri as a slave state?

26. **Connect Geography and History** How did geography affect the way each region developed?

27. **Analyze Primary Sources** This political cartoon shows European nations observing a naval blockade. Explain what the blockade represents as well as what nation caused it to exist, and why.

**✓ TEST PRACTICE**

• **Online Test Practice** @ ClassZone.com
• **Test-Taking Strategies & Practice** at the front of this book

## MULTIPLE CHOICE

**Use the quotation and your knowledge of U.S. history to answer question 1.**

### PRIMARY SOURCE

❝ [The Missouri] question, like a fire bell in the night, awakened and filled me with terror. . . . A geographical line . . . once conceived and held up to the angry passions of men, will never be [erased]; and every new irritation will mark it deeper and deeper. ❞

—Thomas Jefferson, April 22, 1820

1. What did Jefferson fear the growth of?
   A. industry
   B. national unity
   C. sectional tensions
   D. European colonies

**Read each question and choose the best answer.**

2. Which invention had the greatest impact on the spread of slavery?
   A. cotton gin
   B. locomotive
   C. steamboat
   D. steel plow

3. Which was a result of the Missouri Compromise?
   A. Congress established a protective tariff.
   B. The Mason-Dixon Line divided slave states and free states.
   C. Slavery was banned from the Louisiana Territory.
   D. Maine was admitted to the Union as a free state.

4. What was the power source for the first textile mills in America?
   A. slave labor
   B. water
   C. coal
   D. mules and oxen

## YOU BE THE HISTORIAN

28. **Evaluate** How did the Industrial Revolution affect the balance of power among American regions?

29. **Connect to Today** The steamboat and the telegraph were two of the most significant inventions of the early 1800s. What recent inventions have had a similar impact on life today?

30. **Make Inferences** What effect do you think armed rebellions by enslaved people, such as the uprising led by Nat Turner, had on the institution of American slavery?

31. **Form and Support Opinions** Consider what might have happened if the Missouri Compromise had not been passed, and explain whether you think the plan was a wise decision.

32. **Analyze Point of View** Does Marshall's opinion in *McCulloch* v. *Maryland* reflect a strict or a loose interpretation of the Constitution? Explain.

 Answer the
## ESSENTIAL QUESTION
### What forces and events affected national unity and growth?

**Written Response** Write a two- to three-paragraph response to the Essential Question. Be sure to consider the key ideas of each section as well as economic changes in America during the early 1800s. Use the Response Rubric below to guide your thinking and writing.

### Response Rubric
#### A strong response will
• describe the impact of the Industrial Revolution
• explain how new inventions affected the economy in different regions
• analyze the spread of slavery in South
• discuss the impact of nationalism and sectionalism

**12** The Age of Jackson
1824–1840  pages 392–415

**13** Manifest Destiny
1821–1853  pages 416–447

**14** A New Spirit of Change
1830–1860  pages 448–475

# Why It Matters Now

Between 1810 and 1860, the nation had to face
difficult questions about expansion, immigration,
slavery, and the rights of minorities. America is
still wrestling with the imperfect solutions of
those crucial years in its early history.

Difficulty is the excuse history never accepts.
—Edward R. Murrow

# The Age of Jackson

## 1824–1840

1. Jacksonian Democracy and States' Rights

2. Jackson's Policy Toward Native Americans

3. Prosperity and Panic

### ESSENTIAL QUESTION

What impact did Andrew Jackson's presidency have on the nation?

### CONNECT ↻ Geography & History

How did geography affect the settlement of the United States during this period?

**Think about:**

**1** U.S. population growth

**2** reasons why land might be considered valuable

**3** the importance of rivers

Jackson's inauguration

**1824**

Sectional interests divide the Democratic-Republican Party in the 1824 election.

▼

**Effect** John Quincy Adams is elected president.

**1828** Andrew Jackson is elected president.

**1830** Indian Removal Act is passed.

▼

**Effect** Thousands of Cherokees are forced west on the Trail of Tears.

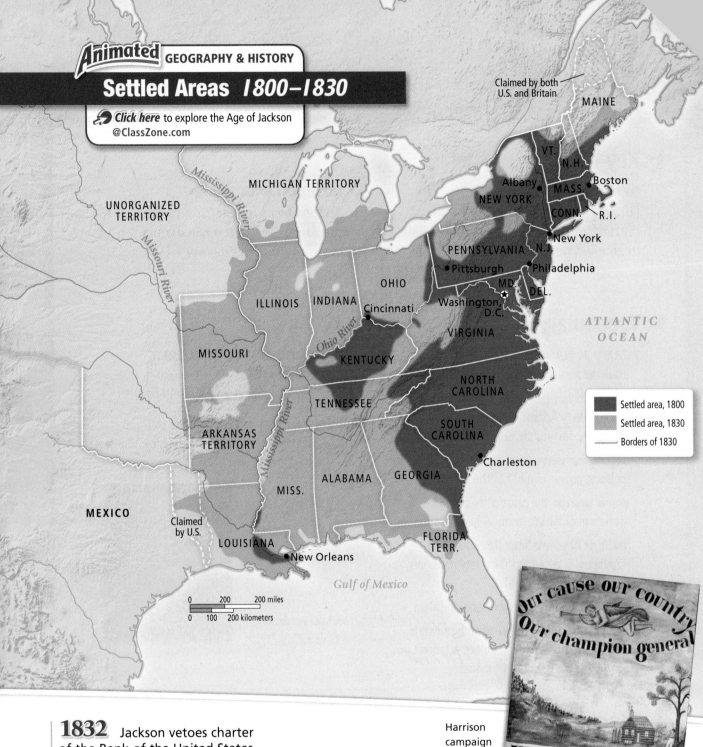

Claimed by both
U.S. and Britain

MAINE

MICHIGAN TERRITORY

VT.
N.H.
Albany
MASS.
Boston
NEW YORK
CONN.
R.I.

UNORGANIZED
TERRITORY

*Mississippi River*

*Missouri River*

PENNSYLVANIA
N.J.
New York

Pittsburgh
Philadelphia

OHIO
MD.
DEL.

ILLINOIS
INDIANA
Cincinnati
Washington,
D.C.

MISSOURI

*Ohio River*

VIRGINIA

ATLANTIC
OCEAN

KENTUCKY

NORTH
CAROLINA

TENNESSEE

ARKANSAS
TERRITORY

SOUTH
CAROLINA

*Mississippi River*

ALABAMA
GEORGIA

Charleston

MISS.

MEXICO

Claimed
by U.S.

LOUISIANA
New Orleans

FLORIDA
TERR.

Gulf of Mexico

| | |
|---|---|
| ■ | Settled area, 1800 |
| ■ | Settled area, 1830 |
| — | Borders of 1830 |

0    200    200 miles
0    100    200 kilometers

**1832** Jackson vetoes charter
of the Bank of the United States.

Jackson is reelected.

Western settlers
clearing land

**1834** Whig
Party is formed.

**1836** Martin
Van Buren is
elected president.

**1837** Panic of
1837 occurs.

▼

**Effect** Many people
lose money and jobs.

Harrison
campaign
poster

*Our cause our country*
*Our champion general*

**Wᴹ H. HARRISON,**
**OUR BRAVE DEFENDER.**

**1840**

William Henry
Harrison is elected
president.

## ▶ Key Ideas

**BEFORE, YOU LEARNED**

Forces and events in the early 19th century both strengthened and threatened national unity and growth.

**NOW YOU WILL LEARN**

Andrew Jackson's election to the presidency in 1828 opened a new era of popular democracy.

## ▶ Vocabulary

**TERMS & NAMES**

**Andrew Jackson** U.S. president from 1829–1837

**John Quincy Adams** 1824 presidential candidate favored by New Englanders

**Jacksonian democracy** the idea of widening political power to more of the people

**spoils system** the practice of giving government jobs to political backers

**Tariff of Abominations** 1828 law that significantly raised tariffs on raw materials and manufactured goods

**John C. Calhoun** Jackson's vice-president

**doctrine of nullification** idea that a state had the right to nullify, or reject, a federal law that it considers unconstitutional

**BACKGROUND VOCABULARY**

**secede** (SIH•SEED) to withdraw

**REVIEW**

**states' rights** the rights of the states to make decisions without interference from the federal government

**Visual Vocabulary**
John Quincy Adams

## ▶ Reading Strategy

As you read and respond to the **KEY QUESTIONS,** use a graphic organizer like the one shown to note the main ideas and important details. Create new diagrams as needed.

 **See Skillbuilder Handbook, page R4.**

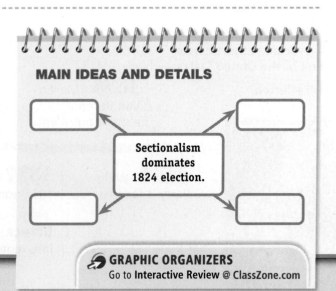

**MAIN IDEAS AND DETAILS**

Sectionalism dominates 1824 election.

**GRAPHIC ORGANIZERS**
Go to **Interactive Review** @ ClassZone.com

# Jacksonian Democracy and States' Rights

**6.2.A.2.** Describe the underlying values and principles of democracy and distinguish these from authoritarian forms of government.
**6.4.F.1.** Describe the political, economic, and social changes in New Jersey and American society preceding the Civil War, . . . .

## One American's Story

Margaret Bayard Smith and her husband were central figures in the political and social life of Washington. Here Smith describes the lively scene at the presidential inauguration of **Andrew Jackson** on March 4, 1829.

**PRIMARY SOURCE**

❝ When the speech was over, and the President made his parting bow, the barrier that had separated the people from him was broken down and they rushed up the steps all eager to shake hands with him. . . . Country men, farmers, gentlemen, mounted and dismounted, boys, women, and children, black and white. Carriages, wagons, and carts all pursuing him to the President's house. ❞

　　—Margaret Bayard Smith, *The First Forty Years of Washington Society*

Margaret Bayard Smith wrote about life in the nation's capital in the first half of the 19th century.

Jackson's election to the presidency set the stage for an era of greater public involvement in government.

## Sectionalism Changes Politics

🔻 **KEY QUESTION** What political divisions appeared during the election of 1824?

By the 1820s, politics were increasingly dominated by sectionalism, or loyalty to the interests of a particular region of the country. In the election of 1824, these sectional interests tore apart the Democratic-Republican Party (the party of Thomas Jefferson). Four men competed to replace James Monroe as president. Their supporters were divided along sectional lines:

- New Englanders liked **John Quincy Adams**, Monroe's secretary of state.
- Westerners backed Henry Clay, "the Great Compromiser," and Andrew Jackson, a former military hero from Tennessee.
- Southerners supported Jackson and William Crawford of Georgia.

*The Age of Jackson* **395**

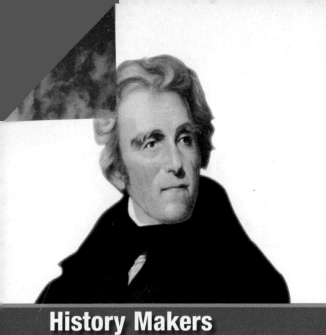

## History Makers

### Andrew Jackson    1767–1845

The son of Scots-Irish immigrants, Jackson grew up in the Carolina backcountry. Jackson's father died shortly before his birth, and his mother and two brothers died during the Revolutionary War. After the war, Jackson moved to Tennessee, built a successful law practice, and bought and sold land. After the War of 1812 broke out, he was appointed as a general in the army. His decisive win against the British at the Battle of New Orleans in 1815 brought him national recognition. He earned the nickname "Old Hickory" after soldiers claimed that he was "tough as hickory." Jackson's humble background, and his reputation as a war hero, helped make him president. Many saw his rise above hardship as an American success story.

#### CRITICAL THINKING

**Connect to Today**  Do you think Andrew Jackson would be a popular presidential candidate today? Record evidence to support your opinion as you read through this chapter.

 **ONLINE BIOGRAPHY**  For more on Andrew Jackson, go to the **Research & Writing Center** @ ClassZone.com

**Adams Defeats Jackson in 1824**  Jackson won the most popular votes in the election. But no candidate received a majority of electoral votes. According to the Constitution, the House of Representatives must choose the president when this happens.

Clay had come in fourth and threw his support to Adams, who then won. Because Adams later named Clay as his secretary of state, Jackson's supporters claimed that Adams gained the presidency by making a deal with Clay. Charges of a "corrupt bargain" followed Adams throughout his term.

Adams had many plans for his presidency. He wanted to build roads and canals, aid education and science, and regulate the use of natural resources. But Congress, led by Jackson supporters, defeated his proposals.

Jackson felt that the 1824 election had been stolen from him and that the will of the people had been ignored. He immediately set to work on gaining the presidency in 1828.

Over the next four years, the division in the Democratic-Republican Party between the supporters of Jackson and of Adams grew wider. Jackson claimed to represent the "common man." He said Adams represented a group of privileged, wealthy Easterners. This division eventually created two parties. The Democrats came from among the Jackson supporters, while the National Republicans grew out of the Adams camp.

▲ **SUMMARIZE**  Describe the political divisions that appeared before and after the 1824 election.

## Jackson Redefines "Democracy"

▼ **KEY QUESTION**  How did American democracy change during Jackson's presidency?

Although the United States had been founded on democratic principles, only white male landowners could vote in many states. In the face of growing calls for reform, Andrew Jackson helped broaden American democracy by advocating the extension of voting rights to more of the population.

**Voting Rights Expand**  The election of 1828 again matched Jackson against Adams. It was a bitter campaign—both sides made vicious personal attacks. Even Jackson's wife, Rachel, became a target. During the campaign,

### EXERCISING THE VOTE

The 1828 presidential election drew more than three times as many voters to the polls as the election of 1824. However, voting was limited to adult white males. Today, all citizens aged 18 and over are eligible to vote.

Citizens under the age of 18 can also participate in the election process. They can educate themselves about the issues, campaign for candidates they support, and practice casting their votes in mock, or pretend, elections. They can also urge eligible voters to cast their ballots, like the student shown here.

### Hold a Mock Election.

**1** Choose issues and candidates. You may focus on the national, state, or local level.

**2** Campaign for the candidates or issues you support.

**3** Set up a mock election in your classroom. Create a polling place, ballots, and other needed materials.

**4** Prepare mock media reports on the election's outcome.

📖 See Citizenship Handbook, page 303.

Jackson crusaded against control of the government by the wealthy. He promised to look out for the interests of the common people. He also promoted the concept of majority rule. The idea of widening political power to more of the people and ensuring majority rule became known as **Jacksonian democracy**.

Actually, the practice of spreading political power had begun before Jackson ran for office. In the early 1800s, many states reduced restrictions on who could vote. This increased the number of voters. Despite the extension of voting rights, however, large segments of the population were still excluded. Women, the enslaved, and free African Americans still could not vote in most places.

**Jackson Wins in 1828** The expansion of voting rights helped Jackson achieve an overwhelming win in the 1828 presidential election. Jackson's triumph was hailed as a victory for the common people. Large numbers of Western farmers as well as workers in the nation's cities supported him. Their vote put an end to the idea that government should be controlled by an educated elite.

Jackson's success in the election came at a high price. Shortly after he won, his wife died of a heart attack. Jackson believed that campaign attacks on her reputation had caused her death. She was a religious person who preferred a more private life. In fact, she had said that she "would rather be a doorkeeper

Jackson's presidency marked a dramatic shift in American politics. Although Jackson's Democrats had grown out of Jefferson's Democratic-Republican Party, ideas of democracy had changed.

| JEFFERSONIAN DEMOCRACY | JACKSONIAN DEMOCRACY |
|---|---|
| Government by an educated few | More public involvement in government |
| Voting restricted to property owners | Voting expanded to all white males |
| Limited government | Limited government with a stronger executive branch |

### CRITICAL THINKING

1. **Draw Conclusions** Which president do you think exercised more power? Why?
2. **Compare and Contrast** What ideas did Jeffersonians and Jacksonians share in common?

in the house of God than . . . live in that palace at Washington."

The tragedy of his wife's death overshadowed Jackson's inauguration. But the capital was full of joy and excitement. Thousands of people attended the ceremony.

A throng followed Jackson to the White House. At the reception, people broke china and glasses as they grabbed for the food and drinks. The rowdiness finally drove Jackson to flee the White House. As Supreme Court Justice Joseph Story observed, "The reign of King Mob seemed triumphant."

**A New Political Era Begins** Jackson's inauguration began a new political era. In his campaign, he had promised to reform government. He started by replacing many government officials with his supporters. This practice of giving government jobs to political backers became known as the **spoils system**. The name comes from the statement "to the victor belong the spoils [possessions] of the enemy." Jackson defended the principle of "rotation in office," noting that it broke up one group's hold on government.

 **CAUSE AND EFFECT** Explain how Jackson helped change American democracy.

## Rising Sectional Differences

▼ **KEY QUESTION** How did economic issues increase sectional tensions?

At the time of Jackson's inauguration, the country was being pulled apart by conflicts among its three main sections. Legislators from the Northeast, the South, and the West disputed three major economic issues:

- the sale of public lands in the West
- federal spending on internal improvements, such as roads and canals
- rising tariffs

**Regional Interests** Westerners wanted the federal government to sell public lands at low prices. They hoped to encourage settlement and give the section more political power. Northeasterners feared that cheap Western land might attract workers who were needed in Northeastern factories.

Better transportation routes would help bring food and raw materials to the Northeast and manufactured goods to Western markets. Southerners opposed federal spending on such projects because they were financed through tariffs.

**Southerners Against Tariffs** Tariffs made imported goods more expensive than American-made goods, which helped protect Northeastern factories from foreign competition. But Southern planters depended on trading cotton in exchange for foreign manufactured goods. Rising tariffs hurt the South's economy.

▲ **MAIN IDEAS AND DETAILS** In what ways did economic issues increase sectional tensions?

## Federal Government vs. the States

▼ **KEY QUESTION** What issues were at stake in the debate over states' rights?

The issue of tariffs fueled the fires of a national debate that had been raging ever since the nation was formed. That debate was over the balance of power between federal and state governments. Some supported a strong federal government. Others defended **states' rights**, or the rights of the states to make decisions without interference from the federal government.

**COMPARING** *Sectional Interests*

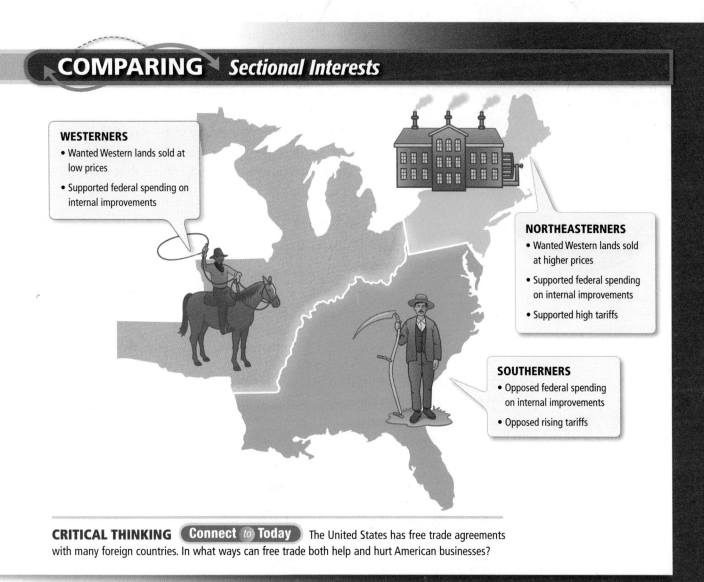

**WESTERNERS**
- Wanted Western lands sold at low prices
- Supported federal spending on internal improvements

**NORTHEASTERNERS**
- Wanted Western lands sold at higher prices
- Supported federal spending on internal improvements
- Supported high tariffs

**SOUTHERNERS**
- Opposed federal spending on internal improvements
- Opposed rising tariffs

**CRITICAL THINKING** (Connect *to* Today) The United States has free trade agreements with many foreign countries. In what ways can free trade both help and hurt American businesses?

John C. Calhoun led the fight for states' rights.

Daniel Webster spoke powerfully in favor of a strong Union.

**The Nullification Crisis** In 1828 Congress passed a bill that significantly raised tariffs on raw materials and manufactured goods. Southerners hated the tariff and called it the **Tariff of Abominations** (an abomination is a hateful thing). Southerners felt that the economic interests of the Northeast were determining national policy.

The Tariff of Abominations hit South Carolina especially hard because the state's economy was in a slump. Some leaders in the state even spoke of leaving the Union over the issue. **John C. Calhoun**, Jackson's vice-president, sympathized with the South Carolinians because he was one himself. However, he wanted to find a way to keep South Carolina from leaving the Union. His solution was the **doctrine of nullification**. A state, he said, had the right to nullify, or reject, a federal law that it considered unconstitutional. He believed that Congress had no right to impose a tariff that favored one section of the country over another.

**The States' Rights Debate** Calhoun's ideas increased controversy over the nature of the federal union. This would remain a major political issue until the Civil War resolved it almost 30 years later.

Senators Daniel Webster of Massachusetts and Robert Y. Hayne of South Carolina debated the doctrine of nullification. Hayne argued that nullification gave the states a lawful way to protest and maintain their freedom. In words that were printed and spread across the country, Webster argued that freedom and the Union go together.

**PRIMARY SOURCE**

❝ When my eyes shall be turned to behold for the last time the sun in heaven, may I not see him shining on the broken and dishonored fragments of a once glorious Union. . . . Liberty and Union, now and forever, one and inseparable! ❞

—Daniel Webster, a speech in the U.S. Senate, January 26, 1830

**Jackson States His Position** Although Jackson supported states' rights, he did not believe that the states should nullify federal law. But he kept his opinion to himself, until a dinner in honor of Thomas Jefferson's birthday. Jackson had learned that Calhoun planned to use the event to win support for nullification.

After dinner, Jackson was invited to make a toast. He stood up, looked directly at Calhoun, and stated bluntly, "Our Federal Union—it must be preserved." As Calhoun raised his glass, his hand trembled. Called on to make the next toast, Calhoun stood slowly and countered, "The Union— next to our liberty, the most dear; may we all remember that it can only be preserved by respecting the rights of the states and distributing equally the benefits and burdens of the Union." From that day, the two men were political enemies.

Henry Clay earned the nickname the "Great Compromiser" for his efforts to end sectional conflicts.

**South Carolina Threatens to Secede** Even though Jackson worked to limit the powers of the federal government, he was dedicated to preserving the Union. He asked Congress to reduce the tariffs, and Congress did so in 1832. Unsatisfied, South Carolina nullified the tariff acts of 1828 and 1832 and voted to build its own army. South Carolina's leaders threatened to **secede**, or withdraw from the Union, if the federal government tried to collect tariffs.

Jackson ran for reelection in 1832, this time without Calhoun as his running mate. After he won, he made it clear that he would use force to see that federal laws were obeyed and the Union preserved.

In the Senate, Henry Clay came forward with a compromise tariff in 1833. Congress quickly passed the bill, and the crisis ended. South Carolina remained in the Union.

 **SUMMARIZE** Identify the issues at stake in the state's rights debate.

---

 **New Jersey Core Curriculum Content Standards** *Review*

**ONLINE QUIZ**
For test practice, go to
**Interactive Review @ ClassZone.com**

### TERMS & NAMES

**1.** Explain the importance of
- Andrew Jackson
- John Quincy Adams
- Jacksonian democracy
- spoils system
- Tariff of Abominations
- John C. Calhoun
- doctrine of nullification

### USING YOUR READING NOTES

**2. Main Ideas and Details** Complete the diagram you started at the beginning of this section. Then create a diagram for each other main idea in this section.

Sectionalism dominates 1824 election.

### KEY IDEAS

**3.** What were the effects of the 1824 election?

**4.** What factors helped Jackson win the 1828 election?

### CRITICAL THINKING

**5. Compare and Contrast** Why did Northeasterners and Southerners disagree over the issue of tariffs?

**6. Problems and Solutions** How was the nullification crisis resolved?

**7. WHAT IF?** What might have happened if states were allowed to nullify federal law?

**8. Connect** *to* **Today** Is the spoils system prevalent in government today?

**9. Math** Research the popular vote totals and percentages of the 1824 and 1828 elections. Then create comparison charts or graphs to display your findings.

*The Age of Jackson* **401**

# Reading for Understanding

## ▶ Key Ideas

**BEFORE, YOU LEARNED**
Andrew Jackson's election to the presidency in 1828 opened a new era of popular democracy.

**NOW YOU WILL LEARN**
During Jackson's presidency, Native Americans were forced to move west of the Mississippi River.

## ▶ Vocabulary

**TERMS & NAMES**

**Sequoya** (sih•KWOY•uh) a brilliant Cherokee who invented a writing system for the Cherokee language

**Indian Removal Act** 1830 law that called for the government to negotiate treaties requiring Native Americans to relocate west

**Indian Territory** an area to which Native Americans were moved covering what is now Oklahoma and parts of Kansas and Nebraska

**Trail of Tears** forced removal of the Cherokee from their homeland to Indian Territory

**Osceola** (AHS•ee•OH•luh) leader during the Second Seminole War

**BACKGROUND VOCABULARY**
**assimilate** to absorb into a culture

**REVIEW**
**literacy** the ability to read and write

**Visual Vocabulary**
Trail of Tears

## ▶ Reading Strategy

As you read and respond to the **KEY QUESTIONS,** use a graphic organizer like the one shown to list causes and effects of the forced removal of Native Americans from their homeland.

 **See Skillbuilder Handbook, page R7.**

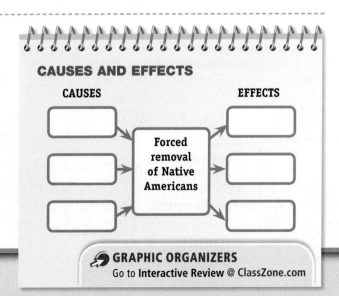

**CAUSES AND EFFECTS**

CAUSES | EFFECTS

Forced removal of Native Americans

**GRAPHIC ORGANIZERS**
Go to **Interactive Review** @ ClassZone.com

# Jackson's Policy Toward Native Americans

**6.4.F.9.** Describe and map the continuing territorial expansion and settlement of the frontier, including the acquisition of new territories and conflicts with Native Americans, . . . .
**6.4.F.10.** Explain how state and federal policies influenced various Native American tribes (e.g., homeland vs. resettlement, Black Hawk War, Trail of Tears).

## One American's Story

In 1821, a brilliant Cherokee named **Sequoya** invented a writing system for the Cherokee language. Using this simple system, the Cherokees soon learned to read and write. A traveler in 1828 marveled at how many Cherokees had learned to read and write without schools or even paper and pens.

**PRIMARY SOURCE**

❝ I frequently saw as I rode from place to place, Cherokee letters painted or cut on the trees by the roadside, on fences, houses, and often pieces of bark or board, lying about the houses. ❞

—Anonymous traveler, quoted in the *Advocate*

Sequoya invented a writing system of 86 characters for the Cherokee language.

Sequoya hoped that by gaining **literacy**—the ability to read and write—his people could share the power of whites and keep their independence. But even Sequoya's invention could not save the Cherokees from the upheaval to come.

## Native Americans Forced West

🔻 **KEY QUESTION** Why did Jackson want native people moved to the West?

By the early 1800s, there were still many Native Americans living east of the Mississippi, despite the fact that white settlers had been pushing them westward for two hundred years. These remaining tribes were viewed by many whites as an obstacle to progress. They debated what to do with the native population.

**Tribes of the Southeast** Some whites hoped that Native Americans could **assimilate**, or be absorbed into white culture. Others wanted Native Americans to move. They believed this was the only way to avoid conflict over land. Also, many whites felt that Native Americans were "uncivilized" and did not want to live near them.

Traditional Creek belt

By the 1820s, about 100,000 Native Americans remained east of the Mississippi River. Most lived in the Southeast. The major tribes were the Cherokee, Chickasaw, Choctaw, Creek, and Seminole. Whites called them the Five Civilized Tribes because they had adopted many aspects of white culture. They held large areas of land in Georgia, the Carolinas, Alabama, Mississippi, and Tennessee.

More than any other Southeastern tribe, the Cherokee had adopted white customs, including their way of dressing. Cherokees owned prosperous farms and cattle ranches. From Sequoya, they acquired a written language, and they published their own newspaper, the *Cherokee Phoenix*. Some of their children attended missionary schools. In 1827, the Cherokees drew up a constitution based on the U.S. Constitution and founded the Cherokee Nation.

**Jackson's Removal Policy** Andrew Jackson had long supported a policy of moving Native Americans west of the Mississippi. He first dealt with moving the Southeastern tribes after the War of 1812. The federal government had ordered Jackson, then acting as Indian treaty commissioner, to make treaties with the Native Americans of the region.

Jackson believed that the government had the right to regulate where Native Americans could live. He viewed them as conquered subjects who lived within the borders of the United States. He thought Native Americans had two choices. They could either assimilate and become U.S. citizens, or they could move into western territories. They could not, however, have their own government within the nation's borders.

In 1828, gold was discovered on Cherokee land in Georgia. Now, not only settlers but also miners wanted to move the Cherokee. Many whites began to move onto Cherokee land. Georgia and other Southern states passed laws that gave them the right to take over Native American lands. When the Cherokee and other tribes protested, Jackson supported the states.

**The Indian Removal Act** Jackson asked Congress to pass a law that would require Native Americans to either move west or submit to state laws. Many Americans objected to Jackson's proposal. Massachusetts congressman Edward Everett warned against forcing Native Americans to a distant land, saying that the "inevitable suffering" would be "incalculable." Religious groups such as the Quakers also opposed moving Native Americans against their will. After heated debate, Congress passed the **Indian Removal Act** of 1830. The act called for the government to negotiate treaties that would require Native Americans to relocate west of the Mississippi.

▲ **CLARIFY** Explain why Jackson wanted Native Americans moved to the West.

# The Trail of Tears

🔻 **KEY QUESTION** What were the effects of the Indian Removal Act?

Jackson immediately set out to enforce the law. He claimed his policy was "just and liberal" and would allow Native Americans to keep their way of life. Instead, his policy caused much hardship and forever changed relations between whites and Native Americans.

**The Forced March** As whites invaded their homelands, many Native Americans saw no choice but to sign treaties. Under the treaties, Native Americans would exchange their current lands for lands in an area that covered what is now Oklahoma and parts of Kansas and Nebraska. This area came to be called **Indian Territory**.

Beginning in 1831, the Choctaw and other Southeast tribes were moved west. The Cherokees, however, appealed to the U.S. Supreme Court to protect their land from being seized by Georgia. In 1832, the Court, led by Chief Justice John Marshall, ruled that only the federal government, not the states, could make laws governing the Cherokees. This ruling meant that the Georgia laws did not apply to the Cherokee Nation. However, both Georgia and President Jackson ignored the Supreme Court. Jackson said, "John Marshall has made his . . . . let him enforce it."

**Connecting History**

**Westward Expansion**
By 1890, the western half of Indian Territory had opened up to white settlement as Oklahoma Territory. Native Americans tried to organize their remaining lands into the state of Sequoya. The federal government rejected this idea, and in 1907 the two territories formed the state of Oklahoma.

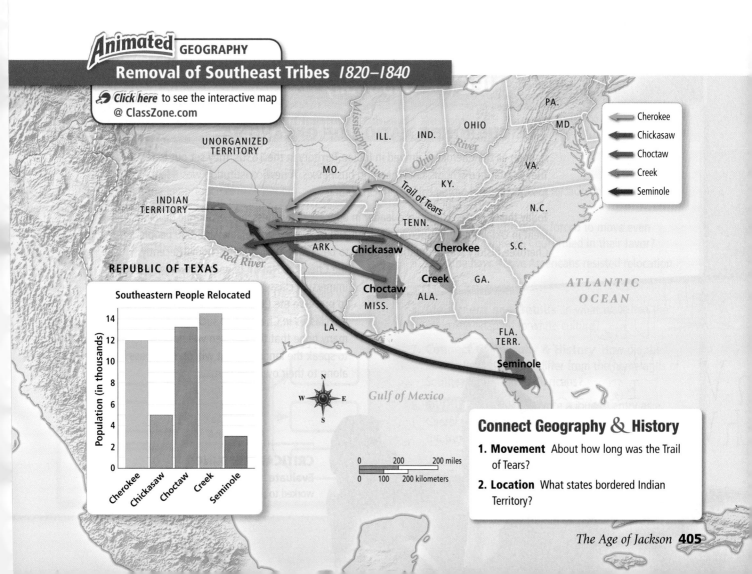

**Animated GEOGRAPHY**

**Removal of Southeast Tribes** *1820–1840*

🖱 *Click here* to see the interactive map @ ClassZone.com

Southeastern People Relocated

**Connect Geography & History**

1. **Movement** About how long was the Trail of Tears?

2. **Location** What states bordered Indian Territory?

*The Age of Jackson* **405**

## ▶ Key Ideas

**BEFORE, YOU LEARNED**

During Jackson's presidency, Native Americans were forced to move west of the Mississippi River.

**NOW YOU WILL LEARN**

After Jackson left office, his policies caused the economy to collapse and affected the next election.

## ▶ Vocabulary

**TERMS & NAMES**

**Martin Van Buren** elected president in 1836 after serving as Jackson's vice-president

**Panic of 1837** widespread fear about the state of the economy that spread after Van Buren took office

**depression** a severe economic slump

**Whig Party** political party formed by Henry Clay, Daniel Webster, and other Jackson opponents

**William Henry Harrison** Whig presidential candidate in 1840

**John Tyler** Harrison's running mate in the 1840 presidential election

**BACKGROUND VOCABULARY**

**inflation** an increase in prices and a decrease in the value of money

**REVIEW**

**charter** a written grant

Visual Vocabulary
William Henry Harrison

## ▶ Reading Strategy

As you read and respond to the **KEY QUESTIONS,** use a graphic organizer like the one shown to record important events in the order in which they happened.

 **See Skillbuilder Handbook, page R5.**

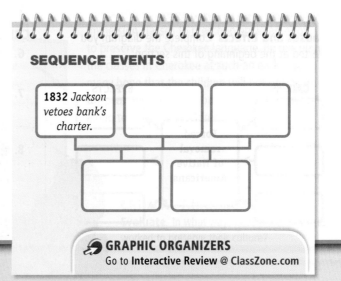

**SEQUENCE EVENTS**

1832 *Jackson vetoes bank's charter.*

**GRAPHIC ORGANIZERS**
Go to **Interactive Review** @ ClassZone.com

# Prosperity and Panic

**6.2.C.3.** Discuss the role of political parties in the American democratic system including candidates, campaigns, financing, primary elections, and voting systems.
**6.4.F.1.** Describe the political, economic, and social changes in New Jersey and American society preceding the Civil War, . . . .

## One American's Story

Most of the nation prospered during Jackson's last years in office. However, shortly after his second term ended, the economy took a turn for the worse. Many people wanted the government to step in and help. Jackson's vice-president, **Martin Van Buren**, who succeeded Jackson as president, disagreed.

### PRIMARY SOURCE

❝ All communities are apt to look to the Government for too much. . . . especially at periods of sudden embarrassment and distress. But this ought not to be. . . . [The framers of the Constitution] wisely judged that the less Government interferes with private pursuits, the better for the general prosperity. ❞

—Martin Van Buren, from a letter to Congress dated September 4, 1837

Jackson and the Democrats opposed many forms of federal power.

Martin Van Buren served as president from 1837 to 1840. He ran unsuccessfully for reelection in 1840 and again in 1848.

## Jackson Targets the National Bank

🔻 **KEY QUESTION** How did Jackson destroy the national bank?

The Second Bank of the United States was the most powerful bank in the country. Jackson declared war on the bank.

**Mr. Biddle's Bank** The bank's president, Nicholas Biddle, set policies that controlled the nation's money supply. Since the bank made loans to members of Congress, Biddle could influence these lawmakers. Jackson believed that the bank was corrupt and had too much power.

To operate, the bank needed a **charter**, or a written grant, from the federal government. In 1832, Biddle asked Congress to renew the bank's charter, even though it would not expire until 1836. He thought Jackson would agree to the renewal rather than risk angering his supporters. But Jackson took the risk.

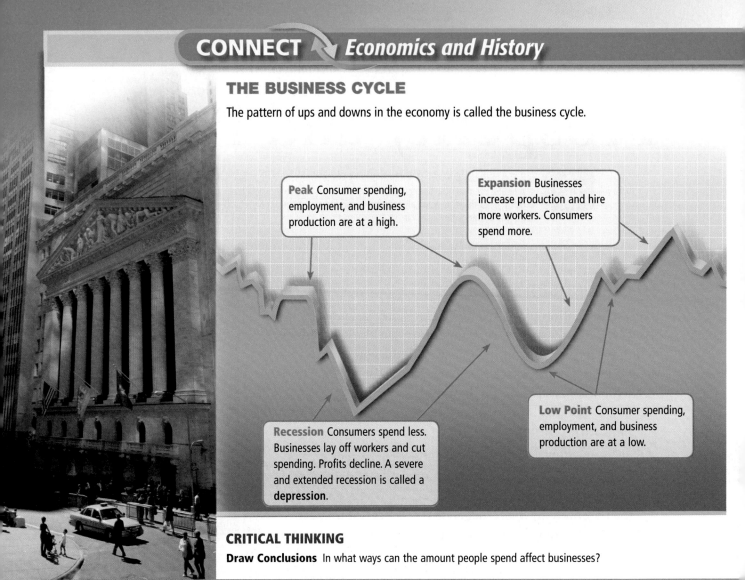

## THE BUSINESS CYCLE

The pattern of ups and downs in the economy is called the business cycle.

> **Peak** Consumer spending, employment, and business production are at a high.

> **Expansion** Businesses increase production and hire more workers. Consumers spend more.

> **Recession** Consumers spend less. Businesses lay off workers and cut spending. Profits decline. A severe and extended recession is called a **depression**.

> **Low Point** Consumer spending, employment, and business production are at a low.

### CRITICAL THINKING

**Draw Conclusions** In what ways can the amount people spend affect businesses?

**Jackson's War on the Bank** When Congress voted to renew the charter, Jackson vetoed the renewal. Although the Supreme Court had ruled that the bank was constitutional, Jackson argued that it was not. He said it was a monopoly that favored the few at the expense of the many.

The bank became the main issue in the presidential campaign of 1832. The National Republican candidate, Henry Clay, called Jackson a tyrant. The Democrats portrayed Jackson as a defender of the people. When he won reelection, Jackson took it as a sign of approval for his war on the bank.

Jackson set out to destroy the bank before its charter ended. He had government funds deposited in state banks. Biddle fought back by making it harder for people to borrow money. He hoped the resulting economic troubles would force Jackson to return government deposits to his bank. Instead, the people supported Jackson. Eventually the bank went out of business. Jackson had won the war, but the economy would suffer for it.

**Prosperity to Panic** Because Jackson's state banks made it easier to borrow money, many people took out loans. The economy boomed. But the banks issued too much paper money, and the rise in the money supply made each dollar worth less. **Inflation,** or an increase in prices and a decrease in the value of money, was the outcome. To fight inflation, Jackson issued an order that required people to pay in gold or silver for public lands.

Jackson left office proud of the nation's prosperity. But it was puffed-up prosperity. Like a balloon, it had little substance. Jackson's popularity helped Van Buren win the presidency in 1836. A few months after Van Buren took office, a panic, or widespread fear about the state of the economy, spread throughout the country. It became known as the **Panic of 1837**.

People began exchanging paper money for gold and silver. Banks quickly ran out of gold and silver. A **depression**, or severe economic slump, followed. Almost all factories in the East closed. Jobless workers had no way to buy food or pay rent. People went hungry and became homeless.

▲ **SUMMARIZE** Explain how Jackson destroyed the national bank.

## CONNECT ⟲ to the Essential Question

### What impact did Andrew Jackson's presidency have on the nation?

| EVENT | IMPACT |
|---|---|
| Election of 1828 | Voting rights expand; Jackson's win hailed as victory for the common people |
| Tariff of Abominations | Sectional tensions grow over tariffs and states' rights; Jackson opposes nullification; South Carolina nullifies tariffs and threatens to secede |
| Indian Removal Act of 1830 | Thousands of Native Americans are removed from their homeland; Cherokees suffer on the Trail of Tears |
| Bank War | Jackson drives the Second Bank out of business; inflation rises |
| Election of 1836 | Jackson's popularity and the nation's prosperity help Vice-President Van Buren win the presidency |

### CRITICAL THINKING

1. **Form and Support Opinions** What do you think was the most important issue in Jackson's presidency? Why?

2. **Evaluate** In what ways did Jackson continue to affect politics after his presidency had ended?

# The Birth of the Whigs

 **KEY QUESTION** In what ways did the Whig Party differ from the Democrats?

Van Buren faced a new political party in his campaign for reelection in 1840. The **Whig Party** had been formed by Henry Clay, Daniel Webster, and other Jackson opponents. It was named after a British party that opposed royal power. The Whigs opposed the concentration of power in the chief executive—whom they mockingly called "King Andrew" Jackson.

This 1840 campaign banner shows a log cabin as a symbol of the frontier. The banner describes Harrison as "The Ohio Farmer" to set him apart from his wealthy opponent, Van Buren.

**Political Beliefs** The Whigs believed that Congress, not the president, represented the will of the people. They also blamed Van Buren—who objected to government "interference"—for not doing more to help the economy during the panic. In 1840 the Whigs chose **William Henry Harrison** of Ohio as a candidate for president and **John Tyler** as his running mate.

**The Election of 1840** The Whigs nominated Harrison, the hero of Tippecanoe and the War of 1812, because of his military record and his lack of strong political views. During the campaign, the Whigs emphasized personalities rather than political issues. They portrayed Harrison as a frontiersman against the wealthy Van Buren. Harrison won the election but he died shortly after his inauguration, and John Tyler became president. The election of 1840 showed the importance of the West in American politics.

 **COMPARE AND CONTRAST** Describe how the Whigs differed from the Democrats.

---

**New Jersey Core Curriculum Content Standards *Review***

**ONLINE QUIZ**
For test practice, go to
**Interactive Review @ ClassZone.com**

### TERMS & NAMES
1. Explain the significance of
   - Martin Van Buren
   - Panic of 1837
   - depression
   - Whig Party
   - William Henry Harrison
   - John Tyler

### USING YOUR READING NOTES
2. **Sequence Events** Complete the diagram to show the major events of this section.

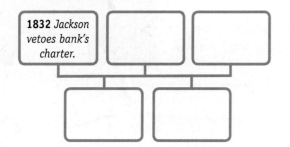

1832 *Jackson vetoes bank's charter.*

### KEY IDEAS
3. Why was Jackson against the Second Bank of the United States?
4. What was Nicholas Biddle's role in the bank war?

### CRITICAL THINKING
5. **Causes and Effects** What role did Jackson's popularity play in the elections of 1836 and 1840?
6. **Connect *to* Today** The percentage of eligible voters who participate in elections today is much lower than it was during Jackson's time. In what ways do you think this influences elections today?
7. **Art** **Campaign Poster** Create a campaign poster representing either the Whig Party or the Democrats in the election of 1840.

## Chapter Summary

**① Key Idea**
Andrew Jackson's election to the presidency in 1828 opened a new era of popular democracy.

**② Key Idea**
During Jackson's presidency, Native Americans were forced to move west of the Mississippi River.

**③ Key Idea**
After Jackson left office, his policies caused the economy to collapse and affected the next election.

For detailed Review and Study Notes go to **Interactive Review** @ **ClassZone.com**

## Name Game

**Use the Terms & Names list to identify each sentence online or on your own paper.**

1. People accused me of making a deal with Henry Clay in the 1824 presidential election. John Quicy Adams

2. I felt that the 1824 election was stolen from me. _____

3. I was Jackson's vice president in his first term. _____

4. I invented a writing system for the Cherokee language. _____

5. South Carolina threatened to secede because of this. _____

6. I led the Seminoles in the fight against removal. _____

7. Shortly after Jackson left office, I spread fear about the state of the economy. _____

8. Many people blamed me for the depression during my presidency. _____

9. This name comes from a British party that opposed royal power. _____

10. I succeeded William Henry Harrison after he died in office. _____

A. Osceola
B. John Quincy Adams
C. John Tyler
D. Whig Party
E. Sequoya
F. Martin Van Buren
G. Andrew Jackson
H. Tariff of Abominations
I. inflation
J. Panic of 1837
K. spoils system
L. doctrine of nullification
M. John C. Calhoun

## Activities

### CROSSWORD PUZZLE

Complete the online crossword puzzle to show what you know about the Age of Jackson.

**DOWN**
**10.** 1840 Whig presidential candidate

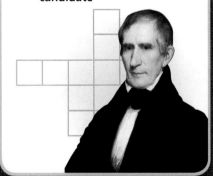

### GEOGAME

Use this online map to reinforce your understanding of the settlement of the United States, including the locations of areas settled between 1800 and 1830. Drag and drop each place name in the list at its location on the map. A scorecard helps you keep track of your progress online.

Missouri

Illinois

Indiana

Tennessee

Kentucky

More items online

## VOCABULARY

**Explain the significance of each of the following:**

1. John Quincy Adams
2. Jacksonian democracy
3. spoils system
4. states' rights
5. Sequoya
6. Osceola
7. Whig Party
8. William Henry Harrison

**Explain how the terms and names in each group are related.**

9. Tariff of Abominations, John C. Calhoun, doctrine of nullification
10. Indian Removal Act, Indian Territory, Trail of Tears
11. Martin Van Buren, Panic of 1837, depression
12. Whig Party, William Henry Harrison, John Tyler

## KEY IDEAS

**1 Jacksonian Democracy and States' Rights (pages 394–401)**

13. What changes in American democracy occurred during Jackson's presidency?
14. What issues divided Northeasterners, Southerners, and Westerners in the 1830s?

**2 Jackson's Policy Toward Native Americans (pages 402–407)**

15. Why did many whites want Native Americans to move west?
16. How did the Indian Removal Act affect Native Americans?

**3 Prosperity and Panic (pages 408–412)**

17. How did Jackson try to destroy the bank before its charter ended?
18. Describe the beliefs of the Whigs.

## CRITICAL THINKING

19. **Compare and Contrast** Create a chart like the one below to show how Jackson portrayed himself against Adams in the 1828 election.

| Jackson | Adams |
|---------|-------|
| *Westerner* | *Easterner* |
| | |

20. **Summarize** How did nullification threaten the nation?

21. **Main Ideas and Details** How did the discovery of gold in Georgia affect policies toward Native Americans?

22. **Synthesize** How did Jackson's policy toward Native Americans show his belief in the power of the presidency?

23. **Causes and Effects** What were the effects of Jackson's war on the national bank?

24. **Draw Conclusions** Based on its economic effects, was Jackson's decision to end the national bank a good one?

25. **Evaluate** How does the campaign poster below portray William Henry Harrison?

Harrison campaign poster

**TEST PRACTICE**

- **Online Test Practice @ ClassZone.com**
- **Test-Taking Strategies & Practice** at the front of this book

## MULTIPLE CHOICE

Use the cartoon and your knowledge of U.S. history to answer question 1.

BORN TO COMMAND.

OF VETO MEMORY.

HAD I BEEN CONSULTED.

KING ANDREW THE FIRST.

1. Why do you think Jackson is portrayed as a king?

   A. He came from a royal family.

   B. He supported a strong alliance with the British.

   C. Many people looked up to him.

   D. His opponents thought he had too much power.

Use the quotation and your knowledge of U.S. history to answer question 2.

**PRIMARY SOURCE**

❝ All communities are apt to look to the Government for too much. Even in our own country, where its powers and duties are so strictly limited, we are prone to do so, especially at periods of sudden embarrassment and distress. But this ought not to be. . . . [The framers of the Constitution] wisely judged that the less Government interferes with private pursuits, the better for the general prosperity. ❞

—Martin Van Buren, from a letter to Congress dated September 4, 1837

2. Why did Van Buren think the government did not need to help the economy during the depression?

   A. It would subject government leaders to embarrassment and distress.

   B. The economy would be better off without government interference.

   C. Any action taken should be made by Congress.

   D. It was the responsibility of the state governments.

## YOU BE THE HISTORIAN

26. **Form and Support Opinions** Do you think Jackson was a champion of the common people? Why or why not?

27. **Recognize Bias and Propaganda** In what ways did Jackson's policy toward Native Americans reflect bias?

28. **Analyze Point of View** Do you think Jackson's use of power during his presidency contradicted his views as a proponent of limited government? Why or why not?

29. **WHAT IF?** What do you think would have happened if Congress had not passed the Indian Removal Act of 1830?

30. **Connect** *to* **Today** **Citizenship** In what ways do you think the changes that have occurred since Jackson's time in voter participation and voter eligibility affect government today?

 Answer the
## ESSENTIAL QUESTION
**What impact did Andrew Jackson's presidency have on the nation?**

**Written Response** Write a two- or three-paragraph response to the Essential Question. Be sure to consider the key ideas of each section as well as the most significant factors that led to changes in the nation. Use the Response Rubric below to guide your thinking and writing.

### Response Rubric
**A strong response will**

- analyze the democratic and political changes
- describe the relocation of Native Americans
- explain the effects of Jackson's policies

1. Trails West
2. The Texas Revolution
3. The War with Mexico
4. The California Gold Rush

# Manifest Destiny

## 1821–1853

 **ESSENTIAL QUESTION**

How did westward expansion transform the nation?

**CONNECT** ⟳ **Geography & History**

How might the geography and topography of the United States have affected westward expansion?

**Think about:**

**1** the highest peak of the **Rocky Mountains**, in Central Colorado, is 14,431 feet high

**2** how people traveled in the early 1800s

**3** the distances covered

This mission, or settlement, is a legacy of Spanish rule.

Oxen yoke

## 1821

Mexico gains independence from Spain. Stephen Austin starts American settlement in Texas.

▼

**Effect** Settlers move to Texas from the United States.

**1824** Jedediah Smith finds South Pass.

▼

**Effect** Pioneers move west on faster trails.

**1836** Texas declares independence from Mexico.

▼

**Effect** Battle of the Alamo; Republic of Texas formed

U.S. military hat

**1849** California gold rush

▼

**Effect** California enters the Union.

# 1853

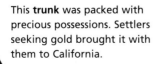

This **trunk** was packed with precious possessions. Settlers seeking gold brought it with them to California.

**1846** Oregon Territory acquired; war with Mexico begins.

▼

**Effect** 1848 Treaty of Guadalupe Hidalgo ends war with Mexico.

## History Makers

### James Beckwourth   1798–?1867

Not much is known about Jim Beckwourth's family history. At the age of 25, he joined a group of fur traders going west and in time became a daring mountain man. For several years, he lived with a Crow tribe and earned the warrior name, "Bloody Arm." Later, he worked as an army scout and gold prospector. In 1850, Beckwourth discovered a mountain pass across the Sierra Nevadas that enabled thousands of pioneers and gold seekers to reach northern California. This pass is still called Beckwourth Pass. The Western Pacific Railway later used this route as a gateway to the West.

**CRITICAL THINKING** Sequence Events How did Beckwourth's discovery of a mountain pass change the future of California and the nation?

 **ONLINE BIOGRAPHY**   For more on on James Beckwourth, go to the **Research & Writing Center @ ClassZone.com**

**Jim Beckwourth**, became famous for their adventures. Although perceived as rugged loners, the men connected economically to the businessmen who bought their furs.

One businessman, William Henry Ashley, created a trading arrangement called the **rendezvous** system. At a prearranged site, trappers met with traders from the East. There, trappers bought supplies and paid in furs. The rendezvous took place every year from 1825 to 1840, when silk came into fashion and the fur trade died out.

Many animals were killed off at the height of the fur trade. This forced trappers to search for new streams where beaver lived. The mountain men's explorations provided Americans with some of the earliest firsthand knowledge of the Far West. This knowledge, and the trails the mountain men blazed, helped later pioneers moving west.

For example, thousands of pioneers used the wide valley through the Rockies called South Pass. Smith learned of this pass, in present-day Wyoming, from Native Americans. Unlike the high northern passes used by Lewis and Clark, South Pass was low, so it got less snow than the higher passes. Also, because South Pass was wide and less steep, wagon trails could run through it.

**The Lure of the West**   To many the West, with its vast stretches of land, offered a golden chance to make money. The Louisiana Purchase had doubled the size of the United States. Some Americans believed it was their right to take land away from Native Americans who inhabited the territory but did not own it.

People called **land speculators** bought huge areas of land. To speculate means to buy something in the hope that it will increase in value. If land value did go up, speculators divided their holdings into smaller sections. They made great profits by selling those sections to the thousands of settlers who dreamed of owning their own farms. Traders also traveled west. Manufacturers and merchants hoped to earn money by making and selling items to settlers and markets opening up in new communities. Others went to find jobs or to hide from the law.

▲ **SUMMARIZE**   Explain what motivated pioneers to undertake the hazardous journey into the rugged west.

# Settling the West

🔻 **KEY QUESTION** How did settlers make the difficult journey west?

The success of early pioneers convinced thousands of families and individuals to make the dangerous journey west. They traveled along a series of routes that led to New Mexico, Oregon, and Utah. Once in these places, the new pioneers claimed the land and established settlements.

**The Santa Fe Trail** In 1821, Mexico gained its independence from Spain. Lands in the Southwest that used to belong to Spain now belonged to Mexico. Spain had kept Americans out of these lands, but Mexico opened its borders to American traders.

One adventurer who took advantage of this new policy was Missouri trader William Becknell. In 1821 he left Missouri for the customary route to Santa Fe, capital of the Mexican province of New Mexico. He made a large profit because the New Mexicans were eager for goods. Back in Missouri, news spread that New Mexico was a place where traders could become rich.

The following year, Becknell left Missouri with a group of traders and pioneered a new route that became the **Santa Fe Trail.** Goods were hauled by covered wagons—rather than by pack animals. Becknell knew he could not haul wagons over the mountain pass he had used on his first trip. Instead, he found a cutoff, a shortcut that avoided steep slopes but it passed through a deadly desert to the south. As his traders crossed the burning sands, they ran out of water and were crazed by thirst. Finally, the traders found a stream

Along with tools, cooking supplies, and a hunting rifle, a tin of gunpowder was an essential item on an overland journey to the West.

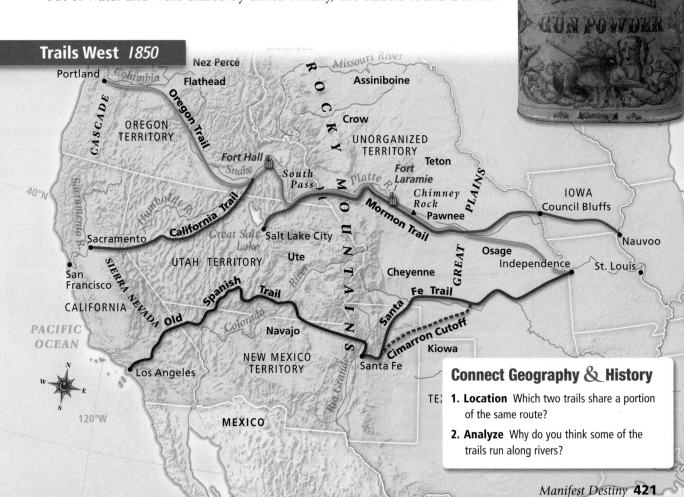

**Trails West** *1850*

## Connect Geography & History

1. **Location** Which two trails share a portion of the same route?

2. **Analyze** Why do you think some of the trails run along rivers?

and pushed on to reach Santa Fe. Becknell returned home with another huge profit. Soon, hundreds of families were braving the cutoff to make the 800-mile journey from Missouri to Santa Fe, New Mexico.

**Oregon Fever** Hundreds of settlers began migrating west on the **Oregon Trail**, which ran from Independence, Missouri, to the Oregon Territory. Among the first settlers to cross the continent to Oregon were missionaries, such as Marcus and Narcissa Whitman in 1836. The Whitmans made few **converts** among the Native Americans, but their glowing reports of Oregon began to attract other American settlers to the region. American settlement eventually led to conflict between Britain and the United States because Oregon was jointly occupied by those two countries.

## Daily Life *On the Trail*

### A Difficult Journey

For pioneers, the western lands held great hope. Following the trails promised new adventures. However, the journey was hazardous and filled with many challenges along the 2,000-mile route.

> ❝ The dust got deeper and deeper . . . Often it would lie in the road fully six inches deep, so fine that a person wading though it would scarcely leave a track. And when disturbed, such clouds! No words can describe it. ❞
>
> —Ezra Meeker, pioneer

### STRANGE BUT TRUE

A glass of water sometimes cost a lot of money on the trail.

**Guess How Much!**

$1   $5   $10   $20   $50   $100

### Data File

**WHO**   350,000 pioneers between 1841 and 1867

**WHAT**   2,000 miles of trail across prairies, rivers, and mountains

**WHERE**   Missouri to Oregon. (There were many other trails including the Santa Fe trail and the Mormon Trail).

**WHEN**   early spring to avoid harsh winters

**WHY**   lure of available land and adventure

#### CHALLENGES OF THE TRAILS

- Wagon trains traveled from dawn to dusk with only a short break for a noontime meal, for nearly six months.
- Wagons were often overloaded with supplies, forcing family members, including children, to travel by foot.
- Children gathered firewood; when none was available they searched for dry buffalo dung.

ANSWER: 001$

Amazing stories spread about Oregon—the sun always shone there and wheat grew as tall as six feet. Such stories lured many people to the 2,000-mile journey to Oregon. In 1843, nearly 1,000 people traveled from Missouri to Oregon. The next year, twice as many came. "The Oregon fever has broken out," observed the *National Intelligencer*, "and is now raging."

**The Mormon Trail** Most pioneers went west in search of wealth, but one large group migrated for religious reasons. Members of the Church of Jesus Christ of Latter-Day Saints, or **Mormons**, also moved west. The church was founded by Joseph Smith in upstate New York in 1830. The Mormons lived in close communities, worked hard, shared their goods, and prospered.

The Mormons also made enemies. Some saw the Mormon practice of polygamy—allowing a man more than one wife at a time—as immoral. Others objected to their policy of holding property in common.

In 1844, an anti-Mormon mob in Illinois killed Joseph Smith. **Brigham Young**, the next Mormon leader, moved his people out of the United States. His destination was Utah, then part of Mexico, where he hoped his people would be left in peace.

In 1847, about 148 Mormon pioneers followed part of the Oregon Trail to Utah. With about 1,700 who soon joined them, they built a new settlement by the Great Salt Lake called Salt Lake City. Because Utah has little rainfall, the Mormons built dams and canals. These structures caught water in the hills and carried it to the farms in the valleys below. During this same period, American settlers were also changing Texas.

▲ **SUMMARIZE** Explain how settlers made the difficult journey west.

**Connecting History**

**Religion in Public Life**
Today the Church of Jesus Christ of Latter-Day Saints thrives in Utah, where Mormons make up about 70 percent of the state's population.

---

**New Jersey Core Curriculum Content Standards** *Review*

 **ONLINE QUIZ**
For test practice, go to
**Interactive Review** @ ClassZone.com

### TERMS & NAMES

**1.** Explain the importance of
- Jedediah Smith
- Jim Beckwourth
- Mountain Men
- Santa Fe Trail
- Oregon Trail
- Mormon
- Brigham Young

### USING YOUR READING NOTES

**2. Main Ideas and Details** Complete the diagram you began at the beginning of this section.

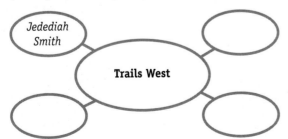

### KEY IDEAS

**3.** How did the mountain men open up the West for future settlement?

**4.** What were some of the reasons settlers chose to live in the West?

### CRITICAL THINKING

**5. Draw Conclusions** Of all the hardships faced by people who went west, what do you think was the most challenging?

**6. Analyze Causes and Effects** How do you think the pioneers' needs affected the local economy of Missouri?

**7. Draw Conclusions** How did the early Mormon settlers adapt to the desert?

**8.** Writing **Letter** Research a pioneer from this section and either write a letter from his or her point of view to a friend or write a journal entry and illustrate it with sights from the journey.

**Click here** to see an animated version of wagon trains @ ClassZone.com

## American Trails West

Most of the trails west took pioneers over rugged mountain ranges and across rivers. The settlers often endured hunger and disease. Some Native American groups were friendly toward the settlers, other groups were hostile to settlers.

**Click here** Pioneers packed carefully for the challenges of the trail.

**Click here** Pioneers experienced varied climate conditions—such as the stark, dry, terrain of the desert.

**Click here** Pioneers had to clear the land to build a home for their families.

## Activity

**Songs on the Trail**

1 Research the music and songs sung by the people going west.

2 Study the lyrics to understand what the journey west was like.

3 Divide the class into groups—narrators and performers.

4 Let each group take turns performing a song or playing recordings of ballads or folk songs from the trails west.

# SECTION 2 Reading for Understanding

## ▶ Key Ideas

**BEFORE, YOU LEARNED**

Thousands of adventurers and pioneers followed trails to the West to make their fortunes and settle the land.

**NOW YOU WILL LEARN**

Conflicts between American settlers and the government of Mexico led Texas to revolt and win independence from Mexico in 1836.

## ▶ Vocabulary

**TERMS & NAMES**

**Stephen F. Austin** founded a colony for Americans in Spanish Texas

**Tejanos** (tay•HAH•nohs) people of Mexican heritage who consider Texas their home

**Antonio López de Santa Anna** Mexican president who led an army against Texas

**Sam Houston** commander of the Texas army at the Battle of San Jacinto; later elected president of the Republic of Texas

**Juan Seguín** (wahn seh•GEEN) a *Tejano* hero of the Texas Revolution

**Battle of the Alamo** battle between Texas and Mexico in 1836

**Lone Star Republic** nickname of the republic of Texas once free from Mexico

**BACKGROUND VOCABULARY**

**Tejas** (tay•HAHS) name the Spanish explorers gave present-day Texas

**annex** join or merge territory into an existing political unit such as a country or state

Visual Vocabulary
Lone Star Republic flag

## ▶ Reading Strategy

Re-create the diagram at right. As you read and respond to the **KEY QUESTIONS**, use the diagram to show important events leading to Texan independence.

 See Skillbuilder Handbook, page R5.

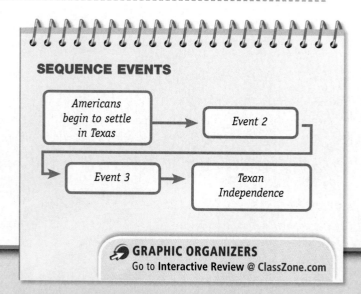

**SEQUENCE EVENTS**

```
Americans
begin to settle  ──▶  Event 2
in Texas                  │
                          │
   ┌──────────────────────┘
   ▼
Event 3  ──▶  Texan
              Independence
```

**GRAPHIC ORGANIZERS**
Go to **Interactive Review** @ ClassZone.com

# The Texas Revolution

 **6.4.F.3.** Explain the concept of the Manifest Destiny and its relationship to the westward movement of settlers and territorial expansion, . . . .
**6.4.F.9.** Describe and map the continuing territorial expansion and settlement of the frontier, including the acquisition of new territories . . . .

## One American's Story

In 1831, Mary Austin Holley visited her cousin Stephen F. Austin in Texas. She decided not to settle there, but published a widely read guide to the territory. Holley's guide was credited with bringing many settlers to Texas territory. Holley wrote approvingly of her cousin's vision.

### PRIMARY SOURCE

❝ When, in the progress of years, the state of Texas shall take her place among the powerful empires of the American continent, her citizens will doubtless regard Col. Austin as their patriarch, and children will be taught to hold his name in reverence. . . . Col. Austin began the work, and was the first to open the wilderness. ❞

—Mary Austin Holley, *Texas: Observations Historical, Geographical and Descriptive* 1833

Mary Austin Holley

Stephen F. Austin's father, Moses Austin, had spent the last years of his life chasing a dream. He had hoped to found a colony for Americans in Spanish Texas. A week after his father's death in 1821, Stephen F. Austin was standing on Texas soil. His father's dream would become his destiny. Austin led the surge of American settlement in Texas.

## Changes in Spanish Texas

🔽 **KEY QUESTION** How did American settlers cause problems in Texas?

Texas—the land the Spanish explorers called **Tejas** (tay•HAHS)—bordered the Louisiana Territory. *Tejas* had lush forests, plains, and rich soil, but relatively few settlers. When Austin arrived, fewer than 5,000 **Tejanos** (tay•HAH•nohs), people of Spanish heritage who thought of Texas as their home, lived in Texas.

**American Settlers in Texas** In 1820, to defend the land from hostile Native Americans, the Spanish government offered huge tracts of land to *empresarios*—people who agreed to find settlers for the land. When Spanish settlers did not respond to their offer of land, the Spanish agreed to let American Moses Austin start a colony there, provided the settlers followed Spanish law. Shortly after Stephen F. Austin arrived in Texas in 1821, Mexico successfully gained its independence from Spain. *Tejas* was now a part of the new nation of Mexico. With the change in government, the Spanish land grant given to Austin's father was worthless.

Stephen F. Austin traveled to Mexico City to persuade the new Mexican government to let him start his American colony. The Mexican government would consent only if the new settlers agreed to become Mexican citizens and members of the Roman Catholic Church.

Between 1821 and 1825, Austin attracted about 300 families to his new settlement. These original Texas settler families are known as the "Old Three Hundred." He demanded proof that each family head worked hard and did not use alcohol. The colony attracted more and more settlers. Some were looking for a new life, some were escaping from the law, and others were looking for a chance to grow rich. By 1830, the population had swelled to about 25,000, with Americans outnumbering the *Tejanos* six to one.

**Rising Tensions in Texas** As more Americans settled in Texas, tensions increased. Americans resented Mexican laws. They were unhappy that offi-

**ONLINE PRIMARY SOURCE**

Hear the perspectives at the **Research & Writing Center** @ ClassZone.com

## COMPARING *Perspectives*

By the 1820s, non-Mexican settlers were a growing presence in Texas. *Tejanos* were quickly outnumbered. Most of the American settlers refused to learn Spanish and resented the Mexican laws they were expected to honor. Different perspectives of the changes in Texas are quoted below.

### Against Settlement

"The Americans . . . have taken possession of practically all the eastern part of Texas, in most cases without the permission of the authorities. They immigrate constantly, finding no one to prevent them, and take possession of the sitio [site] that best suits them without either asking leave or going through any formality other than that of building their homes.

**"**→*attributed to Mexican soldier José María Sánchez, April 1828*

### For Settlement

"My object, the sole and only desire of my ambitions since I first saw Texas, was to . . . settle it with an intelligent, honorable, and enterprising people. . . . Texas should be effectually, and fully, Americanized—that is—settled by a population that will harmonize with their neighbors on the East, in language, political principles, common origin, sympathy, and even interest. **"**

— *Stephen F. Austin, ca.1837*

**CRITICAL THINKING Make Inferences** Why do you think American settlers believed they could Americanize Texas?

cial documents were written in Spanish. Slave owners became angry when Mexico outlawed slavery in 1829. They wanted to maintain slavery so they could grow cotton. Austin persuaded the government to allow slave owners to keep their slaves.

On the other hand, the *Tejanos* found the Americans difficult to live with, too. *Tejanos* thought that the Americans believed they were superior and deserved special privileges. The Americans seemed unwilling to adapt to or to understand Mexican laws.

Responding to warnings of a possible revolution, the Mexican government cracked down on Texas. First, it closed the state to further American immigration. Next, it required Texans to pay taxes for the first time. Finally, to enforce these laws, the government sent more Mexican troops to Texas.

▲ **ANALYZE CAUSES AND EFFECTS**  Explain how American settlers caused problems in Texas.

## Texans Revolt Against Mexico

🔻 **KEY QUESTION**  What events led to Texas's independence from Mexico?

The actions of the Mexican government caused angry protests from Americans and many *Tejanos*. Some Texans talked about breaking away from Mexico. But Austin remained loyal to Mexico.

**War Begins**  In 1833, Austin went to Mexico City to present a list of requested reforms to Mexican officials. The most urgent request was that Texas become a self-governing state within Mexico. Mexican president **General Antonio López de Santa Anna** agreed to most of the reforms. But Santa Anna then learned of a letter Austin had written. If his requests weren't met, wrote Austin, he would support breaking away from Mexican rule. This was rebellion! Santa Anna jailed Austin for almost a year. The furious Texans were ready to rebel.

(*left*) Mexican general Antonio López de Santa Anna liked to be known as the "Napoleon of the West."

Santa Anna sent more troops to Texas. In October 1835, Mexican soldiers marched to the town of Gonzales. They had orders to seize a cannon used by the Texans for protection against Native Americans. Texas volunteers had hung a flag over the big gun that said, "Come and Take It."

The Mexican troops failed to capture the cannon. In December, Texans drove Mexican troops out of an old mission in San Antonio called the Alamo that was used as a fortress. Angered by these insults, Santa Anna and 6,000 troops headed for Texas.

**The Fight for the Alamo**  On March 1–2, 1836, Texans met at a settlement called Washington-on-the-Brazos to decide what to do about Santa Anna's troops. They decided to declare Texas a free and independent republic. **Sam Houston** was placed in command of the Texas army.

## History Makers

### Juan Seguín   1806–1890

Juan Seguín was a *Tejano* who wanted Texas to remain independent and not become part of the United States. He was a hero of the Battle of the Alamo. Seguín was elected to the Texas Senate in 1837 and was mayor of San Antonio twice. However, Seguín was often betrayed and harassed by American newcomers who mistrusted *Tejanos*. Finally he was forced to move to Mexico in 1842. In 1846–1848, Seguín fought against Americans in the War with Mexico.

**CRITICAL THINKING  Compare** In what ways did the goals of Seguín and the Americans in Texas differ?

 **ONLINE BIOGRAPHY**   For more on Juan Seguín, go to the **Research & Writing Center** @ ClassZone.com

**Juan Seguín** (wahn seh•GEEN) led a band of 25 *Tejanos* in support of revolt. Also among the Texas volunteers were free African Americans, but the Texas army hardly existed. There were two small forces ready to stand up to Santa Anna's army. One was a company of some 300 to 400 men, led by James Fannin, stationed at Goliad, a fort in southeast Texas. The second was a company of about 180 volunteers at the Alamo. Headed by James Bowie and William Travis, this small force also included such famous frontiersmen as Davy Crockett.

On February 23, 1836, Santa Anna's troops surrounded San Antonio. The next day, Mexicans began their siege of the Alamo. Two nights later, Travis scrawled a message to the world: "The enemy has demanded surrender. . . . I have answered . . . with a cannon shot. . . . I shall never surrender or retreat." Juan Seguín, a *Tejano*, spoke Spanish, so he was chosen to carry the declaration through enemy lines. Seguín got the message through to other Texas defenders. But when he returned, he saw the Alamo in flames.

The Alamo's defenders held off the Mexican attack for 12 violent days. On the 13th day, Santa Anna ordered over 1,800 men to storm the fortress. The Texans met the attackers with a hailstorm of cannon and gun fire until the Texans ran out of ammunition. At day's end, all but seven Texans were dead and more than 1,000 Mexicans had fallen. The **Battle of the Alamo** was over.

The survivors were executed. A total of 183 Alamo defenders died. Only a few women and children were spared. Hundreds of Mexicans also perished. The slaughter shocked Texans—and showed them how hard they would have to fight for their freedom from Mexico.

**Victory at San Jacinto**  With Santa Anna on the attack, Texans—both soldiers and settlers—fled eastward. Houston sent a message to the troops at Goliad, ordering them to retreat. They were captured by Mexican forces, who executed more than 300. But even in retreat and defeat, Houston's army doubled. Now it was a fighting force of 800 angry men. It included *Tejanos*, American settlers, and many free and enslaved African Americans.

In late April 1836, Houston surprised Santa Anna near the San Jacinto (san juh•SIN•toh) River. The Texans advanced screaming "Remember the Alamo!" and "Remember Goliad!"

In just 18 minutes, the Texans killed more than half of the Mexican army. Santa Anna had to sign a treaty giving Texas its freedom. With the Battle of San Jacinto, Texas was an independent nation.

**Republic of Texas** In December 1836, Texans raised the official flag of the independent nation of Texas, nicknamed the **Lone Star Republic**. Sam Houston was elected president.

Many Texans wanted to be part of the United States. In 1836 the Texas government asked Congress to **annex**, or join, Texas to the Union. Some Northerners objected. Some feared that Texas would allow slavery and upset the balance between free and slave states. Some opposed any expansion of slavery. Others feared that annexing Texas would lead to war with Mexico. In response Congress voted against annexation.

 **SEQUENCE EVENTS** Describe the events that led to Texas's independence from Mexico.

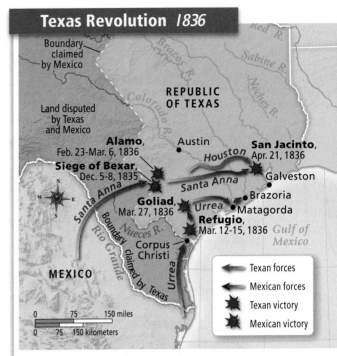

## Texas Revolution 1836

Boundary claimed by Mexico

**REPUBLIC OF TEXAS**

Land disputed by Texas and Mexico

**Alamo,** Feb. 23-Mar. 6, 1836 · Austin · **San Jacinto,** Apr. 21, 1836

**Siege of Bexar,** Dec. 5-8, 1835 · Houston · Galveston

Santa Anna · Brazoria

**Goliad,** Mar. 27, 1836 · Urrea · Matagorda

**Refugio,** Mar. 12-15, 1836 · *Gulf of Mexico*

Corpus Christi · Boundary claimed by Texas

**MEXICO**

Rio Grande · Nueces R.

| 0 | 75 | 150 miles |
| 0 | 75 | 150 kilometers |

→ Texan forces
← Mexican forces
✦ Texan victory
✦ Mexican victory

## Connect Geography & History

1. **Place** What geographic features marked the boundaries of the disputed territory?

2. **Clarify** What does the map show as a major disagreement left unresolved by the war?

---

New Jersey Core Curriculum Content Standards *Review*

**ONLINE QUIZ**
For test practice, go to
**Interactive Review @ ClassZone.com**

### TERMS & NAMES

1. Explain the importance of
   - Stephen F. Austin
   - *Tejanos*
   - Sam Houston
   - Antonio López de Santa Anna
   - Juan Seguín
   - Battle of the Alamo
   - Lone Star Republic

### USING YOUR READING NOTES

2. **Sequence** Complete the diagram you started at the beginning of this section. Then expand the diagram for each of the other important events in this section.

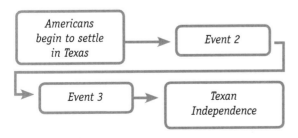

### KEY IDEAS

3. How and why did Texas attract American settlers?

4. How did the Mexican government respond to the Texas rebellion?

### CRITICAL THINKING

5. **Analyze Motives** Why do you think Stephen F. Austin thought it necessary to demand proof of settlers' high morals for his colony?

6. **Recognize Effects** How did losing the Battle of the Alamo serve as a turning point for Texas independence?

7. **Connect Economics & History** Why was Texas a magnet for land speculators and investors?

8. **Writing** **Speech** Write a one-page persuasive speech from Stephen F. Austin to the Mexican government asking for permission to form a colony in Texas.

## ▶ Key Ideas

**BEFORE, YOU LEARNED**

Conflicts between American settlers and the government of Mexico led Texans to revolt and win independence from Mexico in 1836.

**NOW YOU WILL LEARN**

Victory in a war with Mexico allowed Americans to expand the nation across the continent.

## ▶ Vocabulary

**TERMS & NAMES**

**James K. Polk** eleventh president of the United States who was committed to westward expansion

**manifest destiny** belief that the U.S. was meant to expand from coast to coast

**Zachary Taylor** U.S. general who led the battle over the disputed territory of the Rio Grande

**Bear Flag Revolt** rebellion by Americans in 1846 against Mexican rule of California

**Treaty of Guadalupe Hidalgo** (gwah•duh•L OOP•ay hih•DAHL•go) treaty that ended the War with Mexico

**Mexican cession** Mexican territory surrendered to the United States at the end of the war with Mexico

**Visual Vocabulary**
(*above left*) Original 1846 bear flag was replaced by (*above right*) state flag of California in 1911.

## ▶ Reading Strategy

Re-create a diagram like the one shown at right. As you read and respond to the **KEY QUESTIONS**, use boxes to show the sequence of events leading to war with Mexico.

 **See Skillbuilder Handbook, page R5.**

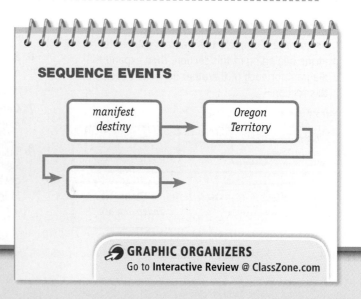

**SEQUENCE EVENTS**

*manifest destiny* → *Oregon Territory* →

⟶ ▢ →

**GRAPHIC ORGANIZERS**
Go to **Interactive Review** @ ClassZone.com

# The War with Mexico

 **6.4.F.1.** Describe the political, economic, and social changes in New Jersey and American society preceding the Civil War, . . . .
**6.4.F.3.** Explain the concept of the Manifest Destiny and its relationship to the westward movement of settlers and territorial expansion, . . . .

## One American's Story

Henry Clay sneered, "Who is **James K. Polk**?" Clay had just learned the name of the Democratic candidate who would run against him for president in 1844. However, Polk wasn't a complete unknown. He had served seven terms in Congress.

Polk was committed to national expansion. He vowed to annex Texas and take over Oregon. Americans listened and voted. When the votes were counted, Clay had his answer. James Knox Polk was the eleventh president of the United States. On the question of Texas, Polk said:

James Polk's presidential campaign emphasized expansion of the United States.

**PRIMARY SOURCE**

❝ To Texas, the reunion is important, because the strong protecting arm of our Government would be extended over her, and the vast resources of her fertile soil and genial climate would be speedily developed. ❞

—James K. Polk, *Inaugural Address*, 1845

Polk's ideas about expanding the country captured the attention of Americans. After his election Polk looked for ways to act on his agenda.

## Americans Support Manifest Destiny

🔻 **KEY QUESTION** How did belief in manifest destiny lead to friction overseas?

Land in the West held great promise for Americans. Although populated by Native Americans and Mexicans, American settlers viewed those lands as unoccupied. And Americans worried about claims by other nations.

**Dispute over Oregon** One country with whom the United States faced conflict was Great Britain. The United States and Britain shared control of the northwest Oregon Territory. Many Americans believed that it was their fate, or destiny, to expand the United States across the continent from ocean to ocean. In 1845, a newspaper editor, John O'Sullivan, gave a name to that belief. He called it **manifest destiny.**

## ▶ Key Ideas

**BEFORE, YOU LEARNED**
Victory in a War with Mexico allowed Americans to expand the country across the continent.

**NOW YOU WILL LEARN**
The discovery of gold in California in 1848 led to a population increase and statehood.

## ▶ Vocabulary

**TERMS & NAMES**

**forty-niner** person who went to California to find gold in 1849

***Californios*** settlers of Spanish or Mexican descent who populated California

**Mariano Vallejo** a prosperous *Californio* who lost a lot of property after American settlement

**James Marshall** carpenter who discovered gold in California in 1848

**California gold rush** migration of thousands of settlers to California in search of gold

**BACKGROUND VOCABULARY**

**migration** movement of people from one country or locality to another

**Visual Vocabulary**
forty-niner

## ▶ Reading Strategy

Re-create the diagram shown at right. As you read and respond to the **KEY QUESTIONS**, use the chart to note important events and their effects. Add boxes or start a new diagram as needed.

 **See Skillbuilder Handbook, page R7.**

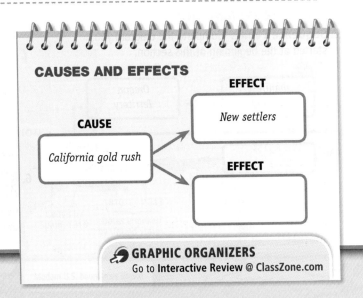

**CAUSES AND EFFECTS**

**CAUSE**

*California gold rush*

**EFFECT**

*New settlers*

**EFFECT**

**GRAPHIC ORGANIZERS**
Go to **Interactive Review** @ ClassZone.com

# The California Gold Rush

**6.4.F.3.** Explain the concept of the Manifest Destiny and its relationship to the westward movement of settlers and territorial expansion, . . . .
**6.4.F.8.** Discuss sectional compromises associated with westward expansion of slavery, such as the Missouri Compromise (1820) and the continued resistance to slavery by African Americans . . . .

## One American's Story

Luzena Wilson said of the year 1849, "The gold excitement spread like wildfire." That year, **James Marshall** had discovered gold in California. Luzena's husband became a **forty-niner**—someone who went to California to find gold, starting in 1849. Luzena went to California with her husband. She found that women were rare in California. Shortly after she arrived, a miner offered her five dollars for her baked biscuits. Shocked, she just stared at him. He quickly doubled his offer and paid in gold. Finding she could make money by taking care of miners, Luzena opened a hotel. The gold rush boosted California's economy and changed the nation's history.

These prospectors were residents of a mining camp in Auburn Ravine, California, in the mid-1800s.

## A Discovery Changes California

▼ **KEY QUESTION** What led to the rapid settlement in California?

Before the forty-niners came, California was populated by as many as 150,000 Native Americans and 6,000 *Californios*—settlers of Spanish or Mexican descent. Many *Californios* lived on huge cattle ranches.

**The Rush for Gold** On January 24, 1848, just one month before Mexico lost California to the United States, a carpenter named James Marshall made an important discovery. While building a sawmill in northern California, he saw a shiny stone in the nearby American River. He later said, "My eye was caught by a glimpse of something shining. . . . It made my heart thump for I felt certain it was gold." It was indeed. Marshall's discovery led to one of the greatest **migrations**—movements of persons from one country or locality to another—in American history, as thousands from all over the world poured into California to make their fortunes.

In 1849, people from all over California and the United States raced to the American River—starting the **California gold rush.** A gold rush occurs when large numbers of people move to a site where gold has been found.

Mariano Vallejo (*inset*), a *Californio*, was the proud owner of a large California estate (*top*). **What major migration changed the *Californio* way of life?**

Miners soon found gold in other streams flowing out of the Sierra Nevada. The military governor of California estimated that the region held enough gold to "pay the cost of the present war with Mexico a hundred times over." He sent this news to Washington with a box of gold dust as proof.

The following year thousands of gold seekers set out to make their fortunes. A forty-niner who wished to reach California from the East had a choice of three routes, all of them dangerous. 1) Sail 18,000 miles around South America and up the Pacific coast—enduring storms, seasickness, and spoiled food. 2) Sail to the narrow Isthmus of Panama, cross overland (and risk catching a deadly tropical disease), and then sail to California. 3) Travel the trails across North America—braving rivers, prairies, mountains, and all the hardships of the trail. Because the venture was so hard, most gold seekers were young men.

**Changes for *Californios*** James Marshall's discovery of gold in 1848 did little to improve the lot of the *Californios*. Before the gold rush, many *Californio* families had prospered when the Mexican government took away the land that once belonged to the Spanish missions in California.

One important *Californio* was **Mariano Vallejo**. He was a member of one of the oldest Spanish families in America, and owned 250,000 acres of land. Vallejo's nephew proudly described the heritage of the *Californios* as "the pioneers of the Pacific coast." The gold rush found *Californios* challenged by a new wave of pioneers.

**The Gold Seekers** About two-thirds of the forty-niners were Americans. Most of these were white men. However, Native Americans, free blacks, and enslaved African Americans also worked the mines.

Thousands of experienced miners came from Sonora in Mexico. Other foreign miners came from Europe, South America, Australia, and China. Most of the Chinese miners were peasant farmers who fled hardships in China. By the end of 1851, one of every ten immigrants was Chinese.

The Chinese would often take over sites that American miners had left because the easy gold was gone. Through steady, hard work, the Chinese made these "played-out" sites yield profits. Some Americans envied the success of the Chinese and made fun of their different customs. As the numbers of Chinese miners grew, American resentment toward them also increased.

The mining camps began as rows of tents along the streams flowing out of the Sierra Nevada. Gradually the tents gave way to rough wooden buildings that housed stores and saloons. Camp gossip told of miners who got rich overnight by finding eight-pound nuggets, but in reality, few miners got rich. Exhaustion, poor food, and disease all damaged the miners' health. Not only was acquiring gold brutally difficult, but the miners had to pay very high prices for basic supplies.

▲ **EVALUATE** Explain the events that led to fast settlement in California.

# Final Impact of the Gold Rush

▼ **KEY QUESTION** What was the final impact of the gold rush on California?

The gold rush peaked in 1852. While it lasted, about 250,000 people flooded into California. This huge migration caused economic growth that changed California permanently.

**Opportunities and Turmoil** By 1849, California had enough people to apply for statehood. It was admitted as a free state in 1850. Its constitution banned slavery, but it did not grant African Americans the right to vote.

For some people, California's statehood proved to be the opportunity of a lifetime. An enslaved woman, Nancy Gooch, gained her freedom because of the law against slavery. Then she worked to buy the freedom of her children in Missouri. Eventually, the Gooch family became so prosperous that they bought Sutter's sawmill, where James Marshall first found the gold that started California's gold rush.

The population explosion ruined many *Californios*. The newcomers did not respect *Californios* or their legal rights. In many cases, Americans seized their property. Mariano Vallejo lost all but 300 acres of his huge estate. Yet the Spanish heritage plays a prominent role in California culture today.

## CONNECT To Today

### ECONOMIC OPPORTUNITY

**The discovery of gold brought tens of thousands of settlers west to find prosperity. Many newcomers chose to open businesses to meet the demands of what became a booming region.**

Today, economic opportunity doesn't necessarily require people to move to another state, region, or country. Instead, many companies use the Internet to communicate with employees and customers at home and overseas. This practice is known as offshoring or outsourcing.

A number of large corporations outsource some or most of their work. Consequently, many overseas economies have ballooned since going into the offshore business. Huge western investments in outsourcing are bringing new prosperity to many developing nations. India is one example of successful offshoring. (*right*) Indian office workers work in a time zone 10.5 hours ahead of Eastern Standard Time. This means more time to conduct business.

### CRITICAL THINKING
1. **Make Inferences** Why might a company hire workers in a different country and/or a different time zone?

2. **Evaluate** How might outsourced programs affect American education and the American workplace?

**Native Americans and Foreigners** Thousands of Native Americans died from diseases brought by the newcomers. Settlers killed thousands more. The impact on the environment also affected Native Americans' use of the land. Rivers that had been their waterways and fishing sites were diverted and polluted. Hunting grounds were taken over by settlers. By 1870, California's Native American population had fallen from 150,000 to about 58,000.

Once the easy-to-find gold was gone, American miners began to force Native Americans and miners such as Mexicans and Chinese out of the gold fields to reduce competition. This practice increased after California became a state in 1850.

**Foreign Miners Tax** One of the first acts of the California state legislature was to pass the Foreign Miners Tax, which imposed a tax of $20 a month on miners from other countries. That was more than most could afford to pay. As the tax collectors arrived in the camps, most foreigners left.

Driven from the mines, the Chinese opened shops, restaurants, and laundries. So many Chinese owned businesses in San Francisco that their neighborhood became known as Chinatown, as it still is today.

# CONNECT ↻ to the Essential Question

## How did westward expansion transform the nation?

| EVENTS | | EFFECTS |
|---|---|---|
| **1820 ▼ 1840** | Westward trails move thousands to new territories | Native Americans are displaced |
| | Austin and others colonize Texas | Earlier settlers are pushed aside |
| | Texans revolt against Mexico | Republic of Texas is proclaimed |
| **1841 ▼ 1848** | Texas annexed as a slave state | War with Mexico |
| | Mexican cession | Almost 50% of Mexican territory is acquired by United States |
| **1849 ▼ 1853** | California Gold Rush | California enters Union as a free state |
| | U.S. transcontinental railroad planned | Gadsden Purchase completes expansion of the United States |

**CRITICAL THINKING** **Clarify** Which event fulfilled the nation's "manifest destiny"?

**Economic Effects of Statehood** The port city of San Francisco grew to become a center of banking, manufacturing, shipping, and trade. Its population exploded from around 400 in 1845 to 35,000 in 1850. And, in response to increasing demand for food, Sacramento became the center of a rich farming region.

The population explosion also created a huge demand for water. California's complicated water system is a legacy of the inventiveness and skill of the forty-niners. The miners needed lots of water to pan for gold. (See chart at right.)

On a national level, California's application for statehood created turmoil. Before 1850, there were an equal number of free states and slave states. Southerners feared that because the statehood of California made free states outnumber slave states, Northerners might use their majority to abolish slavery. Conflict over this issue would threaten the very survival of the Union.

 **CAUSES AND EFFECTS** Describe the events that led to California statehood.

## CALIFORNIA WATER RIGHTS

The forty-niners cleverly diverted water for their needs—laying the groundwork for the complex system of dams and canals serving California today. There are three basic categories of water rights in California: Riparian, Appropriative, and Public Trust uses.

**RIPARIAN RIGHTS**
allows a landowner to use the water flowing past his or her property; takes priority over other claims.

**APPROPRIATIVE RIGHTS**
allows use of water channelled well away from its original source; based on forty-niners' "finders keepers" law

**PUBLIC TRUST DOMAIN**
protects fish and wildlife; public recreation areas— such as parks, streams and lakes.

---

**New Jersey Core Curriculum Content Standards** *Review*

 **ONLINE QUIZ**
For test practice, go to
**Interactive Review @ ClassZone.com**

### TERMS & NAMES

**1. Explain the importance of**
- forty-niner
- *Californio*
- Mariano Vallejo
- James Marshall
- California Gold Rush

### USING YOUR READING NOTES

**2. Causes and Effects** Complete the diagram you started at the beginning of this section.

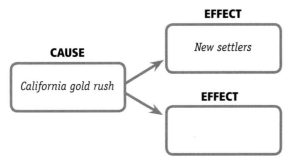

### KEY IDEAS

**3.** Why did the gold rush come to an end?

**4.** Why was California poised to upset the balance of the United States?

### CRITICAL THINKING

**5. Summarize** What were some of the cultural conflicts caused by the influx of new settlers into California?

**6. Evaluate** What impact did the gold rush have on the people who lived in California before 1849?

**7. Recognize Effects** What effect did the gold rush have on the growth of California?

**8. Writing Report** Use the Internet to research women or foreign immigrants during the California gold rush. Write a brief report explaining how they created opportunities and shaped their new communities.

# CALIFORNIA'S GOLD RUSH

Discovery of gold brought thousands of settlers to California from all over the world. What were some of the effects of rapid growth?

## FORTY-NINERS

Water vastly eased the prospectors' work. At first, they waded in streams sloshing water around dirt and gravel in metal pans. Soon they were shoveling gravel into a sluice—a series of long boxes with ridges on the bottom. Rushing water carried lightweight materials along with it. Heavy gold sank to the bottom and was trapped between the ridges. Within two years, forty-niners were damming rivers and erecting simple storage reservoirs for the water so vital to their existence.

## Teens in History

### A YOUNG SETTLER

Elizabeth Keegan arrived in Marysville, California, on September 17, 1852. Two months later, she wrote to her brother and sister still back in St. Louis:

*"See what gold can do (it) brings men from all nations here to this distance shore to make their fortune [and] many go home worse than when they came [but] others have wealth countless wealth . . ."*

### DIVERSITY

Many of the California migrants came to make their fortunes. Most were disappointed, but they stayed to establish thriving communities.

*Chinese miner*

## Activity

## Find the hidden words!

Find the ten words scrambled below—all are connected to the gold rush.

```
B Z R V H B N I  H O N B
N T H I P U S V I Y E N
S M Q P V P A N I R G Z
X L M I N E R U L W O X
D A U S M O R G A L A C
C X X I F N E G E C N L
E X V I C O I E X U B O
R E L T T E S T I V N S
S A W M I L L M M I X A
C R O O W B B J U G P O
```

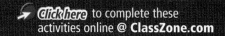

## Chapter Summary

**① Key Idea**
Thousands of adventurers and pioneers followed trails to the West to settle the land and make their fortunes.

**② Key Idea**
Conflicts between American settlers and the government of Mexico led Texas to revolt and win independence from Mexico in 1836.

**③ Key Idea**
Victory in a war with Mexico allowed Americans to expand the nation across the continent.

**④ Key Idea**
The discovery of gold in California in 1848 led to a population increase and statehood.

For detailed Review and Study Notes go to **Interactive Review** @ ClassZone.com

## Name Game

**Use the Terms & Names list to complete each sentence online or on your own paper.**

1. The ⌐Mormons⌐ settled in Utah for religious reasons.

2. _____ discovered the South Pass through the Rocky Mountains.

3. A person who went to California in search of gold was called a _____ .

4. The _____ was a route across the Rocky Mountains.

5. The victorious general at the Battle of the Alamo. _____

6. The _____ was a nickname for the republic of Texas.

7. _____ commanded the Texas Army at the battle of San Jacinto.

8. In the 1820s, people of Mexican heritage living in Texas were called _____ .

9. _____ was elected the eleventh president of the United States in 1844.

10. _____ was the belief that the United States was meant to expand from coast to coast.

A. Santa Fe Trail
B. *Tejanos*
C. Santa Anna
D. Jedediah Smith
E. Manifest Destiny
F. James K. Polk
G. Mormons
H. Jim Beckwourth
I. Forty-Niner
J. Sam Houston
L. California Gold Rush
M. Oregon Trail
N. Lone Star Republic
O. Zachary Taylor
P. Bear Flag Revolt

## Activities

### CROSSWORD PUZZLE

Use the online crossword puzzle to show what you know about western expansion.

**ACROSS**

1. _____ founded American colony in Spanish Texas.

### FLIPCARD

Use the online flipcards to quiz yourself on the terms and names introduced in this chapter.

I was a *Tejano* who fought for Texan independence.

ANSWER
Juan Seguín

## VOCABULARY

**Explain the significance of each of the following.**

1. Mexican cession
2. Sam Houston
3. James K. Polk
4. Brigham Young
5. Mariano Vallejo
6. James Marshall
7. Jedediah Smith
8. Stephen Austin
9. Zachary Taylor
10. Antonio López de Santa Anna

**Choose the best answer from each pair.**

11. Tensions resulted between these people and American settlers in Texas. (*Tejanos/Californios*)

12. This resulted in massive migration to California. (California Gold Rush/Treaty of Guadalupe Hidalgo)

13. American goal reached after post-war settlements with Mexico. (manifest destiny/Mexican cession)

14. William Becknell helped open this trail to pioneers. (Oregon Trail/Santa Fe Trail)

15. This American rebellion was against Mexican rule in California. (Bear Flag Revolt/Gadsden Purchase)

## KEY IDEAS

**1 Trails West 1810–1853 (pages 418–423)**

16. What were three reasons why people moved west?

17. What were the three main trails that led to the West?

**2 The Texas Revolution (pages 426–431)**

18. Why were Texans unhappy with Mexican rule?

19. Why were the Battles of the Alamo and San Jacinto important to the Texas revolution?

**3 The War with Mexico (pages 432–437)**

20. What areas did the United States gain as a result of Americans' belief in manifest destiny?

21. What lands did the United States acquire as a result of the Treaty of Guadalupe Hidalgo?

**4 The California Gold Rush (pages 438–443)**

22. Who were four groups of forty-niners?

23. What were three ways California changed because of the gold rush?

## CRITICAL THINKING

24. **Analyze Causes** How did Mexico's independence from Spain lead to changes in Texas?

25. **Make Inferences** Of the masses of pioneers moving west, in what ways was the Mormon migration unique?

26. **Distinguish Fact from Opinion** How do you think Americans considered Native Americans during the expansion period? How does this relate to the belief in manifest destiny?

27. **Compare and Contrast** Create a table to compare and contrast life in California before and after the Gold Rush.

| | Before Gold Rush | After Gold Rush |
|---|---|---|
| population | Native Americans & Californians | forty-niners & migrants |
| economy | agriculture | |

28. **Make Generalizations** Think about the leaders discussed in this chapter. What characteristics did they have that made them good leaders?

29. **Draw Conclusions** How did the War with Mexico and the California gold rush contributed to the cultural diversity of the United States?

30. **Interpret Graphs** In what year did the population of those living west of the Appalachian Mountains account for about half of the total U.S. population?

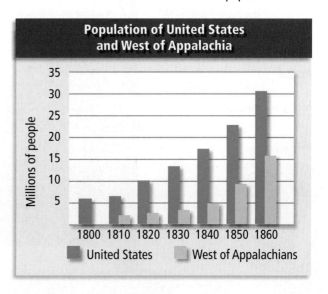

**Population of United States and West of Appalachia**

Millions of people

35
30
25
20
15
10
5

1800 1810 1820 1830 1840 1850 1860

■ United States   ▨ West of Appalachians

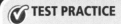
# DOCUMENT-BASED QUESTIONS

## PART 1: Short Answer

Analyze each document, and answer the questions that follow.

### DOCUMENT 1

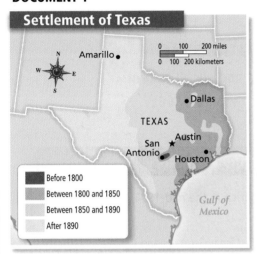

Settlement of Texas

Before 1800
Between 1800 and 1850
Between 1850 and 1890
After 1890

**1.** When did Texas gain the largest expanse of territory?

### DOCUMENT 2

**PRIMARY SOURCE**

❝ The determination of our slaveholding President to prosecute the war, and the probability of his success in wringing from the people men and money to carry it on, is made evident. . . . None seem willing to take their stand for peace at all risks; and all seem willing that the war should be carried on, in some form or other. ❞

—Frederick Douglass in *The North Star*, January 21, 1848

**2.** Why might Douglass have considered the War with Mexico a war against the free states?

## Part 2: Essay

**3.** Using information from the documents, your answers to the questions in Part 1, and your knowledge of U.S. history, write an essay that discusses the American justification for manifest destiny.

## YOU BE THE HISTORIAN

**31. Causes & Effects** Why, after the gold rush ended, did so many people choose to stay in California rather than return to their home state or country?

**32. What If?** Suppose the United States had lost the War with Mexico. How might this have changed the history of the territory gained from Mexico?

**33. Draw Conclusions** How did women and people of different racial, ethnic, or national groups contribute to the California gold rush?

**34. Summarize** How did the War with Mexico escalate the disagreement over slavery?

**35. Connect Geography & History** How did the opening of the West affect the economy of that region?

**36.** **Connect** *to* **Today** Large numbers of settlers moved west in the 1840s and after. What factors cause people to move from one part of the country to another today?

Answer the
## ESSENTIAL QUESTION

**How did westward expansion transform the nation?**

**Written Response** Write a two- to three-paragraph response to the Essential Question. Be sure to consider the key ideas of each section as well as the most important factors that led to the expansion of the United States. Use the Response Rubric below to guide your thinking and writing.

### Response Rubric
**A strong response will include**

• major discoveries and events that led to westward expansion
• discussion of manifest destiny and political issues
• analysis of key leaders
• knowledge of geography and territorial holdings

1. The Hopes of Immigrants
2. Reforming American Society
3. Abolition and Women's Rights

# A New Spirit of Change

## 1830–1860

 **ESSENTIAL QUESTION**

How did immigration and social reform change the nation in the mid-1800s?

---

**CONNECT** ⟳ **Geography & History**

How did immigration affect America in the mid-1800s?

Think about:

**1** how many immigrants came just from Germany and Ireland

**2** the variety of cultures and beliefs they brought to America

**3** where most immigrants settled—Northeastern cities and the Midwest

This early-19th-century image shows stagecoaches in lower Manhattan.

An Irish famine memorial in Westchester County, N.Y.

**1840** The World Anti-Slavery Convention is held in London.

## 1830

**1831** *The Liberator*, an abolitionist newspaper, begins publication.

**1839** Mississippi passes the first U.S. law giving women rights to their own property and wages.

**1843** Dorothea Dix asks the Massachusetts legislature to improve care for the mentally ill.

▼

**Effect** New laws create widespread changes in institutional care.

# Emigration to America *1831–1860*

*Click here* to preview the Era of
Reform @ClassZone.com

**GERMANY**
1,538,747

**NORWAY and
SWEDEN**
36,035

**IRELAND**
940,260

**GREAT BRITAIN**
339,303

*North
Sea*

*ATLANTIC
OCEAN*

**FRANCE**
199,195

**SWITZERLAND**
34,476

A 1978 stamp honoring
Harriet Tubman

*Harriet Tubman*

Black Heritage USA 13c

Women's-rights advocate
Amelia Bloomer promoted
comfortable clothing for
women.

**1848** Women demand
rights at the Seneca Falls
Convention.

**1860**

**1849** Harriet Tubman escapes
from slavery.

▼

**Effect** Tubman aids runaway
slaves on the Underground Railroad.

Abraham
Lincoln is
elected
president.

## ▶ Key Ideas

**BEFORE, YOU LEARNED**

In colonial times, waves of immigrants created a diverse society in America.

**NOW YOU WILL LEARN**

In the mid-1800s, millions of Europeans came to the United States hoping to build a better life.

## ▶ Vocabulary

**TERMS & NAMES**

**"push" factor** a reason or force that causes people to leave their native land

**"pull" factor** a reason or force that causes people to choose to move to a new place

**Know-Nothing Party** political party in the United States during the 1850s that was against recent immigrants and Roman Catholics

**Visual Vocabulary**
Know-Nothing Party flag

**BACKGROUND VOCABULARY**

**emigrant** person who leaves a country

**immigrant** person who settles in a new country

**steerage** the cheapest deck on a ship

**famine** (FAM•ihn) severe food shortage leading to starvation

**prejudice** (PREHJ•uh•dihs) a negative opinion that is not based on facts

**nativist** native-born American who wanted to eliminate foreign influence

## ▶ Reading Strategy

Re-create the diagram shown at right. As you read and respond to the **KEY QUESTIONS**, use the center oval to record the main idea, and use the outer ovals to note important details. Add ovals or start a new diagram as needed.

 **See Skillbuilder Handbook, page R4.**

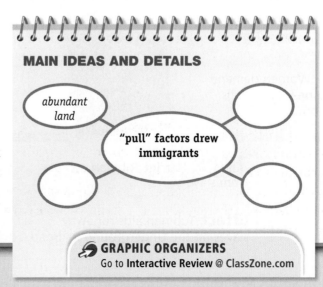

**MAIN IDEAS AND DETAILS**

*abundant land*

**"pull" factors drew immigrants**

**GRAPHIC ORGANIZERS**
Go to **Interactive Review** @ ClassZone.com

# The Hopes of Immigrants

 **6.4.F.1.** Describe the political, economic, and social changes in New Jersey and American society preceding the Civil War, including the early stages of industrialization, the growth of cities, and the political, legal, and social controversies surrounding the expansion of slavery.

## One American's Story

In 1830, English weaver John Downe became an **emigrant**, or person who leaves a country. Downe left England alone to work in New York, where he awaited his family's arrival.

**PRIMARY SOURCE**

❝ You will find a few inconveniences in crossing the Atlantic, but it will not be long, and when that is over, all is over, for I know you will like America.

America is not like England, for here no man thinks of himself as your superior. . . . This is a country where a man can stand as a man, and where he can enjoy the fruits of his own exertions [work], with rational liberty to its fullest extent. ❞

—John Downe, letter to his wife, August 12, 1830

*The Bay and Harbor of New York,* by Samuel B. Waugh

Emigrants—mainly from Europe—flocked to America during the mid-1800s. Like Downe, most left hoping to build a better life. After arrival in America, they became **immigrants**, or people who settle in a new country.

## Patterns of Immigration

🔻 **KEY QUESTION**  What attracted people to America in the mid-1800s?

Most immigrants endured hardships to reach America. Although some brought their families, many men, like Downe, went through the difficult journey alone. Most immigrants made the ocean voyage in **steerage**, the cheapest deck on a ship. In steerage, conditions were crowded and unhealthy. Many passengers became ill or died on the journey.

**Why People Migrated** What drew immigrants to America? Historians talk about **"push" factors** and **"pull" factors**. These forces push people out of their native land and pull them toward a new place. One push factor was population growth—a boom in population had made Europe overcrowded. Another push factor was crop failure. Poor harvests brought widespread hunger. Three main pull factors lured people to America:

- freedom
- economic opportunity
- abundant land

**Germans Pursue Economic Opportunity** The Germans were the largest immigrant group of the 1800s. They settled in cities as well as on farms and the frontier. Many were drawn to the fertile and newly available lands of Wisconsin, which was organized as a territory in 1836. Thousands more formed German-speaking communities in Texas.

Germans opened businesses as bakers, butchers, carpenters, printers, and tailors. Some, like John Jacob Bausch and Henry Lomb, achieved great success. In 1853, they started a firm to make eyeglasses and other lenses. Their company became the world's largest lens maker. Some German immigrants were Jews, many of whom worked as traveling salespeople. They brought pins, needles, pots—and news—to frontier homes and mining camps. In time, some opened their own stores. Many German Jews settled in cities.

German immigrants strongly influenced American culture. Many things we think of as originating in America came from Germany, such as kindergartens, gymnasiums, the Christmas tree, and the hamburger and frankfurter.

## COMPARING  *Push and Pull Factors*

The "push" factors of immigration pushed millions of people out of Europe and elsewhere in the 1800s. "Pull" factors drew many of them to the United States.

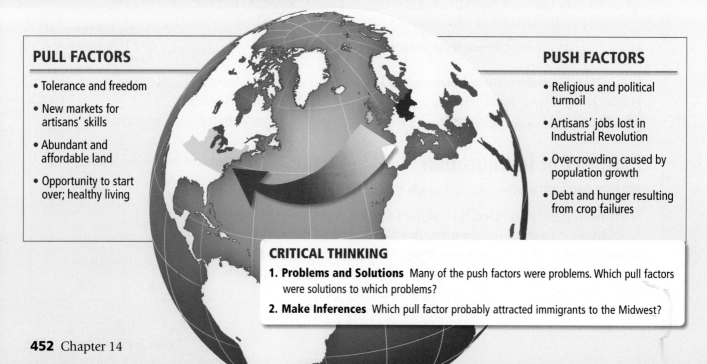

**PULL FACTORS**

- Tolerance and freedom
- New markets for artisans' skills
- Abundant and affordable land
- Opportunity to start over; healthy living

**PUSH FACTORS**

- Religious and political turmoil
- Artisans' jobs lost in Industrial Revolution
- Overcrowding caused by population growth
- Debt and hunger resulting from crop failures

**CRITICAL THINKING**

1. **Problems and Solutions** Many of the push factors were problems. Which pull factors were solutions to which problems?

2. **Make Inferences** Which pull factor probably attracted immigrants to the Midwest?

**Immigrants Move Westward** In the mid-1800s, public land in America was sold for $1.25 an acre. The promise of cheap land lured thousands of European immigrants, especially to territories in the Midwest.

Thousands of Scandinavians fled poverty in their homeland and moved to Minnesota and Wisconsin. Like Scandinavia, these states had forests, lakes, and cold winters. A high proportion of Scandinavian immigrants became farmers. Meanwhile, land shortages in Great Britain motivated thousands of British farmers to seek new opportunities in America. They, too, helped to make the Midwest a region known for farming. Many British artisans who felt squeezed out by the factory system also chose to emigrate.

The mid-1800s brought another major immigrant group: the Chinese. Most of the first Chinese immigrants went to California after the 1849 gold rush. By 1852, there were an estimated 25,000 Chinese in California. Most were miners, but some worked in agriculture and construction.

**The Irish Flee Starvation** Most Irish immigrants were Catholic. Protestant Britain had ruled Ireland for centuries—and controlled the Catholic majority by denying them rights. Irish Catholics could not vote, hold office, own land, or go to school. Because of the poverty produced by Britain's rule, some Irish had emigrated to America in the early 1800s.

In 1845, a disease attacked Ireland's main food crop, the potato. This caused a severe food shortage, or **famine** (FAM•in). The Irish Potato Famine killed 1 million people and forced many to emigrate. By 1855, an estimated 1.5 million people had left Ireland. Most went to North America, although some settled in Australia and Great Britain.

**Connect** *to the* **World**

**The Potato Famine**
In 1846, an Irish newspaper described famine victims "frantically rushing from their home and country, not with the idea of making fortunes in other lands, but to fly from a scene of suffering and death…"

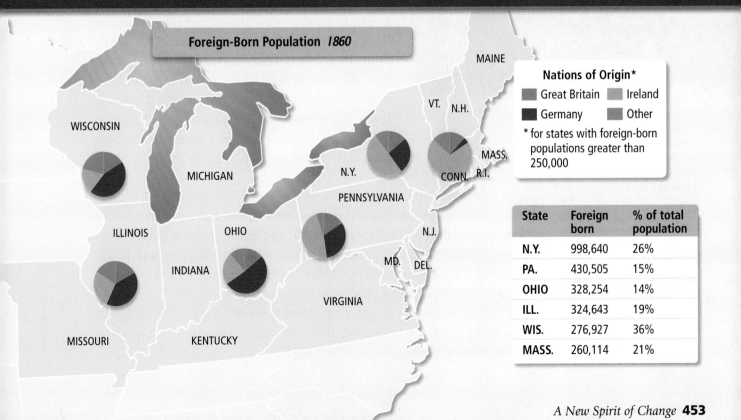

**Foreign-Born Population** *1860*

MAINE

**Nations of Origin***

- Great Britain
- Ireland
- Germany
- Other

*\* for states with foreign-born populations greater than 250,000*

WISCONSIN

VT. N.H.

MICHIGAN

N.Y. CONN. R.I. MASS.

PENNSYLVANIA

ILLINOIS OHIO N.J.

MD. DEL.

INDIANA

VIRGINIA

MISSOURI KENTUCKY

| State | Foreign born | % of total population |
|-------|--------------|------------------------|
| N.Y. | 998,640 | 26% |
| PA. | 430,505 | 15% |
| OHIO | 328,254 | 14% |
| ILL. | 324,643 | 19% |
| WIS. | 276,927 | 36% |
| MASS. | 260,114 | 21% |

*A New Spirit of Change* **453**

In America, Irish farmers became city-dwellers. Arriving with little or no savings, many of these immigrants had to settle in the port cities where their ships had docked. By 1850, the Irish made up one-fourth of the population in Boston, New York, Philadelphia, and Baltimore.

The uneducated Irish immigrants came with few skills and had to take low-paying, back-breaking jobs. Irish women took in washing or worked as servants. The men built canals and railroads across America. So many Irish men died doing this dangerous work that people said there was "an Irish-man buried under every [railroad] tie." The Irish competed with free African Americans for the jobs that nobody else wanted. Both groups had few other choices in America in the 1800s.

▲ **SUMMARIZE** Explain what attracted immigrants to America in the mid-1800s.

During the mid-1800s, thousands of new immigrants settled in the crowded New York City neighborhood known as Five Points.

# America Adjusts to Immigrants

▼ **KEY QUESTION** What was life like for the new immigrants?

The huge numbers of immigrants caused over-crowding in the cities. This population explosion alarmed many Americans. However, some formed organizations to help immigrants adapt to their new country. Soon, like all immigrants before them, the new arrivals began to influence American society and culture.

**Life for the New Arrivals** Immigrants flocked to American cities. So did many native-born Americans, who left rural areas hoping to make a better living in new manufacturing jobs. The North, with its higher wages and greater economic opportunity, attracted many more immigrants than the South. Because the South was a plantation economy based on slave labor, it offered fewer opportunities for free laborers. Between 1800 and 1830, New York's population jumped from 60,489 to 202,589. Both St. Louis and Cincinnati doubled their populations every 10 years between 1800 and 1850.

Rapid urban growth brought problems. Without enough space for new-comers, greedy landlords packed tenants into buildings. Cramped living quarters allowed little sunlight and fresh air, and outdoor toilets overflowed, spreading disease. In such depressing urban neighborhoods, crime flourished. Cities were unprepared for these problems. Most lacked a public police force, fire department, and adequate sewers.

Most immigrant groups set up aid societies to assist newcomers from their country. Many city politicians also offered to help immigrants find housing and work, hoping to earn votes in exchange.

**Opposition to Immigration** Some native-born Americans believed that immigrants were too foreign to learn American ways. Others feared that immigrants might outnumber natives. Immigrants faced anger and **prejudice**—a negative opinion that is not based on facts. For example, some Protestants believed that Catholics threatened democracy. Those Protestants feared that the Pope, the head of the Roman Catholic Church, was plotting to overthrow democracy in America.

People who want to eliminate foreign influence are known as **nativists**. In the mid-1800s, some American nativists refused to hire immigrants and put up signs like "No Irish need apply." In cities such as New York and Boston, nativists formed a secret society. Members promised not to vote for Catholics or immigrants running for political office. If asked about their society, they said, "I know nothing about it."

In the 1850s, nativists started a political party called the **Know-Nothing Party**. It wanted to ban Catholics and the foreign-born from holding office. It also called for a cut in immigration and a 21-year-wait to become an American citizen. The Know-Nothings did get six governors elected. But their Northern and Southern branches couldn't agree on the issue of slavery, and they disappeared quickly as a national party.

A nineteenth-century advertisement for "Know Nothing Soap"
**What might the Native Americans represent?**

 **MAKE GENERALIZATIONS** Describe what life was like for new immigrants.

---

**New Jersey Core Curriculum Content Standards _Review_**

 **ONLINE QUIZ**
For test practice, go to
**Interactive Review** @ ClassZone.com

**TERMS & NAMES**

**1.** Explain the importance of
- "push" factor
- "pull" factor
- Know-Nothing Party

**USING YOUR READING NOTES**

**2. Main Ideas and Details** Use the diagram you started at the beginning of the section to record details about immigration. Note which groups came and why, and where they settled.

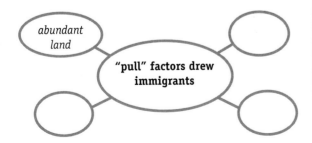

**KEY IDEAS**

**3.** What difficulties did immigrants face in the United States?

**4.** How did the arrival of immigrants affect U.S. cities?

**CRITICAL THINKING**

**5. Make Inferences** Why were immigrants willing to endure the hardships of coming to America?

**6. Analyze Primary Sources** In 1841, British novelist Charles Dickens described the huts in which some Irish railroad workers in New York lived:

> **❝** The best were poor protection from the weather; the worst let in the wind and rain . . . some had neither door nor window; some had nearly fallen down. **❞**

Do you think these immigrants were better off in America than in Ireland? Explain.

**7.** **Writing** **Letter** Research the Irish Potato Famine. Write a letter to friends in America that describes life in Ireland and why you want to join them in America.

*A New Spirit of Change* **455**

## ▶ Key Ideas

**BEFORE, YOU LEARNED**

In the mid-1800s, millions of Europeans came to the United States hoping to build a better life.

**NOW YOU WILL LEARN**

A 19th-century religious revival launched movements to reform education and society.

## ▶ Vocabulary

**TERMS & NAMES**

**Second Great Awakening** renewal of religious faith in the 1790s and early 1800s

**temperance movement** campaign to stop the drinking of alcohol

**Shaker** member of a Christian sect that practiced communal living and did not allow marriage and childbearing

**Horace Mann** reformer who advocated improving education

**Dorothea Dix** reformer who was a pioneer in the movement for better treatment of the mentally ill

**BACKGROUND VOCABULARY**

**labor union** group of workers who band together to seek better working conditions

**strike** to stop work to demand better working conditions

**REVIEW**

**evangelicalism** the doctrine, or belief, that each person can experience a sudden conversion and experience a new spiritual relationship with God

## ▶ Reading Strategy

Re-create the problem-solution chart at right. As you read and respond to the **KEY QUESTIONS**, use the chart to organize the problems reformers identified in society and the solutions they proposed.

 **See Skillbuilder Handbook, page R9.**

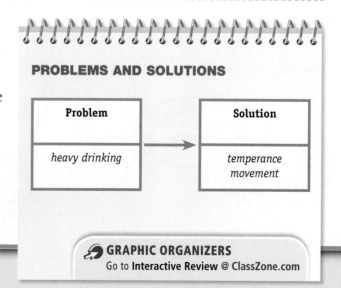

**PROBLEMS AND SOLUTIONS**

| Problem | | Solution |
|---------|---|----------|
| *heavy drinking* | → | *temperance movement* |

**☁ GRAPHIC ORGANIZERS**
Go to **Interactive Review** @ ClassZone.com

# Reforming American Society

 **6.4.F.1.** Describe the political, economic, and social changes in New Jersey and American society preceding the Civil War, . . . .
**6.4.F.2.** Discuss American cultural, religious, and social reform movements in the antebellum period . . . .

## One American's Story

In the mid-1800s, many Americans had ideas for creating a better society in their new nation. Mary Lyon, the founder of Mount Holyoke Seminary in Massachusetts, advocated college-level education for women. Seeing the first building go up at her school gave Lyon a sense of awe.

### PRIMARY SOURCE

❝ . . . The stones and brick and mortar speak a language which vibrates through my very soul. I have indeed lived to see the time when a body of gentlemen have ventured to lay the corner stone of an edifice [building] which . . . will be an institution for the education of females. . . . This will be an era in female education. ❞

—Mary Lyon, letter, October 7, 1836

Mary Lyon

In this section, you will learn how individuals like Lyon called on Americans to reform, or improve, themselves and their society.

## A Spirit of Revival

🔻 **KEY QUESTION** How did religion and philosophy encourage people to improve society?

In the early 19th century, a reform movement swept through American society. This movement was inspired mainly by a religious revival, like the one that had changed American life a century before.

**The Second Great Awakening** The renewal of religious faith in the 1790s and early 1800s is called the **Second Great Awakening**. Unlike Puritans, who believed that only some people would be saved, revivalist preachers insisted that anyone could choose salvation. This idea appealed to Americans' sense of optimism and equality, and offered a new interpretation of Christianity.

Revival meetings—emotionally charged events in which religious leaders hoped to attract followers—spread quickly across the country. Many groups, such as Baptists and Methodists, gained converts during this time. Settlers in the West eagerly awaited revivalist preachers like Peter Cartwright, who spent more than 60 years preaching on the frontier. In Eastern cities, Charles Grandison Finney held large revival meetings. He preached that selfishness was sin and that faith led people to help others.

The spread of evangelical ideas awakened a spirit of reform. Many people began to believe that they could help to right the wrongs of the world.

Temperance pledges often featured inspiring pictures and mottoes. **What does the main picture suggest about the benefits of giving up alcohol?**

**Temperance** Heavy drinking was common in the early 1800s. One response to this problem was the **temperance movement**—a campaign to stop the drinking of alcohol. Some men spent most of their wages on alcohol, leaving their families poor. As a result, many women joined the movement.

Temperance workers handed out pamphlets urging people to stop drinking and gave plays dramatizing the evils of alcohol. They asked people to sign a pledge to not use alcohol. By 1838, a million had signed.

In 1851, Maine banned the sale of liquor. By 1855, 13 other states had passed similar laws. Most of these laws were later repealed. Still, the movement to ban alcohol remained strong, even into the 20th century.

**Creating Ideal Societies** Some people wanted society to start anew. They aimed to build an ideal society, called a utopia.

Religion led to some utopian experiments. The **Shakers** followed the beliefs of English immigrant Ann Lee, who preached that people should live in faith-centered communities. Shakers vowed not to marry or have children. They shared all their goods with each other and treated men and women as equals.

People called them Shakers because they shook with emotion during church services. Shakers set up communities in New York, New England, and on the frontier. Because they did not marry, Shakers depended on converts and adoption to keep their communities going. In the 1840s, Shakers had 6,000 members. In 2005, only four remained.

Not all utopian communities were based on religion. Two well-known experiments in communal living took place in New Harmony, Indiana, and Brook Farm, Massachusetts. However, these communities experienced conflicts and financial difficulties. They ended after only a few years.

▲ **EVALUATE** Explain how religion and philosophy encouraged people to try to improve society.

# Workers' Rights

**KEY QUESTION** How did the labor movement try to improve working conditions?

Factory conditions were often unhealthy, and management could be unjust. By the 1830s, American workers had begun to demand improvements.

**Factory Life** Most factory workers labored 12 or 14 hours a day for six days a week. A typical workday began at five o'clock in the morning. It was not unusual for workers to spend most of the workday in dark, hot, crowded rooms with air so dirty that it was difficult to breathe. In the 1830s, many workers began to call for a ten-hour workday.

Hoping to increase profits, factory owners sometimes cut workers' pay and forced them to increase their pace. It was also legal to pay women and children lower wages than men in similar jobs. Partly for this reason, the majority of workers at the mills in Lowell, Massachusetts, were young women. Some of these women became active in the fight for workers' rights.

**Organizing for Better Conditions** The young women mill workers in Lowell, Massachusetts, started a **labor union**—a group of workers who band together to seek better working conditions. In 1836, the mill owners raised the rent of the company-owned boarding houses where the women lived. About 1,500 women went on **strike**, stopping work to demand better conditions. Eleven-year-old Harriet Hanson helped lead the strikers.

### PRIMARY SOURCE

**❝** I . . . started on ahead, saying, . . . 'I don't care what you do, I am going to turn out, whether anyone else does or not,' and I marched out, and was followed by the others. As I looked back at the long line that followed me, I was more proud than I have ever been since. **❞**

—Harriet Hanson, quoted in Howard Zinn's *A People's History of the United States*

In 1835 and 1836, 140 strikes took place in the eastern United States alone. Some striking workers compared themselves to the American patriots who had fought for freedom in the Revolutionary War. In 1860, one group of workers began a strike on Washington's birthday.

Then the Panic of 1837 brought hard times economically. Jobs were scarce, and workers were afraid to cause trouble. The young labor movement fell apart. Even so, workers achieved a few goals. For example, in 1840 President Martin Van Buren ordered a ten-hour workday for government workers.

**SUMMARIZE** Explain how the labor movement tried to improve working conditions.

**Connect** *to the* **World**

By the 1830s, a labor movement had gathered strength in Great Britain. Like the American labor movement, it sought better conditions and a shorter workday.

About 800 women shoemakers march during a strike in Lynn, Massachusetts, in 1860.

## History Makers

### Horace Mann 1796–1859

Mann is remembered as "the father of the American common [public] school." He believed that education was "the balance wheel of the social machinery." As secretary of the Massachusetts board of education, Mann advanced his cause by reporting to the state legislature, lecturing widely, and writing for various publications. His efforts raised awareness of the value of public education. They also led to dramatic changes in Massachusetts and across the country, with increased public spending on education, higher teacher salaries, better books for students, advanced teacher training, and—ultimately—a more educated population.

**COMPARING** *Leaders*

**Compare and Contrast** As you read through the chapter, look for other reform leaders. Compare Mann's efforts to promote his cause with those of other leaders in this chapter.

 **ONLINE BIOGRAPHY**  For more on Horace Mann, go to the **Research & Writing Center** @ ClassZone.com

# Social Reform

**KEY QUESTION** What aspects of society did reformers try to change?

By the 1830s, the religious revival had sparked the rise of a reform movement. Social reformers campaigned to improve education, establish mental hospitals, and improve prisons.

**Improving Education** In the 1830s, Americans began to demand better schools. Massachusetts set up the first state board of education in 1837. Its leader, **Horace Mann**, called public education "the great equalizer" and argued for improving public educational opportunities. By 1850, most Northern states had opened public elementary schools.

Boston opened the first public high school in 1821. A few other Northern cities soon did the same. In addition, churches and other groups founded hundreds of private colleges in the following decades. Many were located in states carved from the Northwest Territory. These included Antioch and Oberlin Colleges in Ohio, Notre Dame in Indiana, and Northwestern University in Illinois.

**Expanding Opportunities** Women could not attend most colleges. An exception was Oberlin—the first college to accept women. From its founding in 1833, Oberlin admitted students regardless of race or sex. Until the late 1800s, however, it was rare for a woman to attend college.

African Americans also faced obstacles to getting an education. This was especially true in the South. Teaching an enslaved person to read was illegal in most of the Southern states. Enslaved African Americans who tried to learn to read were brutally punished. Even in the North, African-American children were barred from most public schools.

Few colleges accepted African Americans. The first African-American man to receive a college degree was Alexander Twilight in 1823. He later became a Vermont state legislator. Mary Jane Patterson was the first African-American woman to earn a college degree. She graduated from Oberlin in 1862 and became a teacher.

**Care for the Needy** Some reformers sought to improve care for society's most vulnerable members. In 1841 **Dorothea Dix**, a reformer from Boston, was teaching at a women's jail when she discovered that some women were locked up simply because they were mentally ill. Dix learned that the mentally ill often received no treatment, and that some were chained and beaten. Dix lectured widely in the United States and Europe to promote better care. Her efforts led to publicly funded mental hospitals in a number of states.

Some reformers worked to improve life for people with other disabilities. In 1817 in Hartford, Connecticut, educator Thomas H. Gallaudet started the first free school for deaf children in the United States. Reformer Samuel G. Howe directed the New England Asylum for the Blind (now the Perkins School for the Blind), which opened in Boston in 1832.

Reformers also tried to improve prisons. In the early 1800s, debtors, lifelong criminals, and children were put in the same cells. Reformers demanded that children go to special jails. They also called for adult prisoners to be rehabilitated, or prepared to live useful lives after their release.

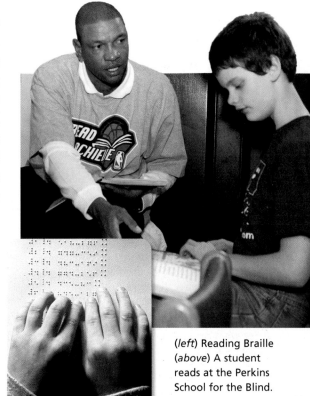

(*left*) Reading Braille (*above*) A student reads at the Perkins School for the Blind.

 **PROBLEMS AND SOLUTIONS** List the problems in society that reformers worked to change.

---

**New Jersey Core Curriculum Content Standards** *Review*

🖰 **ONLINE QUIZ**
For test practice, go to
**Interactive Review** @ ClassZone.com

### TERMS & NAMES

1. Explain the importance of
   - Second Great Awakening
   - temperance movement
   - Shakers
   - Horace Mann
   - Dorothea Dix

### USING YOUR READING NOTES

2. **Problems and Solutions** Complete the chart you started at the beginning of the section. Show the problems reformers identified in society and the solutions they proposed.

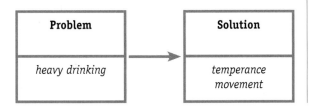

| Problem | | Solution |
|---------|---|----------|
| *heavy drinking* |  | *temperance movement* |

### KEY IDEAS

3. How did the Second Great Awakening influence the reform movement?

4. How did women contribute to social reform?

### CRITICAL THINKING

5. **Main Ideas and Details** How did government work for better schools?

6. **Summarize** What obstacles faced women and African Americans who wanted an education?

7. **Causes and Effects** What factors might have caused utopian communities to fail?

8. **Art** Imagine you are a reformer in the mid-1800s. Choose one of the problems that you read about in this section and make a poster that encourages citizens to become involved and make positive changes.

# Report to the Massachusetts Legislature

**SETTING THE STAGE** After traveling to several places where the mentally ill were kept in terrible conditions, Dorothea Dix wrote a report describing what she had seen. In 1843, she presented her report to lawmakers.

## Advocate of the Helpless

In earlier times, the word *idiotic* did not mean "stupid." It was used to describe someone who was mentally disabled.

**1. For what groups of people is Dix pleading for help?**

## History Makers

### Dorothea Dix
**1802–1887**

Dix began teaching at 14 and opened her own school at 19. Later, she turned her skills as an educator toward improving society. Her bold activism earned her the nickname "Dragon Dix."

Gentlemen: . . . I come to present the strong claims of suffering humanity. I come to place before the Legislature of Massachusetts the condition of the miserable, the desolate, the outcast. I come as the **advocate**[1] of helpless, forgotten, insane, and idiotic men and women; of beings sunk to a condition from which the most unconcerned would start with real horror; of beings wretched in our prisons, and more wretched in our **almshouses**.[2] I must confine myself to a few examples, but am ready to furnish other and more complete details, if required.

I proceed, gentlemen, briefly to call your attention to the present state of insane persons confined within this **Commonwealth**,[3] in cages, closets, cellars, stalls, pens! Chained, naked, beaten with rods, and lashed into obedience.

I offer the following extracts from my notebook and journal.

Springfield: In the jail, one lunatic woman, furiously mad, a state **pauper**,[4] improperly situated, both in regard to the prisoners, the keepers, and herself. It is a case of extreme self-forgetfulness and oblivion to all the decencies of life … In the almshouse of the same town is a woman apparently only needing **judicious**[5] care and some well-chosen employment to make it unnecessary to confine her in solitude in a dreary unfurnished room. Her appeals for employment and companionship are most touching, but the mistress replied "she had no time to attend to her."

Lincoln: A woman in a cage. Medford: One idiotic subject chained, and one in a close stall for seventeen years. Pepperell: One often doubly chained, hand and foot; another violent; several peaceable now. Brookfield: One man caged, comfortable. Granville: One often closely confined, now losing the use of his limbs from want of exercise.

---

1. **advocate:** a person who promotes a cause.
2. **almshouses:** homes for poor people.
3. **Commonwealth:** a term used to refer to certain U.S. states; in this case, Massachusetts.
4. **pauper:** a person who lives on the state's charity.
5. **judicious:** wise and careful.

Charlemont: One man caged. Savoy: One man caged. Lenox: Two in the jail, against whose unfit condition there the jailer protests.

Dedham: The insane **disadvantageously**[6] placed in the jail. In the almshouse, two females in stalls, situated in the main building, lie in wooden bunks filled with straw; always shut up. One of these subjects is supposed curable. The overseers of the poor have declined giving her a trial at the hospital, as I was informed, on account of expense.

Besides the above, I have seen many who, part of the year, are chained or caged. The use of cages is all but universal. Hardly a town but can refer to some not distant period of using them; chains are less common; **negligences**[7] frequent; willful abuse less frequent than sufferings proceeding from ignorance, or want of consideration. I encountered during the last three months many poor creatures wandering reckless and unprotected through the country. . . . But I cannot **particularize**.[8] In traversing the state, I have found hundreds of insane persons in every variety of circumstance and condition, many whose situation could not and need not be improved; a less number, but that very large, whose lives are the saddest pictures of human suffering and degradation.

I give a few illustrations; but description fades before reality. . . .
Men of Massachusetts, I beg, I implore, I demand pity and protection for these of my suffering, outraged sex. . . . Become the benefactors of your race, the just guardians of the solemn rights you hold in trust. Raise up the fallen, **succor**[9] the desolate, restore the outcast, defend the helpless, and for your eternal and great reward receive the benediction, "Well done, good and faithful servants, become rulers over many things!"

------------------------------------------------------------------

6. **disadvantageously:** harmfully.
7. **negligences:** careless actions.
8. **particularize:** to name in detail.
9. **succor:** to help in a time of need.

## I Have Seen Many

Notice that Dix cites evidence from many different towns.

**2. Why do you think she includes so many specific details in her report?**

## Men of Massachusetts

When Dix says "Men of Massachusetts," she is still speaking to the members of the state legislature.

**3. What does Dix want the Massachusetts Legislature to do?**

## DOCUMENT-BASED QUESTIONS
### Short Answer
1. On what evidence did Dorothea Dix base her report about "suffering humanity"?
2. Whom did Dix ask to help improve the care of the mentally ill?

### Extended Answer
3. What do Dix's efforts have in common with other social reform efforts discussed in this chapter?

### ▶ Key Ideas

**BEFORE, YOU LEARNED**

A 19th-century religious revival launched movements to reform education and society.

**NOW YOU WILL LEARN**

The social campaigns to gain freedom for enslaved persons and equality for women were closely linked.

### ▶ Vocabulary

**TERMS & NAMES**

**abolition** the movement to stop slavery

**Frederick Douglass** abolitionist and journalist who became an influential lecturer in the North and abroad

**Sojourner Truth** abolitionist and feminist who spoke against slavery and for the rights of women

**Underground Railroad** a series of escape routes used by slaves escaping the South

**Harriet Tubman** conductor on the Underground Railroad who led enslaved people to freedom

**Elizabeth Cady Stanton** reformer who helped organize the first women's rights convention

**Seneca Falls Convention** the first women's rights convention, held in Seneca Falls, New York

**BACKGROUND VOCABULARY**

**suffrage** the right to vote

Visual Vocabulary
Seneca Falls Convention

### ▶ Reading Strategy

Re-create the diagram shown at right. As you read and respond to the **KEY QUESTIONS**, use the diagram to note important issues and their effects. Add boxes or start a new diagram as needed.

 See Skillbuilder Handbook, page R7.

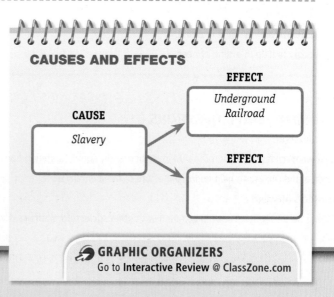

**CAUSES AND EFFECTS**

CAUSE

Slavery

EFFECT

Underground Railroad

EFFECT

 GRAPHIC ORGANIZERS
Go to **Interactive Review** @ ClassZone.com

# Abolition and Women's Rights

**6.4.F.1.** Describe the political, economic, and social changes in New Jersey and American society preceding the Civil War, . . . .
**6.4.F.2.** Discuss American cultural, religious, and social reform movements in the antebellum period . . . .

## One American's Story

African-American poet and reformer Frances Ellen Watkins Harper often wrote about the suffering of enslaved persons, including enslaved mothers.

### PRIMARY SOURCE

❝ They tear him from her circling arms,
Her last and fond embrace.
Oh! never more may her sad eyes
Gaze on his mournful face.
No marvel, then, these bitter shrieks
Disturb the listening air:
She is a mother, and her heart
Is breaking in despair. ❞

—Frances Ellen Watkins Harper, "The Slave Mother"

Frances Ellen Watkins Harper

Harper toured the North as an antislavery speaker. She also spoke out for women's rights and against racism. As this section explains, many individuals in the mid-1800s demanded equal rights for African Americans and women.

## Abolitionists Protest Slavery

🔻 **KEY QUESTION** What methods did abolitionists use to fight against slavery?

In the late 1600s, the Quakers had been among the first to take a stand against slavery. However, **abolition**, the movement to end slavery, did not begin until the late 1700s. During the Revolution, Northern states began passing antislavery laws. By 1804, almost all the Northern states had abolished slavery, and Congress banned the importation of African slaves into the United States starting in 1807. Abolitionists then demanded a law ending slavery in the South, where the economy depended on slave labor. The stage was set for an emotional debate that would tear the nation apart.

**Demanding an End to Slavery** Abolitionists were bold in their statements and reactions to their beliefs were just as fierce. David Walker, a free African American in Boston, printed a pamphlet in 1829 urging slaves to revolt. Copies of the pamphlet appeared in the South. This angered slaveholders. Shortly afterward, Walker died; some believed he had been poisoned.

Some Northern whites also fought slavery. In 1831, William Lloyd Garrison began publishing an abolitionist newspaper, *The Liberator*, in Boston. Of his antislavery stand, he wrote, "I will not retreat a single inch—AND I WILL BE HEARD." Many hated his views. In 1835, a mob in Boston grabbed Garrison and dragged him toward a park to hang him. He was rescued by the mayor.

Two famous abolitionists were Southerners who grew up on a plantation. Sisters Sarah and Angelina Grimké believed that slavery was morally wrong. They moved to the North and spoke out against slavery, even though women at the time were not supposed to lecture in public. Theodore Weld, Angelina's husband, led a campaign to send antislavery petitions to Congress. Proslavery congressmen passed a gag rule to prevent the reading of petitions in Congress.

President John Quincy Adams ignored the gag rule and read the petitions. He also introduced an amendment to abolish slavery. Proslavery congressmen tried to stop him. Such efforts, however, weakened the proslavery cause by showing them to be opponents of free speech. Adams also defended a group of enslaved Africans who had rebelled on the slave ship *Amistad*. He successfully argued their case before the U.S. Supreme Court in 1841, and the Africans returned home immediately.

**Eyewitness to Slavery** Two powerful abolitionist speakers, **Frederick Douglass** and **Sojourner Truth**, spoke from their own experiences of having been enslaved. Douglass had a long career as a lecturer for the Massachusetts Anti-Slavery Society.

People who opposed abolition spread rumors that the brilliant speaker could never have been a slave. To prove them wrong, in 1845 Douglass published an autobiography that vividly narrated his slave experiences. Afterward, he feared recapture by his owner, so he left America for a two-year speaking tour of Great Britain and Ireland. When Douglass returned, he bought his freedom.

## History Makers

### Frederick Douglass   1818–1895

When lecturing on abolition, Douglass—an escaped slave—was often introduced as "a piece of property." Douglass was a popular and eloquent speaker who had few equals on the lecture circuit. Abolitionists welcomed his graphic descriptions of slave life as a way to publicize the injustice of slavery. As his popularity grew, Douglass began to introduce the topic of racial discrimination in the North. In addition to lecturing, Douglass published his autobiography and an abolitionist newspaper, *The North Star*. He said that in the North, people "are far wealthier than any plantation owner—they are rich with freedom."

### CRITICAL THINKING

1. **Draw Conclusions** How might Douglass's life experiences have made him a persuasive speaker?

2. **Make Inferences** What did Douglass mean by Northerners being "rich with freedom"?

 **ONLINE BIOGRAPHY** For more on Frederick Douglass, go to the **Research & Writing Center** @ ClassZone.com

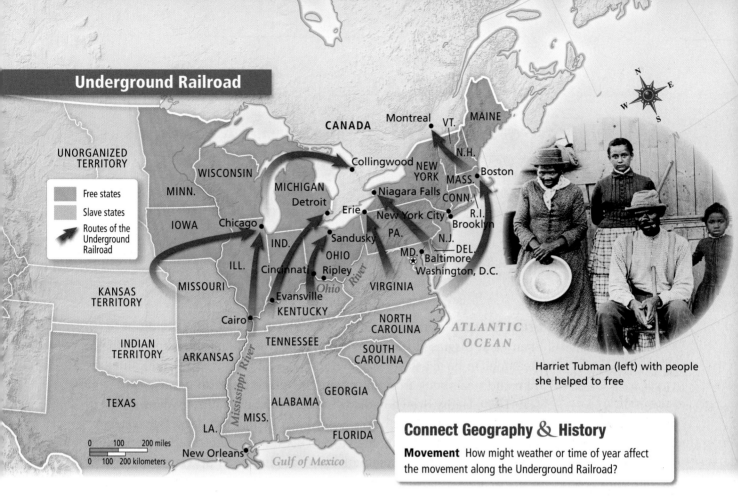

## Underground Railroad

Free states
Slave states
Routes of the Underground Railroad

CANADA
Montreal
VT.
MAINE
N.H.
Collingwood
NEW YORK
MASS.
Boston
Niagara Falls
CONN.
R.I.
New York City
Brooklyn
Erie
PA.
N.J.
Sandusky
DEL.
OHIO
MD.
Baltimore
Cincinnati
Ripley
Washington, D.C.
Ohio River
VIRGINIA
Evansville
KENTUCKY
Cairo
NORTH CAROLINA
TENNESSEE
SOUTH CAROLINA
ARKANSAS
Mississippi River
GEORGIA
TEXAS
ALABAMA
MISS.
LA.
FLORIDA
New Orleans
Gulf of Mexico
ATLANTIC OCEAN

UNORGANIZED TERRITORY
WISCONSIN
MINN.
MICHIGAN
Detroit
IOWA
Chicago
IND.
ILL.
MISSOURI
KANSAS TERRITORY
INDIAN TERRITORY

0    100    200 miles
0   100   200 kilometers

Harriet Tubman (left) with people she helped to free

### Connect Geography & History

**Movement** How might weather or time of year affect the movement along the Underground Railroad?

Sojourner Truth also began life enslaved, in New York State. In 1827, when she was about 30, Truth fled her owners and stayed with a Quaker family. She was originally called Isabella but changed her name in 1843 to reflect her life's work: to sojourn (stay temporarily in a place) and "declare the truth to the people." A bold and captivating speaker, Truth drew huge crowds.

**The Underground Railroad** Some brave abolitionists helped slaves escape to freedom along the **Underground Railroad**. Neither underground nor a railroad, the Underground Railroad was actually a series of aboveground escape routes from throughout the South up to the free North. On these routes, runaway slaves traveled on foot and by wagons, boats, and trains. They usually journeyed by night and hid by day in places called stations. Stables, attics, and cellars all served as stations. At his home in Rochester, New York, Frederick Douglass once housed 11 runaways at the same time.

The people who led the runaways to freedom were called conductors. The most famous was **Harriet Tubman**, who was born into slavery in Maryland. She escaped in 1849 when she learned that her owner was about to sell her. Tubman later described her feelings as she crossed into the free state of Pennsylvania: "I looked at my hands to see if I was the same person now that I was free. There was such a glory over everything."

After her escape, Harriet Tubman made 19 dangerous journeys to free enslaved persons. She carried medicine to quiet crying babies. Her enemies offered $40,000 for her capture, but no one ever caught her. "I never run my train off the track and I never lost a passenger," she proudly declared. Among the people she saved were her sister, brother, and parents.

(top left) In 2004, a visitor to the National Underground Railroad Freedom Center squeezes into a replica of the box in which Henry Brown escaped slavery.
(top right) This 19th-century print from Brown's autobiography shows his arrival in Philadelphia. **What dangers did people such as Brown face in trying to escape from slavery?**

**Great Escapes** Some escapes by enslaved persons became famous. In 1848, Ellen Craft disguised herself as a white man while her husband, William, pretended to be her slave. Together they traveled more than 1,000 miles, by train and steamboat, from slavery in Georgia to freedom in the North.

In 1849, Henry Brown had a white carpenter pack him in a box and ship him to Philadelphia. The box was two and one half feet deep, two feet wide, and three feet long. It bore the label "This side up with care." Nevertheless, Brown spent several miserable hours traveling head down. At the end of about 27 hours, "Box" Brown climbed out a free man in Philadelphia.

▲ **SUMMARIZE** List the methods abolitionists used to fight against slavery.

# The Fight for Women's Rights

▼ **KEY QUESTION** What rights were women fighting for in the mid-1800s?

Some white abolitionist women had begun to realize that their own rights were extremely limited. In 1840, an incident at a major antislavery convention in London helped launch the U.S. movement for women's rights.

**Women Reformers Face Barriers** Lucretia Mott and **Elizabeth Cady Stanton** were two leading women abolitionists. Mott and Stanton were part of an American delegation that attended the World Anti-Slavery Convention in London in 1840. Although the women in the delegation had much to say, they were not allowed to participate in the convention or speak in public. Instead, they had to sit silent behind a heavy curtain.

To show his support, the famed abolitionist William Lloyd Garrison joined them. He said, "After battling so many long years for the liberties of African slaves, I can take no part in a convention that strikes down the most sacred rights of all women."

But most Americans agreed that women should stay out of public life. Women in the 1800s possessed few legal or political rights. Few could vote, sit on juries, or hold public office. Many laws treated women—especially married women—as children. Single women had some freedoms, such as being able to manage their own property. But in most states, a husband controlled any property his wife inherited and any wages she might earn.

**The Seneca Falls Convention** After the World Anti-Slavery Convention, Stanton and Mott decided it was time to demand not only freedom for enslaved people, but equality for women. They made up their minds to plan a convention for women's rights after they returned to the United States.

On July 19 and 20, 1848, Stanton and Mott headed the **Seneca Falls Convention** for women's rights in Seneca Falls, New York. It was the world's first convention on the rights of women. It attracted about 300 women and men, including the well-known abolitionist Frederick Douglass.

Before the meeting opened, a small group of planners discussed how they would present their ideas. The planners wrote a document modeled on the Declaration of Independence. They called it the Declaration of Sentiments and Resolutions. Just as the Declaration of Independence said that "All men are created equal," the Declaration of Sentiments stated that "All men and women are created equal." It went on to list several statements of opinion, or resolutions. Then it concluded with a demand for rights.

### PRIMARY SOURCE

❝ Now, in view of this entire disenfranchisement [denying the right to vote] of one-half the people of this country, their social and religious degradation—in view of the unjust laws above mentioned, and because women do feel themselves aggrieved, oppressed, and fraudulently deprived of their most sacred rights, we insist that they have immediate admission to all the rights and privileges which belong to them as citizens of the United States. ❞

—**Declaration of Sentiments and Resolutions, 1848**

Every resolution won unanimous approval from the group except **suffrage**, or the right to vote. Some argued that the public would laugh at women if they asked for the vote. But Elizabeth Cady Stanton and Frederick Douglass fought for the resolution. They argued that the right to vote would give women political power that would help them win other rights. The resolution for suffrage won by a slim margin.

## History Makers

### Elizabeth Cady Stanton    1815–1902

Stanton (pictured with one of her children) had long known that the world could be unfair to women. Her father was a lawyer who had many women clients. Some faced poverty because laws gave a married woman's money to her husband, who could lose it to drink or gambling. Women who divorced often lost the right to see their children. As an adult, Stanton fought to change laws that affected women, and strongly believed that the ability to vote would help women to ensure their rights. Stanton was a persuasive lecturer and writer. During a career that lasted half a century, she recruited many to her cause.

### CRITICAL THINKING

1. **Draw Conclusions** Why did Stanton want women to have more legal rights?

2. **Form and Support Opinions** Do you agree with Stanton about the importance of voting? Explain.

 **ONLINE BIOGRAPHY** For more on Elizabeth Cady Stanton, go to the **Research & Writing Center** @ ClassZone.com

**Continued Calls for Women's Rights** The women's rights movement of the mid-1800s was ridiculed by many people. Newspaper cartoons and editorials often poked fun at women who wanted equal rights, and suffrage seemed far out of reach.

As women's rights activists continued their efforts, however, they began to see results. Susan B. Anthony, a skilled organizer from the temperance and abolitionist movements, played a key part in building the call for women's rights into a national movement. Anthony argued that women's suffrage would be the foundation on which women would achieve other legal rights. She believed that "there never will be complete equality until women themselves help to make laws and elect lawmakers."

Anthony was an outspoken advocate for equal pay for men and women. She also called for laws that would give married women the right to keep their own property and wages. In 1839, Mississippi passed the first such law. New York passed a property law in 1848 and a wages law in 1860. By 1865, 29 states had similar laws.

▲ **CAUSES AND EFFECTS** Explain what rights women fought for in the mid-1800s.

## CONNECT  to the Essential Question

**How did immigration and social reform change the nation in the mid-1800s?**

| PROBLEM | SOLUTION |
|---|---|
| Overcrowding and lack of opportunity in Europe and elsewhere | Millions of immigrants settle in the United States |
| Poor working conditions | Workers form labor unions and go on strikes<br>Schools founded for children with disabilities |
| Education for only the few | Public schooling becomes more widespread |
| Slavery in the South | Abolitionists demand an end to slavery<br>Underground Railroad helps some enslaved people escape |
| Limited rights for women | Women demand rights to vote and to keep their own property and wages |

**CRITICAL THINKING Causes and Effects** What long-term effects did these solutions have on American society?

# A Changing Nation

 **KEY QUESTION** How did immigration, religious revival, and reform change the nation?

In the early and mid–19th century, America experienced dramatic social and cultural changes. These changes came from forces outside the country as well as from the religious and reform movements within its borders.

**America Transformed** Americans continued to adapt to their growing nation. Immigration had produced a far more diverse population, and cities were dramatically changed in size, culture, and economy. Some people felt threatened by the new face of America and fought to stop immigration. Others launched a reform movement, sparked by the religious revivals, that sought to take control of the forces of change. American reformers advocated such causes as temperance, education, and workers' rights. Soon, some women reformers began to fight for their own rights.

Meanwhile, the issue of slavery continued to tear the nation apart. As the abolitionist movement gathered strength in the North, the economy of the South continued to depend on slave labor—and millions of African Americans remained enslaved.

 **CAUSES AND EFFECTS** Explain how immigration, religious revival, and reform changed the nation.

---

**New Jersey Core Curriculum Content Standards *Review***

**ONLINE QUIZ** For test practice, go to **Interactive Review** @ ClassZone.com

## TERMS & NAMES

**1.** Explain the importance of
- abolition
- Frederick Douglass
- Sojourner Truth
- Underground Railroad
- Harriet Tubman
- Elizabeth Cady Stanton
- Seneca Falls Convention

## USING YOUR READING NOTES

**2. Causes and Effects** Complete the diagram you started at the beginning of this section. Then create a diagram for each of the other main issues in this section.

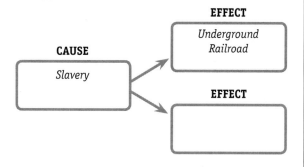

## KEY IDEAS

**3.** How did formerly enslaved persons participate in the abolitionist movement?

**4.** What barriers to equality did women face in the mid-1800s?

**5.** How did women abolitionists help to spark the fight for women's rights?

## CRITICAL THINKING

**6. Make Inferences** Why did the women at the Seneca Falls Convention believe they should have rights?

**7. Analyze Point of View** Runaway slaves risked their lives for freedom. Why do you think some risked their lives and freedom again to help free others?

**8. Draw Conclusions** How did the Underground Railroad reflect a geographic division over slavery in America?

**9. Computer Science** Use the Internet to research the Quakers and their position on slavery. Design a web page that describes their position and how they helped people such as Sojourner Truth.

# The True Confessions of Charlotte Doyle by Avi

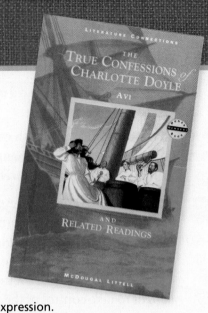

The period in which *The True Confessions of Charlotte Doyle* takes place was one of significant developments in American literature. In the 1830s, several American thinkers including Ralph Waldo Emerson, a poet and essayist, developed a philosophical and literary movement that rejected traditional beliefs and authority in favor of the individual's intuition and insight. Transcendentalism, as this movement came to be called, was part of the romantic movement prominent in England and Germany at that time—a movement of style, literature, and thought that focused on emotional forms of expression.

Henry David Thoreau, another transcendentalist writer of the period, praised self-reliance and individual decision-making. Thoreau believed that people should reject the materialism and greed that, for many, had come to guide American life. In *Walden*, Thoreau puts his beliefs into practice as he writes of his life alone in the New England woods.

Themes of individualism appeared in the works of other writers of the period as well, including Nathaniel Hawthorne, Henry Wadsworth Longfellow, and later Louisa May Alcott, Herman Melville, and Walt Whitman.

*The True Confessions of Charlotte Doyle* takes place in this period of change in America and across the seas. Here, Charlotte Doyle, a thirteen-year-old American girl, confronts uncertainty in the dark hold of the ship that carries her across dangerous seas from England to America.

I was too frightened to cry out again. Instead I remained absolutely still, crouching in pitch blackness while the wash of ship sounds eddied about me, sounds now intensified by the frantic knocking of my heart. Then I recollected that Zachariah's dirk was still with me. With a shaking hand I reached into the pocket where I'd put it, took it out, and removed its wooden sheath which slipped through my clumsy fingers and clattered noisily to the floor.

"Is someone there?" I called, my voice thin, wavering.

No answer.

After what seemed forever I repeated, more boldly than before, "*Is someone there?*"

Still nothing happened. Not the smallest breath of response. Not the slightest stir.

Gradually, my eyes became accustomed to the creaking darkness. I could make out the ladder descending from the deck, a square of dim light above. From that point I could follow the line of the ladder down to where it plunged into the hold below. At that spot, at the edge of the hole, I could see the head more distinctly. Its eyes were glinting wickedly, its lips contorted into a grim, satanic smirk.

Horrified, I nonetheless stared back. And the longer I did so the more it dawned on me that the head had not in fact moved—not at all. The features, I saw, remained unnaturally fixed. Finally, I found the courage to edge aside my fear and lean forward—the merest trifle—to try and make out who—or what—was there.

With the dirk held awkwardly before me I began to crawl forward. The closer I inched the more distorted and grotesque grew the head's features. It appeared to be positively inhuman.

When I drew within two feet of it I stopped and waited. Still the head did not move, did not blink an eye. It seemed as if it were *dead*.

- - - - - - - - - - - - - - - - - - - - - - - - - - - - - -

## ADDITIONAL READING

**Two Years Before the Mast** Richard Henry Dana chronicles his adventures as a crewmember aboard two ships, the *Pilgrim* and the *Alert*, between 1833 and 1855.

## Chapter Summary

**1** **Key Idea**
In the mid-1800s, millions of Europeans came to the United States hoping to build a better life.

**2** **Key Idea**
A 19th-century religious revival launched movements to reform education and society.

**3** **Key Idea**
The social campaigns to gain freedom for enslaved persons and equality for women were closely linked.

🡒 For detailed Review and Study Notes go to **Interactive Review** @ ClassZone.com

## Name Game

Use the Terms & Names list to identify each sentence online or on your own paper.

1. I lived in a community centered on religion. ⌷Shaker 🖑

2. I helped enslaved people reach freedom through the Underground Railroad.

3. This is a work stoppage to demand better conditions.

4. This is the right to vote.

5. I was opposed to recent immigrants.

6. Economic opportunity is an example of this.

7. I was an abolitionist speaker who chose my own name.

8. I worked toward better treatment of the mentally ill.

9. I worked toward improvements in public education.

10. This was the cheapest deck on a ship.

A. Horace Mann
B. Dorothea Dix
C. Elizabeth Cady Stanton
D. steerage
E. suffrage
F. strike
G. nativist
H. Sojourner Truth
I. Harriet Tubman
J. Shaker
K. "push" factor
L. "pull" factor
M. temperance movement

## Activities

### FLIPCARD

Use the online flip cards to quiz yourself on the terms and names introduced in this chapter.

He escaped from slavery and became a famous abolitionist speaker and newspaper publisher.

ANSWER
Frederick Douglass

### CROSSWORD PUZZLE

Complete the online crossword puzzle to show what you know about social change in the early 1800s.

**ACROSS**
1. **Harriet Tubman was a _____ on the Underground Railroad.**

Harriet Tubman
Black Heritage USA 13c

## VOCABULARY

**Match the term on the left with its description on the right.**

1. Know-Nothing Party
2. temperance movement
3. Second Great Awakening
4. Underground Railroad
5. Seneca Falls Convention

A. helped slaves escape
B. called for women's rights
C. opposed immigration
D. revived religious feeling
E. worked to stop the drinking of alcohol

**Choose the term or name that does not belong in each group, and explain why.**

6. Sojourner Truth, Horace Mann, Frederick Douglass

7. nativism, labor union, strike

8. steerage, suffrage, emigrant

Sojourner Truth

## KEY IDEAS

**1** **The Hopes of Immigrants (pages 450–455)**

9. What factors pushed emigrants out of Europe in the mid-1800s?

10. What was the Know-Nothing Party, and what was its stance on immigration?

**2** **Reforming American Society (pages 456–461)**

11. What were the goals of people who fought for workers' rights?

12. How did reformers seek to improve educational opportunities?

**3** **Abolition and Women's Rights (pages 464–471)**

13. How did the Underground Railroad operate?

14. What were the goals of the women's rights movement in the mid-1800s?

## CRITICAL THINKING

15. **Synthesize** Why was America the destination for so many immigrants?

16. **Causes and Effects** How did the rapid increase in immigration during the mid-1800s cause conflicts in society?

17. **Make Generalizations** Why did many factory owners support the temperance movement?

18. **Causes and Effects** Create a chart to show the effects of educational reform in the mid-1800s. After you complete your chart, explain how these efforts have helped to make society more equal.

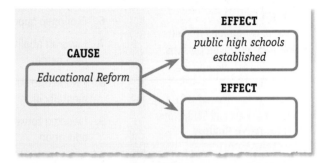

CAUSE

*Educational Reform*

EFFECT

*public high schools established*

EFFECT

19. **Compare and Contrast** How were Frederick Douglass and Sojourner Truth similar as abolitionists?

20. **Make Inferences** Why do you think that some of the people who fought for abolition also fought for women's rights?

21. **Draw Conclusions** The cartoon below shows a husband and wife fighting over "who will wear the pants in the family"—that is, who will rule the household. What do the pants symbolize?

## DOCUMENT-BASED QUESTIONS

### PART 1: Short Answer

**Analyze each document and answer the questions that follow.**

### DOCUMENT 1

1. This nineteenth-century painting shows a revival meeting. Note the figure on the left with the outstretched arms. What is he doing, and how would he have hoped to affect the crowd?

### DOCUMENT 2

**PRIMARY SOURCE**

❝ What, to the American slave, is your Fourth of July? I answer: a day that reveals to him, more than all other days of the year, the gross injustice and cruelty to which he is the constant victim. To him, your celebration is a sham [something false]; . . . your sounds of rejoicing are empty and heartless; . . . ❞

—Frederick Douglass, 1852

2. Frederick Douglass gave this speech at a Fourth of July celebration in New York. Why does he say the sounds of the celebration are "empty and heartless"?

### PART 2: Essay

3. In two or three short paragraphs, explain how individuals in the nineteenth century sought to influence their society. Use information from your answers to Part 1 and your knowledge of U.S. history.

## YOU BE THE HISTORIAN

22. **Connect to Today** Which "pull" factors of the mid-1800s still attract new immigrants to the United States today?

23. **Analyze Point of View** Think of a person in this chapter who exercised leadership by standing up for an unpopular position. Why might this leader have been willing to take such a risk?

24. **Causes and Effects** What were the long-term effects of the nineteenth-century reform movement?

25. **Evaluate** How successful was the women's movement of the mid-1800s?

26. **Form and Support Opinions** Of the reform efforts you learned about in this chapter, which do you consider the most important? Explain.

 Answer the

## ESSENTIAL QUESTION

### How did immigration and social reform change the nation in the mid-1800s?

**Written Response** Write a two- to three-paragraph response to the Essential Question. Be sure to consider the key ideas of each section as well as the most significant problems that faced Americans in the mid-1800s. Use the Response Rubric below to guide your thinking and writing.

### Response Rubric

**A strong response will**

• analyze factors that pulled immigrants to America
• evaluate the impact of social reform movements
• discuss the strategies of leading abolitionists
• describe the goals of the women's rights movement

# A Nation Divided and Rebuilt

## 1846–1877

**15** **The Nation Breaking Apart**
1846–1861  pages 478–507

**16** **The Civil War Begins**
1861–1862  pages 508–533

**17** **The Tide of War Turns**
1863–1865  pages 534–567

**18** Reconstruction
1865–1877  pages 568–591

## Why It Matters Now

The Civil War represented the greatest threat to the survival of the American republic in our history. Why we fought, how the Union won, and how we rebuilt the nation remain enduring matters of discussion and debate.

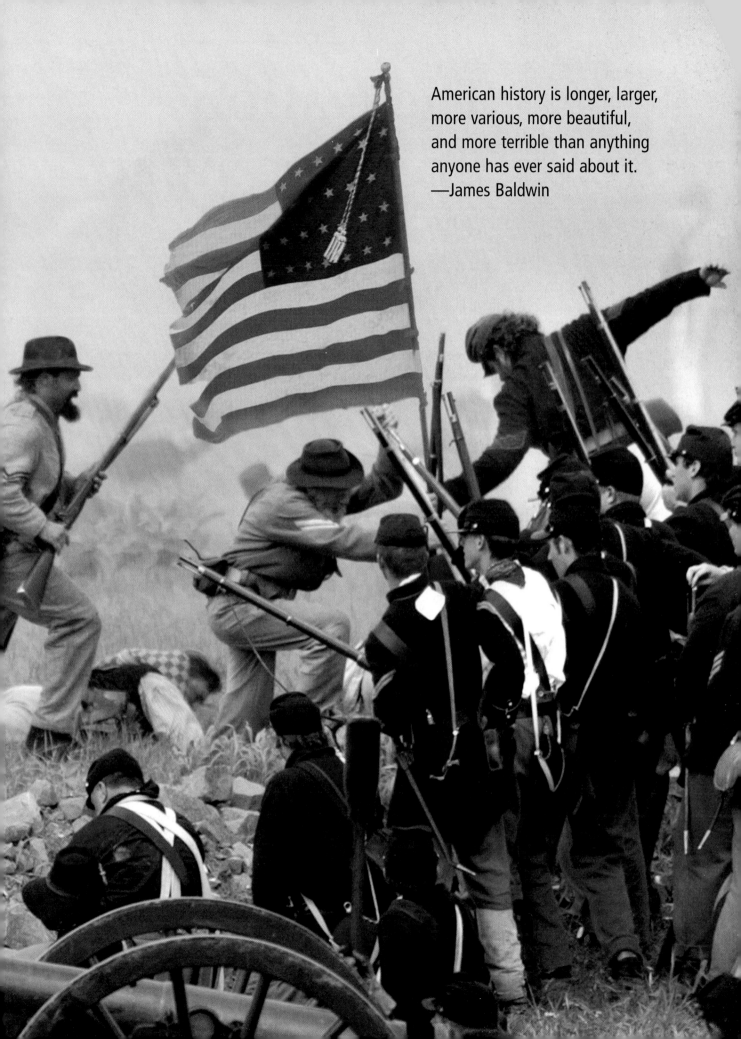

American history is longer, larger, more various, more beautiful, and more terrible than anything anyone has ever said about it.
—James Baldwin

1. Tensions Rise Between North and South

2. Slavery Dominates Politics

3. Lincoln's Election and Southern Secession

# The Nation Breaking Apart

## 1846–1861

 **ESSENTIAL QUESTION**

What issues and events shattered the nation's unity and led to civil war?

---

**CONNECT** 🔄 **Geography & History**

How did geography and climate help create the nation's sectional division?

**Think about:**

**1** the areas where cotton was grown

**2** the difference between the climate of the South and that of the North

**3** why cotton flourished in the South

Playing cards showing American generals in the War with Mexico

## 1846

War with Mexico

Wilmot Proviso introduced

## 1850
Compromise of 1850, including the Fugitive Slave Act, is passed.

▼

**Effect** Abolitionists defy the law by helping slaves escape.

## 1852
*Uncle Tom's Cabin* published

▼

**Effect** The novel increases tension between North and South.

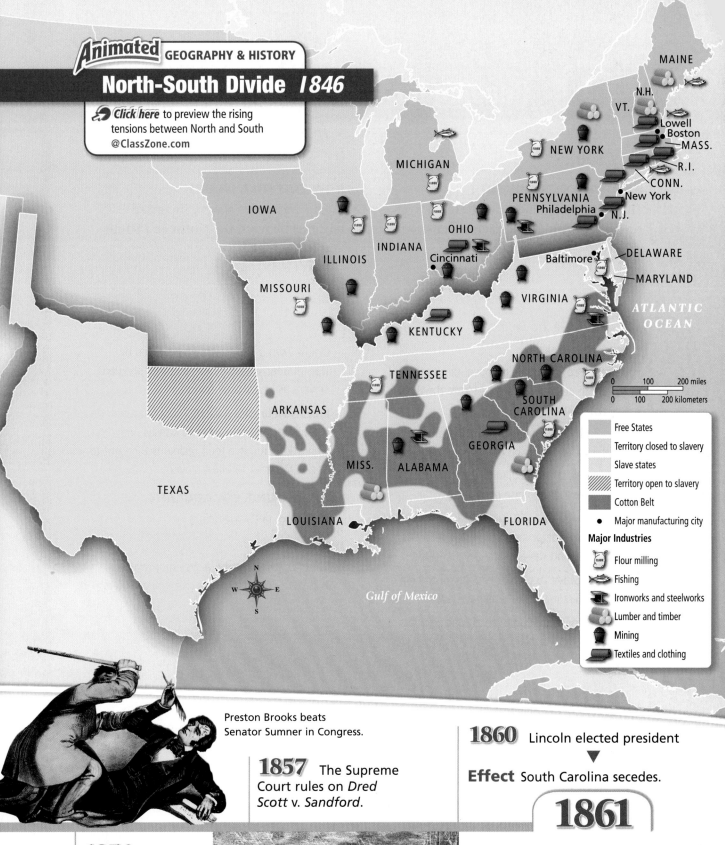

**Click here** to preview the rising tensions between North and South
@ClassZone.com

MAINE

N.H.

VT.

Lowell
Boston
MASS.

R.I.

CONN.

New York

N.J.

NEW YORK

MICHIGAN

PENNSYLVANIA
Philadelphia

IOWA

OHIO

INDIANA

ILLINOIS

Cincinnati

Baltimore

DELAWARE

MARYLAND

MISSOURI

VIRGINIA

ATLANTIC
OCEAN

KENTUCKY

NORTH CAROLINA

TENNESSEE

SOUTH
CAROLINA

ARKANSAS

GEORGIA

TEXAS

MISS.

ALABAMA

LOUISIANA

FLORIDA

Gulf of Mexico

0    100    200 miles
0    100    200 kilometers

| | |
|---|---|
| | Free States |
| | Territory closed to slavery |
| | Slave states |
| | Territory open to slavery |
| | Cotton Belt |
| • | Major manufacturing city |

**Major Industries**

| | |
|---|---|
| | Flour milling |
| | Fishing |
| | Ironworks and steelworks |
| | Lumber and timber |
| | Mining |
| | Textiles and clothing |

Preston Brooks beats
Senator Sumner in Congress.

**1857** The Supreme
Court rules on *Dred
Scott* v. *Sandford*.

**1860** Lincoln elected president
▼
**Effect** South Carolina secedes.

# 1861

The Confederate
States of America is
formed.

**1854**
Kansas-
Nebraska Act is
passed.
The Republican
Party is formed.

Fugitive slaves escaping
from Maryland

## ▶ Key Ideas

**BEFORE, YOU LEARNED**

The North and South tried to reach a compromise in their disagreements over slavery.

**NOW YOU WILL LEARN**

Rising anger over slavery increased tensions between the North and South and led to violence.

## ▶ Vocabulary

**TERMS & NAMES**

**Wilmot Proviso** 1846 proposal that outlawed slavery in any territory gained from the War with Mexico

**Free-Soil Party** political party dedicated to stopping the expansion of slavery

**Stephen A. Douglas** Illinois senator who backed the Compromise of 1850

**Compromise of 1850** series of laws intended to settle the major disagreements between free states and slave states

**Fugitive Slave Act** 1850 law meant to help slaveholders recapture runaway slaves

**Harriet Beecher Stowe** abolitionist; author of *Uncle Tom's Cabin*

*Uncle Tom's Cabin* novel published by Harriet Beecher Stowe in 1852 that showed slavery as brutal and immoral

**Kansas-Nebraska Act** 1854 law that established the territories of Kansas and Nebraska and gave their residents the right to decide whether to allow slavery

**BACKGROUND VOCABULARY**

**bickering** petty quarreling

**REVIEW**

**popular sovereignty** a system in which issues are decided by the citizenry or voters

## ▶ Reading Strategy

Re-create the diagram shown at right. As you read and respond to the **KEY QUESTIONS**, use the diagram to note the difference between the economies of the North and South.

 See Skillbuilder Handbook, page R8.

**COMPARE AND CONTRAST**

| Northern Economy | Southern Economy |
|---|---|
|  | *relied on plantation farming* |

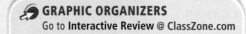

**GRAPHIC ORGANIZERS**
Go to **Interactive Review** @ ClassZone.com

# Tensions Rise Between North and South

 **6.4.F.1.** Describe the political, economic, and social changes in New Jersey and American society preceding the Civil War, . . . .
**6.4.F.11.** Understand the institution of slavery in the United States, resistance to it, and New Jersey's role in the Underground Railroad.

## One American Story

During the 1830s, a French government official named Alexis de Tocqueville (TOHK•vihl) traveled along the Ohio River. The river was the border between Ohio, a free state, and Kentucky, a slave state. Tocqueville noted what he saw on both sides of the river.

### PRIMARY SOURCE

" The State of Ohio is separated from Kentucky just by one river; on either side of it the soil is equally fertile, and the situation equally favourable, and yet everything is different. Here [on the Ohio side] a population devoured by feverish activity, trying every means to make its fortune. . . . There [on the Kentucky side] is a people which makes others work for it and shows little compassion, a people without energy, mettle or the spirit of enterprise. . . . These differences cannot be attributed to any other cause but slavery. "

—Alexis de Tocqueville, *Journey to America*

Alexis de Tocqueville

Foreign observers were often surprised by the cultural and political division between North and South. This division was now widening.

## North and South Follow Different Paths

🔻 **KEY QUESTION** How did the economies of the North and South differ?

The economies of the North and South had been developing differently ever since colonial times. Although both economies were mainly agricultural, there were more small farms in the North. The North had also developed more industry and commerce. By contrast, the Southern economy relied on plantation farming and slave labor rather than industry. The economic differences between the two sections began to divide the nation politically.

**Industry and Immigration in the North** The growing industries of the North attracted many immigrants to Northern cities. As the Northern cities grew, immigrants and Easterners were also moving west. They built farms in the new states carved out of the Northwest Territory. Most canals and railroads ran east and west, strengthening ties between Eastern and Midwestern states.

In the North, some abolitionists believed that slavery was immoral and should be ended immediately. But other Northern opponents of slavery took a different position. Some Northern workers opposed slavery because it was an economic threat to them. Because slaves did not work for pay, wage workers feared that enslaved labor would replace them.

**Agriculture and Slavery in the South** The Southern economy was mostly agricultural. A small class of wealthy planters dominated Southern politics and society. They made great profits from the labor of their slaves. Much of this profit came from trade. Planters relied on exports of cash crops, especially cotton, and invested in land and slaves instead of industry.

Most Southern whites were poor farmers who owned no slaves. Many of these people resented the powerful plantation owners. But some poor whites accepted slavery because it gave them a feeling of social superiority.

**Connecting History**

**Expanding Liberty**
In the late 1700s, slavery was gradually outlawed throughout the Northern states. However, as slavery declined in the North, it continued to spread in the South. *See Chapter 8, page 247.*

## CONNECT  *Economics and History*

### INVESTMENT

The sectional differences between North and South increased partly through investment. Investment is when money is committed to a project in order to create a profit.

Northerners invested in new kinds of machinery that might save them money. This helped fuel the industrial boom in the North.

Southerners, in contrast, invested profits back into land and slaves. Thus, investment strengthened sectional differences: the North became more industrial and "modern" while the South remained agricultural.

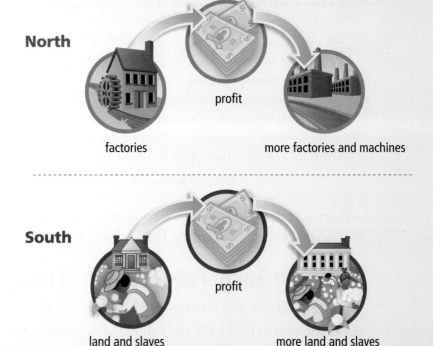

**North**

profit

factories                    more factories and machines

**South**

profit

land and slaves              more land and slaves

**CRITICAL THINKING**  **Connect** *to* **Today**  If you were an investor, in what new industries would you invest?

When Northern criticism of slavery increased, slaveholders defended their way of life. To justify slavery, most offered the openly racist argument that white people were superior to African Americans. Many also claimed that slavery helped slaves by introducing them to Christianity, as well as providing them with food, clothing, and shelter throughout their lives. In time, different attitudes to slavery brought the North and the South into conflict.

▲ **COMPARE AND CONTRAST** Compare the economies of the North and South.

## Slavery and Territorial Expansion

▼ **KEY QUESTION** How did territorial expansion inflame sectional conflicts?

After the Missouri Compromise in 1820, political disagreements over slavery seemed to fade. However, the War with Mexico in 1846 brought the issue of slavery back to the forefront.

**The Wilmot Proviso** Many Northerners suspected that Southerners wanted to take territory from Mexico in order to extend slavery. They feared that this would upset the balance between free and slave states. To prevent this, Representative David Wilmot of Pennsylvania proposed a bill, known as the **Wilmot Proviso**, to outlaw slavery in any territory the United States might acquire from the War with Mexico.

But slaveholders believed that Congress had no right to prevent them from bringing slaves into any of the territories. The Constitution, they claimed, gave equal protection to the property rights of all U.S. citizens. The Wilmot Proviso divided Congress along sectional lines. The bill passed the House of Representatives. But Southerners prevented it from passing the Senate.

Even though the Wilmot Proviso never became law, it had important effects. It led to the creation of the **Free-Soil Party**, a political party dedicated to stopping the expansion of slavery. The party's slogan expressed its ideals—"Free Soil, Free Speech, Free Labor, and Free Men." The Free-Soil Party won ten seats in Congress in the election of 1848. More important, the party made slavery a key issue in national politics.

**The Compromise of 1850** By 1848, the nation's leaders had begun to debate how to deal with slavery in the lands gained from the War with Mexico. The proposed addition of new states threatened the balance of power in Congress between North and South. Both sides worried about what would happen when California became a state.

The discovery of gold attracted so many people to California that there soon would be enough people to qualify for statehood. Most California residents wanted theirs to be a free state. But this would tip the balance of power in favor of the North. Southerners wanted to divide California in half, making the northern half a free state and the southern half a slave state.

In March 1850, California applied to be admitted as a free state. With California as a free state, slave states would become a minority in the Senate just as they were in the House.

Ribbon of the Free-Soil Party worn on supporters' clothing

## IMAGES OF SLAVERY

Supporters of slavery argued that the enslaved were well fed, well clothed, and happy—much as they appear on this tobacco label below. However, the reality of slavery was very different, as the photograph at right reveals. Even the children of the enslaved were forced to labor long hours in dangerous and unhealthy conditions. Slaves suffered violent and cruel punishments. Many enslaved families were broken up when family members were sold to work on distant plantations.

OH CARRY ME BACK

TO OLE VIRGINNY.

### CRITICAL THINKING

**Connect** *to* **Today**  Can you describe any modern advertisements that present life in an unrealistic way?

California could not gain statehood, however, without the approval of Congress. And Congress was divided over the issue. But statesmen sought compromise. Senator Henry Clay of Kentucky crafted a plan to settle the problem.

- To please the North, California would be admitted as a free state, and the slave trade would be abolished in Washington, D.C.
- To please the South, Congress would not pass laws regarding slavery for the rest of the territories won from Mexico, and Congress would pass a stronger law to help slaveholders.

People on both sides felt they had to give up too much in this plan. Others, tired of the sectional **bickering**, just wanted to preserve the Union.

The job of winning passage of the plan fell to Senator **Stephen A. Douglas** of Illinois. By the end of September, Douglas succeeded, and the plan, now known as the **Compromise of 1850**, became law.

Some people celebrated the compromise, believing that it had saved the Union. But the compromise would not bring peace. In the years that followed, sectional tensions continued to rise.

▲ **CAUSES AND EFFECTS**  Explain how the Wilmot Proviso inflamed debate.

# The Crisis Deepens

**KEY QUESTION** How did the Fugitive Slave Act deepen the crisis?

The Compromise of 1850 was an attempt to calm the political situation. However, it contained one bill that heightened, rather than calmed, the crisis. That bill was called the **Fugitive Slave Act**.

**The Fugitive Slave Act** Under this law, accused fugitives could be held without an arrest warrant. They had no right to a jury trial. Instead, a federal commissioner ruled on each case.

Southerners backed the Fugitive Slave Act because they considered slaves to be property. But one aspect of the act especially enraged Northerners: it required them to help recapture runaway slaves. It also placed penalties on people who would not cooperate with the law. Southern slave catchers were allowed to roam the North. Sometimes they captured free African Americans.

The act drew more people to the abolitionist cause. Many decided to defy the act, even though this meant breaking the law.

**Outrage Over the Act** Abolitionist writer **Harriet Beecher Stowe** was outraged by the Fugitive Slave Act. Her anger inspired her to write *Uncle Tom's Cabin* in 1852. The novel presented the cruelty and immorality of slavery. The novel describes the escape of a slave named Eliza and her baby across the Ohio River.

**PRIMARY SOURCE**

❝ Eliza made her desperate retreat across the river just in the dusk of twilight. The gray mist of evening, rising slowly from the river, enveloped her as she disappeared up the bank, and the swollen current and floundering masses of ice presented a hopeless barrier between her and her pursuer. ❞

—Harriet Beecher Stowe, *Uncle Tom's Cabin*

Stowe's book was popular in the North. But white Southerners argued that the book presented a false picture of the South and slavery.

**CAUSES AND EFFECTS** Explain how the Fugitive Slave Act affected the country.

## History Makers

### Harriet Beecher Stowe   1811–1896

Harriet Beecher Stowe came from a family of abolitionists. While Stowe and her family were living in Cincinnati, Ohio, they bravely sheltered slaves fleeing from the neighboring slave state of Kentucky. Outrage at the Fugitive Slave Act of 1850 led Stowe to write *Uncle Tom's Cabin*. This novel, published in 1852, revealed the cruelties of slavery. But it also went a step further—and showed the evil effects that slavery had on slaveholders themselves.

*Uncle Tom's Cabin* made Stowe famous. It was translated into more than 20 languages. Because of its popularity, it drew the world's attention to the injustice of slavery in the South.

**CRITICAL THINKING Draw Conclusions** Why was the novel so unpopular in the South?

 **ONLINE BIOGRAPHY**   For more on Harriet Beecher Stowe, go to the **Research & Writing Center @ ClassZone.com**

# Violence Erupts

▼ **KEY QUESTION** Why did violence erupt in Kansas and Congress?

The Fugitive Slave Act and *Uncle Tom's Cabin* heightened tension between the North and South. As political tensions increased, the issue of slavery in the territories brought bloodshed to the West and even to Congress itself.

**The Kansas-Nebraska Act** In 1854, Senator Douglas drafted a bill to organize the Nebraska Territory. This bill became known as the **Kansas-Nebraska Act**. It proposed to divide the territory into two parts— Nebraska and Kansas.

To get Southern support for the bill, Douglas suggested that **popular sovereignty** should be used to decide whether a territory becomes either slave or free. Popular sovereignty is a system that allows residents to vote to decide an issue. Southerners liked the bill because people would be able to vote for slavery in territories where it had been banned by the Missouri Compromise. However, if the bill passed, it would mean the destruction of the Missouri Compromise.

The bill angered opponents of slavery, but it passed. Few people realized that the Kansas-Nebraska Act would soon turn Kansas into a violent and bloody battleground over the issue of slavery.

## COMPARING *Free States, Slave States, and Territories*

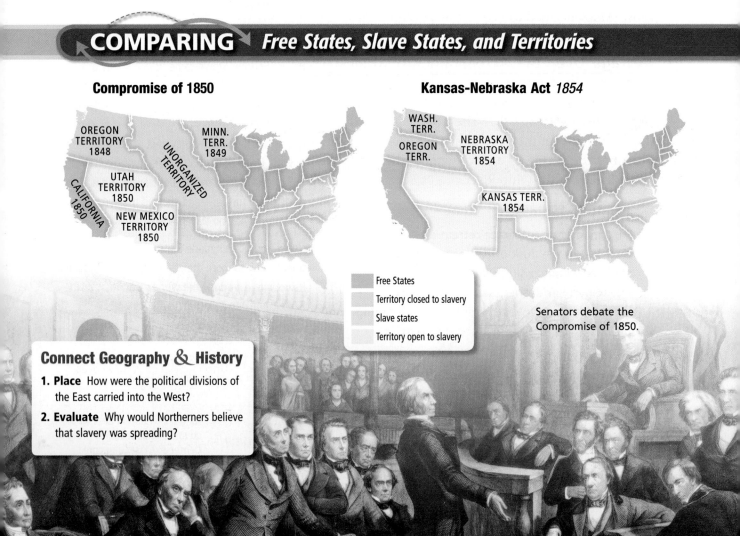

**Compromise of 1850**

OREGON TERRITORY 1848
MINN. TERR. 1849
UNORGANIZED TERRITORY
UTAH TERRITORY 1850
CALIFORNIA 1850
NEW MEXICO TERRITORY 1850

**Kansas-Nebraska Act** *1854*

WASH. TERR.
OREGON TERR.
NEBRASKA TERRITORY 1854
KANSAS TERR. 1854

Free States
Territory closed to slavery
Slave states
Territory open to slavery

Senators debate the Compromise of 1850.

### Connect Geography & History

1. **Place** How were the political divisions of the East carried into the West?

2. **Evaluate** Why would Northerners believe that slavery was spreading?

**Bleeding Kansas** During the election of March 1855, there were more proslavery than antislavery settlers in the Kansas Territory. After five thousand residents of neighboring Missouri came and voted illegally, the Kansas legislature was filled with proslavery representatives.

Antislavery settlers rejected the elected government. Settlers on both sides armed themselves. In May, a proslavery mob looted the town of Lawrence, Kansas. This attack was called the Sack of Lawrence.

In response, John Brown, an extreme abolitionist, led seven other men in a massacre of five of his proslavery neighbors. This attack is known as the Potawatomie Massacre, after the creek near where the victims were found. As news of the violence spread, civil war broke out in Kansas. It continued for three years, and the territory came to be called "Bleeding Kansas."

**Violence in Congress** In May 1856, Senator Charles Sumner of Massachusetts spoke against the proslavery forces in Kansas. In his speech, Sumner insulted A. P. Butler, a senator from South Carolina.

Preston Brooks, a relative of Butler, heard about Sumner's speech. He attacked Sumner, who was sitting at his desk in Congress. Brooks beat Sumner unconscious with his cane, causing severe injuries that disabled him for years.

Brooks was cheered in the South. But Northerners were shocked at the violence in the Senate. "Bleeding Kansas" and "Bleeding Sumner" became rallying cries for antislavery Northerners. In their anger over events, antislavery forces united to create a new political organization—the Republican Party.

 **SUMMARIZE** Describe the events that led to violence in Kansas.

---

**New Jersey Core Curriculum Content Standards *Review***

**ONLINE QUIZ**
For test practice, go to
**Interactive Review @ ClassZone.com**

### TERMS & NAMES

**1.** Explain the importance of

- Wilmot Proviso
- Free-Soil Party
- Stephen A. Douglas
- Compromise of 1850
- Fugitive Slave Act
- Harriet Beecher Stowe
- *Uncle Tom's Cabin*
- Kansas-Nebraska Act

### USING YOUR READING NOTES

**2. Compare and Contrast** Complete the diagram you started at the beginning of this section.

| Northern Economy | Southern Economy |
|---|---|
| | *relied on plantation farming* |

### KEY IDEAS

**3.** What were two ways that the North and the South differed by the 1850s?

**4.** How did the War with Mexico provoke disagreements between the North and the South?

**5.** Why was the Kansas-Nebraska Act so controversial?

### CRITICAL THINKING

**6. Causes and Effects** How did *Uncle Tom's Cabin* affect national politics?

**7. Problems and Solutions** What might have been done to prevent the violence in Kansas?

**8. Art** Research the architecture of the North and South in the 19th century. Then create a travel poster showing the kinds of houses a visitor might see in each section of the country.

## Connect Geography & History

# Land Use and Slavery

In 1850 cotton was the main cash crop of the lower South. But there was a problem: cotton exhausts the fertility of the soil. So planters had to abandon farmland and move west into new land. As planters moved west, they brought hundreds of thousands of enslaved people with them to farm the land.

One of the largest concentrations of cotton plantations was along the Mississippi River. The lower Mississippi offered excellent transportation for the crops. It also provided fertile soil for agriculture.

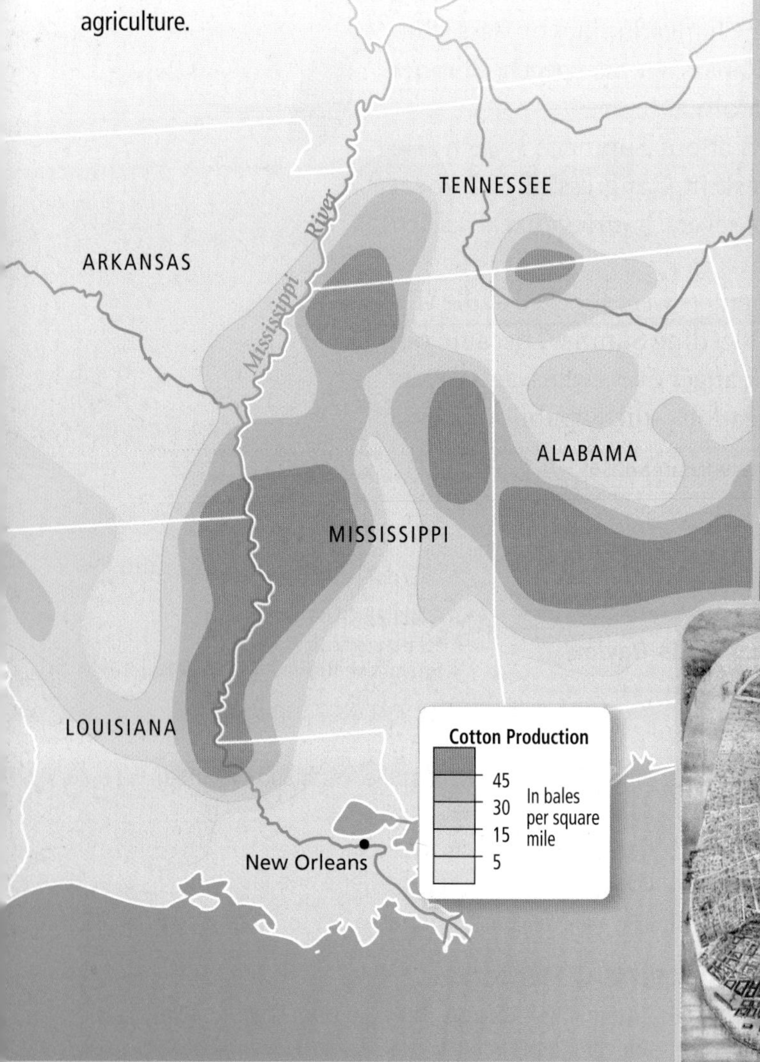

ARKANSAS

TENNESSEE

Mississippi River

ALABAMA

MISSISSIPPI

LOUISIANA

**Cotton Production**

| | |
|---|---|
| 45 | In bales |
| 30 | per square |
| 15 | mile |
| 5 | |

New Orleans

New Orleans, the main port for shipments of cotton on the Mississippi River

In some places along the river, cranes were used to load cotton onto steamboats.

Enslaved people and their children shown outside the plantation slave cabins

**Connect Geography & History**

1. **Make Inferences** Why would this region of the South have had such a large African-American population?

2. **Draw Conclusions** Why did New Orleans become such an important city?

See Geography Handbook, pages A1–A17.

# Reading for Understanding

## ▶ Key Ideas

**BEFORE, YOU LEARNED**
Rising anger over slavery destroyed compromise between the North and South and led to violence.

**NOW YOU WILL LEARN**
The formation of the antislavery Republican Party further divided the country.

## ▶ Vocabulary

**TERMS & NAMES**

**Republican Party** political party formed in 1854 by opponents of slavery

**John C. Frémont** Republican presidential candidate in 1856

**James Buchanan** Democratic presidential candidate in 1856

***Dred Scott* v. *Sandford*** 1856 Supreme Court case in which a slave, Dred Scott, sued for his freedom; the Court ruled against Scott

**Roger B. Taney** (TAW•nee) Supreme Court chief justice who wrote the majority opinion in the case of *Dred Scott* v. *Sandford*

**Abraham Lincoln** Illinois Republican who ran against Stephen A. Douglas in 1858

**Harpers Ferry** federal arsenal in Virginia; captured in 1859 during an antislavery revolt

**REVIEW**

**Whig Party** political party organized in 1834 to oppose the policies of Andrew Jackson

**Know-Nothing Party** anti-immigrant party formed in the 1850s

**Visual Vocabulary**
Harpers Ferry today

## ▶ Reading Strategy

Re-create the diagram shown at right. As you read and respond to the **KEY QUESTIONS**, use the center oval to record the main idea; use the outer ovals to note important details.

 See Skillbuilder Handbook, page R4.

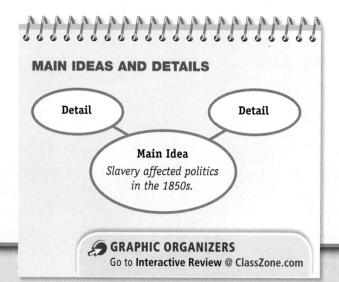

**MAIN IDEAS AND DETAILS**

Detail

Detail

**Main Idea**
*Slavery affected politics in the 1850s.*

**⚡ GRAPHIC ORGANIZERS**
Go to **Interactive Review** @ ClassZone.com

# Slavery Dominates Politics

**6.4.F.11.** Understand the institution of slavery in the United States, resistance to it, and New Jersey's role in the Underground Railroad.

**6.4.G.1.** Explain the major events, issues, and personalities of the American Civil War including the Dred Scott and other Supreme Court decisions.

## One American's Story

Emily Edmondson (standing center behind table) with her sister (in plaid at far left) as well as Frederick Douglass and others at an abolitionist convention, 1850

She was only 13, but her story edged the nation closer to civil war. Emily Edmondson grew up in slavery in Washington, D.C. On April 15, 1848, Emily, her 15-year-old sister Mary, and four of her brothers joined more than 70 other slaves in an escape attempt. Hidden on board a ship, they sailed toward freedom in the North. However, their ship was pursued and captured. Despite a debate in Congress and a public outcry, Emily and her sister were shipped to New Orleans to be resold.

In New Orleans an outbreak of yellow fever forced slave traders to send the girls back to the safety of Virginia. It was then that the girls' parents contacted Harriet Beecher Stowe's brother, who was a famous abolitionist. He raised enough money to buy their freedom. Harriet Beecher Stowe arranged for the girls to attend Oberlin College. (In the photo at right, they appear in plaid dresses.)

Although Mary died young, Emily became a famous abolitionist. Her story motivated various antislavery groups to create the Republican Party—a party dedicated to the elimination of slavery.

## Slavery and Political Division

🔽 **KEY QUESTION** How did the issue of slavery affect political parties?

As you have read, the Kansas-Nebraska Act allowed residents of a new territory to vote either for or against slavery. This act caused a political crisis for the **Whig Party**. The Whig party had been formed in 1834 to oppose the policies of Andrew Jackson. Now the act began to tear the party apart. Southern

Whigs supported the act. Northern Whigs opposed it. There was no room for compromise. As a result, the Whig Party split into two factions.

**The Republican Party Forms** Some of the Southern Whigs joined the Democratic Party. Others looked for leaders who supported slavery and the Union. The Northern Whigs, however, joined with other rivals and formed the **Republican Party**.

The Republican Party was both an antislavery party and a sectional party that sought to protect the interests of the North. Republicans not only used moral arguments against slavery, they also looked down on the South's agricultural system based on enslaved labor.

The Republicans quickly gained strength in the North. "Bleeding Kansas" was the key to the Republican rise. Many blamed the violence on the Democrats. With the 1856 elections nearing, Republicans seized the chance to gain seats in Congress and win the presidency.

The Republicans needed a strong presidential candidate in 1856 to strengthen their young party. They nominated **John C. Frémont**. Frémont was a handsome young hero known for his explorations in the West. He was nicknamed "the Pathfinder."

Republicans liked Frémont because he wanted California and Kansas admitted as free states. Also, he did not have a controversial political past. Even so, the Republican position on slavery was so unpopular in the South that Frémont's name did not appear on the ballot there.

**Election of 1856** The Democrats nominated **James Buchanan** for the presidency in 1856. As ambassador to Great Britain, he had been in England since 1853 and had spoken neither for nor against the Kansas-Nebraska Act.

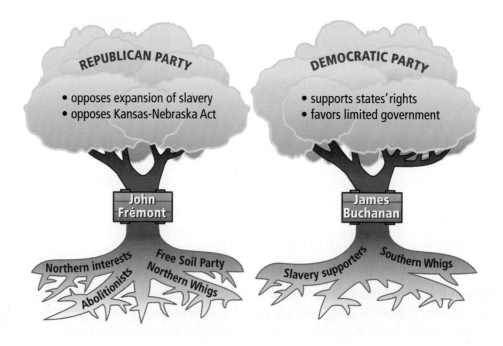

REPUBLICAN PARTY
- opposes expansion of slavery
- opposes Kansas-Nebraska Act

John Frémont

Northern interests
Abolitionists
Free Soil Party
Northern Whigs

DEMOCRATIC PARTY
- supports states' rights
- favors limited government

James Buchanan

Slavery supporters
Southern Whigs

Buchanan said little about slavery and claimed that his goal was to maintain the Union. Buchanan appealed to Southerners, especially to people in the upper South and the border states, and to Northerners who feared that Frémont's election could tear the nation apart.

The American Party, or **Know-Nothing Party**, an anti-immigrant party, nominated Millard Fillmore as presidential candidate in 1856. Fillmore had been president following the death of Zachary Taylor, from 1850 until 1853. But the Know-Nothings were divided over slavery and had little strength.

The 1856 presidential election turned into two separate races. In the North, it was Buchanan against Frémont. In the South, it was Buchanan against Fillmore. Buchanan won. He carried all the slave states except Maryland, where Fillmore claimed his only victory. Buchanan also won several Northern states, such as Pennsylvania and Illinois.

Although he lost the election, Frémont won 11 Northern states. These results showed two things. First, the Republican Party was a major force in the North. Second, slavery was dividing the nation along sectional lines.

🔺 **MAIN IDEAS & DETAILS**  Explain how the issue of slavery affected political parties.

## The Breaking Point

🔻 **KEY QUESTION**  What events brought the nation to a crisis?

The argument over slavery was affecting not only Congressional politics. The slavery debate was forcing its way into another branch of government—the judiciary. In the mid-1850s, a legal case involving an enslaved man named Dred Scott reached the Supreme Court. The Supreme Court's decision in this case divided the country even further.

Article covering the Dred Scott case from *Frank Leslie's Illustrated Newspaper*

**The Case of Dred Scott**  Scott had been an enslaved person in Missouri. However, he had lived for a time in free territories before being taken back to Missouri. After his owner's death, Dred Scott argued that he was a free man because he had lived in territories where slavery was illegal. Scott's wife and their two daughters also sued in court for their freedom. Scott's case, **Dred Scott v. Sandford**, reached the Supreme Court in 1856.

In 1857, the Court ruled against Scott. Chief Justice **Roger B. Taney** (TAW•nee) stated that Dred Scott was not a U.S. citizen. As a result, he could not sue in U.S. courts. Taney also ruled that Scott was bound by Missouri's slave code because he had lived in Missouri.

Taney also argued that banning slavery in the territories would violate slaveholders' property rights, protected by the Fifth Amendment. This meant that legislation such as the Missouri Compromise was unconstitutional.

# Dred Scott v. Sandford (1857)

**KEY ISSUE** citizenship

**KEY PEOPLE**

| | |
|---|---|
| Dred Scott | b. 1795, d. 1858; enslaved to John and Irene Emerson |
| John and Irene Emerson | "owners" of Dred and Harriet Scott; residents of Missouri |
| John Sanford | executor of the Emersons' estate (Sanford's name was misspelled "Sandford" by a court clerk) |
| Roger Taney | Chief justice of the Supreme Court (1836–1864) |

## History Makers

### Roger Taney
### 1777–1864

Roger Taney was born in Maryland, the son of plantation owners. Personally, he abhorred slavery, and upon inheriting his family's plantation, he freed all his slaves.

In 1831 he became President Andrew Jackson's attorney general. In 1836 Taney was appointed chief justice in the Supreme Court.

**ONLINE BIOGRAPHY**

For more on the life of Roger Taney, go to the **Research & Writing Center @ ClassZone.com**

## The Case

John and Irene Emerson lived in Missouri. John worked for the military, so he traveled, and when he did he brought his slave Dred Scott with him. After the Emersons died, Dred Scott sued their estate for his freedom. Scott's lawyers argued that Scott became free when he lived with Emerson in Illinois—a free state—and in Wisconsin, which was made a free territory by the Missouri Compromise.

**The Court's Decision** The court protected and even expanded slavery. It said that, as a slave, Dred Scott was property. He was not a citizen; he would not be a citizen even if he were freed. He had no rights; he could not even file a lawsuit. The court also said that the Congress had no power to limit slavery, because any such limits would violate the Constitutional property rights of slaveholders.

**Historical Impact** The decision meant that the Missouri Compromise was void, because Congress could not limit slavery in the territories. Further, it seemed to imply that no state could be a free state because states could not prohibit their citizens from importing, owning, or buying and selling slaves.

*Dred Scott* thrilled slaveowners, while it outraged free-soilers and abolitionists. By deepening the sectional divide between North and South, the decision helped bring about the Civil War. Following the Civil War, the 14th Amendment to the U.S. Constitution was passed, undoing the Dred Scott decision.

## CRITICAL THINKING

1. **Summarize** What was the basis of Scott's argument, and why did the Taney court disagree?

2. **Make Inferences** How did this decision bring the nation closer to civil war?

**The Lincoln-Douglas Debate** After the Dred Scott decision, the Republicans charged that the Democrats wanted to legalize slavery not only in all U.S. territories but in all the states. They used this charge to attack individual Democrats. Stephen A. Douglas, sponsor of the Kansas-Nebraska Act, was one of their main targets in 1858. That year, Illinois Republicans nominated **Abraham Lincoln** to challenge Douglas for his U.S. Senate seat. In his first campaign speech, Lincoln expressed the Northern fear that Southerners wanted to expand slavery to the entire nation. He laid the groundwork for his argument by using a phrase from the Bible.

### PRIMARY SOURCE

❝'A house divided against itself cannot stand.' I believe this government cannot endure, permanently, half slave and half free. I do not expect the Union to be dissolved; I do not expect the house to fall; but I do expect it will cease to be divided. It will become all one thing, or all the other.❞

—Abraham Lincoln, Springfield, Illinois, June 16, 1858

Later in the year, the two men held debates across Illinois in front of large crowds. The Lincoln-Douglas debates are models of political debate.

## CONNECT To Today

### POLITICAL DEBATE

In the mid-19th century, large crowds listened to candidates debate the issues of the day. Lincoln debated Douglas seven times; thousands of people came to listen.

The first televised presidential debate, in 1960, featured candidates John F. Kennedy and Richard Nixon. Today, millions watch televised debates. These debates have strict rules—about the topics, the length of each debate and its closing arguments, and so forth. In contrast to the Lincoln-Douglas debates, today's live audiences are instructed not to applaud or make any noise while the debate is in progress.

Senator John Kerry (*standing*) debates President George W. Bush (*right, seated*) in a 2004 "town meeting" style debate.

### CRITICAL THINKING
**Make Generalizations** What factors might influence your opinion of a candidate during a political debate?

## REACHING COMPROMISE

Compromise comes when two people or groups each give way a little to settle their dispute. In the mid-19th century, the failure to compromise led to violence and eventually to a civil war in which hundreds of thousands of Americans died.

Today, negotiation and compromise—whether in government or business or in classrooms and on playgrounds—is just as important as it was in the 19th century. Educational programs under the names of peace education, conflict resolution, and negotiation teach compromising skills. The purpose of these programs is not just to resolve conflicts and prevent violence, but to develop skills for citizenship.

**CRITICAL THINKING** **Make Inferences** What factors lead to a successful compromise? Give an example of a time when you've compromised.

See Citizenship Handbook, pages 300–307.

### Activity

## Discuss how to promote compromise in your school.

1 Respect yourself and encourage your friends to respect others.

2 Encourage your friends to be good observers.

3 Help your friends pause a moment if something angers them.

4 During disagreements, encourage others to keep from shouting.

5 Compromise is a form of bargaining. Next time you overhear a dispute, suggest ways that the two parties might reach an agreement.

---

The two men addressed the expansion of slavery. For Lincoln, slavery was "a moral, a social, and a political wrong." But he did not suggest that he wanted to end slavery where it existed. He argued only that slavery should not be expanded.

Douglas agreed that it was the national government's role to prevent the expansion of slavery. But he argued that popular sovereignty was the best way to address the issue because it was the most democratic method of doing so.

Popular sovereignty was a problem for Douglas. The Supreme Court decision in the Dred Scott case had made popular sovereignty unconstitutional. Why? It said that people could not vote to ban slavery, because doing so would take away slaveholders' property rights. (Slaves were considered property.) In a debate at Freeport, Illinois, Lincoln asked Douglas if he thought people in a territory who were against slavery could legally prohibit it—despite the Dred Scott decision.

Douglas replied that it did not matter what the Supreme Court might decide about slavery because "the people have the lawful means to introduce it or exclude it as they please." Douglas won reelection. Lincoln, despite his loss, became a national figure and strengthened his position in the Republican Party.

**John Brown's Raid** In 1859, John Brown, who had murdered proslavery Kansans three years before, added to the sectional tensions. Brown wanted to provoke a slave uprising. To do this, he planned to capture the weapons in the U.S. arsenal at **Harpers Ferry**, Virginia.

On October 16, 1859, Brown and 18 followers—13 whites and 5 blacks—captured the Harpers Ferry arsenal. Brown then sent out the word to rally and arm local slaves. But no slaves joined the fight. U.S. marines attacked Brown at Harpers Ferry. Some of his men escaped, but Brown and six others were captured, and ten men were killed.

*John Brown Going to His Hanging*, by Horace Pippin

Brown was tried for murder and betrayal of his country, or treason. He was also accused of conspiracy to cause a slave revolt. Brown was convicted and sentenced to hang. On the day he was hanged, abolitionists tolled bells and fired guns in his honor. Southerners were enraged by Brown's actions and horrified by Northern reactions to his death. As the nation headed toward the election of 1860, the issue of slavery had raised sectional tensions to the breaking point.

 **SUMMARIZE** Describe the events that brought the nation to a crisis.

---

**New Jersey Core Curriculum Content Standards *Review***

**ONLINE QUIZ**
For test practice, go to
**Interactive Review @ ClassZone.com**

**TERMS & NAMES**

**1.** Explain the importance of
- Republican Party
- Roger B. Taney
- John C. Frémont
- Abraham Lincoln
- James Buchanan
- Harpers Ferry
- *Dred Scott* v. *Sandford*

**USING YOUR READING NOTES**

**2. Main Ideas and Details** Complete the diagram you started at the beginning of this section.

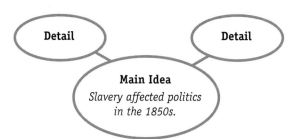

**KEY IDEAS**

**3.** Why was the Republican Party created?

**4.** What were the consequences of the Dred Scott decision for enslaved people?

**5.** How did John Brown's attack on Harpers Ferry increase tensions between the North and the South?

**CRITICAL THINKING**

**6. Make Inferences** How did the opinion in the Dred Scott case threaten the idea of popular sovereignty?

**7. Draw Conclusions** What did the Dred Scott decision reveal about Southern attitudes to slavery?

**8. Writing Speech** Imagine you are a candidate in the 1856 election. Write a speech explaining your political opinions.

# Reading for Understanding

## ▶ Key Ideas

**BEFORE, YOU LEARNED**

The formation of the antislavery Republican Party further divided the country.

**NOW YOU WILL LEARN**

The election of Abraham Lincoln as president in 1860 led seven Southern states to secede from the Union.

## ▶ Vocabulary

**TERMS & NAMES**

**Confederate States of America** confederation formed in 1861 by the Southern states after their secession from the Union

**Jefferson Davis** first president of the Confederate States of America

**Crittenden Compromise** compromise introduced in 1861 that might have prevented secession

**BACKGROUND VOCABULARY**

**platform** statement of beliefs

**secede** to withdraw

**REVIEW**

**states' rights** idea that the states have certain rights that the federal government cannot overrule

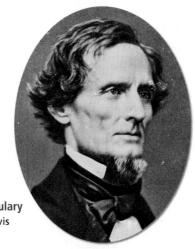

Visual Vocabulary
Jefferson Davis

## ▶ Reading Strategy

Re-create the diagram shown at right. As you read and respond to the **KEY QUESTIONS**, use the diagram to show why the Democratic Party broke apart.

 **See Skillbuilder Handbook, page R6.**

**CATEGORIZE**

| Southern Democrats | Northern Democrats |
|---|---|
| *wanted party to defend slavery* | |

 **GRAPHIC ORGANIZERS**
Go to **Interactive Review** @ ClassZone.com

# Lincoln's Election and Southern Secession

 **6.4.G.1.** Explain the major events, issues, and personalities of the American Civil War including the causes of the Civil War (e.g., slavery, states' rights).

## One American's Story

Mary Boykin Chesnut was born into wealth but died in poverty, one of the many victims of the political events that tore the nation apart.

Born in South Carolina in 1823, Mary grew up in a world of privilege and political power. At the age of 17 she married James Chesnut, a wealthy lawyer who became a senator. James supported slavery and resigned his senate seat at the news of Lincoln's election in 1860. Mary was also upset by this political event, and recorded the moment when she first heard the news.

### PRIMARY SOURCE

❝ CHARLESTON, S.C., November 8, 1860. - Yesterday on the train, just before we reached Fernandina, a woman called out: "That settles the hash." Tanny touched me on the shoulder and said: "Lincoln's elected." "How do you know?" "The man over there has a telegram."

The excitement was very great. Everybody was talking at the same time. One, a little more moved than the others, stood up and said despondently: "The die is cast; no more vain regrets; sad forebodings are useless; the stake is life or death." ❞

—Mary Boykin Chesnut, *A Diary from Dixie*

Wedding photo of Mary and James Chesnut

For Mary Chesnut, Lincoln's election was a threat. Perhaps she foresaw the coming war that would take her from riches to poverty. But like the other Southerners on the train, she knew that Lincoln's election meant there could be no more compromise. Now there was no choice left but to fight.

# The Election of 1860

▼ **KEY QUESTION** How did the 1860 election reveal the divisions in the country?

In April, the Democratic convention was held in Charleston, South Carolina. It was clear that Northern and Southern Democrats had very different ideas about slavery. The Democratic Party began to split along sectional lines.

**The Split in the Democratic Party** The Southerners wanted the party to defend slavery in the party's **platform**, or statement of beliefs. But Northerners wanted the platform to support popular sovereignty as a way of deciding whether a territory became a free state or a slave state. The Northerners won the platform vote, causing many Southern delegates to leave the convention before the Democrats chose a candidate for the presidential election.

The Democrats met again in Baltimore to choose a candidate. Northerners and Southerners remained at odds. Most Southerners left the meeting.

The Northern Democrats backed Stephen A. Douglas and his support for popular sovereignty. Meanwhile, proslavery Southern Democrats nominated vice president John Breckinridge of Kentucky.

The Republicans had already nominated Abraham Lincoln. Also in the race was a fourth party—the Constitutional Union Party. Its members had one aim—to preserve the Union. They nominated John Bell of Tennessee.

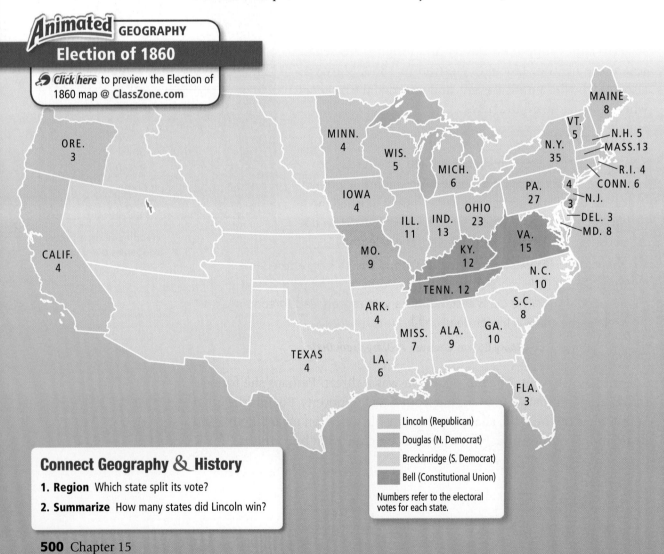

**Animated GEOGRAPHY**

### Election of 1860

🔊 *Click here* to preview the Election of 1860 map @ ClassZone.com

Lincoln (Republican)
Douglas (N. Democrat)
Breckinridge (S. Democrat)
Bell (Constitutional Union)

Numbers refer to the electoral votes for each state.

## Connect Geography & History

1. **Region** Which state split its vote?

2. **Summarize** How many states did Lincoln win?

### FOOTRACE TO THE WHITE HOUSE

In this cartoon from 1860, the rival presidential candidates are competing in a footrace. As they race toward the White House, it is obvious which runner is going to win.

Bell:
"Bless my soul . . . I give up."

Breckinridge:
"That long legged Abolitionist is getting ahead of us after all."

Douglas:
"I never run so in my life."

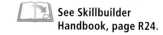
the White House

### CRITICAL THINKING

1. **Make Inferences** What common symbol for a political campaign is used in the cartoon?
2. **Synthesize** What is the basic message of the cartoon?

**See Skillbuilder Handbook, page R24.**

**Two Political Races** The election of 1860 turned into two different races for the presidency—one in the North and one in the South. Lincoln and Douglas were the only candidates with much support in the North. Breckinridge and Bell competed for Southern votes.

Lincoln and Breckinridge were considered to have the most extreme views on slavery. Lincoln opposed the expansion of slavery into the territories. Breckinridge insisted that the federal government be required to protect slavery in any territory. Douglas and Bell were considered moderates because neither wanted the federal government to pass new laws on slavery.

The outcome of the election made it clear that the nation was tired of compromise. Lincoln defeated Douglas in the North. Breckinridge carried most of the South. Douglas and Bell managed to win only in the border states. Because the North had a larger population, Lincoln won the election.

Despite Lincoln's statements that he would do nothing to abolish slavery in the South, white Southerners did not trust him. Many were sure that he and the other Republicans would move to ban slavery. As a result, white Southerners saw the Republican victory as a threat to their way of life.

▲ **CATEGORIZE** Explain the divisions that affected political parties in 1860.

# Southern States Secede

**KEY QUESTION** How did seven Southern states justify their decision to secede?

**Connecting History**

**Federalism**
Many Southerners claimed that their fight for independence from the federal government was an echo of America's fight to separate from British tyranny during the Revolutionary War.

Even before the election, Southerners had warned that if Lincoln won the presidency, Southern states would **secede**, or withdraw, from the Union.

**The Confederate States of America** Southerners based their arguments on **states' rights**, the idea that states have certain rights that the federal government cannot overrule. They argued that since the states had voluntarily joined the Union, they could voluntarily leave it.

On December 20, 1860, South Carolina became the first state to secede. Other states in the Deep South, where the economies depended on slavery and cotton production, also considered secession. Shortly after, Mississippi, Florida, Alabama, Georgia, Louisiana, and Texas joined South Carolina.

In early February 1861, the states that had seceded met in Montgomery, Alabama. They formed the **Confederate States of America**. The convention named **Jefferson Davis** president of the Confederacy.

The convention then drafted a constitution. The Confederate Constitution was modeled on the U.S. Constitution. But there were a few important differences. For example, the Confederate Constitution supported states' rights. It also protected slavery in the Confederacy, including any territories it might acquire.

Having formed its government, the Confederate states made plans to defend their separation from the Union. Some believed that war between the states could not be avoided. But everyone waited to see what the Union government would do in response.

Detail of secession banner with tree representing South Carolina

**The Union's Response** Northerners considered the secession of the Southern states was unconstitutional. President James Buchanan argued against secession. He believed that the states did not have the right to withdraw from the Union because the federal government, not the state governments, was sovereign. If secession were permitted, the Union would become weak, like a "rope of sand." He believed that the U.S. Constitution was framed to prevent such a thing from happening.

In addition to these issues, secession raised the issue of majority rule. Southerners complained that Northerners intended to use their majority to force the South to abolish slavery. But Northerners responded that Southerners were not willing to live with the election results. As Northern writer James Russell Lowell wrote, "[The Southerners'] quarrel is not with the Republican Party, but with the theory of Democracy."

**The Failure of Compromise** With the states in the lower South forming a new government, some people continued to seek compromise. Senator John J. Crittenden of Kentucky proposed that slavery should be protected south of the line established in the Missouri Compromise, that Congress should not abolish slavery in a slave state, and that the federal government should compensate the owners of fugitive slaves. **The Crittenden Compromise** was presented to Congress in early 1861, but it was defeated in the Senate.

With the election of 1860, it was clear that attempts at compromise had failed. The issue of slavery had pulled the nation apart. Every Congressional attempt to reach a compromise only served to enrage one section of the country or the other. The following chart shows how the events and laws of these years brought the nation closer to civil war.

## CONNECT to the Essential Question

**What issues and events shattered the nation's unity and led to civil war?**

| | EVENT | NORTHERN REACTION | SOUTHERN REACTION |
|---|---|---|---|
| 1846 | War with Mexico | fear that slavery would expand into the territories won from Mexico | desire to extend slavery into territory taken from Mexico |
| 1846 | Wilmot Proviso proposes that slavery be outlawed in territory taken from Mexico. | support for Wilmot Proviso<br><br>founding of Free-Soil Party dedicated to stopping expansion of slavery | Southerners fear that more free states will be created and upset the balance of power. Southern senators prevent passage of Wilmot Proviso |
| 1850 | Compromise of 1850 | relief that California would be a free state<br><br>outrage over Fugitive Slave Act | relief that Congress would not ban slavery from territories won from Mexico with the exception of California<br><br>satisfaction with Fugitive Slave Act |
| 1852 | *Uncle Tom's Cabin* is published. | The novel becomes highly popular. | Southerners believe the book gives a false impression of the South and slavery. |
| 1854 | Kansas–Nebraska Act | anger over repeal of Missouri Compromise, which banned slavery in some territories | support for popular sovereignty, which allowed people to vote for slavery in territories where Missouri Compromise had banned it |
| 1854 | Whig Party splits over Kansas–Nebraska Act. | Northern Whigs join other groups to form antislavery Republican Party. | Southern Whigs join Democrats. |
| 1860 | Election of 1860 | satisfaction with election of Republican candidate Abraham Lincoln | Seven Southern states secede from Union. |

**CRITICAL THINKING** **Causes and Effects** Why did this series of laws and events shatter the unity of the nation?

**Lincoln's Inauguration** With the hopes for compromise fading, Americans waited for Lincoln's inauguration. What would the new president do about the crisis? On March 4, Lincoln took the oath of office and gave his First Inaugural Address. He assured the South that he had no intention of abolishing slavery there. But he spoke forcefully against secession. Then he ended his speech with an appeal to friendship.

### PRIMARY SOURCE

❝ We are not enemies, but friends. We must not be enemies. Though passion may have strained, it must not break our bonds of affection. The mystic chords of memory, stretching from every battle-field and patriot grave, to every living heart and hearthstone, all over this broad land, will yet swell the chorus of the Union, when again touched, as surely they will be, by the better angels of our nature. ❞

**Abraham Lincoln,** *First Inaugural Address*

Lincoln did not want to invade the South. But he would not abandon the government's forts that stood on Southern soil. These forts would soon need to be resupplied. Throughout March and into April, Northerners and Southerners waited anxiously to see what would happen next.

▲ **SEQUENCE** Explain how the Southern states justified secession.

---

**New Jersey Core Curriculum Content Standards** *Review*

 **ONLINE QUIZ**
For test practice, go to
**Interactive Review @ ClassZone.com**

### TERMS & NAMES

**1.** Explain the importance of
- Confederate States of America
- Jefferson Davis
- Crittenden Compromise

### USING YOUR READING NOTES

**2. Categorize** Complete the diagram you started at the beginning of this section.

| Southern Democrats | Northern Democrats |
|---|---|
| *wanted party to defend slavery* | |

### KEY IDEAS

**3.** Who were the candidates in the 1860 presidential election, and what policies did each candidate support?

**4.** What attempts did the North and the South make to compromise? What were the results?

### CRITICAL THINKING

**5. Analyze Point of View** Do you think the Southern states seceded to protect slavery or states' rights?

**6.** **Connect** *to* **Today** What can the events in this section teach us about compromise in the political process today?

**7.** **Writing** **News Article** Imagine you are a newspaper reporter covering the 1860 election. Write a short analysis of the election results for either Northern or Southern readers.

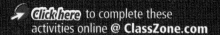

## Chapter Summary

**1** **Key Idea**
Rising anger over slavery increased tensions between the North and South and led to violence.

**2** **Key Idea**
The formation of the antislavery Republican Party further divided the country.

**3** **Key Idea**
The election of Abraham Lincoln as president in 1860 led seven Southern states to secede from the Union.

For detailed Review and Study Notes go to **Interactive Review** @ **ClassZone.com**

## Name Game

**Use the Terms & Names list to identify each sentence online or on your own paper.**

1. I was the first president of the Confederacy. _____
   Jefferson Davis 👆

2. This compromise of 1861 might have prevented secession. _____.

3. I am the Illinois senator who backed the Compromise of 1850. _____

4. I ran for President as a Democrat in 1856. _____

5. I wrote a novel about slavery. _____

6. I presided in the case of *Dred Scott* v. *Sandford*. _____

7. This party's slogan was "Free Soil, Free Speech, Free Labor, and Free Men." _____

8. This 1850 law was meant to help slaveholders recapture runaway slaves. _____

9. I was the Republican candidate in 1856. _____

10. This proposal was meant to outlaw slavery in new territories. _____

A. Harriet Beecher Stowe
B. Free-Soil Party
C. Roger B. Taney
D. Crittenden Compromise
E. Abraham Lincoln
F. James Buchanan
G. Wilmot Proviso
H. Jefferson Davis
I. Confederate States of America
J. Fugitive Slave Act
K. Stephen A. Douglas
L. John Frémont

## Activities

### CROSSWORD PUZZLE

Complete the online puzzle to show what you know about the buildup to the Civil War.

**ACROSS**
**1.** The election of this man frightened the Southern states.

### GEOGAME

Use this online map to reinforce your understanding of the sectional divide. Drag and drop the labels to identify slave states and free states. A scorecard helps you keep track of your progress online.

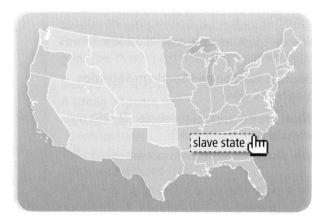

slave state

free state

slave state 👆

1. War Erupts

2. Life in the Army

3. No End in Sight

Detail of a
painting of
Union general
McClellan

# The Civil War Begins

## 1861–1862

### ESSENTIAL QUESTION

What events, leaders, and strategies
shaped the early years of war?

---

**CONNECT** ↻ **Geography & History**

What geographic features would the Union have to seize in order to
defeat the Confederacy?

**Think about:**

❶ how goods and weapons were transported in the South, which did not
have an extensive railway system

❷ the way the Southern economy relied on exporting cotton by ship

❸ the position of New Orleans, the South's largest city

**1861** July:
Confederacy sets up its
capital in Richmond.

Recruitment
posters

## 1861

**April:** Confederate
attack on Fort
Sumter

Detail of a painting
of Bull Run

**1861** July: First Battle of
Bull Run

▼

**Effect** Lincoln realizes he
must raise a national army.

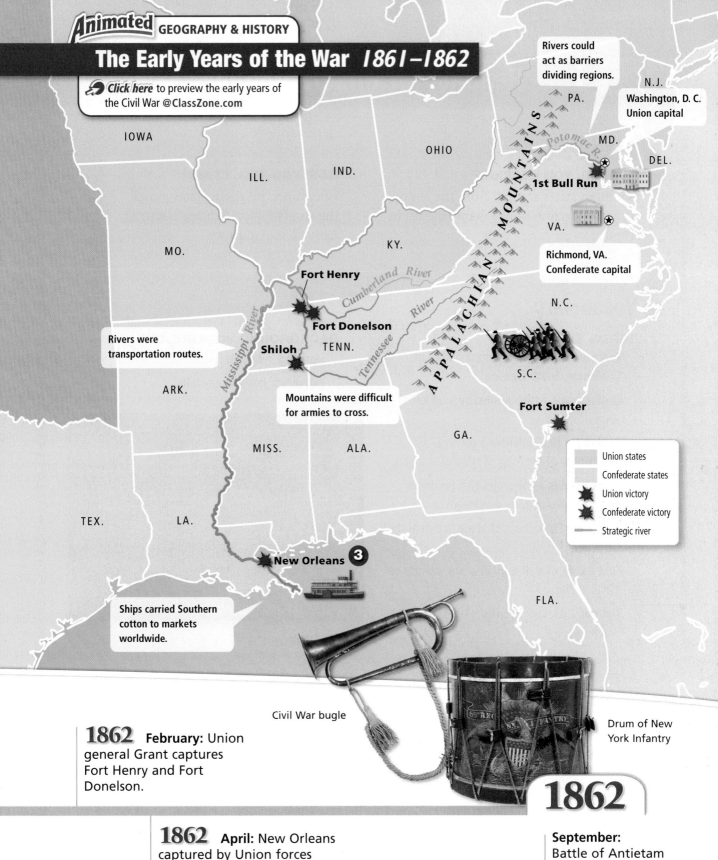

## The Early Years of the War 1861–1862

Click here to preview the early years of the Civil War @ClassZone.com

Rivers could act as barriers dividing regions.

N.J.

PA.

Washington, D. C.
Union capital

MD.

Potomac R.

DEL.

1st Bull Run

VA.

Richmond, VA.
Confederate capital

IOWA

OHIO

ILL.

IND.

N.C.

MO.

KY.

Fort Henry

Cumberland River

Fort Donelson

Tennessee River

APPALACHIAN MOUNTAINS

Shiloh

TENN.

Rivers were transportation routes.

S.C.

ARK.

Mississippi River

Fort Sumter

Mountains were difficult for armies to cross.

GA.

MISS.

ALA.

Union states
Confederate states
Union victory
Confederate victory
Strategic river

TEX.

LA.

New Orleans ③

FLA.

Ships carried Southern cotton to markets worldwide.

Civil War bugle

Drum of New York Infantry

**1862** **February:** Union general Grant captures Fort Henry and Fort Donelson.

**1862**

**1862** **April:** New Orleans captured by Union forces
▼
**Effect** The Confederacy loses its most important city.

**September:** Battle of Antietam
▼
**Effect** 23,000 casualties; Lee retreats

*The Civil War Begins* **509**

## ▶ Key Ideas

**BEFORE, YOU LEARNED**

Southern states seceded from the Union after the election of Abraham Lincoln in 1860.

**NOW YOU WILL LEARN**

After more Southern states joined the Confederacy, fighting began on Confederate territory.

## ▶ Vocabulary

**TERMS & NAMES**

**Fort Sumter** Union fort in the harbor of Charleston, South Carolina

**Confederacy** nation formed by Southern states

**Robert E. Lee** Confederate general, commander of the Army of Northern Virginia

**border states** slave states that bordered states in which slavery was illegal

**Anaconda Plan** Union strategy to defeat the Confederacy

**First Battle of Bull Run** first major battle of the Civil War

**Thomas J. Jackson** Confederate general at Bull Run

**BACKGROUND VOCABULARY**

**uprising** rebellion

**populous** heavily populated

Visual Vocabulary
Attack on Fort Sumter

## ▶ Reading Strategy

Re-create the diagram shown at right. As you read and respond to the **KEY QUESTIONS**, use the diagram to note problems faced by the Union and the Southern states and how they were addressed.

 See Skillbuilder Handbook, page R9.

**PROBLEMS AND SOLUTIONS**

| Problem | Solution |
|---|---|
| *What to do about the federal forts located in the Confederacy?* | |
| | |

**GRAPHIC ORGANIZERS**
Go to **Interactive Review** @ ClassZone.com

# War Erupts

**6.4.F.11.** Understand the institution of slavery in the United States, resistance to it, and New Jersey's role in the Underground Railroad.
**6.4.G.1.** Explain the major events, issues, and personalities of the American Civil War including the course and conduct of the war (e.g., Antietam, Vicksburg, Gettysburg).

## One American's Story

Like other South Carolinians, Emma Holmes got caught up in the passions that led her state to secede. In her diary, she wrote about South Carolina's attack on **Fort Sumter**, a federal fort on an island in Charleston's harbor.

Emma Holmes

### PRIMARY SOURCE

❝ [A]t half past four this morning, the heavy booming of cannons woke the city from its slumbers. . . . Every body seems relieved that what has been so long dreaded has come at last and so confident of victory that they seem not to think of the danger of their friends. . . . With the telescope I saw the shots as they struck the fort and [saw] the masonry crumbling. ❞

—Emma Holmes, *The Diary of Miss Emma Holmes 1861–1866*

Many Southerners expected a short war that they would easily win. Northerners expected the same. In this section, you will learn how Americans slowly realized that the war would be long and difficult.

## First Shots at Fort Sumter

🔻 **KEY QUESTION** What did Lincoln do about the forts in Confederate territory?

As Southern states seceded from the Union, they took control of most of the federal forts located within their borders. President Abraham Lincoln wrestled with a decision that might provoke war—what should he do about the forts that remained under federal control?

**Lincoln's Decision** In Charleston Harbor, Robert Anderson's garrison in Fort Sumter was running out of supplies.

Lincoln faced a difficult decision. If he sent supplies, he risked war. If he surrendered the fort, he would be giving in to the rebels. Lincoln decided to send supply ships and notified the leaders of the **Confederacy**—the nation formed by Southern states. Confederate leaders decided to attack the fort before the supply ships arrived.

## History Makers

### Abraham Lincoln 1809–1865

Today Abraham Lincoln, shown above with his son, is regarded as a national hero. Yet when Lincoln became President, many people in the North did not think he was equal to the enormous task before him.

Lincoln surprised his critics with his vision and his ability to organize and lead the war effort. In the nation's worst crisis, he focused on winning the war and preserving the Union. Throughout the war, Lincoln inspired fellow Americans to "dare to do our duty as we understand it."

**CRITICAL THINKING  Make Inferences**
Why would the ability to inspire people be important in a wartime leader?

 **ONLINE BIOGRAPHY**  For more on Abraham Lincoln, go to the **Research & Writing Center** @ ClassZone.com

On April 12, 1861, the Confederates opened fire. After enduring 34 hours of shelling, Anderson surrendered. No one was killed defending the fort, but the attack on Fort Sumter marked the beginning of the Civil War.

**Lincoln Calls Out the Militia**  Two days after the surrender of Fort Sumter, President Lincoln asked the Union states to provide 75,000 militiamen for 90 days to put down the **uprising**, or rebellion, in the South. Citizens of the North responded with enthusiasm to the call to arms. A New York woman wrote, "it seems as if we never were alive till now; never had a country till now."

In the upper South, however, state leaders responded with defiance. The governor of Kentucky said that the state would "furnish no troops for the wicked purpose of subduing her sister Southern states." In the weeks that followed, Virginia, North Carolina, Tennessee, and Arkansas voted to join the Confederacy.

▲ **PROBLEMS AND SOLUTIONS**  Explain how Lincoln tried to solve the problem of the federal forts.

## Preparing For Battle

▼ **KEY QUESTION**  What strategy did each side hope to pursue?

With Virginia on its side, the Confederacy had a better hope of victory. Virginia was rich and **populous**, or heavily populated. In July of 1861, the Confederacy moved its capital to Richmond.

Virginia was also the home of **Robert E. Lee**, a military leader who became the South's greatest general. When Virginia seceded, Lee resigned from the United States army and joined the Confederacy. Lee's support strengthened the Confederacy.

**Choosing Sides**  After Virginia seceded, all eyes turned to the **border states**. The border states—Delaware, Maryland, Kentucky, and Missouri—were slave states that bordered states where slavery was illegal. Their location and resources were important to both sides.

All four states stayed in the Union. Later in the war, the Union gained territory when the western counties of Virginia broke away from the Confederacy and formed the state of West Virginia in 1863. West Virginia supported the Union. In the end, there were 24 states in the Union and 11 in the Confederacy.

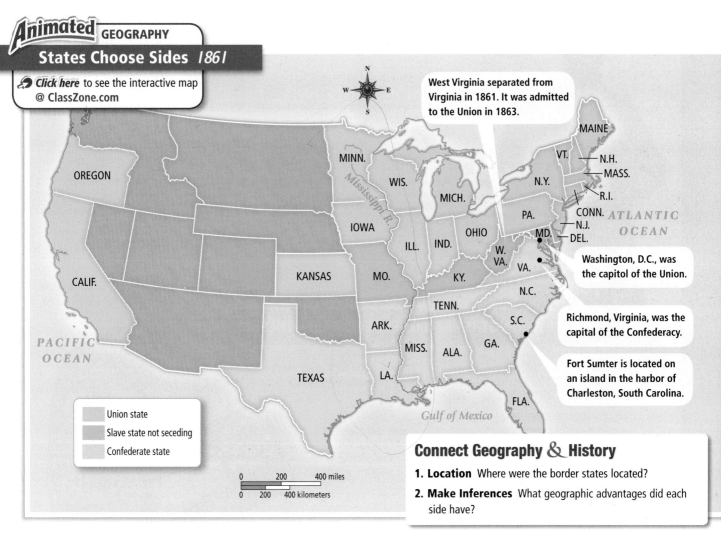

West Virginia separated from Virginia in 1861. It was admitted to the Union in 1863.

Washington, D.C., was the capitol of the Union.

Richmond, Virginia, was the capital of the Confederacy.

Fort Sumter is located on an island in the harbor of Charleston, South Carolina.

Union state
Slave state not seceding
Confederate state

0    200    400 miles
0    200    400 kilometers

**Connect Geography & History**

**1. Location** Where were the border states located?

**2. Make Inferences** What geographic advantages did each side have?

**Planning Strategies** The Confederacy started off with a defensive strategy. Confederate leaders knew that support for the war in the North would weaken if the fighting went on for a long time. They also hoped that foreign dependence on their cotton exports would bring military aid from Great Britain and France. But both European nations had sufficient supplies of cotton. The South adopted a mix of defensive and offensive strategy, invading the North several times.

The Northern strategy was to invade and conquer the South. To do this they adopted the **Anaconda Plan**, developed by General Winfield Scott. This plan was designed to strangle the South's economy like a giant anaconda snake squeezing its prey. The plan called for

- a naval blockade of the South's coastline. In a blockade, armed forces block the traffic of goods or people.
- taking control of the Mississippi River. This would split the Confederacy in two.
- capturing Richmond, Virginia—the Confederate capital.

With Richmond only about 100 miles from Washington, Virginia became the site of many battles during the war.

▲ **CAUSES AND EFFECTS** Explain each side's strategy for winning the war.

# COMPARING North and South

## UNION STRENGTHS

large population (22 million)

85% of nation's factories

70% of the nation's railroad mileage

almost all the nation's naval vessels and shipyards

## UNION WEAKNESSES

had to depend on long supply lines

fewer good military leaders

soldiers fighting an offensive war

Union general
McClellan

Confederate
general Lee

## CONFEDERATE STRENGTHS

vast size of the Confederacy

good generals

soldiers fighting a defensive war to protect their homeland

## CONFEDERATE WEAKNESSES

smaller population (5.5 million free; 3.5 million enslaved)

few factories

fewer railroads

no naval power

**CRITICAL THINKING** **Draw Conclusions** Which strength or weakness might have had the greatest effects?

## First Battle of Bull Run

🔻 **KEY QUESTION** Why was the Union surprised by the outcome of Bull Run?

Many people in the North called for an immediate attack on Richmond. But to take Richmond, the Union army would first have to defeat the Confederate troops stationed at the town of Manassas, Virginia, near Washington, D.C. Many believed the battle, and the war, would be quickly won.

**Intense Fighting** On July 16, 1861, Union forces led by General Irvin McDowell marched to Manassas. They were joined there by hundreds of spectators from Washington who expected a quick and entertaining battle. Both soldiers and spectators were totally unprepared for what followed.

Union forces attacked the Confederates near the creek called Bull Run. In the North this battle is known as the **First Battle of Bull Run**. The Confederates, led by General Pierre Beauregard, were driven back. However, a regiment led

Fighting at Bull Run

by **Thomas J. Jackson** stopped the Union advance. Another officer saw Jackson and said, "There is Jackson standing like a stone wall!" From then on, Jackson was known as "Stonewall" Jackson.

Confederate forces launched a counter-charge while letting out a blood-curdling scream that became known as the "rebel yell." Frightened Union soldiers ran for their lives, along with scared and confused spectators.

The Confederate victory thrilled the South and shocked the North. Casualty figures reached around 2,700 for the Union and 2,000 for the Confederacy. It was obvious that this would be a deadly war.

**Lessons of Bull Run** The First Battle of Bull Run made three points clear:

- The fighting would be bloody.
- The war would not be over quickly.
- Southern soldiers would fight fiercely to defend the Confederacy.

After Bull Run, Lincoln realized the 90-day militias were no match for Confederate forces. He sent them home and called for a real army of 500,000 volunteers for three years. He also appointed George McClellan as commander of the Union army in the east.

 **SUMMARIZE** Explain why the Union was surprised by the outcome of Bull Run.

---

**New Jersey Core Curriculum Content Standards *Review***

 **ONLINE QUIZ**
For test practice, go to
**Interactive Review @ ClassZone.com**

### TERMS & NAMES

**1.** Explain the significance of

- Fort Sumter
- Confederacy
- Robert E. Lee
- border states
- Anaconda Plan
- First Battle of Bull Run
- Thomas J. Jackson

### USING YOUR READING NOTES

**2. Problems and Solutions** Complete the diagram that you started at the beginning of this section.

| Problem | Solution |
|---------|----------|
| *What to do about the federal forts located in the Confederacy?* | |
| | |

### KEY IDEAS

**3.** What were Lincoln's choices in regard to Fort Sumter?

**4.** Why were the border states important to both sides in the Civil War?

**5.** What kind of military strategy did each side develop?

### CRITICAL THINKING

**6. Evaluate** Which side seemed better prepared for the conflict?

**7. Draw Conclusions** Why did the Confederacy adopt a defensive strategy?

**8. Connect Economics and History** How did the Union hope to damage the Southern economy?

**9. Writing Description** Imagine you were a spectator at Bull Run. Describe what you saw and explain how it changed your attitude toward the war.

## Key Ideas

**BEFORE, YOU LEARNED**

The Civil War began on Confederate territory.

**NOW YOU WILL LEARN**

Army life and new technology brought unexpected hardships to millions of soldiers.

## Vocabulary

**TERMS & NAMES**

the *Monitor* Union ironclad ship

the *Merrimack* Confederate ironclad ship, later renamed the *Virginia*

**BACKGROUND VOCABULARY**

**enlist** to join the armed forces

**contractor** private supplier

**hygiene** conditions and practices that promote health

**Visual Vocabulary**
The *Monitor* (below) clashes with the *Merrimack*, or *Virginia* (below left)

## Reading Strategy

Re-create the diagram shown at right. As you read and respond to the **KEY QUESTIONS**, use the boxes to show causes of important events. Create a new diagram for each event.

 See Skillbuilder Handbook, page R7.

**CAUSES AND EFFECTS**

| Cause | |
|---|---|
| African Americans saw the war as a way to end slavery. | **Effect** Many volunteered to fight. |
| **Cause** | |
| **Cause** | |

**GRAPHIC ORGANIZERS**
Go to **Interactive Review** @ ClassZone.com

# Life in the Army

 **6.4.G.1.** Explain the major events, issues, and personalities of the American Civil War including the course and conduct of the war (e.g., Antietam, Vicksburg, Gettysburg).

## One American's Story

In 1862, Peter Vredenburgh, Jr., answered President Lincoln's call for an additional 300,000 soldiers. Nearly 26 years old, Vredenburgh became a major in the 14th Regiment New Jersey Volunteer Infantry. Less than two months after joining the regiment, he wrote a letter urging his parents to keep his 18-year-old brother from enlisting.

### PRIMARY SOURCE

❝ I am glad that Jim has not joined any [regiment] and I hope he never will. I would not have him go for all my pay; it would be very improbable that we could both go through this war and come out unharmed. Let him come here and see the thousands with their arms and legs off, or if that won't do, let him go as I did the other day through the Frederick hospitals and see how little account a man's life and limbs are held in by others. ❞

—Major Peter Vredenburgh, Jr., quoted in *Upon the Tented Field*

Major Peter Vredenburgh, Jr., was an officer in the Union army.

On September 19, 1864, Vredenburgh was killed in battle. He was only one of many young men unprepared for the horrors of the war.

## Civilians Become Soldiers

🔻 **KEY QUESTION** Why did so many volunteer to fight?

Like Peter Vredenburgh, the majority of soldiers in the Civil War were between 18 and 30 years of age. But both the Confederate and Union armies had younger and older soldiers, whose ages ranged from 11 to 83. These soldiers came from cities, towns, and farms across America.

**Joining Up** On both sides volunteers rushed to **enlist**, or join the army. Many were farmers who had never been far from home. Some rode a train for the first time. German and Irish immigrants made up the largest ethnic groups.

(top) Soldiers off duty. (inset) Union jacket and cap.

**How does the crisp, new jacket above compare to those in the larger photograph?**

At the beginning of the war, African Americans wanted to fight. They saw the war as a way to end slavery. However, neither the North nor the South accepted African Americans into their armies—at first. But as the war dragged on, the North finally took African Americans into its ranks.

In all, about 2 million men served in the Union Army and less than 1 million fought for the Confederacy. Most were volunteers. They enlisted for many different reasons. Some fought out of loyalty to their state or country. They also sought excitement and glory. Some soldiers signed up to escape the boredom of their lives in the factory or on the farm. Still others joined for the money.

**Turning Civilians Into Soldiers** After enlisting, volunteers were sent to an army camp for training. They lived in tents and had drill sessions. In winter, the soldiers lived in log huts or in heavy tents positioned on a log base.

Union soldiers were issued blue uniforms. Confederate soldiers wore gray or yellowish-brown. Early in the war, Northern soldiers received clothing of very poor quality. **Contractors,** or private suppliers, often supplied shoddy goods. In the Confederacy, some states had trouble providing uniforms at all. Confederate soldiers sometimes lacked shoes. After battles needy soldiers took coats, boots, and other clothing from the dead.

As the war went on, food became scarce. When soldiers were on the march they were sometimes out of reach of supply trains and had to find food on their own.

▲ **CAUSES AND EFFECTS** Explain why men volunteered for the army.

# A New Kind of War

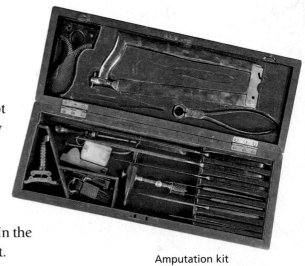

Amputation kit
**Why would equipment like this have helped increase casualties?**

▼ **KEY QUESTION** How was the Civil War different from previous conflicts?

For many soldiers, the experience of army life did not meet their expectations. Advances in military technology brought high casualties. Primitive medical techniques and filthy conditions helped spread disease.

**Unhealthy Conditions** Military camps were filthy and smelled from the odors of garbage and latrines. One Union soldier described a camp near Washington. In the camp, cattle were killed to provide the troops with meat.

### PRIMARY SOURCE

❝ The hides and [waste parts] of the [cattle] for miles upon miles around, under a sweltering sun and sultry showers, would gender such swarms of flies, armies of worms, blasts of stench and oceans of filth as to make life miserable. ❞

—William Keesy, quoted in *The Civil War Infantryman*

Not only were the camps filthy, but so were the soldiers. They often went weeks without bathing or washing their clothes. Their bodies, clothing, and bedding became infested with lice and fleas. Poor **hygiene**—or conditions and practices that promote health—resulted in widespread sickness. Doctors were unaware that dirt carried germs that caused disease. They performed surgery without washing their hands. Because of these conditions, more soldiers died from disease than on the battlefield.

Andersonville prison camp. A prisoner's meal might be little more than a single cracker.

**Civil War Prison Camps** The war was difficult for all soldiers, but prisoners had an especially hard time. At prison camps in both the North and the South, prisoners of war faced terrible conditions.

One of the worst prison camps in the North was in Elmira, New York. In just one year, more than 24 percent of Elmira's 12,121 prisoners died of sickness and exposure to severe weather.

Conditions were also horrible in the South. The camp with the worst reputation was in Andersonville, Georgia. Inmates had little shelter from the heat or cold. Drinking water came from a tiny creek that also served as a sewer. As many as 13,000 died at Andersonville from starvation, disease, and exposure.

## CIVIL WAR TECHNOLOGY

The American Civil War brought startling changes to military warfare.

### Railroads and Cannons

The North's superior railway system gave the Union a distinct advantage. Railways helped move millions of soldiers and supplies quickly and easily to strategic positions. Cannon could also be mounted on railcars, as in the photo above.

### Ironclads

The ironclads transformed naval warfare. Powered by steam, and with their sides protected by iron plates, ironclads were fast and deadly. The Union churned them out in order to create an inland navy to control Southern rivers. Union ironclads like the one above played an important role in Grant's capture of Fort Henry.

### Rifles and Grenades

The rifle and minié ball increased the range of accuracy from 100 to 400 yards. Defenders could shoot down lines of advancing troops. Grenades were thrown by hand and exploded on impact. The days of formal, linear warfare were over.

### Trenches

Soldiers quickly learned to stay low to the ground in order to avoid rifle fire. The new weaponry encouraged soldiers to protect themselves by digging trenches. Massive trench systems were dug by both sides during the war.

---

**CRITICAL THINKING** **Make Inferences** Which aspect of military technology do you think had the most impact on the fighting?

**Changes in Military Technology** Improvements in the weapons of war had far-reaching effects. The new weaponry increased the number of casualties. It also changed battlefield strategies.

One change was the use of rifles and minié balls. A rifle is a gun with a grooved barrel that spins a bullet through the air. The minié ball is a bullet with a hollow base. The bullet expands upon firing to fit the grooves in the barrel. Rifles with minié balls could shoot farther and more accurately than old-fashioned muskets. As a result, mounted charges and assaults did not work as well. Defenders could shoot more of the attackers before they got close.

New technology also changed naval warfare. Ironclads were naval warships covered with iron. They were a vast improvement over conventional warships. Ironclads were faster and better-protected than wooden ships. A witness reported that an ironclad ship's prow cut through a wooden ship "as a knife goes through cheese."

In March 1862, off the coast of Virginia, a Union ironclad named **the** *Monitor*, fought **the** *Merrimack*, a Confederate ironclad renamed the *Virginia*. The day-long battle between the *Monitor* and the *Merrimack* ended in a draw. But the event became famous as the first battle in history between two ironclad ships.

Despite new technology and tactics, in the first two years of the war, neither side was able to defeat its enemy.

 **SUMMARIZE** Describe ways the Civil War differed from previous conflicts.

---

**New Jersey Core Curriculum Content Standards** *Review*

 **ONLINE QUIZ**
For test practice, go to
**Interactive Review** @ ClassZone.com

**TERMS & NAMES**

**1.** Explain the significance of
- the *Monitor*
- the *Merrimack*

**USING YOUR READING NOTES**

**2. Causes and Effects** Complete the diagram that you started at the beginning of this section.

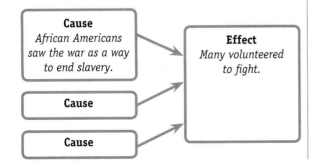

**Cause**
*African Americans saw the war as a way to end slavery.*

**Effect**
*Many volunteered to fight.*

**Cause**

**Cause**

**KEY IDEAS**

**3.** What was life like for the volunteers?

**4.** Why did so many soldiers die of disease?

**5.** How did the use of the rifle and minié ball change combat tactics in the Civil War?

**CRITICAL THINKING**

**6. Draw Conclusions** Why would commanders have to worry about marching too far from supply trains?

**7. Causes and Effects** What caused the high death rates during the Civil War?

**8. Make Inferences** Why were ironclads an improvement over wooden ships?

**9.** **Math** Research the casualty figures of the Civil War. Make a graph to display the information.

## Key Ideas

**BEFORE, YOU LEARNED**

The Union defeat at the Battle of Bull Run shocked the North.

**NOW YOU WILL LEARN**

Both the Union and the Confederacy won important victories in the first years of the war.

## Vocabulary

**TERMS & NAMES**

**George McClellan** commander of Union army in the east

**Ulysses S. Grant** Union general who won battles in the west

**Battle of Shiloh** bloody battle in Tennessee won by Grant

**William Tecumseh Sherman** Union general at Battle of Shiloh

**David Farragut** Union naval commander who captured New Orleans

**Seven Days' Battles** Confederate victory in Virginia, during which Lee stopped Union campaign against Richmond

**Battle of Antietam** battle in Maryland that ended Lee's first invasion of the North

**BACKGROUND VOCABULARY**

**plunder** steal from, ransack

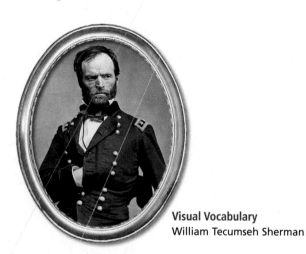

**Visual Vocabulary**
William Tecumseh Sherman

## Reading Strategy

Re-create the diagram shown at right. As you read and respond to the **KEY QUESTIONS**, use the diagram to record the events that support the main idea that the Union was succeeding in splitting the Confederacy in two.

 See Skillbuilder Handbook, page R4.

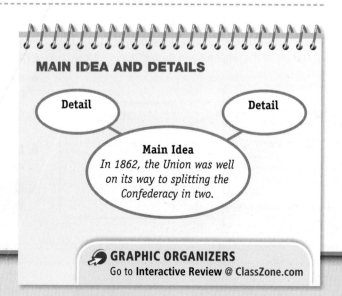

**MAIN IDEA AND DETAILS**

Detail

Detail

**Main Idea**
*In 1862, the Union was well on its way to splitting the Confederacy in two.*

**GRAPHIC ORGANIZERS**
Go to **Interactive Review** @ ClassZone.com

# No End in Sight

🔲 **6.4.G.1.** Explain the major events, issues, and personalities of the American Civil War including the course and conduct of the war (e.g., Antietam, Vicksburg, Gettysburg).

## One American's Story

Twenty-year-old Sarah Morgan was living in the river town of Baton Rouge, Louisiana, when the Yankee gunships arrived. The Union navy had already captured New Orleans. Now Union ships were sailing deep into Confederate territory. When the gunships began shelling the town, the Morgans fled their home.

### PRIMARY SOURCE

Sarah Morgan

❝ As we stood in the door, four or five shells sailed over our heads at the same time, seeming to make a perfect corkscrew of the air—for it sounded as though it went in circles. . . . I [stayed] behind to lock the door, with this new music in my ears. . . . I had heard Jimmy laugh about the singular sensation produced by the rifled balls spinning around one's head, and [here] I heard the same peculiar sound, ran the same risk, and was equal to the rest of the boys, for was I not in the midst of flying shells, in the middle of a bombardment? I think I was rather proud of it. ❞

—Sarah Morgan, *The Civil War Diary of a Southern Woman*

Sarah Morgan had rejoiced at the news of Confederate victories in the east. Now she remained defiant as the Union gained control of the Mississippi River in the west.

## Union Victories in the West

🔽 **KEY QUESTION** In 1862, how close did the Union come to achieving its goals?

In the summer of 1861, President Lincoln gave **George McClellan** command of the Union army in the East. The army had recently been defeated at Bull Run. Within months, McClellan restored the soldiers' confidence and organized and trained an army that could defeat the Confederates. Although McClellan prepared his army well, he seemed reluctant to attack the Southern capital at

Richmond. Instead, he kept drilling his troops. Lincoln, growing impatient, said that McClellan had "the slows." Meanwhile, another Union general was winning victories in the west.

**Grant Opens Up the South** That victorious Union general in the west was **Ulysses S. Grant**. In civilian life, he had failed at many things. But Grant had a simple strategy of war: "Find out where your enemy is. Get at him as soon as you can. Strike at him as hard as you can, and keep moving on."

In February 1862, Grant made a bold move to take Tennessee. Using ironclad gunboats, Grant's forces captured two Confederate river forts. These were Fort Henry on the Tennessee and Fort Donelson on the nearby Cumberland. (See map **A**) The seizure of Fort Henry opened up a river highway into the heart of the South. Union gunboats could now travel by river as far as northern Alabama. A week later, Union troops marched into Nashville.

**The Battle of Shiloh** After Grant's river victories, Albert S. Johnston, Confederate commander on the Western front, ordered a retreat to Corinth, Mississippi. Grant followed. By early April, Grant's troops had reached Pittsburg Landing on the Tennessee River. There he waited for more troops from Nashville. Johnston, however, decided to attack before Grant gained reinforcements. Marching his troops north

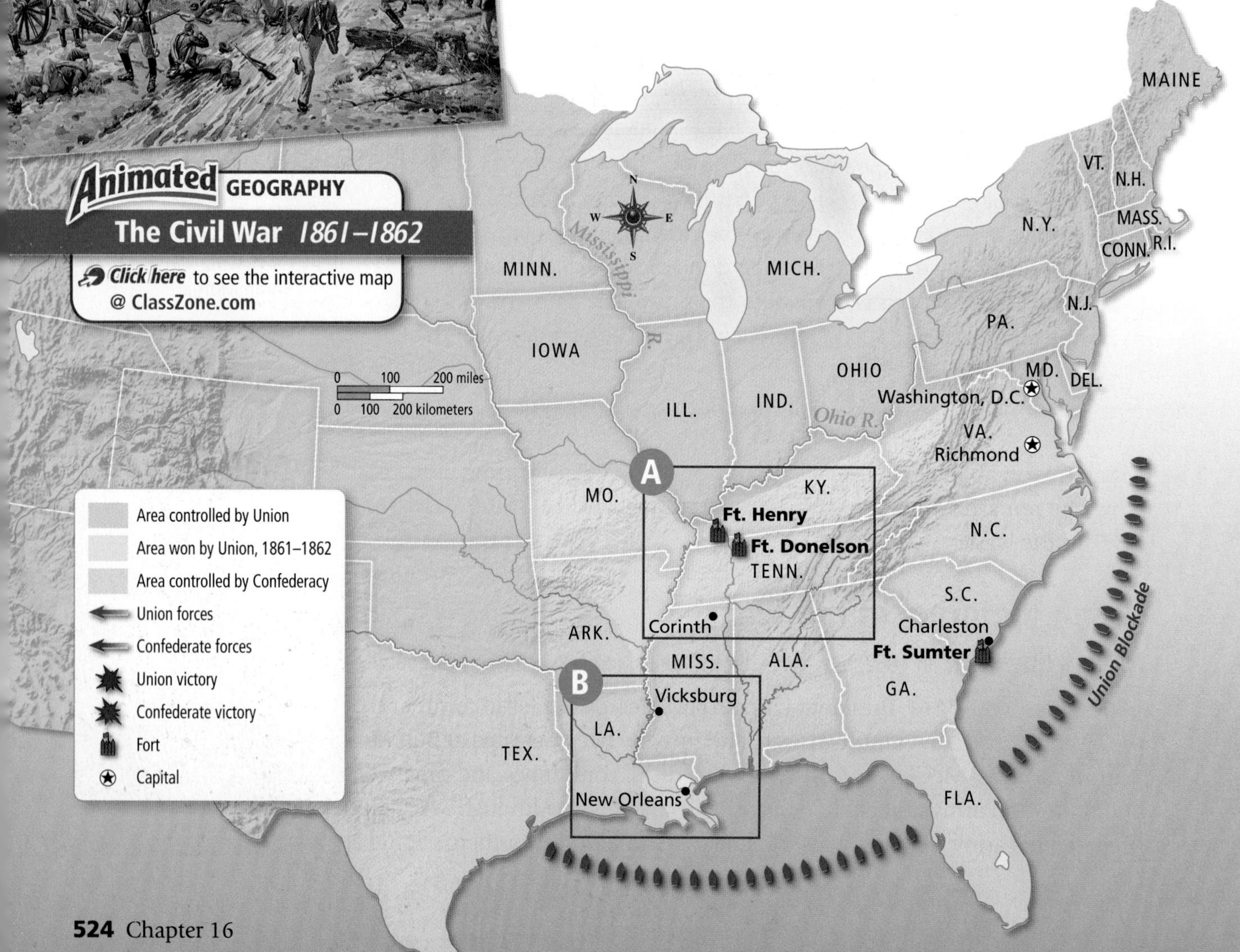

Battle of Shiloh

**Animated GEOGRAPHY**

**The Civil War** *1861–1862*

*Click here* to see the interactive map @ ClassZone.com

MAINE
VT.
N.H.
MINN.
MICH.
N.Y.
MASS.
CONN. R.I.
PA.
N.J.
IOWA
OHIO
MD. DEL.
Washington, D.C.
ILL.
IND.
Ohio R.
VA.
Richmond
MO.
**A**
KY.
**Ft. Henry**
N.C.
**Ft. Donelson**
TENN.
S.C.
ARK.
Corinth
Charleston
**Ft. Sumter**
MISS.
ALA.
**B**
Vicksburg
GA.
LA.
TEX.
New Orleans
FLA.
Union Blockade

Mississippi R.

| | Area controlled by Union |
| | Area won by Union, 1861–1862 |
| | Area controlled by Confederacy |
| ← | Union forces |
| ← | Confederate forces |
| ✹ | Union victory |
| ✹ | Confederate victory |
| 🏰 | Fort |
| ★ | Capital |

0   100   200 miles
0   100   200 kilometers

from Corinth on April 6, 1862, Johnston surprised the Union forces near Shiloh Church. The Battle of Shiloh in Tennessee turned into the fiercest fighting the Civil War had yet seen. (See map **B** below.)

Commanders on each side rode into the thick of battle to rally their troops. One Union general, **William Tecumseh Sherman**, had three horses shot out from under him. General Johnston was killed, and the command passed to General Pierre Beauregard. By the end of the day, each side believed that dawn would bring victory.

That night, there was a terrible thunderstorm. Lightning lit up the battlefield, where dead and dying soldiers lay in water and mud. During the night, Union boats ferried fresh troops to Grant's camp. Grant then led an attack at dawn and forced the exhausted Southern troops to retreat.

The cost of the Union victory was staggering. Union casualties at Shiloh numbered over 13,000, about one-fifth of the 65,000 who had fought. The Confederates lost nearly 11,000 out of 41,000 soldiers. Describing the piles of mangled bodies, General Sherman wrote home, "The scenes on this field would have cured anybody of war." In the North, people were horrified at the slaughter. Members of Congress criticized Grant for the high casualties and urged Lincoln to replace him. But Lincoln replied, "I can't spare this man—he fights."

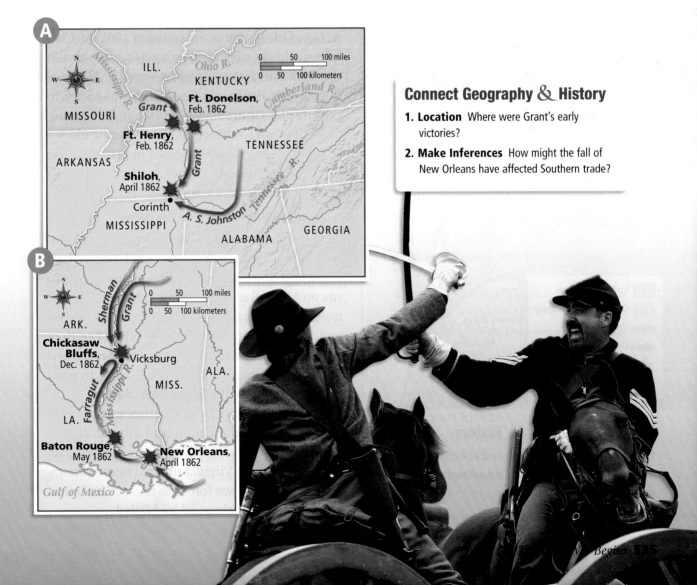

## Connect Geography & History

1. **Location** Where were Grant's early victories?

2. **Make Inferences** How might the fall of New Orleans have affected Southern trade?

# Across Five Aprils
## by Irene Hunt

Irene Hunt's acclaimed historical novel, *Across Five Aprils*, captures the emotions, events, and people of the Civil War era. The book tells the story of Jethro Creighton, a boy of nine who grows into manhood during the four long years of civil war in the United States. Hunt depicts the savagery of battle as well as the difficulties of those who endure the conflict at home. In this scene, Jethro listens to members of his extended family—Wilse, Matt, John, and Bill—debate the issue of slavery and its effects on the Union. Here Jethro's cousin, Wilse Graham, responds to a question about whether slaves in the South should be freed.

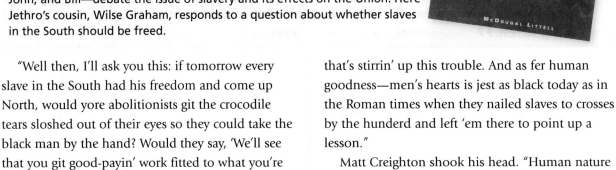

"Well then, I'll ask you this: if tomorrow every slave in the South had his freedom and come up North, would yore abolitionists git the crocodile tears sloshed out of their eyes so they could take the black man by the hand? Would they say, 'We'll see that you git good-payin' work fitted to what you're able to do—we'll see that you're well housed and clothed—we want you to come to our churches and yore children to come to our schools—why, we danged near fergit the difference in the colors of our skins because we air so almighty full of brotherly love!' Would it be like that in yore northern cities, Cousin John?"

"It ain't like that fer the masses of white people in our northern cities—nor in the southern cities either. And yet, there ain't a white man, lean-bellied and hopeless as so many of them are, that would change lots with a slave belongin' to the kindest master in the South."

Then Bill spoke for the first time, his eyes still on the yellow light of the lamp.

"Slavery, I hate. But it is with us, and them that should suffer fer the evil they brought to our shores air long dead. What I want us to answer in this year of 1861 is this, John: does the trouble over slavery come because men's hearts is purer above the Mason-Dixon line? Or does slavery throw a shadder over greed and keep that greed from showin' up quite so bare and ugly?"

Wilse Graham seemed to leap at Bill's question. "You're right, Cousin Bill. It's greed, not slavery, that's stirrin' up this trouble. And as fer human goodness—men's hearts is jest as black today as in the Roman times when they nailed slaves to crosses by the hunderd and left 'em there to point up a lesson."

Matt Creighton shook his head. "Human nature ain't any better one side of a political line than on the other—we all know that—but human nature, the all-over picture of it, *is* better than it was a thousand—five hundred—even a hundred years ago. There is an awakenin' inside us of human decency and responsibility. If I didn't believe that, I wouldn't grieve fer the children I've buried; I wouldn't look for'ard to the manhood of this youngest one."

Jethro felt as if he were bursting with the tumult inside him. The thought of war had given him a secret delight only a matter of hours before . . .

Suddenly he was deeply troubled. He groped towards an understanding of something that was far beyond the excitement of guns and shouting men; but he could not find words to define what he felt, and that lack left him in a turmoil of frustration.

- - - - - - - - - - - - - - - - - - - - - - - - - - - - -

### ADDITIONAL READING

*Carrying the Flag*, by Gordon C. Rhea  Mr. Rhea tells the amazing story of Private Charles Whilden, an unlikely hero of the Confederacy.

*To Be a Slave*, by Julius Lester  Julius Lester presents a wealth of slave narratives that provide important insight into the lives of enslaved African Americans in the early years of America. Paintings by Tom Feelings capture the brutality of the slave experience.

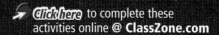

## Chapter Summary

**① Key Idea**
After more Southern states joined the Confederacy, fighting began on Confederate territory.

**② Key Idea**
Army life and new technology brought unexpected hardships to millions of soldiers.

**③ Key Idea**
Both the Union and the Confederacy won important victories in the first years of the war.

For detailed Review and Study Notes go to **Interactive Review** @ ClassZone.com

## Name Game

Use the Terms & Names list to identify each sentence online or on your own paper.

1. I was the Confederacy's greatest general.
Robert E. Lee

2. This Union ironclad fought the *Merrimack*. ____

3. I was a Union general who won battles in the west. ____

4. I was the commander of the Union army in the east. ____

5. This plan was meant to strangle the Confederacy. ____

6. I captured New Orleans. ____

7. This was the first major battle of the Civil War. ____

8. I was a Confederate general at Bull Run. ____

9. During these battles, Lee prevented a Union attack on Richmond. ____

10. The attack on this Union fort marked the beginning of the Civil War. ____

A. Anaconda Plan
B. Thomas J. Jackson
C. *Monitor*
D. George McClellan
E. Seven Days' Battles
F. Fort Sumter
G. Robert E. Lee
H. William Tecumseh Sherman
I. First Battle of Bull Run
J. Ulysses S. Grant
K. Battle of Shiloh
L. David Farragut

## Activities

### CROSSWORD PUZZLE

Complete the online crossword puzzle to show what you know about the early years of the Civil War.

**ACROSS**
1. ____ was a very cautious Union general.

### GEOGAME

Use this online map to reinforce your understanding of the first years of the Civil War, including the locations of important battles and geographic features. Drag and drop each place name in the list at its location on the map. A scorecard helps you keep track of your progress online.

Mississippi River
Shiloh
New Orleans
Bull Run
Tennessee River

More items online.

New Orleans

# CHAPTER 16 Assessment

## VOCABULARY

**Explain the significance of each of the following.**

1. William Tecumseh Sherman
2. Battle of Antietam
3. George McClellan
4. Ulysses S. Grant
5. Robert E. Lee
6. the *Monitor* and the *Merrimack*
7. First Battle of Bull Run
8. Fort Sumter
9. Confederacy
10. Anaconda Plan
11. Battle of Shiloh
12. David Farragut

**Match each military commander on the left with a battle on the right and explain the role he played in that battle.**

13. Grant
14. Sherman
15. Lee
16. McClellan
17. Farragut
18. Jackson
19. Johnston

A. Battle of Shiloh
B. Battle of Antietam
C. Seven Days' Battles
D. New Orleans
E. First Battle of Bull Run

## KEY IDEAS

### 1 War Erupts (pages 510–515)

20. What did the South need to do to win the war?
21. What did the Battle of Bull Run reveal about the future battles of the Civil War?

### 2 Life in the Army (pages 516–521)

22. Why did so many people volunteer to fight in the Civil War?
23. How did the use of rifles and minié balls change military tactics?

### 3 No End in Sight (pages 522–529)

24. What part of the Union strategy did Grant accomplish in 1862? How did he do it?
25. Why did Congressmen criticize Grant and why did Lincoln like him?

## CRITICAL THINKING

26. **Evaluate** Which side came out of the Battle of Shiloh in worse condition? Explain your answer.
27. **Draw Conclusions** Why do you think Confederate forces attacked Fort Sumter when they did?
28. **Make Inferences** What did the Union hope to gain by damaging the Southern economy?
29. **Compare and Contrast** Compare and contrast the Union with the Confederacy by filling in this chart.

|  | Union | Confederacy |
|---|---|---|
| *Reasons for Fighting* | to preserve the Union |  |
| *Advantages* |  |  |
| *Disadvantages* |  |  |
| *Military Strategy* |  |  |
| *Battle Victories* |  |  |

30. **Causes and Effects** Why did the introduction of ironclad warships have such an impact on naval warfare?
31. **Draw Conclusions** Why did the North have such difficulty in capturing Richmond, Virginia?
32. **Make Inferences** What changes in military technology might have surprised new recruits?
33. **Connect Geography and History** Study the map below. Why didn't McClellan take a land route to attack Richmond?

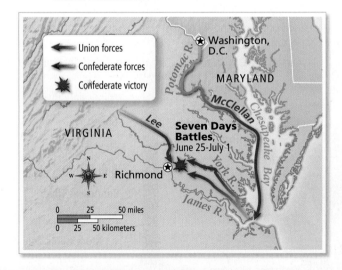

## DOCUMENT-BASED QUESTIONS

### PART 1: Short Answer

**Analyze each document and answer the questions that follow.**

**DOCUMENT 1**

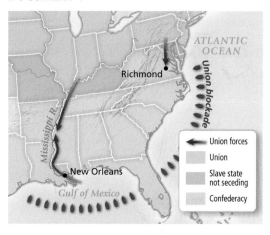

1. Examine this map of the Anaconda Plan. By 1862, which parts of the plan had been successful?

**DOCUMENT 2**

**PRIMARY SOURCE**

**❝** [S]oon as I feel that my army is well organized and well disciplined and strong enough, I will advance and force the Rebels to a battle on a field of my own selection. A long time must elapse before I can do that. **❞**

—General George McClellan, quoted in
*Civil War Journal: The Leaders*

2. What reason does General McClellan give for his slowness in attacking Confederate forces?

### Part 2: Essay

3. Using the information from the documents, your answers to the questions in Part 1, and your knowledge of U.S. history, write an essay that describes the success of the Anaconda Plan in the early years of the war.

## YOU BE THE HISTORIAN

34. **WHAT IF?** In what ways might history have been changed if Lincoln had ordered Major Anderson to turn Fort Sumter over to the Confederacy?

35. **Causes and Effects** How do you think the Civil War affected the lives of civilians who were not in the war zone?

36. **Compare and Contrast** In what ways was the South's strategy in 1861–1862 like the American army's strategy during the American Revolution?

37. **Evaluate** What does the presence of picnickers at the Battle of Bull Run reveal about civilians' attitude to the war?

38. **Make Generalizations** Why is an invading army usually at a disadvantage in a conflict?

39. **Analyze Point of View** What does Lincoln's admiration for Grant reveal about Lincoln?

Answer the
## ESSENTIAL QUESTION
**What events, leaders, and strategies shaped the early years of the war?**

**Written Response** Write a four–paragraph response to the Essential Question. Be sure to consider the key ideas of each section as well as the most significant facts that helped determine your answer. Use the Response Rubric below to guide your thinking and writing.

### Response Rubric
**A strong response will**

• describe each side's strengths and weaknesses
• evaluate how close each side came to achieving its strategic goals
• explain the long-term effects of the events of the first two years of the war

# 17

1. The Emancipation Proclamation
2. War Affects Society
3. The North Wins
4. The Legacy of the War

*The Freedman* by John Quincy Adams Ward

# The Tide of War Turns

## 1863–1865

### ESSENTIAL QUESTION

In what ways did the Civil War transform the nation?

---

**CONNECT** Geography & History

How did the Union make use of Southern geography in order to defeat the Confederacy?

**Think about:**

**1** Union victories during the first two years of the war

**2** the strength of the Union navy

**3** the destructive Union march through Georgia

---

**1863** May
Siege of Vicksburg begins.

## 1863

**January** Lincoln issues the Emancipation Proclamation.

▼

**Effect** Slaves are declared free in Confederate territory.

**1863** July Battle of Gettysburg takes place.
**July** Vicksburg falls.

▼

**Effect** The tide of war turns in favor of the North.

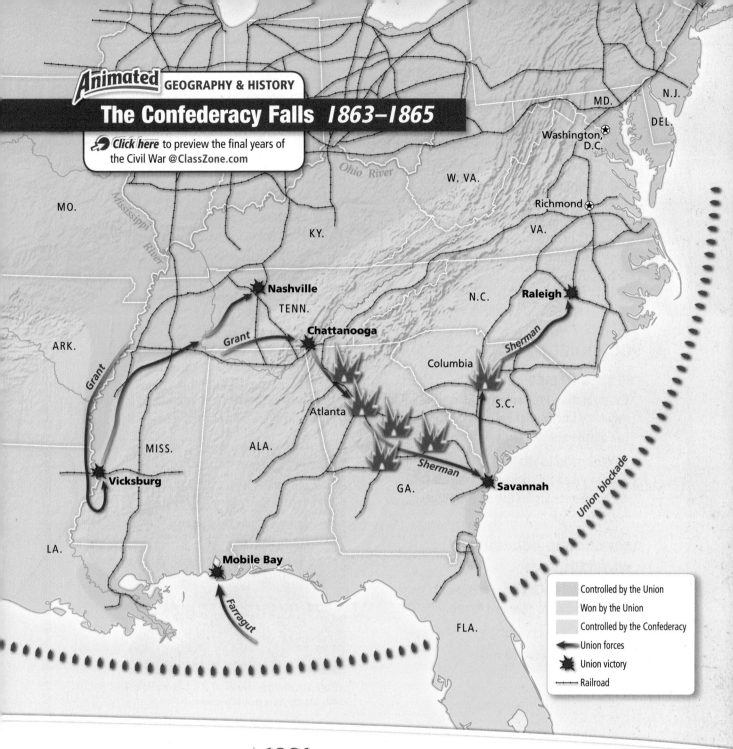

## Animated GEOGRAPHY & HISTORY

# The Confederacy Falls 1863–1865

🖱 **Click here** to preview the final years of the Civil War @ClassZone.com

MO.

MISSISSIPPI River

Ohio River

W. VA.

MD.

N.J.

DEL.

Washington, D.C. ⊛

Richmond ⊛

VA.

ARK.

KY.

TENN.

**Nashville**

Grant

Grant

**Chattanooga**

N.C.

**Raleigh**

Sherman

Columbia

Atlanta

S.C.

MISS.

ALA.

Sherman

**Vicksburg**

GA.

**Savannah**

Union blockade

LA.

**Mobile Bay**

Farragut

FLA.

| | |
|---|---|
| ▨ | Controlled by the Union |
| ▨ | Won by the Union |
| ▨ | Controlled by the Confederacy |
| ← | Union forces |
| ✸ | Union victory |
| ┼┼┼ | Railroad |

**1864** **March**
General Grant is appointed commander of all Union armies.

**1864** **November** Union general Sherman begins his March to the Sea.

▼

**Effect** Southern resources are destroyed; Southern morale sinks.

# 1865

**April** Lee surrenders at Appomattox Court House.

*Lee Surrendering at Appomattox* by Thomas Lovell

# Reading for Understanding

## ▶ Key Ideas

**BEFORE, YOU LEARNED**

Abolitionists had been fighting to end slavery for many decades before the Civil War began.

**NOW YOU WILL LEARN**

The Emancipation Proclamation promised freedom to slaves in the Confederacy and allowed African Americans to join the Union army.

## ▶ Vocabulary

**TERMS & NAMES**

**Emancipation Proclamation** document issued by Lincoln that declared that all slaves in Confederate-held territory were free

**54th Massachusetts Volunteers** regiment of African-American soldiers that gained fame for its courageous assault on Fort Wagner, South Carolina

**BACKGROUND VOCABULARY**

**emancipate** to free

**Commander-In-Chief** the President in his role as commander of all armed forces

**liberation** the act of setting someone free

**prolong** to lengthen (in time)

**REVIEW**

**Battle of Antietam** bloody battle in Maryland that ended Lee's first invasion of the North

**Visual Vocabulary** detail of a sculpture of the 54th Massachusetts Volunteers

## ▶ Reading Strategy

Re-create the diagram shown at right. As you read and respond to the **KEY QUESTIONS**, use the diagram to note the effects of the Emancipation Proclamation.

 See Skillbuilder Handbook, page R7.

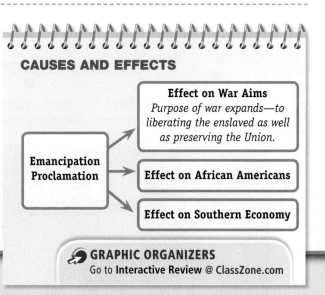

**CAUSES AND EFFECTS**

Emancipation Proclamation

→ **Effect on War Aims**
*Purpose of war expands—to liberating the enslaved as well as preserving the Union.*

→ **Effect on African Americans**

→ **Effect on Southern Economy**

🔗 **GRAPHIC ORGANIZERS**
Go to **Interactive Review** @ ClassZone.com

# The Emancipation Proclamation

 **6.4.G.1.** Explain the major events, issues, and personalities of the American Civil War including the Emancipation Proclamation.

## One American's Story

During the Civil War, abolitionists such as Frederick Douglass continued their campaign against slavery. Douglass urged President Lincoln to **emancipate**, or free, all enslaved Americans.

### PRIMARY SOURCE

❝ To fight against slaveholders, without fighting against slavery, is but a half-hearted business, and paralyzes the hands engaged in it. . . . Fire must be met with water. . . . War for the destruction of liberty [by the South] must be met with war for the destruction of slavery. ❞

—Frederick Douglass, quoted in *Battle Cry of Freedom*

Frederick Douglass

For Douglass there was now a practical as well as a moral purpose for ending slavery. If the Union promised to end slavery, millions of enslaved Americans might help the Union cause. Urged on by Douglass and others, Lincoln decided to act.

## A War of Liberation

🔻 **KEY QUESTION** How did the Emancipation Proclamation affect the war effort?

Arguments over the issue of slavery had brought the nation to war. Now the war was forcing Americans to resolve the slavery question once and for all.

**Abolitionists Demand Action** In parts of the South, slavery began collapsing early in the war. As Union armies swept through Confederate territory, thousands of enslaved people escaped from the plantations.

Meanwhile, abolitionists were pressuring the government to act. They realized that the war provided an opportunity to destroy slavery forever. Lincoln hesitated for several reasons. Although he did not like slavery, he feared that he did not have the constitutional power to abolish slavery in every state.

Most importantly, Lincoln's priority was to preserve the Union. "If I could save the Union without freeing any slave I would do it," he declared. "If I could save it by freeing all the slaves I would do it; and if I could save it be freeing some and leaving others alone, I would also do that."

In his struggle to keep the Union together, Lincoln did not want to anger the border states, the four slave states that remained in the Union. He also knew that many in the North opposed emancipation.

By the summer of 1862, however, Lincoln had decided in favor of emancipation. The war was taking a terrible toll. If freeing the slaves helped weaken the South, then he would do it. Lincoln waited for a moment when the Union was in a position of strength. After General Lee's forces were stopped at the **Battle of Antietam**, Lincoln felt confident enough to act.

**The Emancipation Proclamation** On January 1, 1863, Lincoln issued the **Emancipation Proclamation**, which declared that all slaves in Confederate-held territory were free.

### PRIMARY SOURCE

❝ On the first day of January, in the year of our Lord one thousand eight hundred and sixty-three, all persons held as slaves within any State or designated part of a State, the people whereof shall then be in rebellion against the United States, shall be then, thenceforward, and forever free. ❞

—**Abraham Lincoln, from the *Emancipation Proclamation***

The proclamation made a great impact on the public, but it freed few slaves. The Union army could enforce the proclamation only in the Confederate territory under its control. Most slaves lived in areas far removed from the Union army and remained under the control of plantation owners.

Scene of the Emancipation Proclamation being read in a slave cabin. **Why didn't the artist show the Proclamation being read outside, in daylight?**

## FREEDOM TO THE SLAVE

Political cartoons are images that carry a political message. Older political cartoons, especially those from the 18th and 19th centuries, are often very detailed. First read the words in the banner. Then study the cartoon in order to understand its meaning.

The image shows enslaved African Americans gaining their liberty from a Union soldier as the Union army passes by. On the left-hand side, the cartoonist has imagined what will happen after slavery ends.

freed slaves entering a school

a newspaper, symbolizing literacy

### CRITICAL THINKING

1. **Make Inferences** What does the cartoonist suggest will happen after the abolition of slavery?

2. **Synthesize** What is the overall meaning of the cartoon?

 See Skillbuilder Handbook, page R24.

"Freedom to the Slave" printed in Philadelphia 1863

Why, critics asked, did Lincoln free slaves only in the South? Lincoln believed that the Constitution did not give him the authority to free all slaves. But because freeing slaves in the South weakened the Confederacy, the proclamation could be seen as a military action. According to the Constitution, the President is **Commander-in-Chief** of all armed forces. In this role, Lincoln claimed the military authority to issue the proclamation.

Although the Emancipation Proclamation did not free many enslaved people at the time, it added a great moral purpose to the Union cause. The Northern goal was no longer simply to preserve the Union. The Civil War was now being fought to free millions of Americans from slavery. The conflict had become a war of **liberation**.

**Response to the Proclamation** Abolitionists were thrilled that Lincoln had finally issued the Emancipation Proclamation. "We shout for joy that we live to record this righteous decree," wrote Frederick Douglass. Still, many believed the law should have gone further. They were upset that Lincoln had not freed *all* enslaved people, including those in the border states.

Other people in the North, especially Democrats, were angered by the president's decision. A majority of Northern Democrats opposed emancipat-

### Connecting History

**Expanding Liberty**
During the Revolutionary War, the British had also tried to weaken their opponents by offering to free the enslaved. *See Chapter 7, page 196.*

ing even Southern slaves. They claimed that the proclamation would only **prolong**, or lengthen, the war by further angering the South. A newspaper man in Ohio called Lincoln's proclamation "monstrous, impudent, and heinous . . . insulting to God as to man."

Most Union soldiers welcomed emancipation. One officer noted that, although few soldiers were abolitionists, most were happy "to destroy everything that . . . gives the rebels strength."

White Southerners reacted angrily to the proclamation. Although it had no effect in areas outside the reach of Northern armies, many slaves began escaping to Union lines. At the same time that these slaves deprived the Confederacy of labor, they also began to provide the Union with soldiers.

🔺 **CAUSES AND EFFECTS** Describe how the Emancipation Proclamation affected the war.

## Fighting for Freedom

🔻 **KEY QUESTION** How did African-American soldiers contribute to the Union cause?

In addition to freeing slaves, the Emancipation Proclamation declared that African-American men willing to fight "will be received into the armed service of the United States." Determined to destroy slavery, African-American soldiers brought renewed intensity to the Union cause.

**African-American Soldiers** Frederick Douglass had argued for the recruitment of African-American soldiers since the start of the war. He believed that military service would be the first step to full citizenship. Douglass declared, "Once [you] let the black man get upon his person the brass letters, U.S. . . . there is no power on earth which can deny that he has earned the right to citizenship."

Before the proclamation, the federal government had discouraged the enlistment of African Americans, and only a few regiments were formed. Once the restriction was lifted, African Americans rushed to join the army. Most of these African Americans came from the South. By war's end, about 180,000 black soldiers wore the blue uniform of the Union army.

African-American soldiers were organized in 166 all-black regiments, usually led by white officers. They were paid less than white soldiers. Despite these obstacles, African Americans showed great courage on the battlefield and wore their uniforms with pride. More than one regiment insisted on fighting without pay rather than accepting lower pay.

Recruitment poster to attract African-American volunteers
**Why would an image like this have attracted volunteers?**

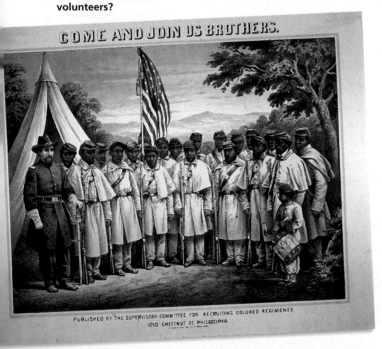

COME AND JOIN US BROTHERS.

PUBLISHED BY THE SUPERVISORY COMMITTEE FOR RECRUITING COLORED REGIMENTS
1210 CHESTNUT ST. PHILADELPHIA

African-American soldiers were determined to destroy slavery, gain self-respect, and prove they deserved equal treatment. Many white officers started out with racist views about their soldiers. After seeing these soldiers' determination and courage on the battlefield, many of these officers changed their minds.

Middle school students, dressed in period uniforms, portray life in the 54th Massachusetts Volunteers.

**The 54th Massachusetts** The **54th Massachusetts Volunteers** was one of the first African-American regiments organized in the North. The soldiers of the 54th—which included two sons of Frederick Douglass—soon made the regiment one of the most famous of the Civil War.

The 54th Massachusetts earned its greatest glory in July 1863, when it led a heroic attack on Fort Wagner in South Carolina. The soldiers' bravery made them famous and increased African-American enlistment.

Soldiers in African-American regiments faced grave dangers if captured. The Confederate government threatened to execute them or return them to slavery rather than make them prisoners of war.

The Emancipation Proclamation was one sign that the war was bringing dramatic change to both North and South. As the fighting continued, it was clear that the war was changing American society in unexpected ways.

 **SUMMARIZE** Describe the contributions of African-American soldiers to the Union cause.

---

**New Jersey Core Curriculum Content Standards** *Review*

🔁 **ONLINE QUIZ** For test practice, go to **Interactive Review @ ClassZone.com**

**TERMS & NAMES**

**1.** Explain the importance of
- Emancipation Proclamation
- 54th Massachusetts Volunteers

**USING YOUR READING NOTES**

**2. Causes and Effects** Complete the chart that you started at the beginning of this section.

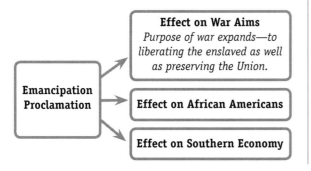

**Effect on War Aims**
*Purpose of war expands—to liberating the enslaved as well as preserving the Union.*

**Emancipation Proclamation**

**Effect on African Americans**

**Effect on Southern Economy**

**KEY IDEAS**

**3.** Why was the Emancipation Proclamation limited in scope?

**4.** How did African Americans help the Union cause?

**CRITICAL THINKING**

**5. Causes and Effects** How did the Emancipation Proclamation change the role of African Americans in the Civil War?

**6. Make Inferences** Why would African-American Union soldiers face greater danger than white Union soldiers?

**7. Draw Conclusions** Why do you think that Lincoln waited until the Union was in a position of strength before issuing the Emancipation Proclamation?

**8.** **Math** Research the number of free and enslaved people in each Confederate state. Then calculate the percentage of slaves in each of those states.

## ▶ Key Ideas

**BEFORE, YOU LEARNED**

The Civil War took millions of men from their homes, disrupting life in both North and South.

**NOW YOU WILL LEARN**

As the war dragged on, social, economic, and political change affected both the Union and the Confederacy.

## ▶ Vocabulary

**TERMS & NAMES**

**Copperheads** Northern Democrats who favored peace with the South

**writ of *habeas corpus*** law that prevents the government from holding citizens without formal charges

**Clara Barton** Civil War nurse who later founded the American Red Cross

**BACKGROUND VOCABULARY**

**conscription** military draft

**income tax** tax on earnings

**greenback** paper money introduced during the Civil War

**REVIEW**

**inflation** increase in prices and decrease in value of money

Visual Vocabulary
greenback

## ▶ Reading Strategy

Re-create the diagram shown at right. As you read and respond to the **KEY QUESTIONS**, use the center box to record the main idea; use the outer ovals to note important details. Add circles or start a new diagram as needed.

 **See Skillbuilder Handbook, page R4.**

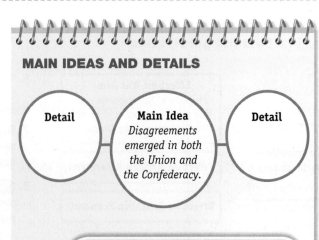

**MAIN IDEAS AND DETAILS**

Detail

**Main Idea**
*Disagreements emerged in both the Union and the Confederacy.*

Detail

**GRAPHIC ORGANIZERS**
Go to **Interactive Review** @ ClassZone.com

# War Affects Society

 **6.4.G.1.** Explain the major events, issues, and personalities of the American Civil War including the role of women.

## One American's Story

On April 4, 1863, a Southern woman named Agnes came upon a group of hungry women and children marching through the streets of the Confederate capital of Richmond, Virginia. The crowd was joined by others angered by the shortage of food.

**PRIMARY SOURCE**

❝ The crowd now rapidly increased, and numbered, I am sure, more than a thousand women and children. It grew and grew until it reached the dignity of a mob—a bread riot. ❞

— Agnes, quoted in *Reminiscences of Peace and War*

The mob broke into shops and stole food and other goods. When President Jefferson Davis appeared, the crowd hissed at him. As the Civil War moved into its third year, American society in both the North and the South began cracking under the strain of war.

Illustration of a food riot in the South, from a Northern magazine

## A Divisive Time

🔻 **KEY QUESTION** What disagreements emerged inside both the Union and the Confederacy?

The fight between the North and the South was not the only conflict of the Civil War. Even within the Union and the Confederacy, disagreements raged.

**Disagreements About the War** Some Southern areas opposed secession. The western counties of Virginia had few plantations or slaves. In 1863, these counties seceded from Virginia and formed a new state—West Virginia. West Virginia then joined the Union.

Disagreements over the war also arose in the North. Lincoln's main opponents were the **Copperheads**, Northern Democrats who favored peace with the South. (A copperhead is a poisonous snake that strikes without warning.) Lincoln had protesters arrested. He also suspended the **writ of habeas corpus**, which prevents the government from holding citizens without formal charges.

Slaves escaping from Southern plantations. **Why would wartime conditions have allowed enslaved people to escape?**

**Slaves Undermine the Confederacy** Enslaved people did their best to weaken the Confederacy. Slaves slowed their work or stopped working altogether. When planters fled advancing Union armies, slaves often refused to join their former "masters." In defiance, they stayed behind, waiting to greet or join the Union armies. One Union officer described a common sight.

### PRIMARY SOURCE

❝ It was very touching to see the vast numbers of colored [African-American] women following after us with babies in their arms, and little ones like our Anna clinging to their tattered skirts. One poor creature, while nobody was looking, hid two boys, five years old, in a wagon, intending, I suppose that they should see the land of freedom if she couldn't. ❞

—Union officer, quoted in *Sherman: Fighting Prophet*

After the Emancipation Proclamation, the number of slaves fleeing Southern plantations greatly increased.

**The Draft Laws** As enthusiasm for the war declined, both the North and the South began passing laws of **conscription**, also known as the draft. These laws required men to serve in the military.

In the South, planters with more than 20 slaves were not required to serve in the army. In both the Union and Confederacy, the rich could pay substitutes to serve in their place. This caused widespread resentment.

The draft was extremely unpopular. In July 1863, anger over the draft and simmering racial tensions led to the four-day-long New York City draft riots. Irish-Americans and others destroyed property and attacked African Americans on the streets. Over 1000 people were killed or wounded. Union troops were brought to the city to put down the uprising.

🔺 **MAIN IDEAS & DETAILS** Describe the disagreements that emerged in both the Union and the Confederacy.

# Economic and Social Change

▼ **KEY QUESTION** What economic and social changes were caused by the war?

In the North and the South, the war brought economic and social change. In the North, free African Americans were now serving in the Union military. Women were taking over jobs in factories and hospitals. At the same time, poverty and hunger spread through the Union and the Confederacy. The suffering was worse in the South.

**Economic Effects of the War** Food shortages were very common in the South. Many farmers were in the army and unable to harvest crops. Transportation was disrupted, preventing food from reaching markets. Additionally, both the Confederate and invading Union armies seized food.

Another problem in the South was **inflation**. Inflation is an increase in the cost of goods and a decrease in the value of money. Over the course of the war, prices rose steadily in the South. Inflation in the North was much lower, but prices still rose faster than wages, making life harder for working people.

During the war, the federal government passed two important economic measures. In 1861, it established the first **income tax**—a tax on earnings. The following year, the government issued a new paper currency, known as

## COMPARING ▸ *Northern and Southern Inflation*

During the Civil War, inflation affected both the North and the South. Inflation occurs when prices rise and the purchasing power of money falls. Wartime inflation was especially severe in the Confederacy, where basic necessities became outrageously expensive.

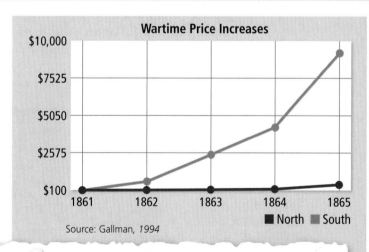

**Wartime Price Increases**

Source: Gallman, *1994*

■ North ■ South

### FOOD PRICES IN THE SOUTH, 1864

**$6.00**
Dozen Eggs

**$6.25**
Pound of Butter

**$10.00**
Quart of Milk

**$12.00**
Pound of Coffee

**$18.00**
Confederate Soldier's
Monthly Pay

**CRITICAL THINKING** **Draw Conclusions** How long would it take a soldier to earn enough to buy some of the items shown above?

greenbacks because of their color. The new currency helped the Northern economy by ensuring that people had money to spend. It also helped the federal government to pay for the war.

**Women Aid the War Effort** With so many men away at war, women in both the North and the South assumed more responsibilities. Women plowed fields and ran farms and plantations. They also took over office and factory jobs that had previously been done only by men.

Thousands of women, such as **Clara Barton**, served on the front lines as volunteer workers and nurses. Susie King Taylor was an African-American woman who wrote an account of her experiences as a volunteer with an African-American regiment. She asked her readers to remember that "many lives were lost,—not men alone but noble women as well."

Relief agencies allowed women to work gathering supplies, washing clothes, and cooking food for soldiers. Also, nursing became a respectable profession for many women. By the end of the war, around 20,000 nurses had worked in Union and Confederate hospitals. Southern women were also active as nurses and as volunteers on the front.

## CONNECTING ↘ History

### WARS AND SOCIAL CHANGE

During the Civil War, many people were presented with opportunities for freedom or advancement. This situation was not unique to the Civil War. In fact, throughout American history, long, deadly wars have helped bring about dramatic social change.

**1700s**

**1775–1783**
**The Revolutionary War**
allowed African Americans to serve in the military.

**1800s**

**1861–1865**
**The Civil War**
freed enslaved people; allowed more women to enter the workforce and take on jobs traditionally done by men.

**1900s**

**1939–1945**
**World War II**
helped desegregate some factories and temporarily created more opportunities for women.

nurse tending to Federal troops

### CRITICAL THINKING

1. **Make Inferences** Why would wartime situations offer more opportunities for women?
2. **Summarize** Why do wars help cause social change?

As in the American Revolution, some women on both sides disguised themselves as men and enlisted. One was an Illinois woman named Jennie Hodgers. She served in a Union regiment as Albert Cashier.

Women also played a key role as spies in both the North and the South. Harriet Tubman served as a spy for Union forces in South Carolina. The most famous Confederate spy was Belle Boyd. Although she was arrested six times, she continued her work through much of the war.

**War Transforms Society** With millions of men absent from their homes and workplaces, the war transformed Northern and Southern societies. In the North, opportunities opened up for those who had traditionally been kept out of public life. Women became active in the war effort and staffed hospitals in large numbers. African Americans gained more rights as several states began repealing discriminatory laws.

In the South, ordinary people began to resent the burden they were forced to bear. Small farmers, reduced to poverty by the war, were growing bitter. Many questioned why they were asked to fight a war for rich slaveowners. As the war dragged on, social resentment, inflation, and food shortages began to destroy Southern morale.

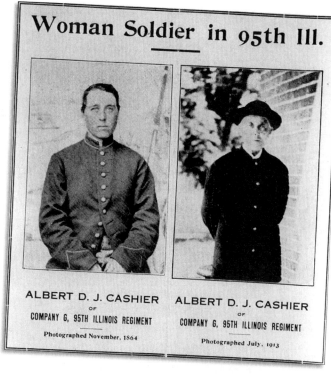

Woman Soldier in 95th Ill.

ALBERT D. J. CASHIER
OF
COMPANY G, 95TH ILLINOIS REGIMENT
Photographed November, 1864

ALBERT D. J. CASHIER
OF
COMPANY G, 95TH ILLINOIS REGIMENT
Photographed July, 1913

Albert Cashier (Jenny Hodgers) was one of hundreds of women who disguised themselves as men in order to fight in the war.

 **SUMMARIZE** Describe the economic and social changes caused by the war.

---

 **New Jersey Core Curriculum Content Standards** *Review*

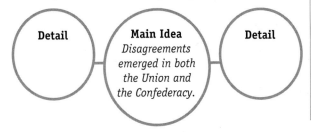 **ONLINE QUIZ**
For test practice, go to
**Interactive Review @ ClassZone.com**

### TERMS & NAMES

1. Explain the importance of
   - Copperheads
   - Clara Barton
   - writ of *habeus corpus*

### USING YOUR READING NOTES

2. **Main Ideas and Details** Complete the diagram that you started at the beginning of this section.

Detail

**Main Idea**
*Disagreements emerged in both the Union and the Confederacy.*

Detail

### KEY IDEAS

3. Why were people in the western counties of Virginia against secession?

4. What hardships did civilians suffer during the war?

### CRITICAL THINKING

5. **Connect Economics and History** Why do you think the economy of the South suffered more during the war than that of the North?

6. **Make Generalizations** Why do you think both sides introduced a draft?

7. **Writing** **Newspaper Article** Suppose you are a journalist for a foreign newspaper. Write an article describing war-time conditions in both the Confederacy and the Union.

## ▶ Key Ideas

**BEFORE, YOU LEARNED**

General Robert E. Lee caused the Union many difficulties in the east.

**NOW YOU WILL LEARN**

After a series of Southern victories, the North began winning battles that led to the defeat of the Confederacy.

## ▶ Vocabulary

**TERMS & NAMES**

**Battle of Gettysburg** battle in 1863 in Pennsylvania when Union forces stopped a Confederate invasion of the North

**George Pickett** Confederate general who fought at Gettysburg

**Pickett's Charge** failed assault on Union positions on final day of Battle of Gettysburg

**Siege of Vicksburg** the surrounding of the city of Vicksburg, Mississippi, by Union forces

**Sherman's March to the Sea** Union general Sherman's destructive march across Georgia

**Appomattox Court House** town in Virginia where Lee surrendered to Grant

**BACKGROUND VOCABULARY**

**dislodge** remove

**Visual Vocabulary** monument on the site of the Battle of Gettysburg

## ▶ Reading Strategy

Re-create the diagram shown at right. As you read and respond to the **KEY QUESTIONS**, use the diagram to show the effects of Union victories at Gettysburg and Vicksburg.

 **See Skillbuilder Handbook, page R7.**

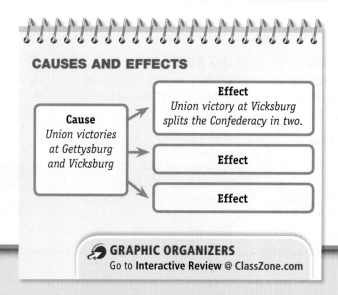

**CAUSES AND EFFECTS**

**Cause**
*Union victories at Gettysburg and Vicksburg*

**Effect**
*Union victory at Vicksburg splits the Confederacy in two.*

**Effect**

**Effect**

**GRAPHIC ORGANIZERS**
Go to **Interactive Review** @ ClassZone.com

# The North Wins

**6.4.G.1.** Explain the major events, issues, and personalities of the American Civil War including the course and conduct of the war (e.g., Antietam, Vicksburg, Gettysburg).

## One American's Story

Tillie Pierce was 15 years old when war came to her doorstep in Gettysburg, Pennsylvania. On July 2, 1863, the second day of the battle, Tillie and her family tried to flee. She later wrote about her memories of the epic battle that took place around her home.

### PRIMARY SOURCE

**"** Hardly had we arrived at our supposed place of refuge, when we were told to hurry back to where we came from . . . So there was no alternative but to retrace our steps about as fast as we came.

During the whole of this wild goose chase, the cannonading had become terrible! . . . Occasionally a shell would come flying over Round Top and explode high in the air over head. It seemed as though the heavens were sending forth peal upon peal of terrible thunder directly over our heads; while at the same time, the very earth beneath our feet trembled. **"**

—Tillie Pierce, quoted in *War Between Brothers*

Tillie Pierce

Tillie Pierce spent the next few days helping care for wounded Union soldiers. Little did she realize that the battle she had just witnessed would be the turning point of the war.

## Union Victories at Gettysburg and Vicksburg

 **KEY QUESTION** Why were the battles of Gettysburg and Vicksburg so significant?

In 1863 the war in the east seemed to be going well for the Confederacy. Confident after a series of victories at Fredericksburg and Chancellorsville, Virginia, General Lee decided to invade the North. It was a fatal mistake.

**Lee Invades the North** For Lee, the victory at Chancellorsville came at a high price. In the confusion after the battle, Confederate guards accidentally shot Confederate General Stonewall Jackson, who died a week later.

After Chancellorsville, Lee decided to head north once again. He hoped that a victory in Union territory would fuel Northern discontent and bring calls for peace. He also hoped that a Southern victory would lead European nations to recognize the Confederacy as an independent nation.

In late June 1863, Lee crossed into southern Pennsylvania. At the town of Gettysburg the Confederates stumbled upon Union troops. Both sides called for reinforcements, and on July 1, the **Battle of Gettysburg** began.

**The Battle of Gettysburg** The fighting raged for three days. On the rocky hills and fields around Gettysburg, 90,000 Union troops under the command of General George Meade clashed with 75,000 Confederates.

During the struggle, Union forces tried to hold their ground on Cemetery Ridge, just south of town, while rebel soldiers tried to **dislodge**, or remove, them. (See map on facing page.) At times, the air seemed full of bullets. "The balls [were] whizzing so thick," said one Texan, "that it [looked] like a man could hold out a hat and catch it full."

The turning point came on July 3, when General **George Pickett** mounted a direct attack on the middle of the Union line. It was a deadly mistake. Some 15,000 rebel troops charged up the ridge into heavy Union fire. One soldier recalled "bayonet thrusts, sabre strokes, pistol shots . . . men going down on their hands and knees, spinning round like tops . . . ghastly heaps of dead men."

**Pickett's Charge**, as this attack came to be known, was a failure. The Confederates retreated and waited for a counterattack. But once again, Lincoln's generals failed to completely defeat Lee's army. The furious Lincoln wondered when he would find a general to defeat Lee once and for all.

Even so, the Union rejoiced over the victory at Gettysburg. Lee's hopes for a Confederate victory in the North were crushed. The North suffered 23,000 casualties, or about one quarter of the army, but Southern losses were even greater. Over one-third of Lee's army, 28,000 men, lay dead or wounded. Sick at heart, Lee led his army back to Virginia.

Although the war would last two years longer, the South never recovered from its defeat at Gettysburg.

Reenactors portray the Battle of Gettysburg.

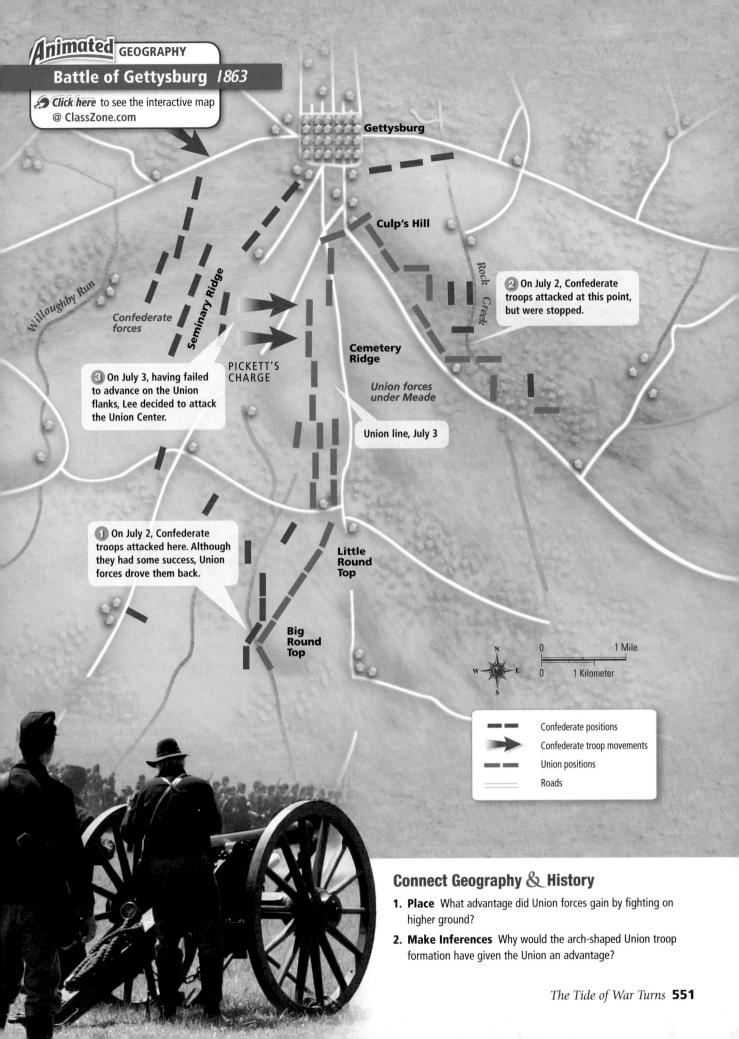

Gettysburg

Culp's Hill

Rock Creek

**2** On July 2, Confederate
troops attacked at this point,
but were stopped.

Willoughby Run

*Confederate
forces*

Seminary Ridge

PICKETT'S
CHARGE

**Cemetery
Ridge**

*Union forces
under Meade*

**3** On July 3, having failed
to advance on the Union
flanks, Lee decided to attack
the Union Center.

Union line, July 3

**1** On July 2, Confederate
troops attacked here. Although
they had some success, Union
forces drove them back.

**Little
Round
Top**

**Big
Round
Top**

N
W    E
S

| 0 | | 1 Mile |
| 0 | 1 Kilometer | |

▬ ▬ ▬  Confederate positions

━━━▶  Confederate troop movements

▬ ▬ ▬  Union positions

━━━  Roads

## Connect Geography & History

1. **Place** What advantage did Union forces gain by fighting on
   higher ground?

2. **Make Inferences** Why would the arch-shaped Union troop
   formation have given the Union an advantage?

*The Tide of War Turns* **551**

**The Siege of Vicksburg** On July 4, 1863, the day after Pickett's Charge, the Union received more good news. Confederate troops at Vicksburg in Mississippi had surrendered to General Ulysses S. Grant.

The previous year, Grant had won important victories in the West that opened up the Mississippi River and allowed Union troops to travel deep into the South. Vicksburg was the last major Confederate stronghold on the river. Grant had begun his attack on Vicksburg in May 1863. When direct attacks failed, he settled in for a long siege.

During the **Siege of Vicksburg**, Grant's troops surrounded the city and prevented the delivery of food and supplies. Eventually, the Confederates ran out of food. The civilian population moved into caves to protect themselves from the constant bombardment. After nearly a month and a half, the city surrendered.

The Union victory fulfilled a major part of the Anaconda Plan. The North had taken New Orleans in April 1862. With the Union now in complete control of the Mississippi River, the South was split in two.

With the victories at Vicksburg and Gettysburg, the tide of war turned in favor of the North. In General Grant, President Lincoln found a man who might be able to defeat General Lee.

 **CAUSES AND EFFECTS** Explain how the Union victories at Gettysburg and Vicksburg affected the course of the war.

**Connect** *to the* **World**

**Crucial Decisions**
After Gettysburg and Vicksburg, the British government dropped discussion of recognizing the Confederacy.

**ONLINE BIOGRAPHY**

For more on Grant and Lee go to the **Research & Writing Center** @ ClassZone.com

---

# History Makers  Civil War Generals

### Ulysses S. Grant   1822–1885

When the Civil War broke out, Ulysses S. Grant was quickly promoted through the ranks and proved to be a brilliant general. Highly focused and cool under fire, Grant won the first major Union victories of the war. Grant was willing to attack Lee's army, even if the costs were high. He told one of his generals, "Wherever Lee goes, there you will go also."

### Robert E. Lee   1807–1870

In General Robert E. Lee, the Confederacy found an unlikely hero. Lee opposed slavery and secession. He did not want to fight the Union, but felt he had to defend his home state of Virginia. "I did only what my duty demanded," Lee said. "I could have taken no other course without dishonor."

During the Seven Days' Battles Lee forced the Union army away from Richmond. After this, his reputation began to rise. By the end of the war, Lee inspired respect and devotion in the South and fear in the North.

**COMPARING** *Leaders*

What qualities did Grant have that helped him defeat Lee?

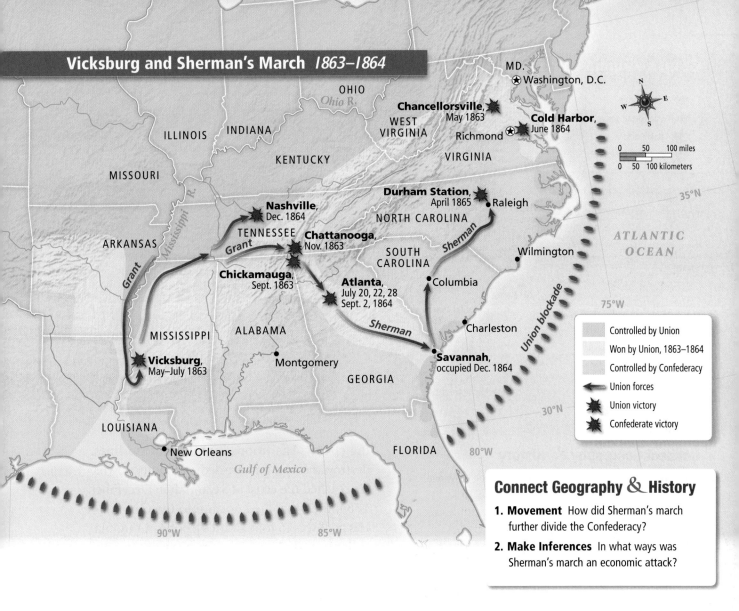

## Vicksburg and Sherman's March *1863–1864*

**Connect Geography & History**

1. **Movement** How did Sherman's march further divide the Confederacy?

2. **Make Inferences** In what ways was Sherman's march an economic attack?

# The Confederacy Falls

🔻 **KEY QUESTION** How did Grant's new strategy defeat the Confederacy?

In March 1864, President Lincoln gave General Grant command of all Union armies. Grant then called for all Union forces to coordinate their attacks. Grant would pursue Lee's army in Virginia, while Union forces under General William Tecumseh Sherman pushed through the Deep South.

**Sherman Takes Atlanta** Battling southward from Tennessee, Sherman took Atlanta in September 1864. Sherman's victory affected the 1864 election. Northerners were tired of war, and Peace Democrats—who had nominated George McClellan—stood a chance of winning on an antiwar platform. But with Sherman's success, Northerners could sense victory. The President won reelection. (See page 564 for Lincoln's Second Inaugural Address.)

In November 1864, Sherman burned Atlanta and set out on a terrifying march to the sea. Sherman's army cut a path of destruction across Georgia that was 60 miles wide and 300 miles long. Sherman waged total war: a war not only against enemy troops, but against everything that supported

## Grant's Virginia Campaign 1864–1865

Union forces
Confederate forces
Union victory
Confederate victory

0    25    50 miles
0    25    50 kilometers

Washington, D.C.    MARYLAND

**Wilderness,**
May 5–6, 1864    • Fredericksburg

Grant

Lee

*Rappahannock R.*

**Spotsylvania,**
May 8–19, 1864

VIRGINIA

*James River*

**Cold Harbor,**
June 3, 1864

Richmond

Lee

Grant

**Appomattox
Court House,**
Apr. 9, 1865
Lee surrenders
to Grant

**Petersburg,**
June 1864–Apr. 1865

The fall of Richmond

## Connect Geography & History

1. **Movement** Why did the opposing forces circle Richmond?
2. **Make Inferences** Why did Lee turn to the West?

the enemy. His troops tore up railroad lines, destroyed crops, and burned and looted towns. He reached the coast at Savannah in December 1864, then marched north into the Carolinas. His goal was to join Grant's troops in Virginia.

**Sherman's March to the Sea**, as it was called, tore into the heart of the Confederacy. Sherman's march also increased the size of the Union army—in Georgia alone more than 19,000 former slaves left plantations and followed the Union army to freedom.

**Grant's Virginia Campaign** In Virginia, Grant pursued Lee's army. Grant had a brutal plan for ending the war: to keep attacking Lee despite the number of casualties that Union forces might suffer. The Union armies could replace fallen soldiers, but the South was running out of men and supplies.

In the Virginia campaign, Lee showed his genius for strategy. Lee's army lacked sufficient manpower and supplies. But Lee excelled at maneuvering his army to fight and then escaping to fight another day. It took Grant a year to corner and defeat Lee.

At the Battle of the Wilderness in May 1864, Union and Confederate forces fought in a tangle of trees and brush so thick that they could barely see each other. Grant suffered over 17,000 casualties, but he pushed on. "Whatever happens," he told Lincoln, "we will not retreat."

At Spotsylvania and Cold Harbor, the fighting continued. Again, the losses were staggering. Grant's attack in June, at Cold Harbor, cost him 7,000 casualties, most in the first few minutes of battle. Some Union troops were so sure they would die in battle that they pinned their names and addresses to their jackets so their bodies could be identified later.

In June 1864, Grant's armies arrived at Petersburg, just south of Richmond. Unable to break through the Confederate defenses, the Union forces dug trenches and settled in for a nine-month-long siege.

**Richmond Falls** At the beginning of April 1865, Lee realized he could hold out no longer. He sent Davis a note advising the government to leave Richmond. Lee hoped to move his army to food supplies and so prolong the war.

On April 2, the Confederate government fled Richmond. Confederate leaders burnt anything that could be of use to the enemy. The fires spread, and the city was in flames when Union forces arrived on April 3, 1865.

Lincoln visited Richmond to see the prize that the Union had pursued for four years. Most white residents stayed indoors. African Americans cheered the president of the United States who had led the fight for freedom.

**Surrender at Appomattox** From Richmond and Petersburg, Lee fled west, while Grant followed in pursuit. Lee wanted to continue fighting, but he knew that his situation was hopeless. He sent a message to General Grant that he was ready to surrender.

On April 9, 1865, Lee and Grant met in the small Virginia town of **Appomattox Court House** to arrange the surrender. Grant later wrote that his joy at that moment was mixed with sadness.

Grant offered generous terms of surrender. After laying down their arms, the Confederates could return home in peace, taking their private possessions and horses with them. Grant also fed the hungry Confederate soldiers.

The Civil War was ending. The conflict had changed the country forever.

 **SUMMARIZE** Explain Grant's strategy for ending the war.

---

**New Jersey Core Curriculum Content Standards** *Review*

 **ONLINE QUIZ**
For test practice, go to
**Interactive Review @ ClassZone.com**

### TERMS & NAMES
**1.** Explain the importance of
- Battle of Gettysburg
- George Pickett
- Pickett's Charge
- Siege of Vicksburg
- Appomattox Court House
- Sherman's March to the Sea

### USING YOUR READING NOTES
**2. Causes and Effects** Complete the diagram that you started at the beginning of this section.

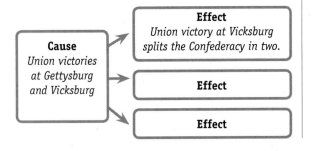

| Cause | | Effect |
|---|---|---|
| Union victories at Gettysburg and Vicksburg | → | Union victory at Vicksburg splits the Confederacy in two. |
| | → | Effect |
| | → | Effect |

### KEY IDEAS
**3.** Why was the Battle of Gettysburg important?

**4.** How did the victory at Vicksburg fulfill a part of the Union strategy?

**5.** How did Sherman's victory at Atlanta affect the election of 1864?

### CRITICAL THINKING
**6. Evaluate** How was Sherman's March to the Sea different from other military campaigns in the Civil War?

**7. Draw Conclusions** Why do you think Grant gave generous terms of surrender to Lee?

**8. Make Inferences** Why was the Confederacy unable to stop Sherman's campaign?

**9. Writing Description** Suppose that you lived on a farm overlooking the battlefield at Gettysburg. Describe what you saw during the battle.

**Click here** to see an animated version of the Union strategy at Vicksburg @ ClassZone.com

## The Struggle for Vicksburg

On April 16, 1863, the Union fleet steamed down the Mississippi past Vicksburg. As the enemy ships sailed south, the Confederate defenders of Vicksburg opened fire. The missiles failed to stop the Union fleet.

General Grant's brilliant strategy to capture Vicksburg had begun.

1. As his fleet sailed south, Grant moved his army down the west bank of the Mississippi.

2. **Next,** He marched north east. The Confederates could not understand why he was cutting himself off from his supplies on the river.

3. **Next,** Grant sent forces to conquer Jackson and turned west. He defeated a Confederate force sent from Vicksburg to stop him.

4. **Finally,** When Grant reached the massive fortifications around Vicksburg, he decided to starve the city into surrender. He surrounded the city with fortifications of his own. The Siege of Vicksburg lasted about six weeks. The city surrendered to the Union on July 4.

## Sharing Perspectives

**1** As a class, divide into 2 groups representing (a) the Confederate defenders and civilians of Vicksburg, and (b) the Union attackers.

**2** Read about the siege of Vicksburg on pages 552 and 556–557.

**3** Discuss how your group would have experienced the siege. For instance: How might a siege affect civilians? In what ways would life be different inside and outside the city?

**4** Prepare a brief presentation or skit to present your group's perspective.

## CRITICAL THINKING

1. **Draw Conclusions** Why do you think the Confederates in Vicksburg were confused by Grant's strategy?

2. **Make Inferences** How did Grant turn the Vicksburg defenses into a trap for the city's defenders?

# Second Inaugural Address (1865)

**SETTING THE STAGE** President Lincoln delivered his Second Inaugural Address just before the end of the Civil War. In this excerpt, he recalled the major cause of the war and vowed to fight for the restoration of peace and unity.

## Slavery in Territories

Before the Civil War, Northern states wanted to prohibit slavery in territories that would eventually become new states. Southern states fought to expand slavery, fearing that outlawing it would threaten slavery where it already existed.

1. **Why did the Southerners fear that prohibiting slavery in new territories might threaten slavery where it already existed?**

## Malice Toward None

As Northerners became more confident in victory, many wanted to punish Southerners, whom they blamed for the war. Lincoln, however, urged citizens to care for one another and work for a just and lasting peace.

2. **Why do you think that Lincoln believed it would be wiser for Americans not to place blame or seek revenge on one another?**

One-eighth of the whole population were colored slaves. . . . These slaves constituted a peculiar and powerful interest. All knew that this interest was, somehow, the cause of the war. To strengthen, perpetuate, and extend this interest was the object for which the **insurgents**[1] would rend the Union, even by war; while the government claimed no right to do more than to restrict the territorial enlargement of it. Neither party expected for the war, the magnitude, or the duration, which it has already attained. Neither anticipated that the cause of the conflict might cease with, or even before, the conflict itself should cease. Each looked for an easier triumph, and a result less fundamental and astounding. Both read the same Bible, and pray to the same God; and each invokes His aid against the other. . . . Fondly do we hope—fervently do we pray—that this mighty **scourge**[2] of war may speedily pass away. Yet, if God wills that it continue until all the wealth piled by the **bondsman's**[3] two hundred and fifty years of **unrequited**[4] toil shall be sunk, and until every drop of blood drawn with the lash, shall be paid by another drawn with the sword, as was said three thousand years ago, so still it must be said, "the judgments of the Lord are true and righteous altogether."

With malice toward none; with charity for all; with firmness in the right as God gives us to see the right, let us strive on to finish the work we are in; to bind up the nation's wounds; to care for him who shall have borne the battle, and for his widow, and his orphan—to do all which may achieve and cherish a just and lasting peace, among ourselves and with all nations.

----

1. **insurgents** one that revolts against civil authority
2. **scourge** a source of suffering and devastation
3. **bondsman** enslaved person
4. **unrequited** not paid for

## DOCUMENT-BASED QUESTIONS

### Short Answer

1. Why might President Lincoln have begun the Gettysburg Address by noting that the country was "dedicated to the proposition that all men are created equal"?
2. According to Lincoln's Second Inaugural Address, why did the Confederacy go to war?

### Extended Answer

3. In 1865, if the South had asked to rejoin the Union without ending slavery, do you think Lincoln would have agreed? Use statements from the two documents and your knowledge of U.S. history to support your position.

## Chapter Summary

**1** **Key Idea**
The Emancipation Proclamation promised freedom to slaves in the Confederacy and allowed African Americans to join the Union army.

**2** **Key Idea**
As the war dragged on, social, economic, and political change affected both the Union and the Confederacy.

**3** **Key Idea**
After a series of Southern victories, the North began winning battles that led to the defeat of the Confederacy.

**4** **Key Idea**
The Civil War transformed the nation.

➜ For detailed Review and Study Notes go to **Interactive Review** @ **ClassZone.com**

## Name Game

**Use the list of terms and names to identify each sentence online or on your own paper.**

1. I shot Abraham Lincoln. ⟨John Wilkes Booth⟩

2. I was a poet who wrote about the Civil War. ____

3. This constitutional amendment ended slavery. ____

4. This was a famous regiment of African Americans. ____

5. I was a nurse who founded the American Red Cross. ____

6. This battle stopped a Confederate invasion of the North. ____

7. We were Northern Democrats who favored peace with the South. ____

8. This document freed all slaves in Confederate territory. ____

9. I was a Confederate general who fought at Gettysburg. ____

10. This law prevents the government from holding citizens without a trial. ____

A. Thirteenth Amendment
B. Clara Barton
C. Emancipation Proclamation
D. John Wilkes Booth
E. writ of habeas corpus
F. Battle of Gettysburg
G. 54th Massachusetts Volunteers
H. Copperheads
I. George Pickett
J. Walt Whitman
K. Siege of Vicksburg
L. Pickett's Charge

## Activities

### FLIPCARD

Use the online flipcards to quiz yourself on the terms and names introduced in this chapter.

Theater in Washington, D.C., where Lincoln was shot.

ANSWER
Ford's Theatre

### GEOGAME

Use this online map to reinforce your understanding of the final years of the Civil War, including the locations of important battles and geographic features. Drag and drop each place name in the list at its location on the map. A scorecard helps you keep track of your progress online.

Nashville

Chattanooga

Richmond

Vicksburg

Raleigh

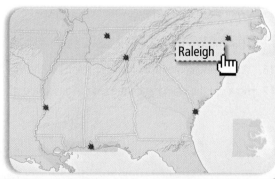

Raleigh

More items online

## VOCABULARY

**Match the term or name on the left with an item on the right.**

1. Clara Barton
2. John Wilkes Booth
3. Copperheads
4. Thirteenth Amendment
5. George Pickett

A. Battle of Gettysburg
B. American Red Cross
C. ended slavery
D. Northern Democrats
E. assassinated President

**Explain how the terms in each group are related.**

6. Battle of Antietam, Emancipation Proclamation

7. George Pickett, Battle of Gettysburg, Pickett's Charge

8. 54th Massachusetts Volunteers, Emancipation Proclamation

9. Thirteenth Amendment, Emancipation Proclamation

## KEY IDEAS

**1 The Emancipation Proclamation (pages 536–541)**

10. What impact was the Emancipation Proclamation meant to have on the Confederacy?

11. In what ways did African-American soldiers aid the war effort?

**2 War Affects Society (pages 542–547)**

12. How did enslaved people help undermine the Confederacy?

13. What economic changes did the war bring about?

**3 The North Wins (pages 548–555)**

14. Why were the Union victories at Gettysburg and Vicksburg a turning point in the war?

15. What was Grant's strategy for defeating Lee?

**4 The Legacy of the War (pages 558–562)**

16. What were some of the positive results of the war?

17. How did the war change the federal government?

## CRITICAL THINKING

18. **Make Inferences** How do you think the assassination of President Lincoln affected the nation?

19. **Categorize** Describe the difference between the tactics of Grant and Lee during the Virginia campaign.

| Grant | Lee |
|---|---|
| *determined to keep attacking Lee* | |

20. **Problems and Solutions** How did Grant help bring the war to an end?

21. **Draw Conclusions** Why do you think Lincoln waited until the Union was in a strong position before he issued the Emancipation Proclamation?

22. **Make Inferences** Why did the federal government expand its powers during the Civil War?

23. **Causes and Effects** How did Sherman's victory in Atlanta affect the election of 1864?

24. **Make Generalizations** At what point did the Civil War become a war of liberation?

25. **Draw Conclusions** Study the casualty charts below. Approximately how many soldiers were wounded in the war?

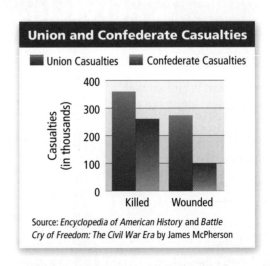

**Union and Confederate Casualties**

■ Union Casualties ■ Confederate Casualties

Casualties (in thousands): 400, 300, 200, 100, 0
Killed | Wounded

Source: *Encyclopedia of American History* and *Battle Cry of Freedom: The Civil War Era* by James McPherson

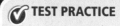 **TEST PRACTICE**

• **Online Test Practice** @ ClassZone.com
• **Test-Taking Strategies & Practice** at the front of this book

## DOCUMENT-BASED QUESTIONS

### PART 1: Short Answer

**Study each document carefully and answer the questions that follow.**

**DOCUMENT 1**

1. Examine this picture called *A Ride for Liberty* by Eastman Johnson. What messages might this painting have conveyed to people who saw it during the war?

**DOCUMENT 2**

**PRIMARY SOURCE**

 The war now being waged in this land is a war for and against slavery; and that it can never be effectually put down till one or the other of these vital forces is completely destroyed. 🙳

—Frederick Douglass, quoted in *Passages to Freedom*

2. According to Frederick Douglass, why was the Civil War fought?

### Part 2: Essay

3. Using information from the documents, your answers to the questions in Part 1, and your knowledge of U.S. history, write an essay that discusses how the Civil War became a fight against slavery.

## YOU BE THE HISTORIAN

26. **Draw Conclusions** Do you think Sherman's tactics were justified? Explain your answer.

27. **WHAT IF?** How might the course of the Civil War have changed if Lincoln had not issued the Emancipation Proclamation?

28. **Causes and Effects** Discuss the impact that Grant and Sherman had on the outcome of the Civil War.

29. **Connect** *to* **Today** What political, social, and economic issues of the Civil War are still relevant today?

30. **Causes and Effects** Why did the Union win the war?

31. **Problems and Solutions** What great national questions were settled by the Civil War?

32. **Draw Conclusions** Why did Confederates believe they might win the war?

Answer the
## ESSENTIAL QUESTION

### In what ways did the Civil War transform the nation?

**Written Response** Write a four-paragraph response to the Essential Question. Be sure to consider the key ideas of each section as well as the most significant forces that transformed the nation. Use the Response Rubric below to guide your thinking and writing.

### Response Rubric
**A strong response will**

• discuss the social and economic transformation brought by the end of slavery
• analyze the effects of four years of war
• describe the increases in the powers of the federal government

# Reconstruction
## 1865–1877

1. Rebuilding the Union
2. Reconstruction and Daily Life
3. The End of Reconstruction

## ESSENTIAL QUESTION
How did a deeply divided nation move forward after the Civil War?

### CONNECT — Geography & History

How might the Civil War have affected the economy of the South?

**Think about:**

**1** how most of the war was fought in the South, including major battles in Virginia, Tennessee, Georgia, and Mississippi

**2** how the amount of Southern farmland before the war compares with the amount after the war

**3** what happened to the region's main system of labor—slavery

Lincoln's funeral train left Washington, D.C., on April 21, 1865, and arrived in Springfield, Illinois, on May 3.

**1868** President Johnson impeached and later acquitted by a single vote

A ticket to Johnson's impeachment proceedings

**1865**

Lincoln assassinated; Johnson becomes president.
▼
**Effect** Johnson pardons white Southerners.

**1866** Fourteenth Amendment
▼
**Effect** Former slaves become citizens.

**1870** Fifteenth Amendment
▼
**Effect** African-American men get the vote.

## Farmland in the South

Click here to preview the Reconstruction years in the South @ClassZone.com

VIRGINIA
31.1*  18.1

TENNESSEE
20.7  19.6

NORTH CAROLINA
23.8  19.8

ARKANSAS
9.6  7.6

SOUTH CAROLINA
16.2  12.1

TEXAS
25.3  18.4

MISSISSIPPI
15.8  13.1

ALABAMA
19.1  15.0

GEORGIA
26.7  23.6

LOUISIANA
9.3  7.0

FLORIDA
2.9  2.4

**Farmland in former Confederate States** (*in millions of acres*)

1860     1870

\* 1860 data include West Virginia.

Hiram Revels (*far left*), the first African-American U.S. senator, with six U.S. representatives

During Reconstruction, federal troops were stationed in the South.

## 1877

**1871** Congress passes anti-Klan legislation.

**1873** Financial panic begins depression.

**1876** Supreme Court rules that the Fifteenth Amendment does not give everyone the right to vote. ▼

**Effect** Southern states stop African Americans from voting.

Federal troops leave the South. ▼

**Effect** Reconstruction ends.

## ▶ Key Ideas

**BEFORE, YOU LEARNED**

The Civil War promoted industry and economic growth in the North, but left the South in ruins.

**NOW YOU WILL LEARN**

During Reconstruction, the president and Congress fought over how to rebuild the South.

## ▶ Vocabulary

**TERMS & NAMES**

**Radical Republican** congressman who favored using federal power to rebuild the South and promote African-American rights

**Reconstruction** period from 1865 to 1877 in which the U.S. government attempted to rebuild Southern society and governments

**Freedmen's Bureau** federal agency set up to help former enslaved people

**Andrew Johnson** Democrat who became president after Lincoln was assassinated

**black codes** laws that limited the freedom of former enslaved people

**Fourteenth Amendment** constitutional amendment that made all people born in the U.S. (including former slaves) citizens

**scalawag** white Southerner who supported Radical Reconstruction

**carpetbagger** Northerner who went to the South after the Civil War to participate in Reconstruction

**BACKGROUND VOCABULARY**

**amnesty** official pardon

**civil rights** rights granted to all citizens

**impeach** to formally accuse the president of misconduct in office

**REVIEW**

**veto** (VEE•to) to prevent from becoming law

## ▶ Reading Strategy

As you read and respond to the **KEY QUESTIONS**, use a graphic organizer like the one shown to compare presidential and Congressional Reconstruction. Record the goals of each plan in the columns. Circle any shared goals.

 See Skillbuilder Handbook, page R8.

**COMPARE AND CONTRAST**

| Presidential Reconstruction | Congressional Reconstruction |
|---|---|
|  | *promote civil rights for freed people* |

 **GRAPHIC ORGANIZERS**
Go to **Interactive Review** @ ClassZone.com

# Rebuilding the Union

**6.4.G.3.** Explain Reconstruction as a government action, how it worked, and its effects after the war.
**6.4.G.4.** Discuss the impact of retaliatory state laws and general Southern resistance to Reconstruction.

## One American's Story

After the Civil War, Pennsylvania congressman Thaddeus Stevens became a leader of the **Radical Republicans**. This group of congressmen favored using federal power to promote full citizenship for freed African Americans.

### PRIMARY SOURCE

❝ We have turned, or are about to turn, loose four million slaves without a hut to shelter them or a cent in their pockets. . . . if we leave them to the legislation of their late masters, we had better have left them in bondage. ❞

—Thaddeus Stevens, the *Congressional Globe*, December 18, 1865

Radical Republicans wanted to make the South a region of small farms, free schools, and equality for all citizens.

Thaddeus Stevens was a passionate opponent of slavery and a strong supporter of the rights of African Americans.

## Presidential Reconstruction

🔻 **KEY QUESTION** Why did presidential Reconstruction fail under Johnson?

Soon after the war ended, the nation began a process called **Reconstruction**. It lasted from 1865 to 1877. During Reconstruction, the federal government faced the challenge of rebuilding Southern society and governments.

**Reconstruction Under Lincoln** In his Second Inaugural Address, in March 1865, President Lincoln promised to reunify the nation "with malice [harm] toward none, with charity for all." Lincoln wanted to treat the South with respect. His plan included pardoning Confederate officials. It also called for allowing the Confederate states to send representatives to Congress.

Congress established the **Freedmen's Bureau**—a federal agency set up to assist former enslaved people. The Freedmen's Bureau set up schools and hospitals for African Americans and distributed clothes, food, and fuel.

**Reconstruction Under Johnson** When Lincoln was killed, Vice-President **Andrew Johnson** became president. Johnson believed that Reconstruction was the job of the president, not Congress. His policies were based on Lincoln's goals. He insisted that the new state governments ratify the Thirteenth Amendment, which banned slavery in the United States. He also insisted that they accept the supreme power of the federal government.

Johnson offered **amnesty**, or official pardon, to most white Southerners. He promised that their property would be returned to them. However, they had to pledge loyalty to the United States. At first, the large plantation owners, top military officers, and ex-Confederate leaders were not included in this offer. But most of them, too, eventually won amnesty.

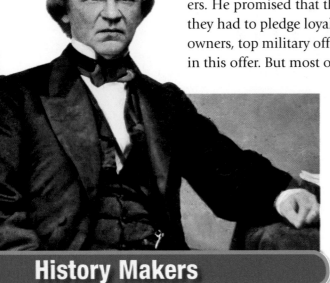

## History Makers

### Andrew Johnson    1808–1875

Andrew Johnson came from humble beginnings. His first career was as a tailor; his wife taught him to write and do arithmetic. In 1857, he was elected to the U.S. Senate from Tennessee. Although he was a Democrat and a former slaveholder, Johnson remained loyal to the Union. As president, he called for a mild program for bringing the South back into the Union. In particular, he let states decide whether to give voting rights to freed African Americans. Johnson's policies led to a break with the Radical Republicans in Congress and, finally, to his impeachment trial. (See page 575.)

**CRITICAL THINKING**

1. **Analyze Point of View** Why would many white Southerners have welcomed Johnson's decision on voting rights?

2. **Analyze Point of View** Why might Johnson have chosen not to punish the South?

 **ONLINE BIOGRAPHY** For more on Andrew Johnson, go to the **Research & Writing Center** @ ClassZone.com

**Johnson's Failure** Congress was not in session when Johnson became president in April 1865. Congress did not reconvene until December. During these eight months, the Southern states rebuilt. As they did so, they set up new state governments that were very much like the old ones. Some states flatly refused to ratify the Thirteenth Amendment. "This is a white man's government," said the governor of South Carolina, "and intended for white men only."

Johnson required only that the Southern states meet the conditions of his Reconstruction plan. His main goal was to have the Southern states readmitted to the Union as quickly as possible. He did not attempt to meet the needs of formerly enslaved people by helping them to gain land, voting rights, or equal protection under the law. Johnson believed the states should have the right to address these matters on their own. This was a relief to many white Southerners.

Southern states passed laws, known as **black codes**, that limited the freedom of formerly enslaved people. These laws were simply updated versions of the rules that had governed Southern African Americans during slavery. In Mississippi, for instance, one law said that African Americans had to have written proof of employment. Anyone without such proof could be arrested or imprisoned. African Americans were forbidden to meet in unsupervised groups or carry guns. Because the black codes were so much like slave codes, many people in the North suspected that white Southerners were trying to bring back the "old South."

 **CAUSES AND EFFECTS** Explain what caused the failure of presidential Reconstruction.

# Congressional Reconstruction

**KEY QUESTION** What were the goals of Congressional Reconstruction?

When Congress finally met again in December 1865, its members first refused to seat representatives from the South. Many of these Southern representatives had been Confederate leaders only months before.

**Congress States Its Intentions** Congress exercised its Constitutional right to decide whether its members are qualified to hold office. It set up a committee to study conditions in the South and decide whether the Southern states should be represented. By taking such action, Congress let the president know that it planned to play a major role in Reconstruction.

Republicans outnumbered Democrats in both houses of Congress. Within the Republican Party, however, opinions differed as to how involved Congress should be in Reconstruction. Moderate Republicans supported the states' right to govern themselves. Radical Republicans wanted the federal government to play an active role in remaking Southern politics and society. Led by Thaddeus Stevens and Massachusetts senator Charles Sumner, the group demanded full and equal citizenship for African Americans.

**Civil Rights for African Americans** Urged on by the Radicals, Congress passed a bill promoting **civil rights**—those rights granted to all citizens. The Civil Rights Act of 1866 said that all people born in the United States (except Native Americans) were citizens. It also stated that all citizens were entitled to equal rights regardless of their race.

"The First Vote," by Alfred R. Waud, appeared on the cover of *Harper's Weekly* on November 16, 1867.

Republicans were shocked when Johnson chose to **veto** the bill, or stop it from becoming law. Johnson argued that federal protection of civil rights would lead to "centralization" of the government. He was also against giving African Americans full citizenship. Two-thirds of the House and two-thirds of the Senate voted to override the veto, and the bill became law.

Republicans wanted equality to be protected by the Constitution itself, and proposed an amendment in 1866. The **Fourteenth Amendment** stated that all people born or naturalized in the United States were citizens, had the same rights, and were to be granted "equal protection of the laws." However, the amendment did not specifically give African Americans the vote. Instead, it declared that any state that kept African Americans from voting would lose representatives in Congress. This meant that the Southern states would have less power if they did not grant black men the vote.

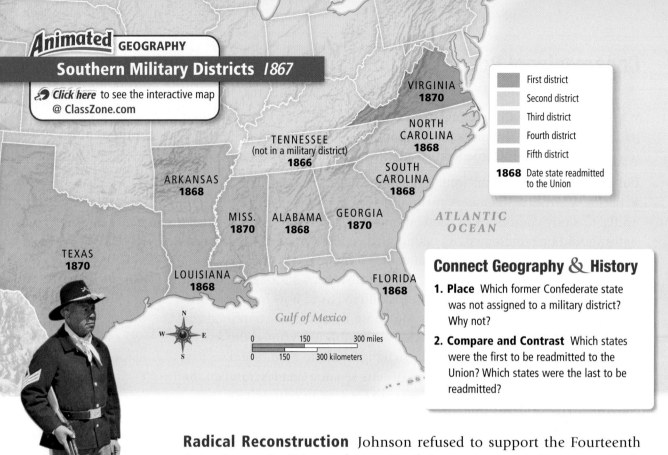

**Click here** to see the interactive map
@ ClassZone.com

VIRGINIA
**1870**

NORTH
CAROLINA
**1868**

TENNESSEE
(not in a military district)
**1866**

SOUTH
CAROLINA
**1868**

ARKANSAS
**1868**

MISS.
**1870**

ALABAMA
**1868**

GEORGIA
**1870**

*ATLANTIC
OCEAN*

TEXAS
**1870**

LOUISIANA
**1868**

FLORIDA
**1868**

*Gulf of Mexico*

N
W    E
S

0        150        300 miles
0    150    300 kilometers

| | First district |
|---|---|
| | Second district |
| | Third district |
| | Fourth district |
| | Fifth district |
| **1868** | Date state readmitted to the Union |

### Connect Geography & History

1. **Place** Which former Confederate state was not assigned to a military district? Why not?

2. **Compare and Contrast** Which states were the first to be readmitted to the Union? Which states were the last to be readmitted?

Under the Reconstruction Acts, the U.S. army governed states in the Southern military districts.

**Radical Reconstruction** Johnson refused to support the Fourteenth Amendment. So did every former Confederate state except Tennessee. Moderate and Radical Republicans were outraged. The two groups joined forces and passed the Reconstruction Acts of 1867. This began a phase, known as Radical Reconstruction, in which Congress controlled Reconstruction.

The Reconstruction Acts divided the South into five military districts. They also said that before Southern states could rejoin the Union, they must:

1. approve new state constitutions that gave the vote to all adult men, including African Americans.
2. ratify the Fourteenth Amendment.

▲ **SUMMARIZE** Summarize Congressional goals for Reconstruction.

## The Impact of Reconstruction

▼ **KEY QUESTION** What were the effects of Congressional Reconstruction?

After the Reconstruction Acts, Southern voters chose delegates to draft state constitutions. Delegates—all Republicans—came from three groups.

**Constitutional Delegates** Many of the Republicans were white farmers, many of them poor, who were angry at planters for starting what they called the "rich man's war." Some Democrats called these delegates **scalawags** (scoundrels) for going along with Radical Reconstruction.

The second group of delegates were known as **carpetbaggers**—white Northerners who rushed to the South after the war. Many Southerners accused them, often unfairly, of seeking only wealth or political power.

African Americans made up the third group of delegates. Of these, half had been free before the war. Most were teachers or other skilled workers.

**New Southern Governments** The new constitutions written by these delegates gave the vote to all adult males. By 1870, voters in all the Southern states had approved their new constitutions. As a result, former Confederate states were let back into the Union and allowed to send representatives to Congress.

During Reconstruction, nearly 700 African Americans served in Southern state legislatures, and 16 served as Southern U.S. congressmen. These included two senators: Hiram Revels and Blanche Bruce, both of Mississippi.

**Johnson Is Impeached** Johnson fought many changes made by Radical Republicans. His conflicts with Congress brought a showdown. In 1867, Congress passed the Tenure of Office Act, which prohibited the president from firing government officials without Senate approval. In February 1868, Johnson fired his secretary of war over disagreements about Reconstruction. Three days later, the House **impeached** the president, or formally accused him of improper conduct while in office.

The case moved to the Senate for a trial. If Johnson were convicted, he would have to leave office. In the end, Johnson was acquitted by a single vote. But much work remained to be done in rebuilding the South.

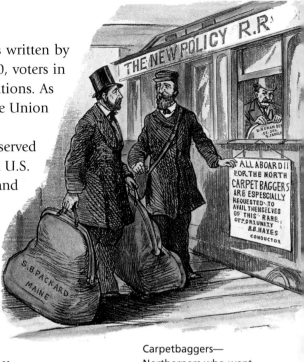

Carpetbaggers—Northerners who went South after the Civil War—were named for a type of luggage, made from old carpet, that was popular at the time.

 **CAUSES AND EFFECTS** Identify the effects of Congressional Reconstruction.

---

**New Jersey Core Curriculum Content Standards *Review***

**ONLINE QUIZ**
For test practice, go to
**Interactive Review @ ClassZone.com**

### TERMS & NAMES

**1.** Explain the importance of

- Radical Republican
- Reconstruction
- Freedmen's Bureau
- Andrew Johnson
- black codes
- Fourteenth Amendment
- scalawag
- carpetbagger

### USING YOUR READING NOTES

**2. Compare and Contrast** Complete the chart to show the goals of presidential and Congressional Reconstruction.

| Presidential Reconstruction | Congressional Reconstruction |
|---|---|
|  | *promote civil rights for freed people* |

### KEY IDEAS

**3.** How did President Andrew Johnson treat the South during Reconstruction?

**4.** Why did Congress decide to take a larger role in Reconstruction?

**5.** What conditions did the Southern states meet in order to rejoin the Union?

### CRITICAL THINKING

**6. Compare and Contrast** How were the black codes similar to the old slave codes?

**7. Draw Conclusions** Did the Fourteenth Amendment truly protect African-American men's right to vote? Explain.

**8. Evaluate** Do you think the House was justified in impeaching President Johnson? Why or why not?

**9. Writing Speech** Research an African American who served in Congress during Reconstruction. Write a speech about his accomplishments.

## ▶ Key Ideas

**BEFORE, YOU LEARNED**

During Reconstruction, the president and Congress fought over how to rebuild the South.

**NOW YOU WILL LEARN**

As the South rebuilt, millions of freed African Americans worked to improve their lives.

## ▶ Vocabulary

**TERMS & NAMES**

**freedmen's school** school set up to educate newly freed African Americans

**sharecropping** system under which landowners gave poor farmers seed, tools, and land to cultivate in exchange for part of their harvest

**Ku Klux Klan** secret group that used violence to try to restore Democratic control of the South and keep African Americans powerless

**BACKGROUND VOCABULARY**

**lynch** to kill by hanging without due process of law

**REVIEW**

**plantation** large farm that raises cash crops

**Visual Vocabulary**
freedmen's school

## ▶ Reading Strategy

Re-create the diagram shown here. As you read and respond to the **KEY QUESTIONS**, use the center box to record the main idea; use the outer ovals to note important details. Add ovals or start a new diagram as needed.

 See Skillbuilder Handbook, page R4.

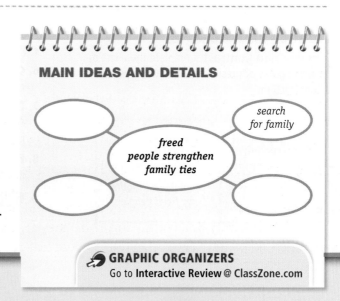

**MAIN IDEAS AND DETAILS**

*search for family*

*freed people strengthen family ties*

**GRAPHIC ORGANIZERS**
Go to **Interactive Review** @ ClassZone.com

# Reconstruction and Daily Life

**6.4.G.3.** Explain Reconstruction as a government action, how it worked, and its effects after the war.
**6.4.G.4.** Discuss the impact of retaliatory state laws and general Southern resistance to Reconstruction.

## One American's Story

After emancipation, many African Americans went in search of family members separated from them by slavery. One observer described a Virginia search party in a letter to an African-American newspaper.

### PRIMARY SOURCE

❝ Aged women and grayhaired men journeyed to Virginia from far-off Georgia hoping to . . . meet sons and daughters whom they bade farewell at the auction block. Many had the good fortune to find those they sought, and their greetings were pathetic [heart-breaking] beyond description. ❞

—B., *The New National Era*, July 23, 1874

Freed people on the South Carolina plantation of former Confederate general Thomas Drayton

Some former slaves walked hundreds of miles to find loved ones. Many placed advertisements in newspapers or with the Freedmen's Bureau.

## Responding to Freedom

🔻 **KEY QUESTION** How did formerly enslaved people first respond to freedom?

Most African Americans' first reaction to freedom was to leave the **plantations**, the large farms that had raised cash crops using slave labor.

**Leaving Plantations** Some former slaves went looking for economic opportunity, while others traveled just because they could—they no longer needed passes to travel. Freedom also allowed African Americans to strengthen their family ties. For the first time, they could marry legally and raise families, knowing that their children could not be sold.

**Connecting History**

**Education**
American education had boomed in the mid–19th century, thanks to the efforts of reformers in both state governments and private organizations.
*See Chapter 14, p. 460.*

**Freedmen's Schools** With freedom, African Americans no longer had to work for an owner's benefit. They could now work to provide for their families. To reach their goal of economic independence, however, most had to learn to read and write. Children and adults flocked to **freedmen's schools,** which were set up to educate newly freed African Americans.

Such schools were started by the Freedmen's Bureau, Northern missionary groups, and African-American organizations. Freed people in cities held classes in warehouses, billiard rooms, and former slave markets. In rural areas, classes were held in churches and private homes. Children who went to school often taught their parents to read at home.

By 1869, more than 150,000 African-American students were attending 3,000 schools. Almost 20 percent of the South's African-American adults could read. Many white Southerners, however, worked against African Americans' efforts to educate themselves. White racists even killed teachers and burned freedmen's schools in some parts of the South. Despite these violent attacks, African Americans kept working toward an education.

▲ **SYNTHESIZE** Explain how freedom changed the lives of formerly enslaved people.

## CONNECT To Today

### RICHMOND, VIRGINIA

During the Civil War, Richmond was the capital of the Confederate States of America. In April 1865, the South faced defeat as Union troops approached the city. The retreating Confederates blew up Richmond's gunpowder supplies in a shattering explosion. Most of the business district and many residential areas were destroyed by fire.

Richmond quickly rebuilt after the war, aided by money from the tobacco industry, of which the city was a hub. Today, Richmond is the capital city of Virginia.

(*right*) A statue of Confederate general Robert E. Lee on Richmond's Monument Avenue. The street was built in the 1880s to honor Civil War veterans. (*inset*) Richmond, April 1865

### CRITICAL THINKING

1. **Make Inferences** Why would the Confederates destroy their own supplies?

2. **Evaluate** What are the advantages and disadvantages of rebuilding a city?

# Working the Land

▼ **KEY QUESTION** What prevented formerly enslaved people from making greater economic advances?

More than anything else, freed people wanted land. To them, land meant economic independence. As one freedman said, "Give us our own land and we take care of ourselves, but without land, the old masters can hire us or starve us, as they please."

**Forty Acres and a Mule** As the Civil War ended, General Sherman suggested that abandoned land in the coastal South be split into 40-acre parcels and given to freedmen. The army also had extra mules that Sherman wanted to loan. The rumor then spread that all freedmen would get 40 acres and a mule. Most freed people thought they deserved at least that much. Said one freedman:

### PRIMARY SOURCE

❝ Our wives, our children, our husbands, [have] been sold over and over again to purchase the lands we now [locate] upon; for that reason we have a divine right to the land. . . . And [then] didn't we clear the land, and raise [the] crops [of] corn, of cotton, of tobacco, of rice, of sugar, of everything? And then didn't . . . cities in the North grow up on the cotton and the sugars and the rice that we made! . . . I say they have grown rich, and my people are poor. ❞

—Bayley Wyat, quoted in *Reconstruction: America's Unfinished Revolution*

In the end, however, most freedmen received no land. Those who did often had to return it later to its former owners—planters who were pardoned by President Johnson.

Radical Republicans Thaddeus Stevens and Charles Sumner pushed for land reform. Stevens proposed a plan that would have taken land from plantation owners and given it to freed people. He argued that civil rights meant little without economic independence. But many other Republicans were against the plan. They believed that civil and voting rights for African Americans were enough, and that the plantation owners had the right to keep their land. As a result, Congress did not pass the plan.

Picking cotton on a Southern plantation, 1870

## COMPARING *Southern Agriculture*

|      | Cotton (bales) | Corn (bushels) | Hay (tons) |
|------|----------------|----------------|------------|
| 1850 | 2.5 million    | 240 million    | 718,997    |
| 1860 | 5.3 million    | 283 million    | 1.1 million |
| 1870 | 3.1 million    | 179 million    | 474,739    |
| 1880 | 5.9 million    | 249 million    | 699,200    |

(Source: *Historical Statistics of the States of the United States*)

**CRITICAL THINKING  Make Inferences** What effects of the Civil War explain the drop in agricultural production in Southern states?

**The Contract System** After the Civil War, planters needed workers to raise cotton—still the South's main cash crop. Without their own land, many African Americans accepted contracts for plantation work.

The contract system was far better than slavery. African Americans were paid for their labor and could decide whom to work for. But even the best contracts paid very low wages. Some landowners abused or cheated workers. As a result, many African Americans turned to sharecropping.

**The Economics of Sharecropping** In the **sharecropping** system, farmers rented land on credit. The landowner provided tools and seed. At harvest time, farmers gave a share of their crops to the landowner as payment.

The sharecropping system had serious problems. Farmers wanted to grow food to feed their families, but landowners forced them to grow cash crops, such as cotton. Meanwhile, most farmers had to buy food, clothing, and other goods on credit—often at inflated prices. By the time they had shared their crops with the landowner and paid their debts, sharecroppers usually had little or no money left. Without money or land of their own, most sharecroppers had no hope of escaping poverty.

▲ **CAUSES AND EFFECTS** Identify the factors that held back the economic advancement of formerly enslaved people.

## COMPARING ⟩ *The Contract System and Sharecropping*

### CONTRACT SYSTEM

- earn wages
- choose whom to work for

### SHARECROPPING

- earn portion of harvest
- supervise own work

**DRAWBACKS**

- low wages
- often cheated by landowner

**BENEFITS**

- families stay together
- landowner provides land, tools, seed

**DRAWBACKS**

- landowner decides what to grow
- farmers often must buy goods on credit from landowner

**CRITICAL THINKING** **Form and Support Opinions** Which do you think offered farmers a better chance of escaping poverty: the contract system or sharecropping? Why?

# Violent Racism

▼ **KEY QUESTION** What were the goals of the Ku Klux Klan?

African Americans in the South faced serious problems besides poverty—including violent racism. Many planters and former Confederate soldiers did not want African Americans to have equal rights.

**The Ku Klux Klan** In 1866, racism in the South spurred the rise of a terrorist group called the **Ku Klux Klan**. Its members came from all walks of life, from poor farmers to former Confederate officers. The Klan's goals were to restore Democratic control of the South and keep former slaves powerless. By 1868, the Klan existed in nearly every Southern state.

The Klan attacked African Americans and white Republicans. Klansmen rode on horseback and dressed in robes and hoods that hid their faces. They beat and tortured people and burned schools, churches, and homes. They even **lynched** some victims—killed them by hanging without a trial as punishment for a supposed crime.

Targets of the Klan had little protection. Military governors in the South often ignored the violence. President Johnson had appointed most of these authorities, and they were against Reconstruction.

The Klan's violence served the Democratic Party. As Klansmen kept Republicans away from the polls, the Democrats' power increased.

▲ **SUMMARIZE** Describe the goals of the Ku Klux Klan.

(top) A former slave trader and Confederate general, Nathan Bedford Forrest led the Klan from 1867 to 1869. (bottom) an 1866 Klan flag.

---

**New Jersey Core Curriculum Content Standards *Review***

 **ONLINE QUIZ**
For test practice, go to
**Interactive Review** @ ClassZone.com

### TERMS & NAMES

**1.** Explain the importance of:
- freedmen's school
- Ku Klux Klan
- sharecropping

### USING YOUR READING NOTES

**2. Main Ideas and Details** Give details about the ways in which newly freed African Americans worked to strengthen family ties.

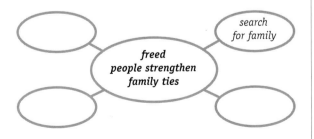

### KEY IDEAS

**3.** How did newly freed African Americans work to improve their lives?

**4.** Why did many African Americans move from the contract system to sharecropping?

**5.** How did the Ku Klux Klan benefit the Democratic Party?

### CRITICAL THINKING

**6. Connect Economics and History** How did the sharecropping system affect African Americans' efforts to achieve economic independence?

**7. Problems and Solutions** What problems did formerly enslaved people face in their efforts to improve their lives?

**8.** **Writing** **Journal** Write a journal entry from the point of view of a sharecropper who was a former contract worker. Describe a day in the life of this person.

## ▶ Key Ideas

**BEFORE, YOU LEARNED**

As the South rebuilt, millions of newly freed African Americans worked to improve their lives.

**NOW YOU WILL LEARN**

As white Southerners regained power in Congress, Reconstruction ended, as did African-American advances toward equality.

## ▶ Vocabulary

**TERMS & NAMES**

**Fifteenth Amendment** constitutional amendment that stated that citizens could not be stopped from voting "on account of race, color, or previous condition of servitude"

**Panic of 1873** financial panic in which banks closed and the stock market crashed

**Compromise of 1877** agreement that decided the 1876 presidential election

**BACKGROUND VOCABULARY**

**stock market** place where shares of ownership in companies are bought and sold

**depression** time of low business activity and high unemployment

**compromise** settlement of differences in which each side gives up something it wants

**REVIEW**

**Ulysses S. Grant** former Union general

**electoral votes** votes made by the members of the Electoral College, which elects the president and vice president

**amendment** formal alteration or addition to the U.S. Constitution

Visual Vocabulary
Panic of 1873

## ▶ Reading Strategy

Re-create the diagram shown here. As you read and respond to the **KEY QUESTIONS**, use the diagram to note important events and their effects. Add boxes or start a new diagram as needed.

 **See Skillbuilder Handbook, page R7.**

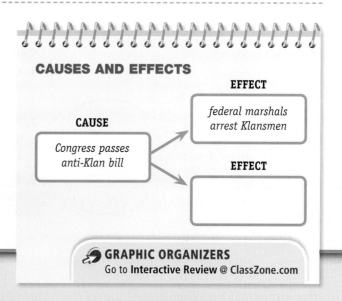

**CAUSES AND EFFECTS**

**CAUSE**

Congress passes anti-Klan bill

**EFFECT**

federal marshals arrest Klansmen

**EFFECT**

**GRAPHIC ORGANIZERS**
Go to **Interactive Review** @ ClassZone.com

**3**

# The End of Reconstruction

 **6.4.G.3.** Explain Reconstruction as a government action, how it worked, and its effects after the war.
**6.4.G.4.** Discuss the impact of retaliatory state laws and general Southern resistance to Reconstruction.

## One American's Story

Robert B. Elliott was elected to the U.S. Congress from South Carolina in 1871. A brilliant orator, he gave a famous speech to Congress in favor of the Civil Rights Act of 1875, which outlawed racial segregation in public services such as restaurants, hotels, and transportation.

### PRIMARY SOURCE

❝ The passage of this bill will determine the civil status, not only of the negro but of any other class of citizens who may feel themselves discriminated against. It will form the capstone of that temple of liberty begun on this continent. ❞

—Robert B. Elliott, quoted in *The Glorious Failure*

In 1877, federal troops left the South. White Southerners quickly took back control of the region, and African Americans lost many hard-earned gains. Even the Civil Rights Act of 1875 was overturned within a decade.

## Protecting African-American Rights

🔻 **KEY QUESTION** How did the Republican Party try to advance civil rights for African Americans?

In 1868, the Republican candidate, former Union general **Ulysses S. Grant**, won the presidency. The Republican Party seemed stronger than ever.

**Grant's Victory** Grant won with 214 **electoral votes**—votes in the Electoral College, which elects the president and vice president. His Democratic opponent received only 80. In the popular count, however, Grant had a majority of only about 305,000 votes. He would not have had this majority without the freedmen's vote. Despite attacks by the Klan, about 500,000 African Americans voted in the South, and most cast their ballots for Grant.

On January 6, 1874, U.S. Representative Robert B. Elliott argued for "equal rights and equal public privileges for all classes of American citizens." This demand was made law in the Civil Rights Act of 1875.

*Reconstruction* **583**

**The Fifteenth Amendment** After Grant's win, Radical Republicans feared that Southern states might try to keep African Americans from voting in future elections. In addition, some states outside the South still prohibited African-American men from voting. To protect African-American suffrage, Radical Republican leaders proposed a constitutional **amendment**—a formal change or addition to the U.S. Constitution.

The **Fifteenth Amendment** stated that citizens could not be stopped from voting "on account of race, color, or previous condition of servitude." (This amendment, like the Fourteenth Amendment, did not apply to Native Americans on tribal lands.) The amendment was ratified in 1870.

The amendment did not apply to women. This made many white women angry, especially those who had fought to end slavery. Suffragist Elizabeth Cady Stanton was opposed to the idea of uneducated immigrants and freedmen "who cannot read the Declaration of Independence . . . making laws for . . . women of wealth and education." But most African-American women, including suffragist Frances E. W. Harper, felt it was important for African Americans to gain voting rights, even if that meant only men at first.

## COMPARING ▸ *Political Representation*

### AFRICAN AMERICANS AND WOMEN IN CONGRESS

(*left*) Jeannette Rankin, elected in 1916, and (*right*) Shirley Chisholm, elected in 1968

These graphs show the number of African Americans and women who served in the U.S. Congress from 1866 onward.

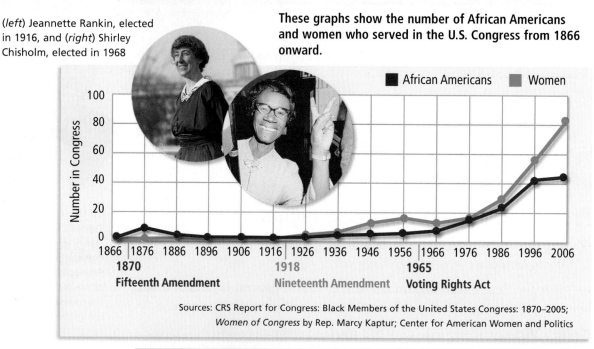

Sources: CRS Report for Congress: Black Members of the United States Congress: 1870–2005; *Women of Congress* by Rep. Marcy Kaptur; Center for American Women and Politics

### CRITICAL THINKING

1. **Draw Conclusions** What happened to African-American representation in Congress after Reconstruction ended?

2. **Make Generalizations** Who made advances in representation more quickly after 1916, African Americans or women?

**Grant Fights the Klan** Despite gaining the vote, African Americans in the South continued to be terrorized by the Ku Klux Klan. In 1871, President Grant asked Congress to pass a tough law against the Klan. Joseph Rainey, a black congressman from South Carolina, had received death threats from the Klan. He urged his fellow lawmakers to support the bill.

**PRIMARY SOURCE**

❝ When myself and colleagues shall leave these Halls and turn our footsteps toward our southern home we know not but that the assassin may await our coming. Be it as it may we have resolved to be loyal and firm, and if we perish, we perish! I earnestly hope the bill will pass. ❞

—Joseph Rainey, quoted in *The Trouble They Seen*

Congress approved the anti-Klan bill. Federal marshals then arrested thousands of Klansmen. Klan attacks on African-American voters declined. As a result, the 1872 presidential election was both fair and peaceful in the South. Grant won a second term.

▲ **PROBLEMS AND SOLUTIONS** Identify the ways Republicans tried to advance rights for African Americans.

# Reconstruction Weakens

▼ **KEY QUESTION** How did Reconstruction lose its strength?

Under President Grant, support for the Republicans and their pro–African-American attitude toward Reconstruction weakened. One major cause of this loss of support was scandal in Grant's administration.

This cartoon from *Puck* magazine shows Grant weighed down by corruption in his administration. **How was Grant burdened by his employees?**

**Scandal in the Republican Party** President Grant did not choose his advisers well. He put his former army friends and his wife's relatives in government positions. Many of these people were unqualified. Some Grant appointees took bribes. Grant's private secretary, for instance, was involved with whiskey distillers who wanted to avoid paying taxes. Grant's secretary of war, General William Belknap, left office after people accused him of taking bribes.

Such scandals angered many Republicans. In 1872, some Republican officials broke away and formed the new Liberal Republican Party. The Republicans, no longer unified, became less able to impose tough Reconstruction policies on the South.

This cartoon by Thomas Nast dramatizes the Panic of 1873: a sudden explosion hits Wall Street, New York's financial center. **What does the image suggest about the effects of the Panic?**

**The Panic of 1873** In 1873, political corruption and quarreling gave way to a more serious problem. Several powerful Eastern banks ran out of money after making bad loans. Worried that the banks would lose their money, people made withdrawals. In the **Panic of 1873**, banks across the land closed. The **stock market** (a place where shares of ownership in companies are bought and sold) temporarily collapsed. The panic caused an economic **depression**, a time of low business activity and high unemployment.

The depression, which lasted about five years, touched nearly all parts of the economy. By 1875, more than 18,000 companies had folded and half a million workers had lost their jobs. Many Americans blamed the crisis on the Republicans—the party in power. As a result, Democrats won victories in the 1874 congressional and state elections. In the middle of the depression, Americans grew tired of hearing about the South's problems. The nation was losing interest in Reconstruction.

**Civil Rights Reversals** To make matters worse for the Republicans, the Supreme Court began to undo some of the progress that had been made for civil rights. In an 1876 case, *U.S.* v. *Cruikshank*, the Court ruled that the federal government could not punish individuals who violated the civil rights of African Americans. Only the states had that power, the Court declared. Southern state officials often would not punish those who attacked African Americans. As a result, violence against them increased.

In the 1876 case *U.S.* v. *Reese*, the Court ruled in favor of white Southerners who barred African Americans from voting. The Court stated that the Fifteenth Amendment did not give everyone the right to vote—it merely listed the grounds on which states could not deny the vote. In other words, states could prevent African Americans from voting for other reasons. States later imposed poll taxes and unfair literacy tests to restrict the vote. These Court decisions weakened Reconstruction and blocked African-American efforts to gain full equality.

▲ **CAUSES AND EFFECTS** Explain what caused Reconstruction to weaken.

## Reconstruction Ends

▼ **KEY QUESTION** What finally led to the end of Reconstruction?

The final blow to Reconstruction came with the 1876 presidential election. In the election, the Democrats chose Samuel J. Tilden, governor of New York. The Republicans nominated Rutherford B. Hayes, governor of Ohio. The election's result forced a **compromise**—a settlement in which both parties gave up some things they wanted. The Republicans gave up the most.

**Compromise of 1877** Victory in the 1876 presidential election depended on three Southern states—South Carolina, Louisiana, and Florida. The votes in those states were so close that both sides claimed victory. A commission of Republicans and Democrats made a deal. Under the **Compromise of 1877**, Republican Rutherford Hayes became president. But the terms were a blow to Republican Reconstruction in the South:

- The government would remove federal troops from the South.
- The government would provide land grants and loans for the construction of railroads linking the South to the West Coast.
- Southern officials would receive federal funds for construction and improvement projects.
- Hayes would appoint a Democrat to his cabinet.
- The Democrats promised to respect African Americans' rights.

**Connecting History**

**Presidential Elections**
The election of 1876 was not the first to be disputed. The election of 1800 had resulted in a tie, which was broken by a compromise in the House of Representatives. *See Chapter 10, pp. 337–339.*

# CONNECT to the Essential Question

How did a deeply divided nation move forward after the Civil War?

| PROBLEM | PRESIDENTIAL SOLUTIONS | CONGRESSIONAL SOLUTIONS |
|---|---|---|
| State governments led by former Confederates | Asked Southern states to ratify the Thirteenth Amendment and accept the supreme power of the federal government<br><br>Offered amnesty and return of property to Confederates who pledged loyalty to the federal government<br><br>✓ SUCCESS | Set up commission to study conditions in the South and determine if Southern states should be allowed representation in U.S. Congress<br><br>✓ SUCCESS |
| Resistance to granting civil rights to formerly enslaved people | Asked Congress to pass anti–Ku Klux Klan legislation<br><br>✓ SOME SUCCESS | Passed Civil Rights Act of 1866<br><br>Proposed Fourteenth and passed Fifteenth Amendments<br><br>Passed anti–Ku Klux Klan legislation<br><br>✓ SOME SUCCESS |
| Formerly enslaved people needing education and employment | None<br>X FAILURE | Freedmen's Bureau<br>✓ SOME SUCCESS |

**CRITICAL THINKING** **Make Inferences** Why might Reconstruction be considered a time in which the presidency was weak?

A statue of educator Booker T. Washington at Hampton University, one of several historically black colleges founded during Reconstruction

Abolitionist Wendell Phillips was against the compromise. He doubted that the South would respect African Americans' rights. "The whole soil of the South is hidden by successive layers of broken promises," he said. "To trust a Southern promise would be fair evidence of insanity."

After the 1876 presidential election, Republican Reconstruction in the South collapsed. The Democrats returned to power.

**The Legacy of Reconstruction** Historians still argue about the success of Reconstruction. The government did achieve its most important goal—the reunification of the nation. However, Reconstruction's effect on African Americans is less straightforward.

African Americans' legal situation changed greatly during Reconstruction. Slavery was outlawed, and African-American men gained the vote and ability to hold office. But the federal government did not enforce the spirit of the Fourteenth and Fifteenth Amendments. In fact, the Supreme Court's rulings in favor of states' rights practically reversed these two amendments. Meanwhile, African Americans continued to face widespread violence and prejudice. White intimidation prevented many African Americans from taking part in politics. Lack of land ownership and economic opportunity meant that most African Americans continued to live in poverty and as second-class citizens.

 **SYNTHESIZE** Explain how Reconstruction ended.

---

 **New Jersey Core Curriculum Content Standards** *Review*

**ONLINE QUIZ**
For test practice, go to
**Interactive Review @ ClassZone.com**

**TERMS & NAMES**

1. Explain the importance of
   • Fifteenth Amendment • Compromise of 1877
   • Panic of 1873

**USING YOUR READING NOTES**

2. **Causes and Effects** Complete the diagram you started at the beginning of this section. Then create a diagram for each of the other main events in this section.

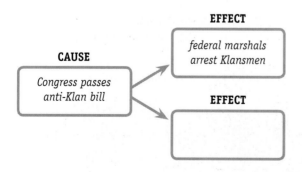

**CAUSE**

*Congress passes anti-Klan bill*

**EFFECT**

*federal marshals arrest Klansmen*

**EFFECT**

**KEY IDEAS**

3. What did the Fifteenth Amendment declare?

4. What effect did scandals in the Grant administration have on the Republican Party?

5. What concessions did the Republicans make in the Compromise of 1877?

**CRITICAL THINKING**

6. **Analyze Point of View** Why did the Fifteenth Amendment anger some white women?

7. **Causes and Effects** Why did the Supreme Court's decisions in favor of states' rights hurt African-American advances toward equality?

8. **Draw Conclusions** Why do you think the Republicans were willing to agree to the Compromise of 1877, even though they knew it would weaken Reconstruction?

9. **Writing** **Essay** Research the presidential election of 2000. Write a one-page essay comparing and contrasting the settlement to that election with that of the presidential election of 1876.

## Chapter Summary

**1** **Key Idea**
During Reconstruction, the president and Congress fought over how to rebuild the South.

**2** **Key Idea**
As the South rebuilt, millions of freed African Americans worked to improve their lives.

**3** **Key Idea**
As white Southerners regained power in Congress, Reconstruction ended, as did African-American advances toward equality.

For detailed Review and Study Notes go to **Interactive Review** @ **ClassZone.com**

## Name Game

Use the Terms & Names list to identify each sentence online or on your own paper.

1. I was a farmer who rented land on credit.

   sharecropper

2. I believed in using Congressional power to rebuild the South.

3. This caused high unemployment.

4. This was set up by Congress to help formerly enslaved people.

5. This used violence to try to restore Democratic control of the South.

6. I was a white Southerner who supported Reconstruction.

7. This stated that citizens could not be stopped from voting on the basis of race.

8. This was a reason that formerly enslaved people had limited legal rights.

9. This was a time in which the U.S. government tried to rebuild Southern society.

10. This removed federal troops from the South.

A. Radical Republican
B. Freedmen's Bureau
C. Fourteenth Amendment
D. Fifteenth Amendment
E. Panic of 1873
F. Compromise of 1877
G. carpetbagger
H. Ku Klux Klan
I. black codes
J. scalawag
K. Reconstruction
L. sharecropper

## Activities

### FLIPCARD

Use the online flip cards to quiz yourself on the terms and names introduced in this chapter.

This president was impeached and later acquitted by a single vote.

ANSWER
Andrew Johnson

### CROSSWORD PUZZLE

Complete the online crossword puzzle to show what you know about Reconstruction.

**ACROSS**
1. Northerner who moved to the South after the Civil War

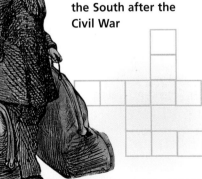

## VOCABULARY

**Explain the significance of each of the following.**

1. Fifteenth Amendment
2. freedmen's school
3. black codes
4. Fourteenth Amendment
5. amnesty
6. Compromise of 1877
7. carpetbagger

**Identify the term that does not belong in each group, and explain why.**

8. stock market, Radical Republican, civil rights
9. depression, Panic of 1873, carpetbagger
10. Andrew Johnson, Fifteenth Amendment, amnesty

## KEY IDEAS

**1 Rebuilding the Union (pages 570–575)**

11. Under the Reconstruction Acts of 1867, what was asked of Southern states before rejoining the Union?

12. Why was Andrew Johnson impeached?

**2 Reconstruction and Daily Life (pages 576–581)**

13. What was a freedmen's school?

14. Why did Congress not pass a land-reform plan?

**3 The End of Reconstruction (pages 582–588)**

15. Why did Republicans lose power in the government?

16. During Reconstruction, how did the Supreme Court weaken African Americans' civil rights?

## CRITICAL THINKING

17. **Synthesize** Why was Reconstruction needed?

18. **Compare and Contrast** How did President Johnson's ideas about Reconstruction differ from those of the Radical Republicans?

19. **Make Inferences** What years included in the chart brought the greatest increase in the national debt? Why might this have been?

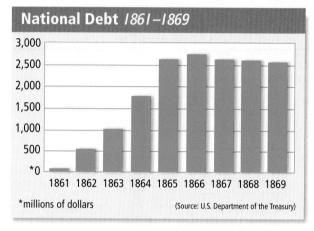

National Debt *1861–1869*

*millions of dollars    (Source: U.S. Department of the Treasury)

20. **Summarize** What impact did the Reconstruction Acts of 1867 have on the South?

21. **Analyze Point of View** Why did African Americans want their own land?

22. **Causes and Effects** How did the Panic of 1873 affect Reconstruction?

23. **Main Ideas and Details** What demands did Southern Democrats make in the Compromise of 1877? What did Republicans gain from the Compromise?

24. **Problems and Solutions** Fill in a table like the one shown to identify the major problems of Reconstruction and how the government attempted to solve them.

| PROBLEMS | PROPOSED SOLUTIONS |
|---|---|
| *State governments led by former Confederates* | |
| *Resistance to granting civil rights to former enslaved people* | |
| *Large numbers of former enslaved people needing education and employment* | |

☑ **TEST PRACTICE**

• **Online Test Practice @ ClassZone.com**
• **Test-Taking Strategies & Practice** at the front of this book

## MULTIPLE CHOICE

**Use the map and your knowledge of U.S. history to answer question 1.**

### Election *1876*

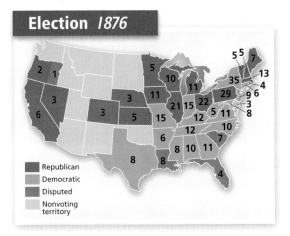

Republican
Democratic
Disputed
Nonvoting territory

**1.** What regions voted mostly Republican?

**A.** the North and East

**B.** the North and West

**C.** the South and East

**D.** the South and West

**Use the quotation and your knowledge of U.S. history to answer question 2.**

### PRIMARY SOURCE

❝ It is a matter of regret to me that it is necessary at this day that I should rise in the presence of an American Congress to advocate a bill which simply asserts equal rights and equal public privileges for all classes of American citizens. ❞

—U.S. Representative Robert Elliott of South Carolina

**2.** Why was it "a matter of regret" to Robert Elliott that he had to speak in support of this bill?

**A.** He wanted Congress to compromise on the bill.

**B.** The failures of Reconstruction filled him with regret.

**C.** Supporting the bill could cause him to lose his job.

**D.** He believed all Americans should already have equal rights.

## YOU BE THE HISTORIAN

**25. Make Generalizations** How did Reconstruction change the lives of most formerly enslaved people?

**26. WHAT IF?** If the Ku Klux Klan had not existed, how might Reconstruction have been different?

**27. Causes and Effects** How did government corruption and misconduct make an impact on Reconstruction?

**28. Citizenship** How did the Fifteenth Amendment promote citizenship for African Americans? How was the amendment limited?

**29. Draw Conclusions** What lasting gains did African Americans make during Reconstruction?

**30. Form and Support Opinions** Do you think African Americans were better off in 1877 than they had been in 1865? Why?

Answer the
### ESSENTIAL QUESTION
**How did a deeply divided nation move forward after the Civil War?**

**Written Response** Write a two- to three-paragraph response to the Essential Question. Consider the key ideas of each section along with the major successes and failures of Reconstruction. Use the Response Rubric below to guide your thinking and writing.

### Response Rubric
**A strong response will**

• compare presidential and Congressional Reconstruction

• explain the obstacles to Reconstruction

• identify the major successes and failures of Reconstruction

• analyze how those successes and failures affected American society

# America Transformed

## 1860–1914

Late 19th-century steam locomotive

## Industrialization and Urbanization

**Key Idea:** New opportunities and challenges developed as America became an industrial power.

America's Gilded Age of industrialization, with its new inventions, corporations, and jobs, helped produce great wealth for a few, spurred the growth of American cities, and made it possible for mass culture to flourish. Industrialization and urbanization also created new problems, such as urban slums and dangerous factories. Progressive reformers worked to solve these and other economic, social, and political problems.

## Changes in the West

**Key Idea:** The nation changed as a result of westward movement after the Civil War.

America's transcontinental railroad opened the way for settlers in the West, many of whom were drawn to the region's booming mining and cattle industries. On the Great Plains, however, Native Americans fought to maintain their ways of life as settlers poured onto their lands, and recently-settled farmers faced many economic problems.

Poster advertising the sale of Native American land

**1860**

Lincoln is elected president; South Carolina secedes.

**1862** Homestead Act

**1865** Civil War ends.

**1869** The transcontinental railroad is completed.

**1877** Reconstruction ends.

**1882** Congress passes the Chinese Exclusion Act.

**1884** Congress organizes Alaska Territory.

**1886** Haymarket Affair

**1887** The Dawes Act distributes reservation land to individuals.

## Immigration and Segregation

**Key Idea:** Immigration transformed American culture, while discrimination continued to plague it.

During the 1800s and early 1900s, millions of immigrants from all over the world added to America's cultural diversity and helped the already booming economy grow. Despite their contributions, immigrants were discriminated against by many native-born Americans. At the same time, whites continued to discriminate against African Americans in the form of poll taxes, segregation, and lynchings. To fight for their civil rights, African American leaders and reformers petitioned Congress and the courts and organized the NAACP.

Immigrants at Ellis Island, New York

## Imperialism

**Key Idea:** America's growing power affected its relationship with other nations.

The United States took major steps in becoming an empire by acquiring Alaska and annexing Hawaii. The nation continued its imperial expansion by gaining territories of Guam, the Philippines, and Puerto Rico in the war with Spain. Government policies such as the Open Door Policy and the Roosevelt Corollary also expanded U.S. influence in China and Latin America.

Queen Lilioukalani, the last Queen of Hawaii

(*above*) Bell telephone and terminal panel, 1877; (*right*) Alexander Graham Bell, inventor of the telephone

**1890** NAWSA formed to win women's right to vote

**1892** Populist Party is founded to support rights of farmers and laborers.

**1893** U.S. annexes Hawaii.

**1894** Pullman Strike

**1896** *Plessy* v. *Ferguson*

**1898** Spanish-American War begins.

**1899** U.S. Open Door Policy

**1909** Founding of NAACP

**1912** Clayton Antitrust Act

**1914**
Panama Canal opens; World War I begins.

*America Transformed* **593**

# World War I & Its Legacy

## 1914–1929

## War in Europe

**Key Idea:** World War I devastated Europe and drew America into a global conflict.

The assassination of Austro-Hungarian Archduke Franz Ferdinand in 1914 ignited the underlying causes of World War I—European imperialism, nationalism, militarism, and alliances between nations. Most of the fighting took place in Europe, although nations from every part of the globe became involved in the war. The United States joined the Allies in 1917 and eventually helped them to defeat Germany in 1918.

I WANT YOU FOR U.S. ARMY
NEAREST RECRUITING STATION

World War I recruiting poster

British soldiers during the Battle of the Lys, April 29, 1918

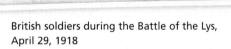

**1915** German U-boat sinks Lusitania.

**1917** The United States declares war against Central Powers; Revolution brings Communists to power in Russia.

**1919** The Treaty of Versailles is signed; the 18th Amendment establishes Prohibition.

**1914**

World War I begins.

**1916** The battles of Verdun and the Somme claim millions of lives.

**1918** Wilson's Fourteen Points; Armistice is declared on November 11, 1918. World War I ends.

**1920** The 19th Amendment grants women the right to vote.

## The Home Front

**Key Idea:** Americans united and made many sacrifices to help the war effort.

Once the United States entered World War I, the federal government built up the military with a draft and sought to control the wartime economy, information, and public opinion. American civilians bought war bonds and economized to help the war effort. Women served in the military and worked in wartime industries, as did African Americans, whose movement to northern cities at this time became known as the Great Migration.

(*above*) Segregated waiting room in train station at Jacksonville, Florida
(*right*) a liberty bond from 1917

Magazine cover from 1926

## The Roaring Twenties

**Key Idea:** American society changed during the 1920s.

After World War I, most Americans were eager for a "return to normalcy" and prosperity, but were divided over foreign policy and domestic issues such as Prohibition. Women won the right to vote, yet their growing independence often clashed with traditional society. African Americans faced new challenges but made great contributions to American culture during the Jazz Age and the Harlem Renaissance.

Louis Armstrong, jazz musician

**1923** Calvin Coolidge becomes president; U.S. economy booms during his administration.

**1925** The Jazz Age and Harlem Renaissance are in full swing; Scopes "Monkey Trial"

**1927** Charles Lindbergh makes first solo flight across the Atlantic.

**1927** *The Jazz Singer*: first commercial "talking" motion picture

**1929**

Americans spend $4 billion on entertainment. Stock market crashes; Great Depression begins.

*World War I & Its Legacy* **595**

# Depression, War, & Recovery
## 1929–1960

## The Great Depression and the New Deal

**Key Idea:** The government enacted various programs to end the Great Depression.

When the prosperity of the 1920s collapsed, President Herbert Hoover struggled to address the country's economic problems. After becoming president in 1933, Franklin D. Roosevelt launched an aggressive program to fight the Great Depression. The hardships of the Great Depression and the policies of the New Deal forever changed American society and government.

$100. WILL BUY THIS CAR MUST HAVE CASH LOST ALL ON THE STOCK MARKET

Migrant worker and her children in California during the Great Depression

Man trying to sell his car after the stock market crash

**1929**

**1930** Dust Bowl conditions

**1932** Bonus Army; FDR elected

**1935** Italy invades Ethiopia.

**1940** Germany conquers France; Battle of Britain begins.

Oct. 29: Black Tuesday—Great Depression begins.

**1931** Japan invades Manchuria.

**1933** Roosevelt's Hundred Days: New Deal begins

**1939** Germany invades Poland, starting WWII.

**1941** U.S. enters WWII after Japan attacks Pearl Harbor.

## The Rise of Dictators and World War II

**Key Idea:** World War II Transformed America and the World.

The rise of dictators in Europe in the 1930s led to World War II. As the war raged in Europe, Americans at home made great contributions to the Allied cause. After five long years of world conflict, the Allies finally defeated the Axis powers in Europe and Africa. Following victory in Europe, and despite early losses in the Pacific, the Allies eventually defeated the Japanese. During the course of the war, America emerged as a major power in the western hemisphere.

(*right*) German dictator Adolf Hitler in 1938
(*below*) German troops riding a tank in 1944

Hydrogen bomb test in 1957

## The Cold War and the American Dream

**Key Idea:** In the years after World War II, America faced Cold War tensions as well as significant domestic changes.

The end of World War II led to prosperity as well as a new kind of war against Communism. The Cold War led to the Korean War, which produced an intense anti-Communism movement in America. From 1945 to the 1960s, economic growth and Cold War tensions caused many changes in American society.

Rock 'n' roll pioneer Chuck Berry

**1942** Battle of Midway; Japanese-American internment begins.

**1944** D-Day: Allied invasion of Europe

**1945** Yalta Conference; Atomic bombs dropped on Hiroshima and Nagasaki; Germany & Japan surrender; Roosevelt dies, Truman becomes president; United Nations created; Nuremburg trials

**1947** HUAC targets communists.

**1948** Marshall Plan begins; Israel created; Berlin airlift begins.

**1949** Communist revolution in China

**1950** Korean War begins.

**1957** Soviet Union launches Sputnik.

**1960** JFK elected

# Civil Rights, Vietnam, & Watergate

## 1954–1975

## The Struggle for Civil Rights

**Key Idea:** Americans responded to discrimination during the civil rights era.

Between the 1870s and World War II, African Americans lost many of the civil rights they had gained during Reconstruction. Their long struggle to regain these rights began in the early 20th century as African-American leaders and white activists organized to fight segregation, voting restrictions, and lynching. In the 1950s and 1960s, Supreme Court rulings against segregation and effective protests by the African-American civil rights movement inspired Hispanics, Native Americans, and women to fight for and win increased civil rights.

Martin Luther King, Jr., and his wife, Coretta, lead a civil rights march in 1965.

Leaders of the United Farm Workers, Dolores Heurta and César Chávez, discuss events during grape pickers' strike.

**1965** Congress passes the Voting Rights Act; many more African Americans register to vote.

**1955** Rosa Parks arrested for refusing to give up her bus seat for a group of white passengers. The Montgomery bus boycott begins.

**1962** Cuban Missile Crisis increases fear that communism might spread.

**1964** Congress passes Civil Rights Act of 1964.

**1954**
▼
*Brown* v. *Board of Education* decided by Supreme Court.

**1960** John F. Kennedy is elected president.

**1963** Lyndon B. Johnson becomes president after Kennedy's assassination; the March on Washington unites the civil rights movement.

## The Vietnam War

**Key Idea:** U.S. involvement in the Vietnam War had lasting effects on America and Southeast Asia.

Fearing the spread of Communism, the U.S. government intensified its military and political interests in Vietnam between 1950 and 1973. Americans expected a quick victory, but soldiers soon grew frustrated by the elusive Viet Cong. As the conflict escalated and dragged on, more Americans protested the war and government misconduct. After the United States pulled out of the war, the Viet Cong gained complete control of Vietnam and Congress limited the president's war-making powers.

American soldiers in Vietnam, 1968

Tourists reading headlines outside the White House in 1974. Richard Nixon is the only U.S. president to resign from office.

## Watergate Changes Politics

**Key Idea:** The Watergate scandal weakened the United States government.

In 1972, President Nixon and his aides illegally tried to cover up a break-in at Democratic Party Headquarters in the Watergate complex in Washington, D.C. The Watergate scandal, as it became known, caused Americans to lose confidence in elected officials and weakened the government, especially the presidency. Facing impeachment, Nixon resigned from office on August 9, 1974.

Poster calling for an end to the war in Vietnam

**1968** Martin Luther King, Jr., is assassinated; the Tet offensive causes Americans to question the war in Vietnam.

**1970** La Raza Unida is founded.

**1972** Members of AIM occupy and Bureau of Indian Affairs. Congress passes the Equal Rights Amendment, but it fails to get ratified.

**1974** Nixon resigns as a result of the Watergate scandal

**1975**

**1969** Richard M. Nixon becomes president.

**1971** The 26th Amendment lowers the voting age from 21 to 18.

**1973** United States withdraws from Vietnam.

The Vietnam War ends after Communists take over South Vietnam.

# America in a Changing World
## 1976–2006

### The Late 1970s

**Key Idea:** The late 1970s were years of doubt for many Americans.

In 1976 it seemed that celebrating the bicentennial of American independence would help the nation to recover from the turmoil of Vietnam, assassinations, the civil rights struggles, and Watergate. But like President Ford, Carter also had little success: while he was able to negotiate peace in the Middle East, his presidency was troubled by an oil shortage, a recession, and the hostage crisis in Iran.

Jimmy and Rosalynn Carter
on Inauguration Day, 1977

America's bicentennial was celebrated around the world with fireworks, parades, and many other events.

**1978** Camp David Peace Accords between Egypt and Israel

**1980** Ronald Reagan elected president

**1986** Iran-Contra affair discovered

**1990** End of Cold War

**1992** Bill Clinton elected president

**1976**

▼
American bicentennial celebrations

**1979** Americans taken hostage in Iran

**1983** IBM releases first desktop "personal computer"

**1989** World Wide Web protocol created; Exxon Valdez oil spill

**1991** Soviet Union breaks apart; Persian Gulf War

## Conservatives Reshape Politics

**Key Idea:** During the 1980s, conservatives reshaped U.S. politics.

Republican President Ronald Reagan pursued conservative goals by increasing military spending. By the time Reagan left office, the economy was growing, and soon thereafter Eastern Europe became free of Soviet control. President Bush won a decisive victory in the Persian Gulf War but could not win re-election. Under President Clinton the nation saw reductions in the federal deficit, inflation, crime, and unemployment.

East and West Berlin reunited in 1989.

## Challenges to Face, Strengths to Build On

**Key Idea:** America's strengths have helped us face the challenges of the past four decades and will help us in the 21st century.

Recent events have tested America's strengths—economic and military leadership, enviable technologies, abundant resources, a robust democracy, and a diverse, educated citizenry. Today the nation faces many complex issues, including growing health care costs, jobs moving overseas, global warming, terrorism, and a changing population. How Americans address these challenges will shape the lives of future generations.

America's future lies in the strengths of its young people.

Hours after this photograph was taken on Sept. 11, 2001, both towers of the New York World Trade Center collapsed.

**1995** Terrorists blow up Federal Building in Oklahoma City

**2000** George W. Bush declared winner of disputed election; More than half of American households have cell phones.

**2002** U.S. leads invasion of Afghanistan

**2004** George W. Bush wins disputed election

**2006**

**1993** NAFTA lowers tariffs; European Union created

**1996** Taliban captures Kabul, Afghanistan; President Clinton impeached, found not guilty

**2001** Sept. 11 attacks; first artificial heart

**2003** Iraq war begins.

**2005** Hurricane Katrina devastates New Orleans

# Reference Section

# American HISTORY

Skillbuilder Handbook ............................... **R1**

Facts About the States ................................ **R40**

Presidents of the United States .......................... **R42**

Gazetteer ........................................ **R45**

English Glossary .................................... **R49**

Spanish Glossary ................................... **R56**

Index ........................................... **R65**

Acknowledgments .................................. **R76**

# Table of Contents

## Reading and Critical Thinking

**1.1** Taking Notes with Graphic Organizers ... R2
**1.2** Summarizing ... R3
**1.3** Finding Main Ideas ... R4
**1.4** Sequencing Events ... R5
**1.5** Categorizing ... R6
**1.6** Analyzing Causes and Effects ... R7
**1.7** Comparing and Contrasting ... R8
**1.8** Identifying Problems and Solutions ... R9
**1.9** Making Inferences ... R10
**1.10** Making Generalizations ... R11
**1.11** Drawing Conclusions ... R12
**1.12** Making Decisions ... R13
**1.13** Evaluating ... R14
**1.14** Analyzing Point of View ... R15
**1.15** Distinguishing Fact from Opinion ... R16
**1.16** Analyzing Primary Sources ... R17
**1.17** Recognizing Bias and Propaganda ... R18
**1.18** Synthesizing ... R19

## Reading Maps, Graphs, and Other Visuals

**2.1** Reading Maps ... R20
**2.2** Reading Graphs and Charts ... R22
**2.3** Analyzing Political Cartoons ... R24
**2.4** Creating a Map ... R25
**2.5** Creating a Model ... R26

## Research, Writing, and Presentation Skills

**3.1** Formulating Historical Questions ... R27
**3.2** Identify and Use Primary and Secondary Sources ... R28
**3.3** Using a Database ... R29
**3.4** Paraphrasing ... R30
**3.5** Outlining ... R31
**3.6** Forming and Supporting Opinions ... R32
**3.7** Essay ... R33
**3.8** Constructed Response ... R34
**3.9** Extended Response ... R35
**3.10** Creating a Multimedia Presentation ... R36

## Using the Internet

**4.1** Using a Search Engine ... R37
**4.2** Evaluating Internet Sources ... R38
**4.3** Recognizing Bias ... R39

# 1.1 Taking Notes with Graphic Organizers

## Defining the Skill

When you **take notes**, you write down the important ideas and details of a paragraph, passage, or chapter. A chart or an outline can help you organize your notes to use in the future.

## Applying the Skill

The following passage describes President Washington's cabinet. Use the strategies listed below to help you take notes on the passage.

### How to Take and Organize Notes

**Strategy ❶** Look at the title to find the main topic of the passage.

**Strategy ❷** Identify the main ideas and details of the passage. Then summarize the main idea and details in your notes.

**Strategy ❸** Identify key terms and define them. The term *cabinet* is shown in boldface type and highlighted; both techniques signal that it is a key term.

**Strategy ❹** In your notes, use abbreviations to save time and space. You can abbreviate words such as *department (dept.)*, *secretary (sec.)*, *United States (U.S.)*, and *president (pres.)* to save time and space.

❶ **WASHINGTON'S CABINET**

❷ The Constitution gave Congress the task of creating departments to help the president lead the nation. The ❷ president had the power to appoint the heads of these departments, which became his ❸ **cabinet**.

Congress created three departments. Washington chose talented people to run them. ❷ For secretary of war, he picked Henry Knox, a trusted general during the Revolution. ❷ For secretary of state, Washington chose Thomas Jefferson. He had been serving as ambassador to France. The State Department oversaw U.S. foreign relations. For secretary of the treasury, Washington turned to the brilliant ❷ Alexander Hamilton.

### Make a Chart

Making a chart can help you take notes on a passage. The chart below contains notes from the passage you just read.

| Item | Notes |
|---|---|
| 1. ❸ cabinet | heads of ❹ depts; ❹ pres. appoints heads |
| a. War Dept. | Henry Knox; ❹ sec. of war; former Revolutionary War general |
| b. State Dept. | Thomas Jefferson; sec. of state; oversees relations between ❹ U.S. and other countries |
| c. Treasury Dept. | Alexander Hamilton; sec. of the treasurey |

## Practicing the Skill

Turn to Chapter 3, Section 3, "The Southern Colonies." Read "The Region of the South" on page 81, and use a graphic organizer to take notes on the passage.

# 1.2 Summarizing

## Defining the Skill

When you **summarize**, you restate a paragraph, passage, or chapter in fewer words. You include only the main ideas and most important details. It is important to use your own words when summarizing.

## Applying the Skill

The passage below tells about Harriet Tubman, a prominent member of the Underground Railroad. She helped runaway slaves to freedom. Use the strategies listed below to help you summarize the passage.

### How to Summarize

**Strategy ❶** Look for topic sentences stating the main idea. These are often at the beginning of a section or paragraph. Briefly restate each main idea—in your own words.

**Strategy ❷** Include key facts and any numbers, dates, amounts, or percentages from the text.

**Strategy ❸** After writing your summary, review it to see that you have included only the most important details.

### HARRIET TUBMAN

❶ One of the most famous conductors on the Underground Railroad was Harriet Tubman. ❷ Born into slavery in Maryland, the 13-year-old Tubman once tried to save another slave from punishment. The angry overseer fractured Tubman's skull with a two-pound weight. She suffered fainting spells for the rest of her life but did not let that stop her from working for freedom. When she was 25, Tubman learned that her owner was about to sell her. Instead, ❷ she escaped.

After her escape, ❷ Harriet Tubman made 19 dangerous journeys to free enslaved persons. The tiny woman carried a pistol to frighten off slave hunters and medicine to quiet crying babies. Her enemies offered $40,000 for her capture, but ❷ no one caught her. "I never run my train off the track and I never lost a passenger," she proudly declared. Among the people she saved were her parents.

## Write a Summary

You can write your summary in a paragraph. The paragraph at right summarizes the passage you just read.

❸ Harriet Tubman was one of the most famous conductors on the Underground Railroad. She had been a slave, but she escaped. She later made 19 dangerous journeys to free other slaves. She was never captured.

## Practicing the Skill

Turn to Chapter 6, Section 2, "Colonial Resistance Grows." Read "The Boston Massacre" on pages 163–164, and write a paragraph summarizing the passage.

# 1.3 Finding Main Ideas

## Defining the Skill

The **main idea** is a statement that summarizes the main point of a speech, an article, a section of a book, or a paragraph. Main ideas can be stated or unstated. The main idea of a paragraph is often stated in the first or last sentence. If it is the first sentence, it is followed by sentences that support that main idea. If it is the last sentence, the details build up to the main idea. To find an unstated idea, you must use the details of the paragraph as clues.

## Applying the Skill

The following paragraph describes the role of women in the American Revolution. Use the strategies listed below to help you identify the main idea.

### How to Find the Main Idea

**Strategy ①** Identify what you think may be the stated main idea. Check the first and last sentences of the paragraph to see if either could be the stated main idea.

**Strategy ②** Identify details that support that idea. Some details explain the main idea. Others give examples of what is stated in the main idea.

---

**WOMEN IN THE REVOLUTION**

① Many women tried to help the army. Martha Washington and other wives followed their husbands to army camps. ② The wives cooked, did laundry, and nursed sick or wounded soldiers. ② A few women even helped to fight. ② Mary Hays earned the nickname "Molly Pitcher" by carrying water to tired soldiers during a battle. ② Deborah Sampson dressed as a man, enlisted, and fought in several engagements.

---

### Make a Chart

Making a chart can help you identify the main idea and details in a passage or paragraph. The chart below identifies the main idea and details in the paragraph you just read.

> **Main Idea:** Women helped the army during the Revolution.
>
> **Detail:** They cooked and did laundry
> **Detail:** They nursed the wounded and sick soldiers
> **Detail:** They helped to fight.
> **Detail:** One woman, Molly Pitcher, carried water to soldiers during battles.

## Practicing the Skill

Turn to Chapter 5, Section 2, "Roots of American Democracy." Read "Parliament and Colonial Government" on page 139, and create a chart that identifies the main idea and the supporting details.

# 1.4 Sequencing Events

## Defining the Skill

**Sequence** is the order in which events follow one another. By being able to follow the sequence of events through history, you can get an accurate sense of the relationships among events.

## Applying the Skill

The following passage describes the sequence of events involved in Britain's plan to capture the Hudson River valley during the American Revolution. Use the strategies listed below to help you follow the sequence of events.

### How to Find the Sequence of Events

**Strategy ①** Look for specific dates provided in the text. If several months within a year are included, the year is usually not repeated.

**Strategy ②** Look for clues about time that allow you to order events according to sequence. Words such as *day*, *week*, *month*, or *year* may help to sequence the events.

> **BRITAIN'S STRATEGY**
>
> Burgoyne captured Fort Ticonderoga in **①** July 1777. From there, it was 25 miles to the Hudson River, which ran to Albany. **②** Burgoyne took three weeks to reach the Hudson. On **①** August 3, Burgoyne received a message from Howe. He would not be coming north, Howe wrote, because he had decided to invade Pennsylvania to try to capture Philadelphia and General Washington. "Success be ever with you," Howe's message said. But General Burgoyne needed Howe's soldiers, not his good wishes. Howe did invade Pennsylvania. In **①** September 1777, he defeated —but did not capture—Washington at the Battle of Brandywine.

### Make a Time Line

Making a time line can help you sequence events. The time line below shows the sequence of events in the passage you just read.

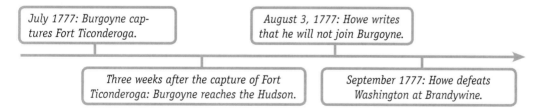

July 1777: Burgoyne captures Fort Ticonderoga.

August 3, 1777: Howe writes that he will not join Burgoyne.

Three weeks after the capture of Fort Ticonderoga: Burgoyne reaches the Hudson.

September 1777: Howe defeats Washington at Brandywine.

## Practicing the Skill

Turn to Chapter 8, Section 1, "The Confederation Era." Read "The Articles Are Ratified" on page 237, and make a time line showing the sequence of events in that passage.

# 1.5 Categorizing

## Defining the Skill

To **categorize** is to sort people, objects, ideas, or other information into groups, called categories. Historians categorize information to help them identify and understand patterns in historical events.

## Applying the Skill

The following passage contains information about the reasons people went west during the mid-1800s. Use the strategies listed below to help you categorize information.

## How to Categorize

**Strategy ①** First, decide what kind of information needs to be categorized. Decide what the passage is about and how that information can be sorted into categories. For example, find the different motives people had for moving west.

**Strategy ②** Then find out what the categories will be. To find why many different groups of people moved west, look for clue words such as *some*, *other*, and *another*.

**Strategy ③** Once you have chosen the categories, sort information into them. Of the people who went west, which ones had which motives?

### THE LURE OF THE WEST

**①** People had many different motives for going west. **②** One motive was to make money. **②** *Some* people called speculators bought huge areas of land and made great profits by selling it to thousands of settlers. **②** *Other* settlers included farmers who dreamed of owning their own farms in the West because land was difficult to acquire in the East. **②** *Another* group to move west was merchants. They hoped to earn money by selling items that farmers needed. Finally, **②** *some* people went west for religious reasons. These people included **②** missionaries, who wanted to convert the Native Americans to Christianity, and Mormons, who wanted a place where they could practice their faith without interference.

## Make a Chart

Making a chart can help you categorize information. You should have as many columns as you have categories. The chart below shows how the information from the passage you just read can be categorized.

**③**

| Motives | Money | Land | Religion |
|---------|-------|------|----------|
| Groups | • speculators<br>• merchants | • farmers | • missionaries<br>• Mormons |

## Practicing the Skill

Turn to Chapter 14, Section 3, "Reforming American Society." Read "Social Reform" on page 460, and make a chart in which you categorize the changes happening in elementary, high school, and college education.

# 1.6 Analyzing Causes and Effects

## Defining the Skill

A **cause** is an action in history that makes something happen. An **effect** is the historical event that is the result of the cause. A single event may have several causes. It is also possible for one cause to result in several effects. Historians identify cause-and-effect relationships to help them understand why historical events took place.

## Applying the Skill

The following paragraph describes events that caused changes in Puritan New England. Use the strategies listed below to help you identify the cause-and-effect relationships.

### How to Analyze Causes and Recognize Effects

**Strategy ❶** Ask why an action took place. Ask yourself a question about the title and topic sentence, such as, "What caused changes in Puritan society?"

**Strategy ❷** Look for effects. Ask yourself, "What happened?" (the effect). Then ask, "Why did it happen?" (the cause). For example, What caused the decline of Puritan religion in New England?

**Strategy ❸** Look for clue words that signal causes, such as *cause* and *led to*.

**Strategy ❹** One way to practice recognizing effects is to make predictions about the consequences that will result from particular actions. Then, as you read, look to see if your predictions were accurate.

❶ **CHANGES IN PURITAN SOCIETY**

❶ The early 1700s saw many changes in New England society. ❷ One of the most important changes was the gradual decline of the Puritan religion in New England. There were a number of reasons for that decline. ❸ One *cause* of this decline was the increasing competition from other religious groups. Baptists and Anglicans established churches in Massachusetts and Connecticut, where Puritans had once been the most powerful group. ❸ Political changes also *led to* a weakening of the Puritan community. In 1691, a new royal charter for Massachusetts granted the vote based on property ownership instead of church membership.

## Make a Diagram

Using a diagram can help you understand causes and effects. The diagram below shows two causes and an effect for the passage you just read.

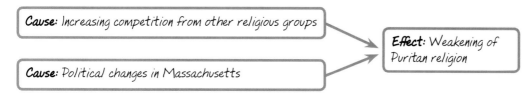

**Cause:** Increasing competition from other religious groups

**Cause:** Political changes in Massachusetts

**Effect:** Weakening of Puritan religion

## Practicing the Skill

Turn to Chapter 4, Section 2, "The Southern Colonies: Plantations and Slavery." Read "Expansion of Plantations Brings Resistance" on pages 106–107, and make a diagram about the causes and effects of slave resistance.

# 1.7 Comparing and Contrasting

## Defining the Skill

**Comparing** means looking at the similarities and differences between two or more things. **Contrasting** means examining only the differences between them. Historians compare and contrast events, personalities, behaviors, beliefs, and situations in order to understand them.

## Applying the Skill

The following paragraph describes the American and British troops during the Revolutionary War. Use the strategies listed below to help you compare and contrast these two armies.

## How to Compare and Contrast

**Strategy ①** Look for two aspects of the subject that may be compared and contrasted. This passage compares the British and American troops to show why the Americans won the war.

**Strategy ②** To contrast, look for clue words that show how two things differ. Clue words include *by contrast*, *however*, *except*, and *yet*.

**Strategy ③** To find similarities, look for clue words indicating that two things are alike. Clue words include *both*, *like*, *as*, and *similarly*.

> ### WHY THE AMERICANS WON
>
> ① By their persistence, the Americans defeated the British even though they faced many obstacles. The Americans lacked training and experience. They were often short of supplies and weapons. ② *By contrast*, the British forces ranked among the best trained in the world. They were experienced and well-supplied professional soldiers. ② *Yet*, the Americans also had advantages that enabled them to win. These advantages over the British were better leadership, foreign aid, a knowledge of the land, and motivation. Although ③ *both* the British and the Americans were fighting for their lives, ② the Americans were also fighting for their property and their dream of liberty.

## Make a Venn Diagram

Making a Venn diagram will help you identify similarities and differences between two things. In the overlapping area, list characteristics shared by both subjects. Then, in the separate ovals, list the characteristics of each subject not shared by the other. This Venn diagram compares and contrasts the British and American soldiers.

*American Soldiers:*
lacked experience and training
short of supplies and weapons
had better leadership
received foreign aid
had knowledge of the land
fought for liberty and property

*Both:*
fought for their lives

*British Soldiers:*
best trained in the world
experienced
well-supplied

## Practicing the Skill

Turn to Chapter 5, Section 1, "Early American Culture." Read "Life of the Young" on pages 129–130, and make a Venn diagram showing the similarities and differences between the roles of boys and girls in colonial America.

# 1.8 Identifying Problems and Solutions

## Defining the Skill

**Identifying problems** means finding and understanding the difficulties faced by a particular group of people during a certain time. **Solutions** are the actions people took to remedy those problems. By studying the solutions to problems in the past, you can learn ways to solve problems today.

## Applying the Skill

The following paragraph describes problems that the Constitutional Convention faced on the issues of taxation, representation, and slavery. Use the strategies listed below to help you identify the Founders' solutions to these problems.

## How to Identify Problems and Solutions

**Strategy ①** Look for the difficulties, or problems, people faced.

**Strategy ②** Consider how the problem affected people with different points of view. For example, the main problem described here was how to count the population of each state.

**Strategy ③** Look for solutions people tried to deal with each problem. Think about whether the solution was a good one for people with differing points of view.

---

### SLAVERY AND THE CONSTITUTION

Because the House of Representatives would have members based on the population of each state, ① the delegates had to decide who would be counted in that population. The Southern states had many more slaves than the Northern states. ② Southerners wanted the slaves to be counted as part of the general population for representation but not for taxation. ② Northerners argued that slaves were not citizens and should not be counted for representation but should be counted for taxation. ③ The delegates decided that three-fifths of the slave population would be counted for both purposes: representation and taxation.

---

## Make a Chart

Making a chart will help you identify and organize information about problems and solutions. The chart below shows problems and solutions included in the passage you just read.

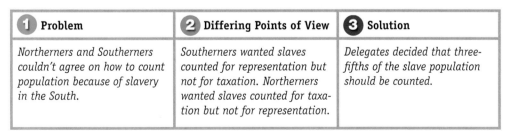

| ① Problem | ② Differing Points of View | ③ Solution |
|---|---|---|
| *Northerners and Southerners couldn't agree on how to count population because of slavery in the South.* | *Southerners wanted slaves counted for representation but not for taxation. Northerners wanted slaves counted for taxation but not for representation.* | *Delegates decided that three-fifths of the slave population should be counted.* |

## Practicing the Skill

Turn to Chapter 8, Section 2, "Creating the Constitution." Read "Some Challenges of the Convention" on pages 245–246, and make a chart that details the problems faced by the delegates at the Constitutional Convention and the solutions they agreed on.

# 1.9 Making Inferences

## Defining the Skill

Inferences are ideas that the author has not directly stated. **Making inferences** involves reading between the lines to interpret the information you read. You can make inferences by studying what is stated and using your common sense and previous knowledge.

## Applying the Skill

The passage below describes the strengths and weaknesses of the North and the South as the Civil War began. Use the strategies listed below to help you make inferences from the passage.

### How to Make Inferences

**Strategy 1** Read to find statements of facts and ideas. Knowing the facts will give you a good basis for making inferences.

**Strategy 2** Use your knowledge, logic, and common sense to make inferences that are based on facts. Ask yourself, "What does the author want me to understand?" For example, from the facts about population, you can make the inference that the North would have a larger army than the South. See other inferences in the chart below.

> ### ADVANTAGES OF THE NORTH AND THE SOUTH
>
> The North had more people and resources than the South. **1** The North had about 22 million people. **1** The South had roughly 9 million, of whom about 3.5 million were slaves. In addition, **1** the North had more than 80 percent of the nation's factories and almost all of the shipyards and naval power. The South had some advantages, too: **1** able generals, such as Robert E. Lee, **1** and the advantage of fighting a defensive war. Soldiers defending their homes have more will to fight than invaders do.

## Make a Chart

Making a chart will help you organize information and make logical inferences. The chart below organizes information from the passage you just read.

| **1** Stated Facts and Ideas | **2** Inferences |
|---|---|
| The North had about 22 million people. The Confederacy had about 9 million. | The North would have a larger army than the South. |
| The North had more factories, naval power, and shipyards. | The North could provide more weapons, ammunition, and ships for the war. |
| The Confederacy had excellent generals. | The Confederacy had better generals, which would help it overcome other disadvantages. |
| The Confederacy was fighting a defensive war | Confederate soldiers would fight harder because they were defending their homes and families. |

## Practicing the Skill

Turn to Chapter 12, Section 1, "Jacksonian Democracy and States' Rights." Read "Voting Rights Expand" on pages 396–397, and use a chart like the one above to make inferences about Jacksonian democracy.

# 1.10 Making Generalizations

## Defining the Skill

To **make generalizations** means to make broad judgments based on information. When you make generalizations, you should gather information from several sources.

## Applying the Skill

The following three passages contain different views on George Washington. Use the strategies listed below to make a generalization about these views.

### How to Make Generalizations

**Strategy 1** Look for information that the sources have in common. These three sources all discuss George Washington's ability as a military leader.

**Strategy 2** Form a generalization that describes Washington in a way that all three sources would agree with. State your generalization in a sentence.

### WASHINGTON'S LEADERSHIP

**1** Washington learned from his mistakes. After early defeats, he developed the strategy of dragging out the war to wear down the British. **1** Despite difficulties, he never gave up.

—*Creating America*

**1** [Washington] was no military genius. . . . But he was a great war leader. Creating an army out of unpromising material, he kept it in being against great odds.

—*The Limits of Liberty*

**1** [Washington] certainly deserves some merit as a general, that he . . . can keep General Howe dancing from one town to another for two years together, with such an army as he has.

—*The Journal of Nicholas Cresswell, July 13, 1777*

### Make a Chart

Using a chart can help you make generalizations. The chart below shows how the information you just read can be used to generalize about people's views of Washington.

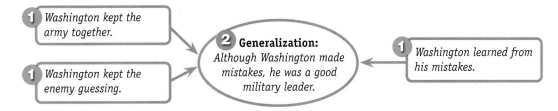

**1** Washington kept the army together.

**1** Washington kept the enemy guessing.

**2 Generalization:** *Although Washington made mistakes, he was a good military leader.*

**1** *Washington learned from his mistakes.*

## Practicing the Skill

Turn to Chapter 16, Section 1, "War Erupts." Read "Planning Strategies" on page 513. Also read "Comparing North and South" on page 514. Then, use a chart like the one above to make generalizations about the two sides on the eve of the Civil War.

# 1.11 Drawing Conclusions

## Defining the Skill

**Drawing conclusions** means analyzing what you have read and forming an opinion about its meaning. To draw conclusions, look at the facts and then use your own common sense and experience to decide what the facts mean.

## Applying the Skill

The following passage presents information about the Intolerable Acts and the colonists' reactions to them. Use the strategies listed below to help you draw conclusions about those acts.

### How to Draw Conclusions

**Strategy ➊** Read carefully to identify and understand all the facts, or statements, that can be proven true.

**Strategy ➋** List the facts in a diagram and review them. Use your own experiences and common sense to understand how the facts relate to each other.

**Strategy ➌** After reviewing the facts, write down the conclusion you have drawn about them.

> **THE INTOLERABLE ACTS**
>
> ➊ In 1774, Parliament passed a series of laws to punish the Massachusetts colony and serve as a warning to other colonies.
>
> ➊ These laws were so harsh that colonists called them the **Intolerable Acts**. One of the acts closed the port of Boston. Others banned committees of correspondence and allowed Britain to house troops wherever necessary.
>
> In 1773, Sam Adams had written, "I wish we could arouse the continent." ➊ The Intolerable Acts answered his wish. Other colonies immediately offered Massachusetts their support.

### Make a Diagram

Making a diagram can help you draw conclusions. The diagram below shows how to organize facts and inferences to draw a conclusion about the passage you just read.

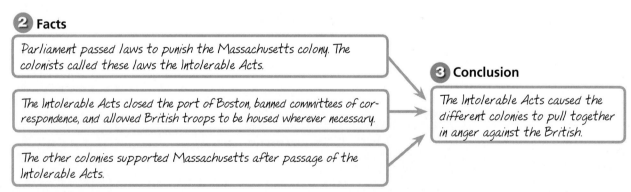

**➋ Facts**

Parliament passed laws to punish the Massachusetts colony. The colonists called these laws the Intolerable Acts.

The Intolerable Acts closed the port of Boston, banned committees of correspondence, and allowed British troops to be housed wherever necessary.

The other colonies supported Massachusetts after passage of the Intolerable Acts.

**➌ Conclusion**

The Intolerable Acts caused the different colonies to pull together in anger against the British.

## Practicing the Skill

Turn to Chapter 3, Section 2, "New England Colonies." Read "Puritans Persecute Quakers" on page 71, and use the diagram above as a model to draw conclusions about Puritans' beliefs.

# 1.12 Making Decisions

## Defining the Skill

**Making decisions** involves choosing between two or more options or courses of action. In most cases, decisions have consequences, or results. Sometimes decisions may lead to new problems. By understanding how historical figures made decisions, you can learn how to improve your decision-making skills.

## Applying the Skill

The following passage describes Lincoln's decisions regarding federal forts after the Southern states seceded. Use the strategies listed below to help you analyze his decisions.

### How to Make Decisions

**Strategy ① Identify a decision** that needs to be made. Think about what factors make the decision difficult.

**Strategy ② Identify possible** consequences of the decision. Remember that there can be more than one consequence to a decision.

**Strategy ③ Identify the deci-** sion that was made.

**Strategy ④ Identify actual** consequences that resulted from the decision.

> ### FIRST SHOTS AT FORT SUMTER
>
> ① Lincoln had to decide what to do about the forts in the South that remained under federal control. A Union garrison still held Fort Sumter, but it was running out of supplies. ② If Lincoln supplied the garrison, he risked war. ② If he withdrew the garrison, he would be giving in to the rebels. ③ Lincoln informed South Carolina that he was sending supply ships to Fort Sumter. ④ Confederate leaders decided to prevent the federal government from holding on to the fort by attacking before the supply ships arrived. No one was killed, but ④ the South's attack on Fort Sumter signaled the beginning of the Civil War.

## Make a Flow Chart

A flow chart can help you identify the process of making a decision. The flow chart below shows the decision-making process in the passage you just read.

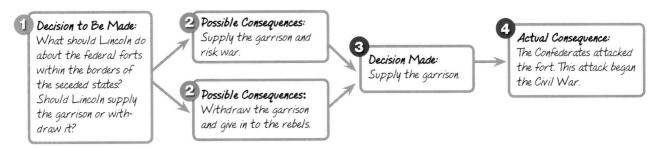

**① Decision to Be Made:** What should Lincoln do about the federal forts within the borders of the seceded states? Should Lincoln supply the garrison or withdraw it?

**② Possible Consequences:** Supply the garrison and risk war.

**② Possible Consequences:** Withdraw the garrison and give in to the rebels.

**③ Decision Made:** Supply the garrison.

**④ Actual Consequence:** The Confederates attacked the fort. This attack began the Civil War.

## Practicing the Skill

Turn to Chapter 12, Section 2, "Jackson's Policy Toward Native Americans." Read "Native American Resistance" on page 407, and make a flow chart to identify a decision and its consequences described in that section.

# 1.13 Evaluating

## Defining the Skill

To **evaluate** is to make a judgment about something. Historians evaluate the actions of people in history. One way to do this is to examine both the positives and negatives of a historical action, then decide which is stronger—the positive or the negative.

## Applying the Skill

The following passage describes Susan B. Anthony's fight for women's rights. Use the strategies listed below to evaluate how successful she was.

### How to Evaluate

**Strategy ❶** Before you evaluate a person's actions, first determine what that person was trying to accomplish.

**Strategy ❷** Look for statements that show the positive, or successful, results of Anthony's actions. Did she achieve her goals?

**Strategy ❸** Also look for statements that show the negative, or unsuccessful, results of her actions. Did she fail to achieve something she tried to do?

**Strategy ❹** Write an overall evaluation of the person's actions.

---

**SUSAN B. ANTHONY**

❶ Susan B. Anthony was a skilled organizer who fought for women's rights. ❷ She successfully built the women's movement into a national organization. An outspoken advocate for equal pay for men and women, she called for laws that would give married women the right to keep their own property and wages. ❷ Mississippi passed the first such law in 1839. New York passed a property law in 1848 and a wages law in 1860.

❸ Anthony also wanted to win the vote for women but failed to convince lawmakers to pass this reform in her lifetime. This reform did go through in 1920, 14 years after her death.

---

### Make a Diagram for Evaluating

Using a diagram can help you evaluate a person's actions and decisions. The diagram below shows how the information from the passage you just read can be organized.

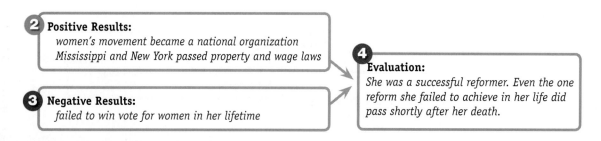

❷ **Positive Results:**
*women's movement became a national organization*
*Mississippi and New York passed property and wage laws*

❸ **Negative Results:**
*failed to win vote for women in her lifetime*

❹ **Evaluation:**
*She was a successful reformer. Even the one reform she failed to achieve in her life did pass shortly after her death.*

## Practicing the Skill

Turn to Chapter 2, Section 3, "The Spanish and Native Americans." Read "The Columbian Exchange" on pages 44–45, and make a diagram in which you evaluate whether the Columbian Exchange had mainly a positive or negative impact on the world.

# 1.14 Analyzing Point of View

## Defining the Skill

**Analyzing point of view** means looking closely at a person's arguments to understand the reasons behind that person's beliefs. The goal of analyzing a point of view is to understand a historical figure's thoughts, opinions, and biases about a topic.

## Applying the Skill

The following passage describes the Panic of 1837 and two politicians' points of view about it. Use the strategies listed below to help you analyze their points of view.

### How to Analyze Point of View

**Strategy 1** Look for statements that show you a person's view on an issue. Van Buren said he believed the economy would improve if he took no action. Clay thought the government should do something.

**Strategy 2** Use information about people to validate them as sources and understand their differences. What do you know about Clay and Van Buren that might explain their biases and disagreements?

**Strategy 3** Write a summary that explains why different people took different positions on the issue.

> **THE PANIC OF 1837**
>
> The Panic of 1837 caused severe hardship. People had little money, so manufacturers had few customers for their goods. Almost 90 percent of factories in the East closed. Jobless workers could not afford food or rent. Many people went hungry.
>
> **1** Whig senator Henry Clay wanted the government to do something to help the people. **1** President Van Buren, a Democrat, disagreed. He believed that the economy would improve if left alone. He argued that "the less government interferes with private pursuits the better for the general prosperity." Many Americans blamed Van Buren for the Panic, though he had taken office only weeks before it started.

## Make a Diagram

Using a diagram can help you analyze points of view. The diagram below analyzes the views of Clay and Van Buren in the passage you just read.

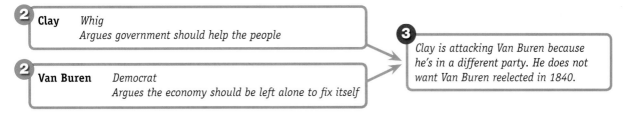

**2 Clay** *Whig*
*Argues government should help the people*

**2 Van Buren** *Democrat*
*Argues the economy should be left alone to fix itself*

**3** *Clay is attacking Van Buren because he's in a different party. He does not want Van Buren reelected in 1840.*

## Practicing the Skill

Turn to the Reading Primary Sources on pages 255 and 256. Read the selections by James Madison and George Mason. Use their language, information from other sources, and information about each man to validate them as sources. Then make a diagram to analyze their different points of view on the Constitution.

# 1.15 Distinguishing Fact from Opinion

## Defining the Skill

**Facts** are events, dates, statistics, or statements that can be proved to be true. **Opinions** are the judgments, beliefs, and feelings of a writer or speaker. By distinguishing fact from opinion, you will be able to think critically when a person is trying to influence your own opinion.

## Applying the Skill

The following passage tells about the Virginia Plan for legislative representation offered at the Constitutional Convention of 1787. Use the strategies listed below to help you distinguish facts from opinions.

### How to Recognize Facts and Opinions

**Strategy** **1** Look for specific information that can be proved or checked for accuracy.

**Strategy** **2** Look for assertions, claims, and judgments that express opinions. In this case, one speaker's opinion is expressed in a direct quotation.

**Strategy** **3** Think about whether statements can be checked for accuracy. Then, identify the facts and opinions in a chart.

> **ANTIFEDERALIST VIEWS**
>
> **1** Antifederalists published their views about the Constitution in newspapers and pamphlets. **1** They thought the Constitution took too much power away from the states and did not protect the rights of the people. They charged that the Constitution would destroy American liberties. As one Antifederalist wrote, **2** "It is truly astonishing that a set of men among ourselves should have had the [nerve] to attempt the destruction of our liberties."

## Make a Chart

The chart below analyzes the facts and opinions from the passage above.

| Statement | **3** Can It Be Proved? | **3** Fact or Opinion |
|---|---|---|
| *Antifederalists published their views in newspapers and pamphlets.* | *Yes. Check newspapers and other historical documents.* | *Fact* |
| *They thought the Constitution took too much power away from the states.* | *Yes. Check newspapers and other historical documents.* | *Fact* |
| *It is astonishing that some Americans would try to destroy American liberties.* | *No. This cannot be proved. It is what one speaker believes.* | *Opinion* |

## Practicing the Skill

Turn to Chapter 11, Section 3, "Nationalism and Sectionalism." Read "The Missouri Compromise" on page 382, and make a chart in which you analyze key statements to determine whether they are facts or opinions.

# 1.16 Analyzing Primary Sources

## Defining the Skill

**Primary sources** are materials written or made by people who lived during historical events and witnessed them. When you **analyze** primary sources, you interpret them, or decide what they tell you about history. Analyzing primary sources will help deepen your understanding of historical events.

## Applying the Skill

The following passage is from a magazine article written by an African American who taught formerly enslaved persons in South Carolina. Use the strategies listed below to analyze it.

### How to Analyze Primary Sources

**Strategy** ① Use the information in the document to make inferences about daily life at the time it was written.

**Strategy** ② Look for evidence that will tell you what the author's purpose may have been, and who was her intended audience.

**Strategy** ③ Identify the author of the primary source and note when it was written. Consider what important historical events were occurring at this time.

> **PRIMARY SOURCE**
>
> ① Many of the grown people are desirous of learning to read. It is wonderful how a people who have been so long crushed to the earth, so imbruted [treated cruelly] as these have been . . . can have so great a desire for knowledge, and such a capability for attaining it. ② One cannot believe that the haughty Anglo Saxon race, after centuries of such an experience as these people have had, would be very much superior to them.
>
> ③ —Charlotte Forten, "Life on the Sea Islands," 1864

## Make a Chart

Making a chart will help you analyze information from primary sources. The chart below provides an analysis of the passage you just read.

| | |
|---|---|
| **Author:** Charlotte Forten | |
| **Type of source:** magazine article | **Title:** "Life on the Sea Islands" |
| **Date:** 1864 | **Historical events:** Civil War |
| **Author's purpose:** Gain support for education of former enslaved persons | |
| **Audience:** Whites, free African Americans | |
| **What it tells you about history:** Enslaved African Americans were prevented from getting an education, but after they were freed, they eagerly pursued education. | |

## Practicing the Skill

Turn to Chapter 11, Section 1, "Early Industry and Inventions." Read "Time Table of the Holyoke Mills" on page 367, and analyze the poster to understand the historical context in which it was written.

# 1.17 Recognizing Bias and Propaganda

## Defining the Skill

**Bias** is a one-sided presentation of an issue. **Propaganda** is communication that aims to influence people's opinions, emotions, or actions. Propaganda is not always factual. Rather, it uses prejudicial language or striking symbols to sway people's emotions. Modern advertising often uses propaganda. By thinking critically, you can avoid being swayed by bias and propaganda.

## Applying the Skill

The following political cartoon shows Andrew Jackson dressed as a king. Use the strategies listed below to help you understand how it works as propaganda.

### How to Recognize Bias and Propaganda

**Strategy ❶** Identify the aim, or purpose, of the cartoon. Point out the subject and explain the point of view.

**Strategy ❷** Identify those images on the cartoon that viewers might respond to emotionally and identify the emotions.

**Strategy ❸** Think critically about the cartoon. What facts has the cartoon ignored?

BORN TO COMMAND.

OF VETO MEMORY.

HAD I BEEN CONSULTED.

KING ANDREW THE FIRST.

## Make a Chart

Making a chart will help you think critically about a piece of propaganda. The chart below summarizes the information from the anti-Jackson cartoon.

| ❶ Identify Purpose | *The cartoon portrays Jackson negatively by showing him as a king.* |
|---|---|
| ❷ Identify Emotions | *The cartoonist knows that Americans like democracy. So he portrays Jackson as a king because kings are not usually supporters of democracy. He also shows Jackson standing on a torn U.S. Constitution—another thing that Americans love.* |
| ❸ Think Critically | *The cartoon shows Jackson vetoing laws. But it ignores the fact that those actions were not against the Constitution. The president has the power to veto legislation. In this case, Jackson was exercising the power of the presidency, not acting like a king.* |

## Practicing the Skill

Turn to Chapter 6, Section 2, "Colonial Resistance Grows," and look at Paul Revere's etching of the Boston Massacre on page 164. Use a chart like the one above to think critically about the etching as an expression of bias or as an example of propaganda.

# 1.18 Synthesizing

## Defining the Skill

**Synthesizing** means bringing together information to create an overall picture of a topic. Historians use synthesis to understand the importance of historical events. Like detectives, they look for "clues" such as facts, explanations, and conclusions. The historian then combines this information with his or her own knowledge to understand the event.

## Applying the Skill

The following passage presents information about agriculture in the Americas prior to 1500. Use the strategies listed below to help you synthesize the information.

### How to Synthesize

**Strategy** ❶ Read the entire passage carefully. Then reread, looking for facts, explanations, conclusions, and other important clues.

**Strategy** ❷ Record the important information in a web. Then review the evidence, looking for the larger idea that ties these pieces of information together.

**Strategy** ❸ Bring together the information you have gathered to create an overall picture of the subject.

### AGRICULTURE IN THE AMERICAS

❶ The first Americans hunted animals and gathered wild seeds, nuts, and berries. ❶ In time, people started to plant the seeds they found. This was the beginning of agriculture. By trial and error, people learned which seeds grew the best crops.

Knowledge of agriculture spread throughout the Americas. ❶ Having a stable food supply changed the way people lived. ❶ Once they no longer had to travel to find food, they built permanent villages. ❶ Farmers were able to produce large harvests, so that fewer people needed to farm. Some people began to practice other crafts, such as weaving or making pottery. A few people became religious leaders. Slowly, some cultures grew complex and became civilizations.

### Make a Web

Making a web can help you synthesize. The web at the right shows how to organize the facts, examples, and conclusions needed to synthesize the information in the above passage.

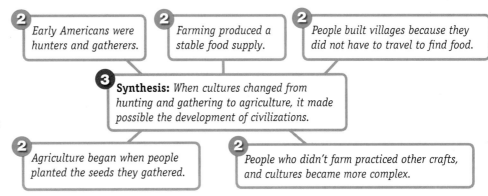

❷ Early Americans were hunters and gatherers.

❷ Farming produced a stable food supply.

❷ People built villages because they did not have to travel to find food.

❸ **Synthesis:** When cultures changed from hunting and gathering to agriculture, it made possible the development of civilizations.

❷ Agriculture began when people planted the seeds they gathered.

❷ People who didn't farm practiced other crafts, and cultures became more complex.

## Practicing the Skill

Turn to Chapter 15, Section 1, "Tensions Rise Between North and South." Read "North and South Follow Different Paths" on page 481, and make a web to synthesize the economic factors that contributed to the division between North and South.

# 2.1 Reading Maps

## Defining the Skill I

**Maps** are representations of features on the earth's surface. Historical maps often show political features, such as national borders, and physical features, such as bodies of water. Reading maps requires identifying map elements and using math skills.

## Applying the Skill

The following map shows the Battle of Yorktown during the Revolution. Use the strategies listed below to help you identify the elements common to most maps.

### How to Read a Map

**Strategy 1** Read the title. This identifies the main idea of the map.

**Strategy 2** Look for the grid of lines on the map. These numbered lines are the lines of latitude (horizontal) and longitude (vertical). They indicate the location of the area on the earth.

**Strategy 3** Read the map key. It is usually in a box. This will give you the information you need to interpret the symbols or colors on the map.

**Strategy 4** Use the scale and the pointer, or compass rose, to determine distance and direction.

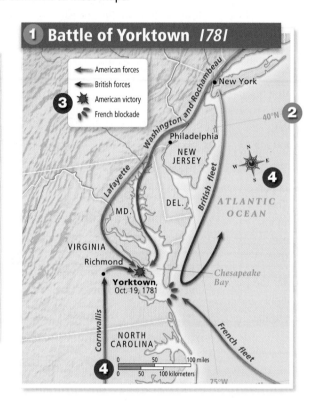

## Make a Chart

A chart can help you organize information given on maps. The chart below summarizes information about the map you just studied.

| Title | Battle of Yorktown, 1781 |
|---|---|
| Location | between latitude 40°N and 35°N, just east of longitude 80°W |
| Map Key Information | blue = American forces,  red = British forces |
| Scale | approx. 3/4 in. = 100 miles; approx. 1/2 in. = 100 km |
| Summary | British forces led by Cornwallis were trapped by American troops and a French naval blockade. |

## Practicing the Skill

Turn to Chapter 3, Section 4, "The Middle Colonies." Read the map entitled "American Colonies, 1740" on page 86, and make a chart to identify information on the map.

# Defining the Skill II

**Special-purpose maps** help people focus on a particular aspect of a region, such as economic development in the South. These kinds of maps often use symbols to indicate information.

# Applying the Skill

The following special-purpose map indicates the exports of the Southern colonies. Use the strategies listed below to help you identify the information shown on the map.

## How to Read a Special-Purpose Map

**Strategy 1** Read the title. It tells you what the map is intended to show.

**Strategy 2** Read the legend. This tells you what each color and symbol stands for. This legend shows the exports that were produced in various Southern colonies.

**Strategy 3** Look for the places on the map where the symbol appears. These tell you the places where the goods were produced.

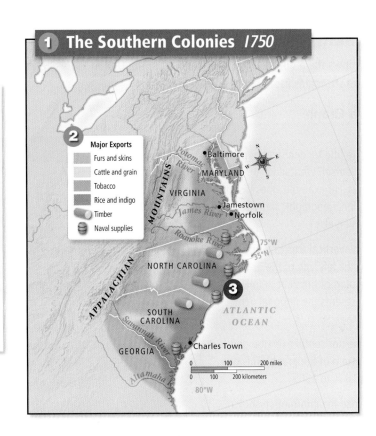

**1** The Southern Colonies *1750*

**2** Major Exports
- Furs and skins
- Cattle and grain
- Tobacco
- Rice and indigo
- Timber
- Naval supplies

## Make a Chart

A chart can help you understand special-purpose maps. The chart below shows information about the special-purpose map you just studied.

|  | Furs and skins | Cattle and grain | Tobacco | Rice and indigo | Timber | Naval stores |
|---|---|---|---|---|---|---|
| Maryland | × | × | × |  |  |  |
| Virginia | × | × | × |  |  |  |
| North Carolina | × | × | × | × | × | × |
| South Carolina | × | × |  | × | × | × |
| Georgia | × |  |  | × |  |  |

# Practicing the Skill

Turn to Chapter 8, Section 2, "Creating the Constitution." Look at the special-purpose map entitled "Slave Poplulation, 1790" on page 246, and make a chart that shows information about the population of slaves soon after the Constitution was ratified.

# 2.2 Reading Graphs and Charts

## Defining the Skill I

**Graphs** use pictures and symbols, instead of words, to show information. Graphs are created by taking information and presenting it visually. The graph on this page takes numerical information on the national debt and presents it as a bar graph. There are many different kinds of graphs. Bar graphs, line graphs, and pie graphs are the most common. Bar graphs compare numbers or sets of numbers. The length of each bar shows a quantity. It is easy to see how different categories compare on a bar graph.

## Applying the Skill

The bar graph below shows the amount of the national debt in the United States between 1861 and 1869. Use the strategies listed below to help you interpret the graph.

### How to Interpret a Graph

**Strategy 1** Read the title to identify the main idea of the graph. Ask yourself what kinds of information the graph shows. For example, does it show chronological information, geographic patterns and distributions, or something else?

**Strategy 2** Read the vertical axis (the one that goes up and down) on the left side of the graph. This one shows the amount of the debt in millions of dollars. Each bar represents the national debt during a particular year.

**Strategy 3** Read the horizontal axis (the one that runs across the bottom of the graph). This one shows each year from 1861 to 1869.

**Strategy 4** Summarize the information shown in each part of the graph. Use the title to help you focus on what information the graph is presenting.

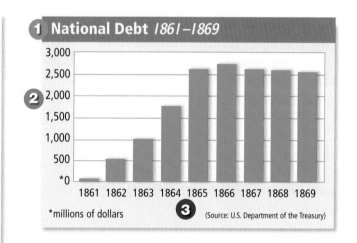

**1** **National Debt** *1861–1869*

*millions of dollars

**3** (Source: U.S. Department of the Treasury)

## Write a Summary

Writing a summary will help you understand the information in the graph. The paragraph to the right summarizes the information from the bar graph.

**4** *The national debt of the United States rose sharply during the years of the Civil War. In 1861 the country owed about $100 million, but by 1865 its debt had surpassed $2.5 billion. The debt peaked in 1866, when it totalled approximately $2.75 billion. By 1869, the U.S. had decreased the national debt by about $200 million.*

## Practicing the Skill

Turn to Chapter 4, Section 2, "The Southern Colonies: Plantations and Slavery." Look at the graph entitled "Slave Populations" on page 105, and write a paragraph in which you summarize what you learned from it.

# Defining the Skill II

**Charts**, like graphs, present information in a visual form. Charts are created by organizing, summarizing, and simplifying information and presenting it in a format that makes it easy to understand. Tables and diagrams are examples of commonly used charts.

# Applying the Skill

The chart below shows a comparison between the Virginia and New Jersey plans for government. Use the strategies listed below to help you interpret the information in the chart.

## How to Interpret a Chart

**Strategy ①** Read the title. It will tell you what the chart is about. Ask yourself what kinds of information the chart shows. For example, does it show chronological information, geographic patterns and distributions, or something else?

**Strategy ②** Read the labels to see how the information in the chart is organized. In this chart, it is organized by plan and branch of government.

**Strategy ③** Study the data in the chart to understand the facts that the chart intends to show.

**Strategy ④** Summarize the information shown in each part of the chart. Use the title to help you focus on what information the chart is presenting.

### COMPARING ⟲ Plans for Government

| | VIRGINIA PLAN | NEW JERSEY PLAN |
|---|---|---|
| **Legislative branch** | Two (branches) houses: representation determined by state population or wealth | One house: one vote for each state, regardless of size |
| | Lower House: elected by the people  Upper House: elected by lower house | Elected by state legislatures |
| **Executive branch** | Appointed by Legislature | Appointed by Legislature |
| **Judicial branch** | Appointed by Legislature | Appointed by Executive |

## Write a Summary

Writing a summary can help you understand the information given in a chart. The paragraph to the right summarizes the information in the chart "Comparing Plans for Government."

**④** The chart compares the Virginia Plan for government with the New Jersey Plan. It focuses on each plan's approach to how the three branches of government should be formed. The main difference between them was in the legislature, with the Virginia Plan calling for two houses and the New Jersey Plan arguing for one house.

## Practicing the Skill

Turn to Chapter 8, Section 1, "The Confederation Era." Study the chart entitled "Powers Granted and Denied Congress" on page 236, and write a paragraph in which you summarize what you learned from it.

# 3.4 Paraphrasing

## Defining the Skill

When you **paraphrase**, you restate a sentence, paragraph, or passage in your own words. Unlike a summary, which includes only the most important ideas, a paraphrase includes all information and is about the same length as the original. When paraphrasing, you change the structure of the sentence, as well as individual words.

## Applying the Skill

The passage below describes the development of the idea of manifest destiny in the mid-1800s. Use the strategies listed below to help you paraphrase the passage.

### How to Paraphrase

**Strategy ❶** Think about the ideas that each sentence is trying to communicate. Then express the same ideas in your own words.

**Strategy ❷** In addition to using different vocabulary, you must use your own sentence structures. Do not copy the grammar of the original.

**Strategy ❸** Paraphrasing is useful in research papers to avoid cluttering your report with too many quotations. But remember always to cite your source, even for a paraphrase.

---

**MANIFEST DESTINY**

Many Americans believed that the United States was destined to stretch across the continent from the Atlantic Ocean to the Pacific Ocean. In 1845, a newspaper editor name John O'Sullivan gave a name to that belief. O'Sullivan wrote, "Our manifest destiny [is] to overspread and possess the whole of the continent which Providence [God] has given us for the development of the great experiment of liberty. . . ." Manifest destiny suggested that expansion was not only good but bound to happen—even if it meant pushing Mexicans and Native Americans out of the way. After James K. Polk's election in 1844, manifest destiny became government policy.

—John Q. Author, in *A History Book*

---

### Write a Paraphrase

Write your paraphrase in the same form as the original. The following paragraph paraphrases the passage above.

The idea that the United States was meant to cover the continent from the east coast to the west coast was a common one among Americans. Newspaper editor John O'Sullivan coined the term "manifest destiny" in 1845. ❶ O'Sullivan believed that God wanted Americans to spread their system of government all across the continent. According to manifest destiny, the widespread growth of America was both positive and unstoppable. ❷ The fact that Mexicans and Native Americans were already occupying parts of the continent did not matter. The U.S. government officially pursued manifest destiny after Polk became president in 1844. ❸ Source: *A History Book*, by John Q. Author

## Practicing the Skill

Turn to Chapter 1, Section 2, "Societies of Africa." Read "One African's Story" on page 11, and paraphrase the section in your own words.

# 3.5 Outlining

## Defining the Skill

An **outline** is a summary of the information you plan to include in a written piece, and how you plan to structure it. A topic outline begins with a shortened version of the thesis statement. Roman numerals identify the major parts of the essay, followed by key ideas and supporting details listed with letters and Arabic numerals. Ways to organize your ideas include chronological order, cause-and-effect, and order of degree.

## Applying the Skill

The outline shown here is a plan for a report on the Lewis and Clark expedition. Use the strategies listed below to help you create an outline.

## How to Outline

**Strategy ①** Write a possible title for the essay, along with your thesis statement, at the top of your outline.

**Strategy ②** The body of the essay is where you discuss the points that support your thesis. List each main point after a capital letter.

**Strategy ③** List supporting details below each main point with Arabic numerals. In general, there should be at least two details that support each main idea. If you have only one detail for a main idea, you may need more research.

---

**①** The Accomplishments of the Lewis and Clark Expedition

**Thesis statement:** The Lewis and Clark expedition made important contributions to the expansion of the U.S. in the 19th century.

I. Introduction

**②** II. **Body:** Three goals accomplished by the Lewis and Clark expedition

   A. Increased knowledge of the geography of the American West

    **③** 1. Learned there was no all-water route across the continent

    2. Made more accurate maps than had previously existed of areas west of St. Louis

   B. Established good relations with Native Americans

    **③** 1. Guidance of Sacagawea and the Shoshone

    2. Assistance of the Nez Perce

   C. Discovered natural resources

    **③** 1. Navigated Missouri, Clearwater, Snake, and Columbia Rivers

    2. Sketched edible plants and animals

III. Conclusion

---

## Practicing the Skill

Prepare an outline for an essay called "The Impact of the Emancipation Proclamation on the Civil War." Refer to Chapter 17, Section 1, "The Emancipation Proclamation" on pages 537–540, as a resource for your outline.

# 3.6 Forming and Supporting Opinions

## Defining the Skill

When you **form opinions**, you interpret and judge the importance of events and people in history. You should always **support your opinions** with facts, examples, and quotes.

## Applying the Skill

The following passage describes events that followed the gold rush. Use the strategies listed below to form and support your opinions about the events.

### How to Form and Support Opinions

**Strategy ① Look for important information about the events. Information can include facts, quotations, and examples.**

**Strategy ② Form an opinion about the event by asking yourself questions about the information. For example, How important was the event? What were its effects?**

**Strategy ③ Support your opinions with facts, quotations, and examples. If the facts do not support the opinion, then rewrite your opinion so it is supported by the facts.**

> ### THE IMPACT OF THE GOLD RUSH
>
> By 1852, the gold rush was over. ① While it lasted, about 250,000 people flooded into California. ① This huge migration caused economic growth that changed California. ① The port city San Francisco grew to become a center of banking, manufacturing, shipping, and trade. ① However, the gold rush ruined many *Californios*. *Californios* are the Hispanic people of California. The newcomers did not respect *Californios*, their customs, or their legal rights. ① In many cases, Americans seized their property.
>
> Native Americans suffered even more. ① Thousands died from diseases brought by the newcomers. ① Miners hunted down and killed thousands more. ① By 1870, California's Native American population had fallen from 150,000 to only about 30,000.

## Make a Chart

Making a chart can help you organize your opinions and supporting facts. The following chart summarizes one possible opinion about the impact of the gold rush.

| ② Opinion | *The effects of the gold rush were more negative than positive.* |
|---|---|
| ③ Facts | *Californios were not respected, and their land was stolen.*<br>*Many Native Americans died from diseases, and others were killed by miners.*<br>*Their population dropped from 150,000 to about 30,000.* |

## Practicing the Skill

Turn to Chapter 11, Section 3, "Nationalism and Sectionalism." Read "The Monroe Doctrine" on page 385, and form your own opinion about the United States' reaction to European colonialism. Make a chart like the one above to summarize your opinion and the supporting facts and examples.

# 3.7 Essay

## Defining the Skill

An **essay** is a written presentation consisting of (1) a thesis, and (2) an argument supported by details and evidence. A thesis is a statement that answers the question you are exploring in your essay. The argument explains why you believe your thesis is true. An argument is based on accurate evidence (facts, examples, statistics, etc.) from which you draw logical conclusions that help prove your thesis.

## Applying the Skill

The page shown here is from an essay on the role of the cotton gin in the growth of slavery. Analyze the writer's use of these strategies in the essay.

### How to Write an Essay

**Strategy ①** Use the introduction to state your thesis and provide important background information.

**Strategy ②** The body of the essay is where you present your argument. Often, you can present each point of your argument in a separate paragraph.

**Strategy ③** Fill out each paragraph with details and evidence that support the main point.

### Practicing the Skill

Turn to Chapter 11, Section 1, "Early Industry and Inventions." Read "One American's Story" on page 365, "The Lowel Mills Hire Women" on page 367, and "Comparing Perspectives" on page 366. Then, write an essay around a thesis statement about the working conditions for women in the Lowell mills.

---

### THE COTTON GIN AND THE GROWTH OF SLAVERY

① A warm climate and fertile soil made the southern states ideal for agriculture. In the late 1700s, cash crops such as tobacco, indigo, rice, and sugar cane were grown on plantations using enslaved labor. The demand for that labor grew dramatically after new technology made cotton the dominant cash crop in the South. Eli Whitney's invention of the cotton gin in 1793 led to an increase in the use of slave labor in the United States at the end of the 18th century.

② Separating seeds and other debris from cotton fibers by hand was slow and very expensive. Whitney's gin made the cleaning process fast and easy. Sold at a lower price, cotton became the most commonly used fiber in textile production. As the demand for cotton grew, so did the demand for labor in the form of slaves.

Many plantations that had grown tobacco, rice, or indigo switched to cotton. From the increased profits on cotton, plantation owners could purchase more slaves. If soiled by storms, cotton was worthless. So many laborers were needed to pick cotton quickly before bad weather could destroy the crop.

Cotton could be grown on smaller plots than sugar cane and still make a profit. As a result, more people began to farm, more land was cultivated, and more labor was needed. ③ In Georgia, for example, from 1790 to 1810 (a period during which the cotton gin was invented), the number of slaves increased 104 percent.

# 3.8 Constructed Response

## Defining the Skill

A **constructed response** requires you to write your own answer to a question, rather than to make a choice among provided answers. A constructed-response item consists of an "exhibit"—a document or artifact, such as a quotation, map, drawing, or photograph—and a series of questions about the exhibit and related history. Often, the answer can be found within the exhibit, but some questions require your own knowledge of the subject.

## Applying the Skill

Shown here are three sample constructed-response items along with answers. Use the strategies listed below to help you answer constructed-response questions.

### How to Answer Constructed-Response Questions

**Strategy ❶** Unless the directions specify otherwise, you do not need to write your answers in complete sentences.

**Strategy ❷** Look for clues to answer a question. One clue for the second question is in the exhibit—the date the magazine was published (1845). The second clue is in the question itself, which provides a description of the Industrial Revolution.

**Strategy ❸** The third question requires you to synthesize your own knowledge about the Industrial Revolution with information in the exhibit. This response refers to specific details in the exhibit and compares them to the student's own knowledge about factory work in the 1800s.

1. Who wrote the articles published in the *Lowell Offering*?

   ❶ *young women who worked in factories*

2. At the time the *Lowell Offering* was published, ❷ what movement was replacing hand tools with machines, and farming with manufacturing?

   *the Industrial Revolution*

3. Does the cover illustration accurately reflect the daily lives of young women employed in factories? Why or why not?

   ❸ *No. In the illustration, the girl is standing in a wooded area holding a book, which makes her daily life look peaceful and leisurely, when factory girls actually worked 12-hour days in noisy, crowded mills.*

## Practicing the Skill

Turn to Chapter 9, Section 3, "The Federalists in Charge." Read the excerpt of the letter from Benjamin Banneker to Thomas Jefferson on page 327, and formulate a constructed response to the following question: Why do you think Banneker wrote these words to Jefferson?

# 3.9 Extended Response

## Defining the Skill

An **extended response** is a detailed answer to a complex question about an exhibit or topic. It requires more time and thought to answer than a constructed response. Many extended-response questions ask you to write an essay on a given topic, using information from the exhibit and your own knowledge.

## Applying the Skill

Shown here is a sample extended-response item along with its answer. Use the strategies listed below to help you answer extended-response questions.

### How to Answer Extended-Response Questions

**Strategy** ① Carefully read or study the exhibit and the question that follows.

**Strategy** ② Take notes or diagram important information on a separate sheet of paper.

**Strategy** ③ Create a rough outline for your essay on a separate sheet of paper. Then use the outline to write your answer.

Read the passage about religion in some of the colonies. How did these colonies' ideas of religious tolerance help shape attitudes about diversity in the United States today?

### RELIGIOUS TOLERATION IN THE COLONIES

William Penn founded Pennsylvania in 1681 when King Charles II gave him a large piece of land in America as repayment for debts to his family. Penn, a Quaker, organized his colony to provide a safe haven for Quakers and other persecuted peoples. Lord Baltimore founded Maryland in 1632 to create a refuge for Roman Catholics fleeing persecution in England. To attract other settlers besides Catholics, Maryland passed the Toleration Act in 1649. Like William Penn and Lord Baltimore, James Oglethorpe also wanted to help people persecuted for their religion, especially Protestants. He founded the Georgia colony, where all religions were welcome.

In response to religious persecution in Europe in the 1600s, the colonies of Pennsylvania, Maryland, and Georgia each offered settlers religious freedom. Whether to provide a safe haven for persecuted people or to attract more settlers, the founders of these colonies believed it important not to exclude anyone from living there based on religion. The ideas of religious tolerance in the Middle and Southern Colonies helped shape attitudes toward religious diversity in the United States today.

Those who had been persecuted for their beliefs in Europe greatly valued the freedom of religion they found in the colonies, where people of many faiths often lived side-by-side. As America developed from individual colonies into a nation, the freedom to worship became an expectation of society. Many states refused to ratify the U.S. Constitution until the founders agreed to add a Bill of Rights, the first of which protected religious freedom.

The toleration that started in the colonies extends today in the United States. . . .

## Practicing the Skill

Turn to Chapter 17, Section 2, "War Affects Society." Read "Economic and Social Change" on pages 545–547, and formulate an extended response to the following question: What impact did the Civil War have on American society?

# 3.10 Creating a Multimedia Presentation

## Defining the Skill

Movies, CD-ROMs, television, and computer software are different kinds of media. To **create a multimedia presentation**, you need to collect information in different media and organize them into one presentation.

## Applying the Skill

Use the strategies listed below to help you create your own multimedia presentation.

### How to Create a Multimedia Presentation

**Strategy 1** Identify the topic of your presentation and decide which media are best for an effective presentation. For example, you may want to use slides or posters to show visual images of your topic. Or, you may want to use CDs or audiotapes to provide music or spoken words.

**Strategy 2** Research the topic in a variety of sources. Images, text, props, and background music should reflect the historical period of the event you choose.

**Strategy 3** Write the script for the oral portion of the presentation. You could use a narrator and characters' voices to tell the story. Primary sources are an excellent source for script material. Make sure the recording is clear so that the audience will be able to understand the oral part of the presentation.

**Strategy 4** Videotape the presentation. Videotaping the presentation will preserve it for future viewing and allow you to show it to different groups of people.

**3**

> **Narrator**
> Lee's plan on July 3 was to attack the middle of the Union line along Cemetery Ridge with 15,000 Confederate soldiers. But General Longstreet disagreed with Lee's strategy.
>
> **Longstreet**
> It is my opinion that no 15,000 men ever arrayed for battle can take that position.
>
> **Narrator**
> Lee refused to change his mind. He wanted to see the battle—and the war—end that day.
>
> **Pickett**
> [to Longstreet] General, shall I advance?
>
> **Narrator**
> Longstreet, foreseeing disaster, could not speak. He only bowed to Pickett in a silent order of "Advance".
>
> **Pickett**
> [shouting] Charge the enemy and remember old Virginia!

## Practicing the Skill

Turn to Chapter 16, "The Civil War Begins" Choose a topic from the chapter, and use the strategies listed above to create a multimedia presentation about it.

# 4.1 Using a Search Engine

## Defining the Skill

A **search engine** is a computer program that looks for, gathers, and reports information available on the Internet. Using a search engine helps you find such information quickly and easily. By entering key words into a search engine, you will generate a list of Web pages and sites that contain those words.

## Applying the Skill

Shown here is a list of results from a search for information on Harriet Tubman's work on the Underground Railroad. Use the strategies listed below to get better results when you search the Internet.

### How to Use a Search Engine

**Strategy 1** Be specific when searching to get more relevant information. Use quotation marks around exact phrases that you want the engine to search for as a whole. Narrow your search with plus and minus signs. For example, to include Harriet Tubman in your search but exclude Levi Coffin, you would enter "+Tubman –Coffin" in the search box.

**Strategy 2** The brief excerpt that appears under the title is actual text from the page. Read it carefully for clues as to whether or not the site contains useful information. The first result, for example, shows a quotation from Tubman, which might indicate that there are more pirmary sources on the Web site.

**Strategy 3** Read the title of the Web site. Although a site might meet the search criteria, sometimes you can tell by reading the title that it will not be useful. The third result, for example, is a quiz that probably will not help your research.

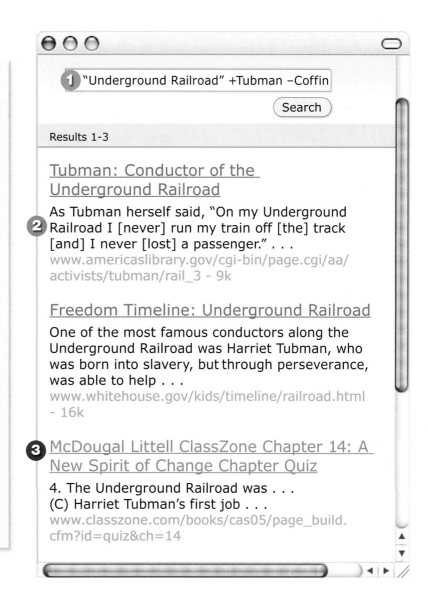

**1** "Underground Railroad" +Tubman –Coffin

Search

Results 1-3

**Tubman: Conductor of the Underground Railroad**

**2** As Tubman herself said, "On my Underground Railroad I [never] run my train off [the] track [and] I never [lost] a passenger." . . .
www.americaslibrary.gov/cgi-bin/page.cgi/aa/activists/tubman/rail_3 - 9k

**Freedom Timeline: Underground Railroad**

One of the most famous conductors along the Underground Railroad was Harriet Tubman, who was born into slavery, but through perseverance, was able to help . . .
www.whitehouse.gov/kids/timeline/railroad.html - 16k

**3** **McDougal Littell ClassZone Chapter 14: A New Spirit of Change Chapter Quiz**

4. The Underground Railroad was . . .
(C) Harriet Tubman's first job . . .
www.classzone.com/books/cas05/page_build.cfm?id=quiz&ch=14

## Practicing the Skill

Turn to Chapter 3, Section 2, "New England Colonies," and read about Anne Hutchinson on page 70. Then look for Web sites about Hutchinson and her trial using an Internet search engine. Jot down the three sites that you feel provide the best information.

# 4.2 Evaluating Internet Sources

## Defining the Skill

Evaluating Internet sources will help you decide if the information you find online is trustworthy. Reliable Internet sources generally:

- are created by a credible author, with the backing of an educational institution or government agency;
- have content that is well-researched and free from bias with sources cited.

## Applying the Skill

Shown here is a Web page about the Lincoln-Douglas debates. Use the strategies listed below to help you evaluate Internet sources.

### How to Evaluate Internet Sources

**Strategy 1** Identify the author of the material and the organization, if any, that supports the site. In the example here, the URL includes ".edu," which means the site is sponsored by an educational institution.

**Strategy 2** Examine the content for accuracy and thoroughness. Are sources cited? Are there signs of bias? How recently was it created or updated?

**Strategy 3** Consider how well the page or site is organized. Is it easy to read and navigate? Do images provide useful information?

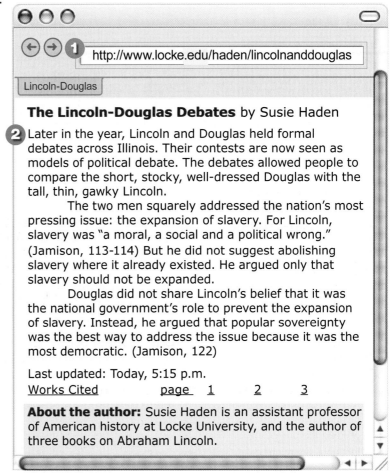

**1** http://www.locke.edu/haden/lincolnanddouglas

Lincoln-Douglas

**The Lincoln-Douglas Debates** by Susie Haden

**2** Later in the year, Lincoln and Douglas held formal debates across Illinois. Their contests are now seen as models of political debate. The debates allowed people to compare the short, stocky, well-dressed Douglas with the tall, thin, gawky Lincoln.

The two men squarely addressed the nation's most pressing issue: the expansion of slavery. For Lincoln, slavery was "a moral, a social and a political wrong." (Jamison, 113-114) But he did not suggest abolishing slavery where it already existed. He argued only that slavery should not be expanded.

Douglas did not share Lincoln's belief that it was the national government's role to prevent the expansion of slavery. Instead, he argued that popular sovereignty was the best way to address the issue because it was the most democratic. (Jamison, 122)

Last updated: Today, 5:15 p.m.
Works Cited          page    1       2       3

**About the author:** Susie Haden is an assistant professor of American history at Locke University, and the author of three books on Abraham Lincoln.

### Make a Chart

Making a chart can help you evaluate Internet sources. The chart below contains notes on the Web page you just read.

| **1** Source | Author | University professor, expert on Lincoln |
|---|---|---|
| | Sponsor | Locke University (.edu) |
| **2** Content | Accuracy & objectivity | Good, no evidence of bias, sources cited |
| | Thoroughness | Good |
| | Up-to-date | Yes |
| **3** Style & Functionality | Organization | Clear |
| | Legibility | Good, easy to read |
| | Ease of navigation | Yes, links provided to each page of site |

### Practicing the Skill

Go to the Library of Congress Web site and find the exhibition on Lewis and Clark. Use the above strategies to evaluate the exhibition's reliability as a historical source about the Corps of Discovery. Create a chart like the one here to organize your evaluation.

# 4.3 Recognizing Bias

## Defining the Skill

**Bias** is the presentation of only one side of an issue. A biased source is not objective: it exhibits a point of view influenced by its author's emotions or personal preferences. Bias can also appear in the form of advertising to try to persuade you to patronize a product or service. Recognizing bias will help you evaluate whether or not a source is reliable.

## Applying the Skill

Shown here is a Web page about Thomas Jefferson's first term as president. Use the strategies listed below to identify words and tone that indicate bias.

### How to Recognize Bias

**Strategy** ① Read the Web page carefully, looking for evidence of the author's point of view. Note places where the author expresses a personal opinion. Consider word choice.

**Strategy** ② Think critically about the text. Decide whether or not it seems balanced. Does it present both sides of an argument?

**Strategy** ③ Use the evidence you have gathered to judge whether or not the material is biased.

### Make a Chart

Making a chart will help you recognize bias in online materials. The chart below shows how bias appears in the Web site.

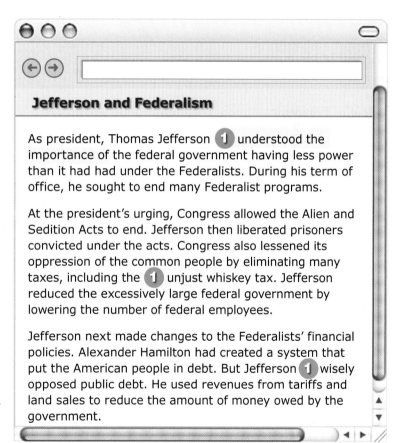

**Jefferson and Federalism**

As president, Thomas Jefferson ① understood the importance of the federal government having less power than it had had under the Federalists. During his term of office, he sought to end many Federalist programs.

At the president's urging, Congress allowed the Alien and Sedition Acts to end. Jefferson then liberated prisoners convicted under the acts. Congress also lessened its oppression of the common people by eliminating many taxes, including the ① unjust whiskey tax. Jefferson reduced the excessively large federal government by lowering the number of federal employees.

Jefferson next made changes to the Federalists' financial policies. Alexander Hamilton had created a system that put the American people in debt. But Jefferson ① wisely opposed public debt. He used revenues from tariffs and land sales to reduce the amount of money owed by the government.

| ① Evidence of Point of View | Author shows his own belief ("the importance of") that the federal government needed to have less power. Word choice: unjust, wisely |
| --- | --- |
| ② Think Critically | Makes all Federalist policies sound bad. Does not tell Hamilton's "side of the story." |
| ③ Bias | Biased in favor of Jefferson and small government. Author's purpose is to persuade reader that Federalism is bad. |

## Practicing the Skill

Search the Web for an article about an event or figure in American history. Using the above strategies, create a chart to identify any instances of bias in the content of the article. If you notice bias, consider how it could be written more objectively.

# Facts About the States

**Alabama**
4,557,808 people
52,218 sq. mi.
Rank in area: 30
Entered Union in 1819

**Florida**
17,789,864 people
59,909 sq. mi.
Rank in area: 22
Entered Union in 1845

**Louisiana**
4,523,628 people
49,650 sq. mi.
Rank in area: 31
Entered Union in 1812

**Alaska**
663,661 people
616,240 sq. mi.
Rank in area: 1
Entered Union in 1959

**Georgia**
9,072,576 people
58,970 sq. mi.
Rank in area: 24
Entered Union in 1788

**Maine**
1,321,505 people
33,738 sq. mi.
Rank in area: 39
Entered Union in 1820

**Arizona**
5,939,292 people
113,998 sq. mi.
Rank in area: 6
Entered Union in 1912

**Hawaii**
1,275,194 people
6,641 sq. mi.
Rank in area: 43
Entered Union in 1959

**Maryland**
5,600,388 people
12,297 sq. mi.
Rank in area: 42
Entered Union in 1788

**Arkansas**
2,779,154 people
53,178 sq. mi.
Rank in area: 29
Entered Union in 1836

**Idaho**
1,429,096 people
83,570 sq. mi.
Rank in area: 14
Entered Union in 1890

**Massachusetts**
6,398,743 people
9,240 sq. mi.
Rank in area: 44
Entered Union in 1788

**California**
36,132,147 people
158,854 sq. mi.
Rank in area: 3
Entered Union in 1850

**Illinois**
12,763,371 people
57,914 sq. mi.
Rank in area: 25
Entered Union in 1818

**Michigan**
10,120,860 people
96,716 sq. mi.
Rank in area: 11
Entered Union in 1837

**Colorado**
4,665,177 people
104,093 sq. mi.
Rank in area: 8
Entered Union in 1876

**Indiana**
6,271,973 people
36,418 sq. mi.
Rank in area: 38
Entered Union in 1816

**Minnesota**
5,132,799 people
86,938 sq. mi.
Rank in area: 12
Entered Union in 1858

**Connecticut**
3,510,297 people
5,543 sq. mi.
Rank in area: 48
Entered Union in 1788

**Iowa**
2,966,334 people
56,271 sq. mi.
Rank in area: 26
Entered Union in 1846

**Mississippi**
2,921,088 people
48,282 sq. mi.
Rank in area: 32
Entered Union in 1817

**Delaware**
843,524 people
2,396 sq. mi.
Rank in area: 49
Entered Union in 1787

**Kansas**
2,744,687 people
82,276 sq. mi.
Rank in area: 15
Entered Union in 1861

**Missouri**
5,800,310 people
69,704 sq. mi.
Rank in area: 21
Entered Union in 1821

**District of Columbia**
550,521 people
68 sq. mi.
Created 1790

**Kentucky**
4,173,405 people
40,409 sq. mi.
Rank in area: 37
Entered Union in 1792

**Montana**
935,670 people
147,042 sq. mi.
Rank in area: 4
Entered Union in 1889

Sources: U.S. Census Bureau, *American Factfinder* online: 2005 Population Estimates. *CIA World Factbook* online.
*Encyclopaedia Britannica Almanac* 2006. *Rand McNally Goode's World Atlas,* 20th ed., 2000.

**Nebraska**
1,758,787 people
77,353 sq. mi.
Rank in area: 16
Entered Union in 1867

**Ohio**
11,464,042 people
44,825 sq. mi.
Rank in area: 34
Entered Union in 1803

**Texas**
22,859,968 people
267,256 sq. mi.
Rank in area: 2
Entered Union in 1845

**Nevada**
2,414,807 people
110,560 sq. mi.
Rank in area: 7
Entered Union in 1864

**Oklahoma**
3,547,884 people
69,898 sq. mi.
Rank in area: 20
Entered Union in 1907

**Utah**
2,469,585 people
84,898 sq. mi.
Rank in area: 13
Entered Union in 1896

**New Hampshire**
1,309,940 people
9,282 sq. mi.
Rank in area: 46
Entered Union in 1788

**Oregon**
3,641,056 people
97,126 sq. mi.
Rank in area: 9
Entered Union in 1859

**Vermont**
623,050 people
9,614 sq. mi.
Rank in area: 45
Entered Union in 1791

**New Jersey**
8,717,925 people
8,214 sq. mi.
Rank in area: 47
Entered Union in 1787

**Pennsylvania**
12,429,616 people
46,055 sq. mi.
Rank in area: 33
Entered Union in 1787

**Virginia**
7,567,465 people
42,328 sq. mi.
Rank in area: 35
Entered Union in 1788

**New Mexico**
1,928,384 people
121,589 sq. mi.
Rank in area: 5
Entered Union in 1912

**Rhode Island**
1,076,189 people
1,231 sq. mi.
Rank in area: 50
Entered Union in 1790

**Washington**
6,287,759 people
70,634 sq. mi.
Rank in area: 18
Entered Union in 1889

**New York**
19,254,630 people
54,077 sq. mi.
Rank in area: 27
Entered Union in 1788

**South Carolina**
4,255,083 people
31,190 sq. mi.
Rank in area: 40
Entered Union in 1788

**West Virginia**
1,816,856 people
24,230 sq. mi.
Rank in area: 41
Entered Union in 1863

**North Carolina**
8,683,242 people
52,670 sq. mi.
Rank in area: 28
Entered Union in 1789

**South Dakota**
775,933 people
77,116 sq. mi.
Rank in area: 17
Entered Union in 1889

**Wisconsin**
5,536,201 people
65,498 sq. mi.
Rank in area: 23
Entered Union in 1848

**North Dakota**
636,677 people
70,699 sq. mi.
Rank in area: 19
Entered Union in 1889

**Tennessee**
5,962,959 people
42,143 sq. mi.
Rank in area: 36
Entered Union in 1796

**Wyoming**
509,294 people
97,813 sq. mi.
Rank in area: 10
Entered Union in 1890

# United States: *Major Dependencies*

American Samoa—62,700 people; 90 sq. mi.
Guam—165,000 people; 217 sq. mi.
Commonwealth of Puerto Rico—3,898,000 people; 5,324 sq. mi.

Virgin Islands of the United States—109,000 people; 171 sq. mi.
Midway Islands—no indigenous inhabitants; 6.2 sq. mi.
Wake Island—no indigenous inhabitants; 6.5 sq. mi.

# Presidents of the United States

Here are some little-known facts about the presidents of the United States:

- First president born in the new United States: **Martin Van Buren** (eighth president)
- Only president who was a bachelor: **James Buchanan**
- First left-handed president: **James A. Garfield**
- Largest president: **William H. Taft** (6 feet 2 inches, 332 pounds)
- Youngest president: **Theodore Roosevelt** (42 years old)
- Oldest president: **Ronald Reagan** (77 years old when he left office in 1989)
- First president born west of the Mississippi River: **Herbert Hoover** (born in West Branch, Iowa)
- First president born in the 20th century: **John F. Kennedy** (born May 29, 1917)

**1** **George Washington**
**1789–1797**
No Political Party
Birthplace: Virginia
Born: February 22, 1732
Died: December 14, 1799

**2** **John Adams**
**1797–1801**
Federalist
Birthplace: Massachusetts
Born: October 30, 1735
Died: July 4, 1826

**3** **Thomas Jefferson**
**1801–1809**
Democratic-Republican
Birthplace: Virginia
Born: April 13, 1743
Died: July 4, 1826

**4** **James Madison**
**1809–1817**
Democratic-Republican
Birthplace: Virginia
Born: March 16, 1751
Died: June 28, 1836

**5** **James Monroe**
**1817–1825**
Democratic-Republican
Birthplace: Virginia
Born: April 28, 1758
Died: July 4, 1831

**6** **John Quincy Adams**
**1825–1829**
Democratic-Republican
Birthplace: Massachusetts
Born: July 11, 1767
Died: February 23, 1848

**7** **Andrew Jackson**
**1829–1837**
Democrat
Birthplace: South Carolina
Born: March 15, 1767
Died: June 8, 1845

**8** **Martin Van Buren**
**1837–1841**
Democrat
Birthplace: New York
Born: December 5, 1782
Died: July 24, 1862

**9** **William H. Harrison**
**1841**
Whig
Birthplace: Virginia
Born: February 9, 1773
Died: April 4, 1841

**10** **John Tyler**
**1841–1845**
Whig
Birthplace: Virginia
Born: March 29, 1790
Died: January 18, 1862

**11** **James K. Polk**
**1845–1849**
Democrat
Birthplace: North Carolina
Born: November 2, 1795
Died: June 15, 1849

**12** **Zachary Taylor**
**1849–1850**
Whig
Birthplace: Virginia
Born: November 24, 1784
Died: July 9, 1850

**13** **Millard Fillmore**
**1850–1853**
Whig
Birthplace: New York
Born: January 7, 1800
Died: March 8, 1874

**14** **Franklin Pierce**
**1853–1857**
Democrat
Birthplace: New Hampshire
Born: November 23, 1804
Died: October 8, 1869

**15** **James Buchanan**
**1857–1861**
Democrat
Birthplace: Pennsylvania
Born: April 23, 1791
Died: June 1, 1868

**16** **Abraham Lincoln**
**1861–1865**
Republican
Birthplace: Kentucky
Born: February 12, 1809
Died: April 15, 1865

**17** **Andrew Johnson**
**1865–1869**
Democrat
Birthplace: North Carolina
Born: December 29, 1808
Died: July 31, 1875

**18** **Ulysses S. Grant**
**1869–1877**
Republican
Birthplace: Ohio
Born: April 27, 1822
Died: July 23, 1885

**19** **Rutherford B. Hayes**
**1877–1881**
Republican
Birthplace: Ohio
Born: October 4, 1822
Died: January 17, 1893

**20** **James A. Garfield**
**1881**
Republican
Birthplace: Ohio
Born: November 19, 1831
Died: September 19, 1881

**21** **Chester A. Arthur**
**1881–1885**
Republican
Birthplace: Vermont
Born: October 5, 1829
Died: November 18, 1886

**22** **24** **Grover Cleveland**
**1885–1889, 1893–1897**
Democrat
Birthplace: New Jersey
Born: March 18, 1837
Died: June 24, 1908

**23** **Benjamin Harrison**
**1889–1893**
Republican
Birthplace: Ohio
Born: August 20, 1833
Died: March 13, 1901

**25** **William McKinley**
**1897–1901**
Republican
Birthplace: Ohio
Born: January 29, 1843
Died: September 14, 1901

**26** **Theodore Roosevelt**
**1901–1909**
Republican
Birthplace: New York
Born: October 27, 1858
Died: January 6, 1919

**27** **William H. Taft**
**1909–1913**
Republican
Birthplace: Ohio
Born: September 15, 1857
Died: March 8, 1930

**28** **Woodrow Wilson**
**1913–1921**
Democrat
Birthplace: Virginia
Born: December 28, 1856
Died: February 3, 1924

**29** **Warren G. Harding**
**1921–1923**
Republican
Birthplace: Ohio
Born: November 2, 1865
Died: August 2, 1923

**Erie Canal** all-water channel dug out to connect the Hudson River with Lake Erie. *363, 381*

**Europe** second smallest continent, actually a peninsula of the Eurasian landmass.

**Florida** 27th state. Capital: Tallahassee. *A34–A35*

**Fort McHenry** fort in Baltimore harbor where 1814 British attack inspired U.S. national anthem. (39°N 77°W) *355*

**Fort Sumter** fort in Charleston, South Carolina, harbor where 1861 attack by Confederates began the Civil War. (33°N 80°W) *509, 524*

**Fort Ticonderoga** fort in New York on Lake Champlain; site of battles during French and Indian War and the Revolutionary War. (44°N 73°W) *145, 178, 200*

**France** nation in western Europe; it aided America in the Revolutionary War. Capital: Paris. *A24–A25*

**Gadsden Purchase** last territory (from Mexico, 1853) added to continental United States. *A38–A39*

**Georgia** 4th state. Capital: Atlanta. *A34–A35*

**Germany** nation in central Europe. Capital: Berlin. *A24–A25*

**Gettysburg** Pennsylvania town and site of 1863 Civil War victory for the North that is considered the war's turning point. (40°N 77°W) *551*

**Ghana** first powerful West African trading empire. *14*

**Great Britain** European island nation across from France; it consists of England, Scotland and Wales. *A24–A25*

**Great Lakes** five connected lakes—Ontario, Erie, Huron, Michigan, and Superior—on the U.S. border with Canada. *A24–A25*

**Great Plains** vast grassland region in the central United States. *A36–A37*

**Guam** Pacific island, possession of United States. *A24–A25*

**Gulf of Mexico** body of water forming southern U.S. boundary from east Texas to west Florida. *A30–A31*

**Haiti** nation sharing the island of Hispaniola with Dominican Republic. Capital: Port-au-Prince. *A30–A31*

**Harpers Ferry** village today in extreme eastern West Virginia where John Brown raided stored U.S. weapons in 1859. (39°N 78°W)

**Hawaii** 50th state. Capital: Honolulu. *A34–A35*

**Hispaniola** West Indies island (shared today by Dominican Republic and Haiti) that Columbus mistook for Asia. *A30–A31*

**Hudson River** large river in eastern New York. *113, 200*

**Idaho** 43rd state. Capital: Boise. *A34–A35*

**Illinois** 21st state. Capital: Springfield. *A34–A35*

**Indiana** 19th state. Capital: Indianapolis. *A34–A35*

**Indian Territory** area, mainly of present-day Oklahoma, that in the 1800s became land for relocated Native Americans. *405*

**Iowa** 29th state. Capital: Des Moines. *A34–A35*

**Ireland** island country west of England whose mid-1800s famine caused more than one million people to emigrate to America. Capital: Dublin. *A24–A25*

**Israel** Jewish nation in the Middle East. Capital: Jerusalem. *A24–A25*

**Italy** nation in southern Europe. Capital: Rome. *A24–A25*

**Jamestown** community in Virginia that was the first permanent English settlement in North America. *59, 80*

**Japan** island nation in east Asia. Capital: Tokyo. *A24–A25*

**Kansas** 34th state. Capital: Topeka. *A34–A35*

**Kentucky** 15th state. Capital: Frankfort. *A34–A35*

**Latin America** region made up of Mexico, Caribbean Islands, and Central and South America, where Latin-based languages of Spanish, French, or Portuguese are spoken. *A30–A31*

**Lebanon** Middle East country on the Mediterranean coast. Capital: Beirut. *A24–A25*

**Lexington** Massachusetts town and site of first Revolutionary War battle in 1775. (42°N 71°W)

**Little Bighorn River** Montana site of Sioux and Cheyenne victory over Custer. (46°N 108°W)

**Little Rock** capital of Arkansas and site of 1957 school-desegregation conflict.

**Los Angeles** 2nd largest U.S. city, on California's coast.

**Louisiana** 18th state. Capital: Baton Rouge. *A34–A35*

**Louisiana Purchase** land west of the Mississippi River purchased from France in 1803. *347, 436*

**Lowell** Massachusetts city built in early 1800s as planned factory town. (43°N 71°W)

**Maine** 23rd state. Capital: Augusta. *A34–A35*

**Mali** early West African trading empire succeeding Ghana empire. *14*

**Maryland** 7th state. Capital: Annapolis. *A34–A35*

**Massachusetts** 6th state. Capital: Boston. *A34–A35*

**Mexico** nation sharing U.S. southern border. Capital: Mexico City. *A30–A31*

**Michigan** 26th state. Capital: Lansing. *A34–A35*

**Middle East** eastern Mediterranean region that includes countries such as Iran, Iraq, Syria, Kuwait, Jordan, Saudi Arabia, Israel, and Egypt.

**Minnesota** 32nd state. Capital: St. Paul. *A34–A35*

**Mississippi** 20th state. Capital: Jackson. *A34–A35*

**Mississippi River** second longest U.S. river, south from Minnesota to the Gulf of Mexico.

**Missouri** 24th state. Capital: Jefferson City. *A34–A35*

**Missouri River** longest U.S. river, east from the Rockies to the Mississippi River.

**Montana** 41st state. Capital: Helena. *A34–A35*

**Nebraska** 37th state. Capital: Lincoln. *A34–A35*

**Nevada** 36th state. Capital: Carson City. *A34–A35*

**New England** northeast U.S. region made up of Maine, New Hampshire, Vermont, Massachusetts, Rhode Island, and Connecticut. *72*

**New France** first permanent French colony in North America. *38*

**New Hampshire** 9th state. Capital: Concord. *A34–A35*

**New Jersey** 3rd state. Capital: Trenton. *A34–A35*

**New Mexico** 47th state. Capital: Santa Fe. *A34–A35*

**New Netherland** early Dutch colony that became New York in 1664. *38*

**New Orleans** Louisiana port city at mouth of the Mississippi River. *355*

**New Spain** former North American province of the Spanish Empire, made up mostly of present-day Mexico and the southwest United States. *42*

**New York** 11th state. Capital: Albany. *A34–A35*

**New York City** largest U.S. city, at the mouth of the Hudson River; temporary U.S. capital, 1785–1790.

**North America** continent of Western Hemisphere north of Panama-Colombia border.

**North Carolina** 12th state. Capital: Raleigh. *A34–A35*

**North Dakota** 39th state. Capital: Bismarck. *A34–A35*

**Northwest Territory** U.S. land north of the Ohio River to the Great Lakes and west to the Mississippi River; acquired in 1783. *240, 320*

**Ohio** 17th state. Capital: Columbus. *A34–A35*

**Ohio River** river that flows from western Pennsylvania to the Mississippi River.

**Oklahoma** 46th state. Capital: Oklahoma City. *A34–A35*

**Oregon** 33rd state. Capital: Salem. *A34–A35*

**Oregon Country** former region of northwest North America claimed jointly by Britain and the United States until 1846. *347, 434*

**Oregon Trail** pioneer wagon route from Missouri to the Oregon Territory in the 1840s and 1850s. *421*

**Pacific Ocean** world's largest ocean, on the west coast of the United States.

**Panama Canal** ship passageway cut through Panama in Central America, linking Atlantic and Pacific oceans. (8°N 80°W) *709*

**Paris** capital city of France. (49°N 2°E)

**Pearl Harbor** naval base in Hawaii. (21°N 158°W)

**Pennsylvania** 2nd state. Capital: Harrisburg. *A34–A35*

**Philadelphia** large port city in Pennsylvania; U.S. capital, 1790–1800. (40°N 76°W) *113*

**Philippine Islands** Pacific island country off the southeast coast of China. Capital: Manila. *701*

**Plymouth** town on Massachusetts coast and site of Pilgrim landing and colony. (42°N 71°W) *69*

**Poland** central European republic on the Baltic coast. Capital: Warsaw. (52°N 21°E) *A24–A25*

**Portugal** nation in southwestern Europe; leader in early oceanic explorations. Capital: Lisbon. *A24–A25, 30*

**Potomac River** river separating Virginia from Maryland and Washington, D.C.

**Puerto Rico** Caribbean island that has been U.S. territory since 1898. *A30–A31*

**Quebec** major early Canadian city; also a province of eastern Canada. *38*

**Rhode Island** 13th state. Capital: Providence. *A34–A35*

**Richmond** Virginia capital that was also the capital of the Confederacy. (38°N 77°W)

**Rio Grande** river that forms part of the border between the United States and Mexico. *435*

**Roanoke Island** island off the coast of North Carolina; 1585 site of the first English colony in the Americas. (36°N 76°W) *59*

**Rocky Mountains** mountain range in the western United States and Canada. *A36–A37*

**Russia** large Eurasian country, the major republic of the former Soviet Union (1922–1991). Capital: Moscow. *A24–A25*

**St. Augustine** oldest permanent European settlement (1565) in the United States, on Florida's northeast coast. (30°N 81°W) *38*

**St. Lawrence River** Atlantic-to-Great Lakes waterway used by early explorers of mid-North America. *38*

**St. Louis** Missouri city at the junction of the Missouri and Mississippi rivers. (39°N 90°W) *363*

**San Antonio** Texas city and site of the Alamo. (29°N 99°W) *431*

**San Francisco** major port city in northern California. (38°N 123°W)

**San Salvador** West Indies island near the Bahamas where Columbus first landed in the Americas. (24°N 74°W)

**Santa Fe Trail** old wagon route from Missouri to Santa Fe in Mexican province of New Mexico. *421*

**Scotland** northern part of the island of Great Britain. *A24–A25*

**Sierra Nevada** mountain range near the Pacific coast.

**Songhai** early West African trading empire succeeding Mali empire. *12*

**South America** continent of Western Hemisphere south of Panama-Colombia border.

**South Carolina** 8th state. Capital: Columbia. *A34–A35*

**South Dakota** 40th state. Capital: Pierre. *A34–A35*

**Spain** nation in southwestern Europe; early empire builder in the Americas. Capital: Madrid. *A24–A25, 30*

**Tennessee** 16th state. Capital: Nashville. *A34–A35*

**Tennessee Valley** area of Appalachian Mountains drained by the Tennessee River. *791*

**Tenochtitlán** Aztec Empire capital; now site of Mexico City. *30*

**Texas** 28th state. Capital: Austin. *A34–A35*

**Timbuktu** city and trading center of ancient Mali. *14*

**Utah** 45th state. Capital: Salt Lake City. *A34–A35*

**Valley Forge** village in southeast Pennsylvania and site of Washington's army camp during winter of 1777–1778. (40°N 75°W) *193, 207, 208*

**Vermont** 14th state. Capital: Montpelier. *A34–A35*

**Vicksburg** Mississippi River site of major Union victory (1863) in Civil War. (32°N 91°W) *553, 556*

**Virginia** 10th state. Capital: Richmond. *A34–A35*

**Washington** 42nd state. Capital: Olympia. *A34–A35*

**Washington, D.C.** capital of the United States since 1800; makes up whole of District of Columbia (D.C.). (39°N 77°W) *274*

**West Africa** region from which most Africans were brought to the Americas.

**Western Hemisphere** the half of the world that includes the Americas. *A6*

**West Indies** numerous islands in the Caribbean Sea, between Florida and South America. *A30–A31*

**West Virginia** 35th state. Capital: Charleston. *A34–A35, 513*

**Wisconsin** 30th state. Capital: Madison. *A34–A35*

**Wounded Knee** South Dakota site that was scene of 1890 massacre of Sioux. (43°N 102°W)

**Wyoming** 44th state. Capital: Cheyenne. *A34–A35*

**Yorktown** Virginia village and site of American victory that sealed British defeat in Revolutionary War. (37°N 77°W) *216*

# English Glossary

**54th Massachusetts Volunteers** regiment of African-American soldiers that gained fame for its courageous assault on Fort Wagner, South Carolina (p. 536)

## A

**abolition** the movement to stop slavery (p. 464)

**Act of Toleration** Maryland law that forbade religious persecution (p. 76)

**Alamo, Battle of the** battle between Texas and Mexico in 1836 (p. 426)

**Albany Plan of Union** first formal proposal to unite the colonies (p. 142)

**Alien and Sedition Acts** series of four laws enacted in 1798 to reduce the political power of recent immigrants (p. 326)

**aliens** immigrants who are not yet citizens (p. 326)

**alliance** people or nations involved in a pact or treaty (p. 26)

**ally** (AL•eye) a country that agrees to help another country achieve a common goal (p. 204)

**amendment** addition to a document (p. 248)

**American System** plan introduced in 1815 to make America economically self-sufficient (p. 378)

**amnesty** official pardon (p. 570)

**Anaconda Plan** Union strategy to defeat the Confederacy (p. 510)

**annex** join or merge territory into an existing political unity such as a country or state (p. 426)

**Antietam, Battle of** battle in Maryland that ended Lee's first invasion of the North (p. 522)

**Antifederalists** people who opposed ratification of the Constitution (p. 248)

**Appalachian Mountains** mountain range stretching from eastern Canada south to Alabama (p. 116)

**Appomattox Court House** town in Virginia where Lee surrendered to Grant (p. 548)

**apprentice** (a•PREN•tis) one who is learning a trade from an experienced craftsperson (p. 126)

**arsenal** place where weapons are kept (p. 234)

**Articles of Confederation** plan for national government ratified in 1781 (p. 234)

**artillery** cannon and large guns (p. 176)

**artisans** skilled craftspeople, such as blacksmiths and cabinet makers (p. 110)

**assimilate** to absorb into a culture (p. 402)

**attorney general** nation's top legal officer; today also the head of the Department of Justice (p. 312)

**Aztec** Native American civilization that spread through what is now Mexico (p. 4)

## B

**Backcountry** the far western edges of the colonies (p. 94)

**Bacon's Rebellion** 1676 rebellion in Virginia (p. 102)

**banish** to force someone to leave a place (p. 66)

**Bear Flag Revolt** rebellion by Americans in 1846 against Mexican rule of California (p. 432)

**bickering** petty quarreling (p. 480)

**Bill of Rights** first ten amendments to the U.S. Constitution (p. 248)

**black codes** laws passed by Southern states that limited the freedom of former slaves (pp. 570)

**Black Death** deadly disease that spread through Europe in the 14th century (p. 16)

**border states** slave states that bordered states in which slavery was illegal (p. 510)

**Boston Massacre** incident in 1770 in which British troops fired on and killed American colonists (p. 160)

**Boston Tea Party** incident in 1773, when colonists protested British policies by boarding British ships and throwing their cargoes of tea overboard (p. 160)

**boycott** refusal to buy (p. 156)

**Bull Run, First Battle of** first major battle of the Civil War (p. 510)

## C

**cabinet** group of Executive department heads that serve as the President's chief advisers (p. 312)

**California Gold Rush** migration of thousands of settlers to California in search of gold (p. 438)

***Californios*** settlers of Spanish or Mexican descent who populated California (p. 438)

**carpetbagger** Northerner who went to the South after the Civil War to help with Reconstruction (p. 570)

**cash crops** crops raised to be sold for money (p. 102)

**Catholics** Christian followers of the Roman Catholic Church (p. 16)

**cede** surrender, or give up (p. 318)

**Charles Town, Battle of** British siege of Charles Town (Charleston), South Carolina, in May 1780, in which the Americans suffered their worst defeat of the war (p. 212)

**charter** written contract giving the right to establish a colony (p. 60)

**checks and balances** the ability of each branch of government to exercise checks, or controls, over the other branches (p. 242)

**citizen** person owing loyalty to and entitled to protection of a state or nation (p. 234)

**civil rights** rights granted to all citizens (p. 570)

**civilization** complex society in which people share key characteristics such as language and religion (p. 4)

**clans** large groups of families that claim a common ancestor (p. 116)

**coercion** (ko•ER•shun) practice of forcing someone to act in a certain way by use of pressure or threats (p. 352)

**Columbian Exchange** transfer of plants, animals and diseases between the Western and Eastern hemispheres (p. 40)

**Commander-In-Chief** the President in his role as commander of all armed forces (p. 536)

**committee of correspondence** organization formed to exchange information about British policies and American resistance (p. 160)

**common** shared land where public activities took place (p. 94)

**compromise** settlement of differences in which each side gives up something it wants (p. 582)

**Compromise of 1850** series of laws intended to settle the major disagreements between free states and slave states (p. 480)

**Compromise of 1877** agreement that decided the 1876 presidential election (p. 582)

**Conestoga wagons** covered wagons introduced by German immigrants (p. 110)

**Confederate States of America** confederation formed in 1861 by the Southern states after their secession from the Union (p. 498)

**Confederation Congress** national legislative body formed by the Articles of Confederation (p. 234)

**congregation** a group of people who belong to the same church (p. 66)

**conquistador** (kahn•KEES•tuh•dawr) Spanish soldier that explored the Americas and claimed land for Spain (p. 26)

**conscription** military draft (p. 542)

**Constitutional Convention** 1787 meeting at which the U.S. Constitution was created (p. 242)

**Continental Army** America's Patriot army during the Revolutionary War (p. 176)

**contractor** private supplier (p. 516)

**converts** people who accept a new religious belief (p. 418)

**Copperheads** Northern Democrats who favored peace with the South (p. 542)

**corps** (kor) a number of people acting together for a similar purpose (p. 344)

**cotton gin** machine that made cleaning seeds from cotton faster (p. 372)

**Crittenden Compromise** compromise introduced in 1861 that might have prevented secession (p. 498)

**D**

**Daughters of Liberty** organization of colonial women formed to protest British policies (p. 160)

**Declaration of Independence** document that declared American independence from Britain (p. 176)

**denomination** distinct religious group (p. 110)

**depression** a severe economic slump (pp. 408, 582)

**desert** (duh•ZERT) to leave military duty without permission (p. 204)

**dislodge** remove (p. 548)

**disputes** (dis•PYOOTS) disagreements (p. 222)

**dissenter** (dih•SEHN•tuhr) a person who disagrees with an official church (p. 66)

**diversity** variety (p. 76)

**doctrine of nullification** idea that a state had the right to nullify, or reject, a federal law that it considers unconstitutional (p. 394)

***Dred Scott v. Sandford*** 1856 Supreme Court case in which a slave, Dred Scott, sued for his freedom; the court ruled against Scott (p. 490)

**duties** taxes placed on imported goods (p. 160)

**E**

**electoral votes** votes made by members of the Electoral College, which elects the president and vice president (p. 582)

**elite** highest-ranking social group (p. 76)

**emancipate** to free (p. 536)

**Emancipation Proclamation** document issued by Lincoln that declared that all slaves in Confederate territory were free (p. 536)

**Embargo Act of 1807** law that forbade American ships from sailing to foreign ports and closed American ports to British ships (p. 352)

**emigrant** person who leaves a country (p. 450)

***encomienda*** grant of Native American slave labor (p. 40)

**English Bill of Rights** 1689 laws protecting the rights of English subjects and Parliament (p. 136)

**Enlightenment** philosophical movement stressing human reason (p. 126)

**enlist** to join the armed forces (p. 516)

**Erie Canal** waterway that connected New York City with Buffalo, New York (p. 378)

**executive branch** government department that enforces laws (p. 242)

**export** to send abroad for trade or sale (p. 40)

**F**

**factory system** method of production using many workers and machines in one building (p. 364)

**fall line** the point at which waterfalls prevent large boats from moving farther upriver (p. 116)

**Fallen Timbers, Battle of** 1794 battle between Native Americans and American forces (p. 318)

**famine** (FAM•ihn) severe food shortage leading to starvation (p. 450)

**Federal Judiciary** (joo•DISH•ee•ER•ee) **Act** 1789 law passed by the first Congress that set up lower Federal courts (p. 312)

**federalism** system of government in which power is shared between the national (or federal) government and the states (p. 248)

***The Federalist* papers** ratification essays published in New York newspapers (p. 248)

**Federalists** people who supported ratification of the Constitution (p. 248)

**Fifteenth Amendment** constitutional amendment that stated citizens could not be stopped from voting "on account of race, color, or previous condition of servitude" (p. 582)

**First Continental Congress** meeting of delegates from most of the colonies, called in reaction to the Intolerable Acts (p. 168)

**Ford's Theatre** theater in Washington, D.C. where Lincoln was shot (p. 558)

**foreign policy** relations with the governments of other nations (p. 326)

**Fort Sumter** a Union fort in the harbor of Charleston, South Carolina (p. 510)

**forty-niner** person who went to California to find gold in 1849 (p. 438)

**Founders** people who helped create the U.S. Constitution (p. 242)

**Fourteenth Amendment** constitutional amendment that made all people born in the U.S. (including former slaves) citizens (p. 570)

**Freedman's Bureau** federal agency set up to help former enslaved people (p. 570)

**freedmen's school** school set up to educate newly freed African Americans (p. 576)

**Free-Soil Party** a political party dedicated to stopping the expansion of slavery (p. 480)

**French and Indian War** war of 1754–1763 between Britain, France, and their allies for control of North America (p. 142)

**French Revolution** revolution overthrowing the government in France that began in 1787 and ended in violence and mass executions (p. 318)

**Fugitive Slave Act** an 1850 law to help slaveholders recapture runaway slaves (p. 480)

**Fundamental Orders of Connecticut** document that has been called the first written constitution in America (p. 66)

**galleon** sailing ship (p. 34)

**Gettysburg, Battle of** battle in 1863 in Pennsylvania when Union forces stopped a Confederate invasion of the North (p. 548)

**Ghana** West African kingdom that prospered between A.D. 700 and 1000 (p. 10)

**Glorious Revolution** events of 1688–1689, during which the English Parliament invited William and Mary to replace James II as monarchs (p. 136)

**Great Awakening** Christian religious movement (p. 126)

**Great Compromise** agreement to establish a two-house national legislature, with all states having equal representation in one house and each state having representation based on its population in the other house (p. 242)

**great famine** a widespread food shortage that killed thousands of Europeans (p. 16)

**Great Migration** the movement of tens of thousands of English settlers to New England during the 1630s (p. 66)

**greenback** paper money introduced during the Civil War (p. 542)

**Greenville, Treaty of** 1795 treaty in which 12 Native American tribes ceded control of much of Ohio and Indiana to the U.S. government. (p. 318)

**Guadalupe Hidalgo** (gwah•duh•LOOP•ay hih•DAHL•go), **Treaty of** treaty that ended the War with Mexico (p. 432)

**guerillas** (guh•RIL•uhz) small bands of fighters who weaken the enemy with surprise raids and hit-and-run attacks (p. 194)

*hacienda* large farm or estate (p. 40)

**Harpers Ferry** a federal arsenal in Virginia captured in 1859 during an antislavery revolt (p. 490)

**headright** land grant given to one who could pay his or her way to the colonies (p. 60)

**heritage** tradition (p. 136)

**House of Burgesses** the Virginia assembly, which was the first representative assembly in the American colonies (p. 60)

**Huguenots** French Protestants (p. 76)

**hygiene** conditions and practices that promote health (p. 516)

**immigrant** person who settles in a new country (p 450)

**impeach** to formally accuse the president of misconduct in office (p. 570)

**impressment** the act of seizing by force; between 1803 and 1812, the British impressed, or kidnapped, about 6,000 American sailors to work on British ships (p. 352)

**inaugurate** (in•AW•gyuh•rate) to formally swear in or induct into office (p. 312)

**Inca** Native American civilization that developed in what is now Peru (p. 4)

**income tax** tax on earnings (p. 542)

**indentured servant** one who worked for a set time without pay in exchange for a free passage to America (p. 60)

**Indian Removal Act** 1830 law that called for the government to negotiate treaties requiring Native Americans to relocate west (p. 402)

**Indian Territory** an area to which Native Americans were moved that covered what is now Oklahoma and parts of Kansas and Nebraska (p. 402)

**indigo** plant that produces a deep blue dye (p. 102)

**Industrial Revolution** the economic changes of the late 1700s, when large-scale manufacturing replaced farming as the main form of work (p. 364)

**inflation** an increase in prices and a decrease in the value of money (p. 408)

**Intolerable Acts** series of laws, known in Britain as the Coercive Acts, meant to punish Massachusetts and clamp down on resistance in other colonies (p. 168)

**investor** person who puts money into a project to earn a profit (p. 60)

**Islam** religion that teaches there is one God, named Allah, and Muhammad is his prophet (p. 10)

**J**

**Jacksonian democracy** the idea of widening political power to more of the people (p. 394)

**Jamestown** the first permanent English settlement in North America (p. 60)

**Jay's Treaty** agreement that ended the dispute with Britain over American shipping during the French Revolution (p. 318)

**joint-stock company** company funded by a group of investors (p. 60)

**judicial branch** government department that interprets laws (p. 242)

**judicial review** principle that states that the Supreme Court has the final say in interpreting the Constitution (p. 338)

**Judiciary Act of 1801** law that let President John Adams fill federal judgeships with Federalists (p. 338)

**K**

**Kansas-Nebraska Act** 1854 law that established the territories of Kansas and Nebraska and gave their residents the right to decide whether to allow slavery (p. 480)

**Kentucky and Virginia Resolutions** Resolutions passed by Kentucky and Virginia in 1798 giving the states the right to declare acts of Congress null and void (p. 326)

**King Philip's War** 1675–1676 Native American uprising against the Puritan colonies (p. 94)

**Know-Nothing Party** political party in the United States during the 1850s that was against recent immigrants and Roman Catholics (p. 450)

**Kongo** Central African kingdom that ruled during the 1400s (p. 10)

**Ku Klux Klan** secret group that used violence to try to restore Democratic control of the South and keep African-Americans powerless (p. 576)

**L**

**labor union** group of workers who band together to seek better working conditions (p. 456)

**Land Ordinance of 1785** law that established a plan for dividing the federally owned lands west of the Appalachian Mountains (p. 234)

**land speculators** (SPEC•yuh•LAY•tors) people who buy land in the hope that it will increase in value (p. 418)

**legislative branch** government department that makes laws (p. 242)

**levy** impose or raise a tax (p. 234)

**Lewis and Clark expedition** group that explored the Louisiana Territory and lands west; also known as the Corps of Discovery (p. 344)

**Lexington and Concord** first battles of the Revolutionary War (p. 168)

**liberation** the act of setting someone free (p. 536)

**literacy** the ability to read and write (p. 126)

**Lone Star Republic** nickname of the Republic of Texas once free from Mexico (p. 426)

**Louisiana Purchase** American purchase of the Louisiana Territory from France in 1803 (p. 344)

**Lowell mills** textile mills located in the factory town of Lowell, Massachusetts (p. 364)

**Loyalists** Americans who supported the British (p. 168)

**lynch** to kill by hanging without due process of law (p. 576)

**M**

**Magna Carta** charter of English political and civil liberties (p. 136)

**majority rule** system of government in which more than one half of a group holds the power to make decisions binding the entire group (p. 248)

**Mali** West African kingdom that ruled from about 1200 to 1400 (p. 10)

**manifest destiny** belief that the U.S. was meant to expand from coast to coast (p. 432)

**maroon** runaway or fugitive slave (p. 48)

**Maya** ancient Native American civilization of Mesoamerica (p. 4)

**Mayflower Compact** document that helped establish the practice of self-government (p. 66)

**mechanical reaper** a device that cuts grain (p. 364)

**mercantilism** (MUR•kuhn•tee•LIHZ•uhm) economic system that increased money in a country's treasury by creating a favorable balance of trade (pp. 26, 60)

**mercenary** (MUR•suh•NAIR•ee) a professional soldier hired to fight for a foreign country (p. 194)

**Merrimack** Confederate ironclad ship, later renamed the *Virginia* (p. 516)

**Mesoamerica** region that stretches from modern-day Mexico to Nicaragua (p. 4)

**Mexican cession** Mexican territory surrendered to the United States at the end of the war with Mexico (p. 432)

**middle passage** middle leg of the triangular trade route that brought captured Africans to the Americas to serve as slaves (p. 48)

**migrate** to move from one region to another (p. 4)

**migration** movement of people from one country or locality to another (p. 438)

**militia** a force of armed civilians pledged to defend their community (p. 168)

**Minutemen** group of armed civilians, trained to be ready to fight "at a minute's warning" (p. 168)

**mission** settlement created by the Spanish church in order to convert Native Americans to Christianity (p. 40)

**missionary** person sent by the Church to convert Native Americans to Christianity (p. 26)

**Missouri Compromise** laws enacted in 1820 to maintain balance of power between slave and free states (p. 378)

*Monitor* Union ironclad ship (p. 516)

**Monroe Doctrine** U.S. policy opposing European interference in the Western Hemisphere (p. 378)

**Mormon** member of a church founded by Joseph Smith in 1830 (p. 418)

**mountain men** trappers and explorers who opened up the western pioneer trails (p. 418)

**Muslim** follower of the religion of Islam (p. 10)

**nationalism** a feeling of pride, loyalty, and protectiveness towards one's country (pp. 378)

**nativist** native-born American who wanted to eliminate foreign influence (p. 450)

**Navigation Acts** laws passed by the English government to ensure that England made money from its colonies' trade (p. 94)

**Ndongo** Central African kingdom that ruled during the 1400s (p. 10)

**neutral** (NEW•truhl) not favoring any one side (p. 194)

**New France** first permanent French settlement in North America (p. 34)

**New Jersey Plan** proposal for a legislature in which each state would have one vote (p. 242)

**New Netherland** first permanent Dutch colony in North America (pp. 34, 82)

**nondenominational** not favoring any particular religion (p. 222)

**nonsedentary societies** people who move continually in search of food (p. 4)

**North Atlantic current** clockwise ocean current that flows between Northern Europe and the Caribbean Sea (p. 16)

**Northwest Ordinance** law that described how the Northwest Territory was to governed (p. 234)

**Northwest Territory** lands northwest of the Appalachians, covered by the Land Ordinance of 1785 (p. 234)

**nullification** idea that a state could cancel a federal law within the state (p. 326)

**Oregon Trail** trail that ran westward from Independence, Missouri, to the Oregon Territory (p. 418)

**outposts** (OWT•posts) military bases, usually located on the frontier (p. 222)

**overseers** people who watch over and direct the work of slaves (p. 102)

**pacifist** (PAS•uh•fist) someone who is opposed to all war (p. 194)

**pact** formal agreement; a bargain (p. 142)

**Panic of 1837** widespread fear about the state of the economy that spread after Van Buren took office (p. 408)

**Panic of 1873** financial panic in which banks closed and the stock market crashed (p. 582)

**Paris, Treaty of (1763)** treaty that ended the war between France and Britain (p. 142)

**Paris, Treaty of (1783)** the 1783 treaty that ended the Revolutionary War (p. 222)

**Parliament** England's chief lawmaking body (p. 136)

**Patriots** Americans who sided with the rebels (p. 168)

**patroon** person rewarded with a large land grant for bringing 50 settlers to New Netherland (p. 82)

**persecute** (PUR•sih•KYOOT) to mistreat (p. 66)

**Philadelphia** settlement on the Delaware River that became the fastest growing city in the colonies (p. 110)

**Pickett's Charge** failed assault on Union positions on final day of Battle of Gettysburg (p. 548)

**Piedmont** the broad plateau that lies at the foot of the Blue Ridge Mountains of the Appalachian range (p. 116)

**Pilgrims** Separatist group that traveled to America to gain religious freedom (p. 66)

**Pinckney's** (PINK•neez) **Treaty** 1795 treaty with Spain allowing Americans to use the Mississippi River and to store goods in New Orleans (p. 318)

**plantation** large farm that raises cash crops (p. 40)

**platform** statement of beliefs (p. 498)

**plunder** steal from, ransack (p. 522)

**political party** group of people that tries to promote its ideas and influence government (p. 326)

**Pontiac's Rebellion** Native American revolt against the British colonies (p. 142)

**populous** heavily populated (p. 510)

**precedent** (PRE•seh•dent) an example that becomes standard practice (p. 312)

**prejudice** (PREHJ•uh•dihs) a negative opinion that is not based on facts (p. 450)

**printing press** device that mechanically printed pages by pressing inked forms onto paper, invented in about 1455 (p. 16)

**privateer** (pry•vuh•TEER) a privately owened ship that has been granted permission by a wartime government to attack an enemy's merchant ships (p. 204)

**Proclamation of 1763** British declaration that forbade colonists from settling west of the Appalachians (p. 142)

**prolong** to lengthen (in time) (p. 536)

**prominent** important and well known (p. 136)

**proprietary colony** colony governed by a single owner, or proprietor (p. 76)

**protective tariff** a tax on imported goods that protects a nation's businesses from foreign competition (p. 378)

**Protestants** Christian group that broke away from the Catholic Church (p. 16)

**Pueblo** Native Americans who built great mud-brick cities (p. 4)

**"pull" factor** a reason or force that causes people to choose to move to a new place (p. 450)

**Puritans** English dissenters who wanted to reform the Church of England (p. 66)

**"push" factor** a reason or force that causes people to leave their native land (p. 450)

**Quakers** group of Protestant dissenters (p. 66)

**Quartering Act** act requiring the colonists to quarter, or house, British soldiers and provide them with supplies (p. 156)

**Quebec, Battle of** battle that led to the British victory in the French and Indian War (p. 142)

**racism** belief that some people are inferior because of their race (p. 48)

**Radical Republican** congressman who favored using federal power to rebuild the South and promote African-American rights (p. 570)

**radical** person who takes extreme political positions (p. 338)

**ratification** act of official confirmation (p. 234)

**ratify** approve (p. 558)

**Reconstruction** period from 1865 to 1877, in which the U.S. government attempted to rebuild the Southern society and governments (p. 570)

**redoubt** (re•DOWT) a small fort (p. 212)

**Reformation** movement that divided the church between Catholics and Protestants (p. 16)

**region** distinct area of land (p. 76)

**Renaissance** a time of increased interest in art and learning in Europe (p. 16)

**rendezvous** (RAHN•day•voo) a meeting (p. 194)

**republic** state, country or nation in which people elect representatives to govern (p. 234)

**Republican Party** political party formed in 1854 by opponents of slavery (p. 490)

**royal colony** colony ruled by the king's appointed officials (p. 60)

**Sahara** a large desert in Northern Africa (p. 10)

**Santa Fe Trail** trail that began in Missouri and ended in Santa Fe, New Mexico (p. 418)

**Saratoga** (sair•uh•TOH•guh), **Battles of** a series of conficts in 1777 near Albany, New York (p. 194)

**savanna** flat grassland with abundant wildlife, thorny bushes and scattered trees (p. 10)

**scalawag** white Southerner who supported Radical Reconstruction (p. 570)

**Scots-Irish** the name give to people from the borderlands of Scotland and England and from the region of northern Ireland (p. 116)

**secede** (sih•SEED) to withdraw (pp. 394, 498)

**Second Continental Congress** America's government during the Revolutionary War (p. 176)

**Second Great Awakening** renewal of religious faith in the 1790s and early 1800s (p. 456)

**sectionalism** loyalty to the interests of one's own region or section of the country (p. 378)

**sedentary societies** people who settled in permanent villages or towns (p. 4)

**sedition** stirring up rebellion against a government (p. 326)

**semisedentary societies** people who settled in villages or towns but moved every few years in search of food (p. 4)

**Seneca Falls Convention** a women's rights convention held in Seneca Falls, New York (p. 464)

**Seven Days' Battles** Confederate victory during which Lee stopped the Union campaign against Richmond (p. 522)

**Shaker** member of a Christian sect that practiced communal living and did not allow marriage and childbearing (p. 456)

**sharecropping** system under which landowners gave poor farmers seed, tools, and land to cultivate in exchange for part of their harvest (p. 576)

**Shays's Rebellion** uprising of Massachusetts farmers who wanted debt relief (p. 234)

**Sherman's March to the Sea** Union General Sherman's destructive march across Georgia (p. 548)

**Shiloh, Battle of** bloody battle in Tennessee won by Grant (p. 522)

**siege** when enemy forces surround a town or city in order to force it to surrender (p. 176)

**Siege of Vicksburg** the surrounding of the city of Vicksburg, Mississippi, by Union forces (p. 548)

**slash-and-burn** process of clearing land by cutting down and burning trees (p. 4)

**slave** someone who is captured for use in forced, unpaid labor (p. 10)

**slave codes** law passed to regulate the treatment of slaves (p. 48)

**slavery** practice of one person being owned by another (p. 48)

**smallpox** highly infectious and often fatal disease (p. 142)

**smuggling** importing or exporting goods illegally (p. 94)

**society** group of people with common interests, customs and way of life (p. 4)

**Sons of Liberty** secret society formed to opposed British policies (p. 156)

**South Atlantic current** counter clockwise current that flows between Africa and South America (p. 16)

**Spanish Armada** large fleet of ships sent to invade England and restore Catholicism (p. 34)

**speculate** to buy as an investment (p. 156)

**spirituals** religious folk songs (p. 372)

**spoils system** the practice of giving government jobs to political backers (p. 394)

**mountain men** [hombres de la montaña] *s.* tramperos y exploradores que abrieron senderos de pioneros en el Oeste (pág. 418)

**Muslim** [musulmán] *s.* seguidor del Islam (pág. 10)

**nativist** [nativista] *s.* persona nacida en EE.UU. que quería eliminar la influencia extranjera (pág. 450)

**Navigation Acts** [Actas de Navegación] *s.* leyes aprobadas por el gobierno inglés para asegurarse de que Inglaterra obtenía dinero del comercio de sus colonias (pág. 94)

**Ndongo** [Ndongo] *s.* reino de África Central que predominó en el siglo XVI (pág. 10)

**neutral** [neutral] *adj.* que no está a favor de ningún bando (pág. 194)

**New France** [Nueva Francia] *s.* primer asentamiento permanente francés en Norteamérica (pág. 34)

**New Jersey Plan** [Plan de New Jersey] *s.* propuesta de una legislatura en la que cada estado tendría un voto (pág. 242)

**New Netherland** [Nueva Holanda] *s.* primera colonia holandesa permanente en Norteamérica (pág. 34, 82)

**nondenominational** [aconfesional] *adj.* que no está a favor de ninguna religión concreta (pág. 222)

**nonsedentary societies** [sociedades nómadas] *s.* personas que se trasladaban continuamente buscando alimentos (pág. 4)

**North Atlantic current** [corriente del Atlántico Norte] *s.* corriente oceánico que circula en el sentido de las agujas del reloj entre Europa y el mar Caribe (pág. 16)

**Northwest Ordinance** [Ordenanza de la Tierra del Noroeste] *s.* ley que describía cómo se gobernaría el Territorio del Noroeste (pág. 234)

**Northwest Territory** [Territorio del Noroeste] *s.* tierras al noroeste de los Apalaches, cubiertas por la Ordenanza de la Tierra de 1785 (pág. 234)

**nullification** [anulación] *s.* idea de que un estado puede cancelar una ley federal dentro de ese estado (pág. 326)

**Oregon Trail** [Ruta de Oregón] *s.* ruta que iba hacia el oeste desde Independence, Missouri, al Territorio de Oregón (pág. 418)

**outposts** [puesto fronterizo] *s.* bases militares, situadas generalmente en la frontera (pág. 222)

**overseers** [capataces] *s.* personas que vigilan y dirigen el trabajo de los esclavos (pág. 102)

**pacifist** [pacifista] *s.* alguien que se opone a todas las guerras (pág. 194)

**pact** [pacto] *s.* acuerdo formal; trato (pág. 142)

**Panic of 1837** [pánico de 1837] *s.* temor extendido sobre el estado de la economía tras la toma de posesión de Van Buren (pág. 408)

**Panic of 1873** [Pánico de 1873] *s.* pánico financiero que provocó el cierre de los bancos y que la bolsa se desplomara (pág. 582)

**Paris, Treaty of, 1763** [Tratado de París, 1763] *s.* tratado que puso fin a la guerra entre Francia e Inglaterra (pág. 142)

**Paris, Treaty of, 1783** [Tratado de París, 1783] *s.* tratado que puso fin a la Revolución (pág. 222)

**Parliament** [Parlamento] *s.* el organismo legislativo más importante de Inglaterra (pág. 136)

**Patriots** [Patriotas] *s.* estadounidenses que se pusieron del lado de los rebeldes (pág. 168)

**patroon** [encomendero holandés] *s.* persona a quien se recompensaba con un gran lote de terreno por llevar 50 colonos a Nueva Amsterdam (pág. 82)

**persecute** [perseguir] *v.* maltratar (pág. 66)

**Philadelphia** [Filadelfia] *s.* asentamiento en el río Delaware que se convirtió en la ciudad de mayor crecimiento de las colonias (pág. 110)

**Pickett's Charge** [carga de Pickett] *s.* asalto fallido a posiciones de la Unión el último día de la batalla de Gettysburg (pág. 548)

**Piedmont** [Piedmont] *s.* la amplia llanura que queda a los pies de las montañas Blue Ridge en los Apalaches (pág. 116)

**Pilgrims** [peregrinos] *s.* grupo separatista que viajó a Norteamérica para conseguir libertad religiosa (pág. 66)

**Pinckney's Treaty** [Tratado de Pinckney] *s.* tratado de 1795 por el que España permitió a los norteamericanos usar el río Mississippi y almacenar mercancías en Nueva Orleáns (pág. 318)

**plantation** [plantación] *s.* granja de gran tamaño donde hay cultivos comerciales (pág. 40)

**platform** [plataforma] *s.* declaración de creencias (pág. 498)

**plunder** [saquear] *v.* robar, piratear (pág. 522)

**political party** [partido político] *s.* grupo de personas que intentan promover sus ideas e influir en el gobierno (pág. 326)

**Pontiac's Rebellion** [rebelión de Pontiac] *s.* revuelta indígena norteamericana contra las colonias británicas (pág. 142)

**popular sovereignty** [soberanía popular] *s.* sistema de gobierno regido por el pueblo (pág. 244)

**populous** [populoso] *adj.* muy poblado (pág. 510)

**precedent** [precedente] *s.* ejemplo que se convierte en práctica habitual (pág. 312)

**prejudice** [prejuicio] *s.* opinión negativa que no se basa en datos (pág. 450)

**printing press** [imprenta] *s.* máquina que imprimía páginas de forma mecánica y que se inventó alrededor de 1455 (pág. 16)

**privateer** [corsario] *s.* barco de propiedad privada a cuyo dueño se ha concedido permiso para atacar a barcos mercantes enemigos en tiempo de guerra (pág. 204)

**Proclamation of 1763** [Proclamación de 1763] *s.* declaración británica que prohibió a los colonos asentarse al oeste de los Apalaches (pág. 142)

**prolong** [prolongar] *v.* alargarse en el tiempo (pág. 536)

**prominent** [prominente] *adj.* importante y muy conocido (pág. 136)

**proprietary colony** [colonia propietaria] *s.* colonia gobernada por un solo propietario (pág. 76)

**protective tariff** [arancel proteccionista] *s.* impuesto sobre productos importados que protege los negocios de una nación frente a la competencia extranjera (pág. 378)

**Protestants** [protestantes] *s.* grupo cristiano que se separó de la Iglesia Católica (pág. 16)

**Pueblo** [pueblo] *s.* indígenas norteamericanos que construyeron grandes ciudades de adobe (pág. 4)

**"pull" factor** [factor de atracción] *s.* razón o fuerza que hace a la gente mudarse a un nuevo lugar (pág. 450)

**Puritans** [puritanos] *s.* disidentes ingleses que querían reformar la Iglesia de Inglaterra (pág. 66)

**"push" factor** [factor de repulsión] *s.* razón o fuerza que hace a la gente abandonar su país de origen (pág. 450)

**Quakers** [cuáqueros] *s.* grupo de disidentes protestantes (pág. 66)

**Quartering Act** [Acta de Alojamiento] *s.* acta que obligaba a los colonos a alojar a soldados británicos y a proporcionarles suministros (pág. 156)

**Quebec, Battle of** [batalla de Quebec] *s.* batalla que condujo a la victoria británica en la Guerra Franco-Indígena (pág. 142)

**racism** [racismo] *s.* creencia de que algunas personas son inferiores debido a su raza (pág. 48)

**radical** [radical] *s.* persona que toma posiciones políticas extremas (pág. 338)

**Radical Republican** [republicano radical] *s.* congresista a favor de usar el poder federal para reconstruir el Sur y promover los derechos de los afroamericanos (pág. 570)

**ratification** [ratificación] *s.* acto de confirmación oficial (pág. 234)

**ratify** [ratificar] *v.* aprobar (pág. 558)

**Reconstruction** [Reconstrucción] *s.* período entre 1865 y 1877 en el que el gobierno de EE.UU. intentó reconstruir la sociedad y el gobierno del Sur (pág. 570)

**redoubt** [reducto] *s.* pequeño fuerte (pág. 212)

**Reformation** [Reforma] *s.* movimiento que dividió a la iglesia en católicos y protestantes (pág. 16)

**region** [región] *s.* área de tierra definida (pág. 76)

**Renaissance** [Renacimiento] *s.* época en la que aumentó el interés por el arte y el conocimiento en Europa (pág. 16)

**rendezvous** [*rendezvous*] *s.* encuentro (pág. 194)

**republic** [república] *s.* estado, país o nación en donde la gente elige representantes para el gobierno (pág. 234)

**Republican Party** [Partido Republicano] *s.* partido político formado en 1854 por opositores a la esclavitud (pág. 490)

**royal colony** [colonia real] *s.* colonia gobernada por funcionarios nombrados por el rey (pág. 60)

**Sahara** [Sahara] *s.* gran desierto en el norte de África (pág. 10)

**Santa Fe Trail** [Ruta de Santa Fe] *s.* ruta que comenzaba en Missouri y terminaba en Santa Fe, Nuevo México (pág. 418)

**Saratoga, Battles of** [batallas de Saratoga] *s.* serie de conflictos en 1777 cerca de Albany, Nueva York (pág. 194)

**savanna** [sabana] *s.* pradera llana con abundante vida animal, arbustos espinosos y árboles dispersos (p. 10)

**scalawag** [*scalawag*] *s.* hombre blanco del Sur que apoyó la Reconstrucción de los radicales (pág. 570)

**Scots-Irish** [escoceses-irlandeses] *s.* nombre dado a la gente que proviene de las tierras en la frontera de Escocia e Inglaterra o de la región de Irlanda del Norte (pág. 116)

**secede** [separarse] *v.* retirarse (pág. 394, 498)

**Second Continental Congress** [Segundo Congreso Continental] *s.* gobierno de Norteamérica durante la Guerra de Independencia (pág. 176)

**Second Great Awakening** [Segundo Gran Despertar] *s.* renovación de la fe religiosa a finales del siglo XVIII y principios del XIX(pág. 456)

**sectionalism** [seccionalismo] *s.* lealtad a los intereses de la propia región o sección del país (pág. 378)

**sedentary societies** [sociedades sedentarias] *s.* personas que se asentaban en pueblos o ciudades estables (pág. 4)

**sedition** [sedición] *s.* provocar una rebelión contra un gobierno (pág. 326)

**segregation** [segregación] *s.* separación racial (pág. 650)

**semisedentary societies** [sociedades semi-sendentarias] *s.* personas que se asentaba en pueblos o ciudades pero se trasladaban a los pocos años en busca de alimentos (pág. 4)

**Seneca Falls Convention** [Convención de Seneca Falls] *s.* convención a favor de los derechos de las mujeres celebrada en Seneca Falls, Nueva York (pág. 464)

**Seven Days' Battles** [batallas de los Siete Días] *s.* victoria Confederada en la que Lee detuvo la campaña de la Unión contra Richmond (pág. 522)

**Shaker** [*Shaker*] *s.* miembro de una secta cristiana que vivía en comuna y no permitía el matrimonio o tener hijos (pág. 456)

**sharecropping** [aparcería] *s.* sistema mediante el cual los propietarios daban a los granjeros pobres semillas, herramientas y tierras para cultivar a cambio de parte de sus cosechas (pág. 576)

**Shays's Rebellion** [rebelión de Shays] *s.* levantamiento de los granjeros de Massachusetts que querían la cancelación de sus deudas (pág. 234)

**Sherman's March to the Sea** [marcha al mar de Sherman] *s.* marcha destructiva del general Sherman a través de Georgia (pág. 548)

**Shiloh, Battle of** [batalla de Shiloh] *s.* batalla sangrienta en Tennessee que ganó Grant (pág. 522)

**siege** [asediar] *v.* cuando las fuerzas enemigas rodean un pueblo o ciudad para obligarla a rendirse (pág. 176)

**Siege of Vicksburg** [asedio de Vicksburg] *s.* rendición de la ciudad de Vicksburg, Mississippi, a las tropas de la Unión (pág. 548)

**slash-and-burn** [tala y quema] *s.* proceso de limpiar la tierra cortando y quemando árboles (pág. 4)

**slave** [esclavo] *s.* alguien que es capturado para usarlo en trabajos forzados sin cobrar (pág. 10)

**slave codes** [códigos de esclavos] *s.* ley aprobada para regular el trato a los esclavos (pág. 48)

**slavery** [esclavitud] *s.* práctica por la que una persona pertenece a otra (pág. 48)

**slum** [barriada] *s.* vecindario superpoblado y con edificios peligrosos (pág. 640)

**smallpox** [viruela] *s.* enfermedad altamente contagiosa y a menudo mortal (pág. 142)

**smuggling** [contrabandear] *v.* importar o exportar productos de forma ilegal (pág. 94)

**society** [sociedad] *s.* grupo de gente con intereses, costumbres y formas de vida comunes (pág. 4)

**Sons of Liberty** [Hijos de la Libertad] *s.* sociedad secreta formada para oponerse a las políticas británicas (pág. 156)

**South Atlantic current** [corriente del Atlántico Sur] *s.* corriente que circula en sentido contrario a las agujas del reloj entre África y América del Sur (pág. 16)

**Spanish Armada** [Armada española] *s.* gran flota enviada para invadir Inglaterra y restaurar el catolicismo (pág. 34)

**speculate** [especular] *v.* comprar como inversión (pág. 156)

**spirituals** [espirituales] *s.* canciones religiosas populares (pág. 372)

**spoils system** [sistema de despojos] *s.* práctica de dar puestos en el gobierno a los partidarios políticos (pág. 394)

**Stamp Act** [Acta del Timbre] *s.* ley que exigía que todos los documentos legales y comerciales llevaran un sello oficial demostrando que se había pagado un impuesto (pág. 156)

**states' rights** [derechos estatales] *s.* idea de que los estados tienen ciertos derechos que el gobierno federal no puede denegar (pág. 326)

**steerage** [tercera clase] *s.* la cubierta más barata de un barco (pág. 450)

**stock market** [bolsa de valores] *s.* lugar donde se compran y venden las acciones de las compañías (pág. 582)

**Stono Rebellion** [Rebelión de Stono] *s.* rebelión de esclavos en 1739 en Carolina del Sur (pág. 102)

**strategy** [estrategia] *s.* plan general de acción (pág. 194)

**strike** [huelga] *s.* dejar de trabajar para exigir mejores condiciones laborales (pág. 456)

**subsistence farming** [agricul... producir sólo alimentos para co...

**suffrage** [sufragio] *s.* derecho al vot... ...sistencia] *s. ...nio (pág. 94)

**Sugar Act** [Acta del Azúcar] *s.* ley que c...64) impuesto sobre el azúcar, la melaza y otro... enviados por barco a las colonias (pág. 156) ...tos

**tariff** [arancel] *s.* impuesto sobre productos importa... (pág. 312)

**Tariff of Abominations** [Arancel de las Abominaciones] *s.* ley de 1828 que aumentaba significativamente los aranceles de las materias primas y de los productos manufacturados (pág. 394)

*Tejanos* [Tejanos] *s.* gente de herencia mexicana que consideran Texas su hogar (pág. 426)

*Tejas* [Tejas] *s.* nombre designado por los exploradores españoles a la tierra que hoy día es Texas (pág. 426)

**temperance movement** [movimiento de la moderación] *s.* campaña para evitar el consumo de alcohol (pág. 456)

**Thirteenth Amendment** [Enmienda Decimotercera] *s.* enmienda que puso fin a la esclavitud (pág. 558)

**Three-Fifths Compromise** [Concesión de los Tres Quintos] *s.* acuerdo por el que los tres quintos de la población de un estado esclavista se contarían para la representación y los impuestos (pág. 242)

**threshing machine** [trilladora] *s.* máquina que separa los granos de trigo de la paja (pág. 364)

**Tidewater** [agua de marea] *s.* zona de llanuras costeras (pág. 76)

**tolerance** [tolerancia] *s.* aceptación de distintas opiniones (pág. 66)

**Tordesillas, Treaty of** [Tratado de Tordesillas] *s.* tratado de 1494 por el cual España y Portugal acordaron repartirse las tierras del hemisferio occidental y trasladaron al oeste la Línea de Demarcación (pág. 26)

**Townshend Acts** [Actas de Townshend] *s.* actas aprobadas por el Parlamento en 1767 para intensificar el control británico de las colonias (pág. 160)

**Trail of Tears** [Marcha de las Lágrimas] *s.* el desplazamiento forzado de los cherokee desde su tierra natal hasta el Territorio Indígena (pág. 402)

**triangular trade** [comercio triangular] *s.* complejo sistema de intercambio transatlántico de esclavos, ron, azúcar y melaza (pág. 94)

**tribute** [tributo] *s.* pago a cambio de protección (pág. 352)

**Uncle Tom's Cabin** [La cabaña del Tío Tom] *s.* novela publicada por Harrriet Beecher Stowe en 1852 que mostraba la esclavitud como una práctica brutal e inmoral (pág. 480)

**Underground Railroad** [ferrocarril subterráneo] *s.* serie de rutas de huida utilizadas por los esclavos para escapar del Sur (pág. 464)

**uprising** [levantamiento] *s.* rebelión (pág. 510)

**V**

[Valley Forge] s. lugar al suroeste de ... donde Washington y su ejército acamparon
**Valley** ... do de 1777-1778 (pág. 204)
Pe...

[veto] v. impedir que se convierta en ley (pág. 570)

...ginia Plan [Plan Virginia] s. propuesta de una legislatura con dos cámaras con representación en cada una según la población o riqueza de cada estado (pág. 242)

**Virginia Statute for Religious Freedom** [Estatuto de Virginia para la Libertad de Culto] s. declaración a favor de la libertad religiosa, escrito por Thomas Jefferson (pág. 222)

**W**

**war hawk** [halcón de guerra] s. persona del Oeste que apoyó la Guerra de 1812 (pág. 352)

**Whig Party** [Partido *Whig*] s. partido político formado por Henry Clay, Daniel Webster, y otros opositores a Jackson (pág. 408)

**Whiskey Rebellion** [Rebelión del Whiskey] s. protesta contra los impuestos del gobierno sobre el whiskey que realizaron los granjeros campesinos (pág. 318)

**Wilderness Road** [*Wilderness Road*] s. sendero que terminaba en Kentucky (pág. 204)

**Wilmot Proviso** [Provisión de Wilmot] s. propuesta de 1846 que ilegalizaba la esclavitud en cualquier territorio ganado en la guerra con México (pág. 480)

**writ of habeas corpus** [escrito de habeas corpus] s. ley que impide al gobierno retener a los ciudadanos sin cargo formal (pág. 542)

**writs of assistance** [escritos de allanamiento] s. orden judicial que se usa para entrar en domicilios o negocios en busca de mercancía de contrabando (pág. 160)

**X**

**XYZ Affair** [Asunto XYZ] s. incidente de 1797 en el que oficiales franceses demandaron de los diplomáticos norteamericanos un soborno (pág. 326)

**Y**

**Yorktown, Battle of** [batalla de Yorktown] s. batalla final de la guerra, en la que fuerzas francesas y estadounidenses lideradas por George Washington derrotaron al general británico Cornwallis (pág. 212)

Page references in **boldface** indicate Key Terms & Names and Background Vocabulary that are highlighted in the main text. Page references in *italics* indicate illustrations, charts, and maps.

abolition, 456–468, *464, 465,* 490
  and Emancipation Proclamation, 537–540
  in Federal period, *325*
  and Fugitive Slave Act, 485
  and Harpers Ferry, 497
  and slave experiences, 466–468
  and Underground Railroad, 467
  *See also* Civil War; slavery.
abridging, **286, 287**
*Across Five Aprils,* 530
Act of Toleration, **76, 78**
Adams, Abigail, 172, *172*
Adams, John, **160, 164,** 165, *165, 311,* **326, 329**–332
  at Constitutional Convention, 244–245
  and election of 1800, 339–340
  as president, 329–332
  as Revolutionary leader, 165, 171, 178, 180
Adams, John Quincy, *394,* **394, 395**–396
  and slavery, 466
Adams, Samuel, **160, 163,** 165, *165*
Adams-Onis Treaty, 384
affirmation, **276, 277**
Africa, early kingdoms of, *11,* 11–13, *12, 14–15,* 17, *19*
African-Americans
  and abolition, 465–468
  at Alamo, 430
  and American Revolution, 196, *201,* 205, 213, *221,* 224, 227
  in California Gold Rush, 440–441
  and civil rights, 547, 573–575, 581, 583–85
  as Civil War soldiers, 518, 537, *540,* 540–541
  in colonies, 63, 64, 79, 81, 99, 105, 113–114, 131–132
  cultural contributions of, 52, 105, 327
  education of, 130, 460, 578
  in Federalist period, 327
  on Lewis and Clark expedition, 346
  during Reconstruction, 573–575, 577–581, 583–585, 588
  and religion, 131
  in Revolutionary War, 196, 205, *205*
  violence against, 581
  voting rights for, 235–236, 245, 573–575, 583–584, 586, 588
  *See also* civil rights; slavery.
African Methodist Episcopal Church, 227
age of discovery, 28
  *See also* exploration.
Age of Jackson. *See* Jacksonian era.
agriculture. *See* farming.
Alamo, Battle of, 120, **426, 429**–**430**
Alaska, 8, 383
Albany Plan of Union, **142, 144**
Alcott, Louisa May, 472
Alexander VI, Pope, 30
Algonquin tribe, 9, 39
Alien and Sedition Acts, **326, 330**–**331**
  and Democratic-Republicans, 339, 343
aliens, **326, 331**
Allen, Ethan, **176, 178**
Allen, Richard, **222, 227,** 227
alliance, **26, 31**
ally, **204, 205**
Al-Umari, 11

amendment, **248, 253, 582, 584**
  *See also* constitutional amendments.
*American Crisis, The,* 199
American Indians. *See* Native Americans.
American Revolution, 154–231, *193, 200, 214, 220*
  and battles of Lexington and Concord, 173–174
  boundary disputes after, *225,* 225–226
  and British restrictions, 157–158, 161–165, 170
  casualties of, 207, 223
  civilian involvement in, 197, 199–200, 207, 215, 217–219
  comparison of sides of, 197–198, 217–218, *218*
  and Continental Army, 197, 207–210, 214–215, 217–218
  costs and debts of, 223–224, *224,* 237, 238, 239, 315–316
  and Declaration of Independence, 180–183
  early years of (1775–1776), 195–203
  end of (1781–1783), 216–217, 219, 224–226
  expansion of (1776–1779), 205–211
  and First Continental Congress, 171
  flags of, *137, 181*
  lead-in to (1763–1776), 154–191
  legacy of, 223–228
  literature of, *175*
  in Middle states (1776), 198–199
  military strategies and campaigns of, 197–201, *198, 200, 202–203,* 205–207, *209,* 209–211, 213–217, *215, 216*
  in Northern states (1777), 198–199
  and siege of Boston, 177–180
  soldiers in, *193, 208, 214, 220*
  in Southern states (1778–1781), 213–216
  support for and opposition to, 195–196, 213, 215–216, 223–225
  and taxes, 158–159, 162–166, 164–166
  and Treaty of Paris, 224–226
  and war debts, 237, 238, 239
Americans with Disabilities Act, 290, *290*
*Amistad,* 466
amnesty, **570, 572**
Anaconda Plan, **510, 513,** 552
ancient world (beginnings–1500), 2–23, *3*
  African, 11–13, *12, 14–15*
  American, 5–9, *7*
  European, 17–20, *18, 19*
Anderson, Robert, 511–512
Andersonville prison camp, 519, *519*
Andros, Edmund, *124,* **136,** *139,* **139**
Anglicans, 100, 131
Angola, **10,** 13
annex, **426, 431**
annexation, **432, 434**
Anthony, Susan B., 470
Antietam, Battle of, **522, 527**–529, *528, 529,* **536, 538**
Antifederalists, **248, 249**–252, 256
Apache tribe, 9
Appalachian Mountains, **116, 117**
appellate, **280**
Appomattox Court House, *535,* **548, 555**
apprentice, *126,* **126,** 129
appropriation, **272, 273**

Arapaho tribe, 610
architecture
  colonial, *134–135*
  early Native American, 6, 8–9, *19*
  Federal period, *325*
  Renaissance, 18
Arizona, 437
Arnold, Benedict, 179, **194, 200**–201, 224
Arnold, Hendrick, 430
arsenal, **234, 239**
art
  of Alamo, 430, *430*
  of colonial period, *100, 195, 205, 217*
  of early Native Americans, *2,* 6, 8–9, *19*
  of Federal period, *324*
  of French Revolution, *322*
  of George Washington, 357
  of Native Americans, *404,* 611, *611*
  of Renaissance, 18
  *See also* cultural contributions.
Articles of Confederation, **234,** *236,* **236**–237
artillery, **176, 178**
artisans, **110, 113,** 114
Ashcroft, John, 261, *261*
assimilate, **402, 403**
Associationists, 366
astrolabe, *29*
Atahualpa, 33
Atlantic Ocean, 11
Attorney General, **312, 314**
Attucks, Crispus, **160,** *161,* **161,** 164
Austin, Moses, 427
Austin, Stephen, **426,** 427–428
Avi, 472
azimuthal projection, *A7*
Aztecs, *2,* **4,** 5, **8,** 31–32, *32*


Backcountry, **94, 95,** 116–120
  in 1790s, 321
  and American Revolution, *182*
  geography of, 117–118
  immigration to, 118–119
  Native Americans in, 120
  *See also* frontier.
Bacon, Nathanial, 104
Bacon's Rebellion, *92,* **102, 104,** *104*
bail, **288**
Balboa, Vasco Núñez de, 31
Baltimore, Lord, **76,** 77–78
banish, **66, 70**
Bank of the United States
  First, 315–316, 379, 380, *380*
  Second, 409–411
  *See also* banking system.
banking system, *316*
  after Civil War, 561
  in Jacksonian era, 409–411
  national, 314–317, 379, 380, *380,* 409–411
Banneker, Benjamin, *327,* **327**
Baptists, 100
  and revival meetings, 131, 458
Barton, Clara, **542, 546**
Battle of Antietam, **522, 527**–529, *528, 529,* **536, 538**
Battle of Bennington, 200
Battle of Bull Run, First, *508,* **510,** **514**–515, *528*

Battle of Charles Town, **212, 214**–215
Battle of Concord, 173–**174**
Battle of Fallen Timbers, **318,** *320,* **320,** 323, 354
Battle of Gettysburg, *548,* **548,** 549–551, **550,** *550, 551*
Battle of Guilford Court House, 216
Battle of King's Mountain, 213, *213*
Battle of Lake Champlain, 357
Battle of Lake Erie, 356
Battle of Lexington, **168,** *169,* 173–174, *192*
Battle of Long Island, 198
Battle of New Orleans, 357–358, *360,* 396
Battle of Quebec, *142,* **142, 146**
Battle of San Jacinto, 430–431
Battle of Shiloh, **522,** *524,* 524–525, *525, 528*
Battle of the Alamo, 120, **426,** 429–**430**
Battle of the Thames, 357
Battle of the Wilderness, 554
Battle of Tippecanoe, *354,* 355
Battle of Yorktown, **212, 216**–217
Battles of Saratoga, **194,** 200–**201**
Bausch, John Jacob, 452
Bayard, James A., 341
Bear Flag Revolt, *432,* **432, 436**
Beauregard, Pierre, 514–515, 525
Becknell, William, 421–422
Beckwourth, Jim, **418,** *420,* **420,** *445*
Belknap, William, 585
Bell, John, 500–501
Bennington, Battle of, 200
Berkeley, William, 104
bickering, **480, 484**
Biddle, Nicholas, 409–410
bill of attainder, **274**
Bill of Rights, **248,** 251–254, **253**
    English, **140,** 236
    state, 236
Billy the Kid, 605
Bingham, Anne Willing, 324
black codes, **570, 572**
Black Death, *2,* **16, 17**
Black Hawk, 407
bleeding Kansas, 486–487, 492
Bloomer, Amelia, *449*
*Bonhomme Richard,* 210–211
Boone, Daniel, 209
Booth, John Wilkes, **558, 560**
border states, **510, 512**
Boston, Massachusetts, 195, A2–A3
    siege of, 177–178, 179–180
Boston Massacre, **160, 161,** 163–164, *164*
Boston Tea Party, **160, 166**
bounties, **290, 291**
Bowie, James, 430
boycott, **156, 159,** *162,* 163, 171–172
Boyd, Belle, 547
Braddock, Edward, 144
Brady, Wes, 374
Brandywine, Pennsylvania, *198,* 200
Brant, Joseph, *125,* **194, 200,** 224, 226, *226*
Breckinridge, John, 500–501
Brent, Margaret, **76,** 77
Britain, 451
    in 1790s, 322–323, 329–330, 332
    attack on Washington D.C. by, *337*
    Bill of Rights of, 236
    and Civil War, 527
    frontier outposts of, 225–226, 320, 322–323
    impact on colonies of, *87*
    and Native Americans, 196, 199, 209–210, 224, 320, 354–355, 357, 358
    and Oregon, 433–434
    post-Revolutionary relations with, 238
    Revolutionary military strategies of, 197–198, 202–203, *202–203,* 210–211, 213–217

and Rush-Bagot Agreement, 383
and War of 1812, 353–358
and war with Spain, 36–37
*See also* American Revolution; colonies, British.
British colonies. *See* colonies, British.
Brook Farm, Massachusetts, 458
Brooks, John, 209
Brooks, Preston, *479,* 487, *503*
Brown, Henry "Box", *468*
Brown, John
    and Harpers Ferry, 496–497
    and Kansas-Nebraska Act, 487
Bruce, Blanche, 575
Buchanan, James, **490, 492**–493, 502
Bull Run
    First Battle of, *508,* **510, 514**–515, *528*
    Second Battle of, 527
Burgoyne, John, **194, 199**–200, 201
Burr, Aaron, *289*
    and election of 1800, 339–341
business cycle, *410*
Butler, A.P., 487
buttes, *A8*

cabinet, 312, 314–315
Cabot, John, **34, 36**
Cabrillo, Juan Rodríguez, 36
Calhoun, John C., **394,** *400,* **400**–401
California, 439, *440*
    Chinese immigrants in, 453
    as free state, 483–484
    state flag of, *432*
    during war with Mexico, 434–435
California Gold Rush, **438, 439**–441
*Californios,* **438, 439**–441
Callender, James, 339
Calvert, Leonard, 47
Canada
    and American Revolution, 179, 224, 225
    boundary with, 383
    exploration and conquest of, 36, 38
    and Oregon, 433–434
canals, 363, 381
Canary Islands, 17
captivity narratives, 130
Caribbean islands, 29, 42
carpetbagger, **570, 574,** *575*
*Carrying the Flag,* 530
Cartier, Jacques, **34, 36**
cartoons, political. *See* political cartoons.
Cartwright, Peter, 458
cash crops, **110, 112**
Catholics, **16, 19**
    and Irish immigrants, 453–454
    prejudice against, 455, 644
cede, **318, 321**
Champlain, Samuel de, **34, 38**
Charbonneau, Toussaint, 351
Charles I (England), 65, 77, *173*
Charles II (England), 79, 84, 139
Charles Town, Battle of, **212, 214**–215
Charles Town (Charleston ), South Carolina, 104
charter, **60, 63, 408, 409**–410
charts, reading, R23
checks and balances, 236, 245–**246,** *264,* **264,** *281*
    and Alien and Sedition Acts, 332
    *See also* executive branch; judicial branch; legislative branch.
Cherokee tribe, *403,* 403–407, *406*
Chesnut, James, 499, *499*
Chesnut, Mary, 499, *499,* 526
Chickasaw tribe, 404
Chimney Rock, *421*
Chinese immigrants
    in 1800s, 453

in California Gold Rush, 440, 442, *444*
Chisholm, Shirley, *584*
Choctaw tribe, 404, 405
Church of Jesus Christ of Latter-Day Saints (Mormon), 423
cities, 112, 454
citizenship, 300–307
    and Bill of Rights, 251–254
    and compromise, 496
    definition of, 300–301
    and freedom of speech, 252
    and making decisions, 305, *305*
    and political debate, 495
    responsibilities of, 303, *303*
    rights of, 302, *302*
    role of, 300, *300, 307*
    and staying informed, 304, *304*
    and taking action, 306, *306*
    and trial by jury, 138
    and voting rights, 64, 235–236, 245, 397
    *See also* Bill of Rights; civil rights; democratic beginnings; voting rights.
civil disobedience, 322
civilization, **4, 6**
civil rights, *260,* **302, 570, 573,** *573*
    of disabled, 290
    and Native Americans, 573
    during Reconstruction, 573–575, 581, 583–585, 588
    and Vietnam War, 322
    *See also* citizenship; *See also under specific rights and freedoms.*
Civil Rights Acts
    of 1866, 573
    of 1875, 583
Civil War, *503, 514*
    1846–1861, 478–504
    1861–1862, 508–533
    1863–1865, 534–567
    and Battle of Antietam, 527–529, *528*
    and Battle of Shiloh, 524–525, *528*
    casualties of, 515, 519, 519, 525, 526, *528,* 529, 550, 554, 559, *560*
    draft riots against, 544
    economic impact of, 543, 545–546, 560, 561
    and Emancipation Proclamation, 537-541, 562
    and fall of Confederacy, 552–557
    and fall of New Orleans, 526, *528*
    and First Battle of Bull Run, 514–515, *528*
    impact of, 543–547, 559–562
    Lee's victories in, 526–527, *528*
    literature of, *530*
    military strategies of, 512–513, *528*
    military technology of, *520,* 521, *561*
    and Siege of Vicksburg, 449–**552,** *553,* 556–557
    soldiers of, 517– 519, *518, 519,* 540–541, 544, 546–547
    *See also* Reconstruction; slavery.
clans, **116, 118**
Clark, George Rogers, **204,** *209,* **209**–210
Clark, William, *344,* **344,** 345
Clark County, Nevada, *A16*
class structure
    in colonial period, 104, *119,* 128
    and Jacksonian democracy, 396–397
    *See also* social structure.
Clay, Henry, **401,** *401,* 433
    and Missouri Compromise, 382
    in presidential elections, 395–396, 410
    and Whig party, 412
Clayman, Jim, 419
cliff dwellings, *A14*
climate, *A10,* A11
    and architecture, *134–135*
    colonial, *119*

coal mining, *A8*
Cobb, Thomas, 382
Cody, William (Buffalo Bill), 524, *524*
coercion, **352, 354**
Coercive Acts, 170
Cold Harbor, Virginia, 554
Collins, James P., 213
colonies, British, *119, 125*
    and Backcountry, 116–120
    common characteristics of, 72–73, 85,
        86–88
    culture of (1689–1763), 124–151
    developing (1651–1753), 92–123
    early, 61–63
    establishment of, 58–91
    exploration of, 35–37
    lead-in to Revolution in (1763–1776),
        154–191
    living and working conditions in,
        129–130
    Middle, 82–86, 110–115
    New England, 66–75, 97–101
    population of, 119
    relations with Native Americans in, 63,
        65, 68, 79
    religious tolerance in, 72, 77–81, 88
    representative government in, 64–65,
        67–69, 71, 73–75
    social structure of, 119, 121
    Southern, 76–81, 102–109
    *See also* Middle colonies; New England
        colonies; Southern colonies;
        *individual colonies.*
Columbian Exchange, **40, 44,** *44*
Columbus, Christopher, 24, *26, 28,* **28**–29
Commander-in-Chief, **536, 539**
commerce
    interstate, 381
    maritime, 96, *108–109*
    in Middle colonies, 112
    in New England colonies, 95–98,
        *108–109*
    in pioneer west, 420–421
    *See also* trade.
committee of correspondence, **160, 165**
common, **94, 96**
common law, **288**
*Common Sense,* 180
compromise, **582, 586**
Compromises
    of 1850, **480,** 483–**484,** *486,* 503
    of 1877, **582, 587**–588
    Crittenden, **502**
    Great, **242, 246**
    Missouri, 381–**382,** *382*
compulsory process, **287**
Concord, Battle of, 173–**174**
Conestoga wagons, **110, 114**
Confederacy, **510, 511**
    *See also* Southern states.
Confederate Constitution, 502
Confederate States of America, **498, 502**
Confederation Congress, **234, 236**–237
    weaknesses of, *236,* 238–239, 253, *253*
Confederation era, 236–240
congregation, **66, 69**
Congregationalists, 69, 73
Connecticut, 71, 366
    Fundamental Orders of, **66, 71,** 75
*conquistador,* **26, 27,** 31
conscription, **542, 544**
Constitution, U.S., *260, 262, 264, 266, 284*
    amending, 253–254, *283*
    creating, 242–247, *245, 253, 285*
    judicial review of, 342, 343
    principles and goals of, 260–265, *263,
        264, 266*
    ratifying, 251–252
    strict and loose interpretations of, 317
Constitution, U.S., text of, 266–297

Amendments 1–10. The Bill of Rights,
    286–288
Amendments 11–27, 289–297
Article 1. The Legislature, 267–275, *268,
    270–271*
Article 2. The Executive, *276,* 276–279,
    *278*
Article 3. The Judiciary, 280–281, *281*
Article 4. Relations Among States, *282,*
    282–283
Article 5. Amending the Constitution,
    283, *283*
Article 6. Supremacy of the National
    Government, 284
Article 7. Ratification, 285
preamble, 266, *266*
constitutional amendments
    Bill of Rights, 251–254, **253**
    Fifteenth, *291,* **584,** 588
    First, 254
    Fourteenth, 290, **573**–574, 588
    Nineteenth, 293
    text of, 286–297
    Thirteenth, **562,** 572
    Twenty-Sixth, *261*
Constitutional Convention, **242**–247, **244,**
    254
Constitutional Union Party, 500–501
constitutions, state, 226–227, 236
Continental Army, **176, 178,** *220*
    formation of, 178–180
    on frontiers, 209–210
    in Southern states, 214–216
    strengths and weaknesses of, 197, 207–
        210, *209,* 217, *218*
    at Valley Forge, 207–209
Continental Congress
    First, **168, 171**
    Second, **176, 178**–179, 180–182
Continental Navy, 210–211
contractor, **516, 518**
contract system of farming, 580
convene, **279**
Convention of 1818, 383
converts, **418, 422**
Copley, John Singleton, 195, *195*
Copperheads, **542, 543**
Cornwallis, Lord, **212, 214**–216, *217*
Coronado, Vázquez de, 36
corps, **344, 346**
Corsi, Edward, 641
Cortés, Hernando, 5, **26,** *27,* **27,** 55
Cotton Club, 766
cotton farming, *373,* 373–374, *375,*
    488–489, *579*
cotton gin, *372*
counsel, **287**
court system. *See* judicial branch.
covered wagon, *422*
Cowpens, South Carolina, 215
Craft, Ellen, 468
Crawford, William, 395
Creek tribe, 404
critical thinking and reading strategies
    analyze point of view, 142, 196, 206,
        316, 572, R15
    analyze political cartoons, R24
    analyze primary sources, 196, R17
    categorize, 4, 34, 222, 312, 498, 558,
        600, R6
    causes and effects, 66, 82, 94, 147, 160,
        194, 344, 402, 438, 464, 470, 516,
        536, 582, R7
    clarify, 442
    compare and contrast, 7, 16, 48, 60, 80,
        102, 116, 156, 218, 329, 330, 398,
        434, 528, 552, 570, 579, R8
    create maps, *A4,* R25
    create models, R26
    distinguish fact from opinion, R16

draw conclusions, 32, 128, 172, 182, 214,
    331, 398, 410, 466, 469, 485, 489,
    514, 522, 545, 557, 560, 561, 584,
    R12
evaluate, 28, 214, 236, 406, 411, 436,
    441, 578, R14
evaluate internet sources, R38
form and support opinions, 411, 469,
    580
main ideas and details, 10, 40, 110, 126,
    204, 338, 394, 418, 450, 490, 542,
    576, R4
make decisions, R13
make generalizations, 162, 168, 173,
    340, 495, 584, R11
make inferences, 18, 32, 51, 62, 71, 128,
    171, 181, 206, 241, 316, 351, 428,
    441, 452, 466, 489, 496, 501, 512,
    520, 539, 546, 557, 560, 578, 579,
    587, R10
problems and solutions, 76, 234, 241,
    452, 456, 510, R9
read graphs and charts, R22
read maps, A4–A8, R20
recognize bias and propaganda, R18,
    R39
sequence, 26, 136, 176, 212, 352, 408,
    420, 426, 432, R5
summarize, 19, 241, 242, 318, 326, 546,
    R3
synthesize, 171, 206, 356, 501, 539, R19
take notes with graphic organizers, R2
use search engines, R37
    *See also* research, writing, and
        presentation skills.
Crittenden, John J., 502
Crittenden Compromise, **498, 502**–503
Crockett, Davy, 430
cultural contributions
    of African-Americans, 52, 105, 327
    of *Californios,* 437, 439–441, 442
    of early African kingdoms, 12, 14–15, *19*
    of early Native Americans, 6, 8–9, *19*
    of European explorers, *18,* 18–19, *19*
    during Federal period, *324–325*
    of German immigrants, 452
    of Jefferson, 341
    of Puritans, 101
    of Scots-Irish, 118–119
    of slave culture, 377
Cumberland Island, Georgia, *A11*


da Gama, Vasco, 28
daily life
    of African-Americans during
        Reconstruction, 577–581
    in colonies, 85, *85, 129,* 129–130, *162*
    at Coney Island, 664, *664*
    of cowhands, 603, *603*
    in Federal period, *324*
    of frontier farming, 618–619
    in late 1800s, 664
    in pioneer west, 422, *424–425*
    at Valley Forge, 208
Danielson, Fort, *528*
Daughters of Liberty, **160, 163,** *167*
Davies, Samuel, 131
Davis, Jefferson, *498,* **498, 502,** 543
Dawes, William, 173–174
Dawes Act, **608, 612**
Debs, Eugene V., **656, 661,** *661,* 679, *679*
de Campo, Diego, 49
Decatur, Stephen, 353, *353*
Declaration of Independence, **176, 180**–
    183, **182,** *184*
    text of, 184–188
Declaration of Sentiments and Resolutions,
    469

declaration of war, 273
Declaratory Act, 161–162
Deere, John, 368, 369
Deganawida, 46
de Kalb, Baron, 207, 214–215
Delany, Elizabeth and Sarah, 651, *651*
Delaware (state), 512
Delaware tribe, 354
democratic beginnings
    British limitation of, 139–140
    and English freedoms, 137–141, *147*
    and Exeter Compact, 70
    and Fundamental Orders of Connecticut,
      71, 75
    and House of Burgesses, 64, 104
    impact of American Revolution on,
      226–227
    in Jamestown, 63–65
    in Jefferson era, 341–343, 356, *398*
    and Mayflower Compact, 68, 74
    in Middle colonies, 84
    and proprietary rule, 79–80
    Puritan, 69, 100
    Southern, 80–81
    and town meetings, 69, 73
Democratic Party
    and executive power, 409
    formation of, 396
    during Reconstruction, 573–575,
      583–587
    and slavery, 492, *492*, 500–501
democratic reform. *See* election reform;
    government structure; voting
    rights.
Democratic-Republican Party, *329*
    and Alien and Sedition Acts, 331–332
    founding of, 328–329
    in Jacksonian era, 395–396
    in presidential election of 1816, 381
denomination, **110, 114**
Denver, Colorado, 601, 606
depression, economic, **408, 411, 582, 586**
desert, **204, 207**
de Soto, Hernando, 36
Dias, Bartolomeu, 28
Diaz del Castillo, Bernal, 27
Dickens, Charles, 366
Dickinson, John, 163, 236
discrimination. *See* African-Americans;
    racism; segregation.
dislodge, **548, 550**
disputes, **222, 225**
dissenter, **66, 67**
District of Columbia, 274, *274*, 295, 491
diversity, **76, 80, 126, 130**
    in California, 439–441, 442
    in colonies, 80–81, 83, 114–115, *119*, 130
    and Constitutional Convention, 245
    and disabled, 290, 461
    in education, 460
    in government, 575, *584*
    in Texas, 427–428, 429, 430, 437
    in West, 433–434, 437
    *See also* cultural contributions.
Dix, Dorothea, **456, 461**, 462, *462*
doctrine of nullification, **394, 400**–401
Donelson, Fort, 524
Douglas, Stephen A., **480, 484**, 486
    and debate with Lincoln, 495–496
    and election of 1860, 500–501
Douglass, Frederick, 376, **464, 466**, 467,
    469, *490*, 537, *537*
    and Emancipation Proclamation, 539,
    540
Downe, John, 451
Drake, Francis, 37
*Dred Scott v. Sandford*, *479*, **490, 493**, *493*,
    *494*, 496
due process of law, **287**

Duquesne, Fort, 144, 146
Dutch colonies, 39, 83–84
Dutch immigrants, 111, 115
duties, **160, 162**
Dyer, Mary, 71, *71*

economic categories and systems
    artisans, 114
    banking, *316*, 409–411
    business cycle, *410*, 411
    cash crops, 112
    contract system and sharecropping, 580,
      *580*
    corporations, 634
    depression, 411, 586
    fur trading, 420
    inflation, 411
    international trade, 96
    joint-stock company, **62**
    land ownership, 128, *147*, 420
    mercantilism, 62, 96–97
    offshoring and outsourcing, 441
    paper currency, 545
    patroons, 84
    plantations, 79–81, 103–107, *108*, 481–482,
      *482*
    seaport trade, 96, *108–109*
    slavery, 481–482
    work ethic, 69, 86, 100
economic depression, **408, 411, 582, 586**
economic reform, 458, 459, *470*
    *See also* taxes.
economy
    before Civil War, 481–482, *482*
    during Civil War, *545*, 545–546, 560–562,
      *561*
    and class systems, 104, 128, *128*
    colonial, 41–42, *119*
    under Jackson, 409, 411
    *See also* commerce; trade.
Edmondson, Emily and Mary, 491, *491*
education
    African-American, 578
    after American Revolution, 227
    Cherokee, 403, 404, 406
    after Civil War, 561
    colonial, 130, *130*
    reform of, 460, *470*
Edwards, Jonathan, **126, 131**
"Elastic Clause," 317
election reform, 396–398
    *See also* voting rights.
electoral college, *276*
electoral votes, **582, 583**
electors, **267**
elite, **76, 79**
Elizabeth I (England), 36–37, *37*, 61
Elliott, Robert B., 583, *583*
Elmira prison camp, 519
emancipate, **536**
Emancipation Proclamation, *534*, **536**, *538*,
    **538**–540, *539*, *540*, 562
Embargo Act of 1807, **352, 354**
Emerson, Ralph Waldo, 174, 472
emigrant, **450, 451**
    *See also* immigration.
*empresarios*, 427
*encomienda*, **40, 41**
England. *See* Britain.
English Bill of Rights, **136, 140**
English colonies. *See* colonies.
Enlightenment, **126, 131**, 132–133
enlist, **516, 517**
enumeration, **267**
environment
    in California Gold Rush, 442–443
    and forests, 96, A9, A15
"equal protection," 290

Equiano, Olaudah, *50*
equity, **288, 289**
Era of Good Feelings, 381
Erie Canal, 378, *381*
eskers, *A8*
ethnic diversity. *See* diversity; immigration.
Europe
    before 1500, *2, 3*, 17–20, *18, 19*
    in 1790s, 322
    impact on Americas of, *51*
evangelicalism, **456**
Everett, Edward, 404
executive branch, **242, 245**
    in Constitution, 253, 276–279
Exeter Compact, 70
exploration
    of Canada, 36, 38
    by Christopher Columbus, 28–29, *29*
    by Europeans, *3, 18, 20*, 24–31, *25, 30*,
      35–37, *38*
    of Great Plains, 349, 350
    of Gulf Coast, 350
    of Louisiana Territory, 346–349, 351
    of Mormon Trail, 423
    by mountain men, 419–420
    of Oregon Trail, 422–423
    of Pacific Northwest, 350
    of Rocky Mountains, 350
    of Santa Fe Trail, 421–422
    seeking route to Asia, 27–29, 36
    of Southwest, 350
    by Zebulon Pike, 349
export, **40, 42**
ex post facto law, **274**

factory system, 365–367, *366, 370–371*
Fallen Timbers, Battle of, **318**, *320*, **320**, 323,
    354
fall line, **116, 118**
families, colonial, 129–130
    *See also* social structure.
famine, **450, 453**
Fannin, James, 430
farming
    in 1790s, 321
    in California, 443
    after Civil War, 560, 562, *569*
    cotton, 373–374, *375*, *488–489*
    in Jefferson era, 341
    in Middle colonies, 111–112
    pre-Civil War, 481–482
    during Reconstruction, *579*, 579–580
    and Scandinavian immigrants, 453
    in Southern colonies, 79, 81, 103, 107
    sugar, 42, 49
    technology of, 368, 369
    tobacco, 63–65, 78
Farragut, David, **522, 526**
fashion, Federal period, *324, 329*
federal courts. *See* judicial branch.
Federal Judiciary Act (1789), **312, 314**
Federal Judiciary Act (1801), **338, 343**
federalism, **248, 250**, *263*, **263**
*Federalist* papers, *The*, **248, 250**
    "Number 51," 255
Federalist Party
    end of, 381
    founding of, 328
Federalist period (1789–1800), 310–335,
    *331*
    and Alien and Sedition Act, 330–331
    geography of, *311*
    and Hamilton's policies, 315–317
    under John Adams, 329–332
    relations with Europe during, 322–323,
      329–330, 332
    and states' rights, 331–332

style and architecture of, 324–325
  under Washington, 313–317, 327–328
  and westward expansion, 319–321
Federalists, **248, 249**–251, 255, **326, 328,** *329*
  and French Revolution, 322
  and Jefferson, 339–341, 343
felonies, **272, 273**
Ferdinand, King, 28
Ferguson, Patrick, 213
Fifteenth Amendment, *291,* **582, 584,** 588
54th Massachusetts Volunteers, *536,* **536,** *541,* **541**
Fillmore, Millard, 493
Finney, Charles Grandison, 458
First Amendment, 254
First Battle of Bull Run, *508,* **510, 514**–515, *528*
First Continental Congress, **168, 171**
First Rhode Island Regiment, 205, *205*
fishing industry, *A1*
Five Civilized Tribes, 404
Florida
  exploration and conquest of, 36
  purchase of, 383–384
Forbes, Esther, *175*
Ford, Gerald, *277*
Ford's Theatre, *558,* **558**
foreign policy, **326, 328**
Forrest, Nathan Bedford, *581*
Fort Danielson, *528*
Fort Donelson, 524
Fort Duquesne, 144, 146
Forten, James, *210*
Fort Henry, 524, *528*
Fort Kaskaskia, 209–210
Fort Necessity, 144
Fort Sackville, 209–210
Fort Sumter, *510,* **510, 511**–512, *528*
Fort Ticonderoga, 178, 199, *200*
Fort Wayne, Treaty of, 354
forty-niner, *438,* **438, 439,** 444, *444*
Founders, **242, 244**
Fourteenth Amendment, 290, **570, 573**–574, 588
Fox, George, 71
Fox tribe, 407
France
  in 1790s, 322–323, 329–330, 332
  and American Revolution, 205–206, 216–217
  and Civil War, 527
  and War of 1812, 353–354, 357
Franklin, Benjamin, **126, 130,** 132, *132, 133*
  during Revolution, 178, 180
Franklin, Sally, 157, *157*
Free African Society, 227
free blacks, 374–375
  *See also* African-Americans.
Freedmen's Bureau, **570, 571,** 577, *577*
freedmen's school, *576,* **576, 578**
freedom of religion. *See* religion, freedom of.
freedom of speech. *See* speech, freedom of.
Freeman, Elizabeth, **222, 227**
Free-Soil Party, **480, 483, 483,** *483*
free states, 483–484, *486,* 486–489, 493–497
  *See also* Civil War; slavery.
Frémont, John C., 436, **490, 492**
French and Indian War, **142, 143**–148, *145, 146, 147*
French colonies, 79, 80, 120
  exploration and conquest of, 38–39
  in Jefferson era, 345–346
  and Native Americans, 39
French Revolution, **318, 322,** *322*

frontier
  in 1790s, 319–321, 323
  in American Revolution, 209–210
  *See also* Backcountry; westward expansion.
Fugitive Slave Act, *479,* **480, 485**
Fundamental Orders of Connecticut, **66, 71,** 75
fur trade, 143–144, 323, 420

Gadsden Purchase, 437
Gage, Margaret Kemble, 177, *177*
Gage, Thomas, 163, 173, 177, 178
galleon, **34, 36**
Gálvez, Bernardo de, 206
Garrison, William Lloyd, 466, 468
Gates, Horatio, **194, 201,** 214–215
gender roles. *See* women's roles.
Geographic Information System (GIS ), *A4*
geography
  gazetteer, R45–R49
  handbook, A1–A19
  human, A14–A17
  human-environmental, A3, A14–A15
  and maps, A4–A8
  and movement, A3, A16–17
  physical, A8–A11
  themes of, A2–A3
George III, *154,* **156,** *156,* **157,** 169, 180
Georgia
  in American Revolution, 214
  colonial, 80–81
  state constitution of, 227
German immigrants, 80, 111, 114, *114,* 452, 517
Geronimo, 610, *610,* 612
Gerry, Elbridge, 329–330
Gettysburg, Battle of, *548,* **548,** 549–551, **550,** *550, 551*
Gettysburg Address, 563
Ghana, **10, 12**
Ghent, Treaty of, 358
*Gibbons* v. *Ogden,* 380
Global Positioning System (GPS ), *A4*
Glorious Revolution, **136, 140**
Gold Rush, *439,* **439**–444, *642*
Gooch, Nancy, 441
government structure
  branches of, 236, 245–246, 253, *281,* 342, 343
  impact of American Revolution on, 226–227
  impact of Civil War on, 561, *561*
  under Jefferson, 341–343
  under Washington, 314
Grant, Ulysses S., **582, 583**–585
  as Civil War general, **522, 524,** *528, 552, 554,* 554–555, *556–557*
graphs, reading, R22
Great Awakening, **126, 131**–132, *147*
  Second, *448,* **456, 457**–458
Great Britain. *See* Britain.
Great Compromise, **242, 246**
"Great Compromiser, The" (Henry Clay), 395
great famine, **16, 17**
Great Lakes, 143
Great Law of Peace, Iroquois, 46–47
Great Migration, **66, 68**
Great Plains
  exploration of, 349, 350, *351,* 356
  settling, 419–420
greenback, **542,** *542,* **546**
Greene, Nathanael, 215
Green Mountain Boys, 178
Greenville, Treaty of, **318, 321**
Grimké, Sarah and Angelina, 466
Guadalupe Hidalgo, Treaty of, **432, 437**

guerrillas, **194**
guerrilla warfare, 215
Guilford Court House, Battle of, 216
Gulf Coast, 350, *351*
Gulf of Mexico, *A15*
Gutenberg, Johannes, 19

habeas corpus, **542, 543**
*hacienda,* **40, 41**
Haiti, 346
Hamilton, Alexander, 244, 250, *315,* *315,* 315–316
  and election of 1800, 339–341
  and federal debt, 343
  and *Federalist* papers, *The,* 250
  and French Revolution, 322
  as secretary of treasury, 314–317
  and Whiskey Rebellion, 321
Hamilton, Andrew, 141
Hamilton, Henry, 209–210
Hancock, John, 172, 173, 178, 182, 183
Hanson, Harriet, 459
Harper, Frances Ellen Watkins, 465, *465*
Harpers Ferry, *490,* **490, 497,** *497*
Harrison, William Henry, *393,* 408, **408,** *412,* **412**
  and Native Americans, 354
  and War of 1812, 356–357
Hawthorne, Nathaniel, 472
Hayes, Rutherford B., 586–587
Hayne, Robert Y., 400
headright, **60, 64**
hemisphere, geographic, *A6, A6*
Henry, Fort, 524
Henry, Patrick, **156, 158,** 250, *250,* 251
  in American Revolution, 209
  and Constitutional Convention, 245
  as Revolutionary leader, 178
Henry the Navigator, 27–28
heritage, **136, 141**
Hessian mercenaries, 198–199
Hispaniola, 29, 42, 49
Hodgers, Jennie, 547
Holley, Mary Austin, 427, *427*
Holmes, Emma, 511, *511*
homolosine projection, *A7*
Hooker, Thomas, 71
House of Burgesses, **60, 64,** 104
Houston, Sam, **426, 429**
Houston, Texas, *A14*
Howe, William, 178, 179, 198, 199–200
Hudson, Henry, **34, 35, 35,** 36
Hudson River valley, 199–201
Huguenots, **76, 79**
human-environment interaction, A3, A14–A15
human geography, A14–A17
Hundred Years War, 17–18
Hunt, Irene, *530*
Huron tribe, 144
Hutchinson, Anne, **66, 70,** 71
hygiene, **516, 519**

immigrant, **450, 451**
immigration, *452–453*
  in mid-1800s, 450–455
  to Middle colonies, 111, 114–115, 119
  to New England colonies, 100, 119
  population of, *449*
  pre-Civil War, 482
  prejudice against, 445
  to Southern colonies, 80, 119
  *See also individual immigrant groups.*
immunities, **282**
impeach, *568,* **570, 575**

impeachment, **267,** *268*
  of Andrew Johnson, 575
  of Clinton, *268*
impressment, *352,* **352, 354**
inaugurate, **312, 313**
Inca, *2,* **4,** *7, 8,* **8,** *32,* 33
income tax, 292, **542, 545**
indentured servant, **60, 64,** 78, 104, 105
Independence Hall, *113, 232*
India, 441
Indian. *See* Native Americans.
Indiana, 209–210
Indian Removal Act, *402,* **402, 404**–407, *405*
Indian Territory, **402, 405**
indictment, **268**
indigo, *102,* **102, 106,** *127*
individual rights, *265,* **265**
  *See also* civil rights.
Industrial Revolution and growth (1800–1844), 362–389, *383*
  and nationalism, 379–381, 383–384
  and rise of factory system, 365–367, *366*
  and sectionalism, 381–382
  and slavery, 373–377, 381–382
  technology of, *368,* 368–371, *370–371,* 373, 381
industry, 482, *561,* 562
inferior courts, **280**
inflation, **408, 411,** *542,* **545, 545,** 621
  during Civil War, 545, *545*
inoperative, **294**
insurrection, **290, 291**
Internet, using
  evaluating internet sources, R38
  recognizing bias, R39
  using search engines, R37
Intolerable Acts, **168,** 169–172, *170,* **170**
Inuit tribe, 8
inventions. *See* technology.
investor, **60, 62**
Irish immigrants, *448,* 453–454, *470*
  in Civil War, 517
Irish Potato Famine, 453
ironclad ships, *520,* 521
Iroquois Great Law of Peace, 46–47
Iroquois nations, 46, 144
  earliest, 9
Iroquois tribe, 199–200
  *See also* Mohawk tribe.
Isabella I, 17, *17,* 28
Islam, **10, 12**
Italy, 28–29

Jackson, Andrew, 278, **394, 395,** 396, 396–398, 411
  at Battle of New Orleans, 357–358
  election of, 395–396, 410
  in Florida, 384
  inauguration of, 392, 395, 398
  opposition to national bank by, 409–410
  removal of Native Americans by, 404–406
  and states' rights, 400–401
  wife of, 396–398
Jackson, Rachel, 396–398
Jackson, Thomas J., **510, 515**
Jacksonian democracy, **394, 397**
Jacksonian era, 392–415, *411*
  and democratic reform, 396–398
  economy of, 409, 411
  and Indian Removal, 403–407
  and Jacksonian democracy, 396–398
  and national bank, 409–411
  and sectionalism, 395, 398–401, *399*
  settlement during, *393*
  and spoils system, 398
  and states' rights, 399–401

and Whig Party, 412
James, Jesse, 605
James I, 62–63, 65, 67
James II, 139, 140
Jamestown, **60,** 63–65, 104
Jay, John, *250,* **312, 314,** 322–323
Jay's Treaty, **318, 323**
Jefferson, Thomas, *176,* **176, 180,** 327, **338, 339**
  and Bill of Rights, 251, 253–254, 286
  and Constitutional Convention, 244–245
  and Declaration of Independence, **180**–184
  and democracy and government, 341–343, 356, *356*
  and election of 1800, *339,* 339–341
  and freedom of religion, 228
  and industrialization, 367
  inventions of, 340
  and Louisiana Purchase, 345–351
  and Native Americans, 348
  as president, 336–341
  as secretary of state, 314, 322, 328
  and slavery, 227
  and treasury policy, 316
  and War of 1812, 353–358
Jesuits, 143–144
Jews
  in American Revolution, 223, *223*
  in colonies, 80, 84
  in mid-1800s, 452
John II (Portugal), 30
*Johnny Tremain,* 175
Johnson, Andrew, *568,* **570,** *572,* **572,** *589*
  impeachment of, 575
  and Reconstruction, 572–574, 581
Johnston, Albert S., 524
joint-stock company, **60, 62**
Jones, John Paul, **204, 210,** *211*
judicial branch, **242, 245,** 383
  in Constitution, 280
  under John Adams, 342–343
  under Washington, 314
  *See also* Supreme Court.
judicial review, **338,** 342, **343**
Judiciary Act of 1789, **312, 314**
Judiciary Act of 1801, **338, 343**
jury trial, *288*

Kansas, 487
Kansas-Nebraska Act, **480,** *486,* **486**–487, *503*
Kaskaskia, Fort, 209–210
Keegan, Elizabeth, *444*
Kennedy, John F., *300*
Kentucky, 512
Kentucky and Virginia Resolutions, **326,** 331–**332**
Key, Francis Scott, 357
King, Martin Luther, Jr., *260,* 322
King Philip's War, **94,** *99,* **99**–100
King's Mountain, Battle of, 213
Know-Nothing Party, *450,* **450, 455,** *455,* **490, 493**
Knox, Henry, 314
Kongo, **10, 13**
Kosciuszko, Tadeusz, 201
Ku Klux Klan, **576,** *581,* **581**

labor movement
  during mid-1800s, 459
  and slavery, 482, 562
labor union, **456, 459**
Lafayette, Marquis de, **204,** *207,* **207**
Lake Champlain, Battle of, 357
Lake Erie, Battle of, 356

land, physical geography of, A8, *A9*
Land Ordinance of 1785, **234, 237,** 240
land speculators, **418, 420**
land use and rights
  and Articles of Confederation, 237
  in colonial period, 128, *147*
  in Jacksonian era, 398
  in mid-1800s, 453
  and Native Americans, 128, 147–148, 354–355, 358, 404–406
  during Reconstruction, 579–580
  and slavery, 481–482, *482,* 488–489
  and tobacco farming, 63
Las Casas, Bartolome de, **40, 43**–44
Latin America and Monroe Doctrine, 383–385
latitude lines, *A5,* A6
Lee, Henry, 321
Lee, Richard Henry, 180
Lee, Robert E., **510, 512,** *514,* 528, 552, *552, 578*
  at Battle of Gettysburg, 549–551
  early military victories of, 526–527
  surrender at Appomattox Court House, 555
  and Virginia Campaign, 554–555
legislation, enacting, 270–271
legislative branch, **242, 245**
  in Constitution, 267–275
Lenni Lenape tribe, 147–148
levy, **234, 239**
Lewis, Meriwether, *344,* **344,** 345
Lewis and Clark expedition, *336, 337,* **344,** *345,* **346**–349
Lexington, Battle of, **168,** 169, 173–**174,** *192*
Liberal Republican Party, 585
liberation, **536, 539**
*Liberator, The,* 466
liberty pole, *220*
Liberty quarter, *324*
Liberty Tree, *159*
limited government, *265,* **265**
Lincoln, Abraham, *278,* **490,** *495,* **495,** *512, 563*
  assassination of, 559, 560, *568*
  and election of 1860, 500–501
  and Emancipation Proclamation, 537–540
  and Fort Sumter, 511–512, *518*
  and Gettysburg Address, 563–564
  inauguration of, 504
  and Lincoln-Douglas debate, 495–496
  and Reconstruction, 571
  at Richmond, 555
  and war with Mexico, 434
  *See also* Civil War.
Lincoln-Douglas debate, 495–496
Line of Demarcation, 30
literacy, **126, 130,** *402, 403,* 650, 652
literature
  of 1830s, *472*
  of Civil War, *530*
  of colonial period, 130, *175*
Literature Connections
  *Across Five Aprils,* 530
  *Carrying the Flag,* 530
  *Johnny Tremain,* 175
  *To Be a Slave,* 530
  *True Confessions of Charlotte Doyle, The,* 472
  *Two Years Before the Mast,* 472
Little Turtle, Chief, 319, *319,* 320
Livingston, Robert, 180
location, geographic, A2
Locke, John, **126, 132,** 163, 182
Logan, Greenbury, 430
Logan, James, 117
Lomb, Henry, 452
London, 157

Lone Star Republic, *426,* **426, 431**
Longfellow, Henry Wadsworth, 472
Long Island, Battle of, 198
longitude lines, *A5,* A6
Louisiana Purchase, **344,** 345–351, **346**
    boundaries of, 383–384
    and Lewis and Clark expedition, *345,* 346–349
Louis XVI, 206
L'Ouverture, Toussaint, 346
Love, Nat, 601
Lowell, Francis Cabot, 367
Lowell, James Russell, 502
Lowell mills, *370–371*
Loyalists, **168, 174,** 195–196, *196,* 223–225
    in Southern states, 213, 215–216
Lucas, Eliza, **102, 106**
Lutherans, 84
lynch, **576, 581**
Lyon, Mary, 457, *457*

Madison, Dolley, 357
Madison, James, **242, 244,** *244, 257, 286*
    and American System, 379
    and *Federalist* papers, 250, 255
    and freedom of religion, 228
    and *Marbury v. Madison,* 342, 343
    as president, 354, 355
    as secretary of state, 328
    and treasury policy, 317
    and U.S. Constitution, 206, 245–246
Magellan, Ferdinand, 31
Magna Carta, *136,* **136, 137**
Maine, 382
majority rule, **248, 252**
Mali, **10,** 11, **12**
Malinche, 27, *27*
Manassas, 514–515
Manhattan island, 39
manifest destiny, **433**
    *See also* westward expansion.
Mann, Horace, **456,** *460,* **460**
maps
    creating, A4, R25
    elements, A5–A6, *A5–A6*
    projections, *A6–A7*
    reading, R20
    types, A4
*Marbury v. Madison,* 342, 343
March on Washington, 260
Marina, Doña (Malinche), 27
Marion, Francis, 215
maroon, **48,** *49,* **49**
Marshall, James, **438, 439**
Marshall, John, 330, **338,** *338, 342,* **343**
    and Indian Removal Act, 405
Martin, Joseph Plumb, 219
Mary, Queen, 140
Maryland, 77–78, 512
    Relation of, 47
Mason, George, 103, *103,* 250, 251, 256
Mason-Dixon Line, 382
Massachusetts, 457
    colonial, 68–69, 71, 86, 139
    and colonial protests, 164–164, 166, 170–174
    during Industrial Revolution, 366–367
    and siege of Boston, 177–178, 179–180
    and Shays's Rebellion, 235, 239
    and slavery, 227
Mather, Increase, 137, *137,* 139
Maya, **4, 6**
Mayflower, 68, *74*
Mayflower Compact, **66, 68,** 74
McClellan, George, **522, 523**
    as Civil War general, *508, 514,* 515, 526–529
    as presidential candidate, 553

McCormick, Cyrus, 368, 369
*McCulloch v. Maryland,* 380, *380*
McDowell, Irvin, 514
McHenry, Fort, 357
Meade, George, 550
Meikle, Andrew, 368, 369
Melville, Henry, 472
mercantilism, **26, 30, 60,** *62,* **62,** 96–97
Mercator projection, A7, *A7*
mercenary, **194, 198,** *199*
*Merrimack,* U.S.S. (C.S.S. *Virginia*), **516, 521**
Mesa Verde, Colorado, *A14*
Mesoamerica, **4, 6,** 8
Metacom, 99
Methodists, 458
Mexican Americans, 427–428, 429, 430, 437
Mexican-American War, 434–437, *478,* 483, *503*
Mexican cession, **432, 437**
Mexican cowboy, *437,* 603
Mexican migrants, 437
Mexico
    European conquest of, 31–32, *32*
    and slavery, 428
    and Texas, 427–431, 434–437
    war with, 434–437, *478,* 483, *503*
Miami, Florida, *A15*
Miami tribe, 319, 320, 354
Middle colonies, 82–86
    and American Revolution, *182, 198,* 198–199
    economy of, 111–112
    geography of, 86, 113
    political institutions of, 86
    religious tolerance in, 83–86, 114–115
    settling of, 83–86
    social structure of, 84–86, 113–115
    *See also* colonies, British.
middle passage, *48,* **48,** 50–51
migrate, **4, 5**
migration, **438, 439,** A3
    1950–2004, A16, *A16*
    to California, 439, A16
    of earliest peoples, 5–6
    of English to New England, 68
    of ideas and information, A17
    to sunbelt, A16, *A16*
Migration, Great, **66, 68**
military, in Constitution, *272–273*
military weapons and technology
    of Civil War, *520,* 520–521, *561*
    communications, *214, 221*
militia, **168, 169,** *272, 273*
Militiaman Flag, *155*
mill system, 365–367, *366, 367,* 370–371
Minnesota, 453
Minutemen, **168, 169**
Miranda rights, 287
misdemeanors, **279**
mission, *40,* **40, 43,** *416*
missionary, **26, 30**
Mississippi River, 346, *488–489*
Missouri, 512
Missouri Compromise, 381–**382,** *382*
Missouri River, 349
Mitchell, John, *940,* 941
Mohawk tribe, 196, 199–200, 224, 226
Mohegan tribe, 99
*Monitor,* U.S.S. **516, 521**
Monroe, James, 384
Montcalm, 146
Montezuma, 5, *5,* 32, 55
Monticello, 340, *340*
Monument Valley Navajo Tribal Park, Utah, *A8*
Morgan, J.P., 635
Morgan, Sarah, 523, *523*
Mormon, **418, 423**

Morris, Gouverneur, *267*
Mott, Lucretia, 468
mountain men, **418,** *419*–420
Mount Holyoke Seminary, 457
movement, geographic, A3, *A16,* A16–A17
    *See also* migration.
Musa, Mansa, 11, *11*
music of slavery, 377
    *See also* cultural contributions.
Muslim, **10, 12**

Napoleon
    and Louisiana Purchase, 346
    and War of 1812, 357
national anthem, 357
national bank. *See* Bank of the United States.
national growth. *See* Industrial Revolution and growth (1800–1844); westward expansion.
nationalism
    during Industrial Revolution, 379–381, 383–384
National Puerto Rican Day parade, *A17*
National Republican Party, 396
Native Americans, *59, 61, 65, 233, 240, 336, 337*
    before 1500, *2, 3,* 5–9, *5–9,* 19
    in 1790s, 319–321
    during American Revolution, 196, 199, 209–210, 224
    assimilation of, 403–404, 406
    and British, 355, 357, 358
    in California, 439, 440, 442
    and European conquest, 31–33, *32,* 39, *41,* 41–44
    and European diseases, 32–33, 44–45, 147–148
    in French and Indian War, 143–148
    and Indian Removal Act, 404–407
    in Jacksonian era, 403–407
    loss of land by, 128
    and Louisiana Purchase, 346, 348, 349–351
    in Middle colonies, 111
    in New England colonies, 99
    of Northwest Territory, 238, 240
    relations with colonists of, 47, 63, 65, 68, 70, 79
    and slavery, *41,* 41–44, 50
    in Texas, 427
    voting rights of, 245
    and War of 1812, 354–355, 357, 358
    wars and uprisings of, 65, 79, 99, 147–148, 355, 357, 358, 407
    and westward expansion, 120, 147–148, 420, 433–434
nativist, **450, 455**
natural-born citizen, **276, 277**
naturalization, **272,** *301*
naturalized, **290**
natural resources
    colonial, *119*
    conserving, 676
    forests, 96, *A15*
    in late 1800s, *632*
    maritime, 96, *108–109*
    in New England, 95–97
    in South, 103
    and water rights, 443, *443*
natural rights, 133, 163, 182, 228
Navajo tribe, 9, 612
Navigation Acts, **94,** 96–**97**
navy. *See* ships.
Nebraska, 486–487
Necessity, Fort, 144
Netherlands. *See* Dutch colonies.

neutral, **194, 195, 318, 322**
New Amsterdam, *25,* 39
New England colonies, 66–75
  and American Revolution, *182*
  characteristics of, 72–73, 101
  commerce and trade in, 95–98, *108–109*
  geography of, 72
  and Native Americans, 99–100
  political institutions of, 63–65, 67–69, 71, 73–75
  religious tolerance in, 66–72, 100–101
  and slavery, 98–99
  social structure of, 69, 72, 96, 100–101
  *See also* colonies, British.
New England Way, 69
New France, **34, 38**–39, *125,* 143
  *See also* French and Indian War.
New Harmony, Indiana, 458
New Jersey, 198–199
New Jersey Plan, **242,** *245,* **246**
New Mexico, 421–422
  and war with Mexico, 434, 437
New Netherland, **34, 39, 82, 83**–84
New Orleans, Louisiana, *238,* 346, *528*
  Battle of, 357–358, *360,* 396
Newport, Rhode Island, 205
new republic. *See* Federalist period (1789–1800).
New York, 223, 451
  in American Revolution, *182,* 199–201
  Civil War draft riots in, 544
  colonial, 84
  exploration of, 35
  and Mormons, 423
  and ratification of Constitution, 252
New York, New York, 113, 115, *451, 454, A17*
*New York Weekly Journal,* 141
Nineteenth Amendment, 293
Noche Triste, La, 32
nondenominational, **222, 227**
nonsedentary societies, **4, 6,** *7*
North, Lord, 217
North Atlantic Current, **16, 20**
North Carolina
  in American Revolution, 213, 215–216
  colonial, 79–80
Northern colonies. *See* New England colonies.
Northern states
  and abolition, 456
  in American Revolution, 199–201, *200*
  architecture of, *134*
  before Civil War, 381–382
  economic system of, 481–482
  in Industrial Revolution, 366–367
  in Jacksonian era, 398, 400, 412
  in mid-1800s, 454
Northwest Ordinance, **234, 238**
Northwest Territory
  during Confederation Era, **234, 236,** 237–**238**
  education in, 460
  during Federalist period, **318, 320**–321
  Native Americans of, 240–241
Norway, 810
nullification, **326, 332, 394, 400**–401

Oberlin College, 460
Oglethorpe, James, **76, 80**
oil industry, *A9, A15*
Oklahoma and Native Americans, 405, 406
"Old Hickory" (Andrew Jackson), 396
Old Three Hundred, 428
Olive Branch Petition, 179
Olmec tribe, 6, *6*
Oregon, 433
  settlement of, 421, 433–434

Oregon Country, 384
Oregon Territory, 433–434, *434*
Oregon Trail, **418, 422**
Osceola, **402,** *407,* **407**
O'Sullivan, John, 433–434
Ottawa, 143
outposts, **222, 225**
overseers, **102, 105**

Pacific Northwest, 350
pacifist, **194, 196,** 322
pact, **142, 146**
Paine, Thomas, **176,** *180,* **180**
  and American Revolution, 199
  and Washington, George, 328
Panic of 1837, **408, 411**
Panic of 1873, **582,** *582, 586,* **586**
Paris, Treaty of, **142, 146, 222, 224**–226
Parker, John, 169, 174
Parliament, British, **136,** 139–140
participatory government. *See* democratic beginnings; government structure.
Paterson, William, 246
Patriot Act, USA, 261, *261*
Patriots, **168, 174,** 195–196, *196,* 213
patroon, 82, 84
Peale, Charles Wilson, 324
Pelham, Henry, 195
Penn, William, 59, **82, 84,** 111, 117
Penn's Treaty, *111*
Pennsylvania, *243*
  colonial, 84–86, 111–112, 114–115, 117, 118
  and slavery, 227
  Valley Forge, 207–209
Pequot tribe, 99
Perry, Oliver Hazard, **352, 356**
persecute, **66, 67**
Peru, *32,* 33
Philadelphia, Pennsylvania, **110,** *112,* **112,** 200
Philip, King (Metacom), *99*
Philip III, 41
Phillips, Wendell, 588
Pickett, George, **548, 550**
Pickett's Charge, **548, 550**
Piedmont, **116, 118**
Pierce, Tillie, 549, *549*
Pietists, 114
Pike, Zebulon, **344, 349**
Pilgrims, **66,** 67–**68**
Pinckney, Charles, 329–330
Pinckney, Eliza Lucas, 127, 130
Pinckney, Thomas, 323
Pinckney's Treaty, **318, 323**
pioneers, 419–423
  in New Mexico, 421–422
  in Oregon, 422–423, 433–434
  in Utah, 423
  *See also* Backcountry; westward expansion.
piracy, 97
Pitt, William, 146, 159
Pizarro, Francisco, **26, 33**
place, geographic, A2
plantation, **40, 42, 576, 577**
plantation economy, 103–107, *108,* 481–482, *482*
  impact of Civil War on, 560, 562
  *See also* slavery.
platform, **498, 500**
plunder, **522, 527**
Plymouth, 68, 99
Pocahontas, 63, *63*
political cartoons
  analyzing, R24
  about Boss Tweed, *539*

about colonial period, *170–171, 206, 220*
about Reconstruction, *585, 586*
political institutions. *See* democratic beginnings; government structure.
political party, **326,** *328,* **328,** *329,* 492
Polk, James K., **432,** *433,* **433,** 434–435
poll tax, *295*
Poma de Ayala, Guamán, 41
Pontiac, Chief, 143, *143*
Pontiac's Rebellion, **142, 143,** 147–148
popular culture. *See* cultural contributions.
popular sovereignty, **242, 244, 262, 480, 486,** 496, 500
populous, **510, 512**
Portuguese colonies, 31, 49
Potawatomie Massacre, 487
Potawatomie tribe, 354
poverty. *See* class structure.
Powhatan tribe, 63, 65
precedent, **312, 313**
pre-contact (pre-Columbian) period, 5–9, *7*
prejudice, **450, 455**
Prescott, Samuel, 174
Prescott, William, 178
presentation skills. *See* research, writing and presentation skills.
president
  list of, *R42–R44*
  role of, *278*
  salary of, 277
  term limits on, 294
presidential elections
  of 1789, 313
  of 1796, 329
  of 1800, 289, 332, 339–341
  of 1808, 354
  of 1824, 395–396
  of 1828, 396–398
  of 1832, 410
  of 1836, 411, 412
  of 1840, 412
  of 1844, 434
  of 1856, 492–493
  of 1860, 499, *500,* 500–501, *503*
  of 1864, 553, 564
  of 1868, 583
  of 1872, 585
  of 1876, 586–587
press, freedom of, 236
  after American Revolution, 227
  in Constitution, 251
  and Federalists, 331
  and Zenger case, 141
primary, **294, 295**
Princeton, N.J., victory at, 199
printing press, *16,* **16, 19**
prison camps, Civil War, 518
prison reform, 461
privateer, *204,* **204, 210**
Proclamation of 1763, **142, 148, 156, 157**–158, *182*
Prohibition, 292, 294
projections, geographic, A6, *A7*
prolong, **536, 540**
prominent, **136, 138**
proprietary colony, **76, 78,** 79–80
pro tempore, **268**
Protestants, **16, 19**
publishing, colonial, *124,* 130, *147*
Pueblo, **4,** *9,* **9**
Puerto Rico, 283, *283,* 702–703
"pull" factor, **450, 452**
Puritans, **66, 68**–69, 79, 100–101, 173
  and dissenters, 69–71
  and Native Americans, 99
  and Salem witch trials, 100–101
  weakening of, 100
"push" factor, **450, 452**

Quakers, **66, 71,** 84–86, 111, 114–115
  and Native Americans, 404
  and slavery, 114, 465
quartered, **287**
Quartering Act, **156, 158**
Quebec, 179
  Battle of, **142, 146**
quorum, **268, 269**

racism, **48, 52,** 581
radical, **338, 340**
Radical Reconstruction, 574
Radical Republican, **570, 571,** 573, 579
railroads, 368, 381
Raleigh, Walter, **60, 61**–62
Randolph, Edmund, 243, *243,* 245, 314
Rankin, Jeannette, *584*
ransom, **126**
ratification, **284, 285**
  of Articles of Confederation, **234, 237**
  of Constitution, 251–252
reading maps, graphs, and other visuals
  analyzing political cartoons, R24
  creating maps, *A4,* R25
  creating models, R26
  reading graphs and charts, R22
  reading maps, A4–A8, R20
reading strategies. *See* critical thinking
  and reading strategies.
Reagan, Ronald, *278*
rebel yell, 515
Reconstruction, 568–591, **570, 571,** *574,*
  *587*
  under Andrew Johnson, 572–574, 581
  under Congressional control, 574–575
  Constitutional amendments during,
    290–291, *291*
  end of, 585–588
  under Grant, 583–586
  under Hayes, 586–588
  under Lincoln, 571
  and stationing of federal troops, 574,
    *574,* 581, 587
redoubt, *212,* **212, 216**
Reformation, **16,** 18–**19**
reform movement, 457–463
  *See also* social reform.
region, **76, 81,** A2
regional growth. *See* Industrial Revolution
  and growth (1800–1844).
regionalism
  in colonial period, 107, 119
  in Jacksonian era, 395, 398–401, *399*
  after Revolution, *227*
  *See also* New England colonies;
    Northern states; Southern
    colonies; Southern states; states'
    rights.
Relation of Maryland, 47
religion, colonial, **66, 67,** *70, 78, 119*
  and dissenters, 69–71
  established, 72, 131
  in Middle colonies, 83–86, 114–115
  in New England colonies, 66–72,
    100–101
  and social change, 131–132
  in Southern colonies, 77–81
  in Spanish colonies, 43–44
  *See also individual denominations.*
religion, freedom of
  after American Revolution, 227, 228
  in Bill of Rights, 251, 253–254, 286
  in Virginia constitution, 236
religion, pre-colonial
  in 14th and 15th century Europe, 18–19,
    *19*

and conquest of Americas, 30, 36–37,
    38, 43–44
  in early Africa, 12, *19*
  Native American, 9, *19*
religious revivals, 131–132, *147,* 457–458,
    471, *475*
Remington, Frederic, 611
Renaissance, **16,** 18–19
rendezvous, **194, 200, 418, 420**
Report to the Massachusetts Legislature,
    462–463
representative government. *See*
    democratic beginnings.
reprieves, **279**
republic, **234, 235**
republicanism, *263,* **263**
  *See also* democratic beginnings.
Republican Party, **490, 492,** *492*
  formation of, 487, 491, 492
  and Reconstruction, 573–575, 583–587
research, writing, and presentation skills
  constructed response, R34
  creating a multimedia presentation, R36
  essay, R33
  extended response, R35
  finding and using primary and
    secondary sources, R28
  forming and supporting opinions, R32
  formulating historical questions, R27
  outlining, R31
  paraphrasing, R30
  using a database, R29
resources, geographic, A8, *A9*
resources, natural. *See* natural resources.
Revels, Hiram, *569,* 575
revenue, **270**
Revere, Paul, *168,* **168, 173**
revivals, religious, 131–132, *147,* 457–458,
    471, *475*
Revolution, American. *See* American
    Revolution.
Rhode Island, 70, 205, 366, *A1*
  First Regiment of, 205
Richmond, Virginia, 513, 526, 543, 555, *578*
rights. *See* citizenship; civil rights;
    individual rights.
rights of Englishmen, 137–141, *147*
Roanoke, 61–63
Robbins, John, 169
Robinson projection, A7, *A7*
Rochambeau, Jean, 216
Rocky Mountains, 350, *351*
Rolfe, John, 63
Roosevelt, Franklin Delano, *278,* *294*
  and term limits, 294
Ross, John, 406
Rowlandson, Mary, 130
royal colony, **60, 65**
Rush-Bagot Agreement, 383
Russian colonies, 383

Sacagawea, 251, *344,* **344,** 345, 348–349,
    351, *351*
Sackville, Fort, 209–210
Sahara, **10, 10, 11**
salaries
  of elected officials, 269, 277
  of members of Congress, 269
Salem witchcraft trials, 100–101, *101*
Salomon, Haym, 223
Sampson, Deborah, 197
Samuel Adams, 165, 171, 173, 178
Sánchez, José María, 428
San Francisco, California, 443
San Jacinto, Battle of, 430–431
San Juan Hill, Battle of, 702
Santa Anna, Antonio López de, **426,** *429,*
    **429,** 436

Santa Fe, New Mexico, 419
Santa Fe Trail, **418, 421**–422
Saratoga, Battles of, **194,** 200–**201**
Satanta, *348,* 349
Sauk tribe, 407
savanna, **10, 11**
Savannah, Georgia, 214
scalawag, **570, 574**
Scandinavian immigrants, 453
science. *See* technology.
Scots-Irish, **116,** *117,* 118–119
Scott, Winfield, 436, 513
  and Trail of Tears, 406
Scottish immigrants, 80
secede, **394, 401, 498,** *502,* **502**–504
Second Continental Congress, **176, 178**–
    179, 180–182
Second Great Awakening, *448,* **456,**
    **457**–458
Second Seminole War, 407
sectionalism
  in colonial period, 107, 119
  in Jacksonian era, 395, 398–401, *399*
  after Revolution, *227*
  *See also* New England colonies;
    Northern states; Southern
    colonies; Southern states; states'
    rights.
sedentary societies, **4, 6,** *7*
sedition, **326, 331**
Seguín, Juan, 430, *430*
self-government. *See* democratic
    beginnings.
Seminole tribe, 383–384, 407, *407*
Seminole War, Second, 407
semisedentary societies, **4, 6,** *7*
Senate rules, 269
Seneca Falls Convention, *464,* **464, 469**–470
separation of church and state. *See*
    religion, freedom of.
separation of powers, *264,* **264**
  *See also* checks and balances.
Separatists (Pilgrims), 67–68
Sequoya, **402,** *403,* **403,** 404
servitude, **290**
Seven Days' Battles, **522, 526,** *528*
Seven Years' War, 146
Shaker, **456, 458**
sharecropping, **576, 580,** 637
Shawnee tribe, 354
Shays, Daniel, 235
Shays's Rebellion, **234, 235,** *235,* 239
Sherman, Roger, 180, 244, 246
Sherman, William Tecumseh, *522,* **522, 525**
  March to the Sea of, **548,** 553–554, *554*
Shiloh, Battle of, **522,** 524–525, *528*
ships
  in 1400s, *3,* 20
  in American Revolution, 198, 210–211
  and colonial maritime commerce, 96 ,
    *108–109*
  on Great Lakes, 383
  as water transportation, 358, 381
Shoshone tribe, 348–349, 351
Shreve, Henry Miller, 368
siege, **176, 178**
Siege of Vicksburg, *534,* **548,** 549–552,
    *553, 556–557*
slash-and-burn, **4, 9**
slave, **10, 13**
slave codes, **48,** 50, **52**
slavery, **48, 49,** *544*
  during American Revolution, 213, 225,
    227
  ancient, 13
  beginnings of, 49–52, 103–107
  in California, 441, 443
  and class structure, 104
  in colonies, 78, 79, 80–81, 84, 99,
    112–114

in Constitution, 246–247
in Declaration of Independence, 183
as economic system, 481–482
and Emancipation Proclamation, 537–541, *562*
in Federalist period, *325*
and Industrial Revolution, 373–377, 381–382
living and working conditions of, 49–52, 105, 106, 373–374, 484, *484*
of Native Americans, 79, 99, 105
population of, 50, 105, 246, 374
resistance and revolts under, 106–107, 114, 376, *376*
slave experiences of, 50–51, 466–468, *468*
and slave trade, 13, 50–52, *93*, 99, 113, 247, 466
and territorial expansion, 483–484, 486–489, 493–497
in Texas, 428–429, 434–435
*See also* abolition; Civil War.
Slidell, John, 434
smallpox, **142, 148**
Smith, Jedediah, **418**, *419*, **419**
Smith, John, **60, 63**
Smith, Margaret Bayard, 395, *395*
Smith, Thomas, 95, *95*
smuggling, **94, 97**
social reform
in mid-1800s, 460–463, *461, 470*
and religious revivalism, 131–132
social structure
in 14th and 15th century Europe, 17–19, *18, 19*
during American Revolution, 226–228
during Civil War, 544, *546*, 546–547, 560–562
in colonies, 128–130
of earliest American peoples, 5–6, *7, 8, 8, 19*
of early African kingdoms, *12*, 12–13, *19*
impact of wars on, *546*
and land ownership, 128
in Middle colonies, 84–86, 113–115
of mill system, 365, 366–367
in New England colonies, 69, 72, 96, 100–101
of slaves, 376–377
in slave states, 374
in Southern colonies, 79–81, 104, 105
utopian, 458
and women's roles, 129–130
society, **4, 5,** 6, 8–9
Sons of Liberty, **156, 158,** 173
South Atlantic Current, **16, 20**
South Carolina, 213, 499, 511, 583
in American Revolution, 214–215
colonial, 79–80
and nullification, 400–401
and secession, 502
Southern colonies, 76–81
and American Revolution, *182*
common characteristics of, 81–82
economy of, 79–81, 103–107, *108*
geography and climate of, 80, 103, 107
religious tolerance in, 77–81
social structure of, 79–81, 104, 105
*See also* colonies, British.
Southern states
agricultural production of, *569, 579*
during American Revolution, 213–216
architecture of, *135*
before Civil War, 381–382
economic system of, 481–482
in Federalist period, 315–316
and immigration in mid-1800s, 454
impact of Civil War on, 560, 562
during Industrial Revolution, 373–377
in Jacksonian era, 398–401

during late 1800s, 637
in Progressive era, 677, 681
and Revolutionary War debts, 315–316
secession by, 502–504
South Pass, 420
Southwest
and earliest American peoples, 9
exploration of, 350
Spain, 17
and American Revolution, 205–206, 225
Spanish Armada, *34*, **34,** 37
Spanish colonies, 120
after American Revolution, 238
defeat by England of, 36–37
economy of, 41–42
exploration and conquest of, 27–28, 30–33, 36–37, 41–45, *42*
and Florida, 383–384
impact of, 44–45
in Jefferson era, 345–346, 349
Native Americans in, *41*, 41–47
organization of, 42–43
religion in, *41*, 43–44
and slavery, 49
and Texas, 427–428
Spanish missionary, *41*
speculate, **156, 158**
speech, freedom of, 252, *286, 287*
and Federalists, 331
spoils system, **394, 398**
Spotsylvania, Virginia, 554
Squanto, 68
St. Lawrence River, 36, 39
St. Leger, Barry, 199–200
St. Louis, Missouri, 348
Stamp Act, **156,** 157, *158,* **158**–159, *167, 182*
Stanton, Elizabeth Cady, **464, 468,** *469,* 584
"Star Spangled Banner, The," 357
state facts, R40–R41
statehood
California, 443
Texas, 431
states' rights, **326, 331, 394, 399**–401, **498, 502**
in Articles of Confederation, 236–237
in Constitution, 245–246, 251, 253, *282,* 282–283, 284, 288
in Jacksonian era, 399–401
and Reconstruction, 572–574, 584–585, 586, 588
*See also* Civil War.
steerage, **450, 451**
Stevens, Thaddeus, 571, *571,* 573, 579
stock market, **582, 586**
Stono Rebellion, **102, 106**–107
Story, Joseph, 398
Stowe, Harriet Beecher, **480,** *485,* **485**
strategy, **194, 199**
strikes, **456,** *459,* **459**
*See also* labor movement.
Stuart, Gilbert, 357
Stuart, Jeb, 526
Stuyvesant, Peter, **82, 83,** *83*
subsistence farming, **94, 96**
suburbs, 643
succession, presidential, 277, 295–296
suffrage, **282, 283, 464, 469**
*See also* voting rights.
Sugar Act, **156, 158**
Sumner, Charles, *479,* 487, *503,* 573, 579
Sumter, Fort, *510,* **510, 511**–512, *528*
Supreme Court, *280*
and Andrew Jackson, 405
*See also* judicial branch.
Supreme Court decisions
*Dred Scott* v. *Sanford,* 494
*Gibbons* v. *Ogden,* 380
on Indian Removal Act, 405

*Marbury* v. *Madison,* 342, 343
*McCulloch* v. *Maryland,* 380
on national bank, 410
on Reconstruction, 586–587
*Schenck* v. *United States,* 494
*U.S.* v. *Reese,* 586
*Surrender of Lord Cornwallis, The,* 217
Susquehannock tribe, 47
"Swamp Fox," 215
Swedish colonies, 84
Swiss immigrants, 80

Taney, Roger B., **490, 493**
tariff, **312, 316**
and nullification, 399–401
*See also* taxes.
Tariff of Abominations, **394, 400**
taxes
in Confederation era, 235, 237, 239
in Constitution, 243–244, 253
income, 292, **542, 545**
in Jefferson era, 343
under Reagan, 948
Stamp Act, **156,** 157, *158,* **158**–159, *167, 182*
Sugar Act, **156, 158**
Tea Act, 164–166
Townshend Acts, **160, 162**–163, *164*
on whiskey, 321
Taylor, Susie King, 546
Taylor, Zachary, **432,** 434, **435**
Tea Act, 164–166
technology
of Civil War, *520,* 521
for creating maps, *A4*
during Industrial Revolution, *366, 368,* 368–371, *370–371,* 373, 381
during Jefferson era, 340
of military communication, *214, 221*
*See also* military weapons and technology.
Tecumseh, *352, 354,* **354**–355, 357
*Tejanos,* **426, 427**
*Tejas,* **426, 427**
telegraph, 368
temperance movement, **456,** *458,* **458**
tender, **274, 275**
Tennessee, 524, 601
Tenochtitlán, 8
term limits, 294
terms of government office, *268,* 292
Texas, 427, 433, *A9*
as American territory, 436–437
and annexation, 431, 434
and immigration, 452
as Lone Star Republic, 431
under Mexico, 428–429, 434–436
settlement of, 427–429, 437
under Spain, 427–428
and war with Mexico, 435–436
Texas War for Independence, 429–431
Thames, Battle of the, 357
Thatcher, Margaret, *278*
Thayendanegea (Joseph Brant), 125, 194, 200, 224, 226, *226*
Thirteenth Amendment, **558, 562**
and Andrew Johnson, 572
Thomson, Charles, 313
Thoreau, Henry David, 322, 472
Three-Fifths Compromise, **242, 247**
Thurmond, Strom, 269
Ticonderoga, Fort, 178, 179, 200
Tidewater, **76, 81**
Tilden, Samuel J., 586
Tippecanoe, Battle of, *354,* 355
tobacco farming, 63–65, 78
*To Be a Slave, 530*
Tocqueville, Alexis de, 481, *481*

tolerance, **66, 67**
Tordesillas, Treaty of, **26, 30**
Tories. *See* Loyalists.
town, colonial, 96, 108
town meetings, 170
Townshend Acts, **160, 162**–163, *164*
trade
    and American Revolution, *182*
    with Caribbean, 323
    in Confederation era, 238
    in Constitution, 243, 253
    interstate, 381
    regulation of, 243–244
    and slavery, 482
    and War of 1812, 354, 358
    *See also* commerce.
Trail of Tears, *402, 402,* 405–407 **406**
trains. *See* railroads.
Trans-Appalachian West, 319–321, *320*
transcendentalism, 472
transportation, *363,* 368, 381
    *See also* railroads.
Travis, William, 430
Treaty of Greenville, **318, 321**
Treaty of Guadalupe Hidalgo, **432, 437**
Treaty of Paris, **142, 146, 222,** 224–226
Trenton, N.J., victory at, 199
triangular trade, **94, 98**
    *See also* slavery.
tribunals, **272, 273**
tribute, **352, 353**
*True Confessions of Charlotte Doyle, The,* *472*
Trumbull, John, 217
Truth, Sojourner, **464, 466,** 467
Tsali, 407
Tubman, Harriet, *449,* **464,** *467,* **467,** *473,* 547
Turner, Frederick Jackson, 623
Turner, Nat, *376*
Tuscarora tribe, 79
Twenty-Sixth Amendment, *261*
*Two Years Before the Mast,* 472
Tyler, John, **408, 412**

unanimous consent, **284, 285**
*Uncle Tom's Cabin,* *478,* **480, 485,** *503*
Underground Railroad, **464, 467**
union movement. *See* labor movement.
United States, geography of
    human, A14–A17
    physical, A8–A11
uprising, **510, 512**
urbanization, 454
USA Patriot Act, 261, *261*
Utah settlement, 421, 423
utopian experiments, 458

Vaca, Cabeza de, 36
Vallejo, Mariano, **438,** *440,* **440**
Valley Forge, Pennsylvania, **204, 207**–209, *208*
Van Buren, Martin, **408,** *409,* **409,** 411, 412, 459
vegetation, A11, *A11*
Vermont, 227
Verrazzano, Giovanni da, **34, 36**
Versailles, *125*
Vespucci, Amerigo, *26,* **26,** *31,* **31**
veto, **570, 573**
vice-presidential elections, 289
Vicksburg, Siege of, *534,* **548,** 549–**552,** *553, 556*–557
Virginia, 313
    during American Revolution, 181, 216–217

    during Civil War, 512–515, 526–527
    colonial, 61–63, 86
    during French and Indian war, 144
    state constitution of, 227, 236
    and U.S. Constitution, 252
*Virginia,* C.S.S. (U.S.S. *Merrimack*), **516, 521**
Virginia Company, 62, 63, 64, 65, 68
Virginia Plan, **242,** *245,* **245**
Virginia Statute for Religious Freedom, **222, 228**
von Steuben, Baron, 209
voting rights, 64
    for African-Americans, 236, 245, 291, 584, 586, 588
    in colonial period, 64–65, 69, 71, 73
    in Constitution, 267, 290–291, 293, 295, 297
    in Declaration of Independence, 183
    in Jacksonian era, 396–397
    for Native Americans, 245, 573, 584
    property qualifications for, 236
    voting age for, 261
    for women, 77, 235–236, 245, *293,* 469–470, 584
    *See also* citizenship.
Vredenburgh, Peter Jr., 517, *517*

Wagner, David R., 205
*Walden,* 472
Walker, David, 466
Wampanoag tribe, 99
warfare, 1200–1500, *18*
war hawk, **352, 355**
War of 1812, 353–358
    impact of, 367
Warren, Mercy Otis, 249, *249*
War with Mexico, 434–437, *478*
    and slavery, 483, *503*
Washington (state), A9
Washington, Booker T., 562, *588*
Washington, D.C., 274, *274,* 295, 491
Washington, George, **194, 197,** *310, 313*
    at Constitutional Convention, 244
    and Continental Army, 178, 179
    and French and Indian war, 120, 144
    and French Revolution, 322, 328
    painting of, *357*
    presidency of, 313–317, 319, 321, 327–328
    in Revolutionary battles, 197–200, 205
    at Valley Forge, 207–209
    and Whiskey Rebellion, 321
Washington, Martha, 197
Wayne, "Mad Anthony," 319, 320
Webster, Daniel, 400, *400,* 412
Weld, Theodore, 466
Western states, 398, 412
    *See also* westward expansion.
West Indies, 98
West Virginia, 512, 543
westward expansion
    in 1790s, 319–321, 322–323
    1810–1853, 416–447
    and Articles of Confederation, 237
    British restriction of, 157–158
    and California Gold Rush, 438–444
    after Civil War, 561
    early pioneers of, 419–425
    and immigration, 453
    and Indian Territory, 404–405
    and Louisiana Purchase, 345–351
    and Mormon Trail, 423
    and Native Americans, 120, 147–148, 420, 443–444
    and Northwest Territory, 237–238, 240–241
    and Oregon, 433–434

    and Oregon Trail, 422–423
    and Santa Fe trail, 421–422
    and Texas, 427–431, 434–437
Wheatley, Phillis, *221*
Wheelwright, John, 70
Whig Party, **408, 412, 490, 491**–492, *503*
Whiskey Rebellion, **318, 321**
White, John, 61
Whitefield, George, **126, 132**
White House, 937
Whitman, Marcus and Narcissa, 422
Whitman, Walt, **558,** *559,* **559**
Whitney, Eli, 367, 368
Wicomiss tribe, 47
Wilderness, Battle of the, 554
Wilderness Road, **204, 209**
Wild West, 605, *624*
William of Orange, 140
Williams, Roger, **66, 70**
Wilmot, David, 483
Wilmot Proviso, **480, 483,** *503*
Wilson, James, 244, 267
Wilson, Luzena, 439
Winthrop, John, **66, 67,** *67*
Wisconsin, 452, 453
witchcraft trials, 100–101, *101*
Wolfe, James, 146
woman suffrage. *See* women's rights; voting rights.
women's movement, and Seneca Falls convention, 469–470
women's rights, *261*
    and abolition, 468–469
    during Civil War, 546–567, 561
    during colonial period, 129–130, *167*
    and Declaration of Independence, 183
    and education, 460
    during mid-1800's, 469–470, *470*
    in military, 261
    in Quaker community, 71
    and Seneca Falls Convention, 469–470
    and voting rights, 77, 235–236, 245, *293,* 469–470, 584
women's roles
    during American Revolution, 197, 207
    during colonial period, *167*
    during Industrial Revolution, 367
workers' rights. *See* labor movement.
*World* (New York), 700
Wright, Patience, *221*
writing skills. *See* research, writing and presentation skills.
writ of habeas corpus, **542, 543**
writs of assistance, **160, 162,** 163

XYZ Affair, 326, 330, 330
Yamasee tribe, 79
Yorktown, Battle of, 212, 216–217
Young, Brigham, 418, 423
Zenger, John Peter, 136, 141

# Acknowledgments

## Text Acknowledgments

**Chapter 6**, page 175: Excerpt from *Johnny Tremain* by Esther Forbes. Copyright © 1943 by Esther Forbes Hoskins, copyright renewed © 1971 by Linwood M. Erskine, Jr., Executor of the Estate of Esther Forbes Hoskins. Reprinted by permission of Houghton Mifflin Company. All rights reserved.

**Chapter 16**, page 530: Excerpt from *Across Five Aprils* by Irene Hunt. Copyright © 1964 by Irene Hunt. All rights reserved. Reprinted by permission of Penguin Putnam.

The editors have made every effort to trace the ownership of all copyrighted material found in this book and to make full acknowledgment for its use. Omissions brought to our attention will be corrected in a subsequent edition.

## Art Credits

All maps, with the exception of World Atlas maps, created by GeoNova LLC.

**Cover and Title Page** *Adams* The Granger Collection, New York; *Chavez* Najlah Feanny/Corbis; *eagle* iStockphoto.com; *flag* PhotoDisc/Getty Images; *Lincoln* Archivo Iconografico, S.A./Corbis; *MLK* Flip Schulke/Corbis; *Sacajawea* Connie Ricca/Corbis; *Washington* The Granger Collection, New York; *Yosemite* Jose Fuste Raga/Corbis; *clouds* PhotoDisc.

**Section & American Spirit Banner** *American flag* PhotoDisc Red/Getty Images; **Historic Decisions of the Supreme Court** *courthouse* Royalty-Free/Corbis; *justice* Royalty-Free/Corbis; **Geography & History Banner** *compass* Harnett/Hanzon/Getty Images; **Interactive Primary Source Banner** *glasses, pen, document* Royalty-Free/Corbis; *quill pen, magnifying glass on letter* Royalty-Free/Corbis; *Constitution with quill pen* Comstock; **Table of Contents Banner** *American flag* Comstock; *Rocky Mountains* Digital Stock; *White House* Comstock; *Constitution* Comstock.

**Table of Contents**
**iii** McDougal Littell/Houghton Mifflin Co.; **vii** *bottom right* Detail, *Benjamin Franklin* (ca. 1785), Joseph Siffred Duplessis. Oil on canvas, 72.4 x 59.6 cm. National Portrait Gallery, Smithsonian Institution, Washington, DC. Gift of the Morris and Gwendolyn Cafritz Foundation/Art Resource, New York; **x** *bottom right* Courtesy of the State Preservation Board, Austin, Texas. CHA 1989.96, Photographer Perry Huston, 7/28/95, post conservation; **xii** *bottom right* The Granger Collection, New York; **xiv** *bottom right* Bettmann/Corbis.

**Special Features & Reading for Understanding**
**xvii** Bill Manns/The Art Archive; **xix** The Granger Collection, New York; **xx** Alexander Gardner (1863)/AP Images; **xxii** *center* Flip Schulke/Corbis; *inset* Hulton Archive/Getty Images; **xxx** *center left* Bizuayehu Tesfaye/AP Images; *bottom center* AP Images; *bottom right* Thinkstock Images/Jupiter Images; *frame* Shutterstock; *stamp* AP Images; **xxxi** *top right* National Museum of American History, Smithsonian Institution Negative # 74-2491; *center left* The Granger Collection, New York; *center inset* California Gold Rush Guide, 1849/The Granger Collection, New York; **xxxii** *top* Pixel Images, Inc./McDougal Littell/Houghton Mifflin Co.

**Geography Handbook**
**S30** *top right* Peter Pearson/Getty Images; *bottom left* Bob Torrez/Getty Images; **A1** *top* Onne van der Wal/Corbis; *bottom* Andy Sacks/Getty Images; **A2** *top* Steve Dunwell/Index Stock Imagery; *bottom* Christopher Pfuhl/AP Images; **A3** Brian Snyder/Reuters/Corbis; **A4** *bottom left* Lockheed Martin; **A8** Lester Lefkowitz/Corbis; *bottom* Tom Bean/Corbis; *center* George Steinmetz/Corbis; **A9** *top* Steve Satushek/Getty Images; *bottom* Keith Wood/Getty Images; **A10** *top* Jessica Rinaldi/Reuters/Corbis; **A11** Michael Melford/Getty Images; **A12** Illustration by Ken Goldammer/McDougal Littell/Houghton Mifflin Co.; **A14** *bottom* Atlantide Phototravel/Corbis; *center right* Bill Pogue/Getty Images; *center left* Walter Rawlings/Getty Images; **A15** *top* Najlah Feanny/Corbis SABA; *bottom* Jeff Greenberg/PhotoEdit; **A16** Brooks Kraft/Corbis; **A17** *left* Gregory Bull, Staff/AP Images; *right* James Leynse/Corbis; **A18** Medioimages/Getty Images.

**World Atlas**
**A20** Image created by Reto Stockli with the help of Alan Nelson, under the leadership of Fritz Hasler/NASA. **A21–A39** All maps © Rand McNally.

**Unit 1**
**1** Corbis; **2** *bottom right* Biblioteca Augusta Perugia/Dagli Orti/The Art Archive; *bottom center* Werner Forman/Corbis; *bottom left* Charles & Josette Lenars/Corbis; **3** *top right* The Granger Collection, New York; *center right* Werner Forman Archive; *center left* Macduff Everton/Corbis; *bottom* Sextant, English (brass), English School, (18th century)/Private Collection/The Bridgeman Art Library International; **5** *top right* Werner Forman/Art Resource, NY; *center right* Palazzo Pitti Florence/Dagli Orti (A)/The Art Archive; **6** *center right* SuperStock; **7** George H. H. Huey/Corbis; **8** *top* The Granger Collection, New York; *inset* Medioimages/Getty Images Royalty-Free; **8–9** Wide Group/Getty Images; **9** *top* George H. H. Huey/Corbis; **10** Illustration by Geoff Kornfeld; *bottom left* Gianna Dagli Orti/Corbis; *top left* Getty Images/Royalty-Free; *center left* Keith Dannemiller/Corbis; **12** *center right* Frans Lemmens/Getty Images; **13** *center right* Erich Lessing/Art Resource, NY; *top right* Sandro Vannini/Corbis; **14** Werner Forman Archive; **16** SSPL/The Image Works; **17** *center right* Stock Montage/Getty Images; *top right* Bibliothèque Universitaire de Mèdecine, Montpellier/Dagli Orti/The Art Archive; **18** The Granger Collection, New York; **19** *center* Sandro Vannini/Corbis; *right* Bibliothèque Universitaire de Mèdecine, Montpellier/Dagli Orti/The Art Archive; *left* Werner Forman/Art Resource, NY; **20** Four pocket compasses (wood & brass) by German School, (15th century) © British Museum, London, UK/© Boltin Picture Library/The Bridgeman Art Library; **21** *top* Werner Forman/Art Resource, NY; *bottom left* Biblioteca Augusta Perugia/Dagli Orti/The Art Archive; **22** North Wind Pictures Archive/Alamy; **23** *The Venetian Ambassador's Interview in an Oriental City or, The Reception of Domenico Trevisani in Cairo in 1512* (oil on panel), Italian School, (16th century)/Louvre, Paris, France, Giraudon/The Bridgeman Art Library International; **24–25** Library of Congress, Washington, DC; **24** *bottom left* Museum of Modern Art Mexico/Dagli Orti/The Art Archive; *bottom right* Inca kero, or wooden beaker, Southern Highlands, Peru, 16th century © British Museum, London, UK/The Bridgeman Art Library; **25** *center* Jeffrey L. Rotman/Corbis; *bottom* The Granger Collection, New York; **26** New-York Historical Society, New York, USA/The Bridgeman Art Library; **27** *top right* Museo de la Torre del Oro Seville/Dagli Orti/The Art Archive; *center* Snark/Art Resource, NY; **28** Monastery of the Rabida, Palos, Spain/Dagli Orti/The Art Archive; **29** Archivo Iconografico, S.A./Corbis; **31** Bildarchiv Preussischer Kulturbesitz/Art Resource, NY; **32** *right* American Museum of Natural History, New York, USA/The Bridgeman Art Library; *left* Gianni Dagli Orti/Corbis; **34** *The Launching of English Fireships on the Spanish Fleet off Calais with Queen Elizabeth I (1533-1603) on Horseback on Shore*, by Flemish School, (17th century) Private Collection/Rafael Valls Gallery, London, UK/The Bridgeman Art Library; **35** *center* Bettmann/Corbis; *top right* Museo de la Torre del Oro Seville/Dagli Orti/The Art Archive; **37** Elizabeth I, Armada portrait, c.1588 (oil on panel), English School, (16th century)/Private Collection/The Bridgeman Art Library; **40** Tom Bean/Corbis; **41** *center right* The Granger Collection, New York; *top right* Museo de la Torre del Oro Seville/Dagli Orti/The Art Archive; **42** Bettmann/Corbis; **43** Helmet and Shield: Collection of the Oakland Museum of California, Gifts of Herbert Hamlin and Dr. W. Michael Mathes. Body Armor: The DeYoung Museum of San Francisco; **48** *Slaves Below Deck of Albanez* (date unknown), Francis Meynell. Copyright © National Maritime Museum Picture Library, London.; **49** *center* Fotomas Index/Bridgeman Art Library; *top right* Museo de la Torre del Oro Seville/Dagli Orti/The Art Archive; **50** *Portrait of a Negro Man*, c.1780 (oil on canvas), Ramsay, Allan (1713-84) (attr. to)/Royal Albert Memorial Museum, Exeter, Devon, UK/The Bridgeman Art Library International; **51** Corbis; **53** *top* Museo de la Torre del Oro Seville/Dagli Orti/The Art Archive; *bottom right* Museum of Modern Art Mexico/Dagli Orti/The Art Archive; *bottom left* Archivo Iconografico, S.A./Corbis; **54** Museo de la Torre del Oro Seville/Dagli Orti/The Art Archive; **55** Museo de America Madrid Dagli Orti/The Art Archive.

**Unit 2**
**56–57** *Old State House*, Boston, 1801 (oil on panel) by Marston, James Brown (1775-1817) Massachusetts Historical Society, Boston, MA, USA/The Bridgeman Art Library; **58** *bottom left* Getty Images; *bottom center* Tobacco plant (nicotiana tabacum) (1633), woodcut from Thomas Johnson's "Herball"/The Granger Collection, New York; **59** *bottom* British Library/HIP/Art Resource, New York, New York; *center* Penn's Treaty With the Indians (1830 - 1840), Edward Hicks. Oil on canvas. The Bayou Bend Collection, gift of Alice C. Simkins in memory of Alice Nicholson Hanszen/Museum of Fine Arts, Houston (B.77.46) Photograph by Francis G. Mayer/Corbis; **61** *top right* Richard T. Nowitz/Corbis; *center* Carolina Algonquin Indians Fishing (ca. 1585), John White. Watercolor. The Granger Collection,

New York; **63** Detail, *Pochahontas, Daughter of Powhatan Chief* (ca 1616), Anonymous, after 1616 engraving by Simon van de Passe. Oil on canvas, 76.8 cm x 64.1 cm. National Portrait Gallery, Smithsonian Institution, Washington, DC/Art Resource, New York; **64** Spencer Platt/Getty Images; **65** New Line/Merie W. Wallace/The Kobal Collection ; **67** *center John Winthrop* (1834), Charles Osgood, after portrait by anonymous artist. Oil on canvas. The Granger Collection, New York; *top right* Richard T. Nowitz/Corbis; **68** Richard T. Nowitz/Corbis; **69** *inset* Tim Wright/Corbis; **70** Culver Pictures/The Art Archive; **71** *The Hanging of Mary Dyer* (1906), Basil King. Lithograph, after Howard Pyle/The Bridgeman Art Library; **73** Toby Talbot/AP Images; **74** Joseph Sohm/The Image Works; **76** Library of Congress Prints and Photographs Division (LC-USZ62-61452); **77** Illustration by Christian Hook; *top right* Richard T. Nowitz/Corbis; **79** The Colonial Williamsburg Foundation; **80** *inset* The Granger Collection, New York; **82** The Granger Collection, New York; **83** *center* Stock Montage/Getty Images; *top right* Richard T. Nowitz/Corbis; **85** Illustrations by Andrew Wheatcroft; *all* The Colonial Williamsburg Foundation; *cap* The Colonial Williamsburg Foundation. Gift of Mrs. Cora Ginsburg; **87** *top right* Richard T. Nowitz/Corbis; *bottom* Mary Evans Picture Library ; *top left* Snark/Art Resorce, New York; **88** Merie W. Wallace/New Line/The Kobal Collection; **89** *top left* Richard T. Nowitz/Corbis; *bottom left John Winthrop* (1834), Charles Osgood, after portrait by anonymous artist. Oil on canvas. The Granger Collection, New York; **91** Public Domain; **92** *bottom left* The Granger Collection, New York; *center left* Howard Pyle/The Granger Collection, New York; **93** *bottom* The Granger Collection, New York; **95** *center Self-Portrait* (ca. 1680),Thomas Smith. Oil on canvas, 24.75 x 23.75 inches. Worcester Art Museum, Worcester, Massachusetts. Museum Purchase (1948.19); *top right* Detail, *Southeast Prospect of the City of Philadelphia* (1720), Peter Cooper. Oil on canvas, 20" x 87". The Library Company of Philadelphia; **97** *right* Mary Evans Picture Library; *left* © 2001, 2006 Stars and Stripes. Used with permission.; **98** *right inset Trade Castles and Forts of West Africa* (Stanford University Press, 1964), A.W. Lawrence. Plate 44; taken from "Tilforladelig Efterretning om Kysten Guinea" ("A reliable account of the coast of Guinea"), Ludwig Romer (Copenhagen, 1760)/Stanford University Press; *left inset* The Granger Collection, New York; *left* Hulton Archive/Getty Images; **100** *right John Freake* (ca.1671-1674), Anonymous. Oil on canvas, 42.5 x 36.8 inches. Worcester Art Museum, Worcester, Massachusetts. Sarah C. Garver Fund (1963.135) ; *left Portrait of Elizabeth Clarke Freake and Baby Mary* (ca. 1671-1674), Anonymous. Oil on canvas, 42.5 x 36.8 inches. Worcester Art Museum, Worcester, Massachusetts. Gift of Mr. and Mrs. Albert W. Rice (1963.134) ; **101** North Wind Picture Archives; **102** *yarn* Dorothy Miller; *indigo plant* The New York Botanical Garden; **103** *center right George Mason of Gunston Hall* (1858), Louis Mathieu Didier Guillaume, after John Hesselius. Oil on canvas, 76.20 x 63.50 cm (30 x 25 inches). (1858.2) Virginia Historical Society; *top right* Detail, *Southeast Prospect of the City of Philadelphia* (1720), Peter Cooper. Oil on canvas, 20" x 87". The Library Company of Philadelphia; **106** Angelo Hornak/Corbis; **108** David Lyons/Alamy; **108–109** Illustration by Sebastian Quigley/Linden Artists Ltd.; **110** The Granger Collection, New York; **111** *center right Penn's Treaty With the Indians* (1830 - 1840), Edward Hicks. Oil on canvas. The Bayou Bend Collection, gift of Alice C. Simkins in memory of Alice Nicholson Hanszen/Museum of Fine Arts, Houston (B.77.46) Photograph by Francis G. Mayer/Corbis; *top right* Detail, *Southeast Prospect of the City of Philadelphia* (1720), Peter Cooper. Oil on canvas, 20" x 87". The Library Company of Philadelphia; **112** Lithograph, 1875/The Granger Collection, New York; **113** Royalty-Free/Corbis; **114** Photograph by John Schilling, Courtesy of Peter Wentz Farmstead, Department of Parks and Heritage Services, Montgomery County PA; **116** Ric Ergenbright; **117** Illustration by Roger Stewart; *top right* Detail, *Southeast Prospect of the City of Philadelphia* (1720), Peter Cooper. Oil on canvas, 20" x 87". The Library Company of Philadelphia; **118** *inset* Michael P. Gadomski/Photo Researchers, Inc.; **121** *top left* Detail, *Southeast Prospect of the City of Philadelphia* (1720), Peter Cooper. Oil on canvas, 20" x 87". The Library Company of Philadelphia; *bottom left* New York Botanical Garden; **124** *both* The Granger Collection, New York; **125** *bottom right* Stuart Dee/Getty Images; *bottom left* The Granger Collection, New York; **126** Colonial Williamsburg Foundation; **127** *center* Illustration from Henry Mouzon, Jr., "Map of the Parish of St. Stephen's in Craven County" (1775), South Carolina Historical Society; *top right* Colonial Williamsburg Foundation; *bottom* Gown, silk textile 1740s, remodeled 1780-1795, silk damask with appliquéd silk. From the collection of Doris Langley Moore. The Colonial Williamsburg Foundation; **129** Colonial Williamsburg Foundation; **130** *top* The Granger Collection, New York; *center, bottom* Library of Congress Prints and Photographs Division; **131** Colonial Williamsburg Foundation; **132** *Benjamin Franklin* (ca. 1785),

Joseph Siffred Duplessis. Oil on canvas, 72.4 x 59.6 cm. National Portrait Gallery, Smithsonian Institution, Washington, DC. Gift of the Morris and Gwendolyn Cafritz Foundation/Art Resource, New York; **133** *Franklin's Experiment, June, 1752* (1876), Currier & Ives. Museum of the City of New York/Corbis; **134–135** Illustrations by Luigi Galante; **135** The Colonial Williamsburg Foundation; **136** British Picture Library; **137** *center Increase Mather* (1688), Jan Van Spriett. Oil on canvas. Massachusetts Historical Society/The Granger Collection, New York; *top right* The Colonial Wiliamsburg Foundation; **138** David Frazier/Getty Images; **139** The Granger Collection, New York; **140** Illustrations by Rogue Element; **142** *Death of General Richard Montgomery* (1865 ), Alonzo Chappel. Oil on canvas. Chicago Historical Museum/The Bridgeman Art Library; **143** *center* The Granger Collection, New York; *top right* The Colonial Wiliamsburg Foundation; **145** *inset* Detail, *Braddock's Defeat* (1903), Edward Deming. State Historical Society of Wisconsin Museum Collection, SHSW #42.488; **147** The Granger Collection, New York; **149** *top left* The Colonial Wiliamsburg Foundation; *bottom left* Detail, *Benjamin Franklin* (ca. 1785), Joseph Siffred Duplessis. Oil on canvas, 72.4 x 59.6 cm. National Portrait Gallery, Smithsonian Institution, Washington, DC. Gift of the Morris and Gwendolyn Cafritz Foundation/Art Resource, New York; **151** *The Death of General Wolfe* (ca. 1771), Benjamin West. Oil on panel, 43.2 x 61 cm. Private collection/The Bridgeman Art Library.

Unit 3

**152–153** Burstein Collection/Corbis; **154** Illustration by Thomas Bayley; *right* Military and Historical Image Bank; *left George III* (ca. 1762), Alfter Allan Ramsay. Oil on canvas. Scottish National Portrait Gallery, Edinburgh, Scotland/The Bridgeman Art Library; **155** *bottom left* Pennsylvania Society of the Sons of the Revolution; *bottom right* Don Troiani/Military and Historical Image Bank; **156** *George III* (1794), David Dodd. Oil on canvas. Private Collection/The Bridgeman Art Library; **157** *center Mrs. Richard Bache (Sarah Franklin)* (1793), John Hoppner. Oil on canvas, 30 1/8 x 24 7/8 inches. (76.5 x 63.2 cm). Catherine Lorillard Wolfe Collection, Wolfe Fund, 1901 (01.20),The Metropolitan Museum of Art, New York; *top right* Colored engraving (1770), Paul Revere. The Granger Collection, New York; **158** *bottom* Emmet Collection, Manuscripts and Archives Division, The New York Public Library; *top* The Granger Collection, New York; **159** The Granger Collection, New York; **161** Illustration by Patrick Faricy; *top right* Colored engraving (1770), Paul Revere. The Granger Collection, New York; **162** *window* Colonial Williamsburg Foundation; *dress* The Granger Collection, New York; *clock* Georgian longcase clock with marquetry case, 18th century/ Private Collection/Bonhams, London/The Bridgeman Art Library; *fabric* Floral design with peonies, lilies and roses for Spitalfields silk (1744), Anna Maria Garthwaite/Victoria and Albert Museum/The Bridgeman Art Library; *book The Constitutions of the Freemasons* (1723), Dr James Anderson, London/Bibliotheque Nationale, Paris/ Archives Charmet/The Bridgeman Art Library; *telescope* Reflecting Table Telescope (18th century), English. Brass and leather. Private Collection/The Bridgeman Art Library; *glasses* Wine glasses, (18th century), English. Private Collection/The Bridgeman Art Library; **164** Colored engraving (1770), Paul Revere. The Granger Collection, New York; **165** *right John Adams after 1783* (Detail) (ca. 1783), Anonymous, after John Singleton Copley. Oil on canvas, 20 1/4 x 13 5/8 inches (51.43 x 34.61 cm). Seth K. Sweetser Fund (23.180), Museum of Fine Arts, Boston; *left Samuel Adams* (Detail) (ca. 1772), John Singleton Copley. Oil on canvas, 49 1/2 x 39 1/2 inches (125.73 x 100.33 cm). Deposited by the City of Boston (L-R 30.76c), Museum of Fine Arts, Boston; **167** *right A Society of Patriotic Ladies* (1775), Philip Dawe. Mezzotint. British Cartoon Collection, (LC-USZC4-4617) Library of Congress; *left* Library of Congress, Prints and Photographs Division (LC-USZC4-1583); *bottom* The Granger Collection, New York; **168** *Paul Revere* (1768), John Singleton Copley. Oil on canvas, 35 1/8 x 28 1/2 inches (89.22 x 72.39 cm). Gift of Joseph W. Revere, William B. Revere and Edward H. R. Revere (30.781), Museum of Fine Arts, Boston; **169** *center* Art Resource, New York; *top right* Colored engraving (1770), Paul Revere. The Granger Collection, New York; **170** Bettmann/Corbis; **171** The Granger Collection, New York; **172** *Abigail Smith Adams* (ca. 1766), Benjamin Blyth. Pastel on paper, 57.3 x 44.8 cm. Massachusetts Historical Society, Boston MA/Corbis; **173** Illustration, Bibby's Annual (1909), Ernest Crofts. Mary Evans Picture Library; **175** McDougal Littell/Houghton Mifflin Co.; **176** Detail, *Thomas Jefferson* (1786), Mather Brown. Oil on canvas, 90.8 x 72.4 cm. Bequest of Charles Francis Adams, National Portrait Gallery, Smithsonian Institution/Art Resource, New York; **177** *center Mrs. Gage* (1771), John Singleton Copley. Oil on canvas. Private Collection/The Bridgeman Art Library ; *top right* Colored engraving (1770), Paul Revere. The Granger Collection, New York; **179** Lauren McFalls/McDougal Littell/Houghton Mifflin Co.; **180** *both*

Acknowledgments **R77**

The Granger Collection, New York; **181** *all* Pennsylvania Society of the Sons of the Revolution; **182** *all* The Granger Collection, New York; **184** The Granger Collection, New York; **189** *top left* Colored engraving (1770), Paul Revere. The Granger Collection, New York; *bottom right* Don Troiani/Military and Historical Image Bank; *bottom left* The Granger Collection, New York; **191** Military and Historical Image Bank; **192** *bottom left* The Granger Collection, New York; **193** *bottom right* National Park Service, Harpers Ferry Center, artist Don Troiani http://www.cr.nps.gov/museum/exhibits/revwar/image_gal/vafoimg//csfront.html; *bottom left* Guilford Courthouse National Military Park; **195** *top right* Bob Krist/Corbis; *center right* *The Copley Family* (1776/1777), John Singleton Copley. Oil on canvas, 1.841 m x 2.292 m (72 1/2" x 90 1/4"). Andrew W. Mellon Fund, © 1999 Board of Trustees, National Gallery of Art, Washington DC; **196** *both* North Wind Picture Archives; **197** Réunion des Musées Nationaux/Art Resource, NY; **199** The Granger Collection, New York; **200** Photo courtesy of the Historical and Military Image Bank www.historicalimagebank.com; **202** *center left* Albert Konschak; *bottom left* Richard T. Nowitz/Corbis; **208** *top left* Albert Konschak; **202–203** Illustration by Sebastian Quigley/Linden Artists Ltd.; **203** *top right* Kelly Culpepper/Transparencies, Inc.; **204** Photograph courtesy Peabody Essex Museum, Joseph Howard, Watercolor 19 3/4 x 27 3/4 in. Built 1799, Salem, MA, 850 tons. ; **205** *center right* www.davidrwagner.com; *top right* Bob Krist/Corbis; **206** British Cartoon Collection, Library of Congress, (LC-USZ62-45442); **207** *Marquis de Lafayette* (1757-1834), c.1781-85 (oil on canvas) by Francesco Giuseppe Casanova (c.1732-1803), New-York Historical Society, New York, USA/Bridgeman Art Library; **208** *top left* Courtesy National Park Service, Museum Management Program and Guilford Courthouse, National Military Park, GUCO 1603 http://www.cr.nps.gov/museum/exhibits/revwar/image_gal/gucoimg/guco1603amputation.html; **208** *top right* Valley Forge National Historical Park ; *bottom left* National Park Service, Harpers Ferry Center, artist Don Troiani, http://www.cr.nps.gov/museum/exhibits/revwar/image_gal/gucoimg/medicalcare.html; *right* North Wind Picture Archives; **209** *George Rogers Clark* (1976), Rosemary Brown Beck. Oil on canvas. From the Collection of the Indiana State Museum and Historic Sites; **210** Historical Society of Pennsylvania (HSP), James Forten, n.d., Leon Gardiner Collection; **211** *top right* The Granger Collection, New York; **212** Robert K. Ander; **213** *center right* Andy Thomas; *top right* Bob Krist/Corbis; **214** *left* The Granger Collection, New York; *right* Heribert Proepper/AP Images; **217** The Granger Collection, New York; **218** Illustrations by Rogue Element; **220** *both* The Granger Collection, New York; **221** *center right* William L. Clements Library, University of Michigan; *center left* National Portrait Gallery, Smithsonian Institution/Art Resource, NY; *top right* The Granger Collection, New York; **222** The Granger Collection, New York; **223** *center right* United States Postal Service. All rights reserved. Used with permisssion/The Granger Collection, New York; *top right* Bob Krist/Corbis; **224** Illustrations by Rogue Element; **226** The Granger Collection, New York; **227** *inset* The Granger Collection, New York; *frame* PhotoDisc/Getty Images; **229** *top* Bob Krist/Corbis; *bottom* The Granger Collection, New York; **230** *Marquis de Lafayette* (1757-1834), c.1781-85 (oil on canvas) by Francesco Giuseppe Casanova (c.1732-1803), New-York Historical Society, New York, USA/Bridgeman Art Library; **231** The Granger Collection, New York; **232** *bottom left* The Granger Collection, New York; *bottom right* American flag, c.1781 (wool & cotton), American School, (18th century)/© Collection of the New-York Historical Society, USA,/The Bridgeman Art Library International; **233** *bottom right* Peggy & Ronald Barnett/Corbis; *bottom left* The Granger Collection, New York; **235** *center right* The Granger Collection, New York; *top right* Bettmann/Corbis; **238** *View of New Orleans from the Plantation of Marigny, 1803* (oil on canvas), Woiseri, J. L. Bouquet de (fl.1797-1815)/© Chicago Historical Museum, USA,/The Bridgeman Art Library International; **240** *center left* The Granger Collection, New York; *bottom right* Ohio Historical Society; **241** Illustration by Roger Stewart; *survey tool* Copyright © John E. Fletcher & Arlan R. Wiler/National Geographic Image Collection; **243** *center inset* The Granger Collection, New York; *center right* Dennis Degnan/Corbis; *top right* Bettmann/Corbis; **244** Corbis; **249** *center right* The Granger Collection, New York; *top* Bettmann/Corbis; **250** *right* *John Jay* (1745-1829) 1786 (oil on canvas), Wright of Derby, Joseph (1734-97)/© Collection of the New-York Historical Society, USA,/The Bridgeman Art Library International; *left* Bettmann/Corbis; **251** Bettmann/Corbis; **252** AP Images; **253** Bettmann/Corbis; **256** *bottom left* Corbis; **257** *top left* Bettmann/Corbis; **259** *The Constitutional Convention, 1787*, by Allen Cox, Negative # 70681. Architect of the Capitol; **260** *center left* The Granger Collection, New York; *bottom right* Bettman/Corbis; **261** *top left* Norm Dettlaff/AP Images; *center right* Karen Kasmauski/Corbis; *bottom left* Mike Lane; **262** J. L. Atlan/Corbis Sygma; **263** Steve Warmowski/Jacksonville Journal-Courier/The Image Works; **264** Illustrations by Rogue Element; **265** *top right* Terry Ashe/Time Life Pictures/Getty Images; *center right*

David Bacon/The Image Works; **266** *top* National Archives; *bottom left* Richard T. Nowitz/Corbis; **267** The Granger Collection, New York; **268** Peter Lennihan/AP Images; **269** Bettman/Corbis; **270–271** Illustrations by Rogue Element; **271** Jay Penni/McDougal Littell/Houghton Mifflin Co.; **272** *bottom left* Ahn Young-Joon/AP Images; *bottom center* U.S. Navy/Handout/CNP/Corbis; *bottom left* George Hall/Corbis; **273** *bottom left* Brownie Harris/Corbis; **273** *bottom right* Reuters/Corbis; **274** Royalty-Free/Corbis; **276** Illustrations by Rogue Element; **277** Bettmann/Corbis; **278** *top right* Library of Congress, Washington, DC (cwpb 01131); *center left* The Granger Collection, New York; *top left* Eric Draper/White House/Handout/CNP/Corbis; *center right* Wally McNamee/Corbis; *bottom* Bettmann/Corbis; **280** Mark Wilson, Staff/Getty Images; **283** Jack Kurtz/The Image Works; **284** Mike Theiler/Reuters/Corbis; **286** *top left* The Granger Collection, New York; **286–287** Tom Dodge/AP Images; **287** *bottom right* Spencer Grant/PhotoEdit; **288** Alan Klehr/Getty Images; **289** The Granger Collection, New York; **290** Getty Images; **291** 1976 Matt Herron/Take Stock; **292** The Granger Collection, New York; **293** Bettmann/Corbis; **294** Bettmann/Corbis; **295** Francis Miller/Getty Images; **296** *bottom center* Wedgwood Slave Emancipation Society medallion, c.1787-90 (jasperware) by William Hackwood (c.1757-1829), © Private Collection/The Bridgeman Art Library; *bottom left* The Granger Collection, New York; *top right* Associated Press, AP Images; **297** *bottom center* The Art Archive/Museum of the City of New York/47.225.12; *bottom right* Franklin D. Roosevelt Library; **299** Bob Lang; **301** Bettmann/Corbis; Seth Wenig/Reuters/Corbis; **303** *bottom* Will & Deni McIntyre/Corbis; *center right* Royalty-Free/Corbis; **304** NewsCom/PR Newswire; **305** Mary Kate Denny/PhotoEdit; **306** Michael Newman/PhotoEdit.

Unit 4

**308–309** Yale University New Haven/The Art Archive; **310** *bottom left* Library of Congress, Washington, DC (cph 3b52213); *bottom center* SSPL/The Image Works; **311** *bottom left* Birthplaces of John Adams and John Quincy Adams, G. Frankenstein (1849). Courtesy of the National Park Service, Adams National Historical Park; *bottom center* Chateau de Blerancourt/Dagli Orti/The Art Archive; **312** Larry Downing/Reuters/Corbis; **313** *top right* The Granger Collection, New York; *center right* New York Times; **314** The Granger Collection, New York; **315** North Wind Picture Archives; **316** Illustrations by Rogue Element; **319** *center right* North Wind Picture Archives; *top right* The Granger Collection, New York; **320** Ohio Historical Society; **322** *The Women of Les Halles Marching to Versailles, 5th October 1789* (watercolor on paper) Jean-Francois Janinet (1752-1814) © Bibliotheque Nationale, Paris, France/Archives Charmet/The Bridgeman Art Library; **324** *bottom right* The Philadelphia Museum of Art/Art Resource, NY; *top right* Library of Congress, Washington, DC (LC-USZ62-88324); *bottom left* American Numismatic Society; **325** *center left* Joseph Sohm/Visions of America/Corbis; *bottom left* Andre Jenny/Alamy; *top right* British Museum/HIP/Art Resource, New York; *center, bottom center* Dagli Orti/The Art Archive; *center right* John Hicks/Corbis; **327** *both* The Granger Collection, New York; **328** Fenimore Art Museum, Cooperstown, NY; **329** Illustration by Andrew Wheatcroft; **330** The Granger Collection, New York; **331** Photos courtesy of the Military & Historical Image Bank www.historicalimagebank.com; **333** *top left* The Granger Collection, New York; **333** *bottom left* Chateau de Blerancourt/Dagli Orti/The Art Archive; **334** *bottom* A Thames Wharf, c1750 Samuel Scott, oil on canvas, Victoria & Albert Museum, London, UK/The Bridgeman Art Library ; **336** *bottom left* Smithsonian American Art Musuem, Washington, DC/Art Resource, NY; *bottom right* The Granger Collection, New York; **336–337** Library of Congress, Prints and Photographs Division (g3300-ct000584); **337** *center left* From the Archives of the Ernst Mayr Library of the Museum of Comparative Zoology, Harvard University; *bottom left* © 2006 Harvard University, Peabody Museum, 99-12-10/53110.2 T3042.1.1; *bottom right* Bettmann/Corbis; **339** *center right* Smithsonian Institution; *top right* Monticello/Thomas Jefferson Foundation, Inc.; **340** *top right* Thomas Jefferson Polygraph, Special Collections, University of Virginia Library (image provided by Monticello/Thomas Jefferson Foundation, Inc.); *all others* Monticello/Thomas Jefferson Foundation, Inc.; **342** *Chief Justice John Marshall* (date unknown). Rembrandt Peale. Oil on canvas. Collection of the Supreme Court of the United States; **344** *both* Independence National History Park; **345** *top right* Monticello/Thomas Jefferson Foundation, Inc.; *center right* The Granger Collection, New York; **347** *top* Sam Abell/National Geographic Image Collection; *center right* Historical Picture Archive/Corbis; *all others* Smithsonian American Art Museum, Washington, DC/(Detail) Art Resource, New York; **348** *right* Library of Congress, Washington, DC; *left* The Granger Collection, New York; **350** *bottom* Navaswan/Taxi/Getty Images; *top* David Muench Photography; **351** *top left* David Muench/Corbis; *top right* Connie Ricca/Corbis; *center left* Annie Griffiths Belt/Corbis; *bottom right* Olivier Cirendini/Lonely Planet Images; **352** The Granger Collection, New York; **353** *center* *right* The Granger Collection, New York; *top right* Monticello/Thomas Jefferson Foundation, Inc.; **354** *both* The Granger Collection, New York; **356** Bettmann/Corbis; **357** Brooklyn Museum/Corbis; **359** *top left* Monticello/Thomas Jefferson Foundation, Inc.; *bottom right* Smithsonian American Art Musuem, Washington, DC/Art Resource, NY; *bottom left* The Granger Collection, New York; **360** *both* The Granger Collection, New York; **361** The Granger Collection, New York; **362** *bottom right Portrait of Euphemia Toussaint,* c.1825 (miniature on ivory) by Meucci, Anthony (fl.1825) © Collection of the New-York Historical Society, USA/The Bridgeman Art Library; *bottom left* Hulton Archive/Getty Images; **363** *bottom center* Collection of The New-York Historical Society, negative number X.48; *bottom right* National Museum of American History, Smithsonian Institution. Negative # 74-2491; **364** Hulton Archive/Getty Images; **365** *both* American Textile History Museum; **366** *background* The Granger Collection, New York; *inset* David H. Wells/Corbis; **367** The Granger Collection, New York; **368** *center* Thomas Kraft/TRANSTOCK INC.; *bottom* Michael Freeman/Corbis; *center left* Photo By Stock Montage/Getty Images; *top* The Granger Collection, New York; **370** *top left, center left* Bettmann/Corbis; *bottom left* Corbis; **370–371** Illustration by Michael Mundy; **372** National Museum of American History, Smithsonian Institution; **373** *center right* Library of Congress, Prints and Photographs Division; *top right* American Textile History Museum; **375** *right* Tim Rand/Getty Images; *left* The Granger Collection, New York; **376** *Nat Turner (1800-31) with fellow insurgent slaves during the Slave Rebellion of 1831* (coloured engraving) by American School, (19th century) © Private Collection/Peter Newark American Pictures/The Bridgeman Art Library; **377** *inset* The Granger Collection, New York; *top right* Art Media/Heritage-Images/The Image Works; **378** Joseph Sohm; ChromoSohm Inc./Corbis; **379** *center right Portrait of Henry Clay (1777-1852)* (oil on canvas) by Jarvis, John Wesley (1780-1840) Private Collection/© Christie's Images/The Bridgeman Art Library ; *top right* American Textile History Museum; **381** SSPL/The Image Works; **383** Hulton Archive/Getty Images; **385** Bettmann/Corbis; **387** *top* American Textile History Museum; *bottom left* National Museum of American History, Smithsonian Institution; *bottom right* Bettmann/Corbis; **388** *right* Bettmann/Corbis; *left* Stock Montage/Getty Images.

### Unit 5

**390–391** *Three American Indian Chiefs, c.1900* (photogravure) (b&w photo) by Curtis, Edward Sheriff (1868-1952) Private Collection/The Bridgeman Art Library; **392** *left* The Granger Collection, New York; **392** *right* Bettmann/Corbis; **393** *left* North Wind Picture Archives/Alamy; *right* The Granger Collection, New York; **394** Chateau de Blerancourt/Dagli Orti/The Art Archive; **395** *center right Margaret Bayard Smith,* Charles Bird King. Oil on canvas. Redwood Library and Athenaem, Newport, Rhode Island, www.redwoodlibrary.com; *top right* Sonda Dawes/The Image Works; **396** Topham/The Image Works; **397** Michael Dwyer/AP Images; **399** Illustration by Vilma Ortiz-Dillon; **400** *top* Corbis; *bottom* The Art Archive/Culver Pictures; **401** *Henry Clay (1777-1852)* (b/w photo) by American Photographer, (19th century) Private Collection/Peter Newark American Pictures/The Bridgeman Art Library ; *frame* PhotoDisc/Getty Images; **402** The Granger Collection, New York; **403** *center right* Library of Congress, Washington, DC (LC-USZC4-2566); *top right* Sonda Dawes/The Image Works; **404** *Sash, c.1820s* (wool and beads) American School (19th century), © Peabody Essex Museum, Salem, Massachusetts, USA/The Bridgeman Art Library ; **406** Billy E. Barnes/PhotoEdit; **407** *Portrait of Osceola (1804-38)* (oil on canvas), George Catlin (1794-1872)/Private Collection/The Bridgeman Art Library; **408** Bettmann/Corbis; **409** *center right* The Art Archive/National Archives Washington, DC; *top right* Sonda Dawes/The Image Works; **410** Panoramic Images/Getty Images; **411** The Granger Collection, New York; **412** The Granger Collection, New York; **413** *bottom left* Bettmann/Corbis; *top left* Sonda Dawes/The Image Works; **414** The Granger Collection, New York; **415** The Granger Collection, New York; **416** *bottom right* Courtesy of the Oakland Museum of California; *bottom left* Smithsonian American Art Museum, Washington, DC/(Detail)Art Resource, New York; **416–417** Ric Ergenbright; **417** *bottom left* Courtesy of the Oakland Museum of California; *bottom center* Photos courtesy of the Military & Historical Image Bank www.historicalimagebank.com; *center right* Gift of Ruth Koerner Oliver/Buffalo Bill Historical Center, Cody, Wyoming/The Art Archive; **419** *inset* The Granger Collection, New York; *center right* William Manning/Corbis; *top right* Robert Y. Ono/Corbis; **420** The Granger Collection, New York; **421** *inset* Museum of the American West/Autry National Center; **422** *bottom left* James L. Amos/Corbis; *top* Royalty-Free/Getty Images; *center right* Museum of the American West/Autry National Center; *bottom right* James L. Amos/Corbis; **424** *top left* North Wind/Nancy Carter/North Wind Picture Archives; *center left* David Muench/Corbis; *bottom left* The Granger Collection, New York; **424–425** Illustration by Steve Weston/Linden Artists Ltd.; **426** Richard Cummins/Corbis; **427** *center right* Prints and Photographs Collection, Mary Austin Holley File, The Center for American History, The University of Texas at Austin; CN00165; *top right* Robert Y. Ono/Corbis; **428** *both* The Granger Collection, New York; **429** The Granger Collection, New York; **430** Courtesy of the State Preservation Board, Austin, Texas (CHA 1989.96). Photograph by Perry Huston; **432** *right* Library of Congress Prints and Photographs Division (LC-USZC2-3798); *left* Courtesy of the California History Room, California State Library, Sacramento, California; **433** *center right* The Granger Collection, New York; *top right* Robert Y. Ono/Corbis; **437** Christie's Images/Corbis; **438** *center right* Courtesy of the Oakland Museum of California; **439** *center right* Courtesy of the California History Room, California State Library, Sacramento, California ; *top right* Robert Y. Ono/Corbis; **440** *inset* Courtesy of The Bancroft Library University of California, Berkeley, General Vallejo. Houseworth & Co. Photographs. Houseworth's Souvenir Photographs: 5; *top left* Courtesy of The Bancroft Library University of California, Berkeley, Shaw, S. W., artist Kuchel & Dresel (active ca. 1853-ca. 1865), lithographer Britton & Rey (active 1851-1902), printer [18--] lithograph, color 53.9 x 68.8 cm. ; **441** Sherwin Crasto/Reuters/Corbis; **442** Courtesy of the Oakland Museum of California; **444** *bottom left* The Granger Collection, New York; *center right* Collection of the Oakland Museum of California, Gift of Anonymous Donor. Photography by Isaac W. Baker; *top right* The Granger Collection, New York; **445** *top left* Robert Y. Ono/Corbis; *bottom right* Courtesy of the State Preservation Board, Austin, Texas. CHA 1989.96, Photographer Perry Huston, 7/28/95, post conservation.; *bottom left* The Granger Collection, New York; **446** The Granger Collection, New York; **448** *bottom right* Stuart Ramson/AP Images; *bottom left View of St. Paul's Chapel and the Broadway Stages, New York* (color litho), American School, (19th century) /, © Collection of the New-York Historical Society, USA /The Bridgeman Art Library International; **449** Emigrant illustrations by Rogue Element; *others* The Granger Collection, New York; **450** Courtesy of the Milwaukee County Historical Society, Milwaukee, Wisconsin; **451** *both* Museum of the City of New York/Corbis; **454** Brown Brothers; **455** Library of Congress, Washington, DC; **457** *center right* The Granger Collection, New York; *top right* Museum of the City of New York/Corbis; **458** Archive Photos/Getty Images; **459** Brown Brothers; **460** Lauren McFalls/McDougal Littell/Houghton Mifflin Co.; **461** *top right* NBAE/Getty Images; *inset* Will & Deni McIntyre/Getty Images; **462** *left* Bettmann/Corbis; **464** *center right* The Granger Collection, New York; **465** *center right* General Research & Reference Division, Schomburg Center for Research and Black Culture, The New York Public Library, Astor, Lenox and Tilden Foundations; *top right* Museum of the City of New York/Corbis **466** Detail, *Frederick Douglass* (1844), Elisha Hammond. Oil on canvas, 69.9 cm x 71.1 cm. National Portrait Gallery, Smithsonian Institution/Art Resource, New York; **467** Hulton Archive/Getty Images; **468** *left* Mike Simons/Getty Images; *right* Library of Congress Prints and Photographs Division (LC-USZC4-4659); **469** *top right* Corbis; **470** *bottom right* Stuart Ramson/AP Images; **472** McDougal Littell/Houghton Mifflin Co.; **473** *top* Museum of the City of New York/Corbis; *bottom right* The Granger Collection, New York; *bottom left* Detail, *Frederick Douglass* (1844), Elisha Hammond. Oil on canvas, 69.9 cm x 71.1 cm. National Portrait Gallery, Smithsonian Institution/Art Resource, New York; **474** *bottom* Copyright © Collection of The New York Historical Society/The Bridgeman Art Library; *center* Bettmann/Corbis; **475** The Granger Collection, New York.

### Unit 6

**476–477** Carolyn Kaster/AP Images; Don Burk/AP Images; **478** *cards* (ca. 1850), American. Color lithograph. Dallas Historical Society, Texas/The Bridgeman Art Library; *bottom right* Schomburg Center/Art Resource, NY; **479** *both* The Granger Collection, New York; **481** *both* The Granger Collection, New York; **482** Illustrations by Rogue Element; **483** David J. and Janice Frent Collection; **484** *top right* Bettmann/Corbis; *center inset* Lithograph, Robertson, Seibert & Shearman, New York, ca.1859. Library of Congress Prints and Photographs Division (LC-USZC2-2356); **485** Stock Montage/Getty Images; **486** The Granger Collection, New York; **488** *bottom inset Bird's-Eye View of New Orleans and Suburbs* (1873), American School. Color lithograph. Collection of the New-York Historical Society/The Bridgeman Art Library; **488–489** Robert Holmes/Corbis; **489** *top left Loading the Steamboat with Cotton Bales from a Plantation* (ca1860), American School. Color engraving. Private Collection. Peter Newark American Pictures/The Bridgeman Art Library; **489** *center right Slave Quarters, Evan-Hall Plantation* (ca. 1860), George Francois Mugnier. Albumen photograph. Louisiana State Museum; **490** Getty Images; **491** *center right FugitiveSlave Law Convention, Cazenovia, New York, August 22, 1850,* Ezra Greenleaf Weld. (Accession number 84.XT.1582.5). Daguerreotype, 1/6 Plate. Image: 6.7 x 5.4 cm (2 5/8 x 2 1/8 in.) ; Mat: 8.1 x 7 cm (3 3/16 x 2 3/4 in.). The J. Paul Getty Museum, Los Angeles; *top right* The Granger Collection, New York; **492** Illustration by Rogue Element; **493** *Frank*

*Leslie's Illustrated Newpaper*, June 27, 1857. Wood engraving after photograph by Fitzgibbon. Library of Congress Prints and Photographs Division (LC-USZ62-79305); **494** The Granger Collection, New York; **495** Rick Wilking/AP Images; **496** Richmond Times-Dispatch/AP Images; **497** *John Brown Going to His Hanging* (1942), Horace Pippin. Oil on canvas, 24 1/8" x 301/4" (61.3 x 76.8 cm). John Lambert Fund (1943.11), Pennsylvania Academy of the Fine Arts, Philadelphia; **498** Brady-Handy Photograph Collection, Library of Congress, Prints and Photographs Division (LC-BH82-2417); **499** *top right, center right* The Granger Collection, New York; *frame* PhotoDisc; **501** Courtesy of the Lloyd Ostendorf Collection; **502** South Carolina Historical Society; **503** The Granger Collection, New York; **505** *top left* The Granger Collection, New York; *bottom left* Bettmann/Corbis; **506** *bottom* The Granger Collection, New York; *top* Frank Leslie's Illustrated Newpaper, June 27, 1857. Wood engraving after photograph by Fitzgibbon. Library of Congress Prints and Photographs Division (LC-USZ62-79305); **508** *bottom left* Library of Congress, Prints and Photographs Division (LC-USZC2-2804); *center left, center right* The Chicago Historical Society; *bottom center* Museum of the City of New York/Corbis; **509** *center* Military and Historical Image Bank; *right* Military and Historical Image Bank ; **510** *Bombardment of Fort Sumter, Charleston Harbour, 12th & 13th April 1861* (ca. 1865), Currier & Ives. Color lithograph. Library of Congress/The Bridgeman Art Library; **511** *center right* Public Domain; *top right* Carolyn Kaster/AP Images; *frame* Jupiter Images; **512** Library of Congress Prints and Photographs Division (LC-USZ62-11897); **514** *left* Library of Congress Prints and Photographs Division (LC-DIG-ppmsca-08386); *right* Library of Congress Prints and Photographs Division (LC-DIG-cwpbh-03116); *left & right insets* Photograph by Hugh Talman/Smithsonian Images; **515** Museum of the City of New York/Corbis; **516** *The 'Monitor' and the 'Merrimac', the First Fight between Ironclads in 1862* (1886), after Julian Oliver Davidson. Lithograph. Published by Louis Prang & Co. Private Collection/The Bridgeman Art Library; **517** *center right* Bureau of Archives and History, New Jersey State Library; *top right* Carolyn Kaster/AP Images; *frame* Jupiter Images; **518** *top* Hulton Archive/Getty Images; *jacket & cap* Military and Historical Image Bank ; **519** *bottom* Bettmann/Corbis; *bottom inset* Hugh Talman/Smithsonian Institute; *top* Military and Historical Image Bank; **520** *top right* Corbis; *top left* Andrew J. Russell/Corbis; *rifle* Photograph by Dave King/Confederate Memorial Hall, New Orleans/Dorling Kindersley ; *bottom right* Time Life Pictures/Getty Images; *grenade* Armed Forces History, Division of History of Technology, National Museum of American History; **522** Bettmann/Corbis; *frame* Jupiter Images; **523** *top right* Carolyn Kaster/AP Images; **524** Library of Congress Prints and Photographs Division (LC-USZC4-1910); **525** *bottom right* Brad C. Bower/AP Images; **527** *Home, Sweet Home* (ca. 1863), Winslow Homer. Oil on canvas, 21 1/2" x 16 1/2", (54.6 x 41.9 cm). Patrons' Permanent Fund (1997.72.1), National Gallery of Art/Christie's Images/The Bridgeman Art Library ; **528** Military & Historical Image Bank ; **529** *top left* Library of Congress Prints and Photographs Division (LC-DIG-cwpb-00238); *top right* George Eastman House; *photograph in viewer Confederate Soldiers as They Fell, Near the Burnside Bridge at the Battle of Antietam, September 1862*, Alexander Gardner. Glass negative, wet collodion process. Library of Congress Prints and Photographs Division (LC-B811- 555); **530** McDougal Littell/Houghton Mifflin Co.; **531** *top left* Carolyn Kaster/AP Images; *bottom left* Library of Congress Prints and Photographs Division (LC-DIG-ppmsca-08386); **534** *bottom left The Freedman* (1863), John Quincy Adams Ward. Bronze, 19 1/2" x 14 3/4" x 9 3/4" (49.5 x 37.5 x 24.8 cm). Gift of Charles Anthony Lamb and Barea Lamb Seeley, in memory of their grandfather, Charles Rollinson Lamb, 1979 (1979.394), Metropolitan Museum of Art, New York; *bottom right Siege of Vicksburg–13, 15, & 17 Corps, Commanded by Gen. U.S. Grant, Assisted by the Navy under Admiral Porter–Surrender, July 4, 1863* (1888), Kurz and Allison, Art Publishers, Chicago. Lithograph. Library of Congress Prints and Photographs Division (LC-USZC4-1754); **535** *bottom Lee Surrendering at Appomattox*, Thomas Lovell, National Geographic Image Collection; **536** Lee Snider Photo Images/Corbis; **537** *center right* Time Life Pictures/Getty Images; *top right The Fall of Richmond, Virginia* (1865), Currier and Ives. Lithograph. Private Collection/The Bridgeman Art Library; **538** *The Hour of Emancipation* (1863), William Tolman Carlton. Oil on canvas. Private Collection/© Christie's Images/The Bridgeman Art Library; **539** *Freedom to the Slave* (1863). Lithograph, Philadelphia. National Museum of American History, Smithsonian Institution; **540** Kean Collection/Getty Images; **541** Jonathan Wiggs/Boston Globe; **542** *both* Courtesy of the Federal Reserve Bank of Atlanta Monetary Museum; **543** *center* The Museum of the Confederacy; **543** *top right The Fall of Richmond, Virginia* (1865), Currier and Ives. Lithograph. Private Collection/The Bridgeman Art Library; **544** The Granger Collection, New York; **546** Corbis; **547** Abraham Lincoln Presidential Library, Springfield, Illinois; **548** Eric Mencher/Getty Images; **549** *center right* Adams County Historical Society, Gettysburg, Pennsylvania; *top right* The Fall of

*Richmond, Virginia* (1865), Currier and Ives. Lithograph. Private Collection/The Bridgeman Art Library; **550–551** Brad C. Bower/AP Images; **552** *right* Time Life Pictures/Getty Images; *left* Detail, *Ulysses S. Grant* (1864), Mathew Brady. Albumen silver print. National Portrait Gallery, Smithsonian Institution/Art Resource, New York; **554** *The Fall of Richmond, Virginia* (1865), Currier and Ives. Lithograph. Private Collection/The Bridgeman Art Library; **556–557** Illustration by Brian Berley; **558** Time Life Pictures/Getty Images; **559** *center right Portrait of Walt Whitman* (ca. 1853), Gabriel Harrison. Quarter plate daguerreotype, 4 1/4" x 3 1/4" (10.8 x 8.3 cm). Humanities and Social Sciences Library/Rare Books Division, New York Public Library; *top right The Fall of Richmond, Virginia* (1865), Currier and Ives. Lithograph. Private Collection/The Bridgeman Art Library; **560** *top right Incidents of the War: Harvest of Death* (Gettysburg,1863), Timothy H. O'Sullivan. Published by Alexander Gardner in "Gardner's Photographic Sketch Book of the War," Vol I, 1866. (LC-B8184-7964-A) Library of Congress Prints and Photographs Division; *top left* The Granger Collection, New York; *frame* PhotoDisc; **561** AP Images; **563** Alexander Gardner (1863)/AP Images; **565** *top left The Fall of Richmond, Virginia* (1865), Currier and Ives. Lithograph. Private Collection/The Bridgeman Art Library; *bottom left* Time Life Pictures/Getty Images; **567** *A Ride for Liberty, or The Fugitive Slaves* (ca. 1862), Johnson, J. Eastman. Oil on paper board, 21 15/16" x 26 1/8" (55.8 x 66.4 cm). Brooklyn Museum of Art, New York (40.59a-b), Gift of Gwendolyn O. L. Conkling/The Bridgeman Art Library ; **568** *bottom center* The Granger Collection, New York; *bottom left* Corbis; **569** Farmland illustrations by Rogue Element; *bottom left* Dorling Kindersley; *bottom right* Carolyn Kaster/AP Images; **571** *center right* The Granger Collection, New York; *top right* Hisham Ibrahim/Getty Images; **572** The Granger Collection, New York; **573** The Granger Collection, New York; **574** Michael Siluk/The Image Works; **575** The Granger Collection, New York; **576** The Granger Collection, New York; **577** *center right* Corbis; *center* Hisham Ibrahim/Getty Images; **578** *right* Medford Historical Society Collection/Corbis; *background* Richard T. Nowitz/Corbis; *background inset* Buddy Mays/Corbis; **579** The Granger Collection, New York; **580** Illustrations by Rogue Element; **581** *top inset* The Chicago Historical Society; *top* The Granger Collection, New York; **582** Bettmann/Corbis; **583** *bottom The Shackle Broken–by the Genius of Freedom.* Color lithograph. Published by E. Sachs & Co., Baltimore, 1874. The Chicago Historical Society; *center* Library of Congress, Washington, DC; *top right* Hisham Ibrahim/Getty Images; **584** *both* Bettmann/Corbis; **585** The Granger Collection, New York; **586** The Granger Collection, New York; **587** Illustration by Rogue Element; **588** Jeff Greenberg/Index Stock Imagery; **589** *top left* Hisham Ibrahim/Getty Images; *bottom right, bottom left* The Granger Collection, New York; **590** © 2006 The Children's Museum of Indianapolis, Inc. Photograph by Wendy Kaveney.

**Epilogue**
**592** *left* Craig J. Brown/Index Stock Imagery; *right* Library of Congress Prints and Photographs Division, Washington, DC; **593** *left* MPI/Hulton Archive/Getty Images; *top right* The Granger Collection, New York; *bottom center* SSPL/The Image Works; *bottom right* Stock Montage/Getty Images; **594** *left* Library of Congress, Prints & Photographs Division, [LC-USZ62-123456]; *right* Bettmann/Corbis; **595** *left* The Granger Collection, New York; *top right* Florida Division of Library and Information; *center right* Library of Congress, Washington, DC; *bottom right* Bettmann/Corbis; **596** *left* Bettmann/Corbis; *right* Library of Congress, Prints & Photograhs Division, FSA/OWI Collection, [LC-USF34-9058-C]; **597** *top right* Mary Evans Picture Library; *top center* Corbis; *left* Joe Raedle/Getty Images; *bottom right* Getty Images; **598** *right* Bettmann/Corbis; *bottom left* Time Life Pictures/Getty Images; **599** *top right* Getty Images; *center left* Bettmann/Corbis; *bottom right* Smithsonian Institution, Washington, DC; **600** *right* Wally McNamee; *bottom left* Corbis; **601** *top right* Wolfgang Rattay/Reuters; *left* Royalty-Free/Corbis; *bottom right* Str Old/Reuters.

**Skillbuilder Handbook**
**R18** Library of Congress, Wahington, DC; **R24** Courtesy of the Lloyd Ostendorf Collection; **R25** McDougal Littell/Houghton Mifflin; **R26** McDougal Littell/Houghton Mifflin; **R34** The Granger Collection, New York; **R36** Christopher Barth/AP Images.

**Presidents of the United States**
Illustrations by Patrick Faricy.

All other illustrations by
McDougal Littell/Houghton Mifflin Co.

# New Jersey Core Curriculum Content Standards for Social Studies Grade 8

## Strands and Cumulative Progress Indicators

**Building upon knowledge and skills gained in preceding grades, by the end of Grade 8, students will:**

**6.1:** ALL STUDENTS WILL UTILIZE HISTORICAL THINKING, PROBLEM SOLVING, AND RESEARCH SKILLS TO MAXIMIZE THEIR UNDERSTANDING OF CIVICS, HISTORY, GEOGRAPHY, AND ECONOMICS.

### A. Social Studies Skills

1. Analyze how events are related over time.
2. Use critical thinking skills to interpret events, recognize bias, point of view, and context.
3. Assess the credibility of primary and secondary sources.
4. Analyze data in order to see persons and events in context.
5. Examine current issues, events, or themes and relate them to past events.
6. Formulate questions based on information needs.
7. Use effective strategies for locating information.
8. Compare and contrast competing interpretations of current and historical events.
9. Interpret events considering continuity and change, the role of chance, oversight and error, and changing interpretations by historians.
10. Distinguish fact from fiction by comparing sources about figures and events with fictionalized characters and events.
11. Summarize information in written, graphic, and oral formats.

**STANDARD 6.2 (CIVICS):** ALL STUDENTS WILL KNOW, UNDERSTAND AND APPRECIATE THE VALUES AND PRINCIPLES OF AMERICAN DEMOCRACY AND THE RIGHTS, RESPONSIBILITIES, AND ROLES OF A CITIZEN IN THE NATION AND THE WORLD.

### A. Civic Life, Politics, and Government

1. Discuss the sources, purposes, and functions of law and the importance of the rule of law for the preservation of individual rights and the common good.
2. Describe the underlying values and principles of democracy and distinguish these from authoritarian forms of government.
3. Discuss the major characteristics of democratic governments.
4. Describe the processes of local government.
5. Discuss examples of domestic policies and agencies that impact American lives, including the Environmental Protection Agency (e.g., clean air and water), the Department of Labor (e.g., minimum wage) and the Internal Revenue Service (e.g., Social Security, income tax).
6. Explain how non-governmental organizations influence legislation and policies at the federal, state, and local levels.

### B. American Values and Principles

1. Analyze how certain values including individual rights, the common good, self-government, justice, equality and free inquiry are fundamental to American public life.
2. Describe representative government and explain how it works to protect the majority and the minority.
3. Describe the continuing struggle to bring all groups of Americans into the mainstream of society with the liberties and equality to which all are entitled, as exemplified by individuals such as Susan B. Anthony, Frederick Douglass, Nat Turner, Paul Robeson, and Cesar Chavez.

### C. The Constitution and American Democracy

1. Discuss the major principles of the Constitution, including shared powers, checks and balances, separation of church and state, and federalism.

2. Compare and contrast the purposes, organization, functions, and interactions of the legislative, executive, and judicial branches of national, state, and local governments and independent regulatory agencies.

3. Discuss the role of political parties in the American democratic system including candidates, campaigns, financing, primary elections, and voting systems.

4. Discuss major historical and contemporary conflicts over United States constitutional principles, including judicial review in Marbury v. Madison, slavery in the Dred Scott Decision, separate but equal in Plessy v. Ferguson, and the rights of minorities in the Indian Removal Act.

5. Discuss major historical and contemporary conflicts over New Jersey constitutional principles (e.g., the impact of the New Jersey School Law of 1881 which required integration in the state's public schools, Hedgepeth and Williams v. Trenton Board of Education, the Mount Laurel Decision, Jackman v. Bodine, Abbott v. Burke).

6. Research contemporary issues involving the constitutional rights of American citizens and other individuals residing in the United States, including voting rights, habeas corpus, rights of the accused, and the Patriot Act.

## D. Citizenship

1. Discuss the rights and responsibilities of American citizens, including obeying laws, paying taxes, serving on juries, and voting in local, state, and national elections.

2. Discuss how the rights of American citizens may be in conflict with each other (e.g., right to privacy vs. free press).

3. Describe major conflicts that have arisen from diversity (e.g., land and suffrage for Native Americans, civil rights, women's rights) and discuss how the conflicts have been addressed.

4. Explain the benefits, costs, and conflicts of a diverse nation.

5. Discuss basic contemporary issues involving the personal, political, and economic rights of American citizens (e.g., dress codes, sexual harassment, fair trial, free press, minimum wage).

## E. International Education: Global Challenges, Cultures, and Connections

1. Analyze ways in which nation-states interact with one another through trade, diplomacy, cultural exchanges, treaties or agreements, humanitarian aid, economic incentives and sanctions, and the use or threat of military force.

2. Discuss factors that lead to a breakdown of order among nation-states (e.g., conflicts about national interests, ethnicity, and religion; competition for territory or resources; absence of effective means to enforce international law) and describe the consequences of the breakdown of order.

3. Compare and contrast the powers the Constitution gives to Congress, the President, the Senate Foreign Relations Committee, and the federal judiciary regarding foreign affairs.

4. Evaluate current United States foreign policy issues and strategies and their impact on the nation and the rest of the world.

5. Discuss the purposes and functions of major international organizations (e.g., United Nations, World Health Organization, International Red Cross, Amnesty International) and the role of the United States within each.

6. Describe how one's heritage includes personal history and experiences, culture, customs, and family background.

7. Analyze how the life, culture, economics, politics, and the media of the United States impact the rest of the world.

8. Discuss how global challenges are interrelated, complex, and changing and that even local issues may have a global dimension (e.g., environmental issues, transportation).

9. Discuss how cultures may change and that individuals may identify with more than one culture.

10. Engage in activities that foster understanding of various cultures (e.g., clubs, dance groups, sports, travel, community celebrations).

11. Discuss the impact of the Internet and technology on global communication.

12. Discuss the impact of stereotyping on relationships, achievement, and life goals.

13. Analyze how prejudice and discrimination may lead to genocide as well as other acts of hatred and violence for the purposes of subjugation and exploitation.

**STANDARD 6.3 (WORLD HISTORY):** ALL STUDENTS WILL DEMONSTRATE KNOWLEDGE OF WORLD HISTORY IN ORDER TO UNDERSTAND LIFE AND EVENTS IN THE PAST AND HOW THEY RELATE TO THE PRESENT AND THE FUTURE.

## A. The Birth of Civilization to 1000 BCE

1. Describe the physical and cultural changes that shaped the earliest human communities as revealed through scientific methods, including:
   - Early hominid development, including the development of language and writing
   - Migration and adaptation to new environments
   - Differences between wild and domestic plants and animals
   - Locations of agricultural settlements
   - Differences between hunter/gatherer, fishing, and agrarian communities

2. Describe how environmental conditions impacted the development of different human communities (e.g., population centers, impact of the last Ice Age).

3. Compare and contrast the economic, political, and environmental factors (e.g., climate, trade, geography) that led to the development of major ancient civilizations including Mesopotamia (e.g., Hammurabi's Code), Egypt, the Indus Valley, the Yellow River, and Kush (Nubia).

## B. Early Human Societies to 500 CE

1. Explain the historical context, origins, beliefs, and moral teachings of the major world religions and philosophies, including:
   - The origins of Judaism and Christianity and the emergence of the Judeo-Christian tradition
   - The influence of Confucianism, Daoism, and Buddhism on the formation of Chinese civilization
   - Hinduism, the Aryan migrations, and the caste system in India
   - The influence of Buddhism in India

2. Describe the political framework of Athenian society and its influence on modern society, including:
   - The influence of Athenian political ideals on public life
   - The importance of participatory government
   - The role of women in Athenian society, their rights under law, and possible reasons why democracy was limited to males

   - Athenian ideas and practices related to political freedom, national security, and justice

3. Describe the social and political characteristics of the Greek city-states, including:
   - Similarities and differences between Athenian democracy and Spartan military aristocracy
   - Location and political structure of the city-states
   - Hierarchical relationships in Greek societies
   - Civic, economic, and social tasks performed by men and women of different classes

4. Describe the significant contributions of ancient Greece to Western Civilization, including:
   - Characteristics of Classic Greek art and architecture and how they are reflected in modern art and architecture
   - Socrates' values and ideas
   - Philosophy, including Plato and Aristotle
   - Greek Drama, including Sophocles and Euripides
   - History, including Herodotus, Xenophon, and Thucydides
   - Greek mythology

5. Discuss the cultural influences of Greece, Egypt, Persia, and India on Mediterranean cultures through assimilation, conquest, migration, and trade.

6. Discuss the origins and social framework of Roman society, including:
   - The geographic location of various ethnic groups on the Italian peninsula and their influence on early Roman society
   - The legends of the founding of Rome and how they reflect the beliefs and values of its citizens
   - Daily life in Rome and Pompeii

7. Describe the political and social framework of Roman society, including:
   - Political and social institutions of the Roman Republic and reasons for its transformation from Republic to Empire
   - The influence of key Roman leaders

8. Analyze how shifts in the political framework of Roman society impacted the expansion of the empire and how this expansion transformed Roman society, economy, and culture.

9. Discuss the political events that may have contributed to the decline of the Roman Empire, including internal divisions, significant battles, invasions, and political changes.

10. Describe the development of the Mayan civilization from agricultural community to an urban civilization, including the influence of the environment on agricultural methods, water utilization, and herding methods.

11. Describe the significant features of Mayan civilization, including the locations of Mayan city-states, road systems, and sea routes, the role and status of elite men and women in Mayan society and their portrayal in Mayan architecture, the role of religion and ceremonial games in Mayan culture, and the structure and purpose of the Mayan pyramids.

## C. Expanding Zones of Exchange and Interaction to 1400 CE

1. Discuss how Western civilization arose from a synthesis of Christianity and classical Greco-Roman civilization with the cultures of northern European peoples.

2. Discuss the spread of Islam in Southwest Asia, the Mediterranean region, and Northern Africa and the influence of Islamic ideas and practices on other cultures and social behavior, including:

   • The origin and development of Islamic law

   • The significance of the Quran and the Five Pillars of Islam

   • The diverse religious, cultural, and geographic factors that influenced the ability of the Muslim government to rule

   • The split into Sunni and Shi'ite factions

   • The importance of Muslim civilization in mediating long-distance commercial, cultural, intellectual, and food crop exchange across Eurasia and parts of Africa

3. Discuss the significance of the developing cultures of Asia, including the Golden Age in China and spread of Chinese civilization to Japan, Korea, and Southeast Asia and the rise of the Mongol Empire and its impact on the Kievan Rus.

4. Analyze the rise of the West African Empires of Ghana, Mali, and Songhay and compare with changes in Asia, Europe, and the Americas.

5. Analyze the relationships between Mesoamerican and Andean societies, including:

   • The growth of urban societies and urban planning

• Religions and rituals

• Governing structure and economy

• The construction of the Mesoamerican calendar

• Similarities in agriculture, societal structures, and artisan crafts

6. Explain the medieval origins of constitutional government in England (e.g., Edward I, Magna Carta, Model Parliament of 1295, Common Law).

7. Discuss the evolution of significant political, economic, social and cultural institutions and events that shaped European medieval society, including Catholic and Byzantine churches, feudalism and manorialism, the Crusades, the rise of cities, and changing technology.

## D. The Age of Global Encounters (1400–1750)

1. Discuss factors that contributed to oceanic travel and exploration in the 15th and 16th centuries, including technological innovations in ship building navigation, naval warfare, navigational inventions such as the compass, and the impact of wind currents on the major trade routes.

2. Describe the significant contributions of the Renaissance and Reformation to European society, including major achievements in literature, music, painting, sculpture, and architecture.

3. Compare the social and political elements of Incan and Aztec societies, including the major aspects of government, the role of religion, daily life, economy, and social organization.

**STANDARD 6.4 (UNITED STATES AND NEW JERSEY HISTORY):** ALL STUDENTS WILL DEMONSTRATE KNOWLEDGE OF UNITED STATES AND NEW JERSEY HISTORY IN ORDER TO UNDERSTAND LIFE AND EVENTS IN THE PAST AND HOW THEY RELATE TO THE PRESENT AND FUTURE.

## A. Family and Community Life

Reinforce indicators from previous grade levels.

## B. State and Nation

Reinforce indicators from previous grade levels.

## C. Many Worlds Meet (to 1620)

1. Discuss factors that stimulated European overseas explorations between the 15th and 17th centuries and the impact of that exploration on the modern world.

2. Trace the major land and water routes of the explorers.

3. Compare the political, social, economic, and religious systems of Africans, Europeans, and Native Americans who converged in the western hemisphere after 1492 (e.g., civic values, population levels, family structure, communication, use of natural resources).

4. Discuss the characteristics of the Spanish and Portuguese exploration and conquest of the Americas, including Spanish interaction with the Incan and Aztec empires, expeditions in the American Southwest, and the social composition of early settlers and their motives for exploration and conquest.

5. Describe the migration of the ancestors of the Lenape Indians and their culture at the time of first contact with Europeans.

6. Compare and contrast historic Native American groups of the West, Southwest, Northwest, Arctic and sub-Arctic, Great Plains, and Eastern Woodland regions at the beginning of European exploration.

7. Analyze the cultures and interactions of peoples in the Americas, Western Europe, and Africa after 1450 including the transatlantic slave trade.

8. Discuss how millions of Africans, brought against their will from Central Africa to the Americas, including Brazil, Caribbean nations, North America and other destinations, retained their humanity, their families, and their cultures during enslavement.

## D. Colonization and Settlement (1585–1763)

1. Analyze the political, social, and cultural characteristics of the English colonies.

2. Describe the political, religious, social, and economic institutions that emerged in Colonial America, including New Netherland and colonial New Jersey.

3. Explain the differences in colonization of the Americas by England, the Netherlands, France, and Spain, including governance, relation to the mother countries, and interactions with other colonies and Native Americans.

4. Examine the interactions between Native Americans and European settlers, such as agriculture, trade, cultural exchanges, and military alliances and conflicts.

5. Describe Native American resistance to colonization, including the Cherokee War against the English, the French and Indian War, and King George's War.

6. Identify factors that account for the establishment of African slavery in the Americas.

7. Discuss Spanish exploration, settlement, and missions in the American Southwest.

## E. Revolution and the New Nation (1754–1820)

1. Discuss the background and major issues of the American Revolution, including the political and economic causes and consequences of the revolution.

2. Discuss the major events (e.g., Boston Tea Party, Battle of Trenton) and personalities (e.g., George Washington, John Adams, John Witherspoon, William Franklin, Benjamin Franklin, Thomas Jefferson) of the American Revolution.

3. Identify major British and American leaders and describe their roles in key events, such as the First and Second Continental Congresses, drafting and approving the Declaration of Independence (1776), the publication of "Common Sense," and major battles of the Revolutionary War.

4. Explain New Jersey's critical role in the American Revolution, including major battles, the involvement of women and African Americans, and the origins of the movement to abolish slavery.

5. Discuss the political and philosophical origins of the United States Constitution and its implementation in the 1790s.

6. Describe and map American territorial expansions and the settlement of the frontier during this period.

7. Analyze the causes and consequences of continuing conflict between Native American tribes and colonists (e.g., Tecumseh's rebellion).

8. Discuss the background and major issues of the War of 1812 (e.g., sectional issues, role of Native Americans).

## F. Expansion and Reform (1801–1861)

1. Describe the political, economic, and social changes in New Jersey and American society preceding the Civil War, including the early stages of industrialization, the growth of cities, and the political, legal, and social controversies surrounding the expansion of slavery.

2. Discuss American cultural, religious, and social reform movements in the antebellum period (e.g., abolitionists, the Second Great Awakening, the origins of the labor and women's movements).

3. Explain the concept of the Manifest Destiny and its relationship to the westward movement of settlers and territorial expansion, including the purchase of Florida (1819), the annexation of Texas (1845), the acquisition of the Oregon Territory (1846), and territorial acquisition resulting from the Mexican War (1846–1848).

4. Explain the characteristics of political and social reform movements in the antebellum period in New Jersey, including the 1844 State Constitution, the temperance movement, the abolition movement, and the women's rights movement.

5. Explain the importance of internal improvements on the transformation of New Jersey's economy through New Jersey's two canals and the Camden and Amboy Railroad.

6. Discuss the economic history of New Jersey, including growth of major industries and businesses, the lives of factory workers, and occupations of working people.

7. Compare political interests and views regarding the War of 1812 (e.g., US responses to shipping harassment, interests of Native Americans and white settlers in the Northwest Territory).

8. Discuss sectional compromises associated with westward expansion of slavery, such as the Missouri Compromise (1820) and the continued resistance to slavery by African Americans (e.g., Amistad Revolt).

9. Describe and map the continuing territorial expansion and settlement of the frontier, including the acquisition of new territories and conflicts with Native Americans, the Louisiana Purchase, the Lewis and Clark expedition, and the California gold rush.

10. Explain how state and federal policies influenced various Native American tribes (e.g., homeland vs. resettlement, Black Hawk War, Trail of Tears).

11. Understand the institution of slavery in the United States, resistance to it, and New Jersey's role in the Underground Railroad.

### G. Civil War and Reconstruction (1850–1877)

1. Explain the major events, issues, and personalities of the American Civil War including:
   - The causes of the Civil War (e.g., slavery, states' rights)
   - The course and conduct of the war (e.g., Antietam, Vicksburg, Gettysburg)
   - Sectionalism
   - The Dred Scott and other Supreme Court decisions

   - The role of women
   - The role of African Americans
   - The Gettysburg Address
   - The Emancipation Proclamation
   - Juneteenth Independence Day

2. Analyze different points of view in regard to New Jersey's role in the Civil War, including abolitionist sentiment in New Jersey and New Jersey's vote in the elections of 1860 and 1864.

3. Explain Reconstruction as a government action, how it worked, and its effects after the war.

4. Discuss the impact of retaliatory state laws and general Southern resistance to Reconstruction.

5. Discuss the Dawes Act of 1887, how it attempted to assimilate Native Americans by converting tribal lands to individual ownership, and its impact on Native Americans.

**STANDARD 6.5 (ECONOMICS):** ALL STUDENTS WILL ACQUIRE AN UNDERSTANDING OF KEY ECONOMIC PRINCIPLES.

### A. Economic Literacy

1. Discuss how needs and wants change as one ages and the impact of planning, spending and saving.

2. Explain the law of supply and demand.

3. Compare ways to save money, including checking and savings accounts, stocks and bonds, and the relationship between risk and return in investments.

4. Describe the role credit plays in the economy and explain the difference in cost between cash and credit purchases.

5. Discuss the economic growth of a nation in terms of increasing productivity, investment in physical capital, and investment in human capital.

6. Describe how private industry acquires material and energy resources, provides jobs, raises financial capital, manages production processes, and markets goods and services that create wealth in order to meet consumer and industrial requirements.

7. Discuss how innovation, entrepreneurship, competition, customer satisfaction, and continuous improvement in productivity are responsible for the rise in the standard of living in the United States and other countries with market economies.

8. Compare and contrast the characteristics of the three basic economic systems: traditional or barter and trade, market capitalism, and command (e.g., communism).

9. Explain what taxes are, how they are collected, and how tax dollars are used by local, state, and national governments to provide goods and services.

## B. Economics and Society

1. Discuss how meeting the needs and wants of a growing world population impacts the environment and economic growth.

2. Describe the many ways federal, state, and local governments raise funds to meet the need for public facilities and government services.

3. Discuss how societies have been affected by industrialization and by different political and economic philosophies.

4. Describe how inventions and innovations have improved standards of living over the course of history.

5. Compare and contrast various careers, examining educational requirements and costs, salary and benefits, longevity, impact on society and the economy, and demand.

6. Analyze and give examples of how business and industry influence the buying decisions of consumers through advertising.

7. Discuss the need for ethical behavior in economic decisions and financial transactions

**STANDARD 6.6 (GEOGRAPHY):** ALL STUDENTS WILL APPLY KNOWLEDGE OF SPATIAL RELATIONSHIPS AND OTHER GEOGRAPHIC SKILLS TO UNDERSTAND HUMAN BEHAVIOR IN RELATION TO THE PHYSICAL AND CULTURAL ENVIRONMENT.

## A. The World in Spatial Terms

1. Distinguish among the distinct characteristics of maps, globes, graphs, charts, diagrams, and other geographical representations, and the utility of each in solving problems.

2. Translate maps into appropriate spatial graphics to display geographical information.

3. Explain the spatial concepts of relative and absolute location and distance.

4. Estimate distances between two places on a map using a scale of miles, and use cardinal and intermediate directions when referring to a relative location.

5. Use geographic tools and technologies to pose and answer questions about spatial distributions and patterns on Earth.

6. Distinguish among the major map types, including physical, political, topographic, and demographic.

7. Explain the distribution of major human and physical features at country and global scales.

8. Use thematic maps to describe places (e.g., patterns of population, diseases, rainfall).

9. Describe and distinguish among the various map projections, including size, shape, distance, and direction.

10. Describe location technologies, such as Geographic Information Systems (GIS) and Global Positioning Systems (GPS).

11. Describe the significance of the major cities of New Jersey, the United States, and the world.

## B. Places and Regions

1. Compare and contrast the physical and human characteristics of places in regions in New Jersey, the United States, and the world.

2. Describe how regions change over time.

3. Compare the natural characteristics used to define a region.

4. Explain how regional systems are interconnected (e.g., watersheds, trade, transportation systems).

5. Discuss how the geography of New Jersey impacts transportation, industry, and community development.

6. Discuss the similarities and differences among rural, suburban, and urban communities.

7. Describe the types of regions and the influence and effects of region labels including:

   • Formal regions: school districts, states

   • Functional regions: marketing area of a newspaper, fan base of a sport team

   • Perceptual regions: the Bible Belt, the Riviera in southern France

## C. Physical Systems

1. Describe the characteristics and spatial distribution of major Earth ecosystems.

2. Discuss how ecosystems function locally and globally.

3. Predict effects of physical processes and changes on the Earth.

4. Discuss how the community and its environment function as an ecosystem.

5. Describe how the physical environment affects life in different regions (e.g., population density, architecture, transportation systems, industry, building materials, land use, recreation).

## D. Human Systems

1. Discuss how technology affects the ways in which people perceive and use places and regions.

2. Analyze demographic characteristics to explain reasons for variations between populations.

3. Compare and contrast the primary geographic causes for world trade.

4. Analyze the patterns of settlement in different urban regions of the world.

5. Discuss how and why people cooperate, but also engage in conflict, to control the Earth's surface.

6. Compare the patterns and processes of past and present human migration.

7. Explain and identify examples of global interdependence.

8. Describe how physical and human characteristics of regions change over time.

## E. Environment and Society

1. Discuss the environmental impacts or intended and unintended consequences of major technological changes (e.g., autos and fossil fuels, nuclear power and nuclear waste).

2. Analyze the impact of various human activities and social policies on the natural environment and describe how humans have attempted to solve environmental problems through adaptation and modification.

3. Compare and contrast conservation practices and alternatives for energy resources.

4. Compare and contrast various ecosystems and describe their interrelationship and interdependence.

5. Describe world, national, and local patterns of resource distribution and utilization, and discuss the political and social impact.

6. Analyze the importance of natural and manufactured resources in New Jersey.

7. Delineate and evaluate the issues involved with sprawl, open space, and smart growth in New Jersey.